Introduction to Air Law

Introduction to Air Law

Tenth Edition

Pablo Mendes de Leon

Wolters Kluwer

Published by:
Kluwer Law International B.V.
PO Box 316
2400 AH Alphen aan den Rijn
The Netherlands
Website: www.wolterskluwerlr.com

Sold and distributed in North, Central and South America by:
Wolters Kluwer Legal & Regulatory U.S.
7201 McKinney Circle
Frederick, MD 21704
United States of America
Email: customer.service@wolterskluwer.com

Sold and distributed in all other countries by:
Quadrant
Rockwood House
Haywards Heath
West Sussex
RH16 3DH
United Kingdom
Email: international-customerservice@wolterskluwer.com

Printed on acid-free paper.

ISBN 978-90-411-9136-6

e-Book: ISBN 978-90-411-9208-0
web-PDF: ISBN 978-90-411-9209-7

Printed in the United Kingdom.

Table of Contents

Table of Contents

Foreword

Since the adoption of the Chicago Convention on 7 December 1944, the International Civil Aviation Organization (ICAO) has served as the principal forum for States to develop air law treaties as well as Standards and Recommended Practices (SARPs). In this regard during the past seven decades, ICAO has made an outstanding contribution to global aviation by adopting more than forty international air law treaties as well as over 12,000 SARPs. Its Member States benefit greatly from this harmonised legal framework which allows for the development of air transport in a 'safe and orderly manner', as enjoined by the Preamble of the Chicago Convention.

As a specialised field of international law, air law has at the same time, links with a great number of other fields of law, filtering them through the lens of aviation activities. In this connection, a large number of books and articles have been published in the past decades on the important work of ICAO as well as on the various aspects of air law, including safety and security, competition, liability of airlines and other entities involved with air transport and related product liability and insurance questions, regional and institutional arrangements, the protection of the environment, and aircraft financing. At the same time, aviation is recognised as being a cross-border activity. Hence, the role of international law in bringing together cultures and viewpoints on its development is critical.

Comprehension for these developments, the intertwining of fields of law, and the compromises which have to be made between States and international organisations involved with them are challenging tasks. Multifaceted and complex legal and policy questions have to be addressed in order to find solutions, moving air transport yet another step forward. For that purpose, we need the law addressing those developments, and publications explaining them.

It is with great pleasure that I accepted the invitation to write a foreword to the tenth edition of *Introduction to Air Law* which serves as a guide through the various fields of air law as divided into twelve chapters. They explain the state of the art in each field, and demonstrate how they interact.

Obviously, I am happy to see that due attention is paid to subjects which are dedicatedly initiated and closely examined by ICAO, such as safety, security, the protection of the environment and 'fair competition'. ICAO is doing its utmost to reach global understanding on these subjects, and publications can greatly help to promote that.

Last but not least, this tenth edition has been drawn up by the current Director of the International Institute of Air and Space Law of Leiden University, The Netherlands, where I followed the advanced LLM programme air and space law before starting my international professional career. I wish that ICAO, and academic institutions such as Leiden University, will continue to work together in order to contribute to the promotion and advancement of knowledge in the field of air law, thereby supporting the development of global aviation 'to create and preserve friendship and understanding among the nations and peoples of the world' as dictated by the Preamble of the Chicago Convention.

With these words in mind, I hope that this book forms a source of inspiration for all those who are interested in this fascinating area of international law.

Dr Fang Liu
Secretary General of ICAO

Preface

The first edition of 'An Introduction to Air Law' drawn up by Isabella Diederiks-Verschoor appeared in 1974, in Dutch *Inleiding tot het luchtrecht*. It encompassed 170 pages and eleven chapters which were different from the chapters listed in the present, tenth edition. The 1973 edition included subjects such as search and rescue, precautionary arrest of aircraft and Dutch legislation concerning air transport which are not discussed as separate subjects in the present edition.

Much has happened since 1973. The operation of air services has been liberalised in the US and subsequently in the EU, which is playing an important role in the regulatory development of aviation activities. This role is also reflected in the organisation of chapters, two of which are devoted to the regulations and case law established by this organisation, to wit, Chapter 5 regarding Passenger Protection and Chapter 7 on Safety Regulation with special reference to the EU.

The world of aviation has also moved on rapidly since the appearance of the ninth edition in 2012. Those developments pertain to market access and market behaviour by air carriers, case law in the area of airline liability, the growing importance of environmental concerns, new perceptions of security and safety in relation to transparency of accident investigation and the rights, and obligations of passengers, and methods for financing aircraft.

I have made an attempt to update the former edition and to contextualise cases and events which have taken place in this extremely dynamic field of law. As this book is designed as an Introduction to Air Law it does not pretend to exhaustively analyse the multifaceted facets of international air law and policy. The current edition has been provided with references to myriad sources including references to the most recent case law and publications. They should give further guidance.

The texts of treaties and international agreements can be found on the internet. The website of ICAO provides useful information regarding the adherence of States to multilateral air law treaties.

This edition keeps up the tradition of previous versions of this book as it is the result of a collaborative effort. To begin with, I am very grateful to Benjamyn Scott, LLM Leiden University, for spontaneously offering his most valuable help with respect to the writing of a new chapter on Safety Regulation in the EU, and Berend Crans,

Partner at the law firm Norton Rose Fulbright, Amsterdam, for revising yet again the Chapter on Rights in Aircraft. I am also indebted to my distinguished alumni Rishiraj Baruah, Andrea Trimarchi, Peter Neenan and Annemarie Schuite who deserve praise for their efforts to improve the quality of various chapters. I acknowledge that the present work would not have been accomplished without the skilful help of the above and other persons who are mentioned in this book.

I hope that the present edition enriches knowledge on air law and encourages the reader to further explore this fascinating and dynamic field of international law.

Pablo Mendes de Leon
April *2017*

List of Abbreviations and Acronyms

ACAC	Arab Civil Aviation Commission
ACAS	Airborne Collision Avoidance System
ACCA	Air Charter Carriers Association
ACCs	Area Control Centres
ACI	Airport Council International
AEP	Aircraft Equipment Protocol
AFCAC	African Civil Aviation Commission
AICG	Aviation Insurance Clauses Group
AIRs	Airborne Image Recorders
AJIL	American Journal of International Law
ALTA	Latin American and Caribbean Air Transport Association
AMC	Acceptable Means of Compliance
ANSP	Air Navigation Service Provision
AOC	Air Operator Certificate
APEC	Asian Pacific Co-operation
ASEAN	Association of South East Asian Nations
ASECNA	Agence pour la Sécurité de la Navigation Aérienne en Afrique et Madagascar
ASU	Aircraft Sector Understanding
ATA	Air Transport Association of America
ATConf	Air Transport Conference (ICAO)
ATFM	Air Traffic Flow Management
Avi	Aviation Cases (Commerce Clearing House)
AVN/AVS	Aviation Policy Clauses (insurance)
AVSECP	Aviation Security Panel
ASA	Air Services Agreement

BASA	Bilateral Aviation Safety Agreement (EASA)
BIBA	British Insurance Brokers Association
CAA	Civil Aviation Authority
CAAC	Civil Aviation Authority of China
CAB	Civil Aeronautics Board
CACAS	Civil Aviation Council of Arab States
CAEP	Committee on Aviation Environmental Protection (ICAO)
CANSO	Civil Air Navigation Services
CASSOS	Caribbean Aviation Safety & Security Oversight System
CITEJA	Comité International Technique des Experts Juridiques Aériens
CJEU	Court of Justice of the European Union (formerly ECJ)
CNS/ATM	Communication Navigation and Surveillance/Air Traffic Management System
CoA	Certificate of Airworthiness
COCESNA	Corporación Centroamericana de Servicios de Navigación Aerea
COMESA	Common Market for East and South Africa
CORSIA	Carbon Offsetting and Reduction Scheme for International Aviation
COSCAP	Cooperative Development of Operational Safety and Continuing Airworthiness Programme
CRS	Computerised Reservation System (see also GDS)
CTC/AEP	Cape Town Convention/Aircraft Equipment Protocol
CVR	Cockpit Voice Recorder
DOHSA	Death on the High Seas Act (US)
DVT	Deep Vein Thrombosis
EAC	East African Community
EALA	European Air Law Association
EASA	European Aviation Safety Agency
ECA	Export Credit Agency
ECAC	European Civil Aviation Conference
ECHR	European Court of Human Rights
ECJ	European Court of Justice(now CJEU)
ECSC	European Coal and Steel Community
Eds	Editors
EEA	European Economic Area (EU plus Norway, Iceland and Liechtenstein)
(E)EC	European Economic Community (now EU)
EFTA	European Free Trade Association

ER	English Reports
EU	European Union
EUROCAE	European Organisation for Civil Aviation Equipment
EU ETS	EU Emission Trade Scheme/System
FAA	Federal Aviation Administration
FABs	Functional Airspace Blocks
FANS	Future Air Navigation System (ICAO)
FDR	Flight Data Recorder
FNC	Forum Non Conveniens
GARA	General Aviation Revitalization Act (US Product Liability Law)
GATS	General Agreement on Trade in Services
GATT	General Agreement on Tariffs and Trade
GDS	Global Distribution Systems (formerly CRSs)
GNSS	Global Navigation Satellite Systems
GPS	Global Positioning System
HP55	Hague Protocol amending the Warsaw Convention (WC) (29)
IAC	Interstate Aviation Committee
IACA	International Air Charter Association
IAEA	International Atomic Energy Agency
IAG	International Consolidated Airlines Group
IASA	International Aviation Safety Assessment (FAA)
IATA	International Air Transport Association
ICAO	International Civil Aviation Organization
IFALPA	International Federation of Air Line Pilots' Associations
IFSOs	Flight Security Officers
ICJ	International Court of Justice
IIA	Intercarrier Agreement on Passenger Liability (IIA)
ILA	International Law Association
ILM	International Legal Materials
ILO	International Labour Organization
IMF	International Monetary Fund
ITA	Institut du Transport Aérien
IUA	International Underwriting Association
IUAI	International Union of Aerospace Insurers
JAA	Joint Aviation Authorities
JALC	Journal of Air Law and Commerce
JARs	Joint Aviation Requirements

JARUS	Joint Authorities for Rulemaking on Unmanned Systems
LACAC	Latin-American Civil Aviation Commission
LASU	Large Aircraft Sector Understanding
LCC	Low Cost Carrier
LNTS	League of Nations Treaty Series
MALIAT	Multilateral Agreement on the Liberalisation of International Air Transport (Pacific region)
MAP	Montreal Additional Protocol
MC99	Montreal Convention on air carrier liability (1999)
MIA	Agreement on Measures to Implement the IATA Intercarrier Agreement (IIA)
MoC	Memorandum of Cooperation
MoU	Memorandum of Understanding
MRO	Maintenance Repair and Overhaul
MRV	Monitoring Verification and Reporting
NACA	National Air Carrier Association
NASU	New Aircraft Sector Understanding
NTSB	National Transportation Safety Board (US)
OAA	Open Aviation Area
OAU	Organisation of African Unity
OECD	Organisation for Economic Co-operation and Development
OJ	Official Journal of the EU
OJEU	Official Journal of the European Union
PANS	Procedures for Air Navigation
PNR	Passenger Name Records
PSO	Public Service Obligations
REIO	Regional Economic Integration Organisation
RFDA(S)	Revue française de droit aérien (et spatial)
RSOO	Regional Safety Oversight Organizations
SAARC	South Asian Association for Regional Cooperation
SACA	Safety Assessment of Community Aircraft (EU/EASA)
SADC	South African Development Community
SAFA	Safety Assessment of Foreign Aircraft (EU/EASA)
SARI	South Asian Regional Initative
SARPs	Standard and Recommended Practices (ICAO)
SAS	Scandinavian Airline System
SDR	Special Drawing Right (IMF currency)
SES	Single European Sky

SESAR	Single European Sky ATM Research
SGWI	Special Group on Aviation War Risk Insurance
SHGA	Standard Ground Handling Agreement
Stat	United States Statutes
TCAS	Traffic Collision Avoidance System
TEU	Treaty on European Union
TFEU	Treaty on the Functioning of the European Union
TIAS	Treaties and other International Agreements of the United States
TiSA	Trade in Services Agreement
TS	United States Treaty Series
UA[S]	Unmanned Aircraft [System]
UAV	Unmanned Aerial Vehicles
UNTS	United Nations Treaty Series
UPU	Universal Postal Union
USAvR	United States Aviation Reports
USOAP	Universal Safety Oversight Audit Programme (ICAO)
UST	United States Treaties
USTS	United States Treaty Series
WC 29	Warsaw Convention (1929)
WL	Westlaw
WMD	Weapons of Mass Destruction
WTO	World Trade Organization
ZLW	Zeitschrift für Luft-und Weltraumrecht

CHAPTER 1

The Regime of International Civil Aviation

1 DEFINITION OF AIR LAW

Air law can be defined as "…. a body of rules governing the use of airspace and its benefits for aviation, the travelling public, undertakings and the nations of the world." The term 'aeronautical law' is also used, especially in the Roman languages, where expressions like *droit aéronautique* and *diritto aeronautico* are commonly employed side by side with *droit aérien* and *diritto aereo*. In the present book the term 'air law' has been adopted.

The study of air law is particularly important for a number of reasons:[1]

(1) Aviation is still in a continuous phase of development and arouses interest in ever larger circles. For many persons and organisations it is a matter of practical importance to gather at least basic knowledge of the subject. When a person purchases a ticket for air transport he/she notices that the provisions of, for instance, the Montreal Convention on air carrier liability of 1999[2] apply to the transportation. It is useful to appreciate the advantages and disadvantages of the rules to which passengers have become bound.

(2) Air law is increasingly intertwined with other areas of law. It is a part of public international law and involves aspects of constitutional law, trade law,

---

1. Appendix D of ICAO Assembly Resolution A39-11 (2016) entitled *Teaching of air law*, emphasises:

> the undoubted importance for the Organization and the States of the specialized teaching of air law and the desirability of fostering knowledge of this important subject: Invites the Council to take all possible action to promote the teaching of air law in those States where it is not yet available; Urges the States to adopt appropriate measures which would further the achievement of the above objective;

2. Official title: *Convention for the Unification of Certain Rules for International Carriage by Air*, (Montreal 1999); *see further*, Chapter 4.

1

competition law, European Union law, administrative law, civil law, corporate and commercial law, criminal law, consumer protection law, environmental law and increasingly of labour law and tax law. Also, it is closely linked with maritime law and space law. Due to the cross border nature of this activity, its international element is always paramount.

(3) Air law offers a striking example of how existing rules can be swiftly adapted to impressive technological progress and other developments. For instance, in the present era information is disseminated digitally, it is stored, and wanders inside virtual clouds, but who is controlling those intangible movements in i-clouds? A new field of law is emerging, that is, *cyberspace law*, which involves the protection of privacy pursuant to human rights in that space. Jurisdictional questions will be mostly related to private international law, including choice of law regulating the information contained in websites, the competency of courts, and enforcement.[3] Air law[4] comes in when, for instance, passengers use air services, transmit their personal data laid down in Passenger Name Records (PNR) to airlines. These data may be stored because they are employed to enhance aviation security while they are also susceptible to be accessed by third parties in an open, not always protected cyberspace. Thus, privacy rights of individuals may have to be balanced against, among others, aviation security concerns.[5] The International Civil Aviation Organization (ICAO) is also addressing the subject.[6]

(4) Air law is generally divided into public air law, governing the interactions between States, and, increasingly so, States and international organisations, or among international organisations, whereas private air law, including the law on the financing of aircraft, regulate contractual and non-contractual relations between private parties, including but not limited to airlines, their passengers, cargo forwarders, and other service providers such as operators of airports and ground handling services, and lessors and lessees of aircraft. All of these categories of air law will be concisely addressed in this book.

Hence, the scope of air law is broadened, whilst it is increasingly impacted by other fields of law. The following chapters will illustrate this tendency, and the guiding role of the ICAO in this respect.

---

3. *See*, K. Ziolkowski (ed.), *Peacetime Regime For State Activities in Cyberspace: International Law, International Relations and Diplomacy* (2013), and D.J.B. Svantesson, *The New Phenomenon of Cyber Law*, in: S. Hobe (ed.), *Air Law, Space Law, Cyber Law*, Proceedings of the conference held on the occasion of the 90th birthday of the Cologne Institute of Air and Space Law 123–136 (2016).
4. *See*, R. Abeyratne, *Aviation Cyber Security: A Constructive Look at the Work of ICAO*, 41(1) Air & Space Law 24–40 (2016).
5. *See also*, section 3.4 of Chapter 5.
6. *See*, ICAO Resolution A39-19 (2016): *Addressing Cybersecurity in Civil Aviation* in which States are called upon to encourage the development of a common understanding among Member States of cyber threats and risks, and of common criteria to determine the criticality of the assets and systems that need to be protected; and to adopt a flexible, risk-based approach to protecting critical aviation systems through the implementation of cybersecurity management systems based on a common understanding of cyber threats and risks.

2 THE DEVELOPMENT OF AIR LAW

2.1 Origin

As early as the 1900s the French jurist Fauchille suggested that a code of international air navigation be created by the '*Institut de droit international*'. Interestingly, this was one of the rare instances where legal process went ahead of technology. In 1903 the discussions were given a new impetus: aviation had become a matter of topical interest and concern because the Wright Brothers had just successfully carried out their first engine-powered flight. However, it is possible to go back even further into the past when one takes into account the national rules and regulations in various countries. In France, for instance, a police directive was issued on 23 April 1784, aimed directly and exclusively at the balloons of the Montgolfier Brothers: flights were not to take place without prior authorisation. The purpose of this measure was of course to protect the population.

The first concerted attempt at codification on an international scale took place before 1910, when German balloons repeatedly made flights above French territory.[7] The French Government was of the opinion that, for safety reasons, it would be desirable for the two governments involved to try and reach an agreement to resolve the problem. As a result, the Paris Conference of 1910 was convened. Contrary to general assumption, this Conference did not adopt the 'freedom of the air' theory. At that time the general tendency was already in favour of the principle of the sovereignty of States in the space above their territories. This is borne out by the text of the draft Convention approved at the plenary session of the Conference.[8]

However, due to political rather than legal disagreements the Conference ended without achieving any tangible results; its only useful effect was that States had had an opportunity of exchanging views on this new area of law. In contrast, maritime law knows a long historical evolution whereby the influential opinions of scholars like Hugo Grotius in his *Mare liberum* had led to a large measure of freedom on the high seas. A similar evolution is conspicuously lacking in air law. The influence of custom in air law is also considerably less evident than in maritime law.

Following the First World War, on 8 February 1919, the first scheduled air service between Paris and London came into operation. It was considered necessary for existing regulations to be incorporated into a Convention. A choice had to be made between a free airspace analogous to the principle of maritime law, and an airspace governed by the sovereignty of the underlying states. Due to the aftermath of the War there were strong tendencies in favour of defending the national interest so that the latter principle prevailed.

---

7. Earlier, at the time of the Hague Peace Conference of 1899, aerial warfare – a quite different aspect of aviation which will not be considered in this treatise – had already been the subject of international codification.
8. *See*, J.C. Cooper, *The International Air Navigation Conference, Paris 1910*, Journal of Air Law and Commerce 127–143 (1952).

2.2 The Autonomy of Air Law

The point has been raised as to whether it was necessary to introduce a special body of rules to govern the airspace. This line of thinking led, in turn, to the question of whether air law was to be regarded as an area of law *sui generis*, consisting of rules of a typically distinctive nature, or, alternatively, whether it was to be made subject to rules already existent to regulate other means of conveyance such as transport by rail, road or sea.

However, whatever their merits, the best approach will be to strike a balance between the two opposing viewpoints. Thus, air law covers an area which is determined by the special characteristics and demands of aviation, especially so in the areas of safety, security and environmental protection,[9] and economic regulation comprising market access and market behaviour of airlines. Also, its cross border nature, illustrated in law by the fact that aircraft moves from one jurisdiction to another, marks this branch of law. At the same time, and as stated above, air law is increasingly influenced by other fields of law and technological developments.

2.3 Sources of Air Law

A closer look at the definition recorded above leads almost automatically to the question: what exactly does this 'body of rules', which governs the airspace and makes up air law, consist of? The following classification may provide useful guidance:

- multilateral conventions;
- bilateral and other international Air Services Agreements (ASAs);
- general principles of international law;
- norms made by international aviation organisations such as ICAO;
- national law and regulations;
- judicial decisions;
- regional arrangements as to which see the EU and other regional regimes;
- resolutions and conditions drawn up by private bodies such as the International Air Transport Association (IATA);
- contracts between airline companies; between airlines and passengers; and between other parties involved with air transport and air navigation.

Multilateral conventions, also referred to as treaties in the following section, are the highest source of air law, and are thus governed by the provisions of the Vienna Convention on the Law of Treaties of 1969, as to which *see also* the following section. Due to the rapid developments in aviation and with the law-makers attempting to keep

---

9. *See,* P. Fitzgerald, *In Search of Greener Commercial Aviation,* 13(1) Issues in Aviation Law and Policy 99–138 (2013), and section 3.3.8 below.

pace, custom has largely been bypassed as a source of law, the result being that air law today consists almost exclusively of written law.

The most characteristic feature of an aircraft is its speed, in addition to the fact that it moves in three dimensions. Speed enables an aircraft *en route* to a particular destination to pass through the airspace of several countries, each having its own national laws and customs. Consequently, it passes from one legal sphere of influence to another. Principally, those who are involved in aviation – for instance, the State, the owner and the operator of the aircraft, the passengers, the owner of the goods carried on board, the mortgage holders – must be sure that their rights are properly safeguarded and responsibilities and liabilities effectively established.

Achieving this objective is one of the most important elements in air law. The implementing measures are all to be found in international agreements and conventions.

Another classification concerns the distinction between *State aircraft* and *civil aircraft*. This book focuses on *civil* aircraft and *civil* aviation while State aircraft will be concisely addressed in section 3.3.2.2 of this chapter.

In view of the relevance of treaties for the development of international civil aviation and air law, the next section will discuss the Law of Treaties.

2.4 The Law of Treaties

2.4.1 Treaties as Sources of International Law

Treaties are the most important source of international law. They represent the principal way in which States may create binding legal obligations in a deliberate and conscious manner. Therefore, international law has developed a specific set of rules the sole purpose of which is to regulate the creation, operation and termination of treaties. The law of treaties deals with the procedural and substantive rules governing treaties as a source of international law.

The law of treaties covers a wide spectrum. There are rules dealing with entry into force, termination, interpretation, reservations or derogations and the relationship of treaty law to custom.

The treaty is the vehicle through which international relations are conducted. The need for certainty and clarity is the primary reason why the International Law Commission has made great efforts to codify treaty law.[10]

---

10. *See,* R.Y. Jennings, *Recent Developments in the International Law Commission: Its Relation to the Sources of International Law,* 13 International and Comparative Law Quarterly 385–397 (1964); M.E. Villiger, *Commentary on the 1969 Convention on the Law of Treaties* (2009); A. Aust, *Modern Treaty Kaw and Practice* (2007); A. Orakhelashvili and S. Williams (eds), *40 Years of the Vienna Convention on the Law of Treaties* (2010).

2.4.2 Concept of a Treaty

Under the Vienna Convention on the Law of Treaties of 1969, a 'treaty' is regarded as a legally binding agreement deliberately created by, and between, two or more subjects of international law who are recognised as having treaty-making capacity, that is, States and international organisations.

A treaty is an instrument governed by international law. Once it enters into force, the parties thereto have legally binding obligations in international law. In this sense, a treaty creates rights and obligations distinct from those arising under the national law of any party. Obviously, the majority of treaties will be made between States, but there is an increasing number of examples of other persons or subjects endowed with international legal personality – such as international organisations – entering into international arrangements either with States or with each other. Treaties are thus made between those international legal persons recognised as having treaty-making capacity.

There are no obligatory formal requirements that must be satisfied before a 'treaty' can come into existence, although the Vienna Convention on the Law of Treaties 1969 applies to treaties in written form. Under general international law, treaties can be oral, in a single written instrument or in several written instruments.[11] Similarly, a treaty may arise from the deliberations of an international conference, direct bilateral negotiations, informal governmental discussions, an 'exchange of notes', an 'exchange of letters' or any other means which the parties choose. This may be relevant for determining the legal force of, for instance, resolutions made by ICAO.

2.4.3 The Vienna Convention on the Law of Treaties 1969

The *Vienna Convention on the Law of Treaties* was adopted in 1969 but it did not enter into force until January 1980.[12] It applies only to treaties concluded after its entry into force and for States that have become bound by the Vienna Convention itself. However, this does not prevent any customary rules, similar to those found in the Convention, from applying to pre-Convention treaties.

The conclusion of the Vienna Convention is a success, among others, because many of its provisions reflect customary law, while courts often use them as sources for their decisions.[13] For the parties to it, it has settled many areas of considerable difficulty but, as with other treaties, many of its provisions reflect compromises. Consequently, a number of the provisions of the Convention are deliberately open-ended and flexible and may give way to different rules where such are expressed in a treaty to which the Convention is said to apply.

---

11. *See*, Art. 2(a).
12. It has 114 States parties per 2016.
13. As recognised by the International Court of Justice in various decisions made by this court as to which *see*, A. Aust, *Vienna Convention on the Law of Treaties*, Max Planck Encyclopedia of Public International Law (2009).

The Vienna Convention does not apply to all international treaties. Articles 1 and 2 provide that the Convention applies only to treaties between States and only to treaties "in written form ... governed by international law."

A separate Convention made in 1986 deals with treaties made between international organisations or between States and international organisations containing provisions which are similar to those of the above Vienna Convention of 1969 between States.[14] Likewise, the Vienna Convention does not deal with State succession to treaties as this is also governed by a separate convention, namely, the *Vienna Convention on Succession of States in respect of Treaties* (1978).[15]

The Vienna Convention has eight parts and consists of eighty-five articles plus an annex. It establishes five fundamental principles with regard to the law of treaties.

The first two principles are *free consent* and *good faith* that ought to be always followed by States in the course of their dealings with each other. The other three major principles, which emanate from Roman law traditions, relate to the conclusion of treaties and the interpretation or application thereof. The first provides that *a treaty is binding upon the parties (pacta sunt servanda)*. The second recognises that *a fundamental change of circumstances jeopardises the validity of a treaty* (Article 18). Finally, the *'favor contractus'* principle is recognised, namely that it is preferable to seek the maintenance rather than the termination of a treaty.

For the study of air law, reference is also made to Article 27 in conjunction with Article 46 of the Vienna Convention (1969), dictating that a State may not rely on its domestic law in relation to other States in order to escape its obligations made under a treaty.

2.4.4 *Procedural Conditions*

The Vienna Convention provides that every State possesses capacity to conclude treaties. However, the person representing a State for the purpose of adopting or authenticating the text must demonstrate that he has appropriate power and authority to do so. The adoption of the text of a treaty takes place by the consent of all of the States participating in its creation except that the adoption of a treaty at an international conference takes place on the vote of two-thirds of the States present and voting or such other percentage as shall be agreed.[16]

The consent of a State to be bound by a treaty is expressed by signature, exchange of instruments constituting the treaty and by ratification, acceptance, approval or accession or other appropriate means.[17] Pursuant to Article 18, a State is obliged to refrain from acts that would defeat the object and purpose of a treaty when it has signed the treaty but prior to ratification thereof or its coming into force in accordance with its terms.

---

14. *See,* The Vienna Convention on the *Law of Treaties between States and International Organizations or between International Organizations* (1986) which is not yet in force.
15. It has twenty-two parties (2017) and entered into force on 6 November 1996.
16. *See,* Art. 9.
17. *See,* Arts 11–17.

When signing, ratifying, accepting, approving or acceding to a treaty a State may enter a reservation unless prohibited from doing so by the treaty. This means that a State will not adhere to all of the provisions of the treaty but is otherwise bound by it. However, depending upon the circumstances, such a reservation may require the consent of all of the other parties.

Treaties may be amended by agreement between the parties and the rules relating to conclusion and entry into force of a treaty apply equally to amendments made thereto.[18] Treaties may only be terminated or denounced in accordance with their terms or in accordance with the provisions of the convention. Termination, renunciation or suspension may be in respect of part only of a treaty. A State may consider its consent to be bound by a treaty as invalidated by the existence of an error of fact upon which it relied, fraud, corruption or coercion of its representative by another State.[19]

2.5 The First Public Air Law Conventions

The Paris Convention relating to the Regulation of Aerial Navigation of 1919[20] was the first legal instrument to enter into force in the province of air law. It was ratified by thirty-two nations. Complete and exclusive sovereignty of states over the airspace above their territory was recognised, in conformity with the Roman adage: *'Cujus est solum, ejus est usque ad coelum et ad inferos'*.

In order to achieve a degree of uniformity technical annexes were added to the Paris Convention dealing with such matters as standards of airworthiness and certificates of competency for crew members. The above Paris Convention also established, in its Article 34, the CINA, the *Commission Internationale de la Navigation Aérienne*,[21] which was granted far-reaching regulatory powers chiefly directed towards technical matters. Other functions listed in Article 34 are: centralised gathering and publication of information on air navigation; and the rendering of advice on matters submitted by Member States.

The Paris Convention contained the first generally accepted definition of the term 'aircraft', which read as follows: *'Le mot aéronef désigne tout appareil pouvant se soutenir dans l'atmosphère grâce aux réactions de l'air.'* This rather sweeping definition included aircraft, airships, gliders, free balloons, barrage balloons and helicopters. The criterion which should have been given preference is whether the machine has any lift.

The Paris Convention was followed by the Ibero-American Convention, concluded at Madrid in 1926. The latter contained provisions largely similar to those of the Paris Convention, provisions which were also recognised, however, by several Latin-American states invited for the purpose by the Spanish Government.

---

18. *See,* Part IV.
19. *See,* Arts 54–62.
20. *Convention Portant Réglementation de la Navigation Aérienne* (Convention Relating to the Regulation of Aerial Navigation), Paris, 13 October 1919; hereinafter cited as the *Paris Convention. See,* for this first air law convention I.H.Ph. Diederiks-Verschoor and H.A. Wassenbergh, *Dr. J.F. Lycklama à Nijeholt (1846–1947),* 19 Air & Space Law 8–14 (1994), and the sources cited there.
21. In English: ICAN, *International Commission for Air Navigation.*

In 1927, the United States initiated the drafting of an air navigation Convention for the Americas, that is, the Pan-American Convention. This Convention was signed at Havana in 1928.

All of the above sources, developments and conventions have influenced and continue to influence the coming into being of international air law. These public air law conventions are now replaced with the well-known Chicago Convention *on international civil aviation* of 1944.

3   THE CHICAGO CONVENTION ON INTERNATIONAL CIVIL AVIATION (1944)

3.1   The Central Role of Sovereignty in the Air

Sovereignty plays a central role in aviation, as demonstrated by the two conventions laying the foundations for civil aviation, namely, the above Paris Convention relating to the Regulation of Aerial Navigation of 1919 which was replaced by the Chicago Convention on international civil aviation of 1944, hereinafter also referred to as the Chicago Convention or the Convention. The two conventions start with the unequivocal proclamation of the principle of sovereignty.

The unequivocal proclamation of the principle of sovereignty in these two conventions[22] has a military background. The rise of military aircraft during the two major world wars in the twentieth century – dropping bombs while flying in what had become foreign national airspace – caused a need for strict control. Indeed, airspace has no 'natural', that is, physical boundaries; there are no physical obstacles for aircraft when flying from the airspace of one country into the airspace of another country. Thus, reliance on sovereignty served as a legal tool to safeguard national airspace and security, in the absence of physical boundaries.

While the Second World War had emphasised the military importance of aviation, the period between 1919 and 1940 had equally demonstrated the enormous potential for civil aviation, both for economic and political purposes. By the end of the twenty-year period between 1919 and 1939, international aviation had become of global importance. Air services were operated around the world. Airlines of Western European countries, such as Britain, France, the Netherlands, Germany and Italy, operated air routes within Europe and established communications with their respective overseas colonies. The United States had pioneered services in the Western Hemisphere, across the Atlantic and the Pacific. Apart from developing an

---

22. Paris Convention, Art. I: "The High Contracting Parties recognise that every power has complete and exclusive sovereignty over the air space above its territory", whereas Art. 1 of the Chicago Convention stipulates in Art. 1 that: "The contracting States recognize that every State has complete and exclusive sovereignty over the airspace above its territory."; *see*, P.P.C. Haanappel, *The Law and Policy of Air Space and Outer Space: A Comparative Approach* 15–23 (2003); P.P.C. Haanappel, *The Transformation of Sovereignty in the Air*, 20 Air & Space Law 311 (1995); *see also*, E. von den Steinen, *National Interest and International Aviation* (2006); F. Fiorelli, *International Air Transport Economic Regulation: Globalization vs Protection of National Interest*, X(3) Aviation and Space Journal 18–24 (2011).

international network, the United States had been able to build transport planes during the Second World War. European States were engaged in building and operating largely military aircraft.

Against this background, different positions were taken at the conference preparing the Chicago Convention. The views of the United States and British delegations were diametrically opposed as to the regulation of the *economic* side of civil aviation. The United States insisted on maintaining the sovereignty of airspace, but, subject to that sovereignty, desired that restrictions on the economic operation of air services be kept to a minimum. For reasons pertaining to the protection of national safety and security, the British delegation agreed upon the point of sovereignty over airspace, but was strongly committed to regulation, in the economic field as well. The result was the confirmation of 'complete and exclusive' sovereignty over national airspace. Thus, national airspace was *de iure* closed for foreign aircraft and their operators, that is, airlines operating international air services unless and until it is opened up by an international agreement allowing access to the airspace for foreign airlines, illustrating the relevance of such agreements in air law.[23]

3.2 The Conclusion of the Chicago Convention

On 7 December 1944, fifty-two States signed the Chicago Convention,[24] together with two agreements annexed to it, that is, the International Air Services Transit Agreement and the International Air Transport Agreement.[25] In 2016, 191 States had ratified or acceded to the Convention. Regional Economic Integration Organizations (REIOs) cannot become a party to this Convention unless it is amended.[26] In 2011, the EU, a 'REIO', concluded a Memorandum of Cooperation (MoC) with ICAO designed to create a framework for closer cooperation in the fields of safety, security, air traffic management and the environment.[27]

---

23. *See also*, section 1.1 of Chapter 2.
24. *Convention on International Civil Aviation*, Chicago, 7 December 1944. Originally, fifty-five States were invited by the United States Government to the Chicago Conference. Saudi-Arabia did not accept the invitation, while at the last minute the USSR did not participate due to objections against the presence at the Conference of certain other States (Portugal, Spain and Switzerland). The USSR resented the policies followed by these countries during the Second World War not yet ended at that time. *See*, on the establishment of the Chicago Convention, D. Goedhuis, *Problems of Public International Law*, 81(11) Recueil des Cours 205–307 (1952); H.A. Wassenbergh, *Post-War International Civil Aviation Policy and the Law of the Air* (1962); P.S. Dempsey, *Public International Air Law* (2008).
25. *International Air Services Transit Agreement*, Chicago, 7 December 1944; hereinafter cited as *Transit Agreement* (also known as the Two-Freedoms Agreement), and the *International Air Transport Agreement*, Chicago, 7 December 1944, also known as the *Five Freedoms Agreement*.
26. *See*, Arts 92, 93 and 93*bis* in conjunction with Art. 94 of the Convention.
27. *See*, http://eur-lex.europa.eu/LexUriServ/LexUriServ.do?uri = OJ:L:2011:232:0002:0007:EN: PDF

The provisions of the Chicago Convention are directed to States; they form rules under public international law.[28] However, certain provisions including Article 33 of this convention,[29] are 'self-executing': depending on the objective and formulation of the provision in question, private persons may rely on those provisions in court. Reference is also made to the 'direct effects'[30] doctrine in European law and to the applicability of Standards and Recommended Practices (SARPs) of the ICAO Annexes in cases between private individuals.[31]

The International Air Services Transit Agreement has been ratified by 131 States.[32] Only eleven States, not including important aviation States, are a party to the International Air Transport Agreement under which the Freedoms I-V of the Air[33] are exchanged. Hence, this agreement has only marginal value for the practice of international civil aviation.

On 24 September 1968, a Protocol was concluded at Buenos Aires and attached to the Chicago Convention, whereby both French and Spanish texts were added with the status of authentic language. In 1977 the same status was accorded to a Russian text, resulting in four texts of equal authenticity.[34] Since then Arabic and a Chinese text of the Convention have also been given authentic status. Currently there are six texts with equal standing.

Since 14 November 2013, nineteen Annexes are added to the Convention. They provide technical rules, comprising Standards and Recommended Practices, in implementation of its Articles.[35]

3.3 Basic Principles

3.3.1 Application to International Civil Aviation Only

The Chicago Convention applies to *international* – civil – aviation only. The term 'international civil aviation' is not defined but supposes that an international element must be present in the operation of air navigation or the air service. For instance,

---

28. *See*, for an excellent analysis of this question, L. Weber, *Convention on International Civil Aviation – 60 Years*, 53 Zeitschrift für Luft- und Weltraumrecht 310–311 (2004); *see also*, R. Abeyratne, *Convention on International Civil Aviation – A Commentary* (2014).
29. *See*, section 3.3.6 of this chapter and section 2.1 of Chapter 6 discussing the legal force of Standards and Recommended Practices (SARPS) of ICAO.
30. *See*, for instance, P. Craig and D. de Burca, *EU Law, Text, Cases and Materials* (2015).
31. *See* section 3.3.6 of this chapter and case law mentioned there.
32. Status per March 2017; *see*, for an interesting analysis of a practical case, E. Carpanelli, *The 'Siberian Overflights' Issue*, 11(1) Issues in Aviation Law and Policy 23–66 (2011), and J. Baur, *EU-Russia Aviation Relations and the Issue of the Siberian Overflights*, 35(3) Air & Space Law 225–247 (2010).
33. As explained in section 3.7 of Chapter 2.
34. *See*, ICAO Doc. 8876/LC-160 (Minutes and Documents of the 1968 Buenos Aires Conference) and 9256/LC-181 (1977 Montreal Conference).
35. *See*, section 3.3.6 of this chapter.

Article 96(b) defines an international air service" "as an air service which passes through the airspace over the territory of more than one State."[36]

The operation of aircraft on domestic services is generally not covered by its provisions as those are governed by the law and regulations of the State in which they are operated. The operation of domestic services by foreign airlines comes under Article 7 of the Chicago Convention as explained in section 3.7 of Chapter 2.

3.3.2 Application to Civil Aircraft Only

3.3.2.1 Definition

On 6 November 1967, ICAO brought out a new definition of aircraft reading:

> Aircraft is any machine that can derive support in the atmosphere from the reactions of the air other than the reactions of the air against the earth's surface.

Its distinctive feature was that the words "other than the reactions of the air against the earth's surface"[37] had been added. These additional words ensured that hovercraft was now excluded from the definition of 'aircraft'. The term 'aircraft' is divided into lighter than air and heavier than air aircraft as to which see the following scheme:

---

36. *See*, Dr J. Huang, *Aviation Safety and ICAO* (2009) (PhD, Leiden University) explains in section 2.25 that, after the 9/11 tragedy, Annex 17 also encompasses security standards which are applicable to domestic operations. However, this is an exception to the rule.
37. Revised and amended text of Annex 7 to the Chicago Convention.

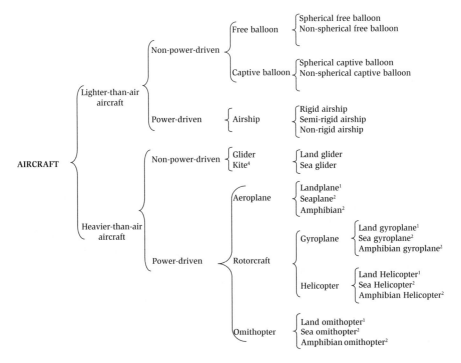

Also, the term 'aircraft' has a different meaning in various air law conventions, according to the context. It is debatable whether rockets fall within the scope of the definition just quoted. Cruise missiles do not derive support in the atmosphere from the reactions of the air, unlike the Second World War flying bombs (V-1). They will not be considered in this treatise as they are subject to special rules of military law. According to the *Multilingual Aeronautical Dictionary*[38] the definition of a rocket (motor) is as follows: "device for producing thrust by the ejection of matter, usually in gaseous form, the thrust being generated by a propellant carried in the system."

A relatively recent development concerns the use of Unmanned Aircraft Systems (UAS) which are more commonly known as 'drones' and were previously referred to as Unmanned Aerial Vehicles (UAV). Those vehicles are employed in a variety of circumstances by both State and private entities and for a variety of purposes; especially, for example, in the field of surveillance, and also, be it limitedly, in transportation.[39] Section 3.6 of Chapter 6 and section 2.6.2, from an EU law perspective, of Chapter 7 explain how such equipment is regulated.

---

38. *Multilingual Aeronautical Dictionary* (Advisory Group for Aerospace Research and Development, North Atlantic Treaty Organization (AGARD/NATO), 1980.
39. *See,* B. Scott, *The Law of Unmanned Aircraft Systems: An Introduction to the Current and Future Regulation under National, Regional and International Law* (2016).

3.3.2.2 The Distinction Between Civil and State Aircraft

Article 3 of the Chicago Convention makes a distinction between State aircraft and civil aircraft.[40] It states that it only applies to civil aircraft, and not to State aircraft. An indication of its meaning – but probably no more than that – is given by the following:

> Aircraft used in military, customs and police services shall be deemed to be State aircraft.

To begin with, it would seem that the aircraft used for the above purposes are to be considered as State aircraft. State aircraft can – but not necessarily has to – mean that the aircraft is registered in the non-civil aircraft registry of a State; or belongs to, or is owned by the State; or is operated by the State. The European air traffic management organisation Eurocontrol has defined State aircraft.[41]

The above quoted formulation of the Chicago Convention appears to make room for other aircraft than aircraft used in military, customs and polices services to be included in the same category.[42] This is confirmed by national laws, international practices and the opinion of authors.[43] Under national – rather than international – legal regimes, the following categories of operations and services *may*, under specified circumstances, fall under the term aircraft used for public – including but not limited to military, customs and police – services:

- coast guard;
- search and rescue;

---

40. *See*, R. de Oliveira, *The Distinction Between Civil and State Aircraft: Does the Current Legal Framework Provide Sufficient Clarity of Law with Regard to Civil and State Aircraft in Relation to Aviation Practicalities?* 41(4/5) Air & Space Law 329–344 (2016).
41. *See*, Principle 1 drawn up by the Provisional Council of Eurocontrol:

    > For ATM purposes and with reference to Art. 3(b) of the Chicago Convention, only aircraft used in military, customs and police services shall qualify as State Aircraft. Accordingly: Aircraft on a military register, or identified as such within a civil register, shall be considered to be used in military service and hence qualify as State Aircraft; Civil registered aircraft used in military, customs and police service shall qualify as State Aircraft; Civil registered aircraft used by a State for other than military, customs and police service shall not qualify as State Aircraft.

42. *See*, ICAO Secretariat Study on *Civil/State Aircraft – Comments from States and International Organisations*; ICAO Doc. LC/29-WP/2-2 (1992/3); ICAO Resolution 22/1: *Consolidated statement of continuing ICAO policies and associated practices related specifically to air navigation,* Appendix P: *Coordination of civil and military air traffic,* laid down in ICAO Doc. 9845 A35-TE (2004), and Resolution A32-14 adopted in 1998 by ICAO; *see also,* M. Schadebach, *Luftraumverletzungen durch Militärflugzeuge. Der griechisch-türkische Konflikt in der Ägäis* (Airspace violations by military aircraft and the Greek Turkish Conflict), 52 Zeitschrift für Luft- und Weltraumrecht 355 (2003); M. Haeck and L. Bourbonniere, *Military Aircraft and International Law: Chicago Opus 3,* 66 Journal of Air Law and Commerce 885 (2000/2001).
43. Although Professor Bin Cheng notes that the Chicago Convention "limits aircraft solely to aircraft used in military, customs and police services while it may have intended no more than to provide that only these categories of aircraft are *to be excluded from the* application of the convention." *See,* Bin Cheng, *State Ships and State Aircraft,* 2 Current Legal Problems 225, 233 (1958); *see also,* M. Milde, 'Redention Flights' and International Air Law, 57 Zeitschrift für Luft- und Weltraumrecht 330 (2008), and *International Air Law and ICAO* 73–79 (2016).

- emergency assistance;
- humanitarian flights;
- geological survey services;
- carriage of heads of States and official personalities in special aircraft;
- carriage of remote station supplies;
- carriage of prisoners (of war), or persons travelling in custody.

Despite the provisions of Article 3(a) of the Chicago Convention stating that the Convention does not apply to State aircraft, Articles 3(b), 3(c) and 3(d) do contain rules on their operation. Article 3(d) states that States, when issuing regulations regarding the operation of State aircraft, should have due regard for the safety of navigation of civil aircraft. ICAO has further explained these provisions in a number of SARPs and Resolutions, as to which *see* further below. A somewhat unexpected provision appears in Article 35 of the Chicago Convention. It reads as follows:

> no munitions of war or implements of war may be carried in or above the territory of a State in aircraft engaged in international navigation, except by permission of such State. Each State shall determine by regulations what constitutes munitions of war or implements of war for the purposes of this Article, giving due consideration, for the purpose of uniformity, to such recommendations as the International Civil Aviation Organization may from time to time make.

If an aircraft carrying munitions of war qualifies as 'State aircraft' or as aircraft engaged in military services, the operation of such aircraft is excluded from the scope of the Convention.[44]

It follows from the above that the classification of an aircraft as 'State' or 'civil' will depend upon the use to which the aircraft is being put from time to time. The interpretation of the term 'use' cannot be objectively determined but depends on an appreciation of the prevailing circumstances and facts, and the interpretation of the applicable international law, for instance, Red Cross and European Human Rights conventions, dealing with State aircraft, and national law and regulations.

3.3.2.3 *Nationality of Aircraft*

For safety reasons, nationality of aircraft occupies a prominent place in the Chicago Convention. That is one of the principal reasons for which an aircraft must have nationality marks on it, confirming its nationality and, as a corollary the State which is responsible for safety supervision.

As confirmed by Article 17, aircraft has the nationality of the State in which it is registered,[45] in accordance with the provisions of Article 20 of the Chicago Convention. National rules provide conditions for registration. Thus they may state that the aircraft which is entered by the operator into the aircraft registry must have the nationality of the State, or its principal place of business there. Pursuant to the Chicago Convention,

---

44. *See*, M. Milde, *International Air Law and ICAO* 68 (2016).
45. "Aircraft have the nationality of the State in which they are registered."

the State of registry is internationally responsible for the issuance of a Certificate of Airworthiness (CoA) of aircraft registered in its national registry, and of personnel licences serving on such aircraft.[46] Article 18 of the Chicago Convention stipulates that:

> An aircraft cannot be validly registered in more than one State, but its registration may be changed from one State to another.

The latter option, that is, change of registration, facilitates the use of aircraft by operators established in different States. Another option is provided by Article 83*bis* of the Chicago Convention.[47]

In air law, due to the Chicago Convention's safety provisions based on nationality of the aircraft in conjunction with provisions of bilateral ASAs stipulating requirements of 'substantial ownership and effective control' for designated airlines operating the agreed international air services under such agreements,[48] civil aviation does not come across the same problems as in the maritime sector. ICAO's Assembly declared that each "individual State's responsibility for safety oversight is one of the tenets of the Chicago Convention."[49]

The State of registry is internationally responsible for the issuance of a CoA of aircraft registered in its national registry, and of personnel licences serving on such aircraft.[50] In the 1970s and 1980s, international transactions among airlines concerning leasing, interchange or charter of aircraft based in different States, increased the flexibility for the use of aircraft. Thus, an aircraft registered in one State was used in another. In turn, the State of registry of the aircraft was not capable of adequately carrying out safety oversight as it was used in another country or even in another part of the world. This practice led to the adoption of Article 83*bis* of the Chicago Convention in 1980; it entered into force on 20 June 1997 for the States which have ratified it.[51] This provision has been considered as an exception to the 'genuine link' which normally, that is, via national law provisions, exists between an aircraft and the State of registry.[52]

---

46. *See*, Arts 31 and 32, as further explained in ICAO, Doc 9734 – AN/959, *Safety Oversight Manuel*, Part A *The Establishment and Management of a State's Safety Oversight System* (2006).
47. Which is discussed in section 2.6 of Chapter 6.
48. On nationality criteria for airlines, *see*, section 1.2.3 of Chapter 2.
49. *See*, Arts 31 and 32, as further explained in ICAO, Doc 9734 – AN/959, *Safety Oversight Manuel*, Part A *The Establishment and Management of a State's Safety Oversight System* (2006); *see also*, M. Milde, *Aviation Safety Oversight Audits and the Law*, XXVI Annals of Air and Space Law 105 (1986), and M. Milde, *Enforcement of Aviation Safety Standards – Problems of Safety Oversight*, 45 Zeitschrift für Luft- und Weltraumrecht 1 (1996); J.S. Ignarski, *Flags of Convenience*, in: R. Bernhardt (ed.), II *Encyclopedia of Public International Law* 404 (1995), and A.I. Mendelsohn, *Flags of Convenience: Maritime and Aviation*, 13(1) The Aviation & Space Journal 2–7 (2014); *see further*, section 2.6 of Chapter 6.
50. *See*, Arts 31 and 32, as further explained in ICAO, Doc 9734 – AN/959, *Safety Oversight Manuel*, Part A *The Establishment and Management of a State's Safety Oversight System* (2006).
51. 170 States per March 2017.
52. *See*, Dr J. Huang, *Aviation Safety and ICAO* 42 (2009): "The amendment to the Chicago Convention through Art. 83*bis* reinforces the principle that the concept of 'flags of convenience' has no place within the ICAO system. Had 'flags of convenience' been acceptable, it would not have been necessary for ICAO to spend several decades in negotiating and adopting Article 83*bis* and to bring it into force."; *see also*, section 2.6 of Chapter 6.

'Flags of convenience', or more appropriately 'flags of non-compliance' are to be avoided, and are avoided by the afore-mentioned Article 83*bis*, safety oversight conducted in the context of bilateral ASAs,[53] ICAO, the US Federal Aviation Administration (FAA) and, in Europe, the European Aviation Safety Agency (EASA).[54] However, safety standards made by ICAO under the Convention are not always implemented or enforced.[55] To some extent, this point has been addressed by the introduction on the part of ICAO of the mandatory Universal Safety Oversight Audit Programme (USOAP).[56]

As regards the question whether an aircraft is part of the territory of the State of nationality of the aircraft it may belong to the national territory in cases when so designated in conventional rule. An example is to be found in Article 23(2) of the 1952 Rome Convention which reads as follows:

> For the purpose of this Convention a ship or an aircraft on the high seas shall be regarded as part of the territory of the State in which it is registered.

The Chicago Convention lacks such a rule.[57] Consequently, a State cannot claim territorial jurisdiction with respect to aircraft flying over the high seas, where it is, as far as the *Rules of the Air* are concerned, subject to ICAO rules laid down in Annex 2 as explained above. This is different for events taking place on board aircraft where, subject to international treaties on aviation security which are discussed in Chapter 10,[58] the law of the State of registration of the aircraft applies. These events concern, for instance, the prohibition of smoking or gambling on board aircraft, birth and death, and the consumption of alcohol and other substances.

Nationality and registration of aircraft, viewed in conjunction with the joint operation of aircraft by several States, may give rise to both political and legal entanglements.[59] The point was at issue in the context of the establishment of *multinational airlines*. The question was whether this form of multinational airline

---

53. *See*, section 3.3 of Chapter 2.
54. *See*, section 2 of Chapter 7.
55. *See*, section 3.3.6 of this chapter.
56. *See*, J. Huang, *Aviation Safety and ICAO* 69–71 (2009); *see also*, section 2.3 of Chapter 6.
57. *See*, F. Videla Escalada, *Nationality of Aircraft: A Vision of the Future*, in: T.L. Masson and P.M.J. Mendes de Leon, *Air and Space Law: De Lege Ferenda*, Essays in Honour of Henri A. Wassenbergh 71–80 (1992).
58. Thus, for offences committed on board, jurisdiction has been provided to a certain extent in the Tokyo Convention, The Hague Convention as amended by the Beijing Protocol of 2011, the Montreal Convention and the Beijing Convention of 2011 as to which *see also*, Chapter 12.
59. *See*, ICAO Resolution A 24-12: *Practical measures to provide an enhanced opportunity for developing States with community of interest to operate international air transport services*, adopted by the ICAO Assembly during its 24th Session (ICAO Doc. 9414, A-24 Res.) *see also*, B. Cheng, *Nationality and Registration of Aircraft – Art. 77 of the Chicago Convention*, 32 Journal of Air Law and Commerce 551 (1966); M. Milde, *Nationality and Registration of Aircraft Operated by Joint Air Transport Operating Organizations or International Operating Agencies*, X Annals of Air and Space Law 133–135 (1985); K. El-Hussainy, *Registration and Nationality of Aircraft operated by International Agencies in Law and Practice*, 10 Air Law 15–27 (1985); and G. FitzGerald, *Nationality and Registration of Aircraft Operated by International Operating Agencies and Art. 77 of the Convention on International Civil Aviation of 1944*, Canadian Yearbook of International Law 193 (1967).

operation was in line with the provisions of Articles 17–21 and Articles 77 and 79 of the Convention, all of which are relevant to cooperation. The ICAO legal committee which was asked to address this question concluded that the Chicago Convention did not need modifying, provided that certain conditions were met.[60] In short, the fact remains that there still has to be a State of registration, as recognised by Article 17 of the Chicago Convention.

Another question pertaining to the interpretation and application of the provisions of the Chicago Convention in the context of multinational airlines was addressed to the ICAO Council when the Consortium Agreement of the Scandinavian Airline System (SAS) was drawn up by the national carriers of three Scandinavian States.[61]

3.3.2.4 References to State Aircraft in International Conventions

References to State aircraft can be found in the following international agreements:

- The Warsaw Convention for the *Unification of Certain Rules Relating to International Carriage by Air* (1929):[62] according to Article 2(1), the Convention is applicable to carriage performed by a State. Nevertheless, an additional protocol with reference to Article 2 provides that States may reserve to themselves the right to declare that "the first paragraph of Article 2 of this Convention shall not apply to international carriage by air performed in State," and The Hague Protocol amending the Warsaw Convention (HP55) stipulates in Article 26 that States may declare this Convention, as amended by the Hague Protocol, to be inapplicable to military transport as confirmed by the Guadalajara Convention[63] which follows, in so far as State aircraft concerned, the provisions of the Warsaw Convention and the Hague Protocol.[64]

- The *Convention for the Unification of Certain Rules Relating to the Precautionary Attachment of Aircraft*,[65] declares that aircraft used exclusively in the service of a State, including the postal service, but excluding commercial service, are not subject to precautionary arrest (Article 3).

---

60. As to which *see* ICAO Doc. 8722-C/976 of 20 February 1968, and ICAO Council Resolution on *Nationality and Registration of Aircraft by International Operating Agencies* of 14 December 1967.
61. Pursuant to which Denmark, Norway and Sweden created a consortium for the operation of commercial air traffic and other business in connection therewith under one name (SAS) and for their joint account, *see* ICAO Circular 99-AT/20 (1970): *Scandinavian Airline System – Consortium Agreement and Related Agreements.*
62. *See,* section 1 of Chapter 4.
63. Convention Supplementary to the Warsaw Convention, for the Unification of Certain Rules Relating to International Carriage by Air Performed by a Person Other than the Contracting Carrier, Guadalajara, 18 September 1961.
64. Protocol to Amend the Warsaw Convention, Guatemala City, 8 March 1971.
65. The Convention for the Unification of Certain Rules Relating to the Precautionary Attachment of Aircraft, Rome, 29 May 1933. Instead of 'attachment' the term 'arrest' may be used.

- The *Convention on the International Recognitions of Rights in Aircraft*[66] provides in Article XIII that the Convention shall not apply to military, customs or police aircraft. Accordingly the Convention is applicable to other State aircraft.

- The *Convention on Damage Caused to Third Parties on the Surface*,[67] replaced by the Rome Convention (1952),[68] had a similar provision in Article 21. This Convention is also applicable to other categories of State aircraft.

- The Tokyo Convention,[69] The Hague Convention as amended by the Beijing Protocol of 2010,[70] the Montreal Convention[71] and the Beijing Convention of 2010 do not apply to military, customs or police aircraft either.

- The Montreal Convention for the *Unification of Certain Rules for International Carriage by Air* (1999) applies to carriage performed by the State (Article 2(1)).

- The *Treaty on Open Skies* establishes a programme for the use of unarmed aircraft for the purpose of surveillance flights over the entire territory of its participants. This Treaty is not related to civil aviation open skies agreements.[72]

Most of the above conventions are discussed in greater detail in the following chapters of this book, in particular Chapters 4, 9, 11 and 12. Reference is made to the relevant sections of those chapters.

3.3.2.5 Joint Registration of Aircraft

Under Article 77 of the Chicago Convention, States may set up a 'joint operating organization' or an 'international operating agency', but such organisations and agencies remain subject to the provisions of this Convention. It continues to prescribe that the Council must determine "in what manner the provisions of this Convention relating to nationality of aircraft shall apply to aircraft operated by international operating agencies."

Article 77 can be viewed as the most 'regionally' oriented provision of the Chicago Convention as it allows for cross border cooperation between States on an institutionalised basis. While aircraft may be operated by a joint operating organisation or an international operating agency this is not to say that they may be registered by such organisations and agencies. However, 'joint registration' is an option as an ICAO Document refers to:

---

66. Convention on the International Recognition of Rights in Aircraft, Geneva, 19 June 1948.
67. Convention on Damage Caused to Third Parties on the Surface, Rome, 29 May 1933.
68. Convention on Damage Caused by Foreign Aircraft to Third Parties on the Surface, Rome, 7 October 1952.
69. *See,* Art. 1(4) of the Tokyo Convention (Chapter 12).
70. *See,* Art. 3(2) of The Hague Convention (Chapter 12).
71. *See,* Art. 4(1) of the Montreal Convention (Chapter 12).
72. Signed at Helsinki on 24 March 1992; it came into force on 1 January 2002. This Treaty currently has thirty-four States Parties, as to which *see https://www.state.gov/t/avc/cca/os/*.

that system of registration of aircraft according to which the States constituting an international operating agency would establish a register other than the national register for the joint registration of aircraft to be operated by the agency[73]

That said, the establishment of a joint register does not imply the disappearance of a national register; on the contrary, a joint register cannot be a substitute for a national register as the said organisations and agencies remain subject to the provisions of the Chicago Convention including those pertaining to the registration of aircraft in a national register.[74]

The above cross border ventures have been tried in the 1950s and 1960s by Arab States in the context of the 'Pan Arab Airline' in 1959,[75] and African States when creating Air Afrique two years later.[76] In both cases the ICAO Council was invited to determine in what manner the provisions relating to the nationality of aircraft should apply to aircraft operated by these ventures. It decided that civil aircraft must have a nationality whether they are operated by an international agency or not.[77]

3.3.2.6 Concluding Remarks

The above picture shows a piecemeal approach towards the status of State aircraft under the various regimes. The regulation and solutions on questions regarding the status of aircraft must be made by reference to international and European conventions and agreements, national law, case law and very importantly, the prevailing circumstances including those pertaining to the use of the aircraft in question. Hence, solution of problems and answers to questions can only be obtained on an ad hoc basis as evidenced by a number of cases on State aircraft accident investigation and payment of damages caused by the operation of State aircraft.

One of such instances concerned the crash near the Russian town of Smolensk on 10 April 2010. All 96 persons on board the aircraft perished, including the Polish President, his wife, and Polish public officials including military chiefs. The aircraft was a State aircraft, but the Polish and Russian Presidents agreed to apply the civil rules laid down in Annex 13 of the Chicago Convention for establishing the cause of the accident.[78]

---

73. *See*, ICAO Doc. 8722-C/976 of 20 February 1968; *see also*, Pablo Mendes de Leon, *Cabotage in Air Transport Regulation* 128–129 and 166–167 (1992).
74. *See*, ICAO Doc. 8106-3, C/927-3 of 8 December 1960.
75. *See*, ICAO Doc C-WP/3091 of 24 February 1960.
76. *See*, ICAO Circular 98/AT/19 (1970).
77. *See also*, B. Cheng, *Nationality and Registration of Aircraft – Article 77 of the Chicago Convention*, 32 Journal of Air Law and Commerce 551–563 (1963); Professor Cheng points out that the major difficulty in the ventures falling under Art. 77 of the Chicago Convention is not Art. 17 but Art. 18 of the same convention.
78. *See*, Dr Piotr Kasprzyk, *Legal Ramifications of the Polish President's Aircraft Accident*, 36 Air & Space Law 201–2016 (2011).

3.3.3   Cooperation on the Basis of Equality

One of the fundamental principles underlying the Convention is the fact that all States should be able to participate in air transportation on the basis of equality. It is linked to the principle of sovereignty which also proceeds from the equality of States under international law. The Convention's Preamble provides a pointer in that direction since it refers to the good faith of States in their dealings with each other and to the regard for equal opportunity and participation.[79]

The implementation of this principle is hampered by the limitations of rights States can impose upon each other, limitations which find their origin in the principle of sovereignty of the State over the airspace above its territory as expressed in Article 1 of the Convention. Governments wished, above all, to urge their own airlines to satisfy the demand for air transport to and from their countries independently. They therefore showed a tendency to impose major limitations on foreign airline companies. These limitations concern the number of passengers to be carried, the flight frequency and other vital matters pertaining to market access, as evidenced by restrictive provisions in bilateral ASAs as to which *see*, sections 2 and 3 of Chapter 2.

3.3.4   Territorial Jurisdiction

The Chicago Convention proceeds from territorial jurisdiction in national airspace. Among others, this follows from the combined effect of Articles 1, as explained in section 3.1 above, and 2 of the Convention.[80] Article 2 of the Convention states:

> For the purpose of this Convention the territory of a State shall be deemed to be the land areas and territorial waters adjacent thereto under the sovereignty, suzerainty, protection or mandate of such State.

The following areas of jurisdiction may be distinguished: the airspace above the national territory, the territorial waters and the high seas. State sovereignty extends to the airspace above national territory and the territorial waters.[81] There is an important qualification to this basic rule in respect of the airspace above the territorial waters,

---

79. In the words of the Preamble: "…. that international air transport services may be established on the basis of equality of opportunity and operated soundly and economically;…" *See also*, Pablo Mendes de Leon, *The Dynamics of Sovereignty and Jurisdiction in International Aviation Law*, in: G. Kreijen et al. (eds), *State, Sovereignty and International Governance*, Liber Amicorum Peter H. Kooijmans 483–495 (2002), and M. Milde, *ICAO: A History of International Civil Aviation* (2010).

80. *See also*, T. Brisibe, *Aeronautical Public Correspondence by Satellite* 91–96 (2006) (PhD Leiden University).

81. *See*, J. Ming, *The US/China Aviation Collision Incident at Hainan in April 2001 – China's Perspective*, 51 Zeitschrift für Luft- und Weltraumrecht 557 (2002); for an exceptional judiciary case on the question of sovereignty, *see*, M. Franklin, *Sovereignty and the Chicago Convention: English Court of Appeal Rules on the Northern Cyprus Question*, 36(2) Air & Space Law (2011); M. Chatzipanagiotis, *Establishing Direct International Flights to and from Northern Cyprus*, 60(3) Zeitschrift für Luft- und Weltraumrecht (2011).

where no right of innocent passage for aircraft exists like there is for ships in the territorial waters. Territorial waters do not include the Exclusive Economic Zones.[82]

Under the United Nations Convention on the Law of the Sea[83] the territorial sea limit was extended to 12 miles.[84] Consequently many of the sea straits thus far considered as belonging to the high seas may now come under the rules and regulations governing the territorial waters: overflying such straits without permission of the States involved will no longer be allowed. In the light of this new situation Article 38 of this Convention (UNCLOS) establishes a right of transit passage in the straits for all ships and aircraft, including military vessels and aeroplanes.[85]

Jurisdiction above the high seas is governed by Article 12 of the Chicago Convention. This article should be read in conjunction with Annex 2 of the Chicago Convention containing the *Rules of the Air*. These *Rules of the Air* are applicable to aircraft during its flight above the high seas without exception, thus creating uniformity of regulation. Disputes concerning the use of the airspace above the high seas may, however, arise in connection with military exercises and nuclear testing; they may also occur in respect of the Air Defence Identification Zones.[86]

Neither the Chicago Convention nor any other international agreement, including any of the treaties regulating outer space and activities related to it, defines the upper borders of airspace. Consensus appears to exist on delimitation between 80 and 120 kilometres above the surface of the earth.[87] In an exceptional case, namely, Australia, national law defines the demarcation between airspace and outer space – in this case at 100 kilometres above the surface of the earth.[88]

---

82. As to which *see* P.M.J. Mendes de Leon and E.J. Molenaar, *Still a Mile too Far? International Law Implications of the Location of an Airport in the Sea*, 14 Leiden Journal of International Law 234–245 (2001).
83. Concluded in Montego Bay, 10 December 1982 and entered into force on 16 November 1994.
84. *See,* Art. 3.
85. In such straits "…all … aircraft enjoy the right of transit *passage, which shall not be impeded;… "* See P. de Vries Lentsch, *The Right of Overflight over Strait States and Archipelagic States: Developments and Prospects,* XIV Netherlands Yearbook of International Law 165–225 (1983); *see also,* for the legal status of the airspace above the maritime areas regulated under UNCLOS, M. Milde, *International Air Law and ICAO* 37–43 (2016).
86. *See,* P.P. Heller, *Flying over the Exclusive Economic Zone,* 27 Zeitschrift für Luft-und Weltraum-recht 15–17 (1978); E. Cuadra, *Air Defense Identification Zones – Creeping Jurisdiction in the Airspace,* 18 Virginia Journal, of International Law 485-5:12 (1978/9); P.P.C. Haanappel, *The Law and Policy of Air Space and Outer Space: A Comparative Approach* 18–19 (2003); Peter A. Dutton, *Caelum Liberum: Air Defense Identification Zones Outside Sovereign Airspace,* 103 American Journal of International Law 691–709 (2009); S.A. Kaiser, *The Legal Status of Air Defense Identification Zones: Tensions over the East China Sea,* 63 Zeitschrift für Luft und Weltraumrecht 386–410 (2014), and C.K. Lamont, *Conflict in the Skies: The Law of Air Defence Identification Zones,* 39(3) Air & Space Law 187–202 (2014).
87. *See,* P. Fitzgerald, *Inner Space: ICAO's New Frontier,* 79(1) Journal of Air Law and Commerce 3–34 (2014), and J. Sin, *The Delimitation Between Airspace and Outer Space en the Emergence of Aerospace Objects,* 78(2) Journal of Air Law and Commerce 355–380 (2013); M.T. King, *Sovereignty's Gray Area: The Delimitation of Air and Space in the Context of Aerospace Vehicles and the Use of Force,* 81(3) Journal of Air Law and Commerce 377–500 (2016).
88. *See,* the Australian *Space Activities Act* No. 123 of 1998, as amended by the *Space Activities Act* No. 100 of 2002.

3.3.5   Scheduled and Non-scheduled Air Services

International air law also makes a distinction between 'scheduled' and 'non-scheduled' flights or services. Article 6 of the Chicago Convention provides that:

> No scheduled air service may be operated over or into the territory of a contracting State, except with special permission or other authorization of that State, and in accordance with the terms of such permission or authorization.

Therefore, each State is free to impose such limitations as it deems fit on the services operated by a foreign airline as evidenced by bilateral ASAs as to which *see* Chapter 2 on Economic Regulation of Air Transport.

On 28 March 1952, the ICAO Council adopted the following definition of scheduled international services:

> A scheduled international air service is a series of flights that possesses all the following characteristics:
>
> (a) it passes through the airspace over the territory of more than one State;
> (b) it is performed by aircraft for the transport of passengers, mail or cargo for remuneration, in such a manner that each flight is open to use by members of the public;
> (c) it is operated so as to serve traffic between the same two or more points, either 1: according to a published timetable, or 2: with flights so regular or frequent that they constitute a recognizable systematic series.[89]

Hence, scheduled and non-scheduled air services differ in that the latter are not carried out according to a published timetable, and were not subject to the rates and tariffs that were applicable to regular scheduled air traffic. Non-scheduled air transport is performed by aircraft not engaged in the operation of regular air services.[90]

The operation of non-scheduled services is subject to Article 5 of the Chicago Convention. It was drafted to guarantee non-scheduled air traffic freedom and flexibility. The grant of those freedoms laid down in Article 5, may be made subject to the permission of the State into whose territory the non-scheduled service is operated.

The regulatory distinction scheduled and non-scheduled services is now fading away in the more developed air transport markets. Reference is made to the regulation of the EU internal air transport market, discussed in section 3.2 of Chapter 3, and the EU-US agreement on air transport, discussed in section 10.3 of Chapter 2. Both regimes apply to the operation of scheduled and non-scheduled services.

---

89. *See,* ICAO Doc. 7278-C/841, at 3.
90. *See also,* ICAO Doc. 7278-C/841 (10 May 1952), *Definition of a Scheduled International Air Service.*

3.3.6   Safety Regulation (ICAO)

The protection of safety is the principal objective of the Chicago Convention. The rule-making power for safety is vested in the central and multilateral level of ICAO.[91] ICAO is responsible for the establishment of technical rules which are laid down in nineteen Annexes attached to the Chicago Convention, comprising Standards and Recommended Practices, and are also referred to as SARPs.[92] They are designed to implement the articles of the Convention and regulate the following subjects:

    (1) Personnel Licensing
    (2) Rules of the Air
    (3) Meteorological Service for International Air Navigation
    (4) Aeronautical Charts
    (5) Units of Measurement to be Used in Air and Ground Operations
    (6) Operation of Aircraft
    (7) Aircraft Nationality and Registration Marks
    (8) Airworthiness of Aircraft
    (9) Facilitation
    (10) Aeronautical Telecommunications
    (11) Air Traffic Services
    (12) Search and Rescue
    (13) Aircraft Accident Investigation
    (14) Aerodromes
    (15) Aeronautical Information Services
    (16) Environmental Protection
    (17) Security
    (18) Safe Transport of Dangerous Goods by Air
    (19) Safety Management.

The Annexes contain a great number of definitions to explain the meaning of terms used in the 'Standards' and the 'Recommended Practices'. 'Standards' are any specifications 'the uniform application of which is recognized as necessary for the safety or regularity of international air navigation'. 'Recommended practices' are not of a mandatory nature but are considered as desirable.

Departures from Standards must be notified to the ICAO Council under Article 38 of the Convention. States do not always comply with this obligation: they may depart from, that is, not implement and enforce a Standard without notifying ICAO of such a move.

SARPs do not have treaty status. For SARPs to have legal force they must be implemented in national law, in accordance with national, including constitutional, procedures for the implementation of international rules in national regulations.

---

91. *See*, section 4.1 of this Chapter.
92. *See*, J. Huang, *Aviation Safety and ICAO* 43–68 (2009).

The legal status of SARPS has raised questions in courts,[93] in literature[94] and in practice. Standards have been attributed binding force; this is especially so if national law treats them as part of the Chicago Convention and attaches them, for instance, to their national aviation codes as secondary regulations. In yet other cases they are regarded as guidance material or 'soft law', as States may choose not to comply with them. Indeed, Article 54(l) of the Chicago Convention dictates that the ICAO Council must, as a 'matter of convenience', adopt SARPs and attach them to this Convention.

While safety standards are made on the global level, ICAO's sanction mechanism is limited.[95] That said, ICAO powers contain certain enforcement powers. In 2001, the ICAO General Assembly adopted a resolution encouraging ICAO Contracting States to implement SARPs "by all available means."[96] Safety oversight must help to strengthen the legal force of ICAO SARPs which are so vital for the 'safe and orderly' development of international civil aviation.[97] As remarked in section 3.3.2.3 above, this concern has to some extent been addressed by the introduction on the part of ICAO of the mandatory Universal Safety Oversight Audit Programme USOAP.[98] Thus, whereas ICAO powers contain certain enforcement powers, the US and the EU have established policies and regulations designed to enforce safety standards internationally.[99]

There is an increasing tendency to go beyond the level of minimum standards, and to better monitor the surveillance system.[100] The result is a growing number of authorities engaged in safety regulation and enforcement thereof. Another concern is that a balance must be found between the promotion of safety and the protection of the environment. For instance, the Single European Sky (SES) of the EU attempts to resolve that dilemma by promoting at the same time safety and the protection of the environment.[101]

---

93. *See, British Caledonian Airways Ltd* v. *Langhorne Bond, Federal Aviation Administration and others,* United States Court of Appeals, District of Colombia, Decision of 2 September 1981; 665 F.2d 1153 (*British Caledonian* v. *Bond,* C.A.D.C. 1981); Cour d'appel de Colmar (Court of Appeals of Colmar), decision of 9 April 1998, Case No. 09700470, Public prosecutor (*Ministère public*) c *Michel Asseline et autres* on the Air France crash at the Mont Saint Odile; *De Vereniging Bewonersgroep tegen Vliegtuigoverlast* v. *Gemeente Rotterdam,* Rechtbank (District court) Rotterdam (The Netherlands), Case No: APV 98/2091-S1; *B.A.R. Belgium, NV Sabena and Deutsche Lufthansa* v. *De Gemeente* (Community) *Zaventem*; Raad van State (Belgium State Council), decision of 5 May 2005; Case Nos 69.837/XII-2441; 69.876/ XII-2442; 74.820/XII-755; 74.821/XII-754; &76.712/XII-795.
94. *See,* J. Huang, *Aviation Safety and ICAO* 58–66 (2009) (PhD thesis Leiden University).
95. *See,* J. Huang, *Aviation Safety and ICAO* 163–238 (2009).
96. *See,* ICAO GA 33d Session, ICAO Doc. 9797 A33-TE; for the implementation of SARPs *see,* sections 2.1 and 2.2 of Chapter 6.
97. *See,* Preamble of the Chicago Convention.
98. *See,* J. Huang, *Aviation Safety and ICAO* 69–71 (2009); *see also,* section 2.3 of Chapter 6.
99. The US FAA supervising the US International Aviation Safety Assessment (IASA) programme, whereas the EU has its 'black listing' legislation as to which *see,* section 2.5.2 of Chapter 7.
100. *See,* section 3.2 of Chapter 6.
101. *See,* section 5.2 of Chapter 3, and: D. Calleja Crespo and P.M.J. Mendes de Leon, *Achieving the Single European Sky* (2011).

3.3.7 Security Regulation (ICAO)

3.3.7.1 The Establishment of Prohibited and Restricted Areas

In special circumstances contracting States to the Chicago Convention have the right to restrict or prohibit flying over their territory. Article 9 concerns bans and restrictions in exceptional circumstances and for reasons of public safety or military necessity; this provision reads as follows:

> (a) Each contracting State may, for reasons of military necessity or public safety, restrict or prohibit uniformly the aircraft of other States from flying over certain areas of its territory …;
> (b) Each contracting State reserves also the right, in exceptional circumstances or during a period of emergency, or in the interest of public safety, and with immediate effect, temporarily to restrict or prohibit flying over the whole or any part of its territory …;
> (c) Each contracting State, under such regulations as it may prescribe, may require any aircraft entering the areas contemplated in subparagraphs
> (a) or (b) above to effect a landing as soon as practicable thereafter at some designated airport within its territory.

Article 9 is interesting because it highlights the tendency of States to put their own interests first in certain circumstances like political aspirations, military necessity or public safety.[102] This point was also put forward in connection with the tragic accident of flight MH17 on 17 July 2014, killing 298 people on board the aircraft. While Ukraine had closed its airspace for civil aircraft till FL320, the question has been raised whether this State should not have prohibited flying in the entire airspace column above the area where rebels were controlling it.[103] Article 9, like Article 1, clearly and unmistakably reflects both the old principle of the sovereignty of a State over the airspace above its territory and the priority given by States to safeguarding their interests. In 2010, the Icelandic volcano, Eyjafjallajökull, erupted on 15 April. This event led to closure of the national airspace, extending to a height of 80 to 100 km, in several EU Member States. Airspace, or part thereof to the extent necessary in the interest of public safety, should then be closed to all traffic.

The above-mentioned provision pertaining to the sovereign power of a State to close – or not to close – its airspace, placed in an *international law* context, is mitigated

---

102. *See also*, section 3.3.7.2 of this Chapter discussing the India-Pakistan dispute on the establishment of a prohibited areas in the period between 1914 and 1947 in areas located between the two countries; *see also*, D.S. Bhatti, H. Drion and P.P. Heller, *Prohibited Areas in International Civil Aviation*, U.S. and Canadian Aviation Reports 109 (1953).
103. *See*, Stefan A. Kaiser, *Legal Considerations about the Loss of Malaysia Airlines Flight MH17 in Eastern Ukraine*, 40 Air & Space Law 107–121 (2015); N. Knittlmayer, *International Obligation to Close the Air Space over 'Conflict Zones'?* 65(1) Zeitschrift für Luft- und Weltraumrecht 44 (2016).

by the introduction of so-called 'no-fly orders' by the UN Security Council.[104] These orders forbid States to make use of the airspace above their territory, or parts thereof, and are issued for certain areas of armed conflict for reasons of humanitarian intervention. Their aim is to prevent or diminish aerial aggression against groups of the population in those areas. By special decision of the UN Security Council military aircraft operating on behalf of the UN may be allowed to enforce the no-fly orders. However, the legal basis for these orders is to be found in the UN Charter and not in the Chicago Convention.[105] Reference is made to Article 89 of the Chicago Convention,[106] allowing States to disregard the provisions of this Convention in case of war or emergency. In 2011, the UN Security Council decided to establish a ban on all flights, except for humanitarian flights, in the airspace of the Libyan Arab Jamahiriya in order to help protect civilians.[107]

National authorities, for instance, the US Federal Aviation Authority (FAA) publish lists of countries which have established prohibited areas which are communicated to airlines through Notice to Airmen (NOTAM).[108] They may impose sanctions in case airlines fly through prohibited areas.[109] ICAO is coordinating work in this field as it has endorsed updated editions of the Global Aviation Safety Plan and the Global Air Navigation Plan as the global strategic directions for safety and air navigation.[110]

---

104. *See,* S. Hobe and M. Lysander Fremuth, '*No Fly Zones*': *Connectivity Between International Law and Air Law in Case of Libya* (in German; English summary); and S. Kaiser, *No Fly Zones Established by the United Nations Security Council,* both published in 60(2) Zeitschrift für Luft- und Weltraumrecht 2011.

105. *See,* P. Malanczuk, *Humanitarian Intervention and the Legitimacy of Force* (1993); M. Milde, *Aeronautical Consequences of the Iraqi Invasion of Kuwait,* 16 Air Law 63–75 (1991); and H.A. Wassenbergh, *Iraq/Kuwait and International Civil Aviation Relations,* 63 ITA Magazine 8–15 (September-October 1990). The Treaty on Open Skies of 24 March 1992 of the Conference on Security and Co-operation in Europe which allows States Parties to carry out aerial monitoring of other States Parties in the cause of prevention of armed conflicts and weapons control. Here air sovereignty is thus made subordinate to the promotion of peace.

106. Art. 89: "In case of war, the provisions of this Convention shall not affect the freedom of action of any of the contracting States affected, whether as belligerents or as neutrals. The same principle shall apply in the case of any contracting State which declares a state of national emergency and notifies the fact to the Council."

107. *See,* SC/10200 adopted at the 6489th Meeting of the UN Security Council on 17 March 2011, at: http://www.un.org/News/Press/docs/2011/sc10200.doc.htm; *See* S. Hobe and M. Lysander Fremuth, '*No Fly Zones*': *Connectivity Between International Law and Air Law in Case of Libya* (in German; English summary); and S. Kaiser, *No Fly Zones Established by the United Nations Security Council,* both published in 60(2) Zeitschrift für Luft- und Weltraumrecht 2011.

108. For the US FAA, *see,* https://www.faa.gov/air_traffic/publications/us_restrictions/.

109. On 14 November 2015, Up in the Sky announced that the US Department of Transportation (DoT) imposed a fine of USD 185,000 because this airline flew through a prohibited area which was announced as such in the concerned *Notice to Airman* (NOTAM).

110. *See,* ICAO Assembly Resolution A39-12, *ICAO global planning for safety and air navigation* (2016); *see also,* R.I.R Abeyratne, *Flight MH370 and Global Flight Tracking: The ICAO Reaction,* 63 Zeitschrift für Luft- und Weltraumrecht 544–558 (2014), and S. Kaiser, *Legal Considerations about the Missing Malaysia Airlines Flight MH370,* 39(4/5) Air & Space Law 235–244 (2014); R. Abeyratne, *Outcome of the 39th Session of the International Civil Aviation Organization,* 42(1) Air & Space Law 13–28 (2017).

3.3.7.2   Attacks Against Aviation[111]

Following the shooting down of Korean Air flight KE 007 in (then) Soviet airspace Article 3*bis* was added to the Chicago Convention. This provision recognises among other things that every State must refrain from resorting to the use of weapons against civil aircraft in flight.[112] Naturally, it only applies to *international* civil aviation. Hence, it was not applicable to US efforts to safeguard their national interests following the attacks on the World Trade Centre towers on '9/11'.

The above-mentioned Article 3*bis* whilst being approved in 1984 did not come into effect until 1998 on receipt of the ratifications of Guinea and Cuba. This latter was ironic in that Cuba itself had been the subject of a UN Security Council Resolution (1067) in 1996 condemning it over the shooting down of two US civil aircraft by the Cuban Air Force. The Security Council held that the downing violated international law and the principle that States must refrain from using weapons against civil aircraft and called upon Cuba to join with other States in complying with their obligations under the Chicago Convention.[113]

The 9/11 (2001) tragedies in New York and Washington DC placed security oversight very much higher on the agenda of policy makers. In 2003, ICAO started to draw up an audit programme designed to organise mandatory, systematic and harmonised aviation security audits promoting global aviation security, also referred to as *Universal Aviation Security Audit Programme* (USAP). The USAP programmes are based on the approach made in safety audits. They are targeted at identifying – rather than 'overseeing' – deficiency in a national security system, and to provide recommendations for improvement. ICAO Annex 17 on Aviation Security forms the basis for the audits; whereas the principle of confidentiality is respected.[114]

---

111. *See,* M. Milde, *Law and Aviation Security,* in: T.L. Masson and P.M.J. Mendes de Leon, *Air and Space Law: De Lege Ferenda,* Essays in Honour of Henri A. Wassenbergh 93–98 (1992).
112. *See,* ICAO Doc. 9436 and 9 Air Law 190 (1984); *see also,* B. Cheng, *The Destruction of KAL Flight KE007, and Art. 3bis of the Chicago Convention,* in: J.W. Storm van 's Gravesande and A. van der Veen Vonk (eds), *Air Worthy* 47–74; M. Kido, *The Korean Airlines Incident on September 1, 1983, and Some Measures Following It,* 62 Journal of Air Law and Commerce 1049 (1997); A.A. van Wijk; *Visual and Oral Signals Between Aircraft in Flight as a Means to Convey Instructions by a State,* Air Worthy 235–289; and I. Awford, *Civil Liability concerning Unlawful Interference with Civil Aviation,* in: *Aviation Security: How to Safeguard International Air Transport* (proceedings of a conference held at the Peace Palace, The Hague, 22–23 January 1987), 47–73 (1987); *see also,* A.F. Lowenfeld et al., *Agora: The Downing of Iran Air Flight 655,* 83 American Journal of International Law 318–341 (1989). Art. 3 *bis* entered into force on 1 October 1998; *see,* J. Huang, *Aviation Safety and ICAO* 85–114 (2009); B.E. Foont, *Shooting Down Civilian Aircraft: Is There an International Law?* 72 Journal of Air Law and Commerce 695 (2007).
113. *See,* M. Milde, *Interception of civil aircraft* vs. *misuse of civil aviation,* XI Annals of Air & Space Law 105–130 (1986).
114. *See,* J. Huang, *Aviation Safety and ICAO* 72–73 (2009).

3.3.7.3   Concluding Remarks

Various sections of this chapter addressed the principal importance of security for the safe operation of international air services. The Chicago Convention and ICAO rules and policies continue to address its relevance.[115]

Article 9 of the Chicago Convention forms a clear expression of the sovereignty principle laid down in Article 1. States remain free to close, or not to close, the airspace under the circumstances mentioned in this provision, and to judge the existence of such circumstances. The restriction to their jurisdictional powers lies in the obligation to apply the non-discrimination principle with respect to the nationality of the aircraft. Finally, neither ICAO nor other States or public bodies can force another State to close its airspace for security reasons.

The same is true for Article 3bis of the Chicago Convention which has also been referred to in connection with the above-mentioned accident involving the MH17 flight. It is to be hoped that States have at least a legal provision to point at when these attacks occur, and can thus blame the responsible State. As always, sanctions remain a sensitive remedy under international law because they are surrounded by, yet again, political motives and factors rather than legal considerations.

3.3.8   The Protection of the Environment

The protection of the environment is not regulated in the Chicago Convention. Annex 16, referred to above in section 3.3.6, contains SARPs on noise and emissions. Moreover, ICAO addresses this subject, among others, in the context of the Committee on Aviation Environmental Protection (CAEP), which carries out studies on the mitigation of noise and emissions caused by civil aircraft.

In October 2016,[116] the General Assembly of ICAO adopted a resolution for the establishment of Global Market Based Measures (GMBM) to offset CO_2 emissions from international aviation and contribute to carbon neutral growth from 2020 onwards; thus, an increase of emissions ought to be offset as the emitting airline should buy and surrender emission units generated by activities carried out in other economic sectors that will reduce CO_2 emissions. The scheme is also referred to as the *Carbon Offsetting and Reduction Scheme for International Aviation* (CORSIA). In the first phase, from 2021–2026, sixty-five countries including eighteen out of the top twenty 'emitting'

---

115. *See*, ICAO Resolution A39-18: *Consolidated statement of continuing ICAO policies related to aviation security*. This resolution stresses the urgent need for ICAO States to accede to the aviation security conventions which are examined in Chapter 12, below, and to implement measures for the prevention of unlawful acts which are commensurate with the current threat to international civil aviation, while keeping track with the new methods of threatening it, such as cyber-attacks, and the SARPs laid down in Annex 17 on this matter.

116. *See*, U. Erling, *International Aviation Emissions Under International Civil Aviation Organization's Global Market Based Measure: Ready for Offsetting?* 42(1) Air & Space Law 1–12 (2017); R. Abeyratne, *Climate Justice and COP21 – The Aviation Perspective*, 65(2) Zeitschrift für Luft- und Weltraumrecht 192 (2016), and F. Gaspari, *Aviation and Environmental Protection after the 2015 Paris Agreement: From Regulatory Unilateralism Toward International Cooperation*, 15(2) Issues in Aviation Law and Policy (2016).

States, that is, the European countries, the US and Canada, China, Japan, Singapore, Mexico, Australia and New Zealand and Turkey, will participate on a voluntary basis. Apart from a couple of small, land locked and developing States, participation will be mandatory in the second phase running from 2027 and 2035.[117] Meanwhile new Standards, including those on Monitoring Verification and Reporting (MRV), will be drawn up and included in Chapter IV of ICAO Annex 16 on the Environment.

As yet a number of questions have not yet been answered. Among them are the fate and the scope of the EU Emission Trade Scheme/System (EU) ETS, and enforcement of the new regime.

3.3.9 Dispute Settlement under the Chicago Convention

3.3.9.1 The Role of ICAO

Chapter XVIII of the Chicago Convention regulates *Disputes and Default*. In the words of the International Court of Justice (ICJ): "[a] dispute is a disagreement on a point of law or fact, a conflict of legal views or of interests between two persons" and stresses that "its determination must turn on an examination of the facts."[118] If the object of the dispute is the interpretation or application of the Convention, and the dispute cannot be resolved by negotiation, the ICAO Council is charged with the task of deciding the matter.[119]

The Rules for the *Settlement of Differences* which were adopted by the ICAO Council in 1957 contain an option for what is termed an 'expert opinion'.[120] When a case is brought to the attention of the Council, it may, during the procedure, entrust any individual, body, bureau, commission or other organisation that it may select, with the task of carrying out an enquiry or giving an expert opinion. So far, no use has been made of this possibility. Moreover, it is confined to the conditions set out in the said rules: an expert opinion, be it legal or not, can only be asked for by the Council if a case has been submitted to it by the parties to the dispute. Hence, the parties in disagreement about a legal question cannot do so.[121]

---

117. *See*, ICAO, Resolution A39-3 (2016): *Consolidated Statements continuing ICAO policies and practices related to environmental protection – Global Market-based Measure (MBM) scheme*; *see also*, H. Hameed, *Cutting Global Aviation Emissions – How Important Is a Global Market Based Measure in Mitigating Aviation's Carbon Footprint?* 63 Zeitschrift für Luft- und Weltraumrecht 518 (2014).
118. *See*, ICJ, Press Release Unofficial, No. 2011/9 1 April 2011, *Application of the International Convention on the Elimination of All Forms of Racial Discrimination* (*Georgia* v. *Russian Federation*), Preliminary objections.
119. Art. 84 of the Chicago Convention; *see also*, ICAO Assembly Resolution, *Authorization to the Council to Act as an Arbitral Body*, ICAO Do 9848; *see further*, Pablo Mendes de Leon, *Settlement of Disputes in Air and Space Law*, in: C.-J. Cheng (ed.), Proceedings of the International Conference on *Air Transport and Space Applications in a New World* (Tokyo, 2–5 June 1993) 329–339 (1995); M. Milde, *International Air Law and ICAO* 198–209 (2016).
120. ICAO Doc. 7782/2 (1959) as amended on 10 November 1975.
121. *See*, M. Milde, *International Air Law and ICAO* 185–195 (2016); L. Weber, *International Civil Aviation Organization – An Introduction* (2007); E. Berisha, *At the Boundaries of the Chicago*

3.3.9.2   Cases Before the ICAO Council

In 1958, a dispute between Jordan and the United Arab Republic on the imposition of air navigation charges had an outcome which was similar to that detailed in the India-Pakistan case which is discussed below.

A well-known case concerns that between India and Pakistan in which India claimed that Pakistan was denying her aircraft the right to fly over certain parts of Pakistan's territory in violation of Articles 5, 6 and 9 of the Chicago Convention and the International Air Services Transit Agreement of 1944; hereafter also referred to as the Transit Agreement. Pakistan had declared a certain part of its territory a 'prohibited area' under Article 9 of the Chicago Convention. This area was located under an air route from India to Pakistan. According to India, the 'prohibited area' was unreasonable and unnecessary, and a non-uniformly supervised prohibition. Moreover, an Iranian air carrier was allowed to fly through what was declared a 'prohibited area'. This was in violation of the non-discrimination provision which was contained in the mentioned Article 9. The ICAO Council invited parties to enter into direct negotiations. A few months later, representatives of the two countries announced that the dispute had been settled by agreement in an amicable atmosphere of extreme cordiality, and that the decision was a triumph of reason and goodwill to see the other's point of view.[122] The dispute was resolved upon negotiations between the parties, helped by an intervention on the part of a Working Group of the ICAO Council.[123]

The President of the ICAO Council mediated in a dispute between Cuba and the United States in a dispute on the transit rights of aircraft registered in Cuba through the airspace of the United States. The ICAO Council confirmed the mediation efforts of its President.[124]

Another case also involved India and Pakistan. India had unilaterally suspended overflight of Indian territory by Pakistani civil aircraft, on and from 4 February 1971, as a consequence of a hijacking incident involving the diversion of an Indian aircraft to Pakistan. There had been hostilities between the two countries in 1965, and after cessation they adopted the Tashkent Declaration of 1966. According to that Declaration, overflights could be resumed. India maintained that overflights could be performed, not on the basis of the Chicago Convention and the Transit Agreement, but of a 'special regime'. Pakistan was of the opinion that, since the adoption of the Tashkent Declaration, the Chicago Convention and the Transit Agreement were indeed applicable. Pakistan had submitted it to the ICAO Council, to hear and determine its claim. India, however, denied Pakistan's right to place the case before the Council, because its

---

Convention – ICAO's Role in Civil Aviation Affairs in Kosovo, 13(1) Issues in Aviation Law and Policy 159–176 (23016); and T. Buergenthal, Law Making in the International Civil Aviation Organization 123 (1969).

122. ICAO Bulletin of January/February 1953 at 26 and R.T. Dicker, The Use of Arbitration in the Settlement of Bilateral Air Rights Disputes, The Vanderbilt International Law Journal 131–132 (1967/1968); see also, B. Cheng, The Law of International Air Transport 101–103 (1962).
123. ICAO Doc. 7367 (A7-P1), (1953) at 74–76 ICAO.
124. ICAO Press Release P10 05/98.

substance was covered by the Chicago Convention and the Transit Agreement. These treaties were not revived by the Tashkent Declaration.

The ICAO Council has been involved in yet other cases. They include, amongst others, the case of *Jordan v. UAR*, concerning a ban on overflying UAR territory.[125]

In 2001, the ICAO Council also helped to solve a dispute between the US and 15 EU Member States on the legality of an EU regulation on the admissible level of noise production of aircraft which was designed to ban the operation of hush-kitted aircraft into and from EU airports. In March 2000, the US challenged the EU Regulation before the ICAO Council and claimed that the EU measures exceeded those of Annex 16 laid down in ICAO resolutions. The said EU regulation affected US aviation and aircraft manufacturing interests. The EU withdrew the contested regulation and replaced it with a 'milder' but perhaps 'noisier' regulation, with intervention from the Secretary General of ICAO.[126]

3.3.9.3 Appeal Procedure Before the ICJ

The Convention also provides for an appeal procedure, either before an ad hoc arbitration tribunal or before the ICJ of the UN.[127] Moreover, there are sanctions if a State does not abide by a decision of either the tribunal or the ICJ. The ICJ can be involved with aviation disputes in three ways:

(1) Directly, that is if States have accepted the Court's jurisdiction pursuant to Article 36(2) of the Court's Statute.
(2) Via the provisions pertaining to dispute settlement of the Convention of Tokyo (1963), The Hague ('hijacking') (1970) and Montreal ('sabotage') (1970).
(3) As an appellate body following the procedure foreseen in Article 84 of the Chicago Convention, and section II(2) of the International Air Services Transit Agreement of 1944, after the ICAO Council has taken a decision on the question put before it.

---

125. Before the disagreement became a dispute under the Chicago Convention, parties settled this matter among themselves, with informal assistance from the ICAO Council ICAO Doc. C-WP/2788 (1958) at 5.
126. *See*, S.D. Murphy, *Contemporary Practice of the United States Relating to International Law*, which appeared in 95(2) American Journal of International Law (April 2001), accessible via: http://www.abanet.org/adminlaw/fall02/aijl_intl_artical.pdf; *see also*, Christian Kaufmann, *Hushkits: Another Dispute Between Europe and the United States*, 50 Zeitschrift für Luft- und Weltraumrecht 330 (2001).
127. Art. 84 of the Chicago Convention, third sentence. *See*, G. Guillaume, *Les affaires touchant au droit aérien devant la Cour internationale de justice*, in: Mariette Benkö and Walter Kröll, *Air & Space Law in the 21st Century*, Liber Amicorum for Karl-Heinz Böckstiegel 75–87 (2001); *see, also*, S. Shubber, *The Contribution of the International Court of Justice to Air Law*, in: V. Lowe and M. Fitzmaurice (eds), *Fifty Years of the International Court of Justice: Essays in honour of Sir Robert Jennings* Part III, Chapter 16 (2007).

Since the early 1950s, the ICJ has been seized a number of times following the second procedure mentioned above. Most of these cases were dismissed due to lack of jurisdiction, or because the parties had reached a settlement just before the oral hearings. Only one case, that is, *Libya v. United States*, following the Lockerbie accident of the bombing of flight PanAm 103 on 21 December 1988, the ICJ declared that it had jurisdiction, and the claims from Libya admissible,[128] but the two cases brought before ICJ were removed from the Court's List on 10 September 2003, at the joint request of the Parties, as Libya had agreed that the two accused, be tried by five Scottish Judges sitting in a neutral court, in the Netherlands.[129]

3.3.9.4 Sanctions

When a State does not comply with the decision of the ICAO Council pursuant to the above dispute settlement mechanism provided by the Chicago Convention, airlines of the disobedient State may be denied operation through the airspace of other contracting States.[130] The drafters of the Chicago Convention even went one step further. If there are contracting States which, despite the final and binding decision of the arbitration tribunal or the ICJ, still allow airlines of the disobedient State to operate through their airspace, the voting power of the State allowing operation of the airline of the disobedient State through its airspace may be suspended in the ICAO Assembly.[131]

Do those provisions have any practical use? In the purview of public international law in general, political interests more often than not prevent States from submitting themselves to binding legal procedures. That may explain why the dispute settlement procedure of the Chicago Convention has hardly been applied while the sanctions mechanism has never been used.

3.3.9.5 Concluding Remarks

While the task of the interpretation of the provisions of the Chicago Convention is a legal one, it is entrusted to a body consisting of representatives of its contracting States. This state of affairs casts doubt on the quality of a legal indication which is assigned to the Council.[132]

The above section also shows that States prefer to solve their disagreements by negotiations rather than legal procedures. Concerns about losing face, and the wish to achieve a result via diplomatic remedies through compromising, appear to support the

---

128. *See*, International Court of Justice, Case concerning *Questions of Interpretation and Application of the 1971 Montreal Convention arising from the Aerial Incident at Lockerbie* (*Libyan Arab Jamahiriya v. United States of America*), Judgment of 27 February 1998.
129. *See*, Agreement between the Government of the United Kingdom of Great Britain and Northern Ireland and the Government of the Kingdom of the Netherlands Concerning *a Scottish Trial in The Netherlands*, Treaty No. 35699, 2062 UNTS 82–99 (1988).
130. Art. 86 of the Chicago Convention.
131. Art. 87 of the Chicago Convention.
132. *See also*, M. Milde, *International Air Law and ICAO* 209 (2016).

view that international civil aviation must be performed by preservation "of friendship and understanding among the nations and peoples of the world" in "order to avoid friction" as dictated by the Preamble of this convention.

4 INTERNATIONAL ORGANISATIONS (WORLDWIDE)

4.1 ICAO (the International Civil Aviation Organisation)[133]

4.1.1 Objectives

ICAO became a Specialised Agency of the United Nations Organisation on 13 May 1947, and is for that reason invested with special powers, pursuant to Article 64 of the Chicago Convention.[134]

The objectives of ICAO are laid down in the Chicago Convention as to which *see* Article 44. ICAO has as its principal objectives the promotion of safety and the orderly development of civil aviation throughout the world.[135] ICAO must also contribute to taking measures regarding aviation security and the protection of the environment. Since the 9/11 events in the US, and the debate around global warming, these latter tasks receive special attention from ICAO and its bodies.

ICAO's tasks in the economic field are limited. The Chicago Convention stipulates that "economic waste caused by unreasonable competition"[136] must be prevented, whereas the Preamble dictates that international air transport services should be established "on the basis of equality of opportunity and operated soundly and economically." However, these principles are not elaborated by ICAO in binding agreements or standards. Economic regulation of international air transport services is basically but not exclusively dealt with under bilateral ASAs between States and between States and regional organisations, and arrangements made by regional organisations such as the EU.[137]

ICAO is mandated to regulate and introduce measures for the benefit of *civil* aircraft and *civil* aviation.[138] As explained in section 3.3.2.2, above, State aircraft are

---

133. *See,* R.D. van Dam, *Regulating International Civil Aviation – An ICAO Perspective,* in: T.L. Masson and P.M.J. Mendes de Leon (eds), *Air and Space Law: De Lege Ferenda,* Essays in Honour of Henri A. Wassenbergh 11–26 (1992); P.M.J. Mendes de Leon, *The International Civil Aviation Organization* (ICAO), 5 The Max Planck Encyclopedia of International Law 413–417 (2012).

134. *See,* M. Milde, *International Air Law and ICAO* 185–195 (2016); L. Weber, *International Civil Aviation Organization – An Introduction* (2007); T. Buergenthal, *Law Making in the International Civil Aviation Organization* 123 (1969); A.D. Groenewege, *The Compendium of International Civil Aviation* 183–218 (2003); G. Guillaume, *ICAO At The Beginning of the 21st Century* 33(4/5) Air & Space Law 313–317 (2008).

135. *See,* section 3.3.6 above; *see also,* J.A. Urban, *International Civil Aviation Organization Initiatives Versus Industry Initiatives: A Look at How Commercially Motivated Transactions Increase Aviation Safety,* 81(4) Journal of Air Law and Commerce 683 (2016).

136. *See,* Art. 44(e).

137. *See,* the EU Commission Officer O. Onidi, *A Critical Perspective on ICAO,* 33 Air and Space Law 38 (2008).

138. *See,* section 3.3.2.2, above.

subject to other regimes, including national law and international regulations. Domestic civil aviation is generally, but not always, is a matter of State responsibility, without intervention from ICAO.

4.1.2 The Assembly

The principal and sovereign body of ICAO is the Assembly.[139] The Assembly meets at least once every three years. The Assembly is convened by the Council, in accordance with Article 48. All Member States have an equal right to representation whereby each State has one vote. The Assembly's functions are summarised in Article 49. An important task concerns the adoption of Resolutions on all aspects of international civil aviation, including but not limited to constitutional and general policy matters; membership and relations with Contracting States; air navigation; airworthiness; accident and incident investigation; licensing of personnel; air transport; establishment of charges; taxation and facilitation; financing of the organisation; unlawful interference with international civil aviation; and organisation and personnel.[140] The legal effect of Assembly Resolutions must be determined in accordance with international law principles on the legal force of resolutions adopted by the supreme bodies of other organisations, including the UN.[141]

Decisions are taken by majority vote, or, preferably, by consensus. Each contracting State has one voice. In special cases, such as admission of new members, an amendment of the Chicago Convention decisions must be taken by a qualified majority. Membership of ICAO, and consequently, participation in the work of the Assembly, is open for States. There is no provision regarding membership of Regional Economic Integration Organisations (REIO).

4.1.3 The Council

The Council is a permanent body whose head office is located in Montreal, Canada. It may be regarded as the Organisation's executive committee.

At present thirty-six States are represented in the Council pursuant to an election by the General Assembly for a period of three years. Council members are elected in

---

139. *See,* P.A. Fossungu, *The ICAO Assembly: The Most Unsupreme of Supreme Organs in the United Nations System? A Critical Analysis of Assembly Sessions,* 26 Transportation Law Journal 1 (1998).

140. *See,* ICAO Secretary General, *ICAO Assembly Resolutions in Force* (as of 8 October 2010); ICAO Doc. 9958 (2010), and R. Abeyratne, *Outcome of the 39th Session of the International Civil Aviation Organization,* 42(1) Air & Space Law 13–28 (2017).

141. *See,* H.G. Schermers and N.M. Blokker, *International Institutional Law* 757 (2003); K. Skubiszewski, *Enactment of Law by International Organizations,* XLI British Yearbook of International Law 226 (1965–1966); H. Mossler, *The International Society as a Legal* Community 88–89 (1980); R. Higgins, *The Development of International Law Through the Political Organs of the United Nations* 2–5 (1963); N.D. White, *The Law of International Organizations* 174 (2005); J. Huang, *Aviation Safety and ICAO* 182–207 (2009).

accordance with geographical and professional qualification criteria. States that make a significant contribution to the development of air transport are adequately represented in this body.

Council decisions are taken by a normal majority vote of its members. The Council elects its President for a period of three years. He/she is not a member of the Council and has no voting power, but must convene meetings of the Council and represent it.

A principal function of the ICAO Council concerns the adoption of *Standards and Recommended Practices* (SARPs) which are laid down in the nineteen technical Annexes to the Chicago Convention and Procedures for Air Navigation Services (PANS). Also, the Council has a judicial function as is it is tasked by the Chicago Convention to settle a dispute between two or more Contracting States by way of a decision as to which *see* above.

4.1.4   The Air Navigation Commission

Another important ICAO body is the Air Navigation Commission, which is also created by the Chicago Convention. The Air Navigation Commission assists the Council with respect to the development of the above-mentioned SARPs and PANS. The Air Navigation Commission makes proposals for SARPs before their adoption by the Council and advises the Council regarding all matters which may help to advance air navigation.

The Air Navigation Commission is composed of nineteen members[142] who are appointed by the Council on the basis of professional expertise while taking into account geographical representation. The members of the Air Navigation Commission carry out their tasks in accordance with personal technical and professional expertise rather than by virtue of a mandate of a State. The Council also appoints the President of this Commission.

4.1.5   The Secretariat

The *Secretariat* is headed by the Secretary General. The Chicago Convention does not mention the Secretariat. The Secretariat must provide technical, legal and administrative support to the Council. It is sub-divided into five departments called *Bureaux*, to wit:

■ the Air Navigation Bureau;
■ the Air Transport Bureau;
■ the Technical Cooperation Bureau;

---

142. Membership increased from fifteen to nineteen by resolution of the Council of 25 May 2010 adopted at General Assembly on 8 November 2010 (amendment to Art. 56 of the Convention; ICAO Doc. 7162-C/825 revised).

- the Legal and External Relations Bureau;
- the Bureau for Administration and Services.

The Legal Bureau is charged with the codification of international public and private air law. It makes proposals for new conventions and amendments of the Chicago Convention. It is also responsible for the establishment of Standards and Recommended Practices providing technical rules designed to improve aviation safety, security and the protection of the environment.

4.2 The International Air Transport Association (IATA)

This organisation occupies an important place in the world of international air transport. Unlike ICAO, IATA is not an intergovernmental body, but a private organisation of scheduled airlines. It was originally set up by six airline companies, on 28 August 1919, as the 'International Air Traffic Association'. IATA's objectives are set out in its incorporating Act; they are to:[143]

(a) promote safe, regular and economical air transport for the benefit of the peoples of the world, to foster air commerce and to study the problems connected therewith;
(b) provide means for collaboration among the airline enterprises engaged directly or indirectly in international transport service;
(c) co-operate with ICAO and other international organisations.

IATA's main purposes lie in the technical, regulatory and commercial sector. Its technical duties were designed from the beginning to achieve safer, more regular and more economical air traffic; in the commercial sector, IATA's activities were expected to create the best possible conditions for all categories of customers. An important function is performed by IATA's *Clearing House,* which operates under the ultimate responsibility of its Financial Committee. This Organisation was originally established in London in 1947, but later transferred to Geneva. It acts as a clearing institute for accounts between airlines, including those accumulated from ticket sales and other sources. Non-IATA members can also qualify for admission to the Clearing House.
As Haanappel mentions:

> Most of IATA's activities find their expression in Resolutions and Recommended Practices adopted by the Traffic Conferences. IATA Traffic Conference Resolutions can be defined as agreements adopted by the *unanimous* vote of the Traffic Conference members. They become binding on the members when approved by interested governments.[144]

IATA's *Conditions of Carriage and of Contract* and *Standard Ground Handling Agreement* (SHGA) designed to draw up uniform provisions for the contractual

---

143. *See also,* A.D. Groenewege, *The Compendium of International Civil Aviation* 219-270 (2003).
144. *See,* P.P.C. Haanappel, *Ratemaking in International Air Transport* 57 (1978).

relationship between airline and passenger, airline and shipper of cargo, and airline and provider of ground handling services are adopted and used worldwide in airline contracts, airlines' contractual arrangements with providers of ground handling services and regional (EU) or domestic rules on slot allocation respectively.

IATA's *Worldwide Scheduling Guidelines* for slot allocation are used as a basis for domestic and regional (EU) rules on the subject. The scheduling process governs the allocation and exchange of slots at congested airports worldwide, on a fair, transparent and non-discriminatory basis, in consultation with the airline and airport coordinator communities.

Practically all airline companies involved in scheduled air transport have a seat in the organisation. It maintains or at least maintained close ties with the government authorities of Member States. Competition-related concerns have contributed to loosening those ties as governments increasingly promote consumer protection rather than the interests of 'their' airlines. Nonetheless, IATA's recommendations to governments, ICAO and other international organisations are always received with due respect and consideration. IATA's support for a multilateral agreement is meaningful.[145]

4.3 Other Organisations

Other important organisations are:

- The Airport Council International (ACI) has no less than 580 member airports operating 1650 airports in 179 countries.[146] ACI endeavours to enhance safety, security, economics, facilitation, technical standards, IT, economic and quality of service of its members.
- IFALPA, the International Federation of Airline Pilots' Association.
- CANSO, the Civil Air Navigation Services Organisation.
- OECD, the Organisation for Economic Cooperation and Development, based in Paris, which conducts studies into the benefits of liberalisation of air transport services.

5 REGIONAL ORGANISATIONS AND ARRANGEMENTS

5.1 European Civil Aviation Conference (ECAC)

European Civil Aviation Conference (ECAC), which is based in Paris, is an intergovernmental, pan-European organisation founded in 1955. It is composed of forty-four Member States. It offers a forum for discussion and decisions.

---

145. *See*, P.P.C. Haanappel, *The Law and Policy of Air and Outer Space: A Comparative Approach* 33–36 (2003).
146. *See further*, A.D. Groenewege, *The Compendium of International Civil Aviation* 271–278 (2003).

The objective of ECAC is to promote the continued development of a safe, efficient and sustainable European air transport system by seeking to harmonise civil aviation policies and practices amongst the Member States and to promote understanding on policy matters between them, and other parties.

At a 145th Directors General of Civil Aviation meeting, which was held on 3 December 2015, the policy statement on 'ECAC's Strategy for the Future' noted that ECAC, being Europe's largest and longest-standing aviation organisation, should cooperate with the European Union (EU), Eurocontrol and industry associations, and prioritise its role in order to:

- act as a pan-European aviation think-tank;
- support its Member States in developing harmonised pan-European positions and solutions; and
- serve as a centre of expertise for its Member States.

ECAC establishes arrangements, understandings and contacts with other regional organisations and States on civil aviation issues of common interest. It issues resolutions, recommendations and policy statements which are brought into effect by its Member States.

The main bodies of the ECAC are: the Plenary Conference in the form of Triennial Sessions and Special Plenary Sessions (meetings once every three years in Strasbourg); the meetings of Directors General of Civil Aviation (usually three times each year); groups established from time to time by Directors General of Civil Aviation to carry out specific tasks under the work programme. They are assisted by the ECAC's Secretariat under the direction of its Executive Secretary.

The ECAC Co-ordinating Committee (CC) coordinates the work of ECAC's bodies and associated bodies. It is headed by the President of ECAC, elected for a three-year term of office, a maximum of three Vice-Presidents and other members of the Committee, up to a maximum total of eleven.[147]

The President of ECAC serves as a Focal Point for External Relations. He is responsible for the conduct of relations with other European organisations, including the EU, in particular the Commission and EASA, and Eurocontrol, in order to achieve the coordination of policies of these European aviation organisations in regard to the region's external partners and in global aviation fora. Furthermore, the President of ECAC maintains relations with ECAC's sister organisations, namely, the Arab Civil Aviation Commission (ACAC), the African Civil Aviation Commission (AFCAC) and Latin American Civil Aviation Commission (LACAC),[148] and other governmental and non-governmental organisations in the civil aviation field, and with States world-wide.[149]

ECAC plays a key role in harmonising, in close cooperation with the EU, the pan-European position at major ICAO meetings. Such positions are developed at

---

147. *See*, Art. 10 of the constitution of ECAC and ECAC's Rules of Procedure.
148. *See*, briefly, section 5.3, below.
149. *See*, Terms of Reference: *Focal Point for External Relations*; adopted by the 163rd meeting of the Coordinating Committee on 20 March 2012.

ECAC/EU coordinating meetings. Consequently, forty-four ECAC Member States speak with one voice and develop common positions on issues of common interest as to which see for instance the pan-European approach towards the regulation of aircraft emissions as discussed in section 5.3.2 of Chapter 3.

In 1996 ECAC created the Legal Task Force which is composed of experts nominated by ECAC Members States. Its main objective is to examine legal questions and develop proposals for their solution. Furthermore, the Legal Task Force has been given a mandate to study and make recommendations on matters relating to public international air law; to discuss legal issues relevant to the work of ICAO with a view of facilitating and supporting the participation of ECAC Member States in the legal work of ICAO, for instance, in the ICAO Legal Committee, and coordinating ECAC common positions including but not limited to the preparation and implementation of international legal instruments, and submit reports and recommendations thereon to Directors General of Civil Aviation of ECAC Member States.

All in all, ECAC plays a prominent role in furthering the interests of European aviation at large. However, this role is sometimes overshadowed by the more articulated presence of the EU.

5.2   Eurocontrol

The European Organisation for the Safety of Air Navigation, known as Eurocontrol, has been created in 1960 pursuant to an international convention, and is tasked with the safety and management of air traffic operating in the airspace of its Member States, and States with which Eurocontrol has concluded agreements to that effect. It is, "committed to building, together with its partners, a SES that will deliver the Air Traffic Management (ATM) performance required for the twenty-first century and beyond." Eurocontrol has more members than the EU, that is, forty-one compared to twenty-eight.

Over time, Eurocontrol has made major achievements in the field of air traffic management. Examples of these include the organisation of air traffic in the combined airspaces of its Contracting States and the provision of air traffic services in the higher layers of the Benelux States and Northern Germany. Within the airspace of its Member States, Eurocontrol is also responsible for the establishment, billing and collection of route charges. The unit rate used for the calculation of route charges must be approved by Eurocontrol's Member States.[150]

In 1997, the Member States conceived the revised Convention in order to more efficiently cope with the growth of air traffic both in airspace and around airports. The amended Convention of 1981, referring to a European system organised jointly by the contracting States for the control of general air traffic in the upper airspace, had a more limited aim. The expansion of Eurocontrol's tasks is exemplified by the objective pertaining to the provision of a seamless system of air navigation services for both civil and military users. The Preamble mentions the establishment of 'standards' as one of

---

150. *See, Multilateral Agreement relating to Route Charges*, Art. 8.

the means to achieve the efficient organisation and safe management of European airspace. The amended Convention of 1981 was silent on both that objective and such means. In the meantime, the EU became involved with safety and efficiency of air traffic management so that the mandates of the two organisations began to overlap as evidenced by the EU's initiative to create a SES.[151]

Thus, the EASA[152] is now exercising rulemaking functions. EASA can use the enforcement powers and remedies which Eurocontrol does not possess.

Since 2011, Eurocontrol performs the role of Network Manager under the SES programme of the EU Commission.[153] The Network Manager is tasked to deal with performance questions strategically, operationally and technically. Its overarching mission is to contribute to the delivery of air traffic management's performance in the pan-European network in the areas of safety, capacity, environment/flight efficiency and cost-effectiveness.

On 12 December 2012, Eurocontrol and the EU signed an agreement establishing a new and stable framework for enhanced cooperation in matters such as Functional Airspace Blocks, international coordination, with special reference to ICAO and non-member States, data and statistics pertaining to air transport, airport policies and UAS. Also, it confirms Eurocontrol's role as the technical and operational arm of the EU in the development and implementation of its SES programme, including the promotion of civil-military coordination in which Eurocontrol possesses expertise, while positioning the EU as the single regulator. It is also designed to facilitate a smooth relationship between EASA and Eurocontrol in order to avoid duplication of tasks.

5.3 Other Regional Organisations

Apart from ECAC and Eurocontrol, the following regional organisations of ICAO are mentioned:

- AFCAC, the African Civil Aviation Commission.[154] This Commission is a branch of the Commission on economic, social, transport and communicational affairs, which is itself an affiliation of the Organisation of African Unity (OAU). Membership is open to African States which are members of the Economic Commission for Africa, ECA, or the OAU.
- CACAS, the Civil Aviation Council of Arab States.[155] CACAS has translated the main air law treaties into Arabic and established the Arabic Services Transit Agreement as well as an agreement to create a Pan-Arabic airline.

---

151. See, section 5.2 of Chapter 3; on the role of the Network Manager, see, K. Arnold, Z. Papp and I. Arnold, *The Difficult Present and Uncertain Future of the Single European Sky Network Manager: The Challenges We Are Facing and Why They Matter*, 42(2) Air & Space Law (2017).
152. See, section 2 of Chapter 6.
153. See, section 5.2 of Chapter 3.
154. AFCAC was the result of the Addis Ababa Conference of 1969; *see* II Annals of Air and Space Law 202–203 (1977).
155. The agreement on the CACAS came into force in October 1967; *see* C.N. Shawcross and K.C. Beaumont, 1 *Air Law* para. 138.

- LACAC, the Latin American Civil Aviation Commission.[156] LACAC has held a number of conferences,[157] concentrating on non-scheduled air transport tariff structures and a '*Code de la navigation aérienne latinoamericaine.*'
- ASECNA, *l'Agence pour la Sécurité de la Navigation Aérienne en Afrique et Madagascar*;[158] and
- COCESNA, the *Corporacion Centroamericana de Servicios de Navigacion Aerea.*[159]

Cooperative arrangements are also developing in the Caribbean Region, under the auspices of CARICOM. They purport to harmonise requirements in order to facilitate the sharing of technical resources.[160] The main effect of intergovernmental co-operation for greater air safety lies in the harmonisation of procedures and the standardisation of equipment.

In Asia, the Association of South East Asian Nations (ASEAN) is becoming more active in the field of air transport as it promotes to the safety and liberalisation of air transport in the region. ASEAN is achieving this goal by drawing up intra-regional arrangements.[161]

In Africa the East African Community (EAC), the South African Development Community (SADC) and the Common Market for East and South Africa (COMESA) aim at liberalising intra-regional air services and implementing competition provisions. These ventures are placed under the umbrella of the Yamoussoukro Decisions drawn up by the African Union and are designed to liberalise air traffic among its Member States and to achieve greater cooperation in the technical field.[162]

6 CONCLUDING REMARKS

The history of international civil aviation is a rich one. This chapter gives insight into the principal regulatory and institutional developments which have taken place during the past century.

---

156. LACAC was founded at a meeting in Mexico City in 1973; *see* J.C. Bogolasky, *Air Transport in Latin America: the Expanding Role of LACAC*, Journal of Air Law and Commerce 75–107 (1978).
157. For instance: Buenos Aires, 1974; Montevideo, 1976; Santiago de Chile, 1978; and Bogotá, 1980.
158. ASECNA Convention, Saint Louis du Sénégal, 12 December 1959.
159. Convention on the Central American Air Navigation Corporation, Tegucigalpa, 26 February 1960.
160. *See*, the Multilateral Agreement Concerning the *Operation of Air Services within The Caribbean Community* (1996) which is to improve the level, quality and efficiency of air services within and beyond the Caribbean Community.
161. *See*, A.K.J. Tan, *Aviation Policy in the Philippines and the Impact of the Proposed Southeast Asian Single Aviation Market*, 44(4/5) Air & Space Law 285–308 (2009), and *The 2010 ASEAN – China Air Transport Agreement: Much Ado over Fifth Freedom Rights?* 14(1) Issues in Aviation Law and Policy 19–32 (2014).
162. *See*, C.E. Schlumberger, *Open Skies for Africa: Implementing the Yamoussoukro Decision* (2010) available on the internet.

Traditionally, air law focused on the regulation of airspace, safety, security and market access. Since the 1960s and 1970s, criminal law, liberalisation of the operation of domestic and international air services, and the protection of the environment and consumers marked the development of international air law. Courts in jurisdictions around the world also apply provisions of national civil and criminal codes in cases where international air law instruments provide for balanced tools for resolving the case.

As stated in the introduction, air law is increasingly influenced by other fields of law. Criminal law as to which *see* Chapter 10 affected the formation of international air law in the 1970s. The 1980s were marked by processes of deregulation in the US and liberalisation in the EU marking the economic deregulation of air transport services. Air law received a green shade in the 1990s and the first decade of the twenty-first century when environmental concerns were introduced into the conduct of aviation policies and the formation of air law.

Meanwhile, competition law, taxation and the organisation of labour relations, prime aviation and the development of air law, as illustrated in the following chapters of this book.[163]

Other fields of law introduce concepts and principles into the regulatory framework governing civil aviation, for instance, the term 'principal place of business. International organisations, principally ICAO, supervise this tendency and aim at achieving a balance between aviation and other interests. The place of Europe in the context of air law development is manifest as many initiatives occur in Europe as explained in Chapter 3 of this book.

It shows the steady role of the Chicago Convention whose provisions continue to be relevant.[164] Its emphasis on sovereignty, territorial jurisdiction, the principal importance of safety of air transport, the relevance of nationality of aircraft, the cooperation between States and equality of opportunity continue to be relevant principles in the twenty-first century. The responsibility of the Chicago Convention and ICAO is limited to *international* civil aviation. The operation of State aircraft falls outside the scope of this regime. However, in light of the uncertainty as to the definition of State aircraft and the consequent lack of regulatory transparency, thought could be given to the application of civil regulations and practices, also in relation to air traffic management, to State aircraft. The status of aircraft under Article 3 could be further explained by studies, based on practical experiences

The role of ICAO can hardly be underestimated. ICAO implements the safety provisions of the Chicago Convention in technical safety regulations but lacks enforcement powers, especially in the area of safety and security. This is sometimes felt as a shortcoming of the current system because ICAO is a principal legislator lacking such powers.

---

163. *See*, B. Havel and G. Sanchez, *The Principles and Practice of International Aviation Law* (2014).
164. *See*, B. Havel and J.Q. Mulligan, *International Aviation's Living Constitution: A Commentary on the Chicago Convention's Past, Present and Future*, 15(1) Issues on Aviation Law and Policy (2015); B. Havel & G. Sanchez, *Do We Need a New Chicago Convention?* 11(1) Issues on Aviation Law and Policy 7–22 (2011).

Also, the role of the ICAO Council as an adjudicating body should be further examined as the Council is an intergovernmental body. ICAO's role in the field of economics of air transport is limited, but may be expanded in the next few years.[165]

The Chicago Convention is not all-encompassing and has shortcomings, some of which have been addressed in the course of time. Certain provisions have become obsolete.[166] Apart from the establishment of airport charges,[167] economic regulation of the operation of air services is not dealt with under the Chicago Convention but under the regime made up by international ASAs, as to which *see* the following chapter. The protection of the environment in terms of noise and emissions has now been addressed in Annex 16 of the Chicago Convention, and in ICAO Resolutions which may lead to further instruments.

Despite these weaknesses,[168] the Chicago Convention is still regarded as the constitution of international civil aviation. Its provisions form the basis for the operation and navigation of international air services as the relevant provisions can be flexibly interpreted so as to meet the needs of time. As noted, the Convention is supplemented by other agreements, arrangements and policies which will be discussed below.

ICAO is aware of regional initiatives not only in the economic but also in the technical and safety field.[169] Regional organisations, especially in Europe, are carrying out tasks which are also exercised by ICAO. In the light of its active role in air transport, and its special tasks in that respect, the EU has not been discussed in this Chapter.[170] Hence, the challenge is to synchronise the activities of the various actors, stakeholders and regions, and to harmonise a multilevel jurisdictional world. Governments and courts have a special function in aligning and combining initiatives, with due regard for the principal role of international law.

This book is designed to increase awareness of those instruments so as to provide guidance for all those who have an interest in, or are engaged with, the formation or application of air law. The following chapters will indicate areas which deserve special attention in this respect.

---

165. *See* the ICAO Air Transport Symposium (IATS) held in Montreal on 31–31 March 2016, *Addressing Competition Issues: Towards A Better Operating Environment*, the results of which are available at http://www.icao.int/Meetings/iats2016/Pages/default.aspx.
166. *See*, M. Milde, *Future Perspectives of Air Law*, in: K.-H. Böckstiegel (ed.), *Perspectives of Air Law, Space Law and International Business Law for the Next Century*, 15 Schriften zum Luft- und Weltraumrecht 13–18 (Proceedings of an international colloquium, held in Cologne, June 1995).
167. *See*, ICAO Doc 9082 – *ICAO's Policies on Charges for Airports and Air Navigation Services*.
168. *See also*, M. Milde, *The Chicago Convention – Are Major Amendments Necessary or Desirable 50 Years Later?* XIX(I) Annals of Air and Space Law 401 (1994), and L. Weber, *Convention on International Civil Aviation – 60 Years*, 53 Zeitschrift für Luft- und Weltraumrecht 298–311 (2004); M. Milde, *International Air Law and ICAO* 198–222 (2016).
169. *See*, A. Trimarchi, *From the Chicago Convention to Regionalism in Aviation. A Comprehensive Analysis of the Evolving Role of the International Civil Aviation Organization*, 15(1) The Aviation & Space Journal 26 (2016).
170. Its achievements will be explained in Chapters 3 and 7, the latter discussing aviation safety as managed by the EU and its safety agency EASA.

CHAPTER 2

Operation of Air Services under International Law

1 THE NEED FOR INTERNATIONAL AIR SERVICES AGREEMENTS (ASAs)

1.1 Opening National Airspace Through Bilateral ASAs

As stated in section 3.1 of Chapter 1, the Chicago Convention confirmed 'complete and exclusive' sovereignty over national airspace. As a corollary, it was *de iure* closed for foreign aircraft and their operators, that is, airlines operating international air services. In the economic field, this starting point is laid down in Article 6 of the Chicago Convention, which states that 'special permission' must be granted for the operation of scheduled international air services. Such 'special permission' is traditionally given in *bilateral ASAs* between States, opening each other's national airspace and market for the operation of international air services. There are at present over 4000 bilateral air agreements.

In light of reliance on the principle of sovereignty, States have not transferred national competencies in the *economic* field to international organisations such as International Civil Aviation Organization (ICAO) or World Trade Organization (WTO) as they wished to keep control of 'their' air transport markets by determining the market share for their national carriers.[1] Generally, security, safety and economic, including social policy concerns explain why States wish to determine who flies in their national airspace, and, if so, under what terms and conditions.

---

1. *See*, M. Andersson, *How Economic History Can Guide Aviation Policy*, 15(2) Issues in Aviation Law and Policy (2016) and F. Fiorelli, *International Air Transport Economic Regulation: Globalization vs Protection of National Interest*, X(3) Aviation and Space Journal 18–24 (2011).

1.2 Licensing of Carriers

1.2.1 Licensing Procedures

For carriers to be designated for the performance of the international air services agreed upon in the ASA they must be licensed by the designating State under the licensing regulations of that State. Licensing is of course a matter of national law, and includes compliance with safety requirements as evidenced by the possession of an Air Operator's Certificate (AOC), environmental standards, and liability and insurance conditions.

For an airline it is not possible to engage in commercial air transport operations unless it has in possession of a valid Air Operator Certificate (AOC) issued by the State of the Operator of the airline.[2] The operator of the aircraft must comply with standards pertaining to adequate organisation, method of control and supervision of flight operations, training programme as well as ground handling and maintenance arrangements[3] which are specified in Annex 6 and must implemented in national law. The State of the Operator must check from time to time the continued validity of an AOC.[4]

Importantly, while Article 33 of the Chicago Convention does not regulate mutual recognition of AOC's, Contracting States of ICAO shall recognise as valid an AOC issued by another Contracting State, provided that the requirements under which the certificate was issued are at least equal to the applicable Standards specified in Annex 6. Hence, this obligation for mutual recognition stems from Annex 6, if it is implemented in national law, and not from the Chicago Convention. States must also establish a programme with procedures for the surveillance of operations in their territory by a foreign operator and for taking appropriate action when necessary to preserve safety.[5]

As to EU carriers, such conditions are laid down in EU Regulation 1008/2008 which will be discussed in section 3.2 of Chapter 3.[6]

1.2.2 Compliance with Safety Standards

National laws vary as to the content of licensing conditions; for instance, for safety they may refer to the minimum standards adopted by ICAO, or set higher standards. The US Federal Aviation Authority (FAA) and the European Aviation Safety Agency (EASA) are known for setting higher standards.

As is the case with nationality requirements which are analysed below, safety standards under domestic licensing procedures may be higher than those set under ASAs. In order to allow access to carriers from all parts of the world to the air transport

---

2. *See*, Standard 4.2.1.1 of Annex 6 – *Operation of Aircraft*.
3. *See*, Standard 4.2.1.3 of Annex 6 – *Operation of Aircraft*.
4. *See*, Standard 4.2.1.4 of Annex 6 – *Operation of Aircraft*.
5. *See*, Standard 4.2.2 of Annex 6 – *Operation of Aircraft*.
6. *See*, in particular, Arts 4–7.

market, such carriers must comply with the minimum safety standards for certification and personal licensing.[7] Safety standards are discussed in Chapter 5.

1.2.3 Nationality Requirements

Domestic licensing regulations will normally also encompass rules on the nationality of the air carrier which wishes to be licensed to operate air services by the local authorities. For instance, EU Regulation 1008/2008[8] and US law contain rather strict definitions regarding allowing shareholding and control by foreign entities. Thus, Regulation 1008/2008[9] replaced the expression 'substantial ownership and effective control' by '*majority* ownership and effective control' – which casts no doubt on the level of allowed foreign ownership which is less than 50 per cent.[10] The term ownership refers to the ownership of shares of the company, that is, the airline, or, as the case may be, the holding company.[11]

In the US, 'substantial ownership' is narrowly defined as 75 per cent voting rights subject to waiver for public policy reasons, such as the presence of an Open Skies' agreement benefitting US passengers and shippers of cargo, which must be in the hands of US citizens.[12] Most shareholders are 'common' shareholders. Common shareholders have limited voting rights with respect to influencing the management of the company, and thus controlling it. However, each company determines the rights of its shareholders in its articles of association, which are, at its turn, subject to national law provisions. For instance, under Japanese commercial law, a shareholder with over three per cent of the equity has the right to demand resignation of the board members of a Japanese company.

---

7. *See*, Art. 33 of the Chicago Convention which has been discussed in section 3.2 of Chapter 1. *See also*, a bilateral clause which reads as follows:

> Certificates of airworthiness, certificates of competency and licenses issued, or rendered in reciprocity, by one Contracting Party and still valid, shall be recognized as valid by the other Contracting Party for the purpose of operating the Agreed Services on the Specified Routes, provided that the requirements under which such certificates and licenses were issued, or rendered in reciprocity, are equal to or higher than the minimum requirements which are, or may be in the future, established under the Convention. Each Contracting Party, however, reserves the right to refuse to recognize, for flights above its Territory, certificates of competency and licenses granted to or validated for its own nationals by the other Contracting Party.

8. Which will be discussed in section 3.2 of Chapter 3; *see also*, U. Schulte-Strathaus, *EU Market Access Developments – 10 Years 'Open Skies' – How to Proceed from Here?* 62(1) Zeitschrift für Luft- und Weltraumracht 75–81 (2012).
9. *See*, Art. 4(1)(f).
10. As explained by the EU Commission in its Decision 95/404/EC quoted above.
11. *See*, Pablo Mendes de Leon, *A New Phase in Alliance Building: the Air France/KLM Venture as a Case Study*, 53 Zeitschrift für Luft- und Weltraumrecht 359–385 (2004).
12. *See*, Title 49 U.S.C. § 40102(a)(15)(C) as amended, and as explained in the landmark case *Willey Daetwyler, D.B.A. Interamerican Airfreight* (CAB Docket 22214 (1971)).

The test of 'effective control' is even more elusive than that of 'substantial ownership'. Control may embrace every form of control, that is, actual or legal, direct or indirect, negative or affirmative. In practice, control can be equated with "influence", as exemplified by the definition employed in EU Regulation 1008/2008.[13]

Under US licensing law, the president of the airline and at least two thirds of its board of directors and other managing officers must be US citizens. Thus, the US government can waive the legal conditions pertaining to ownership and control in certain cases for non-US carriers operating to/from the US. Decisions pertaining to 'effective control' are influenced by subjective factors, and are 'fact specific', facts which must be ascertained by national aviation authorities.[14] Decisions based on legal provisions receive a 'policy touch' by taking into account the 'public interest', such as 'international comity' and the presence of an *Open Skies* agreement between the US and the State granting nationality – in terms of ownership and control – to the forewing airline investing airline investing in the US carrier. Such was the case in the DOT decisions on KLM/Northwest and other intercarrier-US alliances.[15]

Determination of the nationality of airlines has also had to be made in other parts of the world, in particular in South East Asia where, for instance, Malaysian based airline Air Asia has set up airlines in, among others, Indonesia, Philippines, and India.[16] These ventures raise nationality questions under domestic licensing policies.[17]

---

13. *See*, Art. 2(9) of EU Regulation 1008/2008, defining effective control as: "a relationship constituted by rights, contracts or any other means which, either separately or jointly and having regard to the considerations of fact or law involved, confer the possibility of *directly or indirectly* exercising *a decisive influence* on an undertaking, in particular by: (a) the right to use all or part of the assets of an undertaking; (b) rights or contracts which confer a decisive influence on the composition, voting or decisions of the bodies of an undertaking or otherwise confer a decisive influence on the running of the business of the undertaking;" *See*, the Swissair/Sabena case referred to in section ... of Chapter 3.
14. *See*, David T. Arlington, *Liberalisation of Restrictions on Foreign Ownership in U.S. Carriers: the United States Must Take the First Step in Aviation Globalization*, 59 Journal of Air Law and Commerce 133–192 (1993).
15. *See*, Pablo Mendes de Leon, *Before and After the Tenth Anniversary of the Open Skies Agreement Netherlands-US of 1992*, 28(4/5) Air & Space Law 280-312 (2002); DoT Order 89-9-51 of 29 September 1989; *see also*, the DoT's decisions in *United Airlines/Lufthansa* (Order 96-5-12, Docket OST-96-1116 of 9 May 1996), and *United Airlines/Lufthansa/SAS* (Order 96-11-1, Dockets OST 96-1411 and OST-96-1646) and *American Airlines/Canadian Airlines* (Order 96-5-38, Docket OST-95-792).
16. *See*, Jae-Woon Lee and M. Dry, *Mitigating 'Effective Control' Restriction on Joint Venture Airlines in Asia: Philippine AirAsia Case*, 40(3) Air & Space Law 231–254 (2015), A. Khee-Jin Tan, *The 2010 ASEAN-China Air Transport Agreement: Much Ado over Fifth Freedom Rights?* 14(1) Issues in Aviation Law and Policy 19–32 (2014), and Jae-Woon Lee, *The U.S.'s New Divide-and-Conquer Strategy in Northeast Asia*, 14(1) Issues in Aviation Law and Policy 83–102 (2014).
17. For India, *see*, the Notification from the Foreign Exchange Department of the Reserve Bank of India, No. FEMA.362/2016-RB dated 15 February 2016 and published on 25 November 2016, allowing 49 per cent foreign ownership of undertakings performing scheduled air transport services and domestic scheduled passenger airlines, and 100 per cent 'foreign' ownership of undertakings managed by Non Resident Indians, including undertakings performing non-scheduled air transport services and helicopter services.

These questions will continue to be raised when important aviation nations such as Canada and India[18] are rethinking their policies pertaining to allowance of foreign investment by broadening it.[19]

Broader foreign investment opportunities are thought to create fiercer competition and enhanced choices for consumers. Latin American countries such as Chile and Columbia have abolished ownership and control conditions as it suffices that the airline has its principal place of business in those countries in order to obtain an AOC.[20] ICAO is also contributing to the debate by proposing the criterion 'principal place of businesses for the nationality of an airline from where 'effective regulatory control' must be exercised.[21]

1.3 Terms of Bilateral ASAs

Those terms and conditions include but are not limited to:

- definitions of terms, with reference to terms used in the Chicago Convention;
- designation of airlines, that is, which airlines and how many airlines may operate the agreed services;
- nationality requirements for designated airlines, for economic and security reasons, as alluded to above;
- the routes which designated airlines are entitled to fly, that is grant of rights for market access;
- revocation and suspension of the operating permit granted to the designated airline(s) in case of non-compliance with defined provisions of the agreement;
- the applicability of local air navigation rules as confirmed by Article 11 of the Chicago Convention;[22]

---

18. The Air Asia case has become quite convoluted due to petitions filed by *Federation of Indian Airlines* v. *Union of India* (WP (Civil) No. 1373/2014). The final decision of the High Court on the nationality of Air Asia is pending. *See also*, the questions raised about the nationality of Air Asia in the case of *Subramanian Swamy* v. *Union of India* (WP(Civil) No. 5909/2013 & CM.No.13039/2013 & 14134/2013) after which the High Court of Delhi rejected claims to suspend the operating license of Air Asia. The case is in appeal before to the Supreme Court of India. *See also*, L. Braun, *Liberalization or Bust: A Double Step Approach to Relaxing the Foreign Ownership and Control Restrictions in the Brazilian Aviation Industry*, 39(6) Air & Space Law 341–364 (2014), J.I. Garcia-Arboleda, *Transnational Airlines in Latin America Facing the Fear of Nationality*, 37(2) Air & Space Law 93–118 (2012); A. Khee-Jin Tan, *India's Evolving Policy on International Civil Aviation*, 36(3) Air & Space Law 439–462 (2013).
19. In 2016, the Indian government has raised the 49 per cent allowable foreign investment limit to 100 per cent, with foreign direct investment up to 49 per cent permitted automatically, and FDI beyond 49 per cent through Government approval; *see*, Press Information Bureau, Government of India, Prime Minister's Office, *Major impetus to job creation and infrastructure: Radical changes in FDI policy regime*; *Most sectors on automatic route for FDI*, 9 September 2016.
20. *See*, section 1.2.1, above.
21. *See*, ICAO, Air Transport Conference/5, *Model Air Services Agreement* clause (2003).
22. "..., the laws and regulations of a contracting State relating to the admission to or departure from its territory of aircraft engaged in international air navigation, or to the operation and navigation of such aircraft *while within its territory*, shall be applied to the aircraft of all contracting States

- the capacity that designated airlines may offer, that is, the size and the configuration of the aircraft;
- the prices the designated airlines may quote;
- the maintenance of minimum safety and security standards pursuant to Article 33 of the Chicago Convention and in accordance with minimum Standards and Recommended Practices drawn up and updated from time to time by ICAO as laid down in the Annexes to the Chicago Convention;
- operational opportunities and restrictions, for instance, change of gauge, that is, equipment or aircraft;
- recognition of the 'fair competition' principle designed to ensure the establishment of a level playing field between the designated carriers;
- commercial activities including code-sharing and the establishment of sales offices in the territory of the other State;
- the protection of the environment including noise and emissions;
- user charges for the operation of the agreed international air services;
- taxation, including exemptions from taxes;
- access to infrastructure, that is, airports and airport related facilities;
- dispute settlement;
- termination of the agreement;
- registration of the agreement with ICAO and entry into force.

The above conditions are laid down in bilateral ASAs, and, increasingly so, in plurilateral or multilateral agreements. The principal terms will be discussed in this chapter whereas the clarification of others can be found in the publications mentioned in the footnotes.[23]

Bilateral or multilateral ASAs are concluded by *States* which may have to be ratified in accordance with the procedures of national law. The pro-active role of the EU in such international agreements is discussed in Chapter 3 below.

States are represented by delegations of Ministries: the Transport Ministry, including the Director General of the Civil Aviation Authority (CAA) and/or his or her representatives, and representatives of the Ministry of Foreign Affairs in the US and other States, as chairman of the delegation, and representatives of the Ministry of Economic Affairs; airline representatives; and nowadays also representatives of airports and other concerned parties.

---

without distinction as to nationality, and shall be complied with by such aircraft upon entering or departing from or while within the territory of that State." *Italics added.*

23. *See,* B. Cheng, *The Law of International Air Transport* 289–490 (1962); *see also,* H.A. Wassenbergh, *Post-War International Civil Aviation Policy* 3–28 (1962); R.J. Fennes, *International Air Cargo Transport Services: Economic Regulation and Policy* 85–97 (1997) discussing the 'Bermuda Principles'; P.P.C. Haanappel, *The Law and Policy of Air Space and Outer Space: A Comparative Approach* 109–123 (2003), and P.M.J. Mendes de Leon, *Air Transport as a Service under the Chicago Convention,* XIX(II) Annals of Air and Space Law 523–566 (1994).

2 FROM BERMUDA I TO OPEN SKIES

2.1 The Bermuda I and II Agreements

Since the conclusion of the Chicago Convention, States followed a pattern which was modelled on the Bermuda Agreement between the US and the UK of 1946, now also referred to as the *Bermuda I Agreement*. The Bermuda I Agreement was proclaimed by the US and the UK as a standard agreement that was to serve as a pattern for all their aviation agreements. This standard agreement was also accepted by a majority of other States and became the vehicle for the operation of air services internationally in the second half of the twentieth century.[24]

The wording of the Bermuda I Agreement was rather vague and therefore could be termed as a compromise. At one extreme there were States, led by the US, who felt that a liberal interpretation should be adopted as to the economic conditions under which air services were exchanged; that is, there should be no predetermination of capacity, freedom of pricing, and no restrictions as to access to routes. The opposite view, represented by the UK, held that capacity, tariffs and access to routes should be laid down beforehand in the bilateral agreement so as to pre-determine the economic parameters of the operation of the services.

Under the compromise agreement, tariffs were to be established by the airlines within the framework of the International Air Transport Association (IATA),[25] subject to approval of both parties. Capacity was to be determined by the airlines subject to certain agreed principles; for instance, capacity on the agreed services should primarily be used for the carriage of traffic between the two countries,[26] and only in a secondary way for 'third country' traffic.[27]

While the Bermuda I Agreement became a model for many bilateral air agreements, a more restrictive interpretation of the capacity clauses was often adopted. A large number of agreements employed predetermination of capacity. An example of a restrictive agreement is the detailed and complex Bermuda II Agreement of 1977, replacing the Bermuda I Agreement. The Bermuda II Agreement as subsequently amended did not have the same exemplary role as the Bermuda I Agreement.[28]

2.2 Objectives of a Bilateral ASA

The Preamble of a bilateral ASA refers to the Chicago Convention of 1944 and sets forth the reasons for the conclusion of the agreement. It confirms the national air policies

---

24. *See*, B. Cheng, *The Law of International Air Transport* 238–238 (1962) and P.P.C. Haanappel, *Pricing and Capacity Determination in International Air Transport* 27–34 (1984).
25. *See*, section 4.2 of Chapter 1.
26. Also referred to as 'third' Freedom and 'fourth Freedom' traffic as to which *see* section 3.7, below.
27. Also referred to as 'fifth' Freedom traffic; *see*, section 3.7, below.
28. *See*, P.P.C. Haanappel, *Pricing and Capacity Determination in International Air Transport* 40–42 (1984).

governing the relations between the two countries, which may vary from restrictive to very liberal. For instance, 'Open Skies' agreements formulate such objectives as:

- the promotion of international air transport based on 'fair competition' among airlines in the marketplace with minimum governmental interference;
- the expansion of international air transport opportunities;
- the development of an air transport system catering to all segments of demand and providing a wide and flexible range of services;
- the offering of a variety of service options at the lowest prices that are not predatory or discriminatory and do not represent abuse of dominant position, and:
- the encouragement of innovative and competitive pricing, whereas also
- cargo operations should be conducted in a 'deregulated environment',
- taking into account the highest safety, security and environmental standards.

The first Article typically contains definitions, which more often than not are standard definitions in each bilateral agreement. They refer to the definitions of terms employed in the Chicago Convention. The principal goal of the ASA is to provide the opportunity for designated air carriers to operate the agreed international air services, in other words, to form the legal vehicle for market access as to which *see* the next section.

3 MARKET ACCESS RIGHTS

3.1 Designation of Air Carriers

For carriers to operate the agreed international air services they must be so designated by the aeronautical authorities of the designating State. For instance, if Druk Air, the national carrier of the Royal Government of Bhutan wishes to operate services from its capital Thimphu to Delhi, the Bhutanese aeronautical authorities must designate it under its bilateral ASA with India. The Bhutanese authorities will do so if it has licensed that carrier, and can convince the Indian authorities that its carrier complies with the requirements set by the mentioned ASA. Nationality requirements are an important factor in this regard, and so are safety requirements.

Once the aeronautical authorities have designated a carrier, it sends its decision regarding the designation to the aeronautical authorities of the other party, which has to accept it, or may have questions on the designation. For this purpose, diplomatic channels are mostly used.

3.2 Nationality Requirements

Access to international air transport markets is also subject to possession of the nationality of the designating State which may, but does not have to be identical with, nationality requirements laid down in domestic licensing procedures as explained in section 1.2.3 above.

The nationality clause laid down in ASAs[29] is the chosen instrument for defining the link between a State and "its" designated airline. Bilateral agreements stipulate that one State will grant "appropriate authorisations and permissions" for the operation of international air services "provided ... substantial ownership and effective control ... are vested in the Party designating the airline, nationals of that Party, or both ..." The 'formula' of 'substantial ownership and effective control' was generally acceptable because of the vague wording. Thus, aeronautical authorities of States keep the discretionary powers to interpret it, and use, or not use it in their consultations and negotiations.

A State *may* but is not obliged to, revoke, suspend, or limit the operating authorisations or technical permissions of an airline designated by the other party where substantial ownership and effective control are not vested in the other party, the other party's nationals, or both.[30] If parties disagree on the meaning or implications of the "ownership and control" clause, they may hold consultations in order to resolve the disagreement. If the disagreement gives rise to a dispute under the bilateral agreement, either party to the agreement may request arbitration in accordance with the terms set forth by the bilateral agreement. There has been no arbitration on the interpretation of the nationality clause, but it has been interpreted under EU law in the *Swissair/Sabena* case.[31]

Thus, the market access conditions explained above are one of those fields in air law were law and policy are closely intertwined. States may waive the application of the nationality requirements, and do so in practice. Moreover, many jurisdictions are reviewing their licensing conditions and, with that, the interpretation of the bilateral clauses on nationality of designated airlines, in order to give more room for foreign

---

29. *See also*, Art. I(5) of the *International Air Services Transit Agreement* of 1944: "Each contracting State reserves the right to withhold or revoke a certificate or permit to an air transport enterprise of another state in any case where it is not satisfied that *substantial ownership* and *effective control* are vested in nationals of a contracting state, ... " (*italics added*), and Art. I(6) of the International Air Transport Agreement of 1944, containing an identical clause.

30. *See*, B. Wood, *Foreign Ownership of International Airlines: A European View*, in: Prof. Chia Jui Cheng and P.M.J. Mendes de Leon (eds), *The Highways of Air and Outer Space over Asia* 311–327 (1992); *See* A.I. Mendelsohn, *Myths of International Aviation*, 68(3) Journal of Air Law and Commerce 519–535 (2003); H.P. van Fenema, *Substantial Ownership and Effective Control as Airpolitical Criteria*, in: T.L. Masson-Zwaan and P.M.J. Mendes de Leon (eds in chief), *Air and Space Law*: De Lege Ferenda, Essays in Honour of Henri A. Wassenbergh 27–42 (1992); P.P.C. Haanappel, *Airline Ownership and Control, and Some Related Matters*, 26(2) Air & Space Law 90–103 (2001); B. Cheng, *The Law of International Air Transport* 37–379 (1962); H.A. Wassenbergh, *Principles and Practices in Air Transport Regulation* 158 (1992); Pablo Mendes de Leon, *The Future of Ownership and Control Clauses in Bilateral Air Transport Agreements; Current Proposals and Legal Objections*, S. Hobe et al. (eds), *Consequences of Air Transport Globalization* 19–36 (2003); (same author) *The Verdict of the European Court of Justice in the Open Skies Cases: Inside Out?*, in: P.D. Dagtoglou and S. Unger (eds), 18 Proceedings of the Fourteenth Annual Conference of the European Air Law Association 69–80 (2003); 53 Zeitschrift für Luft- und Weltraumrecht 359–385 (2004); I. Leleur, *Law and Policy of Substantial Ownership and Effective Control of Airlines – Prospects for Change* (2003).

31. Decision 95/404/EC: Commission decision of 19 July 1995 on a procedure relating to the application of Council Regulation (EEC) No. 2407/92 (*Swissair/Sabena*).

investment. However, it remains a sensitive subject as States also realise that air transport is a public policy tool which must be preferably controlled by own nationals in order to assure links, by the exercise of traffic rights, to, from and via their territories. To find a balance between the two is a challenging task.

3.3 Compliance with International Safety and Security Standards

Compliance with ICAO's safety Standards[32] is a prerequisite for the exercise of traffic rights by an air carrier under an ASA and States reserve the right to ensure that these Standards are indeed being met. The designated carriers must comply with national air navigation regulations on the footing of Article 11 of the Chicago Convention.[33] Those regulations pertain to entry, clearance, security, immigration, passport control, customs regulations, and, in the case of air cargo, postal regulations.

The bilateral partner normally proceeds from the point of view that the designated carrier meets the standards of ICAO regarding aircraft certification and personnel licensing as to which *see* Article 33 of the Chicago Convention.[34] Those standards are minimum standards. States may set higher standards for their own carriers but not for foreign carriers. Experience shows that those standards not only regard safety but also security and the protection of the environment. Imposition of higher standards than those agreed upon in ICAO to foreign carriers had led to litigation[35] and policy and legal repercussions.[36]

ASAs may contain a clause reading as follows:

> the Designated Airline is qualified to meet the conditions prescribed under the laws and regulations normally applied to the operations of international air transportation by the Contracting Party considering the application or applications.

These regulations may be construed in a broad sense as the term used here is 'operation' – which is the term formulated in Article 6 of the Chicago Convention[37] –

---

32. *See*, section 3.3.6 of Chapter 1.
33. "Subject to the provisions of this Convention, *the laws and regulations of a contracting State relating to the admission to or departure from its territory of aircraft engaged in international air navigation*, or to the operation and navigation of such aircraft *while within its territory*, shall be applied to the aircraft of all contracting States without distinction as to nationality, and shall be complied with by such aircraft upon entering or departing from or while within the territory of that State." (*italics added*).
34. "*Certificates of airworthiness and certificates of competency and licenses issued* or rendered valid by the contracting State in which the aircraft is registered, shall be recognized as valid by the other contracting States, provided that the requirements under which such certificates or licenses were issued or rendered valid are *equal to or above the minimum standards* which may be established from time to time pursuant to this Convention." (*italics added*).
35. *See*, the case of the – then – British carrier British Caledonian against the US FAA, referred to in section 3.3.6 of Chapter 1.
36. *See*, the 'hushkit' dispute between the US and the US, mentioned in section 3.3.7.2 of Chapter 1, and the EU ETS *saga* discussed in section 5.3.2 of Chapter 3.
37. "No scheduled international air service may be *operated* over or into the territory of a contracting State, except with the special permission or other authorization of that State, and in accordance with the terms of such permission or authorization." (*italics added*).

rather than 'navigation' which is the language employed in, for instance, Article 11 of the Chicago Convention. For instance, States may require foreign carriers to satisfy norms outside the areas of safety, security and the protection of the environment such as local noise regulations, the regime regarding emissions, and, increasingly so in the future, labour conditions.[38] The question is, for instance, whether domestic competition rules can be made to apply to the operation of the services of the designated foreign carriers, making use of the 'effects' doctrine,[39] or whether the application of such rules must be agreed upon in a separate provision of the bilateral ASAs. These questions are intensively debated by policymakers in the EU, US and other parts of the world, and analysed in publications.[40]

ASAs also contain a provision on aviation security, in which States express adherence to the security Conventions, namely:

- the *Tokyo Convention* of 1963 on Offences and Certain Other Acts Committed on Board Aircraft;
- the *Hague Convention* of 1970 for the Suppression of Unlawful seizure of Aircraft;
- the *Montreal Convention* of 1971 for the Suppression of Unlawful Acts against the Safety of Civil Aviation, as amended in 1989 by the '*Airports Protocol*'.[41]

The Beijing Convention and Protocol of 2010 are not yet referred to in current bilateral or other ASAs as they are not yet in force.[42]

Moreover, ICAO has an Annex on Security (Annex 17),[43] and adopted a model clause on aviation security for the use of Contracting States in their bilateral agreements.[44] Since '9/11' and the terrorist attacks in Europe in 2015 and 2016 also involving airports, attention for security has yet again increased. The standards laid

---

38. *See also*, section 10.3.2 of this Chapter.
39. *See*, section 3.3.3 of Chapter 3; *see also*, J.A. Silversmith, *The Long Arm of the DOT: The Regulation of Foreign Air Carriers Beyond US Borders*, 38(3) Air & Space Law 173–226 (2013).
40. *See*, P.P. Fitzgerald, *A Level Playing Field for 'Open Skies'* (2016); R. Abeyratne, *Competition and Investment in Air Transport: Legal and Economic Issues* (2016); B. Havel& G. Sanchez, *The Principles and Practice of International Aviation Law* (2014); J.D. Goetz and S.L. Thompson, *The Trans-Pacific Partnership and Its Effect on International Aviation*, 15(2) Issues in Aviation Law and Policy 281–305 (2016); D.T. Duval, *Air Transport in the Asia Pacific* (2014).
41. *See*, sections 2, 3 and 4 of Chapter 12 on *Criminal air law*.
42. *See*, section 5 of Chapter 12 on *Criminal air law*.
43. *See*, B. Cheng, *International Legal Instruments to Safeguard International Air Transport: The Conventions of Tokyo, The Hague, Montreal, and a New Instrument Concerning Unlawful Violence at International Airports*, T.L. Masson and P.M.J. Mendes de Leon (eds), *Aviation Security*, Proceedings of an international conference held in The Hague, 23–46 (1987).
44. ICAO Model Clause on Aviation Safety:

   1. Each Party may request consultations at any time concerning the safety standards maintained by the other Party in areas relating to aeronautical facilities, flight crew, aircraft and the operation of aircraft. Such consultations shall take place within thirty days of that request.
   2. If, following such consultations, one Party finds that the other Party does not effectively maintain and administer safety standards in the areas referred to in paragraph 1 that meet the Standards established at that time pursuant to the *Convention on International Civil Aviation* (Doc 7300), the other Party shall be informed of

down in Annex 17 of ICAO on aviation security and other measures have been sharpened in particular in relation to airports, passengers and their baggage and on board aircraft as well as the safe carriage of cargo. The US takes the lead when it comes to enhancing aviation safety and security. The US Transport Security Administration (TSA) is mandated to conduct a comprehensive security risk assessment of all last point of departure airports with nonstop flights to the US, by providing equipment at foreign last point of departure airport and implementing security measures there. Such measures will be drawn up in an agreement with the foreign government.[45]

3.4 Single or Multiple Designation

Market access may be granted to one, two or more designated carriers on each side. Thus, the *beneficiaries* of the exchange, in other words the designated air carriers who shall be allowed to exercise the traffic and other rights as laid down in the ASA and as explained in the next sections, may be subject to:

- *single designation*, that is one carrier on each side; or
- *dual designation*, that is, two carriers on each side; or
- *multiple designation*, that is, unlimited designation, meaning each side/party to the agreement may designate as many carriers as it deems fit, or, in other words, carriers on each side may enter the market as agreed upon in the agreement unlimitedly,

---

such findings and of the steps considered necessary to conform with the ICAO Standards. The other Party shall then take appropriate corrective action within an agreed time period.

3. Pursuant to Art. 16 of the Convention, it is further agreed that, any aircraft operated by, or on behalf of an airline of one Party, on service to or from the territory of another Party, may, while within the territory of the other Party be the subject of a search by the authorized representatives of the other Party, provided this does not cause unreasonable delay in the operation of the aircraft. Notwithstanding the obligations mentioned in Art. 33 of the Chicago Convention, the purpose of this search is to verify the validity of the relevant aircraft documentation, the licensing of its crew, and that the aircraft equipment and the condition of the aircraft conform to the Standards established at that time pursuant to the Convention.

4. When urgent action is essential to ensure the safety of an airline operation, each Party reserves the right to immediately suspend or vary the operating authorization of an airline or airlines of the other Party.

45. *See*, H.R.4698 – 114th Congress (2015–2016), *Securing Aviation from Foreign Entry Points and Guarding Airports Through Enhanced Security Act* of 26 April 2016. The so-called preclearance programme pursuant to which passengers are screened before they embark the aircraft destined for a point in the US. The foreign airport is responsible for many of the program's costs, including the construction and maintenance of the space dedicated to the effort inside the airport. Passengers departing those airports are treated the same as domestic travellers, and do not have to go through customs when they arrive in the United States. The US Transport Security Administration (TSA) has more than 500 people stationed at fifteen airports, including facilities in Canada, Bermuda, the Bahamas, Aruba, Abu Dhabi and Ireland; *see*, The New York Times, *Preclearance at Foreign Airports Seen as a Necessity to Fight Terrorism,* 24 July 2016.

provided of course that the above requirements pertaining to nationality, safety, security, protection of the environment and compliance with national rules including domestic navigation rules are met by the multiple carriers so designated.[46]

Hence, *single designation* regimes may exclude competition between the designated carriers as they may make arrangements on the operation of the agreed international air services, whereas a *multiple designation* regimes open the door for competition. The latter regime is the one adopted under *Open Skies* agreements.

3.5 Operational Rights

Designated carriers will normally need operational rights, and at any rate traffic rights. Operational rights may not be needed if the flights are operated between adjacent countries only. These concern the right to fly through the airspace of another State, without making a stop there, in order to exercise the agreed traffic rights. The other operational right regards the right to make a technical stop in the territory of another State, without rights for putting down or embarking traffic there, that is, for instance, for refuelling or in case of emergency.

These operational rights are exchanged under the multilateral regime of the *International Air Services Transit Agreement* of 1944, adherence to which is confirmed in the ASA if the parties to it are also a party to the mentioned multilateral agreement. If not they must agree on the grant of these operational rights on a bilateral agreement, and they may ask benefits for the grant of such rights in return, on *quid pro quo* basis. Countries with a big airspace including but not limited to the Russian Federation, Indonesia, Canada and Brazil prefer not to accede to the International ASA as they wish to keep their airspace as an asset in bilateral negotiations. On the other hand, other States with a large airspace such as China, India and the US, are a party to this agreement. For the operation of non-scheduled services, the operational rights are granted by virtue of the multilateral regime of Article 5 of the Chicago Convention which has been ratified by 191 States.

3.6 Traffic Rights

Traffic rights refer to the right of the carriers to operate the agreed international services once they have been designated as such by their governments, in many cases represented in this matter by their CAA or Department of Foreign Affairs. The designation must be accepted by the bilateral partner who may but is not obliged to whether the criteria for designation, that is, the designated carrier or carriers complies or comply with nationality requirements and the minimum safety standards by ICAO.

Traffic rights are rights which are exchanged under bilateral ASAs and employed by designated carriers to operate the agreed international services. This topic is a

---

46. For instance, according to the *Guidelines for Grant of Permission to Indian Air Transport Undertakings for Operation of Scheduled International Air Transport Services* (2016), File No. 5/251/2008-IR, an Indian airline must deploy twenty aircraft or 20 per cent of the total capacity, whichever is higher, for domestic operations.

complex one as traffic rights are 'route specific' that is, they may only be exercised on the routes which have been agreed upon in the ASAs. The regime of an Open Skies agreement is a liberal one as to the exchange of traffic rights, as to which *see* below.

Operational and traffic rights have been termed 'Freedoms of the Air' which are actually 'un-Freedoms of the Air' as they must be obtained through negotiations. Those – operational – rights which have been explained in the previous section are termed the first two Freedoms of the Air, and are illustrated in the next section.

So far,[47] there are nine Freedoms in total. The Freedoms three to nine concern the commercial operation of air services, that is, the carriage of traffic including passengers and cargo on the agreed routes. The agreed routes are specified in the Freedoms of the Air. The higher the 'Freedom number' the more difficult it is to acquire that Freedom through negotiations. Thus, the eighth and ninth Freedoms of the Air, also referred to as cabotage rights,[48] or the operation of domestic services by a foreign carrier, are very rarely granted or exchanged in international ASAs. One exception to this rule concerns EU Regulation 1008/2008, but that special situation must be seen in light of the close relationship between the EU States in the context of the EU treaties and the creation of the internal air transport market.[49] Chile also permits the operation of domestic services in its own territory while applying the national treatment principle, and without requiring reciprocity.[50] Other countries such as Indonesia and India allow the operation of domestic legs by foreign registered aircraft which is not the same as foreign airlines as airlines based in the last mentioned countries may lease aircraft from abroad.[51]

Traffic rights and other commercial arrangements between the parties, including but not limited to frequencies of services, passenger quotas and royalties may be included in 'Memoranda of Understanding' (MoU) which are concluded either by the aeronautical authorities or between the designated airlines. Since they contain sensitive information, MoUs are not registered or published because of secrecy and confidentiality arguments.

3.7 The Freedoms of the Air

The fact that States can impose limitations on flights of foreign airlines stems from the principle embodied in the Paris Convention of 1919, namely that each State has

---

47. *See*, B.I. Scott who, in his article *International Suborbital Passenger Transportation: An Analysis of the Current Legal Situation of Transit and Traffic Rights and Its Appropriate Regulation,* 14(2) Issues in Aviation Law & Policy 277–312 (2015) at 298, identifies the Tenth Freedom of the Air for the operation of cabotage services with suborbital vehicles.
48. *See*, Pablo Mendes de Leon, *Cabotage in Air Transport Regulation* 102–106 (1992).
49. *See*, section 3.2 of Chapter 3.
50. *See*, Resolution 63 (2012) (Resolución Exenta 63, Decreto Ley 2, 564, *Dicta Normas Sobre Aviación Comercial,* Ministerio de Transporte y Telecomunicaciones de República de Chile (21 March 1979) in which Chile unilaterally initiated its Open Skies policy, recorded in an unpublished paper on *Open Skies Policies in Chile,* made in May 2016 by Rodrigo Fernández Navarette, available in the office of the author of this book.
51. Under the – emergency – conditions laid down in this regulation; *see*, PM 109/2015 as amended by PM 109/2016 (Ministerial Regulation), reported by Bahar and Partners on 27 November 2016.

complete and exclusive sovereignty over the airspace above its national territory. This fundamental rule has been repeated and sanctioned in the Chicago Convention. Hence there is no Freedom of the Air as airspace is closed for the operation of international scheduled air services.

The absence of Freedom of the Air can be turned into a more or less articulated Freedom of the Air pursuant to the terms of bilateral or other international ASAs, opening up the airspaces of the parties to the agreement for the operation of international air services and turning it into a market under the most liberal ASAs, to wit Open Skies agreements. Multilaterally, the possibility of allowing greater freedom of movement has been made explicit in two Agreements annexed to the Convention, which divide the Freedom of the Air into five categories.

As stated above, the first two freedoms concern privileges for technical operations; they are laid down in the *International Air Services Transit Agreement*, and they concern the freedom to fly over a foreign State or to make a technical landing there.[52] The freedom to make a technical stop in another State encompassed by the second Freedom of the Air, as to which *see* section 3.7 below, loses relevance at times when aircraft can fly longer distances. For instance, the Australian carrier Qantas considers non-stop flights between Sydney and Paris, and Melbourne and Rome. This development will also affect the attractiveness of traditional hubs for transit traffic.

Transport related freedoms are listed in the *International Air Transport Agreement* laying down three more freedoms, that is, the third, fourth and fifth Freedoms of the Air as explained in section 3.7, below. Only eleven States have ratified this agreement;[53] its significance in practice is very limited.

The third Freedom enables the airline of a State to carry passengers and cargo from its own territory to a foreign State, whereas the fourth concerns the transport of passengers and cargo from a foreign State to the home State of the carrier. The right to carry passengers and cargo between two foreign States is contained in the fifth Freedom if the concerned service is linked to a service originating from or destined for the territory of the home State of the carrier. The latter causes air policy questions to arise, as consent from two foreign States must be obtained for this right to be exercised, explaining why it is not easy to execute fifth Freedom rights in practice, and many States are reluctant to adhere to the *International Transport Agreement* as they wish to control traffic destined for and leaving points in their territories.[54] Thus, if Thailand and South Korea would agree on the grant of fifth Freedom rights for Thai carriers on services beyond Seoul, for instance, Bangkok-Seoul-Tokyo including the right for Thai carriers flying from Bangkok to Seoul to pick up traffic in Seoul and put it down in Tokyo, and *vice versa*, that is, Tokyo-Seoul, with a connecting flight of the Thai carrier from Seoul to Bangkok, not only the Thai and Korean authorities must agree on this fifth Freedom operation between Seoul and Tokyo, but also the Japanese authorities. If

---

52. Per March 2017, 131 States are a party to this agreement.
53. Bolivia, Burundi, Costa Rica, El Salvador, Ethiopia, Greece, Honduras, Liberia, the Netherlands, Paraguay and Turkey.
54. B. Cheng, *The Law of International Air Transport* 21 and 405–409 (1962); H.A. Wassenbergh, *Principles and Practices in Air Transport Regulation* 171–174 and 240–241 (1993).

Japan would be a party to the *International Air Transport Agreement* its authorities had 'given away' this fifth Freedom right *a priori* under a multilateral regime and could not object the operation of the Thai carrier on the Seoul-Tokyo service. On the other hand, adherence to the *International Air Transport Agreement* would have yielded similar fifth Freedom benefits for its – Japanese – carriers. However, at the end of the day States wish to stay in control on these fifth Freedom operations, and make a decision on their allowance on an ad hoc basis.

The remaining transport related Freedoms which are described below, that is, Freedoms six to nine, are not laid down in a multilateral agreement. They have emerged in the decades after the coming into being of the above multilateral agreements encompassing the Freedoms one to five, and are regulated under ASAs.

Under the sixth Freedom of the Air, the home carrier of a State has the right to fly from a foreign State through its home State, defined as the State which has licensed and designated the carrier to another foreign point under the combined effect of fourth and third Freedom rights awarded under a combination of two ASAs. For instance, The Dubai-based carrier carries traffic from Beijing, via Dubai to Nairobi under the China-United Arab Emirates ASA, and the United Arab Emirates-Kenya ASA respectively. Carriers with a small home market, excellent airport facilities and/or a strategic geographical location such as Singapore International Airlines (SIA), KLM, Emirates, Etihad, Qatar Airways and Turkish Airlines are making use of this Freedom.[55]

The Seventh Freedom concerns the right for a carrier operating entirely outside the territory of the flag-State, to fly into the territory of the grantor State and there discharge, or take on, traffic coming from, or destined for, a third State or States. For instance, the US cargo carrier FedEx carries traffic between Dubai and Singapore, without linking this service to a point in the US which is the home State of this carrier. This Freedom is not often practiced in passenger services but cargo carriers find it a useful privilege as their operations are organised differently. Again, the two foreign States, in the above case the United Arab Emirates and Singapore, must give their consent to the said operation.[56]

The eighth and ninth Freedoms of the Air are also referred to as 'cabotage', a term which is derived from maritime law.[57] In air law, it can be defined as the right of an airline to perform services between two points in a foreign territory.

Cabotage privileges are mostly excluded under the rights granted under ASAs as, again, States wish to stay in control of their domestic operations. Allowance of cabotage privileges have been made in exceptional cases only. Thus, for the time being, the ninth Freedom of the Air is at the bottom of the scale, and, consequently, the least

---

55. *See,* H.A. Wassenbergh, *Principles and Practices in Air Transport Regulation* 100–102 (1993); (same author): *The 'Sixth' Freedom Revisited*, 21 Air & Space Law, 285–294 (1996).

56. *See,* H.A. Wassenbergh, *Principles and Practices in Air Transport Regulation* 173–175 (1993); this author mentioned orally that KLM operated in the 1960s flights between Kabul, Afghanistan, and Karachi, Pakistan, as there was no alternative. Also, he said that the Israeli carrier El Al enjoyed seventh Freedom rights between Amsterdam and New York in the 1970s.

57. *See,* B. Cheng, *The Law of International Air Transport* 15 (1962), and Pablo Mendes de Leon *Cabotage in International Air Transport Regulation* 1–4 (1992) who makes a distinction between the two variations on the operation of cabotage services as to which *see* the cited book at 104.

negotiable one. Examples can be found in the EU, for EU carriers only, the Tasman Pact between Australia and New Zealand, for Australian and New Zealand carriers only, whereas Chile's liberal policy in this regard has been briefly alluded to at the end of the previous section.

Cabotage is regulated under Article 7 of the Chicago Convention. Article 7(2) of this Convention requires clarification because of its ambiguous formulation: no exclusive cabotage privileges may be specifically granted to operators of other States.[58]

The following examples may clarify the above descriptions.

1st FREEDOM

The right to fly across foreign territory without landing
For instance: Air Canada flies over the United States to Mexico without landing.

2nd FREEDOM

The right to land in foreign territory for non-traffic purposes
For instance: Iberia flies from Madrid to Tokyo and makes a stop in Anchorage, Alaska for technical purposes.

3rd FREEDOM

The right to carry traffic either from the territory of the State whose nationality the airlines possesses or where the airline is established, into a foreign territory
For instance: Air France flies and carries traffic from Paris to New Delhi.

4th FREEDOM

The right to carry traffic from the territory into the territory of the State whose nationality the airlines possesses or where the airline is established.
For instance: Aer Lingus flies and carries traffic from New York to Dublin.

5th FREEDOM

The right to carry traffic from one point in a foreign territory into a point in another foreign territory and vice versa, which carriage is linked is with a third and fourth freedom traffic right respectively.
For instance: SIA flies and carries traffic from Manila to Seoul, connecting to its service from Singapore to Manila, and *vice versa*.

6th FREEDOM

The right to carry traffic from one point in a foreign territory into a point in another foreign territory via the State whose nationality the airlines possesses or where the airline is established.

---

58. The Swedish delegation has asked the ICAO Council to clarify the second paragraph of Art. 7. Years of debate passed without result. No consensus could be reached among the delegates, basically because both political and economic interests played too big a role. *See* ICAO Doc. 8629-11, C/967-11 (1967), and *see also*, R.C. Hingorani, *Dispute Settlement in International Civil Aviation*, 14(1) The Arbitration Journal 14–25 (1959), and Pablo Mendes de Leon, *Cabotage in Air Transport Regulation* 41–46 (1992).

For instance: KLM flies and carries traffic from Istanbul to Chicago via Amsterdam, and *vice versa*.

7th FREEDOM

The right to carry traffic from one point in a foreign territory into a point in another foreign territory and vice versa, which carriage is not linked with a third and fourth freedom traffic right respectively
For instance: Austrian Airlines flies and carries traffic back and forth between St. Petersburg and Osaka, and *vice versa*, without linking this service to a point in Austria.

8th FREEDOM

The right to carry traffic between two points in a foreign territory, which carriage is linked with third or fourth freedom carriage
For instance: TAP Portugal flies and carries traffic between Milan to Rome, connecting to its service between Lisbon and Milan, and *vice versa*.

9th FREEDOM

The right to carry traffic between two points in a foreign territory, which carriage is not linked with third or fourth freedom carriage
For instance: SAS flies and carries traffic back and forth between Paris and Toulouse.

Meanwhile, an author has identified a tenth Freedom of the Air. It concerns the carriage of space tourists on suborbital flights operated by a foreign company between two points which are mostly the same points in the territory of a State. For instance, Virgin Galactic, a UK based company with strong financial and operational ties to the US, UK and United Arab Emirates, plans to operate a suborbital flight from a point in New Mexico, US, via the edge of outer space, and then back to the same point in New Mexico .[59] Such 'cabotage' flights have, however, not yet been commercially operated.

3.8   Concluding Remarks

Market access conditions are in constant development. States are step by step liberalising nationality requirements by allowing increasing foreign investment in 'their' national airlines. This development raises questions on the nationality of airlines as the traditional requirements pertaining to ownership and control of the airline are being affected by the said trend. One option is to introduce the principal place of business as a link between State and airline, and this criterion has been practiced in ASAs. However, it raises another question, namely, the definition of this term, which is dictated by national law and its link to safety and security oversight in order to avoid 'flags of convenience'.

Another trend pertains to the acquisition of the Freedoms of the Air, and market access generally, outside the regime of bilateral agreements. Unilateral policies

---

59. *See*, B.I. Scott, *International Suborbital Passenger Transportation: An Analysis of the Current Legal Situation of Transit and Traffic Rights and Its Appropriate Regulation*, 14(2) Issues in Aviation Law & Policy 277–312 (2015).

conducted by, for instance, Lebanon, and regional or plurilateral agreements form a vehicle for the exchange of traffic rights. Examples are found in the quoted EU internal air transport market, the Agreement on Air Transport between the EU and the US of 2007 as amended in 2010, the Tasman Pact between Australia and New Zealand, the ASEAN arrangements between South East Asian Nations, the South Asian Association for Regional Cooperation (SAARC),[60] the Yamoussoukro Decision in Africa and Mercosur in Latin America. These agreements liberalise traffic rights, and hence, turn restrictions pertaining to market access based on sovereignty in the air into Freedoms of the Air. However, those regional agreements are not always implemented, and may continue to give room for the simultaneous maintenance of bilateral air service agreements which may even supersede such liberal regional agreements. Domestic interests sometimes prevent governments from moving forward with the process of liberalisation. This is different for the EU with its strongly implemented internal air transport market which is backed by EU institutions and EU law.[61]

In Latin America interesting developments take place via constructions pertaining to the de-nationalisation of airlines in terms of ownership and control, with LAN Airlines and AviancaTaca as the engines behind this. Chile is also a stimulator of liberalisation of international and domestic air services.[62]

4 FROM COOPERATION TO COMPETITION

In restrictive bilateral agreements, aeronautical authorities wanted to shield the designated airlines from competition. They stimulated cooperation between the airlines from the two sides or at least wished to prevent their own carriers from losing market shares as result of competitive forces in the market place because the survival of the national carriers was, and, in certain parts of the world, still is seen as a national interest of the State designating it or them. For instance, States sanctioned or even stimulated designated airlines to conclude 'pool arrangements', which were aimed at sharing the expenses and/or the revenues of the operated international services.

Such restrictive agreements permit and/or encourage coordination of capacity, route planning and pricing. In extreme cases, such coordination is mandated; indeed traffic rights are made contingent on airline-to-airline agreements. Single designation, on routes if not across the entire market, is also typical of such agreements.

This attitude has resulted in 'hard core' economic regulation setting *a priori* standards for the operations undertaken by the designated carriers on the agreed international services. Such agreements require designated carriers to:

■ File schedules specifying routes, frequencies and equipment for approval each traffic season, based on prior coordination with the designated airline of the other Party.

---

60. Including Afghanistan, Bangladesh, Bhutan, India, Nepal, the Maldives, Pakistan and Sri Lanka.
61. *See,* section 2.1 of Chapter 3.
62. *See,* J.I. García-Arboleda, *Transnational Airlines in Latin America Facing the Fear of Nationality,* 37(2) Air & Space Law 93–118 (2012).

- File all fares proposed to be charged, also following coordination, often with lead times of up to ninety days.
- Request approval for exercise of fifth Freedom traffic rights on operations already specified in the agreed air services schedule.
- Provide, through its aeronautical authorities, statistics that document the traffic actually being carried in order to keep track of market requirements.

In this context, virtually the only norm binding such authorities is, however, the concept of *balance of benefits*. That concept gives the aeronautical authorities large discretionary powers to conduct aviation policies, as opposed to competition authorities which have to apply stricter norms when making their decisions.

However, the above restrictive stance was not the letter or spirit of the original 1946 Bermuda I Agreement between the United States and the United Kingdom which contained provisions that are a verbatim feature of many ASAs to the present day. These provisions can be characterised as formulae for *managed competition*. They aimed to create a "fair and equal opportunity", implying balanced opportunities for the designated air carriers from the two sides, to provide the agreed international services. Standards for price setting were established designed to ensure reasonable profits. Airlines, when planning their schedules, were given guidance that they should not "unduly affect" the opportunities of their competitors. Separate principles were established for fifth as opposed to 3rd and 4th Freedom traffic; that is, the latter was to be subordinated to take into account the predominant interest of one of the partners and a third country could have on the routing.

Importantly, the capacity controls were hortatory rather than hard; that is, they provided for *ex post facto* review rather than so-called 'pre-determination' of capacity. Pre-determination meaning schedules and capacities were subject to advance approval and also single designation limiting market access and thus competition to one airline of each party, however, became a feature of many subsequent agreements concluded by other states which otherwise relied heavily on Bermuda language.

In the traffic conferences of IATA, minimum fares for passenger traffic and rates for cargo traffic were agreed upon by the member airlines. IATA had its own compliance office to prevent undercutting of the agreed minimum tariffs. The following principal regimes are applied, varying from restrictive to liberal:

- *double disapproval* of tariff filings by designated air carriers by the aeronautical authorities of the two sides;[63]
- *national approval of country of origin pricing*;
- *free pricing*, with safeguards for excessively low or high pricing is adopted by countries engaged in 'Open Skies' relations, and in the EU regime. When governments withdraw from controlling pricing, competition authorities, applying competition (EU) and anti-trust (US) laws, assume this role.

---

63. *See*, B. Cheng, *The Law of International Air Transport* 441–453 (1962).

Pricing coordination, for example, in the classical Bermuda case, emphasised multi-lateral as opposed to bilateral tariff coordination, often expressly defined as IATA tariff coordination, for which a consumer-friendly argument could be made. In a period when interlining was a dominant feature of passenger itineraries, a formal system was needed to coordinate pricing and allocate so-called pro-rates to providers of partial itineraries.

In certain jurisdictions, to begin with the US and after that the EU, the IATA system of price coordination and other cooperative commercial arrangements between airlines was subject to review by competition authorities of these jurisdictions and operated under conditioned exemptions made by them. However, application of anti-trust (US) and competition (EU) legislation to IATA tariff coordinating practices ended its role in this area.[64] Currently these exemptions do not apply anymore as the entire range of commercial activities carried out by airlines is subject to, naturally *ex post facto*, review conducted by said authorities.

The *open skies* regimes are discussed in section 5.2, creating a market for the operation of air services subject to review by competition authorities.[65]

5   COMMERCIAL OPPORTUNITIES

ASAs also address commercial, or so called 'doping business' rights for the airlines. They are designed to help these airlines to market their services also in the territory of the contracting party. They include but are not limited to:

- the establishment and extent of foreign staffing of airline offices as well as use of agents abroad;
- sales of tickets in local or convertible currency in the other country;
- ground handling opportunities, that is opportunities for 'self' handling by the foreign airline(s) providing a choice between two or more providers of ground-handling services;
- currency conversion and remittance of funds including revenues from tickets and profits by airlines to their home countries;
- non-discriminatory and unrestricted access to and use of Global Distribution Systems (GDSs) assuring the sale of the air services by an airline in the other country through computers and electronic channels.

The above rights are important for the revenues of the airline, and for structuring the operations in the territory of the other country. Restrictions on these rights can have serious consequences including discontinuation of the operation of air services as evidenced by the current situation in Venezuela where many airlines do not operate

---

64. *See*, P.P.C. Haanappel, *The Law and Policy of Air Space and Outer Space* 118–120 and 124–129 (2003).
65. *See*, H.E. Cline, *Hijacking Open Skies: The Line between Tough Competition and Unfair Advantage in the International Aviation Market*, 81(3) Journal of Air Law and Commerce 529–560 (2016).

anymore because of problems with currency remittance of ticket sales proceeds sold in local currency, and other commercial opportunities.[66]

6 USE OF INFRASTRUCTURE

States are obliged to provide the necessary infrastructure for the safe operation of air services.[67] The provision of infrastructure is subject to the principle of non-discrimination as to the nationality of the aircraft whose operator uses the infrastructural facilities.[68]

Infrastructural facilities are airports and all related facilities, such as runways, platforms, navigation aids for landing and take-off and navigation services for *en route* traffic. Access to these facilities is subject to the availability of slots allowing operators to use runways and gates at a certain time, as to which *see* the IATA Worldwide Slot Guidelines which may have been implemented in national law.[69]

Economic regulation of access to infrastructure is regulated on a multilateral basis, with implementation and variations at the national or regional (EU) level.[70] The establishment of airport charges, also referred to as *user charges,* is subject to a number of principles defined by ICAO.[71] They are to:

- Prohibit non-discrimination as to the nationality of the aircraft.
- Create transparency of and consultations with the users on the establishment of the charge.
- Foster cost-relatedness, that is, there must be a relationship between the level of the charge and the cost of the service provided by the operator of the airport and the operator of the navigation services.[72]

The ICAO principles are implemented and elaborated in ASAs,[73] national aviation acts and regulations. ICAO Resolutions remind ICAO States of their exclusive

---

66. *See,* IATA, *IATA Calls on Venezuela to Address Issue of Blocked Funds,* at: www.iata.org/pressroom/pr/Pages/2015–06-08-04.aspx. KLM also decided to discontinue its flights to Cairo, Egypt, because of the restrictions imposed by the Egyptian government with respect to the transfer of foreign currencies from Egypt; *see,* www.upinthe sky.nl of 14 September 2016.
67. *See,* for instance, Art.'s 15, 28 and 68 of the Chicago Convention; States must also implement the standards laid down in Annex 6, Operation of Aircraft, Annex 11, Air Traffic Services, Annex 14, Aerodromes and Annex 15, Aeronautical Information Services.
68. *See,* S. Hobe and W. Müller-Rostin, *Legal Relationship between the Airport Operator and the Air Carrier – A Regulatory Grey Area?* 62(2) Zeitschrift für Luft- und Weltraumrecht 169–184 (2013).
69. The implementation of these Guidelines in EU law is discussed in section 5.5.1 of Chapter 3; for Latin America *see,* J.I. Garcia-Arboleda, *Airport Slot Allocation Regulation in Latin America: Between Building Fortresses and Protecting Newcomers,* 12(3) Issues in Aviation Law and Policy 573–614 (2013).
70. *See,* Art. 15 of the Chicago Convention; as to EU law *see* section 5.1 of Chapter 3.
71. *See also,* ICAO Doc. 9082, *ICAO's Policies on Charges for Airports and Air Navigation Services,* ninth edition (2012); *see also,* M. Tonelli, *Flying in the Dark: How a Legal Loophole Endangers Critical Infrastructure,* 80(4) The Journal of Air Law and Commerce 693 (2015).
72. *See,* L. Brockhoeft, *Transparency of Airline Ancillary Fees: Market Incentives for an Industry-Based Solution,* 80(4) Journal of Air Law and Commerce 749 (2015).
73. A clause on *User Charges* reads:

responsibilities for the provision of infrastructure while recognising that tasks coming under those international State responsibilities may be carried out by other entities, including privatised entities.[74] This responsibility regards the operation of airports and the provision of air navigation services pursuant to the terms of Article 28 of the Chicago Convention. ICAO stimulates increased efficiency and improved cost-efficiencies in the provision of airports and air navigation services, including the foundation for a sound cooperation between providers and users.[75]

The ICAO principles also apply to *en route* or air navigation charges. Questions on the level, especially the cost relatedness of such charges have been raised by European airlines passing through Russian airspace. The question is still on the agenda of EU and Russian policymakers.

The above disagreement shows that the question of charges is a topical and sensitive one. Charges form expenses which airlines have to pay providers of infrastructure for their use of it. It is not always easy to draw up the precise costs of the use

---

1. User Charges that may be imposed by the competent charging authorities or bodies of each Contracting Party on the Airlines of the other Contracting Party shall be just, reasonable, not unjustly discriminatory, and equitably appointed among categories of users. In any event, any such Users Charges shall be assessed on the Airlines of the other Contracting Party on terms not less favorable than the most favorable terms available to any other Airline at the time the charges are assessed.
2. User Charges imposed on the Airlines of the other Contracting Party may reflect, but shall not exceed, the full cost to the competent charging authorities or bodies of providing the appropriate airport, airport environmental, air navigation, and aviation security facilities and services at the airport or within the airport system. Such full cost may include a reasonable return on assets, after depreciation. Facilities and services for which charges are made shall be provided on an efficient and economic basis.
3. Each Contracting Party shall encourage consultations between the competent charging authorities or bodies in its Territory and the Airlines using the services and facilities, and shall encourage the competent charging authorities or bodies and the Airlines to exchange such information as may be necessary to permit an accurate review of the reasonableness of the charges in accordance with the principles of paragraphs (1) and (2) of this Article. ...

74. *See* Standard 2.1 of ICAO Annex 11: Confirming State responsibility for the provision of air navigation services while leaving the option for performance by private entities, licensed by States, open, *see:*

> *2.1 Establishment of authority* 2.1.1 Contracting States shall determine, in accordance with the provisions of this Annex and for the territories over which they have jurisdiction, those portions of the airspace and those aerodromes where air traffic services will be provided. They shall thereafter arrange for such services to be established and provided in accordance with the provisions of this Annex, except that, by mutual agreement, a State may delegate to another State the responsibility for establishing and providing air traffic services in flight information regions, control areas or control zones extending over the territories of the former.

> *See also*, F. Schubert, *The Corporatization of Air Traffic Control: Drifting between Private and Public Air Law* XXII-II Annals of Air and Space Law 224–242 (1997).

75. *See* ICAO Doc. 9082, *ICAO's Policies on Charges for Airports and Air Navigation Services* (2012). As to the emerging contractual relationship between air transport and air navigation service providers, *see*, V. Stamatis, *Airport Competition Regulation in Europe*, section 2.1, and the last paragraph of section 5.1 of Chapter 3 (2016).

of infrastructure in an unbiased and non-discriminatory manner as relations between airports and airlines are multifaceted in which context the payment of charges is one, albeit an important factor.[76]

7 CHARGES AND TAXES

The provision on customs duties and taxes is not about payment, but exemption from them. This is different from the previous section where charges are due for the use of infrastructure.

The difference between charges and taxes is not always clear, because the terms are used interchangeably. Charges are deemed to be cost-related; they are recovered as compensation for a service rendered or damage done. Taxes are general costs assessed on, for instance, aviation, which generate income for the taxing authority. The distinction is becoming blurred.[77]

A customs duties and taxes Article in ASA requires each party to exempt from duties, taxes and charges regular equipment, ground equipment, aircraft fuel, consumable technical supplies, spare parts including engines, stores and supplies, including but not limited to such items as food, beverages and liquor, tobacco and other products destined for sale to or use by passengers in limited quantities during the flight, provided such equipment and supplies remain on board aircraft engaged in international services.[78] Import duties are therefore not imposed because the said goods are in transit on an international service. The measure purports to facilitate international air transport.

There is also a provision exempting from all fees, charges and taxes:

- aircraft stores introduced into or supplied in the territory of the other State;
- ground equipment and spare parts including engines introduced into the territory of the other State for the servicing, maintenance or repair of aircraft;
- fuel, lubricants and technical supplies introduced into or supplied in the territory of the other State for use in the agreed international services, even when these supplies are to be used on a part of the journey performed over the territory of the State where such supplies are taken on board.[79]

---

76. Section 9.4 of this Chapter illustrates the sensitivity of this topic in an arbitration case mentioned there.
77. *See,* Pablo Mendes de Leon and S. Mirmina, *Protecting the Environment by Use of Fiscal Measures: Legality and Propriety,* 62(3) Journal of Air Law and Commerce 791–821 (1997); R. Abeyratne, *A Critical Look at ICAO Policies on Charges Levied for Airports and Air Navigation Services,* 34(3) Air & Space Law 177–188 (2009).
78. *See also,* Art. 24 of the Chicago Convention, ICAO Doc. 8632, *ICAO's Policies on Taxation in the Field of International Air Transport,* ICAO Assembly Resolution A37-18, Consolidated statement of continuing ICAO policies and practices related to environmental protection, as confirmed in: ICAO Doc. 9082, *ICAO's Policies on Charges for Airports and Air Navigation Services,* Resolution A37-20, Appendix E, *Taxation,* ICAO Doc. 9958 (2012).
79. *See,* the following standard clause: "There shall also be exempt, on the basis of reciprocity, from the taxes, levies, duties, fees and charges referred to in paragraph 1 of this article, with the exception of fees and charges based on the cost of the service provided: fuel, lubricants and consumable technical supplies introduced into or, supplied in the territory of a Party for use in

The latter exemption is an exception to the general rule that goods and services are taxed in the country where they are consumed, or taken on board as to which *see*, for instance, fuel for cars. This exemption is designed to facilitate international air transport.

Under pressure from environmental groups, the exemption of fuel from taxation has been questioned. Proposals are being made to terminate this exemption. The conclusion so far is that ICAO must take such a measure at a global level. ICAO has indeed always promoted the tax freedoms for air transport by maintaining the tax exempt status to at least certain aspects of the operations of international air transport.[80]

8 SETTLEMENT OF DISAGREEMENTS

8.1 Method of Settlement of Disagreements and Disputes

Disagreement is not the same as dispute. When a disagreement reaches a degree of definition and clarity where negotiations and consultations have failed to achieve consensus. Consequently, the views of the two sides concerning the performance or non-performance of treaty obligations are clearly opposed, necessitating methods of dispute settlement including arbitration and adjudication.[81]

If the two parties do not succeed in resolving their dispute, it shall be submitted to arbitration. Arbitration clauses are found in most bilateral agreements.[82]

In the history of Post Second World War aviation, the following disputes have been settled by arbitration.[83] Here is a summary description of those.

---

an aircraft of an airline of the other Party engaged in international air transportation, even when these supplies are to be used on a part of the journey performed over the territory of the Party in which they are taken on board".

80. *See,* ICAO Resolution A36-55 Appendix E: *Taxation*, ICAO Doc. 9902, Assembly Resolutions in force as of 27 September 2007.

81. *See,* ICJ, *Interpretation of the Peace Treaties with Bulgaria, Hungary and Romania,* Advisory opinion of 30 March 1950 (first phase), 1950 IC7 Reports 65, at 74.

82. Dispute settlement:

   1. Any dispute arising between the Parties relating to the interpretation or application of this Agreement, ... the Parties shall in the first place endeavour to settle it by consultations and negotiation.
   2. If the Parties fail to reach a settlement through consultations, the dispute may, at the request of either Party, be submitted to arbitrations in accordance with the procedures set forth below.

83. This list is not exhaustive; *see also,* B. Cheng, *The Law of International Air Transport* 454–464 (1962), R. Fennes, *International Air Cargo Transport Services: Economic Regulation and Policy* 99–127 (1997) who also analyses State practice generally with respect to the solution of international disagreements; *see also,* R.T. Dicker, *The Use of Arbitration in the Settlement of Bilateral Air Rights Disputes,* The Vanderbilt International 131–132 (1967/1968) and P.S. Dempsey, *Flights of Fancy and Fights of Fury: Arbitration and Adjudication of Commercial and Political Disputes in International Aviation,* 32(2) Georgia Journal of International and Comparative Law 231–305 (2004).

8.2 The US-France (1964): *Interpretation of 'Near East'*

The arbitration of this dispute evolved around the interpretation of the term 'Near East' as used in the bilateral agreement between France and the US of 1946. France granted the US as Route One from the US to Paris and beyond via intermediate points including Istanbul and Teheran, to China and beyond. Route Two goes from the US over Spain to Marseille and then via Milan and Budapest to Turkey and beyond. At stake was PanAm's wish to exercise fifth Freedom rights between Paris and Istanbul, and between Paris and Teheran.

The arbitration tribunal decided that US airlines had the right to serve Turkey via Paris, but without traffic rights. It also ruled that US airlines are entitled to exercise fifth Freedom rights between Paris and Teheran.[84] The tribunal did not rely so much on an interpretation of the term Near East as it was mentioned in Route One of the bilateral, but on French consent to purposes and subsequent practice.[85]

8.3 US-Italy (1965–1967): *Interpretation of Cargo/Mail*

Carriage of cargo had become an important feature of air transport. American carriers had all-cargo planes, but Alitalia did not have similar equipment. Section III of the Annex to the US-Italy bilateral agreement stated that technical and commercial freedoms are granted to the parties to transport 'passengers, cargo and mail'. The question here was whether all-cargo services were permitted under the US-Italy agreement of 1948.

Again, there was a high commercial interest at stake. Consultations failed to provide a result. Both parties agreed to arbitrate. It was ruled that the 1948 Agreement permitted all-cargo services. Arbitrator Monaco from Italy dissented. This fact, of course, weakened the enforcement process of the decision.[86]

8.4 US-UK (1992): *On Heathrow User Charges*

In November 1979, two and a half years after the conclusion of the Bermuda II Agreement referred to above, the British Airports Authority announced large increases in user charges for the year 1980/81. The increase had the effect (de facto) of raising

---

84. Decision of the Arbitration Tribunal, Established pursuant to the Arbitration Agreement, signed at Paris on 22 January 1963, between the United States of America and France, decided at Geneva on 22 December 1963, and published in International Legal Materials 668 (1964); *see also*, 4 International Legal Materials 974 (1965) and 60 American Journal of International Law 413 (1966).
85. *See*, P.B. Larsen, *Arbitration of the United States-France Air Traffic Rights Dispute*, 30 Journal of Air Law and Commerce 231–247 (1964).
86. *See*, P.B. Larsen, *The United States-Italy Air Transport Arbitration: Problems of Treaty Interpretation and Enforcement*, 61(2) American Journal of International Law 496–520 (1967), and S.D. Metzer, *Treaty Interpretation and the United States-Italy Air Transport Arbitration*, 61 American Journal of International Law 1007–1011 (1967), supporting a *textual* Interpretation of the US-Italy agreement.

charges to the US carriers operating at London Heathrow Airport, especially PanAm and TWA, but also Flying Tigers, by some 60 to 70 per cent. According to the charging system which was set up by the British Airports Authority in 1979, a rather sharp differentiation was made between aircraft movements in *peak* hours and in *off-peak* hours. As a result, American carriers were particularly affected by the new charging system. Of course, in law, no distinction was made between UK and non-UK carriers. The American carriers contended that the British Airports Authority was bound to make Heathrow Airport available to all operators – or all aircraft of other States party to the Chicago Convention – on equal terms. Also, they relied on a provision of the Bermuda II Agreement that the charges must be *cost related*.[87]

The arbitration tribunal found that the UK government had failed to monitor the pricing system of the British Airports Authority. Its sharply differentiated peak/off-peak charging system was in practice working "inequitably" to the detriment of the US designated airlines. It was argued that British Airways was enjoying advantages that were denied to US airlines, in relation to rescheduling flights out of peak hours. The UK government was required to pay the US government about USD 30 million.[88]

8.5 Concluding Remarks

As explained in section 3.3.8 of Chapter 1, the above methods of dispute settlement are rarely used as negotiations are the preferred option. Thus negotiations are the most practiced and effective methods of settlement: there is no final award as in the case of legal proceedings, embarrassing one of the two States; the result forms a compromise which both parties are interested in living with, and it is expedient.

Negotiations and consultations may also take place with a view to amending the bilateral air agreement. The tool of termination, as to which *see* below, has also been used in rare instances only in light of the broader policy and possibly political repercussions of such an act for the trade relations between the States.

---

87. Art. 10 of Bermuda 2: "User charges may reflect, but shall not exceed, the full cost to the competent charging authorities of providing appropriate airport and air navigation facilities, and may provide for a reasonable rate of return on assets, after depreciation. In the provision of facilities and services, the competent authorities shall have regard to such factors as efficiency, economy, environmental impact and safety of operations. User charges shall be based on sound economic principles and on the generally accepted accounting practices within the territory of the appropriate Contracting Party."

   See also, ICAO, Statement by the Council to contracting States on Charges for Airports and Air Navigation Services (1992), ICAO Doc. 9082/4 at 3: "The cost basis for airport charges", and ICAO's Policies on Charges for Airports and Air Navigation Services (ICAO Doc. 9082, as updated), and ICAO Assembly Resolution A36-15, Appendix F.

88. *See*, XXIV Reports of International Arbitral Awards 3–334 (1992): *United States-United Kingdom Arbitration concerning Heathrow Airport User Charges* (United States-United Kingdom): Award on the First Question (revised 18 June 1993), at: http://untreaty.un.org/cod/ riaa/cases/ vol_XXIV/3-334.pdf; Samuel Witten, *The US-UK Arbitration Concerning Heathrow Airport User Charges*, 89 The American Journal of International Law 174–192 (1995).

9 REGISTRATION AND TERMINATION

Bilateral agreements must be registered with the Council of ICAO, which shall publish the agreement "as soon as possible."[89] Since MoUs mentioned at the end of section 4.6 above contain sensitive information, they are not registered or published.

Termination of the bilateral agreement requires giving notice in writing through diplomatic channels to the other party and to ICAO, in which case the agreement shall terminate in six months or one year after the date when the notice has been received by the other party.

The Italy-US agreement has been denounced by Italy following the arbitral decision referred to in section 9.3, above. In the 1990s, the US and Thailand cancelled their agreement. The UK, French and Brazilian governments terminated their bilateral agreements over differences in the interpretation of the provisions on designation and capacity in the 1970s and 1980s. Canada and the UK had a disagreement on the exercise of fifth freedom rights beyond the London Heathrow airport, following which Canada gave the twelve months' notice of termination to the UK because of UK efforts to move Canada's designated carrier from the London Heathrow airport to Gatwick. The disagreement was resolved within this twelve months period, but Canada renounced the International Air Services Transit agreement in order to obtain leverage in relation to the UK as transit rights were not multilaterally available.

The announcement of termination of the ASA has more than once served as a political tool to re-negotiate the points of disagreement. Terminations have rarely been effectuated in practice, because of fear of a trade war between the two countries, and escalation on the political level.

10 OPEN SKIES AGREEMENTS

10.1 Launching the Open Skies Policy

The term 'Open Skies' indicates a shift from the traditional exchange of traffic rights towards a system under which regulation of competition between designated airlines forms the core element. As freedom is inherent to such a system, it would seem more appropriate to list what should *not* be allowed under such a regime instead of the present situation of a non-exhaustive list of what *is* allowed. The US DoT uses the term 'Open Skies' to designate a liberal approach towards the operation of international air services. The term therefore is more of a marketing tool than a legal concept. Parties to an Open Skies agreement have to translate the policy into legal terms. As will be seen below, such terms may – even slightly – vary from one agreement to another.

Open Skies agreements may contain the following elements:

- Freedom of each country's airline to operate air transport services between any point or points in the countries of the contracting parties, or via the home

---

89. *See,* Art. 83 of the Chicago Convention; *see also,* B. Cheng, *The Law of International Air Transport* 471–473 (1962).

country of each country's airline, that is, the operation of sixth Freedom traffic, including to intermediate and beyond points, subject to a third State's approval, and to customs, technical, operational or environmental restrictions.

- Multiple designation of airlines.
- No capacity limitations.
- Option of seventh Freedom for the operations of all-cargo and in exceptional cases, passenger services.
- Unrestricted charter provisions.
- Subject to intervention from competent competition authorities designed to prevent monopolies, predatory pricing and artificially low prices due to government subsidies, freedom with respect to pricing.
- Promotion of liberalisation in the field of charter flights, cargo and Global Distribution Systems (GDS).
- Performance of support functions at airports located in the territory of the other party.

The exercise of the above rights is subject to national and local rules regarding safety, customs, security, and the environment. Also, slot scarcity can place restrictions on the exercise of traffic rights.[90]

States, whose 'flag' carrier is engaged in an alliance with a US carrier, are likely to receive *anti-trust immunity* by the US for such an alliance when concluding an Open Skies agreement with the US. Apart from the legal element, the grant of anti-trust immunity has an important *policy* element.[91] Whereas the US grants anti-trust immunity only if an Open Skies agreement has been concluded, partner countries may only be willing to conclude an Open Skies agreement if anti-trust immunity will be granted to an alliance involving their designated carrier.

Open Skies does not mean that all elements falling under economic regulation of international air transport services are liberalised under the agreement.[92] The following restrictions remain, or may be made subject to further negotiation:

- national ownership and control clauses for designated air carriers;[93]
- seventh Freedom operations for passengers, and in some cases for cargo;
- cabotage;
- commercial opportunities in the other country, including the requirement that code-sharing must be based on traffic rights for all partners;
- (wet-) leasing arrangements in which area restrictions are also gradually being lifted as evidenced by India's decision made in 2016 to allowing its

---

90. *See*, section 5.5.1 of Chapter 3.
91. *See*, Pablo Mendes de Leon, *Before and After the Tenth Anniversary of the Open Skies Agreement Netherlands-US of 1992*, 28(4/5) Air & Space Law 280–312 (2002); *see also*, the alliance cases explained in section 3.3.4 of Chapter 3.
92. *See*, B. Havel and G. Sanchez, *The Principles and Practice of International Aviation Law* (2014).
93. *See* C. Grau Tanner, *New Proposals to Break the Foreign Ownership Deadlock in the Airline Industry*, 34(2) Air & Space Law 127–134 (2009).

airlines to use foreign registered aircraft which move may be governed by Article 83*bis* of the Chicago Convention,[94] and designed to lower costs for Indian airlines, promote regional air traffic and to facilitate the return of the aircraft to its foreign owner.

- restrictions pertaining to currency remittance as referred to in section 5, above.

Apart from the EU-US agreement on air transport[95] and the EU-Canada agreement on air transport (2009),[96] neither the Open Skies policy nor the subsequent Open Skies agreements make provision for the conduct of a harmonised competition policy. Absent a global competition law regime, States, and competent regional organisations, such as the EU, dictate the terms of these regimes which may be applied extra-territorially in cross-border provision of air services.[97] ICAO is asking attention for the role of 'fair competition' in air transport while promoting cooperation between competition authorities across the world, and attempts to establish understanding principles governing competition by conducting research.[98]

The US also targeted countries in the Pacific, Latin-America and Africa for shaping its Open Skies policy. Without going into differences regarding, for instance the grant of seventh Freedom rights for all-cargo operations, these Open Skies agreements contain similar clauses as mentioned above.[99] The total number of Open Skies agreements concluded by the US amount to approximately 120.

The US is not the only country engaging into Open Skies relations with another country. For instance, the UK and Singapore have concluded an agreement which is more liberal than the US Open Skies agreements as the UK-Singapore agreement grants

---

94. *See*, Art. 83*bis*(a) *Transfer of certain functions and duties:*

   when an aircraft registered in a contracting State is operated pursuant to an agreement for the lease, charter or interchange of the aircraft or any similar arrangement by an operator who has his principal place of business or, if he has no such place of business, his permanent residence in another contracting State, the State of registry may, by agreement with such other State, transfer to it all or part of its functions and duties as State of registry in respect of that aircraft under Arts 12, 30, 31 and 32a. The State of registry shall be relieved of responsibility in respect of the functions and duties transferred.

95. *See*, section 10.3 below.
96. *See*, http://ec.europa.eu/transport/air/international_aviation/country_index/canada_en.htm.
97. *EU Air Transport Liberalisation: Process, Impacts and Future Considerations.* Co-authors: Prof. Jaap de Wit and Dr Guillaume Burghouwt. International Transport Forum/OECD, Discussion Papers 2015-04, 1–55, http://internationaltransportforum.org/jtrc/Discussion Papers/DP201504.pdf.
98. *See*, ICAO Air Transport Symposium, held in Montreal on 30–31 March 2016, as to which *see*, http://www.icao.int/Meetings/iats2016/Pages/default.aspx; *see also*, Joanna R. Shelton, Deputy Secretary-General of the OECD, *Competition on Policy. What Chance for International Rules?*, available at http://www.oecd.org/competition/mergers/1919969.pdf.
99. *See*, B.F. Havel, *Beyond Open Skies: A New Regime for International Aviation* (2007).

cabotage rights to Singaporean carriers in the UK.[100] Capacity and other restrictions under an agreement which has also been termed as an Open Skies agreement have been lifted in 2016 between China and Australia; this agreement also includes unlimited code share opportunities for carriers which have agreements thereto with Chinese and Australian carriers.

10.2 Regional Liberalisation Developments

In 2001, six members of the Asian Pacific Co-operation (APEC), namely, the US, Brunei, New Zealand, Chile, Peru and Singapore concluded a plurilateral agreement called the *Multilateral Agreement on the Liberalisation of International Air Transport* (MALIAT).[101] The agreement is designed to relax the airline nationality clause in a plurilateral fashion; however, nothing in the agreement affects each party's laws and regulations concerning ownership and control of airlines. Market access opportunities in terms of the first six Freedoms of the Air, with seventh Freedom rights for cargo services, and the option for the provision of seventh Freedom passenger rights and/or cabotage rights are included. There are no restrictions on pricing or capacity arrangements whereas commercial opportunities for airlines, including third country code-sharing have been expanded.

In Africa, the *Yamoussoukro Declaration* on air transport liberalisation (2000) abolishes restrictions on the operation of the first, second, third and fourth Freedom of the Air, and a gradual removal of restrictions on the operation of the fifth Freedom of the Air, as well as liberalisation of pricing, for airlines designated by one of the countries having adhered to this declaration. The African Union is further promoting the implementation of this decision. Regional African organisations such as the Common Market for East and South Africa (COMESA), the South African Development Community (SADC) and the East African Community (EAC) crafted liberalisation policies, including sometimes a competition law regime which is applicable to the operation of air services in the region. Many African bilateral air services have been inspired by the principles of the Yamoussoukro Declaration and have been concluded

---

100. *See*, A. Tan, *Singapore's New Air Services Agreements with the E.U. and the U.K.: Implications for Liberalization in Asia*, 73(2) Journal of Air Law and Commerce 101–132 (2008).

101. *See*, B. Havel and G. Sanchez, *The Principles and Practice of International Aviation Law* 113 (2014). "MALIAT makes some minor but interesting modifications to the open skies template, such as replacing the traditional ownership and control benchmarks in favor of a more plastic standard of 'effective control' by citizens of the designating contracting State accompanied by (instead of substantial ownership) incorporation and principle place of business in that State. The revised standard might allow a foreign investor to take a large equity stake in a MALIAT-party airline, but otherwise the agreement does little more than regulate the bilateral aviation relations of its signatories. For instance, an authentically multilateral feature, such as collective enforcement of the treaty's terms against a scofflaw party, does not exist within the agreement. Similarly, MALIAT does not provide an open investment regime among its members, nor does it facilitate cross-border regulatory harmonization. In reality, MALIAT amounts to little more than a 'pooled' open skies accord."

under the auspices of the ICAO Air Services Negotiations Conference (ICAN),[102] for instance the South Africa-Zambia agreement of 2013.

Twenty-two Arab States concluded the so-called *Damascus Agreement for the Liberalisation of Air Transport*. This is a relatively comprehensive agreement encompassing not only relaxation of market access that also provisions on smoking on-board aircraft, consumer protection and fair competition. In 2016 the Damascus Agreement, which is concluded under the auspices of the Arab Civil Aviation Commission (ACAN), has been ratified by eight States.[103]

In South East Asia, the Association of South East Asian Nations (ASEAN) is liberalising intra-ASEAN traffic. In 2015, ASEAN States engaged into an Open Skies Agreement covering passenger and cargo services. If this agreement is successfully implemented, there will be no regulatory limits on the frequency or capacity of flights between international airports across the ten ASEAN States. The agreement liberalises third, fourth and fifth Freedom traffic in the region, subject to limitations in terms of timing, and participation of States, as, for instance, Indonesia only reluctantly appears to take part in this liberalisation process, amongst other, because of the size and the complexity of its market. Moreover, not included in the current agreement are steps towards opening up ASEAN aviation to common ownership, in an area where airlines are still for the greater part government owned.[104]

	Restrictive Bilateral Agreements	Open Skies Agreements	Tasman Pact (2000) Australia – New Zealand	APEC (2001)	EU Internal Market
Nationality requirements airlines	Applicable	Applicable; EU-US agreement: EU clause	None, subject to the establishment of a daughter company[1]	Multilateral 'APEC' formula, subject to national law	Community requirements[2]
Designation	Single	Multiple	Multiple	Multiple	Multiple[5]

---

102. The objective of the conference is to facilitate ICAO Member States in their bilateral or multilateral air service negotiations and to improve the efficiency of the process by providing a central meeting place for States to gather and conduct such negotiations at one location; *see*, the ICAO ICAN website.

103. Namely Jordan, the United Arab Emirates, Syria, Oman, Lebanon, Morocco and Yemen, as to which *see*, A. Tan, *The 2004 Damascus Agreement: Liberalizing Market Access and Ownership Rules for Arab Air Carriers*, 35 Annals of Air and Space Law 1–13 (2010).

104. *See*, A. Tan, *Toward a Single Aviation Market in ASEAN: Regulatory Reform and Industry Challenges* (2013) ERIA Discussion Paper Series; *The Proposed E.U.-ASEAN Comprehensive Air Transport Agreement: What Might It Contain and Can It Work?* (2015) 43 Transport Policy 76–84 (2013).

	Restrictive Bilateral Agreements	Open Skies Agreements	Tasman Pact (2000) Australia – New Zealand	APEC (2001)	EU Internal Market
Traffic rights[4]	I-IV, V subject to conditions	I-VI, VII in exceptional cases[5]	I-VI, VII, VIII, IX for cargo; Options for VII/pax	I-VI, VII for cargo; Option for VII/pax	I-IX
Pricing	Double approval	Free	Free	Free	Free
Capacity	Subject to conditions	Free	Free	Free	Free
Code-sharing	Sometimes permitted, and subject to conditions	Allowed	Allowed; including third country code-sharing	Allowed; including third country code-sharing	Allowed without restrictions
Scheduled/ Non-scheduled services	Scheduled (including cargo services	All services (scheduled/ non-scheduled/ cargo)	All services	Scheduled, including cargo; non-scheduled to be included	All service

1. With the exception of Qantas pursuant to the terms of the Qantas Sale Act (1992): http://www.austlii.edu.au/au/legis/cth/consol_act/qsa1992120/.

2. Including that nationality of airlines operating under the EU internal market regime (Article 4 of EU Regulation 1008/2008) are 'substantially owned' and 'effectively controlled' by nationals of the EU, and have their principal place of business in a Member State of the EU.

3. The term 'designation' does not apply to the regime set forth by the European Community; access to intra-EU routes is free for Community airlines if the conditions drawn up by the said Regulation 1008/2008 are satisfied.

4. In terms of Freedoms of the Air; see the Annex to this report.

5. For instance, on specified cargo flights.

In Latin America, the *Mercosur Agreement* is aimed at achieving free trade in air services between the participating countries along the lines of the above-mentioned *Yamoussoukro Declaration*. This said, all bilateral agreements are still in place, and have not been replaced by a regional framework. The same is true for the multilateral regime prevailing in Africa.

A real sign on the wall constitutes the *Tasman Pact*,[105] concluded on 20 November 2000, liberalising air traffic between Australia and New Zealand. The Tasman Pact goes further than Open Skies agreements as nationality requirements for airlines flying under the Tasman Pact, apart from the Australian carrier Qantas, have

---

105. *See,* http://www.executive.govt.nz/gosche/open_skies/.

been abolished thus promoting 'international airlines' in the most genuine meaning of the term. Foreign airlines are allowed to set up daughter companies. Airlines flying under the Tasman Pact may exercise all freedoms of the Air. All of these relaxations may be seen as reflections of the position adopted by Australia and New Zealand during the Conference preparing the Chicago Convention. These countries expressed a strong commitment towards a liberal regulation of air services.[106]

In 2016, India has introduced a 'selective' open skies regime, that is, it adopted an Open Skies agreement with the countries belonging to the South Asian Association for Regional Cooperation (SAARC)[107] and those situated beyond the 5000 kilometres radius from New Delhi.[108] Hence, this policy does not include, for instance, Singapore and the Gulf States.

The above regional and plurilateral arrangements are definitely designed to promote liberalisation of air services, and have, in varying degrees, yielded results. However, it would appear that relaxation of regulatory conditions impeding progress cannot be achieved in the same manner as in the EU, among others, because supra-national institutions such as a regional court of justice and a strongly equipped executive body such as the EU commission, mandated with enforcement powers, are lacking in these arrangements.

10.3 The EU-US Agreement on Air Transport

10.3.1 The Agreement of 2007

The EU-US Agreement[109] is essentially an 'Open Skies' type of agreement as it provides for the operation of unlimited third and fourth Freedom rights,[110] and also fifth Freedom rights on beyond routes, for the airlines of each side, with freedom of pricing. The operation of seventh Freedom rights, that is, the right for an EU airline to carry traffic between a point in the US and a point in a third country, and the right for a US airline to operate between a point in the EU and a point in a third country, is more restricted.

EU airlines can operate combination passenger services between any point in the US and any point in not only the EU but also the European Common Aviation Area,[111] including Norway, Iceland, Albania and the States that were formerly part of Yugoslavia. Unrestricted seventh Freedom rights for all-cargo services are given to EU airlines, but to US airlines only in respect of services involving a point in one of eight named

---

106. See, J. Schenkman, *International Civil Aviation Organization* 81–92 (1955) and J.C. Cooper, *The Right to Fly* 157–174 (1947).
107. Including Afghanistan, Bangladesh, Bhutan, India, Nepal, the Maldives, Pakistan and Sri Lanka.
108. Civil Aviation Authority of India, *National Civil Aviation Policy 2016*, paragraph 9, at: http://www.civilaviation.gov.in/sites/default/files/Final_NCAP_2016_15-06-2016.pdf.
109. In this section also referred to as the Agreement. For the text *see* Council Decision 2007/339.
110. Subject to some special provisions in the case of Ireland: *see* Annex 1, Section 4.
111. See, A.S. Thorsteinsson, *Air Transport and the Agreement on the Agreement on the European Economic Area*, 40 Air & Space Law 229–230 (2015) at 326–327.

Member States – the Czech Republic, France, Germany, Luxembourg, Malta, Poland, Portugal and Slovakia. The scope of these rights in relation to the carriage of cargo between Columbia and Germany via a point in the US, and the Netherlands has been argued before a court in The Netherlands.[112]

Most significantly, the US has accepted the 'Community clause' as it will allow any EU/ European Economic Area (EEA) airline to operate between any point in the US and any point in the EU/EEA, thus remedying the illegality in the present bilateral agreements identified by the European Court of Justice (ECJ). EU/EEA airlines are allowed to commence services, and have in fact done so, between points in the US and points in a Member State other than their own, although the lack of slots at major airports may reduce the practical effects of this. The acceptance of the 'Community clause' facilitates cross-border mergers and acquisitions between Community airlines, as the US will no longer be able to threaten to refuse or take away traffic rights on the basis that the carrier is not substantially owned and effectively controlled by the airline's home State and/or its nationals.

Also, there will be greater flexibility for wet-leasing, code-sharing and franchising, opportunities for self-handling or to select among competing suppliers of handling services, facilitation of the combination of air services with surface transport, the ability for providers of computer reservation systems from one side to provide their services in the other, and the right for EU airlines to carry certain categories of US government traffic under the Fly America programme.

The Agreement contains no provisions on slots. The availability and allocation of slots at congested airports will continue to be governed by the applicable local rules, in the case of the EU, Regulation 95/93 as variously amended.[113] As a consequence, although US airlines will have in theory unlimited rights to operate air services from Heathrow, they will only be able to do so in practice if they can acquire slots there through the allocation process or trading.

The Agreement is different from typical open skies agreements in its provisions for cooperation in a number of areas: security, safety,[114] environment, competition law,[115] State aid and questions of ownership and control.

Furthermore, a Joint Committee has been established to resolve questions relating to the interpretation and application of the Agreement, to review its implementation and to facilitate greater cooperation, particularly by consulting on issues

---

112. As clearly explained by P. van Fenema, *Lufthansa Cargo 'Flower Flights' Columbia/Ecuador-Amsterdam: Netherlands Court Judgement on the Applicability of the EU-US Agreement on 'Establishment'*, 41(3) Air & Space Law 167 (2016).

113. *See*, section 5.5.1 of Chapter 3.

114. On 15 March 2011, the EU and the US concluded an cooperation agreement on safety which entered into force on 1 May 2011. The agreement is to enable the reciprocal acceptance of findings of compliance and approvals, promote a high degree of safety in air transport and ensure regulatory cooperation and harmonisation between the United States and the EU as regards airworthiness approvals and monitoring of civil aeronautical products, environmental testing and approvals of such products, and approvals and monitoring of maintenance facilities.

115. Including detailed provisions on cooperation in Annex 2.

dealt with in international organisations and in relations with third countries, including considering whether to adopt a joint approach.

Finally, third countries may be allowed to join the Agreement.[116] This may be an option for the UK when it decides to leave the EU. That is why it is called a plurilateral rather than a multilateral agreement – although there are no official legal definitions of these terms.

10.3.2 The Protocol of 2010 (Stage II)

The Protocol of 2010 has made the following amendments to the Agreement of 2007:

- Cooperation for the protection of the environment has been expanded as the parties intend to "jointly advancing global solutions" whereas procedures for the introduction of environmental measures have been aligned.[117]
- A closer cooperation in matters on aviation security leading to avoidance of duplication of work in this regard by reliance on each other's security measures.
- The procedure for accepting the designation of air carriers by the other Party in terms of compliance with safety and nationality requirements has been facilitated because that designation will be accepted without further questions, and be regarded as if such a designation "had been made by its own aeronautical authorities" unless specified circumstances occur.[118]
- The 'social dimension' has received a prominent place in the Agreement, as amended, as the Parties are committed to "recognise the importance of the social dimension" while respecting existing labour standards.[119]
- The powers of the Joint Committee have been broadened as it is now more specifically tasked to consider the impact of regulatory measures in the field of security, the environment, infrastructure and labour standards on the market access rights laid down in the Agreement.[120]
- The Parties endeavour to expand market access opportunities, including enhancing access of airlines to capital markets, in specified cases as mentioned in this provision, overseen by a more transparent cooperation between competition authorities.[121]
- Finally, Annex 3 pertaining to US Government Procured Transportation has been replaced as EU airlines now have the right to transport passengers and cargo on flights which the US government procures as indicated in this article.

---

116. Pursuant to the provisions of Art. 18(5) of the Agreement.
117. See, Art. 15 as amended by Art. 3 of the Protocol of 2010.
118. See, Art. 6bis as amended by Art. 2 of the Protocol of 2010.
119. See, Art. 17bis as amended by Art. 4 of the Protocol of 2010.
120. See, Art. 18 as amended by Art. 5 of the Protocol of 2010.
121. See, Art. 21 as amended by Art. 6 of the Protocol of 2010.

The case of Air Norwegian identifies the relevance of social conditions playing an increasingly prominent role in air transport. On 2 December 2016, Norwegian Air International received final approval from the US Department of Transportation to fly between points in the EU, to begin with Barcelona, Spain, and the US, to begin with Newark, despite objections raised by US Congress, principal US airlines and labour unions who contended that Norwegian Air International's business model violated workers' protections embedded in the U.S.-EU agreement that ended most barriers to trans-Atlantic flights.[122]

The Protocol of 2010 introduced new features into the air transport relations between the two parties, notably in the field of labour and the environment. Except for the liberalisation of US procured transportation, existing market opportunities have been maintained but not expanded. There are no plans to modify the current Agreement but the work of the Joint Committee as briefly explained below helps to enhance mutual understanding of the various questions.

10.3.3   The Working of the Joint Committee

The Joint Committee which has been established under the EU-US Agreement is doing its work, and gets together two times per year, discussing a broad range of regulatory issues. They include the following:

- Environment/emissions as to which *see* the previous subsection, on EU ETS, and the introduction of new CO_2 standards by ICAO.
- Environment/noise as the US but also other States such as India claim that opening markets and the imposition of noise restrictions especially at night do not go together.
- Airline alliances as to which *see* the next section.
- Safety arrangements between the US FAA and EASA.
- 'Fair competition' in which context reference is made to ICAO's efforts in this respect as briefly referred to in section 10.1, above.
- Security, with special reference to security with respect to the carriage of cargo.
- Taxation, for instance taxes on energy consumption in individual EU States, which, says the US, infringes the achievement of global measures and the introduction of passenger taxes in the EU.
- Regulation of Unmanned Aircraft.
- Customs, with the US insisting on pre-clearance, and the US differentiated visa waiver program among EU States.
- Sanctions imposed on third countries.
- The preservation of Passenger Name Records (PNR) which is a US concern.

---

122. *See*, Department of Transportation, Docket DOT-OST-2013-0204, Order 2016-11-22, Application of Norwegian Air International Limited for an exemption under 49 U.S.C. §40109 and a foreign air carrier permit under 49 U.S.C. §41301.

- Wet leasing where financial interests are considerable but EU internal procedures and the need to reform the internal market regulation 1008/2008 impede progress.

Formally the Joint Committee has decision making powers in restricted areas only such as fuel taxation and nationality requirements which are regulated in Annex 4 of the EU-US agreement. However, it also takes decisions on wet-leasing, whereas otherwise it is mandated to consider and discuss all matters falling under the scope of this agreement as to which *see* above, and foster consultations with international organisations and third countries.

10.3.4   Brief Evaluation

Generally speaking, the EU-US air transport agreement can be called a success. Meanwhile it is also referred to as 'the mother of all agreements', because of a high regulatory convergence of the two parties, namely in terms of safety and competition law. Another question is whether the airlines of the two sides are making profits on those routes but the agreement allows airlines to compete without destroying each other.

The US has maintains its national regulations on ownership and control, whereas the US domestic market is reserved for US carriers. There is an 'uneven' relationship as the US sticks to its 25 per cent foreign investment standard whereas the EU side allows 75 per cent.

As most EU States already had Open Skies agreements with the US, no substantially increased market access opportunities were achieved through this agreement, with the exception of the US-UK market which was previously governed by the restrictive Bermuda II agreement, as to which *see* section 3.1, above, and the operation of seventh Freedom rights for air cargo carriers, including now (*see* below) between points in Norway and Iceland and beyond. The EU sees the enjoyment of intra-EU-fifth Freedom rights of US carriers in the internal EU market without similar – cabotage – privileges for EU carriers in the US domestic market as an imbalance. Otherwise, routes into and from the EU and US markets are served in combination, that is, by code shares and other marketing tools which are available in and regulated under alliance agreements.

The competition authorities on the two sides are working together in order to achieve a harmonised approach towards the transatlantic alliances including Skyteam, oneworld and Star Alliance. This appears to be working well as they share visions on how to regulate 'mature' markets where consumer benefits have to be balanced with global standards in other fields such as safety, security and the environment, and the interests of the undertakings which must increasingly compete in a global environment. The rise of Gulf carriers which are said to benefit from large State investments has brought the transatlantic partners closer together, and reinforced the existing bonds, under this common transatlantic regime.

As to safety, EASA and FAA gave concluded an agreement on the harmonisation of common safety standards. The consolidated version of the 'Agreement between the USA and the EU on cooperation in the regulation of civil aviation safety' Bilateral Aviation Safety Agreement (BASA) has been prepared by EASA in order to provide stakeholders with an updated and easy-to-read publication. It is designed to combine the officially published corresponding text of the BASA, and all amendments to the BASA annexes adopted so far by the Bilateral Oversight Board.[123]

For the time being, it would seem that the fierce discussions regarding the protection of the environment through the EU ETS regime have been stopped now that ICAO has drawn up a global resolution on this matter. The EU announced that the current restricted scope of the EU ETS to intra-EEA[124] will end on 31 December 2016 and be extended to include all international flights into and from points in the EEA unless global arrangements are made in ICAO before that. Reference is made to section 3.3.8 of Chapter 1.

In the field of security, the EU and the US are also cooperating, mostly through ICAO. Generally, the US will give higher priority to security than to passenger protection, or privacy rights, whereas the EU tries to balance the two policy objectives, to wit, promotion of security and protection of privacy. Meanwhile, they have reached an agreement on the sensitive issue of PNR containing information on passengers, as to which *see* the bilateral PNR Agreements with the United States, Canada and Australia.[125] PNR data pertain to information provided by passengers during the reservation and booking of tickets and when checking in on flights as well as collected by air carriers for their own commercial purposes. PNR data can be used by law enforcement authorities to fight serious crime, terrorism and unruly passengers. The use of PNR data for law enforcement purposes involves the processing of personal data. The transfer of PNR data from the EU to third countries must be governed by a bilateral agreement that provides for a high level of personal data protection.

Another question is whether it allows carriers to make profits on transatlantic routes. At any rate it allows carrier to compete without destroying each other and this may be in no small part due to the concerted action points which are developed in the Joint Committee.

Finally, The Agreement of 2007 and the Protocol of 2010 have formally not yet entered into force but are provisionally applied since 30 March 2008 and 24 June 2010 respectively.

---

123. *See*, www.easa.europa.eu/document-library/bilateral-agreements/eu-usa, and section 2.5.3 of Chapter 7.
124. The European Economic Area, that is, the territories of the twenty-eight EU States plus those of Norway, Iceland and Lichtenstein, with a special position of Switzerland in this respect.
125. *See*, ec.europa.eu/justice/data-protection/international-transfers/pnr-tftp/pnr-and-tftp_en.htm.

Meanwhile, Norway and Iceland requested to accede to this agreement pursuant to the procedure laid down in Article 18(5). Due to procedural errors pertaining to the legal basis of the accession, this accession has not yet been formalised.[126]

11   INTER-AIRLINE COOPERATION

11.1   From Traditional Forms of Cooperation to Foreign Investment

Traditionally, cooperation between airlines included pooling of costs and revenues, coordination of tariffs, scheduling of services, ground handling and maintenance. Within the framework of such international cooperation, the identity of each of the airlines in terms of ownership and control were not affected. This said airlines such as LAN Chili, Etihad from UAE and Air Asia from Malaysia try to find ways and means to circumvent or match nationality conditions drawn up in local and international regulations when buying shares in foreign airlines or setting up daughter companies. The situation is different for relations between airlines bearing the same nationality. It has happened more than once that an airline has lost its independence as a consequence of investments made by airlines of the same nationality.[127] As stated in section 4.2 above, important aviation countries like India, Mexico and Canada are reconsidering their national requirements for their airlines in order to make room for broader foreign investment.

Since airlines were and still are internationally limited in their investment opportunities because of the nationality requirements in bilateral ASAs, they have sought other alternatives in order to enhance their market presence either in those parts of the world where they are not flying or to be more prominently present in parts of the world where they are already operating services. Those tools concern code-sharing and franchising both of which are discussed in the following section.

11.2   Code-Sharing and Franchising

One of the most used – and also simplest – devices to ensure a maximum presence is code-sharing. Code-sharing can be defined as an agreement between two or more airlines according to which either their combined codes or the code of one of the airlines are used on a route flown by one of these airlines.[128]

Normally, a key element in these co-operative arrangements is that the airlines concerned integrate their operations in varying degrees, so that they can offer, under

---

126. On 6 September 2016, the EU Commission has made an amended proposal for a Council Decision on the signature and provisional application of the EU-US Agreement on Air Transport, and the Agreement between the EU, its Member States and Norway and Iceland; *See*, Com(2016) 525.
127. For instance, in the late 1980s, British Caledonian has been purchased by British Airways; in 1992 Air France took over another French carrier (UTA), whereas American Airlines acquired TWA in 2001.
128. *See* H.A. Wassenbergh, *Principles and Practices in Air Transport Regulation* 165–169 (1993).

their own names, a streamlined product which includes flights operated with their partners' aircraft. This practice can take different forms depending on the commercial objectives of the airlines concerned.

Weber identifies two main variants in code-sharing.[129] In the first variant two successive carriers utilise the same flight number and carrier code in a situation where the passenger has to change aircraft and carrier at a stopover. In the second variant the same flight carries two codes and two flight numbers even though the flight is operated by only one of the airlines. In a number of cases variant one can be combined with variant two.

The fundamental issue related to consumer information in code-sharing is one of *transparency*: the nature of the code-shared flight should be made absolutely clear to the customer, not only at the time of purchasing of the ticket but as early as possible during the customer's travel enquiry process.[130]

Code-sharing is finding its way into bilateral ASAs under the heading 'Commercial opportunities'. Most States require the airline using the code of another airline to possess the underlying traffic rights for the operation of the code shared service. For instance, if British Airways would like to attach its code to an Air India flight between New Delhi and Bangkok, BA will be required by the competent authorities of India and Thailand to have the fifth Freedom Rights on the New Delhi-Bangkok sector.

Code-sharing has become a common practice between air carriers. It has raised questions regarding the attribution of liability among the code-sharing carriers. Competition authorities have expressed concerns pertaining to the arrangements between code share partners which can go beyond the 'naked' code-sharing.

11.3   Franchising

Franchising is another tool for cooperation by airlines with the purpose of marketing their services. It is used mostly in the Asia-Pacific region.

Franchisor and franchisee do not always code-share. Under a franchise agreement, one airline licenses its intellectual property and business system to another airline subject to controls imposed by franchisor.[131]

Major franchising variants used in the aviation industry are the business format model, for instance Comair of South Africa which is a franchise unit of British Airways and joint venture arrangements, mostly utilised by AirAsia of Malaysia and Jetstar of Australia with its franchisees.

The hallmark elements of a franchise relationship are '*control and assistance by the franchisor*' and the '*use of the franchisor's brand by the franchisee*'. This raises various questions regarding grant of traffic rights, substantial ownership and effective

---

129. *See*, L. Weber, *Legal Activities of the International Air Transport Association* (IATA) 1993–1994, 20 Air & Space Law 32–34 (1995); *see also*, J.E.C. de Groot, *Code-Sharing. United States' Policies and the Lessons for Europe*, 19 Air & Space Law 62–74 (1994).
130. *See, Code Sharing, A Study into the Consequences for the Internal European Air Transport Market*, European Commission, Directorate General for Transport, 1996.
131. *See*, UNIDROIT Secretariat, *UNIDROIT Franchising Guide*, xxxi (2007).

control, principal place of business, intellectual property protection and labour laws. One author has suggested that it is important for franchisors to create a delicate balance between exercising *'sufficient control'* in order to protect the goodwill of its brand image while at the same time limiting the extent of control in order to fulfil the *'effective control'* test.[132]

11.4 Airline Cooperation under Competition Scrutiny

Government intervention and approval are not required when two or more separate airlines cooperate in such fields as the conclusion of interline agreements, through-ticketing and handling, ground handling, maintenance, schedule coordination, frequent flyer program links and joint advertisements. These fall under the heading of relatively simple marketing arrangements.

The next step is to expand the simple marketing arrangement with, for instance, joint marketing and sales, shared terminal facilities and blocked-space and code-sharing arrangements. Government approval will then be required under the applicable competition or anti-trust laws. Government approval is even more strictly required if the pooling of revenues, network planning, the sharing of marketing data, fares control and limited investment in the partner's stock are part of the cooperation agreement. According to the degree of coordinated activities and the scope of the investment, including control, airlines are approaching a merger as between them. Full mergers need approval from the competent authority. A 'true' international airline merger or takeover is not possible or at least difficult under the present legal regime, with the exception of the special case of the EU.[133]

In 2008, the US Department of Transportation authorised Virgin Nigeria to operate to the United States based on the limited waiver of the nationality clause for certain African countries in the new bilateral agreement. Virgin Nigeria is an air carrier designated by Nigeria but with a very substantial ownership and control stake by the UK based Virgin group.[134] The Open Skies agreement between the US and Nigeria supports this authorisation, including a waiver from the traditional nationality requirements.

Airline behaviour may give rise to concerns from competition authorities. Airlines may engage in co-operative agreements and in unilateral conduct involving the abuse of a dominant position. When airlines are entering into cross-border joint ventures and other co-operative agreements in order to rationalise their operations, increase their market coverage, and strengthen their competitive position in the

---

132. *See,* R. Baruah, *Legal Issues of Franchising in the Airline Industry,* 41(4/5) Air & Space Law 361–386 (2016).
133. As explained in section 3.3.5 of Chapter 3.
134. *See,* http://useu.usmission.gov/Dossiers/Open_Skies/May1308_Byerly_EAC.asp.

market, they face different competition regulations and policies of individual States and of inter-governmental organisations, which may apply simultaneously to co-operative ventures.[135]

Inquiries into alleged anti-competitive behaviours of major world airlines were started in 2006 by competition authorities from several jurisdictions. These airlines were accused of conspiracies regarding the coordination of fuel surcharges levied on the rates for the carriage of cargo.[136]

Anti-trust and competition authorities in the US, Korea, India, Australia, New Zealand, South Africa and the EU investigated and imposed penalties ranging to billions and various civil litigations ensued for settlement of damages caused by the alleged cartelisation.[137] In the US, twenty-two airlines pleaded guilty and criminal fines of USD 1.8 billion were imposed by enforcement agencies, and several civil actions were instituted by private parties at various courts in the US for violations of national anti-trust legislations.[138]

Competition authorities imposed high fines. However, the General Court of the EU overturned the penalties in 2016, arguing that the EU Commission had wrongly accused of the airlines of running a single cartel.[139]

12 CONCLUSIONS

For the time being, the economic side of air transport will continue to be regulated by international agreements concluded between States. States have an interest in promoting national policy objectives through the air transport sector. It is trade and policy wise, a sensitive sector. Agreement on the economic side of the operation of international air services is reached by the achievement of a level playing field created by States for their designated air carriers. Disagreements are solved through negotiations rather than judicial means.

The involvement of third countries under the system of 'bilateralism' can be reduced by adherence to the Air Services Transit Agreement giving rights of overflight to carriers of a substantial number of States over an increasing number of States. As technology progresses, aircraft have more range to operate point-to-point traffic, avoiding the need to make intermediate stops. 'fifth Freedom' sectors may be operated

---

135. *See*, E. Campanelli, *Cooperation Ventures between Air Carriers: Time to Reform International Rules?* 15(2) Issues in Aviation Law and Policy (2016).
136. *See*, S. Truxal and S. Harris, *Air Freight: Regulatory Environment Encourages or Purposes Price Coordination?* 78(3) Journal of Air Law and Commerce 541–583 (2013).
137. *See*, R. Baruah, *Analyzing Legal Concepts of Air Cargo Cartel Litigations*, XLI Annals of Air and Space Law (2016).
138. *See*, *US cartel case settlements break the USD 1 billion mark*, AIRCARGONEWS (30 April 2015); *See also*, In *re Air Cargo Shipping Services Antitrust Litigation*, No. 06-MD-1775 (JG)(VVP), (E.N.D.Y. 10 July 2015); In *re Air Cargo Shipping Services Antitrust Litigation*, No. 06-MDL-1775, 2009 WL 3443405, (E.N.D.Y. 21 August 2009).
139. *See*, General Court of the European Union, Press Release No. 147/15 of 16 December 2016, "The General Court annuls the decision by which the Commission imposed fines amounting to approximately € 790 million on several airlines for their participation in a cartel on the airfreight market."

on the basis of code-sharing and other commercial agreements rather than on the basis of traffic ('hard') rights exercised by the designated carriers under the bilateral agreement. Finally, liberalisation of air transport services will no longer restrict the carriage of traffic, to begin with, within regions such as the EU, and the open market between the EU and the US, and the EU and Canada as they are replaced by 'plurilateral' agreements on the establishment of an Open Aviation Area (OAA).[140] Meanwhile, the EU-ASEAN and the EU-Gulf States negotiations may also lead to liberalised market opportunities for the air services operated under the plurilateral agreements between the mentioned parties when they are concluded.

Other regions in the world, including ASEAN and sub-regions in Africa, are following suit. With the creation of associations of States around the world, including Mercosur and the Andean Pact in South America, the African Union, COMESA, the Tasman Pact and ASEAN arrangements) further liberalisation may be further stimulated on a step by step basis as States wish to carefully weigh the advantages and disadvantages of opening 'their' markets.

Thus, deregulation and liberalisation of international air transport as evidenced by, for instance, a relaxation of nationality requirements under national licensing regulations and the increasing number of Open Skies agreements, go hand in hand with the application of competition regimes in different jurisdictions. These developments lead to a restructuring of the airline industry as designated airlines do not enjoy any more traditional protection, prevailing under the restrictions of 'Bermuda type' bilateral ASAs. In traditional air transport relations, the role of civil aviation departments or authorities was more prominent than that of competition authorities. However, this trend is due to change as shown by, for instance, the above worldwide air cargo fuel surcharge cases, and WTO discussions.

For the time being, air transport to a large extent is excluded from the application of the general principles of the WTO General Agreement on Trade in Services (GATS) Agreement. The Annex on Air Transport attached to the GATS only covers aircraft repair and maintenance services, computer reservations system services and selling and marketing of air transport services.[141] Traffic rights and services directly related to the exercise of traffic rights are excluded from GATS coverage, and this unique exclusion results from the negotiating process of the Uruguay Rounds Negotiations.[142]

General principles of the GATS, for instance the Most Favored Nation or National Treatment principles are in contrast to the existing regime on air transport which is based on reciprocity and balancing of benefits/opportunities between countries. The current exclusion of air transport from GATS seems unlikely to change in the future, however principles enshrined in the GATS could be examined and analysed for application to air transport under the existing regime of bilateral and plurilateral agreements for further liberalisation initiatives.

---

140. For a forward looking view, *see* B.F. Havel and G.S. Sanchez, *Restoring Global Aviation's* 'Cosmopolitan mentalité', 29(1) Boston University International Law Journal 1–40 (2011).
141. General Agreement on Trade in Services, (15 April 1994) 1869 UNTS 183; Annex on Air Transport.
142. GATS Annex on Air Transport, para. 2 excludes the application of GATS to measures affecting 'traffic rights' and services directly related to the exercise of traffic rights.

A new development has been the ongoing negotiations of the Trade in Services Agreement (TiSA). The TiSA is a plurilateral agreement currently under negotiation between twenty-three WTO Member States with an aim to liberalise supply to services in member countries.[143] The TiSA negotiations on air transport services include a much broader scope of the sector than the GATS Annex on Air Transport, as it aims to liberalise aircraft repair and maintenance, the sale and marketing of air transport services, computer reservation services, airport operations and ground handling services such as catering, crew administration and flight planning, passenger and baggage handling. It remains to be seen how the negotiations evolve and if successful, it will liberalise a whole gamut of ancillary air services. However, traffic rights would still be excluded from the TiSA due the existing bilateral system.

This state of affairs does not prevent aviation lawyers from studying General Agreement on Tariffs and Trade (GATT) and GATS principles and procedures, which have significantly contributed to enhancing transparency of transactions, lowering trade barriers and solving disputes between States and undertakings established in those States.

---

143. *See*, European Parliament resolution of 4 July 2013 on the opening of negotiations on a plurilateral agreement on services (2013/2583(RSP)); *See*, Office of United States Trade Representative, *Interagency Trade Policy Group Holds Public Hearing on Negotiating Objectives for International Service Agreement Negotiations*, USTR Press Release (3 March 2013).

CHAPTER 3

Operation of Air Services under EU Law

1 SCOPE OF EU LAW

It is appropriate to start this chapter with a quote from Lord Denning, a famous English judge, who described the influence from European law as follows:

> Our sovereignty has been taken away by the European Court of Justice ... Our courts must no longer enforce our national laws. They must enforce Community law ... No longer is European law an incoming tide flowing up the estuaries of England. It is now like a tidal wave bringing down our sea walls and flowing inland over our fields and houses – to the dismay of all.[1]

For some years after that tide, so far as aviation was concerned, was not very strong but began to increase in strength since the mid-1980s onwards. Prior to that time, there were continuing debates as to the extent to which the EU had competence in the field of air transport. Once that question was finally resolved, and particularly since 1990, EU legislation in this field has developed at a rapid pace.[2] Space does not permit a detailed examination of the whole body of EU aviation law, but allows merely a summary of the principal elements.

The reason for including a summary of EU legislation is primarily because of the impact of EU law on European and international aviation. This role is articulated in the areas of market access and market behaviour, competition and State aid, safety and security regulation, infrastructure including access to airports, distribution and selling of air services, Air Traffic Management (ATM), external policies, including relations with non-EU States and with international organisations such as International Civil Aviation Organization (ICAO), European Civil Aviation Conference (ECAC) and

---

1. Lord Denning, *Introduction to The European Court of Justice: Judges or Policy Makers?* (1990).
2. *See*, J.M. Balfour, *European EU Air Law* (1995).

Eurocontrol, the protection of the environment, including noise and emissions and social policies. Airline liability and passenger protection will be discussed in Chapter 4, and insurance in Chapter 8.

The heavy involvement of the EU institutions[3] with all these areas is explained by European Treaty objectives stating that those institutions must establish an air transport market in which the free movement of goods, persons, services and capital is assured on a level playing field for operators. Unified or harmonised conditions must level that playing field for providers of services and goods.

EU law is not all-encompassing. For instance, it does not regulate aircraft registration and aircraft financing, whereas it has no mandate for the regulation of State aircraft. The EU is an international organisation with unique and specified supranational powers in the field of legislation, jurisdiction, enforcement and competition. As early as 1962, the European Court of Justice (ECJ) now referred to as the Court of Justice of the EU (CJEU), as to which *see* further below, set out the concept of direct effect of EU law, implying that individuals, whether undertakings or national persons, are entitled to invoke EU law in their national courts.[4] Moreover, in case of conflict between EU law and national law, EU law prevails.[5] This hierarchical order is known as the *supremacy of EU law*. It found its way through decisions made by the ECJ but has not been confirmed in the EU Treaties.

As the EU is not a State, its ability to enact legislation depends upon the powers that are attributed to it by the Member States through the legal texts adopted by them, in cooperation with the European Parliament. Its legislative powers have been enhanced following the entry into force of the Treaty on the Functioning of the European Union (TFEU) on 1 December 2009. Secondary EU legislative acts are enacted by the EU Council and the EU Parliament. The TFEU also changed the numbering of the Treaty provisions, and the names of the European Courts.

The EU Treaty expresses the determination of the parties "to lay the foundation of an ever closer union amongst the peoples of Europe."[6] This Treaty provides a framework for the process of integration and establishes an internal market ... based on balanced economic growth and price stability, a highly competitive social market economy, aiming at full employment and social progress, and a high level of protection and improvement of the quality of the environment..."[7] These objectives must be accomplished in accordance "with the principle of an open market economy with free competition."[8]

Chapter 2 has shown that an 'open market'[9] is not *de iure* available in the air transport sector whereas 'free competition' is a subject which needs to be adapted to

---

3. The principal EU institutions, to wit the European Council, the European Commission, the Court of Justice of the EU and the EU Parliament are referred to in section 2.1. For reasons of simplicity and consistency, reference will be made to the acronym EU unless EEC or EC is more appropriate.
4. *See*, ECJ decision of 5 February 1963 in Case 26/62 *Van Gend en Loos*; *see also*, for instance: M. Horspool and M. Humphreys, *European Union Law* 171–175 (2006).
5. *See*, to begin with, ECJ decision of 15 July 1964 in Case 6/64 *Costa* v. *Enel*.
6. Preamble to the Consolidated Treaty establishing the European EU.
7. *See*, Art. 3(3) TEU.
8. *See*, Art. 119 TFEU; *see also*, section 3.1, below.
9. *See*, sections 1.1 and 3.7 of Chapter 2.

the regulatory and other circumstances prevailing in this sector, as illustrated by the discussion on the introduction of 'fair competition'.[10]

Article 5(2) of the TFEU states:

> Under the principle of conferral, the Union shall act only within the limits of the powers conferred upon it by the Member States in the Treaties to attain the objectives set out therein. Competences not conferred upon the Union in the Treaties remain with the Member States.

The article goes on to state that in areas that do not fall within the exclusive competence of the EU, it shall take action only if, and insofar as the objectives of the proposed action cannot be sufficiently achieved by the Member States and can therefore, by reason of the scale or effects of the proposed action, be better achieved by the EU. This principle is also referred to as the principle of 'subsidiarity'.

The powers of the EU institutions, to legislate and conduct policies have grown considerably since its inception and have been widened by each successive Treaty in addition to which further expansion of their application has occurred through the interpretation of the powers by the European Court, since 1 December 2009, also referred to as the CJEU.[11] In its interpretation of the Union powers, policies and law, the European Court has recognised general principles of EU law which must be applied by the Member States while sometimes leaving aside principles and rules of international law, even if they are binding on the EU and its Member States.[12]

2 SOURCES OF EU LAW

2.1 Supranational Features of the EU

The EU is an international organisation created by States with specific features under international law, as it has distinct supranational elements. Among them are the treaty-based and practiced responsibilities of the EU Commission, the EU Parliament and the CJEU. The EU Commission is tasked with, among others, the preparation of legislation, and the surveillance of the execution of the provisions of the EU Treaties by the Member States and other subjects of EU law, including other public bodies and undertakings, and the management of competition rules. As the last mentioned task is carried out independently of the EU States, it is a genuine supranational activity. As a corollary, the EU Commission and the CJEU possess strong enforcement powers which differentiate the EU from other international organisations.

The above features and many other facets of the EU are laid down in the principal sources, to wit the Treaty on European Union (TEU) and the Treaty on the Functioning of the European Union (TFEU). According to the CJEU, the EU legal order constitutes the basis for:

---

10. *See*, section 10.1 of Chapter 2.
11. Henceforth also referred to as: 'the Court', the 'Court of the EU or 'the CJEU'.
12. *See*, for instance, the 'Open Skies' decisions referred to in section 6.1 of this Chapter and the 'IATA' and 'Sturgeon' decisions mentioned in sections 2.3.1 and 2.3.6 respectively of Chapter 4.

[...] a new legal order of international law for the benefit of which States have limited their sovereign rights, albeit within limited fields.[13]

This decision refers to the supranational character of the EU which was set up in a spirit of cooperation and integration in the decades after the Second World War. The current political and economic climate is different for reasons which are unrelated to the subject of this book. However, as air transport is part of the economic activities falling under the regime of the EU treaties, it is also affected by this trend.

2.2 Principal Legal Acts

The law of the EU is based upon specific sources. EU law is not universal as its scope is limited to the territories of the EU States and activities as specified by the above Treaties.

Articles 293–300 of the TFEU govern the adoption of legislation in the EU. Power is conferred upon the European Parliament acting jointly with the Council, or the Council acting alone, and the Commission.[14] The Treaty confers only limited power on the Commission[15] but the Council frequently delegates power to the Commission in order that it might fulfil its executive functions. The Treaty of Lisbon replaced the term 'co-decision procedure' with 'Ordinary Legislative Procedure' to describe the process whereby the proposals and the decision on those proposals are made. It also renamed the specific decision making procedures as 'Special Legislative Procedures'. 'The term illustrates a procedure which is specifically used in the area of Foreign and Security policies where the Council, after consulting the European Parliament, is empowered to take decisions.

There are three principal sources of EU law, as follows:

(1) *Primary legislation*: The EU treaties, that is, the TFEU and the TEU as referred to above and below. For the present book, the TFEU is most important. Conventions drawn up by the EU fall outside the scope of this discussion.

(2) *Secondary legislation*:[16] The binding EU acts are Regulations, Directives and Decisions. There are also non-binding acts in the form of recommendations or opinions that may, however, be of persuasive value:

- A *Regulation* has general application and is 'directly applicable' in all Member States.[17] A regulation will therefore apply directly in all Member States without it having to be incorporated by national legislation. They come into force solely by virtue of their publication in the Official Journal of the European Union (OJEU) and from the date specified in them or, in

---

13. *See*, Case 26/52, *Van Gend & Loos*, judgment of 5 February 1963.
14. *See*, in particular, Arts 289, 293 294 and 297 TFEU.
15. *See*, Art. 290 TFEU delegating the power to adopt non-legislative acts to the EU Commission under scrutiny of the EU legislator.
16. *See*, Arts 288, 293 and 297 TFEU.
17. *See*, Art. 288 in conjunction with Art. 291 TFEU.

the absence thereof, as from the date provided for in the Treaty that is generally as from the twentieth day following their publication.

■ *Directives* are binding as to the effect to be achieved but leaves the choice of form and method of their implementation to the Member States.[18] Directives therefore need to be incorporated into national law before a specified date. They are thus more flexible than regulations that leave no discretion for the introduction of national differences and needs. Inevitably, directives may give rise to problems of interpretation and the improper exercise of discretion. The large majority of Directives is binding on all Member States and is published in the OJEU in the same manner as regulations.

■ *Decisions* are made by the EU Council, and the EU Parliament, or the EU Commission; they contain specific measures issued by the EU that are binding upon those to whom they are addressed. The Commission makes extensive use of such decisions especially in the field of competition. The decision of the Commission in relation to Ryanair and the payment of subsidies by the local authorities and the Charleroi airport in Belgium is a good example of the use of such an instrument.[19]

(3) *Other sources:* international agreements, general principles of law, case law of the CJEU and 'soft law' comprising memoranda, statements and resolutions.

2.3 Division of Competencies

The activities of the EU, including air transport, are based on the TFEU. It draws up the competencies of the EU in the various fields, some of which are *exclusively* dealt with on the EU level. Among them are the establishment of a customs union and the conduct of a competition policy, a monetary policy for the Euro area countries, a common commercial policy and the conclusion of international agreements under specified circumstances. The EU may have exclusive competencies to conclude international agreements, or such competency may be mixed between the EU and EU Member States.[20]

EU law may prevent Member States from acting independently in the case of international agreements. The EU may have the power to conclude international agreements in areas covered by the Treaties where it has internal powers. Pursuant to the *'implied powers'* doctrine[21] the extent to which the EU can negotiate or conclude

---

18. *See also,* Art. 288 TFEU.
19. *See,* section 3.3.6 below.
20. *See* Art. 218 TFEU setting out the procedure for the conclusion of such international agreements.
21. The EU derives external competence in civil aviation matters from the Treaty provisions on transport, in particular Art. 84(2) TEC (now Art. 100(2) TFEU) which was cited by the ECJ in its AETR judgement. This established the principle that once there is EU law in a field, such as air transport, the EU has exclusive competence to negotiate in this field. This is known as the doctrine of *implied powers:* "Each time the EU, with a view to implementing a common policy [...] adopts provisions laying down common rules [...] the Member States no longer have the

agreements next to, or instead of Member States, depends upon the interpretation of the powers contained in the Treaties. If the EU has exclusive power to act under the Treaties, the Member States will be precluded from acting themselves. The powers of the EU must be assessed on a case-by-case basis, which sometimes confuses third parties, including third States, and even EU States and their nationals.

Shared competencies are competencies in which EU institutions work together with EU States in order to achieve the envisaged results. They include but are not limited to the completion of the internal market, transport, with a specific place for air transport as to which *see* below, the protection of the environment, consumer protection, security and immigration, and the creation of Trans-European Networks. The division of powers sometimes lead to questions as to who has to take the lead in a certain field. More than once has the Court intervened in these quests for competencies not least in the field of external air transport relations as alluded to in section 6.1 of this chapter.

The EU Commission has argued before the CJEU that transport falls under the commercial policies conducted by the EU, and that, hence, it has exclusive competencies in this area. However, the court did not agree with the EU Commission. The Court held that international agreements in the field of transport are excluded from the scope of the common commercial policy because, as further explained below, transport was the subject of a separate and specific title of the Treaty.[22] Thus, air transport, as far as the conduct of external relations is concerned, has become a shared competence. The Court has yet again discussed this matter in the *Open Skies* decisions of 2002, as to which *see* section 6.1 below. This is also true for the completion of the internal air transport market as laid down in EU Regulation 1008/2008, as to which *see* section 3.2 below, which also comes under the shared competence between the EU institutions, including the European Parliament and the EU States, upon a proposal made by the EU Commission.

The *Open Skies* agreements on air transport between the EU, its Member States and the US, and the EU and its Member States and Canada, are examples of mixed agreements in which competencies are shared between the EU and its Member States.[23] Moreover, the EU has concluded an international agreement with international organisations, such as, for instance, the one with ICAO on safety and security.[24]

---

right, acting individually or even collectively, to undertake [...] obligations with third countries which affect those rules [...] the Member States lose their right to assume obligations with non-member countries as and when common rules which could be affected by those obligations come into being." Case 22/70, *ERTA*, European Court Reports 1971, 274–276. This standpoint has been confirmed in Opinion 1/76, ECR 1977 at 758, Opinion 1/94 (*WTO Agreement*); European Court Reports I-5267 and Opinion 1/03 (*Lugano Convention*), European Court Reports I-1145.

22. *See, Opinion of 1/94*, Opinion of the – then – ECJ of 15 November 1994.
23. *See*, section 6.1, below.
24. In 2011, a Memorandum of Cooperation (MOC) between the EU and ICAO was signed. The MOC addresses cooperation in the areas of aviation safety, aviation security, air traffic management and environmental protection. A third Annex on Air Traffic Management is being prepared.

3 THE CREATION OF MARKET CONDITIONS FOR AIR TRANSPORT

3.1 Progressing Liberalisation

Within the legal framework of EU law, air transport retains a unique position; it is not firmly enshrined in the Treaty. Air transport is specifically mentioned only once in Article 100(2) TFEU to specify that measures on air transport policy are to be taken as and when the Council so decided. Hence, the Council has discretionary powers in this respect. Yet, the Court held that 'general rules' apply to air transport.[25] General rules encompass the competition rules; they can be applied to this sector even in the absence of implementing regulations and enforced, under certain conditions, by the Commission and by the competition authorities in Member States.[26] The operation of air services is also subject to the general principles of non-discrimination, and the objectives pertaining to environmental and consumer protection. These principles and goals are implemented in the air transport regulations and policies, as to which *see* below. Also, the Freedoms of the EU Treaties apply to the operation of air services. The most relevant are the free movement of services and the right of establishment, as to which *see also* below.

The view holding that competition rules should be applied to the operation of air transport services was not necessarily in line with the traditional approach towards the operation of services which were, as explained in Chapter 2, safeguarded from the application of competition rules under restrictive bilateral air services agreements (ASAs) to begin with. Hence, the EU view was quite revolutionary in those days.

The existence of these agreements, concluded by States, including EU States, accounted, among other factors, for the delay with respect to the establishment of an air transport policy at the EU level which was in those days dominated by EU States. The supranational institutions of the EU, namely, the European Commission, European Parliament and the CJEU, have considerably influenced a more market-oriented approach towards the operation of services by relying on the Treaty rules proclaiming an "open market with free competition."[27] As mentioned in section 6.1, events which have taken place abroad such as the deregulation policy of the US also helped to liberalise European air transport.

An air transport policy was eventually formulated and implemented in the form of three packages designed to liberalise the EU internal air transport market. The First Package dates back to 1987, the Second to 1990 and the implementation of the Third Package commenced on 1 January 1993. From 1 April 1997, the operation of domestic routes in one Member State by air carriers of other EU Member States ('cabotage') was permitted, whereby the aim of the Third Package to establish a fully liberalised *internal*

---

25. *See,* Case 167/73, *French Seamen,* European Court Reports 371 (1974).
26. *See* Cases 209-213/86; *Ministère Public* v. *Lucas Asjes et al.,* European Court Reports 1425–1475 (1986); on the applicability of the provisions on the abuse of a dominant position to air services to points outside the EU (then EEC); *see also,* Case 66/86, *Ahmed Saeed Flugreisen,* European Court Reports 803 (1989).
27. *See,* Art. 4 of the EC Treaty, version of 2006.

air transport market was realised. The three mentioned Packages and underlying regulations are since 2008 replaced with one Regulation, namely, EU Regulation 1008/2008.

This Regulation (1008/2008) sweeps away the barriers for new entries by, for instance, harmonising air carrier licensing conditions. Many of the old restrictions on market entry and behaviour, that is, designation, capacity, pricing and frequencies prevailing under the bilateral ASAs between the Member States have been abolished. Following the principles of the European treaties, room was given for a more market-oriented approach towards the operation of EU services on a level playing field as maintained under applicable Treaty competition rules. They were supplemented by implementing rules for the air transport sector, including exemptions from the scope of those competition rules.

At the same time, the distinction between scheduled and non-scheduled services has been removed so as to enable all types of air carriers holding EU operating licences to provide services anywhere within the EU internal market, according to demand. Demand has substantially increased since the 1990s, resulting in an impressive growth of air traffic in the intra-EU air transport market.[28]

3.2 The Completion of the Internal Air Transport Market

3.2.1 Licensing

As said, the EU internal market is now governed by EU Regulation 1008/2008 on *common rules for the operation of air services in the EU.*

In order to complete the creation of a 'level playing field', the Regulation lays down rules on substantial ownership and effective control on the licensing of air carriers which must be in the hands of EU States or their nationals.[29] The principal place of the business of the EU air carrier so licenced must be located in the State granting the operating licence. This regulation establishes specific criteria, including financial criteria, for the granting of licences to air carriers.

Aeronautical authorities of Member States, and not an EU institution such as the EU Commission, issue an Operating Licence as evidence of the carrier's fitness and financial resources in order to meet liabilities. Carriers must have air transport as their main occupation; have their principal place of business in a Member State and submit a two-year business plan to the authorities and demonstrate their ability to meet their operating costs for a period of three months without the receipt of any revenue. Carriers must have liability insurance[30] and a technical licence, that is, an Air

---

28. *See*, Mott MacDonald, *Annual Analyses of the EU Air Transport Market 2015*, Final report prepared for the EU Commission, available at the website of the EU Commission.
29. *See* Art. 4 of Regulation 1008/2008.
30. In accordance with the provisions of Regulation 784/2004 on *insurance requirements for air carriers and aircraft operators*, as amended by EU Commission Regulation 285/2010, as to which *see also*, section 3.6.1.3 of Chapter 4 and section 2.1 of Chapter 10.

Operator's Certificate (AOC).[31] The possession of an EU Operating Licence enables that air carrier to provide service anywhere within the internal market and if relevant international agreement so permits on external, that is, points outside the EU, routes.[32]

EU Regulation 1008/2008 takes a somewhat cautious approach when imposing restrictions to the use of aircraft registered in non-EU States.[33] National legislation may also limit the transfer for a period exceeding six month in duration.[34] In this context, reference is made to the discussion regarding the transfer of safety oversight in section 2.6 of Chapter 6 where it was concluded that neither Article 83*bis* nor the rest of the Chicago Convention provide for the transfer of jurisdiction, and that EU Regulation 216/2008 is harmonised with this in which Regulation similar wording is used.[35]

3.2.2 Access to Routes

Hence, subject to the availability of slots as discussed in section 5.5.1 below and absent restrictions caused by safety and environmental concerns,[36] any EU national air carrier in possession of an EU Operating Licence can fly anywhere within the internal market and to charge what the market would pay for the type of service offered. The result of these market conditions has been the disappearance of some long-established national airlines such as Sabena from Belgium and Swissair from Switzerland. Their disappearance was offset by the rapid growth of many new budget air carriers such as easyJet,

---

31. *See,* Art. 6 of Regulation 1008/2008.
32. *See,* section 6.2 below.
33. *See,* recital 8: "In order to avoid excessive recourse to lease agreements of aircraft registered in third countries, especially wet lease, these possibilities should only be allowed in exceptional circumstances, such as lack of adequate aircraft on the Community market, and they should be strictly limited in time and fulfill safety standards equivalent to the safety rules of Community and national legislation."; *see also,* Art. 13 allowing leasing among EU air carriers, and section section 2.4.2 of Chapter 7.
34. *See,* section 31(1) of the UK *Air Navigation Order* (2016):

    The Secretary of State may, by regulations, adapt or modify the foregoing provisions of this Part as the Secretary of State deems necessary or expedient for the purpose of providing for the temporary transfer of aircraft to or from the United Kingdom register, either generally or in relation to a particular case or class of cases.

35. *See,* next section (2.4.3.1); Art. 4(1) of Regulation 216/2004:

    Aircraft, including any installed product, part and appliance, which are: ...
        (d) registered in a third country, or registered in a Member State which has delegated their regulatory safety oversight to a third country, and used by a third-country operator into, within or out of the Community.

36. *See,* Arts 19 and 20 of EU Regulation 1008/2008. In its Decision regarding *access to Karlstad Airport,* the EU Commission held that the Swedish authorities were not entitled to impose operational restrictions at Karlstad airport going beyond those which are drawn up in EU law (*see* Directive 92/14 which has been repealed by Regulation 925/1999 – the '*hushkit* regulation' which has in turn been repealed by Directive 2002/30) as such restrictions hamper the freedom of market access; *see* Commission Decision 98/523/EC of 22 July 1998.

Vueling and Ryanair to the point at which the distinction between 'full service' and 'low cost' carriers has disappeared as both categories are subject to exactly the same rules, and, as a corollary, harmonising their services in the internal market. In consequence of the liberalised internal EU market, the number of air carriers operating scheduled routes has grown since 1992, as has the number of direct connections between airports in EU Member States.[37]

The most important policy and regulatory tool to actively promote market access under Regulation 1008/2008 concerns Public Service Obligations (PSO). This tool enables EU governments to secure the maintenance of services that are deemed essential for the harmonious development of their territory.[38] International routes are usually not supported by PSO. A Member State makes known the PSOs that air carriers must fulfil in terms of capacity, frequency and fares. If no carrier comes forward to provide the service, the Member State may limit access to that route to one carrier only and reimburse the carrier some or all of the cost of carrying out the PSOs. Examples of air transport PSOs currently in operation in Europe are routes from Dublin to secondary points in Ireland, services between the Italian mainland and Sardinia, and the French Mainland and Corsica, between Athens and Greek islands, domestic routes in Scandinavian countries and links between points in Scotland and Scottish islands. They are published in the Official Journal of the EU.

3.2.3   Freedom of Pricing

The same regulation (1008/2008) also continues to largely remove the restrictions and controls on pricing so that air carriers are free to set fares in accordance with market forces in competition with each other. Subject to reciprocity, non-EU air carriers also enjoy freedom of pricing.[39] Under this regulation carriers are no longer required to file their fares with the national authorities prior to them being introduced.

The final price or the fare must, as a matter of consumer protection, include all charges, including airport charges, surcharges, fees and taxes.[40] On 15 January 2015, the Court of the EU decided that the final price shown on the bookings via the internet must, at all times, be the final price to be paid by the customer.[41]

3.2.4   Global Distribution Systems

Access to Global Distribution Systems (GDSs), formerly known as Computerised Reservation Systems (CRSs), is now governed by EU Regulation 80/2009 replacing

---

37. *See*, Mott MacDonald, *Annual Analyses of the EU Air Transport Market 2015*, Final report prepared for the EU Commission, available at the website of the EU Commission.
38. *See*, Art. 16 of EU Regulation 1008/2008.
39. *See*, Art. 22(1) of EU Regulation 1008/2008.
40. *See*, Art. 23 of EU Regulation 1008/2008.
41. *See*, Case C-573/13, *Air Berlin* v. *Verbraucherzentrale Bundesverband.*

Regulation 2299/89 and simplifying the latter regulation. The principle of non-discriminatory access,[42] including unbiased display of the services of such airlines in relation to other airlines has been maintained. Operators of GDSs may not abuse their dominant position in their relations with travel agents; smaller travel agents must be entitled to terminate their arrangements with a GDS operator. Airlines are obliged to provide accurate and compliant data pertaining to their services. GDS operators may sell Marketing Information Data Tape (MIDT) on a non-discriminatory basis provided it does not identify the travel agent.

Also, the EU Commission may permit discrimination against airlines coming from jurisdictions which discriminates against EU airlines. Again, this confirms the enforcement of the principle of reciprocal treatment which is also applied in the field of third country pricing and slot allocation.[43] The EU Commission can investigate infringements of the Regulation, it may require information and impose fines up to 10 per cent of the annual turnover of the operator in question.[44]

3.2.5 Concluding Remarks

The internal air transport market of the EU has now been completed. All of the Freedoms of the Air which have been discussed in section 3.7 of Chapter 2 are available for EU carriers and this on an exclusive basis. Those Freedoms are used, especially by new entrant, so called Low Cost Carriers (LCCs) who started their operations in the 1990s. Incumbent flag carriers attempt to survive in this market, not by using the same Freedoms as the more flexible and lenient LCCs but by matching prices for air services.

Thus, the EU internal air transport market is probably the most mature market worldwide. While it is called an internal market, the routes between the intra-EU city pairs are still international routes unless the city pair is located within one State, such as Madrid-Barcelona. The route Helsinki-Athens is international under the Chicago Convention, while internal under the unified EU regime. At the same time, the operation of the services is subject to a unified competition regime as to which *see* the next section.

---

42. As to non-discriminatory access to CRSs *see* the following case: London European who used to operate on the Luton Brussels route lodged a complaint against the then Belgian national flag carrier (Sabena). Sabena denied the complainant airline access to its own CRS, called Saphir, on the grounds that London European fares were too low. Consequently London European was denied access to 80 per cent of the market and, in practice London European was kicked out of that market. In 1988, the EU Commission obliged Sabena to display these flights on Saphir.
43. *See,* section 5.5.1, below.
44. For further explanations, *see* Mia Wouters, *Simplification of the European Code of Conduct for Computer Reservation Systems (CRS)*, 36(1) Air & Space Law 49–62 (2011), and Steer Davies Gleave, *Mid-Term Evaluation of Regulation 80/2009 on a Code of Conduct for Computerised Reservation Systems and Repealing Council Regulation 2299/89, report prepared for the EU Commission* (2012).

3.3 Competition

3.3.1 European Competition Rules[45]

As briefly explained in section 2.1 above, the Court of the EU has decided that the 'general rules' of the EU treaty apply to air transport.[46] As general rules encompass the competition rules, they can be directly applied to this sector even without implementation rules, and enforced by the EU Commission and the competent authorities of the EU Member States.[47]

Article 101(1) TFEU prohibits all agreements between undertakings, decisions by associations of undertakings and concerted practices which may affect trade between Member States and which have as their object or effect the prevention, restriction or distortion of competition in the common market. The term "undertakings" is not defined by the EU treaty law but by the CJEU and the EU Commission; it:

> encompasses every entity engaged in an economic activity regardless of the legal status and the way it is financed.[48]

The three principal elements of this provision are the following:

- A *form of collusion* in the context of an oral or written agreement between undertakings, basically airlines, or an association of undertakings such as IATA, or a concerted practice, which is a form of cooperation without having achieved an agreement.[49]
- Which behaviour may *affect trade between EU States* in which regard reference is made to the 'effects' doctrine in section 3.3.3, below.
- Which behaviour must have as its object or effect, that is, potentially result in, the p*revention, restriction or distortion of competition in the EU market*, including but not limited the fixation of prices, that is, fares (passengers) or rates (cargo), the limitation of the production of the (air) services and the division of markets which may occur in so called 'vertical agreements' that is, agreements between different levels of trade, for instance, between airports and airlines.

Pursuant to Article 101(3) the EU Commission can exempt agreements or decisions from the application of the prohibitions laid down in the EU competition rules

---

45. *See*, J. Milligan, *European Union Competition Law in the Airline Industry* (2017).
46. *See*, Case 167/73, *French Seamen*, ECR 371 (1974).
47. *See*, Cases 209/213/86, *Ministère Public* v. *Lucas Asjes et al.*, ECR 1425 (1986); on the applicability of the provisions on the abuse of a dominant position to points outside the EU, *see also*, case 66/86, *Ahmed Saeed Flugreisen*, ECR 803 (1989), as to which, J. Dutheil de la Rochère, *Contribution of the European Court of Justice to the Implementation of the EEC Treaty bin the field of Air Transport, Past and Future*, in: Tanja L. Masson-Zwaan and Pablo Mendes de Leon. (eds), *Air and Space Law: De Lege Ferenda*, *Essays in Honour of Henri A. Wassenbergh* 161–172 (1992).
48. *See*, Case C-41/90 *Höfner and Elser* (1991).
49. *See*, Cases 48, 49 and 51-57/69, *Dyestuffs* (1972).

when they generate objective economic benefits that outweigh the negative effects of the restriction of competition. Since 1 May 2004, when EU Regulation 1/2003 came into force, the regime of specific and most block exemptions has been abolished by this new regulation encompassing the implementing rules for the EU competition law regime, including Articles 101 and 102 (*see* below) TFEU. Practices which have been considered to be anti-competitive by the EU Commission in its enforcement procedures are the following:

- Revenue sharing.
- Capacity or frequency sharing.
- Market sharing.
- Concerted practices on pricing including the exchange of sensitive information expect possible in the context of alliances and joint ventures for new and so called 'thin routes', that is, routes with relatively low traffic volumes.

Thus, enforcement has been de-centralised from the EU Commission to the undertakings, a network of competition authorities in the EU Member States working together, and courts of the EU States.

Under Article 102 TFEU, any abuse of a dominant position by one or more undertakings within the EU market is prohibited, again, in so far as it affects trade between Member States. This prohibition is again followed by a list of possible abuses. They include but are not limited to:

- The imposition of unfair prices, or other unfair trading conditions.
- The limitation of production to the prejudice of consumers.
- The application of unnecessary supplementary contractual obligations to other parties.

Dominance per se is not prohibited; its abuse is. According to the Court of the EU, abuse is an "objective concept."[50] A merger between two undertakings holding a market share above 60 per cent means dominance.[51] It relates to the behaviour of an undertaking in a dominant position which is such as to influence the structure of a market where, as a result of the presence of the 'abusing' undertaking, the level of competition is weakened because this undertaking takes recourse to measures which are different from those which would create normal conditions of competition, for instance, in the field of the operation of air services, impeding market growth.[52]

---

50. *See*, ECJ, Case 85/76, *Hoffman-La Roche*, decision of 13 February 1979 as to which *see* para. 38: " ... the dominant position ... relates to a position of economic strength enjoyed by an undertaking which enables it to prevent effective competition being maintained on the relevant market by affording it the power to behave to an appreciable extent independently of its competitors, its customers and ultimately of the consumers."
51. *See*, Commission Decision of 25 November 1998, Case M.1225 *Enso/Stora*, paragraphs 84–97.
52. Dominance includes the possession and use of a 'leading position'; 'substantial market power'; or the power to 'increase prices'; *see*, EU Commission, Communication from the Commission – *Guidance on the Commission's enforcement priorities in applying Article 82 of the EC Treaty to abusive exclusionary conduct by dominant undertakings* (2009); NB: Art. 82 EC Treaty is now numbered Art. 102 TFEU.

Dominance has to be determined in relation to a particular, relevant market. The relevant market has been divided into two categories: the relevant product, or, in this case, – air – *services* market, and the geographical market. The geographic market has been defined as "an area where the objective conditions of competition applying to the product in question are the same for all traders."[53] The above concepts have been explained by the EU Commission and the CJEU in case law.[54]

Competition rules are applied to cases, including air transport cases, by the Court of the EU and national courts. They are notably enforced on the basis of the supra-national enforcement powers of the EU Commission, and it has done so in cases which are concisely discussed in the sections below.

3.3.2 Application to the Aviation Sector

While in many States the operation of air transport services, and especially so the operation of *international* air transport services, is exempt from the application of a competition law regime, this is different in the EU, the US and other jurisdictions such as Australia, New Zealand and Canada. This exemption has been justified by the governance of these services by *ex ante* public rules, that is, government dictated and mandated behaviour by the airlines in ASAs, *predetermining* the economic features such as pricing, capacity and frequencies of the operation of the agreed international air services. Such behaviour may be anti-competitive but it is sanctioned because of its 'public service' character. Competition rules are designed to remedy that anti-competitive behaviour by *ex post* rules, that is, after the moment the behaviour, for instance, anti-competitive pricing, has taken place. As a corollary, frictions may arise between said *ex ante*, that is, traditional bilateral provisions, and *ex post* – competition – rules, as demonstrated in the *Air Freight Cartel* cases which are discussed below.

Both provisions, namely, Articles 101 and 102 TFEU, but also State aid which is governed by Article 107 TFEU and is discussed in section 6, below, have been applied to air transport. The definition of 'undertaking' has relevance for the air transport sector as airlines, at least EU airlines, are "undertakings" pursuant to Article 2 of EU Regulation 1008/2008, and so are airports following the decision of the CJEU in, among others, the case of *Aéroports de Paris*.[55] However, Air Navigation Service Providers (ANSPs) are not subject to the EU rules on competition,[56] and neither is Eurocontrol which is not an undertaking.[57] The designated entities under ASAs are *airlines*, without reference to 'undertaking'.

---

53. *See*, ECJ, Case 27/76, *United Brands* v. *Commission of the European Communities*, Judgment of 14 February 1978.
54. *See*, sections 3.3.2, 3.3.4 and 3.3.5 below.
55. *See*, ECJ, Case C-82/01 P, *Aéroports de Paris* v. *Commission of the European Communities*, decision of 24 October 2002.
56. *See*, Consideration 5 of EU Regulation 550/2004 as amended in 2009: "The provision of air traffic services, as envisaged by this Regulation, is connected with the exercise of the powers of a public authority, which are not of an economic nature justifying the application of the Treaty rules of competition."
57. *See*, Case C-364/92, *Eurocontrol* v. *SAT Fluggesellschaft*, para. 89/90 in which the court referred to the above definition of 'undertaking':

IATA and the Airport Council International (ACI) are associations of undertakings which are liable to fall under the term 'association of undertakings' in the field of air transport. Airlines working together in IATA must be careful to respect US anti-trust and EU competition rules in compliance procedures. This is why IATA has created an innovative multilateral interlining system based upon market-driven interlineable,[58] and online coordinated flex fares. This system replaces the former passenger tariff conferences which were scrutinised under competition and anti-trust regimes.

Article 101 TFEU has been applied to the air transport sector, as discussed in the context of airline alliances in section 3.3.4, below. Under the former regime, a specified number of airline practices had been exempted under a 'block exemption regulation'. Since the entry into force of EU Regulation 1/2003, the air transport sector is fully subject to the general EU rules on competition.

There is relatively little case law on Article 102 TFEU which has been enforced in a couple of cases which go back to the twentieth century. They involve airline or airport behaviour,[59] principally in relation to pricing of airport services, that is, charges, market behaviour in relation to interlining, or access to CRSs.[60]

In Italy, the obligation to use of flight coupons in the order in which they are ticketed does not constitute anti-competitive behaviour of the airline as the no show rule is lawful, but the rule must strike a balance between the commercial needs of airlines, including the tariff freedom, and the interests of the passengers.[61]

The alleged anti-competitive behaviour, where concerted practices (Article 101 TFEU) or abuse of dominant position (Article 102 TFEU), must be assessed in a *relevant*

> Taken as a whole, Eurocontrol's activities, by their nature, their aim and the rules to which they are subject, are connected with the exercise of powers relating to the control and supervision of air space which are typically those of a *public authority*. They are *not of an economic nature* justifying the application of the Treaty rules of competition. Accordingly, an international organization such as Eurocontrol does not constitute an undertaking subject to the provisions of Articles 86 and 90 of the Treaty. (*italics added*).

58. Interline refers to the use of one ticket for two or more services operated by different airlines, facilitating international airline connections, with clear consumer benefits. For instance, a passengers books an interline ticket when s/he buys a ticket London-Jakarta via Bangkok whereby the London-Bangkok service is operated by British Airways and the connecting service Bangkok-Jakarta is operated by Thai Airways.

59. *See*, Commission Decision 1999/198 of 10 February 1999 regarding *airport charges at Finnish airports*; Commission decision 95/364/EC of 28 June 1995 regarding *landing fees at Brussels airport*; Commission decision 1999/199/EC of 10 February 1999 on *landing charges in use at Portuguese airports*.

60. *See*, a notable case on the refusal to interline in *British Midland/Aer Lingus* (1992). As to predatory pricing below-cost price by KLM on the Amsterdam-London route *see*, the case EasyJet/ KLM; this case was settled between the parties with the intervention from the Commission in 1997 (*see* http://www.flightglobal.com/articles/1996/08/07/12225/easyjet-threatens-klm.html). In the Case *London European/Sabena* (1992), London European who used to operate on the Luton Brussels route lodged a complaint against the then Belgian national flag carrier (Sabena) as Sabena denied the complainant access to its own CRS, called Saphir, on the grounds that London European fares were too low. Consequently London European was denied access to 80 per cent of the market and, in practice London European was kicked out of that market. In 1988, the EU Commission obliged Sabena to display these flights on Saphir.

61. *See*, L. Pierallini, *No-Show Rule and Round Trip Tickets*, posted on www.internationallawoffice on 25 January 2017.

services market. The determining factor consists of *interchangeability*: air services which are interchangeable fall within one services market. Hence, in the market for the operation of air services, the question is whether direct air services can be substituted with indirect air services, and air transport with surface transport. Whether one of those alternatives forms an alternative for the direct air route depends on a multiplicity of factors, such as the overall travel time, frequency of services and the price of different alternatives. This must be decided on a case-by-case basis.[62]

The *relevant geographical air transport* market is deemed to comprise an area where the objective conditions of competition applying to the operation of air services are the same for all airlines. For instance, the relevant geographic market in intra-European routes of air cargo transport can be defined as European-wide and includes alternative modes of transport, notably road and train transport.[63] The Commission found that the relevant geographic market for Maintenance Repair and Overhaul (MRO) services is worldwide.[64]

Before the entry into force of EU Regulation 1/2003, undertakings, including airlines, were entitled to apply for individual exemptions. However, since 1 May 2004 this is no longer possible; undertakings must conduct a self-assessment of their own practices to determine their compliance with EU competition law.[65]

EU Council Regulation 487/2009 on *the application of Article 101(3) of the TFEU to certain categories of agreements and concerted practices in the air transport sector* is the only air transport specific regulation still in place.[66] It empowers the EU Commission to exempt specified practices from the scope of Article 101 TFEU on the prohibition of concerted practices. So far, the Commission has not adopted any specific exemption and there are no indications that it intends to do so. Hence, the operation of air services is fully subject to the general competition law regime of the EU, and airlines and other undertakings have to manage their competitive behaviour themselves, under compliance procedures. If not, they may be exposed to *ex post facto* review by the EU Commission or national competition authorities, with the risk of imposition of fines.

---

62. *See*, Commission Notice on the *definition of the relevant market*, paragraph 13; EU Commission, Case No. COMP/M.3280 – *AIR FRANCE / KLM* merger procedure, at 9; *see also*, Case No. COMP/M.6447 – *IAG/ BMI*, at 31.
63. *See*, Commission decision of 11 February 2004, COMP/M.3280, *Air France/KLM*, para 36; Commission decision of 28 August 2009, COMP/M.5440, *Lufthansa/Austrian Airlines*, para. 29; Commission decision of 8 September 2010, COMP/M.5747, *Iberia/British Airways*, para. 41.
64. *See*, Commission decision of 11 February 2004, COMP/M.3280, *Air France/KLM*, para. 40.
65. *See*, Art. 2 of Regulation 1/2003, dictating that the undertaking or association claiming exemptions from the competition regime shall bear the burden of proof; *see also*, S. Sharma, *To What Extent Has the Self-Assessment Principle, Introduced in Regulation 1/2003, Affected, Whether Positively or Negatively, the Undertakings in Air Transport Sector in the European Union*, 41(4/5) Air & Space Law 345–359 (2016).
66. Pursuant to Art. 2 of EU Regulation 487/2009 the following practices may be exempted:

   ■ Joint planning and coordination of airline schedules.
   ■ Consultations on tariffs for the carriage of passengers, baggage and freight on scheduled air services.
   ■ Joint operations on new, less busy scheduled air services.
   ■ Slot allocation at airports and airport scheduling.
   ■ Joint purchase, development and operation of Computer Reservation Systems relating to timetabling, reservations and ticketing by air transport undertakings.

Pursuant to decisions of the Commission, technical arrangements on maintenance of aircraft, aircraft and engine leasing or pooling, as well as operational arrangements including but not limited to interlining, successive carriage agreements and clearing house arrangements are permitted. Depending on the circumstances, such as the effects on pricing, code sharing and blocked space agreements may or may not be allowed. The same is true for joint ventures which may be justified for the operation of new or thin routes.

The next sections will give further illustrations of enforcement of the competition rules in this sector.

3.3.3 The External Competence of the EU in Competition Cases

As stated above, the then ECJ acknowledged that the EU competition rules applied extraterritorially because the operation of international air services may have an effect on the functioning of the internal market. This line of reasoning has led to the recognition of the so-called 'effects' doctrine.[67]

Agreements with States and undertakings outside the EU could also be made subject to scrutiny of the EU institutions, to begin with the EU Commission. As this decision created uncertainty about the legality of these agreements, the Commission made proposals for block exemptions from the competition rules for the air transport sector, including its extra-territorial application.[68]

The question of the Commission's external competence on airline competition has now been resolved on the EU regulatory level by the establishment of the above-mentioned EU Regulation 1/2003 as amended by EU Regulation 411/2004 extending the EU competition rules to air transport between the EU and third countries. As a result, the EU Commission has enforcement powers concerning air services between points in the EU and points outside the EU. To that effect, the Commission may have to rely on the 'effects' doctrine developed mainly by US courts in their anti-trust cases, pursuant to which those US courts asserted jurisdiction over acts of foreign nationals committed abroad but having effects in the US marketplace. It is an extended form of the objective territorial principle. While it has long been controversial, the principle of territoriality is the only principle on which competition law jurisdiction can reasonably be based. It plays a significant role in the air transport sector because the cross border character of the operation of air services, and, as a corollary, the foreign places in which airline transactions are made. Hence, the operation of all air transport services having an effect on the EU market is subject to EU competition rules, following which non-EU undertakings may be made subject to the

---

67. *See* Case 66/86, *Ahmed Saeed Flugreisen*, European Court Reports 803 (1989), and below.
68. *See* further, J. Dutheil de la Rochère, *Contribution of the European Court of Justice to the Implementation of the EEC Treaty in the Field of Air Transport – Past and Future*, in: T.L. Masson-Zwaan and P.M.J. Mendes de Leon (eds in chief), *Air and Space Law: De Lege Ferenda, Essays in Honour of Henri A. Wassenbergh* 161–172 (1992).

EU competition law regime.[69] Meanwhile, the 'effects' doctrine is adopted by many States across the world applying their competition law regimes to the operation of international air services.

The *Air Cargo Fuel Charges* cases form an illustration of the extraterritorial application of competition laws, including the EU competition rules as the alleged anti-competitive acts were carried out outside the EU. The investigation started in 2006 with dawn raids, also involving non-EU airlines who had been accused of colliding with respect to the coordinated imposition of surcharges on the price for the carriage of cargo shipments and other trading conditions, in breach of Article 101 TFEU. On 9 November 2010, the EU Commission imposed fines of almost EUR 800 million on eleven airlines for operating a cartel on cargo fuel and security charges.[70] Hence, price fixing has been punished severely because pricing must be made in an independent fashion by the undertakings. The EU Commission warned that "the existence of an alliance agreement cannot give a *blank cheque* for naked price coordination among the members." On the other side, the Commission showed comprehension for the existence of the regulatory regime prevailing in international air transport encouraging in some cases airlines to behave in an anti-competitive manner because of government dictated trade in air services; this comprehension resulted in some cases to a 15 per cent reduction of fines.[71] The freight forwarders and shippers, and their customers, that is, the undertakings whose goods were carried, are now seeking compensation of their civil damages before courts in Germany, the Netherlands, Norway, the US and the UK. Liability claims amount to several hundred million Euros. The procedures include questions on the admissibility of the claimants and secrecy of information held by the EU Commission.

All of the airlines apart from Qantas airlines appealed the decision.[72] The appealing airlines claimed that the level of the fines was disproportionate to the relatively low profitability of the airline sector; the European Commission's decision infringed the principle of equal treatment in applying different standards of proof; the decision failed to correctly define the relevant market, and that it violated the principles of non-interference or comity between States; the European Commission exceeded its

---

69. In Case 89/85 *Wood Pulp*, ECR 5193 (1988) the Court ruled that agreements concluded outside of the EU, even by undertakings which are established outside of the EU, may be considered to have an effect upon trade between the Member States if they are implemented within the EU so as to having an effect on the functioning of the EU market.
70. *See,* the *Airfreight cartel* case COMP/39.258, decision of 9 November 2010.
71. *See,* Clyde & Co, *Aviation Bulletin* 2–3, February 2003. The problematic relationship between the *ex ante* bilateral air services agreements and the *ex post* competition law regimes is sharply articulated in an article by S. Truxal and S. Harris, *Airfreight: Regulatory Environment Encourages or Imposes Price Co-ordination?* 78(3) Journal of Air Law and Commerce 541–582 (2013).
72. Case T-9/11 – *Air Canada* v. *Commission,* Case T-28/11 – *Koninklijke Luchtvaart Maatschappij* v. *Commission,* Case T-36/11 – *Japan Airlines* v. *Commission,* Case T-38/11 – *Cathay Pacific Airways* v. *Commission,* Case T-39/11 – *Cargolux Airlines* v. *Commission,* Case T-40/11 – *LAN Airlines and LAN Cargo* v. *Commission,* Case T-43/11 – *Singapore Airlines and Singapore Airlines Cargo PTE* v. *Commission,* Case T-46/11 – *Deutsche Lufthansa and Others* v. *Commission,* Case T-48/11 – *British Airways* v. *Commission,* Case T-56/11 – *SAS Cargo Group and Others* v. *Commission,* Case T-62/11 – *Air France – KLM* v. *Commission,* Case T-63/11 – *Air France* v. *Commission,* Case T-67/11 *Martinair Holland* v. *Commission.* Appeals brought in January 2011, as to which *see below.*

jurisdiction with respect to activities regulated and managed outside the EU jurisdiction;[73] the decision infringed the principle of proportionality as it only reduced the fines by 15 per cent on account of the prevailing principles of cooperation in the established regulatory framework. The airlines/claimants also used procedural arguments.[74] Moreover, airline managers who have been involved with these cases have faced imprisonment, especially in the US and the UK where there are criminal regimes for cartel offences. Also, the US Department of Justice is conducting a criminal price fixing investigation of certain airlines. The investigation has resulted in seventeen guilty pleas and over USD 1.6 billion in fines to date, the largest fine ever imposed in a single criminal anti-trust investigation. Following the announcement of criminal investigations, purchasers of air cargo services filed anti-trust class actions seeking treble damages from the airlines for price fixing.[75]

On 16 December 2015, the General Court (GC) of the EU annulled the Commission's fining decision holding twenty-one carriers liable for an infringement of the their alleged collusive conduct. The court found that the grounds of the decision were inconsistent with the operative part of the Commission's decision which it found insufficiently clear whereas the grounds contained substantial internal inconsistencies infringing the defence rights of the carriers and preventing the GC from exercising its power of review. Hence, the court emphasised that the principle of *effective judicial protection* required that the decision made by the Commission should comply with the standard of *legal certainty*, which it did not. As a result, the decision in which fines amounted to approximately EUR 790 million was overturned.[76]

EU Regulation 868/2004 on *unfair pricing policies causing injury to EU air carriers in the supply of air services from countries not members of the European EU* lays down a procedure to be followed to provide protection against subsidisation and unfair pricing practices in the supply of air services from countries not members of the EU in so far as injury is thereby caused to the EU airline industry.[77] Subsidies may consist of financial contributions made by governmental or public authorities in the form of direct transfers of funds, assumption of liabilities and non-collection of charges or other duties. The regulation also prohibits unfair pricing practices, that is, where an airline benefits from non-commercial advantages and charges predatory prices. Procedures are laid down for the making of a complaint; for establishing the existence of injury and the carrying out of an investigation and for the taking of 'repressive measures', which would normally take the form of duties imposed upon the non-EU carrier concerned.

Regulation 868/2004 differs from internal EU law on State aid as it does not take into account the 'market investor' principle whereas there is no scope for exemption in

---

73. *See*, the above comments on reliance on the 'effects doctrine'.
74. Concerning the admissibility of the evidence; breach of the rights of defence and breach of the right of fair trial.
75. *See*, Katten Muchin Rosenman LLP, *Air Transport in 40 Jurisdictions Worldwide* 247 (2011).
76. *See*, General Court of the European Union, Press Release No. 147/15 Luxembourg, 16 December 2015.
77. *See*, A. Trimarchi, *EU Regulation 868/2004: Report of a Unilateral Approach on Regulating Unfair Subsidies and Unfair Pricing Practices and its Failure*, 38(2) European Competition Law Review 72–79 (2017).

case of development of economic activities or rescue aid. Enforcement of this regulation may stand square with provisions of bilateral air agreements providing for the economic regulation of air services between an EU and non-EU State. This is probably the reason why the practical value of this regulation is limited,[78] and has never been enforced in relation to air carriers from third countries, in particular those who are targeted by this practice, that is, carriers from Gulf States. The EU Commission intends to regulate 'fair competition' in the context of vertical agreements between the EU and third States, and discussions on this subject in ICAO.[79]

3.3.4 Airline Alliances

A next step with respect to cooperative arrangements between airlines regards the formation of airline alliances. The EU Commission has built a wealth of experience in this field.[80] It distinguishes between product or services and geographical markets and between business/time sensitive and leisure/price sensitive passengers in relation to the dominance on those markets. If needed, airlines participating in the alliance are requested to remedy their potentially anti-competitive behaviour by surrendering slots at hub airports, freezing capacity and/or fares and granting interline opportunities to new entrants. Generally speaking, the EU Commission supports consolidation, with due regard for global developments in this field. The anti-competitive effects of such alliance agreements must now be self-assessed by airlines.[81]

Remedies offered by the parties and approved by the EU Commission may consist of freezing of frequencies on the appearance of a new entrant airline on a certain route, engagements with respect to enter into intermodal arrangements with surface transport operators (for instance, the High Speed Train permitting interlining between air and rail), the grant of grant of fifth freedom traffic rights to other EU air carriers flying to a destination outside the EU and the prohibition pricing on long haul routes. An important measure concerns the surrendering of slots. In the *British Airways/Iberia/ American Airlines* case (2010) concerning the oneworld alliance, the EU Commission implicitly opened the door for slot trading as parties are not prevented from requesting compensation for surrendering slots.[82]

On 23 May 2013, the EU Commission had accepted commitments offered by *Star Alliance* members, namely, Air Canada, United and Lufthansa, to address its concerns

---

78. *See*, Sean McGonigle, *Past Its Use-by Date*: *Regulation 868 Concerning Subsidy and State Aid in International Air services*, 38(1) Air & Space Law 1–20 (2013) at 5.

79. *See*, section 10.1 of Chapter 2.

80. *See*, for instance, *Lufthansa/SAS/United Airlines*, COMP/D-2/36.201, 36.076 and 36.078 – IP/02/1569 of 29 October 2002; KLM/NorthWest, COMP. 36.111 IP/02/1569 of 29 October 2002; *see also*, M. Mohan, *Ray of Hope for Airline Alliances: Consideration of Out of Market Efficiencies by the European Commission*, 39 Air & Space Law 155–162 (2014).

81. *See*, S. Simon, *Consolidation in Europe's Airline Industry – The Role of the EU Competition Watchdog*, XIII(2) The Aviation and Space Journal 2–9 (2014).

82. *British Airways/Iberia/American Airlines* – COMP/39569, decision of 14 July 2010.

that the alliance agreement including a revenue-sharing joint venture was liable to infringe EU competition rules, by prejudicing passengers on the Frankfurt-New York route. In order to address these concerns, the parties offered to make slots available at Frankfurt and New York airports and to enter into agreements with competitors, allowing them to offer more attractive services.[83] Two years after, that is, on 12 May 2015, the Commission approved the alliance arrangements between Air France/KLM, Alitalia and Delta, all members of the *SkyTeam* Alliance, to lower barriers to entry or expansion on three transatlantic routes by making available slots at Amsterdam, Rome and/or New York airports on the Amsterdam-New York, Paris-New York and Rome-New York routes, by entering into agreements enabling competitors to offer tickets on the parties' flights on the three routes, by entering into agreements facilitating access to the parties' connecting traffic on the mentioned routes and by providing access to their frequent flyer programmes on these routes.[84]

Following the entry into force of EU Regulation 1/2003, the EU Commission has made its decisions in relation to the above three alliance agreements by making the commitments proposed by the alliance members legally binding. The Commission warns that this decision does not conclude whether there has been an infringement of EU competition rules. If the alliance partners would break their commitments, the Commission could impose a fine of up to 10 per cent of each company's total annual turnover without having to prove a violation of the competition rules. This, however, has not yet happened.

Mergers go yet again one step further than alliance agreements as the two parties get more closely involved, among others, by deeper integration of corporate structures and of activities carried out by them jointly. The level of integration will of course vary from one merger to another; it will depend on the circumstances and conditions under which it is concluded whether one speaks of a cooperative agreement, an alliance or a merger. Mergers are not examined under Articles 101 or 102 TFEU but are dealt with in a special regulation as to which *see* the next section.

3.3.5 Merger Control

Merger control is a special issue in international air transport as it bears a close relationship with the relevance of nationality requirements under which international air transport operates for the purpose of designation under bilateral ASAs. Moreover, national laws frequently impose restrictions upon the licensing of air carriers on the basis of their nationality.[85]

---

83. *See*, Press Release of 23 May 2013, EU Commission, Antitrust: Commission renders legally binding commitments from Star alliance members Air Canada, United and Lufthansa on transatlantic air transport passenger market.
84. *See*, EU Commission, Press Release of 15 May 2015, *Antitrust: Commission accepts commitments by SkyTeam members Air France/KLM, Alitalia and Delta on three transatlantic route.*
85. *See*, section 1.2.3 of Chapter 2.

EU merger regulation is laid down in EU Regulation 139/2004 on *the control of concentrations between undertakings*.[86] It applies to mergers that have an EU dimension, that is, where there is an acquisition of control in relation to a venture involving: (i) a world-wide turnover of the merging partners of at least EUR 5 billion plus an individual EU wide turnover of at least each of at least two parties of over EUR 250 million; *or* (ii) a total worldwide turnover of more than EUR 2.5 billion plus a rather detailed test pertaining to the EU based turnover. This condition will most probably always be met in airline mergers. The concerned undertakings must notify anticipated mergers to the EU Commission which can either prevent them from being implemented or approve them with or without attaching conditions to the approval. The Commission can prevent the merger from being implemented or attach conditions to its implementation if it creates or strengthens a dominant position impeding competition in the EU. Mergers are cleared rather than self-assessed as they are under cooperative agreements between airlines and airline alliances cases. Most cases are handled relatively rapidly, that is, within the statutory deadlines. The approval in terms of assessment of dominance on the relevant market is similar to that adopted in alliances cases.[87]

There are also guidelines on the assessment of mergers between competing firms.[88] The objective is to provide guidance to companies as to which mergers might be challenged. The substantive test upon which the Commission can block a transaction is if it:

> would significantly impede effective competition, in the common market or in a substantial part of it, in particular as a result of the creation or strengthening of a dominant position.

Otherwise, national competition authorities are entrusted with the task of judging the concentration.

Since the adoption of the Merger Regulation, the EU Commission has reviewed some thirty airline mergers. The first mergers were domestic mergers, including Air France/UTA and KLM/Transavia.[89] Air France/Sabena[90] and Swissair/Sabena[91] were the first international, but still European mergers. In *Swissair/Sabena* (1995),[92] Swissair acquired 49.5 per cent of the voting shares of Sabena. The Commission was of the opinion that the ownership standard is met if 50 per cent plus one share are owned by such EU nationals. That being the case, Swissair's investment in relation to ownership

---

86. Implementing Regulation: Commission Regulation 802/2004 implementing Council Regulation 139/2004 amended by Commission Regulation 1033/2008 including Annexes listing forms for notification of mergers, and Notices and Guidelines explaining procedures, assessment and market definitions.
87. *See*, section 3.3.4, above.
88. *See*, http://ec.europa.eu/competition/mergers/legislation/legislation.html.
89. These cases have not been published.
90. Case M. 157.
91. Non-opposition to a notified concentration under Art. 6(1)(b) of the Merger Control Regulation, at 10.
92. Commission decision 95/404/EC of 19 July 1995 on a procedure relating to the application of Council Regulation (EEC) No. 2407/92 (*Swissair/Sabena*), OJ L 239/19-28 (1995).

has been approved.[93] Even lengthier was the analysis of the 'effective control' test as defined in the Regulation on licensing of air carriers,[94] implying that there is less room for interpretation based on policy criteria. However, the final question is to determine who has the ultimate decision-making power in the management of the carrier concerned. In sum, the Commission found that Belgian nationals held 'effective control' of Sabena.

Acknowledging that ownership and control are separate elements and that both have to be met to achieve compliance with EU law, the Commission defined effective control as "the power, direct or indirect, actual or legal, to exercise decisive influence on an airline."[95] In other words, in order to assess compliance against the *de facto* condition of 'effective control', what matters is taking into account all of the legal and actual circumstances cumulatively. Among these, the composition of the airline's management, the legal and factual power to appoint the members of the Board of Directors and the Chief Executive, as well as the impact of these factors on the day-to-day management of the airline are crucial. Despite the fact that Swissair held evident and concrete powers to appoint members of the Board of Directors and to elect the Chairman of Sabena, the Commission, perhaps due to political considerations,[96] cleared the merger.[97]

Meanwhile, these first international mergers have been dissolved. Other cross border mergers involved transactions in which the taken over airline only operated intra-EU flights. Consequently, its change in ownership following the takeover did not matter as bilateral air agreements with restrictive nationality requirements did not apply.[98]

The Merger Regulation also apply to mergers with a 'Community dimension' between non-EU airlines. Thus, the European Commission has reviewed the United/USAir,[99] Delta/PanAm,[100] Singapore Airlines/Virgin,[101] and Swissair/South Africa[102] joint ventures under the EU regime.

---

93. Subject to the following conditions: the scale of the third country investment; the distribution of the shares within each group of shareholders; and the effect of ownership upon control of the EU company; *see*, section X of the *Swissair/Sabena* Decision (1995).
94. In this respect, it does not matter whether appointments have been made directly or indirectly, but it is relevant to find out who has 'the final say' on key questions as the carrier's business plan, its annual budget or any major investment or cooperation project; *See also*, Art. 2(9) of EU Regulation 1008/2008 defining the term 'effective control'.
95. *See*, Section XI of the *Swissair/Sabena* decision (1995).
96. The *Swissair/Sabena* decision (1995) preceded the referenda held a little less than two years later on the accession of Switzerland to the EU; in 1995, it was perhaps hoped that this decision would help the Swiss to vote in favour of accession by demonstrating good will by allowing Swiss control of an EU airline.
97. *Ibid.* Swissair held the power to appoint half of the members of Sabena's Board of Directors and to appoint, in the case a decision could not be made, the Board's Chairman.
98. *See* for example the takeover of BA of the French domestic carrier TAT.
99. Case M. 2041.
100. Case M. 130.
101. Case M. 1855.
102. Case M. 1626.

Significant cross border merger activity started to take place in the twenty-first century with the merger between Air France and KLM. In *Air France/KLM* (2004),[103] the EU Commission found that the airlines' networks were basically complimentary. However, competition would be affected on fourteen intra-EU and intercontinental routes on which they currently compete, either actually or potentially. The parties offered remedies pertaining to the surrendering of slots; the freezing of frequencies on the appearance of a new entrant on one of the above routes; the engagement into commitments with surface transport operators, for instance, the High Speed Train between Paris and Amsterdam permitting interlining between air and rail; the grant by Dutch and French governmental authorities of fifth freedom traffic rights to other EU air carriers flying via Amsterdam or Paris to a destination outside the EU, while keeping in mind that those authorities are not allowed to regulate pricing on long haul routes. The US authorities approved the Air France/KLM merger on the same day as the EU Commission that is, on 11 February 2004, allowing the combination to go forward. Apart from the EU Commission and the US DoT, a number of countries, including but not limited to Brazil, Japan, Israel, South Africa, the Czech Republic, Poland and Rumania have explicitly approved the deal.

In *Lufthansa/Austrian Airlines*,[104] the EU Commission requested the parties to give up slots at specified airports in Germany and Austria, to engage into interline agreements and other arrangements on, for instance access to frequent flyer programmes, with new entrants and into intermodal agreements with surface in carriers, in particular the operators of high speed trains.

On 14 July 2010, the Commission approved the merger between *British Airways* and *Iberia*.[105] The Commission opined that the merged entity would continue to face competition in the various markets, including those for short haul and long haul services, and passenger, cargo and ground handling services.

On 9 October 2013, the Commission approved the acquisition of Olympic Air by Aegean Airlines, both Greek air carriers because Olympic Air would be forced to exit the market due to financial difficulties if not acquired by Aegean. Once Olympic would be out of business, Aegean would become the only significant domestic service provider and would capture Olympic's current market shares. Therefore, with or without the takeover, Olympic would disappear as a competitor to Aegean. Thus, the merger caused no harm to competition that would not have occurred anyway.

One of the interesting features of the *Etihad/Alitalia* merger of 2014 concerned the analysis of overlapping routes which are flown by carriers in which Etihad has a stake, including Air Berlin, Air Serbia, Darwin Airline and Jet Airways. The Commission concluded that the marketing carrier does not exert more than a residual constraint on the operating carrier. The proximity of Dubai airport was considered in the light of the relevant services market test, in which the substitutability of the airports

---

103. *See,* Prior notification of a proposed concentration that the Commission received on 18 December 2003 pursuant to Art. 4 of Council Regulation 4064/89 as amended and corrected; Case No. COMP/M.3280 – *Air France/KLM,* decision of 11 February 2004.
104. Case M.5440; decision of 28 August 2009.
105. Case M. 5747; decision of 14 July 2010.

is checked.[106] The Commission examined the anti-competitive effects of the *Etihad/Alitalia* merger and concluded that the transaction does not raise any serious competition concern on all of the affected routes, with the exception of the Rome-Belgrade route, mainly because of the competitive pressure exerted by other carriers. Thus, the Commission approved the merger in 2014 while Alitalia and Air Serbia were required to release daily slots at both Rome Fiumicino Airport and Belgrade Airport.[107]

Because this investment is made by a non-EU carrier scrutiny of nationality conditions of Alitalia under EU Regulation 1008/2008 is called for.[108] A number of factual aspects of the merger, among which the intention of opening new strategic routes and the composition of the board of directors are decisive in identifying who has the effective control of the airline.[109]

While in terms of nationality requirements the *Etihad/Alitalia* and the *Swissair/Sabena* mergers have been similarly assessed, the analysis of their anti-competitive effects differs insomuch as, with respect to the former, the Commission had to take into account the relevant network constituted by the carriers in which Etihad maintains a stake, and its partners. Both cases are characterised by the presence of a predominant foreign shareholder. The largest single foreign shareholder has a particular influence, especially where other shareholders are thinly spread and cannot exercise their voting powers in concert.[110]

On 14 November 2014, the EU Commission has also cleared the *International Consolidated Airlines Group* (IAG)/*Aer Lingus* take over, subject to conditions. IAG had to offer slots at London Gatwick airport and concessions pertaining to the carriage of passengers connecting to long haul flights to competing carriers in order to take away competition concerns.[111]

Hence, the Commission imposes restrictions on the merger with the purpose of remedying the potential anti-competitive effects of the venture. The approach is similar to that adopted in alliances cases.[112]

Remedies used by the European Commission include the slot divestiture at congested airports at one of the two or the two origin and destination airports. As practice shows that slot divestiture has not always yielded the desired pro-competitive results, the Commission adopts a more interventionist role with respect to the implementation of such remedies. Other remedies concern: freezing of capacity by the airlines which are subject to competition review; price constraints so as to avoid predatory pricing; introduction of requirements on mandatory engagement into blocked space agreements and interlining with new entrant airlines; access to Frequent

---

106. *See*, EU Commission decision of 14 November 2014.
107. *See*, EU Commission Case No. COMP/M.7333 *Etihad/Alitalia* (2014).
108. *See*, the above *Swissair/Sabena* case.
109. *See*, A. Trimarchi, *A Comparative Critique of the Laws on Ownership and Control of Airlines. Is Commercial Aviation still at the Crossroads?*, LL.M. Thesis, Leiden University (2016).
110. *See*, *Swissair/Sabena* Decision (1995) at 6.
111. *See*, EU Commission, Press Release of 14 November 2014. Similar conditions, that is, the surrender of slots at London Heathrow and the provision of connections to competing airlines, were agreed upon in the acquisition of British Midland (BMI) by IAG, on 30 March 2013.
112. *See*, the overview of EU competition developments published twice per year in the magazine Air & Space Law.

Flyer Programmes and CRS (now GDS) by new entrant airlines or competitor airlines; relaxation of limitations with respect to the performance of fifth and sixth freedom rights on services from within the EU to points outside the EU and *vice versa*.

Merger and take over activities are increasing in an era of consolidation of the airline industry. This trend is fuelled by the need for investments. Consolidation starts receiving a global touch by the stakes purchased by non-European airlines into European airlines. Competition and other authorities are challenged to examine these transactions from a competition law but also from a broader strategic point of view.

The Commission's *Aviation Strategy for Europe*, which was published on 7 December 2015, addresses these challenges by highlighting the objective of accessing growth markets by improving market access, services and investment opportunities with third countries. As to the latter, the EU Commission has made proposals to negotiate vertical, that is, all-encompassing aviation agreements with the Members of the Association of the South East Asian Nations (ASEAN), the Gulf States assembled in the Gulf Cooperation Council, and with Armenia, China, Mexico and Turkey. These vertical agreements are designed to achieve regulatory convergence, with specific attention for competition and State aid related matters. In this regard, 'fair competition' on a level playing field supported by the adoption and implementation of harmonised rules, also in the field of competition, is a high point on the agenda.

While the above *Aviation Strategy for Europe* promotes the efficiency of airport services and recognises that competitive airport services are critical for the competitiveness of the EU aviation sector and the service quality experience of passengers, it does not address cooperation between airports and investments made into airports as a means of achieving these objectives. Meanwhile, airports are also pursuing investments in other airports as exemplified by the controlling interest taken by *Aéroports de Paris* and Aviation Netherlands into Zagreb International Corporation (ZAIC), Croatia. The Commission cleared this takeover, as it would generate negligible repercussions for the EU market.[113]

3.3.6 State Aid

The financial and economic crises in the last decade of the twentieth century, and at the end of the first decade of the twenty-first century, forced many airlines to restructure their operations. The acute fall-off in demand exposed many failings in the industry: overcapacity, low productivity, high costs and undercapitalisation. Successful restructuring required public money, particularly on the part of those airlines that were wholly or partially owned by their governments. Hence, next to mergers and takeovers, undertakings, including airlines and airports, tried to compensate for losses by taking recourse to State aid.

The EU is one of the very few jurisdictions regulating State aid by subjecting it to conditions. Article 107 TFEU prohibits aid by Member States or through publish

---

113. Decision of 8 September 2014; *see*, Case No. COMP/M.7327 – ADP/ BBI / IFC / MARGUERITE / TAV / ZAIC.

resources which distorts or threatened to distort competition by favouring a particular undertaking or undertakings and which affects EU trade. Exemption from the prohibition may be made for air service which is designed to "facilitate the development of certain activities" where such aid "does not adversely affect trading conditions to an extent contrary to the common interest."[114] The EU Commission must supervise compliance with the EU Treaty provisions and, where required, take appropriate measures or impose sanctions. The proposed aid must be notified to the Commission (*ex ante*). Aid which is granted without prior notification is unlawful per se.

The EU Commission can prohibit a State aid case, or approve it, and make its decision subject to conditions, taking into account the *market investor* principle, the *proportionality* principle and, in the case of airports, the achievement of a *well-defined common interest*. When carrying out its examination, the Commission must also apply the so-called *de minimis* rule under which small aid amounts of State aid, basically amounts below EUR 200,000, are exempted from the mentioned prohibition.[115]

The *market investor* principle allows aids made under terms and conditions that would be similar to those carried out by a private investor operating under normal market economic conditions. Under the *proportionality* principle, the aid must be proportional to its purpose, for instance, the restructuring of the undertaking. Aid of a social character benefiting specified categories of passengers including children, persons with disabilities, people on low incomes, students and elderly people is held compatible with the functioning of the internal market.[116]

The EU Commission has monitored State aid granted to airlines since 1989. Aid was in most cases given to the national 'flag' carrier for rescuing it from bankruptcy. In line with the provisions of the EU treaty and secondary legislation, the Commission has authorised aid to airlines as 'exceptional measures' designed to assist the restructuring of the airlines concerned, with a view to completing the liberalisation of the single market.[117] Most of the airlines needing to restructure have done so and the Commission considers that State aid is no longer either necessary or warranted. The Commission decisions involving the aid for Air France,[118] Alitalia[119] and Olympic Airways[120] were challenged before the CJEU.

In 2014, the Commission published its *Guidelines on State aid to airports and airlines*, analysing the role of airports and airlines for connectivity of the region and the functioning of the internal market, including the maintenance of a 'level playing field'

---

114. *See*, Art. 112(3) TFEU.
115. *See*, EU Commission Regulation 1998/2006.
116. *See*, Art. 107(2)(a) TFEU.
117. Relevant cases concerned aid granted by their respective governments to the former Belgium carrier Sabena (1989 and 2001); Air France (1991 and 1994); Aer Lingus (1993); TAP – Air Portugal (1994); Olympic (1994; 2002; 2005 and 2008); Alitalia (1997; 2004 and 2008); the German carrier LTU (2003); Austrian Airlines (2009) and Air Malta (2010).
118. *See*, Case T-358/94, judgment of 12 December (1996).
119. *See*, *Alitalia I*, Case T-296/97, judgement of 12 December 2000; *Alitalia II*: Case T-301/01, judgement of 9 July 2008.
120. *See*, Case C-415/03, judgement of 12 May 2005, in which the court ordered the Greek government to recover State aid granted by it to its – then – flag carrier in the period between 1998 and 2000, upon request of the EU Commission.

for the concerned undertakings. While acknowledging that State aid, in particular operating aid, may yield negative effects on competition and trade between EU States, certain categories of aid to regional airports and airlines using those airports can be justified in exceptional circumstances. For the EU Commission to apply State aid rules to airports and airlines, it does not matter whether they are publicly or privately owned,[121] as long as they are qualified as 'undertakings' which they are, as to which *see* above. However, because not all activities of airports are "of an economic nature" such as Air Traffic Control (ATC), police, customs, security services and fire fighting, a distinction between these activities, and the way they are funded, may have to be made.[122] State aid may take many forms, and must therefore be interpreted in a broad fashion.[123]

In most cases, involving major airlines and flag carriers such as Air France,[124] Sabena,[125] TAP Portugal,[126] Aer Lingus,[127] Austrian Airlines,[128] Alitalia,[129] Adria Airways,[130] airBaltic,[131] SAS[132] and LOT Polish Airlines[133] the aid was approved, subject to conditions, which may include:

- the establishment of a restructuring plan for the undertaking which must be focused on the core business of transport of passengers on the most profitable routes, including reduction or elimination of loss making activities, and synergies to be exploited on the basis of their geographical locations, a more unified fleet, reduction of catering costs in economy class and minimising personal, thus streamlining the operations of the airline;
- the obligation of air carriers to contribute to the restructuring;
- the allowance of 'temporary restricting support' only, limited in both amount and time;

121. *See*, Art. 345: "The Treaties shall in no way prejudice the rules in Member States governing the system of property ownership."
122. *See*, Airport Council International (ACI) Europe, *European airports: a competitive industry*, Policy Paper (2009).
123. Including direct grants, tax rebates, soft loans or other types of preferential financing conditions and subsidies services such as airport services. Recourses can be made available on national, regional or local level.
124. As contested by a number of EU air carriers, as to which *see*, *BA, SAS, KLM, Air UK, Euralair, TAT and British Midland, supported by the Scandinavian and UK governments v. the Commission, supported by the French government;* Cases T-371/94 and T-394/94, decided on 25 June 1998.
125. Case N636/2001.
126. Case N132_2002.
127. Case SA_29064.
128. Case NN72_2008.
129. Case N318; *see also,* EU Commission, *Commission closes preliminary investigation into alleged aid to Alitalia*, Daily News of 6 February 2015.
130. *See*, EU Commission Press Release of 9 July 2014, *Commission approves restructuring aid for Slovenian airline Adria Airways.*
131. *See*, EU Commission Press Release of 9 July 2014, *Commission approves restructuring aid for Latvian airline airBaltic.*
132. *See*, EU Commission Press Release of 9 July 2014, *Commission concludes that Scandinavian Airlines (SAS) did not receive state aid.*
133. *See*, EU Commission Press Release of 29 July 2014, *Commission approves restructuring aid for LOT Polish Airlines.*

- the obligation to pay back the loan which was received from the Government;
- the recapitalisation of the airline;
- the imposition of the 'one time last time' condition, implying that an EU Member State may use public funding of a certain undertaking once every ten years.

On the other side, the proposed aid for Cyprus Airways[134] and Estonian Air[135] has been held illegal, because these two airlines had not put in place the agreed restructuring plan, giving it an undue advantage over its competitors in breach of EU state aid rules, and keeping it artificially in the market to the expense of the tax payers. Meanwhile, European flag carriers have disappeared as a consequence of bankruptcies. They include Swissair (2001), Sabena (2001) and Malev (2009).

The above *State Aid Guidelines* (2014) also focus on financing of airports and start up aid to airlines departing from regional airports. While major hub airports such as London Heathrow and London Gatwick, Paris/Charles de Gaulle, Frankfort and Amsterdam are congested, Europe knows overcapacity when it comes to regional airports which often fulfil a social function in terms of provision of connectivity for the area in which they are located. Those regional airports are mostly public owned and managed under local or regional administration, which have a public interest in attracting traffic, and therefore subsidise those airports they serve, under the mentioned State aid Guidelines, a 'General Economic Interest'. The Court of the EU has explained this notion in the well-known '*Altmark*' judgment[136] pursuant to which public authorities may define activities of general economic interests for which public funding, under specified conditions, may be permitted by EU law.

In an airline-airport related case, the Commission ruled that financial support and assistance given by the regional authorities in south Belgium and the Charleroi airport authority to the Irish airline Ryanair constituted, in part, State aid and was unlawful. It ordered that part of the funds received by the airline should be repaid to the authorities

---

134. *See*, EU Commission, Press Release of 9 January 2015, *Commission orders Cyprus to recover incompatible aid from national air carrier Cyprus Airways*.
135. *See*, EU Commission, Press Release of 7 November 2015, *Commission orders Estonia to recover incompatible aid from national air carrier Estonian Air*.
136. Case C-280/00, *Altmark Trans GmbH and Regierungspräsidium Magdeburg* v. *Nahverkehrsgesellschaft Altmark GmbH*; In case T-271/03 *Deutsche Telekom AG* v. *Commission*, decision of 24 May 2008, the CJEU held that the EU competition articles "…. apply *only* to anti-competitive conduct engaged in by undertakings *on their own initiative*. If anti-competitive conduct is required of undertakings by *national legislation* or if the latter creates a legal framework which itself eliminates any possibility of competitive activity on their part," such provisions do not apply. It went on by stating that "In such a situation, the restriction of competition is *not attributable*, as those provisions implicitly require, to the *autonomous conduct of the undertakings*." (*italics added*); *see also*, CJEU, Case 322/81 *Nederlandsche Banden Industrie Michelin* v. *Commission* decision of 9 November 1983, in which the court stated that:

> an undertaking has a dominant position is not in itself a recrimination but simply means that, irrespective of the reasons for which it has such a dominant position, the undertaking concerned has a special responsibility not to allow its conduct to impair genuine undistorted competition on the common market. (par. 57)

concerned.[137] On 17 December 2008, the Court annulled the above Commission's Decision as the Commission had not correctly applied the above 'market investor' principle. Among others, the Court found that the Commission had wrongly decided that this principle could not be invoked as the aid had been granted by a public authority, namely, the Walloon Region, which did not act as an economic operator.[138]

As a consequence, cases concerning mostly regional airports in Portugal, France, Italy, Poland, Germany, Belgium, Spain, the Czech Republic, Denmark and Finland have been dealt with by the EU Commission. Under the above Guidelines, public funds may be pursued by such regional airports to attract price-sensitive airlines, enhancing connectivity and accessibility of the region, and mobility of EU citizens, thus providing a valuable contribution to regional development, without impeding competition in the EU market.

3.3.7 Concluding Remarks on Competition Matters

Whereas the EU Member States were in the beginning hesitant to subject their carriers, in particular their 'flag' carriers, to the EU competition rules in a free market environment, the EU Commission, helped by the Court of the EU, has strongly promoted the application of these rules to the air transport sector. The Commission has explained them in documents, especially Guidelines. The Guidelines on State aid to airports and airlines serve as a policy tool to monitor State aid cases in the aviation sector. This State aid policy targeting also flag carriers and the demise of Swissair, Sabena and Malev, illustrate the objective of de-linking State and commercial interests, and creating an open market environment. The EU Commission has built an impressive amount of case law, and developed remedies for mitigating the anti-competitive effects of concerted actions and mergers. Thus, the Commission helps to achieve an internal air transport market based on a level playing field for operators and with distinct benefits for consumers.

---

137. *See*, EU Commission decision 2004/393/EC of 12 February 2004 concerning *advantages granted by the Walloon Region and Brussels South Charleroi Airport to the airline Ryanair in connection with its establishment at Charleroi.*

138. *See*, Case T-196/04, *Ryanair v. Commission* because the court found that the Commission's refusal to examine together the advantages granted by the Walloon Region and to apply the private investor principle to the measures adopted by the Walloon Region was not justified on legal grounds. European Commission Decision number DN: IP/04/157 of 3 February 2004 in which the Commission ruled that certain elements of the financial assistance given by the Brussels South Charleroi Airport and the Walloon Region (Belgium) constituted State aid under Art. 87(1) of the EC Treaty (now Art. 107 TFEU), being incompatible with the 'private market investor principle'; *see also*, Commission decision 2016/2069 of 1 October 2014 concerning *measures implemented by Belgium in favour of Brussels South Charleroi Airport and Ryanair* in which the Commission decided that certain aid measures granted to Ryanair by the Walloon Government do not constitute State aid whereas specified measures granted by Belgium must be deemed unlawful State aid whereas others are compatible with the internal market provisions laid down in Art. 107(3)(c) of the TFEU under mentioned time restrictions. For a comment, *see*, S. Stadlmeier and B. Rumersdorfer, *The Ryanair/Charleroi Case Before the European Court*, 34(4/5) Air & Space Law 309–318 (2009); *see also*, M. Geisler and J.P. Schmidt, *State Aid Issues in the Air Transport Sector. The Charleroi/Ryanair Decision of the European Commission*, 53 Zeitschrift für Luft- und Weltraumrecht 347–358 (2004).

The same is true for State aid to airlines. EU Member States remain concerned about the fate of their 'national' carriers and continue to fight with the EU Commission on the application of rules and principles.

Last but not least, the EU Commission pays attention to the international dimension of the EU air transport sector. This dimension is illustrated by the application of the 'effects' doctrine, cooperation between the EU Commission with its non-EU counterparts, and the establishment of Regulation 886/2004 which is nowadays frequently referred to in the context of, for instance, relations with Middle East countries and their airlines. However, as is often the case, international relations and international law do not facilitate the objectives and principles of EU law and policy in a global air transport environment which is one of the reasons why this regulation is being reconsidered.

3.4 Concluding Remarks

The internal market can be regarded as a success, if not the principal achievement of the EU Commission and other European institutions. Its rules function well and have created a liberalised market in which airlines received a high degree of freedom of action, and consumers distinctly more choices. This result would not have been possible by the strong backing of these supranational institutions and the governing treaties of the EU dictating the freedom of services and the freedom of establishment.

Safeguards with respect to access to infrastructure and restrictions for full liberalisation have been and had to be introduced for reasons of safety, security, congestion and the protection of the environment all of which are also high priorities for the European policymakers. These objectives appear to have matched well with the starting point of the internal market which is a market without internal frontiers where services can be feely offered subject to the application of competition rules. Also, apart from a limited number of exceptions, application of these latter rules appears to have functioned well in practice.

4 THE REGULATION OF SAFETY AND SECURITY

4.1 Safety

A very high level of safety is not only an achievement but also a continued objective of the EU. Moreover, as the internal market proceeds from a level playing field between the service providers, that is, the airlines, airports and air navigation service providers, harmonisation of safety standards is a tool to attempt to reach that goal. This is an important reason why the European Aviation Safety Agency (EASA), which is described in Chapter 7, was created in 2004.

In light of the cross border nature of air transport, safety regulation has a global basis. It is discussed in Chapter 6 on Safety in international civil aviation.

4.2   Security

4.2.1   The Introduction of Security Measures

Prior to 2001, the level of EU action in the field of aviation security was relatively low. The events of 11 September 2001, with the attacks on New York and Washington using hijacked aircraft, changed this situation. Following the events in the USA in September 2001, the EU Council met in emergency session within a few days and launched a series of actions that led to the development of more effective security regulations within Europe. The principal regulation now is EU Regulation 300/2008 on *common rules in the field of civil aviation security, and repealing EC Regulation 2320/2002*. This basic Regulation has been implemented and supplemented by Commission Regulations.[139]

Provisions contained in the Regulations may reflect the terms of Annex 17 to the Chicago Convention in order to make use of the expertise of ICAO in this regard and achieve the necessary harmonisation for service providers on the internal air transport market. EU security measures are constantly updated. They pertain to the conduct of procedures in the field of civil aviation security, the establishment, verification and effectiveness of national civil aviation security programmes; methods including technologies for the detection of liquid explosives; the carriage of prohibited articles, and liquids on board aircraft, and the identification of security sensitive parts in the airport. Security measures are contained in confidential Annexes to the regulations which are not published because of secrecy.

The EU security measures apply to airports in EU States and carriage between EU States. As security is a sovereignty sensitive issue, States wish to protect the integrity of their aviation system pursuant to their national policy objectives, with due regard for their international obligations stemming from their adherence to the security conventions which are discussed in Chapter 10 and ICAO Annex 17.

By virtue of provisions laid down in the ECAA agreements[140] the EU Commission is in a position to monitor and enforce compliance with EU aviation security requirements.[141]

---

139. *See*, Commission Regulation 272/2009 amended by Commission Regulation 297/2010, and further amended by Commission Regulations 720/2011, 1141/2011 and 245/2013; *see also*, Commission Regulations 1245/2009 *setting criteria to allow Member States to derogate from the common basic standards on civil aviation security and to adopt alternative security measures*, and 18/2010 amending Regulation (EC) No. 300/2008 as far as *specifications for national quality control programmes in the field of civil aviation security are concerned; see also*, Commission Regulations 72/2010 and 1198/2015 amended by Commission Regulation 2426/2015, and Commission Implementing Regulation 2015/1998 laying down *detailed measures for the implementation of the common basic standards on aviation security*; it applies as from 1 February 2016, and contains detailed measures for the implementation of common standards for safeguarding civil aviation against acts of unlawful interference that jeopardise aviation security.
140. *See*, section 6.2 of this Chapter.
141. *See*, the Study on *The Legal Situation Regarding Security of Flights from Third Countries to the EU* carried out by Innovative Compliance and DLA Pieper, November 2010.

4.2.2 The Protection of Aviation Security in Relation to Privacy

The national sensitivity towards security related questions is illustrated by the relationship between security and human rights. Both need to be protected. However, governments may give different priorities to the protection of these values. Generally speaking, the US would rank security higher because of its fights against terrorism whereas the EU and its Member States stress the protection of human rights as an overriding policy objective.[142]

The discussion of data protection laid down in Passenger Name Records (PNR) gives evidence of this dilemma. Data protection laws of the EU and its Member States do not permit airlines operating services from airports in the EU to transmit the PNR details of their passengers to third countries which do not ensure an adequate level of protection of personal data without adequate safeguard. The EU and the US attempt to bridge their differences in transatlantic agreements on the subject.[143] In order to help air carriers, protect privacy and promote aviation security, the EU made agreements with Australia and Canada designed to fostering privacy while keeping in mind the objective of fighting international terrorism.

The drawing up for a PNR legal measure in the EU also dragged for years, that is, since 2007. Discussions about the application of the proportionality principle and procedural questions caused a delay until the terrorist attacks in Paris in 2015 urged policymakers to move on. In 2016, the PNR Directive was adopted, obliging European States to set up a PNR system and to harmonise their national legislations. EU States must establish a Passenger Information Unit (PIU) for the prevention, detection, investigation or prosecution of terrorist offences and of serious crime or a branch of

---

142. So far the EU and the US have reached four agreements have been on this subject, the first one of which dates back to 2004 which appeared to have the wrong legal basis in EU law; the CJEU agreed in Cases C-317 & 318/04. The US side also showed procedural mistakes. An interim agreement was signed in 2006 failing which airlines would not have been able to operate their services. It was followed by an Agreement made in 2007, which changed the legal basis on the EU side, but, according to the EU Parliament, it did not sufficiently protect the rights of the EU citizens and passengers. In consequent, a fourth agreement was concluded in 2012 regulating the transfer of Passenger Name Records by air carriers to US authorities, namely, the *Agreement between the United States of America and the European Union on the use and transfer of passenger name records to the United States Department of Homeland Security* (2012). In it, the purpose of data collection has been considerably extended as they can be used by US authorities in case of a serious threat or if so ordered by a US court. It also contains restrictions on the use of data. However, doubts has been expressed as to whether all of the privacy rights have even correctly addressed. *See*, W.M. Grossman, *The Great Passenger Name Records Sell Out* (2007), D.R. Rasmussen, *Is International Travel* Per Se *Suspicion of Terrorism? The Dispute Between the United States and European Union over Passenger Name Record Data Transfers*, 26(2) Wisconsin International Law Journal 585 (2008), v. Papkonstantinou & P. De Hert, *The PNR Agreement and Transatlantic Anti-terrorism Co-operation: No Firm Human Rights Framework on Either Side of the Atlantic*, 46 Common Market Law Review 885–919 (2009) at 909; *see also*, Pablo Mendes de Leon, *The Fight Against Terrorism Through Aviation: Data Protection versus Data Production*, 31 Air & Space Law 320–331 (2006).
143. *See*, W.M. Grossman, *The Great Passenger Name Records Sell Out* (2007), D.R. Rasmussen, *Is International Travel* Per Se *Suspicion of Terrorism? The Dispute Between the United States and European Union over Passenger Name Record Data Transfers*, 26(2) Wisconsin International Law Journal 585 (2008).

such an authority.[144] The PIU is responsible for the collection of PNR data from air carriers, storing and processing those data and transferring those data or the result of processing them to the competent authorities through the 'push' method and for the exchange of both PNR data and the result of processing those data with the PIUs of other Member States and with Europol.[145]

For further discussion, reference is made to section 3.5 of Chapter 6.

4.2.3   Concluding Remarks

The promotion of aviation safety and security is essential for the operation of air services. They have a strong technical component whereas aviation security may also affect privacy rights. Those facets contribute to its dynamic development in light of developments and events, such as '9/11' and the attacks against premises, including airports, in Europe in 2015 and 2016.

The EU has become aware of the need to constantly adapt its measures in light of these circumstances while taking into account the global regime governing these fields. At the same time local security measures which are not necessarily air law related must supplement international and European rules as the afore-mentioned events of 2015 and 2016 demonstrate the need for them.

5   INFRASTRUCTURE

5.1   Use of Infrastructure

5.1.1   Charges for the Provision of Airport Services

In 2009, the EU adopted Directive 2009/12 on airport charges. It is a non-exclusive regulation; Member States are entitled to implement additional regulatory measures as long as they are not incompatible with the provisions of this Directive, and Member States have done so,[146] leading to what has been termed as an 'uneven implementation'. The chosen instrument, namely a directive, has contributed to the emergence of disparities in EU Member States with respect to the process of consultations, refinancing of infrastructural project and the introduction of 'airport networks'.[147] Thus, the Directive can hardly be said to move on in terms of harmonisation from the ICAO principles laid down in Doc. 9082.[148]

---

144. *See*, EU Directive 2016/681.
145. Europol is the EU's law enforcement agency whose main goal is to enhance security in the fight of the EU States against serious international crime and terrorism.
146. *See*, EU Commission, *Report on the Evaluation of Directive 12/2009 on Airport Charges* (2013).
147. *See*, Centre for Aviation, *Airport Charges: EC reports increased transparency in setting charges but uneven implementation* (2014).
148. *See*, S. Varsamos, *Airport Competition Regulation in Europe*, Chapter 3 (2016).

The Directive applies to airports in the EU with annual traffic of over 5 million passenger movements per year. It prohibits discrimination among airport users, although they may be modulated on the basis of relevant, objective and transparent criteria for reasons of public and general interests, including protection of the environment. Airport charges must be set in a transparent fashion, following consultations between the airport operator and users, resulting into an agreement between the two parties whereas Member States must establish procedures for resolving disagreements between these parties.

Airport operators must provide information on the system and level of the charges and may engage into service level agreements with users so as to agree on tailor made services, such as the provision of access to a dedicated terminal, in which case charges may be differentiated according to transparent, non-discriminatory and objective criteria.[149] EU Member States have established an independent supervisory authority to guarantee the implementation of the Directive.[150]

The long awaited Directive has not produced dramatic changes. The non-discrimination principles, consultation procedures and service level agreements are already in place. New items are the establishment of a dispute resolution scheme and a Supervisory authority.

Cases have not yet been brought under this directive while the conduct of airport operators as undertakings remains subject to EU rules on competition, including those on State aid.[151]

5.1.2 Slot Allocation

One of the difficulties that might be encountered by air carriers seeking new route opportunities in the liberalised market is the availability of landing and take-off slots at congested EU airports such as London, Paris, Frankfurt and Amsterdam. Thus, the availability, allocation and distribution of slots became one of the most crucial subjects of the last decades. Congestion at airports as a consequence of increase of air traffic, coupled with environmental concerns, has led to a shortage of slots.

For many years, the major 'home' or incumbent air carriers at the larger EU airports had enjoyed what had become known as *grandfather rights* in respect of slots at those airports. Frequently, the major carrier headed up the slot committee at an airport that allocated slots to the various airlines. Consequently, such carriers exercised a great deal of control over who could obtain slots, including potential competitors. Hence, slots became a scarce commodity, which had to be allocated either by imposition on the basis of government regulation or by free trading. Policy makers are faced with the dilemma of striking a balance between the interests of the 'incumbent'

---

149. *See*, S. Hobe and W. Müller-Rostin, *Legal Relationship Between the Airport Operator and the Air Carrier – A Regulatory Grey Area?* 62(2) Zeitschrift für Luft und Weltraumrecht 169–184 (2013).
150. *See*, EU Directive 2009/12 on *airport charges*.
151. In the 1990s, the European Commission made three decisions involving airport charges as the airport operators applied discriminatory charges, favouring the local carrier; they have been referred to in section 3.3.2, above.

carriers, which have for years invested in developing their presence at slot-limited airports, and the interests of start-up airlines. Start-up airlines should be given access to a 'level playing field' in the air transport market in order to promote competition in that 'field'.

The EU has tried to resolve this dilemma in its Regulation 95/93 on *slot allocation* as variously amended. The question of 'slot-trading' is neither expressly allowed nor expressly excluded under the EU regulation.[152] The EU Regulation applies not only to intra-EU services operated by EU air carriers, but also to non-EU air carriers operating within the EU.

Regulation 95/93 on slot allocation, along with its amendments, forms the legal basis of the present process on slot allocation. Under this Regulation, a slot is defined as "the scheduled time of arrival or departure available or allocated to an aircraft movement on a specific date at an airport co-ordinated under the terms of this Regulation."[153] An EU Member State may designate an airport as a coordinated airport or as fully co-ordinated airport in order to facilitate the operations of air carriers operating or intending to operate at an airport in its territory. A *co-ordinated airport* is an airport where a slot co-coordinator has been appointed in order to facilitate operations from and to that airport.[154] The slot coordinator must be functionally and financially independent from the airport, the airlines, the local authorities or any other interested party.[155] A *fully co-ordinated airport* is defined as an airport "where, in order to land or take off, during the periods for which it is fully co-ordinated, it is necessary for an air carrier to have a slot allocated by a co-ordinator."[156] Designation as a fully co-ordinated airport takes place upon a thorough capacity analysis with respect to the airport in question.[157] If a Member State designates an airport as co-ordinated or as fully co-ordinated, it must take into account the principles of transparency of the slot allocation mechanism, neutrality of the slot coordinator, and non-discrimination between air carriers in the context of the slot allocation process.

There is an operational link between the exercise of traffic rights and the availability of slots. Regulations 95/93 and 1008/2008 acknowledge this by cross-references occurring in the two regulations.[158]

---

152. *See*, EU Regulation 95/93 *on the allocation of slots*. *See*, as to 'slot-trading', the case *Regina* v. *the Airport Co-ordination Limited* ex Parte *The States of Guernsey Transport Board*, Case No. CO/0722/98, decision of the Swansea Crown Court of 25 March 1999; *see also*, EC Regulation 894/2002.

153. *See*, Art. 2(a) of Regulation 95/93 as amended.

154. *See*, Art. 2(f) of Regulation 95/93 as amended.

155. *See*, Art. 4(2) of Regulation 95/93 as amended, and as interpreted by the CJEU in Case C-205/14, *European Commission* v. *Portuguese Republic*, decision of 2 June 2016.

156. *See*, Art. 2(g) of Regulation 95/93 as amended.

157. *See*, Art. 3(3) of Regulation 95/93 as amended.

158. *See*, Art. 19(2) of Regulation 1008/2008, referring to the availability of slots but not to Regulation 95/1993 which did not yet exist in 1992, and Art. 9(1)(b) of Council Regulation 95/93 as amended, referring to the matter of *Public Services Obligations* formulated in Regulation 2408/1992, now Art. 16 of Regulation 1008/2008.

The present system of slot allocation, including the respect for grandfather rights and the 'use it or lose it rule', contains inherent barriers to entry into and exit from the aviation market which is marked by increasing congestion at airports.[159] As said, slots have become a scarce resource.

Slot trading could remedy current market entry problems.[160] Slot trading refers to transfers of slots as between airlines, which exchanges are accompanied by payment of a price reflecting the economic value of the slots.[161] The somewhat cryptic formulation of Regulation 95/1993 opened the door for private transactions between air carriers. It is clear from the wording of Article 8(4) of Regulation 95/93 that one carrier with another may only exchange a slot if it receives a slot in return. There has been much debate as to whether it is allowed to exchange a slot for another one involving payment of money.

The UK High Court[162] interpreted Article 8(4) in such a fashion that an airline is entitled to be allocated slots pursuant to the system of grandfather rights regardless of whether that airline intends to use them, and that the provisions allowing airlines to exchange slots permit exchanges regardless whether an airline party to the exchange intends to use them or whether financial considerations accompany the exchange.

Under the present regime, it has to be decided on a case-by-case basis whether the parties involved with the exchange have satisfied the requirement pertaining to exchange. A French judge may take a different view than the UK court did, and so may the CJEU, who has not yet been confronted with the question. Although slot transactions may have private elements, that is, when they are exchanged between air carriers, such transactions are subject to the scrutiny of public law. Under the adopted Proposal from the EU Commission of 2011 for a new Slot Regulation, airlines are allowed to trade slots.[163]

The EU Regulations give priority to airlines that have used slots in the preceding scheduling period for at least 80 per cent of the time.[164] Subject to justifications pertaining to the existence of exceptional circumstances as formulated in the

---

159. *See*, UK Office of Fair Trading, *Competition issues associated with the trading of airport slots*, A paper prepared for DG TREN by the UK Office of Fair Trading and the Civil Aviation Authority 10–17 (2005); NERA, *Study to Assess the Effects of Different Slot Allocation Schemes* 250–251 (2004) and P.S. Dempsey, *Airport Landing Slots: Barriers to Entry and Impediments to Competition*, 26(1) Air & Space Law 20–148 (2001).

160. *See*, J.M. Balfour, *Slot Trading in the European Union*, 53(2) Zeitschrift für Luft-und Weltraumrecht 145–151 (2004).

161. For instance, Croatia Airlines received USD 19 million from Delta Airlines for five slots at London Heathrow early January 2017, which helped to remedy its financial situation; *see*, www.upinthesky.nl of 2017/01/13.

162. *See*, *R* v. *Airport Coordination Ltd*, ex parte *States of Guernsey Transport Board*, judgement of High Court (Queens Bench Division) of 25 November 1999.

163. This proposal has not yet been adopted. *See*, COM(2011) 827 final, dated 1 December 2011; *see also*, Steer Davies Gleaves, Impact assessment of revisions to Regulation 95/93 (2011), and C. Neumann, New *Proposal to Amend the System of Airport Slot Allocation in the European Union*, 37(3) Air & Space Law 185–211 (2012), and S. Truxal, *The 'Legalisation' of European Airport Slot Exchange: Abuses of Dominance in Slots?* European Competition Law Review 10 (2014).

164. *See*, Art. 8 (2) of EU Regulation 793/2004 in conjunction with Art. 10 of EU Regulation 793/2004.

Regulations on slot allocation, an airline will lose slots if it cannot demonstrate the required use. Effectively, the position of grandfather rights was reinforced.

In reaction to the 2008/2009 financial crisis and its impact on air carriers, the Commission proposed to temporarily suspend the *'use-it-or-lose-it'* rule. Further, Regulation 545/2009 allowed air carriers to keep their grandfathered slots for the summer season of 2010 as attributed to them for the summer season of 2009, even if the slots are used less than 80 per cent.

Regulation 793/2004 made a *'technical revision'* to Regulation 95/93.[165] The minor changes primarily helped to make the slot system more flexible in terms of both allocation and use; they also strengthened the coordinator's role and the monitoring of compliance. On 30 April 2008, the EU Commission adopted a Communication on the application of the slot allocation Regulation, which aims to clarify the existing rules.

In particular, the interpretation of *'slot exchanges'* was of great interest as *'secondary trading'* of airport slots between air carriers had been taking place in the United Kingdom.[166] The EU Commission acknowledged for the first time the possibility of secondary trading whereas it does not intend to pursue infringement proceedings regarding secondary trading. As Ms Katja Brecke concludes:

> The European Slot Regulation has remained nearly unchanged since its coming into force in 1993. Change is as vital element of progress and should not be regarded as a threat to stability, but should be perceived as a chance to create sustainable growth and to foster competition.[167]

5.1.3 The Provision of Ground Handling Services

The second piece of legislation pertaining to infrastructure comprises *Council Directive 96/67/EC of 15 October 1996 on access to the ground handling market at EU airports*. This Directive provided that at the larger airports in the EU ground handling of aircraft should be provided by more than one supplier so as to remove the previous monopoly position held by the airport authority or the resident, principal carrier. Self-handling by airlines must be allowed for baggage, ramp, fuel and freight, including mail ait airports with no less than 1 million passenger movements or 25,000 tonnes of freight per year; however, the number of providers may be limited to two or more airport users.

---

165. Regulation 95/93 was further amended in the years 2002, 2003 and 2009. *See*, EU Regulation 894/2002 in force since 1 June 2002, Regulation 1554/2003; and, for the time being, the last one, Regulation 545/2009.
166. Other issues addressed in the Communication were the independence of the coordinator, new entry, transparency of scheduled data, local guidelines and the consistency between slots and flight plans. *See*, Communication from the Commission to the European Parliament, the Council, the European Economic and Social Committee and the Committee of the Regions on the application of Regulation (EEC) No. 95/93 on *common rules for the allocation of slots at EU airports*, as amended, Brussels COM(2008) 227; *see also*, Press release IP/08/672.
167. *See*, Katja Brecke, LLM Leiden University, *Slot Allocation in the EU and the US: A Comparative Analysis*, 36(3) Air & Space Law 183–200 (2011); this publication was based on a paper which was awarded the first IATA prize for the best air law paper written in 2010; *see also*, v. Seabra Ferreira, *The Anticompetitive Effects of Slot Allocation in the EU*, 14(1) Issues in Aviation Law and Policy 103–124 (2014).

Self-handling must also be allowed for other types of handling at all airports. Third parties are entitled to provide ground handling services at airports with no less than 2 million passengers per year or 50,000 tonnes freight per year, but the number of providers may be limited to two or more for the most essential services. Subject to review by the EU Commission, exemptions based on safety or capacity arguments may be made.[168]

In the second half of the 1990s, the German authorities had asked for exemptions from the obligation to introduce more competition. In some cases, the EU Commission granted temporary derogations from the Ground Handling Directive 96/67. The decisions were based on technical arguments related to capacity and safety problems, and require substantial factual and local investigation.[169]

In general, the experiences with this Directive are positive: competition between suppliers has increased whereas prices have decreased.[170] At the same time, ground handling service providers and airlines are still discussing the scope Article 8 of the IATA Standard Ground Handling Agreement (SGHA) making the airline the principal liable person for compensation of damages arising out of this activity.

5.1.4   The EU Airport Package of 2011

The EU Commission is examining further needs for improvement of aviation infrastructure. This examination will be part of the work regarding the establishment of the Airport Package which is designed to improve not only the slot allocation process but also the provision of ground handling services in which sector monopolisation at certain airports should be avoided.

In its Communication, the Commission announces five key actions. These actions are to make better use of existing airport capacity; to draw up a consistent approach to air safety operations at airports; to promote 'co-modality', that is, the integration and collaboration between modes of transport; to improve the environmental capacity of airports and the planning framework for new airport infrastructure; and to develop and implement cost-efficient technological solutions.

---

168. See, T. Soames, *Ground Handling Liberalization*, 3(2) Journal of Air Transport Management 83–94 (1997); C. Dussart-Lefret and C. Federlin, *Ground Handling Services and EC Competition Rules*, 19(2) Air & Space Law 50–61 (1994).
169. See, Commission decision 98/387/EC *On the application of Art. 9 of Council Directive 96/67/EC to Frankfurt airport*; Commission decision 98/630/EC *On the application of Art. 9 of Council Directive 96/67/EC to Stuttgart airport*; Commission decision 98/631/EC *On the application of Art. 9 of Council Directive 96/67/EC to Cologne/Bonn airport*, and Commission decision 98/632/EC *On the application of Art. 9 of Council Directive 96/67/EC to Hamburg airport*.
170. See, Steer Davies Glear, *Possible Revision of EC Directive 96/67/EC on Access to the Ground Handling Market at Community Airports* (2010); *see also*, same author, *Study on Airport Ownership and Management and the Ground Handling Market in Selected Non-EU Countries* (2016).

In 2014, the EU Commission published Guidelines designed to enhance connectivity for airports located in regions with specific air transport needs. That goal justified public funding, despite rules on State aid.[171]

5.2 Air Traffic Management: The Single European Sky (SES)

5.2.1 Purposes

Air Traffic Management (ATM) in Europe is a swiftly developing field of air transport. This development is supported by the regulatory framework governing the SES. The SES regime has been set up in 2004, and forms the starting point for the EU's involvement with ATM. Under the European Common Aviation Area (ECAA) agreement,[172] the SES includes western Balkan States, Norway, Switzerland and Iceland.

Its purposes are to create a "more integrated operating airspace" by the establishment of a harmonised regulatory framework and to set up a more efficient air traffic management system, more closely based on direct flight patterns and operational efficiency than present arrangements which are based largely on national boundaries and national airspaces. The SES regime is designed to reduce delays caused by inefficiencies due to a myriad of national control centres and to the existence of military purposes creating complex and indirect flight patterns, to reduce costs and to create additional capacity for airspace users.[173]

5.2.2 The Regulatory and Institutional Framework

The SES regime had been initiated in late 2001 as a result of the congestion in the airspace of European countries which was, in part, caused by the liberalisation forces.[174] The SES regulatory framework of 2004 comprised four regulations covering the essential elements for a seamless European ATM system.[175] The legislation is designed to increase cross-border co-ordination, to remove administrative and

---

171. *See*, EU Commission, *Guidelines on State Aid to Airports and Airlines* (2014/C99/03); *see also*, D. Grespan, *The New European Commission Guidelines for State Aid to Airports and Airlines*, 13(2) The Aviation and Space Journal 10–19 (2014).

172. *See*, section 6.2.

173. *See*, Dr F. Schubert, *Legal Aspects of Cross-Border Provision in the Single European Sky*, 35(2) Air & Space Law 113–155 (2010).

174. *See*, section 6.1.

175. *See*, Regulation (EC) No. 549/2004 of the European Parliament and of the Council of 10 March 2004 laying down *the framework for the creation of the single European sky* (the 'Framework Regulation'); Regulation (EC) No. 550/2004 of the European Parliament and of the Council of 10 March 2004 *on the provision of air navigation services in the single European sky* (the 'Service Provision Regulation'); Regulation (EC) No. 551/2004 of the European Parliament and of the Council of 10 March 2004 on *the organisation and use of the airspace in the single European sky* (the 'Airspace Regulation') and Regulation (EC) No. 552/2004 of the European Parliament and of the Council of 10 March 2004 on *the interoperability of the European Air Traffic Management network* (the 'Interoperability Regulation').

organisational bottlenecks in the area of decision-making, and to enhance enforcement in ATM. A fundamental facet of the SES initiative concerns the establishment of Functional Airspace Blocks (FABs).[176]

The SES regime is now covered by Regulation 1070/2009 – *Improving the Performance of European Aviation System*, amending and supplementing the four basic regulations of 2004. Regulation 1070/2009 is designed to improve the performance and sustainability of the European aviation system,[177] to improve the performance of the European aviation system in the key areas of safety, environment, capacity and cost-efficiency. It was also necessary to adapt the SES legislation to technical progress and create a single safety framework in the EU. This second legislative package also includes Regulation (EC) 1108/2009 extending EASA remit to airports, ATM and ANS. This second legislative package became known under the heading SES II.

The SES regulations are complemented by implementing regulations. As a step towards the achievement of its objectives, the Commission introduced on 23 December 2005 EU Regulation 2150/2005 laying down *common rules for the flexible use of airspace*. This Regulation establishes a series of principles (Article 3) governing the concept of flexible use of airspace and defines in Article 4 a number of actions required on the part of Member States in terms of strategic airspace management. These actions include approving activities which require airspace reservation or restriction; defining temporary airspace structures and procedures; developing cross-border airspace use with neighbouring Member States where needed by traffic flows and users' activities and coordinating airspace management policy with those neighbouring States. The EU approach to airspace is reflected in the area of service provision. It will be possible for air traffic service providers to operate across national borders and for one Member State to designate an organisation in another Member State to assume the responsibility for ATC in its airspace. This may lead in time to integrated service providers operating over large areas such as FABs (*see* below).[178]

A fundamental element of the regulatory structure is the EU certification mechanism. Each Member State is required to set up a National Supervisory Authority, separate from the service provider, to ensure compliance of the service providers established in their territory with a set of harmonised requirements designed to ensure continuity, safety and quality of service. To that end, EU Regulation 2096/2005 laying *down common certification requirements* under which all air navigation service providers must be certified in order to be able to continue to provide services beyond 31 December 2006.[179] The cross-border service provision arrangements will be supported

---

176. *See*, section 5.2.4, below.
177. *See*, EU Commission Decision of 21 February 2011, setting *the European Union wide performance and alert thresholds for the provision of air navigation services for the years 2012 and 2014*, and EU Commission Implementing Decision of 11 March 2014 setting *the Union-wide performance targets for the air traffic management network and alert thresholds for the second reference period 2015–19*.
178. *See*, B. de Wit et al., *FABEC: Structure Follows Performance or Performance Follows Structure?* in: D. Calleja and P.M.J. Mendes de Leon (eds), *Achieving the Single European Sky: Goals and Challenges* 17–32 (2011).
179. *See*, M. Baumgartner, *Air Traffic Controller License Come into Force*, X(3) The Aviation and Space Journal 2–7 (2011).

by air traffic controller mobility. This will be achieved by the Commission setting up a mechanism for a common air traffic controller's curriculum and a common licensing process facilitating the movement of controllers between centres and countries.[180]

5.2.3 Governance

The EU Commission, assisted by the SES Committee, must adopt implementing regulations, and has indeed done so many times since 2004. However, the EU cannot realise its SES without the help and input from other parties, including the EU Member States, among others, as the SES Regulations stipulate that the SES "does not cover military operations and training", which continues to be subject to intergovernmental cooperation between the EU Member States.[181]

As the EU Commission does not yet possess the technical expertise in the field of ATM which, for instance, Eurocontrol,[182] ICAO[183] and EU Member States have built up during the past fifty years or more, cooperation among those parties remains essential. As stated above, EASA is expected to carry out ATM related tasks in the future in which context the role of Eurocontrol will be reconsidered.[184] In 2011, the European Commission nominated Eurocontrol as the Network Manager with a mandate that runs until the end of the Performance Scheme's second Reference Period – that is, until 31 December 2019. The Network Manager's priority is to achieve the performance targets in the areas of airspace design and flow management as well as scarce resources such as transponder code allocations and radio frequencies.[185]

Since air transport is not only a European but also a global activity, attention should be paid to the international dimension of ATM relations. This is in relation to non-EU and non-ECAA States, and to relevant organisations such as ICAO. The SES regime recognises the commitments of EU States in relation to the global framework set by the Chicago Convention and ICAO.[186]

---

180. *See*, Art. 8 of EU Regulation 1070/2009.
181. *See*, L. Tytgat, *Governance of the Single European Sky: The Single Sky Committee (SSC) and the Involvement of the Industry Consultation Body (ICB)*, in: D.Calleja and P.M.J. Mendes de Leon (eds), *Achieving the Single European Sky: Goals and Challenges* 95–106 (2011).
182. *See*, D. McMillan and R.D. van Dam, *EUROCONTROL and the EU Single European Sky*, in: D. Calleja and P.M.J. Mendes de Leon (eds), *Achieving the Single European Sky: Goals and Challenges* 67–78 (2011).
183. *See*, L. Fonseca de Almeida, *ICAO and the Pan European Dimension: The Single European Sky from a Global Perspective*, in: D. Calleja and Pablo Mendes de Leon (eds), *Achieving the Single European Sky: Goals and Challenges* 95–106 (2011).
184. *See*, Pablo Mendes de Leon, *The Relationship Between Eurocontrol and the EC: Living Apart Together*, International Organizations Law Review 302–321 (2008).
185. *See*, EU Commission Regulation 677/2011 laying down detailed rules for *the implementation of air traffic management (ATM) network functions* and amending EU Regulation 691/2010; on the functions of the Network Manager and the relationship between the EU and Eurocontrol as international organisations, *see*, K. Arnold, Z. Papp and I. Arnold, *The Difficult Present and Uncertain Future of the Single European Sky Network Manager: The Challenges We Are Facing and Why They Matter*, 42(2) Air & Space Law (2017), and section 5.2 of Chapter 1.
186. *See*, for instance, the Preamble of the SES Regulations of 2009: "(22) In view of the creation of functional airspace blocks and the setting up of the performance scheme, the Commission should determine and take into account the necessary conditions for the EU to create a Single

5.2.4 Principal Instruments and Purposes of the SES Regime[187]

Airspace should no longer be organised along national boundaries but pursuant to efficiency criteria. Thus, FABs, defined as:

> an airspace block based on operational requirements and established regardless of State boundaries, where the provision of air navigation services and related functions are performance driven and optimized with a view to introducing, in each functional airspace block, enhanced cooperation among air navigation service providers, or, where appropriate, an integrated service provider;[188]

need to be developed based on operational needs while taking into account safety, airspace capacity, cost reduction objectives and environmental improvements through increased flight efficiency.

Achievement of these objectives requires political commitment and monitoring at the highest level. The EU Commission is mandated to set and monitor performance parameters to be achieved by the various FAB initiatives.[189] Those FABs had to be established by 4 December 2012.[190]

European Flight Information Region (SEFIR), to be requested by the Member States *from the ICAO in accordance with both the established procedures of that organisation and the rights, obligations and responsibilities of Member States under the Convention on International Civil Aviation, signed in Chicago on 7 December 1944* (the Chicago Convention)." (*italics added*).

187. *See also*, Association of European Airlines (AEA), *Air Traffic Management* (ATM): *The AEA Vision of the Single European Sky* (SES), adopted by the AEA Presidents Committee on 29 March 2007.

188. *See*, Art. 1(h), point 25 of EU Regulation 1070/2009.

189. *See also*, EFTA (European Free Trade Association) Surveillance Authority Decision No. 83/15/COL of 18 March 2015 concerning the consistency of certain targets included in the national or functional airspace block plans submitted pursuant to Regulation (EC) No. 549/2004 of the European Parliament and of the Council with the Union-wide performance targets for the second reference period (2016/1418).

190. *See*, G. Jarzembowski, *The Coordinator for the Functional Airspace Blocks System: The Task and the Report* in: D. Calleja and P.M.J. Mendes de Leon (eds), *Achieving the Single European Sky: Goals and Challenges* 179–188 (2011).

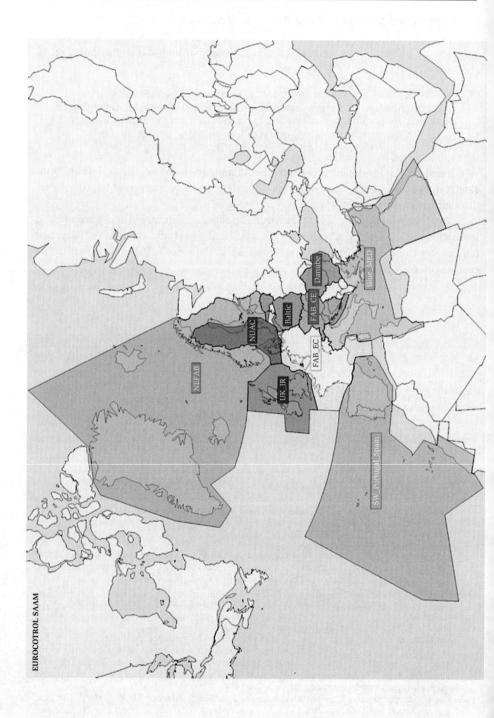

Two out of nine FABs, to wit those established by the UK and Ireland and Sweden and Denmark, are – partially – operational. Other FABs have been drawn up in agreements regulating the governance of the FABs. The EU Commission considers starting infringement procedures against the Member States. The functioning of the first mentioned FAB may be influenced by the implications of 'Brexit'.[191]

The number of service providers in European ATM should be reduced if efficiency objectives are to be met. In consequence, privatisation is key to achieve this objective which pertains to reduction of costs for the users, that is, the airlines.[192] The number of Area Control Centres (ACCs) in Europe will need to be adapted strictly to the operational needs, irrespective of national borders, to make a cost effective SES. In the USA there are only eight ACCs compared to sixty-six in Europe.

Meanwhile, institutional, labour and security have yet to be solved. They form the principal obstacles towards creating the political will of the Member States to move forward while the pressure on the realisation of FABs is increasing as air traffic continues to grow.

The SES process must be underpinned by the implementation of the Single European Sky ATM Research (SESAR) programme.[193] SESAR forms the technical component of the SES which must also contribute to the successful introduction of the performance scheme.[194]

Cooperation between civil and military service providers is crucial in the further development of SES and for the elimination of the most important capacity bottlenecks in core Europe. Admittedly, the military will continue to require airspace sufficient to meet their operational and training requirements which demand flexibility of dimensions and allocation.[195]

In 2009, the SES II regime articulated the interest of drawing up *Performance schemes*. A performance scheme for air navigation services and network functions

---

191. *See*, L. Vrbaski, *Flying into the Unknown: The UK's Air Transport Relations with the European Union and Third Countries Following 'Brexit'*, 41(6) Air and Space Law 421–444 (2016).

192. In September 2016, the German air traffic control provider *Deutsche Flugsichering* (DFS) has taken over air traffic control in Edinburg, Scotland, in a procurement procedure; *see*, www.upinthesky.nl of 16 September 2016.

193. *See*, EU Council Regulation 219/2007 on *the establishment of a Joint Undertaking to develop the new generation European air traffic management system* (SESAR) calling for the development and implementation of an ATM Master Plan. "The implementation of the ATM Master Plan requires regulatory measures to support the development, introduction and financing of new concepts and technologies. It should result in a system composed of fully harmonised and interoperable components, which guarantee high performance air transport activities in Europe." – *see*, Consideration (6) of the Preamble of EU Regulation 1070/209; *see also*, Commission Implementing Regulations 409/2013 (*SESAR Deployment Framework*) and 616/2004 (*Pilot Common Project*).

194. *See*, P. Ky, *SESAR: The Technological Arm of the Single European Sky*, in: D. Calleja and P.M.J. Mendes de Leon (eds), *Achieving the Single European Sky: Goals and Challenges* 239–244 (2011).

195. *See*, G. Fartek and F. Rivet, *The Introduction of the Military Dimension into the SES: A New Paradigm for the European Commission*, in: D. Calleja and P.M.J. Mendes de Leon (eds), *Achieving the Single European Sky: Goals and Challenges* 129–136 (2011).

must include performance targets in the areas of safety, environment,[196] capacity and cost-efficiency; national plans or plans for the establishment of functional airspace blocks;[197] periodic review, monitoring and benchmarking of the performance of air navigation services and network functions.[198] Further provisions specify the responsible bodies, processes and procedures for the operation of the performance scheme.[199] ATM services should – wherever feasible – be performed in competition or after a transparent tender procedure and funded by locally specific fees. Where no competition is possible, mandatory independent economic regulation should be put in place. Unbundling of ancillary ATM services should be accelerated. Ancillary services should become subject to market conditions (full competition) in order to ensure a more cost efficient service. The lack of meaningful competition for ancillary services, that is, Communication/Navigation/Surveillance (CNS), Training and Meteorology Services is now artificially inflating costs.

5.2.5   Concluding Remarks

Inevitably, the development of the SES regulations has not been without its difficulties and serious concerns have been raised with regard to certain aspects of the proposals. Not least has been the concern to reconcile the position of Member States, with regard to sovereignty over their airspace under the Chicago Convention, with the need for willingness to transfer decision-making powers over that same airspace to the EU institutions and to move beyond the traditional national approach to air traffic management.[200] Other concerns were expressed by air traffic services unions in some countries at the prospect of service providers from other States gaining the right to provide air traffic services in their country's sovereign airspace.[201] As a corollary, most ATC agencies have not yet been privatised, with the exception of National Air Traffic Services (NATS) from the UK, which has been partially privatised in 2000, and manages fifteen airports in the UK while offering its services around the world.

The reluctance of EU States to move forward results in the continued fragmentation of the European airspace, divided between sovereign States. While FABs have been established on paper, their implementation is not yet operational in terms of

---

196. *See*, P. Steele, *SES Environmental and Efficiency Benefits: Reduction of Emissions*, in: D. Calleja and P.M.J. Mendes de Leon (eds), *Achieving the Single European Sky: Goals and Challenges* 167–178 (2011).
197. *See*, Commission Regulation 176/2011 on *the information to be provided before the establishment and modification of a functional airspace block*.
198. *See also*, Commission decision 2011/121/EU setting *European Union-wide performance targets and alert thresholds for the provision of air navigation services for the years 2012–2014*.
199. *See*, A. Lambert and T. Johnson, *Performance Review: Implementation*, in: D. Calleja and P.M.J. Mendes de Leon (eds), *Achieving the Single European Sky: Goals and Challenges* 137–146 (2011).
200. *See*, F.P. Schubert, *The Corporatization of Air Traffic Control: Drifting Between Private and Public Law*, XXII-II Annals of Air and Space Law 223–242 (1997).
201. *See*, F. Ballestro and M. Baumgartner, *The Human Factor and the Role for the Human Being in the Single European Sky*, in: D. Calleja and P.M.J. Mendes de Leon (eds), *Achieving the Single European Sky: Goals and Challenges* 267–280 and 299–314 (2011).

optimisation of airspace and resources, which is, says the EU Commission, costs are still relatively high. On the other side, the safety record is good.[202]

In the coming decade, the Performance Review scheme of the SES regime is designed to introduce a more contractual relationship based on a collaborative effort between the principal service providers, to wit, airlines, airport operators and the providers of air navigation services (ANSPs). This scheme must enhance efficiency of the flight by stressing the punctuality and adequacy, that is, agreed performance of the tasks assigned to each actor.[203] Promoting efficiency and increasing punctuality of flights have also been principal causes for putting in place the SES regime, as supported by SESAR.[204]

5.3 Environmental Protection

5.3.1 A 'Balanced Approach' Towards Noise Regulation

The oldest air transport related legislative measure of the EU, then EEC, concerned protection of the. This piece of legislation was designed to reduce the number of noisy aircraft operating at EU airports.[205]

A next step concerned the introduction of the controversial Regulation 925/99 relating to the registration and operation within the EU of certain types of civil subsonic jet aircraft that had been modified and re-certificated so as to meet Chapter 3 standards. Effectively, the Regulation prevented the registration within the EU of aircraft that had been 'hush-kitted' to meet Chapter 3 standards and prevented the operation of such aircraft at EU airports with effect from 1 April 2002. In essence therefore, hush-kitted aircraft were to be dealt with in the same manner as Chapter 2 aircraft. This last Regulation was strenuously contested by the US because it affected US aviation and aircraft manufacturing interests, as well as by local and international operators. The US Government took the disagreement with the EU to ICAO and requested the ICAO Council to rule on the grounds that the EU Regulation went beyond the scope of the internationally accepted restrictions embodied in the ICAO regime.[206] With

---

202. See, European Commission, Report to the European Parliament and the Council on *the implementation and progress of the Single European Sky during the 2012–2016 period*, dated 16 December 2015, COM(2015) 663 final.
203. See, A. Masutti, *Single European Sky – A Possible Regulatory Framework for System Wide Information Management* (SWIM), 36(4/5) Air & Space Law 275–292 (2011).
204. See, P. Ky, *SESAR: The Technological Arm of the Single European Sky*, in: D. Calleja and P.M.J. Mendes de Leon (eds), *Achieving the Single European Sky: Goals and Challenges* 239–244 (2011).
205. See, Directive 80/51/EEC on limitation of noise emissions from subsonic aircraft that prohibited the addition of non-noise certified aircraft to the aircraft registers of Member States and the removal of such aircraft from the registers.
206. See, section 3.3.8 of Chapter 1, and Sean D. Murphy, *Contemporary Practice of the United States Relating to International Law*, which appeared in Vol. 95(2) American Journal of International Law (April 2001), see also, Christian Kaufmann, *Hushkits: Another Dispute Between Europe and the United States*, 50 Zeitschrift für Luft- und Weltraumrecht 330 (2001).

intervention from the Secretary General of ICAO, the EU withdrew the contested regulation and replaced it, as to which *see* below.[207]

The question of the compatibility of the 'hushkit' Regulation with ICAO law arrived at the ICAO General Assembly in Montreal in September/October 2001. The Assembly adopted a Resolution (A33-7) and incorporated into a Consolidated Statement of continuing ICAO policies relating to environmental protection. The policies included the introduction of a more stringent Chapter 4 to Annex 16 of the Convention for new-build aircraft but at the same time recommended a more flexible approach to dealing with Chapter 3 aircraft by the adoption of a 'balanced approach' to aircraft noise management. This 'balanced approach' is intended to recognise that solutions to noise problems need to be tailored to specific characteristics of airports concerned, which necessitate an airport-by-airport approach to be applied. In the light of the adoption of the ICAO Resolution, the EU has now brought forward new legislation, namely Directive 2002/30/EC *on the establishment of rules and procedures with regard to the introduction of noise-related operating restrictions at EU airports* repealing Regulation 925/99, and introduced a new regime under which restrictions on Chapter 3 and marginally compliant aircraft would be adopted by Member States on an airport-by-airport basis. In 2014, the EU adopted Regulation 598/2014 on *the establishment of rules and procedures with regard to the introduction of noise-related operating restrictions at Union airports within a Balanced Approach and repealing Directive 2002/30/EC*. Thus, hush-kitted aircraft that meet Chapter 3 standards is no longer subject to a blanket ban but will be subject to limitations or restrictions at EU airports at which noise is a particularly sensitive issue.[208]

The Directive is supplemented by Directive 2002/49 on *the assessment and management of environmental noise*. This Directive was introduced under (then) Article 80(2) of the Treaty as it aims at introducing a harmonised basis to be applied at airports in the EU in pursuit of harmonised internal market conditions. The objective of the Directive is to lay down rules to facilitate the introduction of operating restrictions in a consistent manner at the airport level so as to help prevent a worsening of the noise climate and to reduce the number of people affected by the harmful effects of aircraft noise. To that end, the Directive seeks to ensure that similar solutions are applied to similar problems at EU airports and that sustainable development of airport capacity is facilitated.

The Directive requires Member States to designate an independent authority responsible for implementing the Directive. Member States are required to ensure that

---

207. This Regulation was also challenged by Omega Air and others on a reference for a preliminary ruling by the High Court of Justice of England and Wales and the High Court in Dublin to the CJEU. The challenge resulted in the delivery of an Opinion by the Advocate General Alber to the Court of the EU to the effect that Regulation 925/99 was indeed invalid but the Court did not agree. *See*, Opinion of Advocate General Alber on Joined Cases C-27/00 and C-122/00 *The Queen* v. *Secretary of State for the Environment, Transport and the Regions,* ex parte *Omega Air Ltd and Omega Air Ltd, Aero Engines Ireland Ltd, Omega Aviation Services Ltd* v. *Irish Aviation Authority.*

208. *See*, EC Directive 2006/93 on *the regulation of the operation of aeroplanes covered by Part II, Chapter 3, Volume 1 of Annex 16 to the Convention on international civil aviation, second edition* (1988).

competent authorities adopt a *balanced approach* developed by ICAO by considering the available measures to address the noise problem at an airport, including reduction of noise at source, land-use planning and management, operational procedures and other noise management methods such as economic incentives and operational restrictions.[209] The authorities are required to take into account the likely costs and benefits of any proposed measures and to ensure that such measures are not more restrictive than is necessary in order to achieve environmental objectives established for the airport. Any decision must be based upon the information specified in Annex 2 to the Directive. The definition of 'airport' excludes airports with less than 50,000 movements *per annum* (excluding flights for training purposes on light aircraft).

Presumably, therefore, such airports will not be affected by the requirement to introduce operating restrictions and may continue to be used by marginally compliant aircraft. However, this point will need to be confirmed once the final legislation is introduced at the national level in each Member State. There are special rules to cover 'city airports' which are listed in Annex 1.

5.3.2 Regulation of Emissions: Towards a Global Approach?

The EU Commission has chosen for a market based trade mechanism in order to combat global warning as a consequence of aircraft emissions.[210] The 'permit to emit' greenhouse gasses should be made subject to an Emission Trade System (ETS). Hence, when airlines operate clean and increasingly cleaner aircraft while not increasing their frequencies, they may find themselves on the 'seller's' side. Airlines who cannot afford to, or do not find it opportune to purchase new aircraft will be on the buyer's side, and have to pay for their allowances unless they decrease the number of their flights.[211]

A principal reason for the introduction of an ETS into for instance the aviation sector comes from the principal that the polluter must pay the damages he causes. This principle is firmly embedded in international environmental law and European law as confirmed by the CJEU.[212]

For the purpose of applying the Kyoto Protocol and Chicago Convention notions to intra-EU schemes,[213] the operation of intra-EU flights are regarded as *international* flights. Moreover, certain intra-EU flights, for instance, from Lisbon to London, transit through the airspace above the high seas, coming under the exclusive jurisdiction of ICAO.[214] The Kyoto Protocol was approved by the EU.[215] The EU Emission Trading

---

209. *See*, www.icao.int/env/noise.htm; the recommended practices for balanced approach are contained in ICAO Doc 9829 – *Guidance on the balanced approach to aircraft noise management*.
210. For ICAO, *see*, the 33rd ICAO Assembly of 2001 endorsing the 'development of an open emissions trading system for international civil aviation', and for the EC Commission, *see*, Communication CONM(2005) 459 *Reducing the Climate Change Impact of Aviation*.
211. *See*, A. Macintosh, *Overcoming the Barriers to International Aviation Greenhouse Gas Emissions Abatement*, CCLP Working Papers 2008/2.
212. *See*, for instance, Case C-188/07, *Commune de Mesquer* v. *Total France SA*, judgment of 24 June 2008.
213. *See*, section 3.3.8 of Chapter 1.
214. *See*, Art. 12 of the Chicago Convention.

Scheme is the largest multi-national Green House Gas – henceforth referred to as GHG – cap and trade scheme. It has been created under EU Directive 2003/87.[216] In 2008, as the EU did not want to await global consensus, the ETS Directive was amended by EU Directive 2008/101[217] – hereafter referred to as the amended ETS Directive – so as to include aviation activities in the scheme for greenhouse gas emission allowance trading within the Community. The EU ETS scheme is designed to operate as an activity under the Kyoto Protocol and the UNFCC, so as to allow a controlled use of GHG reductions and Clean Development Mechanisms activities. As from 1 January 2012, all flights arriving at or departing from an airport located in an EU State had been included within the scope of the amended ETS Directive. Hence, not only flights within the EU, but also a flight from a point in a third State, for instance, Tokyo, overflying Russia to a point in the EU, for instance, Vienna, are subject to the provisions of the amended ETS Directive. The Commission could exempt flights from third States "where necessary."[218]

In October 2010, the ICAO General Assembly adopted a Resolution following which ICAO's leadership on environmental issues relating to international civil aviation including the establishment of policies and regulations regarding the emissions of Greenhouse gasses was re-affirmed.[219] It was also put forward that certain matters relating to neutral carbon growth, the establishment of market based mechanisms to combat climate change and the *de minimis* exception exempting operators performing international air services between a specified threshold should be referred to the ICAO Council for further study.

In light of the policy measures and resolutions adopted by ICAO, the EU's moves in the area of ETS have met with resistance. Third States argued that the EU ETS measures affect the level playing field between the aircraft operators, whereas the argument has also been made that the EU ETS legal framework infringes international law, in particular provisions of the Chicago Convention, ICAO resolutions and bilateral ASAs providing for the maintenance of a level playing field between the concerned States. As a consequence of the international policy and regulatory considerations, the EU had to limit the scope of the Directive of 2008 to intra-EU flights.

The reach of this directive has raised questions with respect to the territorial jurisdiction of the EU and its Member States, especially under the Chicago Convention. In December 2009, three major US airlines and the Air Transport Association of America (ATA) submitted a claim pertaining to the legality of the measures to a court in the UK, which asked for a preliminary ruling to the Court of Justice of the EU. The ATA base their claims on among others, infringement of provisions of the ASA between

---

215. *See*, Council Decision 2002/358.
216. EU Directive 2008/2009 *establishing a scheme for greenhouse gas emission allowance trading within the Community*, as variously amended as to which *see* Directives 2008/1010 and 2009/29, and below.
217. As and implemented by EU Commission Regulation 748/2009 and EU Commission De Directives 2008/1010 and 2009/29, decision of 8 June 2009.
218. *See*, Art. 25a of the amended Directive.
219. ICAO Resolution A37-17/2 containing a *Consolidated Statement of continuing ICAO Policies and Practices related to Environmental Protection – Climate Change*.

the US and the EU which is discussed in the following section, and Articles 1 in conjunction with Article 2 (confirming sovereignty in national airspace), twelve (designating ICAO as the legislator in the airspace above the high seas), fifteen (prescribing the imposition of taxes and charges exclusively for the use of infrastructure) and twenty-four (prohibiting duties on fuel consumed by aircraft while in transit through the airspace of another State) of the Chicago Convention. In a rather surprising, and not very convincing decision, the CJEU decided that Directive 2008/101 did not infringe international law, including provisions of the Chicago Convention and ASAs.[220]

The reactions to the EU ETS proposals have been rather vehement. Not only the US, but also other important aviation states and trading partners of the EU and its Member States, have criticised these proposals which they consider as unilateral actions infringing international law.[221] Confronted with the risk of a trade war on a global scale, and retaliation measures, the EU Council and Parliament Decision decided on 26 April 2013 to *stop the clock*, that is, to temporarily exempt international flights from some of the EU ETS obligations.[222] The said decision temporarily suspends the inclusion of international flights from the EU emissions trading system (ETS), while negotiators try to agree on a global market-based system to reduce aviation emissions at the ICAO. However, the full extent of the scheme remains in place for intra-EU flights whether they are operated by EU or by non-EU air carriers. Hence, as an interim measure, that is, from 1 January 2013 to 31 December 2016, the scope of Directive 2003/87 is limited to the operation of intra-European Economic Area (EEA) flights only, that is, flights between airports located in the territory of EEA States.[223]

Meanwhile ICAO has prepared a global agreement, named CORSIA.[224] The EU institutions consider continuing the 'stop the clock' regime by extending the exclusion of foreign airlines from its intra-EU ETS regime which may stand square with the agreement made by ICAO.

5.3.3 Concluding Remarks

The protection of the environment is a complex subject of regulations as myriad interests and legal regimes are involved with it. It has a very high ranking on the agenda of EU policymakers but that interest must be, and, as the above cases have shown,

---

220. *See*, CJEU in Case C-366/10, *Air Transport Association of America, American Airlines Inc., Continental Airlines Inc., United Airlines Inc.* v. *Secretary of State for Energy and Climate Change*, decision of 21 December 2011.
221. *See*, Pablo Mendes de Leon, *Enforcement of the EU ETS: The EU's Convulsive Efforts to Export Its Environmental Values*, 37(4/5) Air & Space Law 287–306 (2012) and B.F. Havel and J.Q. Mulligan, *The Triumph of Politics: Reflections on Judgment of the Court of Justice of the European Union Validating the Inclusion of Non-EU Airlines in the Emissions Trading Scheme*, 37(1) Air & Space Law 3–33 (2012).
222. *See*, EU Decision 377/2013, and EU Regulation 2014/2014 amending Directive 2003/87 *in view of the implementation by 2020 of an international agreement applying to a single global market-based measure to international aviation emissions*.
223. EEA States are the twenty-eight EU States plus Norway, Iceland and Lichtenstein.
224. *See*, section 3.3.8 of Chapter 1.

matched with existing international law provisions laying down the interests of third States, who may think differently and set priorities in another order.

For the time being, it would appear that the EU institutions are learning their lessons. In the field of noise regulation, the ICAO-based 'balanced approach' has been implemented in EU law. As to emissions, which has by its nature a more global than local character, it would seem that ICAO has taken the lead again, whether inspired by the EU moves going back to 2008 or not.

6 EXTERNAL RELATIONS

6.1 From the Open Skies Judgments to a Three Pillar Policy

On the back of the experience gained in the field of liberalisation and deregulation,[225] the EU Commission took steps to complete the jigsaw by introducing new criteria into the area of economic air transport operations from EU Member States to third countries. As noted in Chapter 2, the traditional bilateral agreements contain a clause that gives a State the right to refuse the designation of an air carrier by another State if that air carrier is not majority owned and effectively controlled by nationals of the State by which it is designated.[226] This nationality provision acts as a brake on the development of cross-border partnerships and mergers between air carriers of different nationalities, and thus to the operation of traffic rights outside the homeland of the air carrier. There is always a danger that if an air carrier acquired a majority stake in a foreign air carrier that foreign carrier's bilateral traffic rights could be lost on the basis of the nationality provisions in the bilateral agreements.[227]

The Commission eventually decided to take a hand in the situation and brought an action against eight Member States before the Court of the EU on a complaint that, pursuant to the '*implied powers*' concept,[228] it now had the exclusive competence to conduct the external air transport relations of the EU, whereas it held that the nationality provision in their bilateral agreements was contrary to the Treaty of Rome provisions on freedom of establishment pursuant to which that establishment in another EU State is entitled to enjoy the same rights as nationals of the State of establishment. Hence, Air France should not only be allowed to operate the agreed international air services as the designated carrier between Paris and New Delhi under the bilateral agreement concluded between France and India, but also to operate air services between Rome and New Delhi, when Air France has an establishment in Rome.

---

225. *See*, section 6.1 of this chapter.
226. *See*, section 1.2 of Chapter 2; and: H.P. van Fenema, *Substantial Ownership and Effective Control as Airpolitical Criteria*, in: T.L. Masson-Zwaan and P.M.J. Mendes de Leon (eds in chief), *Air and Space Law*: De Lege Ferenda, Essays in Honour of Henri A. Wassenbergh 27–42 (1992).
227. *See*, B. Cheng, *EEC Aviation Policy: An International Law Perspective*, in P.D. Dagtoglou, A. Giardina and J.M. Balfour (eds), Proceedings of the European Air Law Association (EALA) Conference Papers 105–130 (1993).
228. *See*, section 2.3 of this chapter.

The – identical – judgments were given in November 2002.[229] The Court argued that pursuant to the freedom of establishment enshrined in the EU Treaties air carriers should also enjoy the right to provide not only internal but also external air services from there, that is, services operated by Air France between Rome and Delhi, as the Freedom of establishment is based on the national treatment principle. Hence, if Italian carriers may operate those services, other EU carriers should be entitled to do the same by virtue of this principle. However, it dismissed the claims pertaining to the conduct of external relations on an exclusive basis, apart from three minor facets of these relations, to wit, pricing of intra-EU services, slot allocation and access to CRSs in which areas the EU possessed exclusive competencies because the regulations regulating these activities also applied to air carriers of non-member countries. This was not the case with traffic rights as these were governed by bilateral ASAs concluded by the EU States, whether they were restrictive or were identified as 'Open Skies' agreements. Because of the mandatory applicability of the Freedom of establishment, the Member States concerned were informed that they must seek to remove the nationality restrictions stemming from their ASAs.

6.2 The Three Pillars

Consequent upon the judgment of 2002,[230] the EU Commission issued a document commenting upon the decision of the CJEU[231] and sought a mandate to enter into negotiations with third countries. From this point onwards, the Commission based its external air transport policy on three pillars, to wit:

- The EU Council mandated the EU Commission to bring the bilateral agreements in conformity with EU law concerning the above nationality requirements, as well as agreed EU law based provisions on taxation of fuel, pricing and ground handling. In particular efforts had to be made to removing the above traditional nationality restrictions in order to conform them with the primary EU principle on the Freedom of establishment with a view to putting in place 'horizontal agreements' between the EU and those third countries. Horizontal agreements purport to override the nationality provisions in the bilateral agreements between those third countries and the Member States concerned.[232] In 2016,[233] Member States, assisted by the EU Commission, had

---

229. European Court of Justice Judgments of 5 November 2002 in Cases C-466, 467, 468, 469, 471, 472, 475 and 476/98; *Commission* v. *United Kingdom, Denmark, Sweden, Finland, Belgium, Luxembourg, Austria, Germany.*

230. *See*, Pablo Mendes de Leon, *The Verdict of the European Court of Justice in the Open Skies Cases: Inside Out?*18 Proceedings of the Fourteenth Annual Conference of the European Air Law Association (Prof. P.D. Dagtoglou and S. Unger (eds) 69–80 (2003).

231. COM(2002) 649 final: Communication from the Commission on *the consequences of the Court judgments of 5 November 2002 for European air transport policy.*

232. COM(2003) 94 final: Communication from the Commission on *relations between the EU and third countries in the field of air transport* and a Proposal for a European Parliament and Council Regulation on *the negotiation and implementation of air service agreements between Member States and third countries.*

succeeded in aligning around 1000 out of 1500 bilateral air agreements with 122 States under this policy, including those with key trading partners such as Brazil (*see also* below), Indonesia, Japan, Singapore and the United Arab Emirates (UAE). The joint effort of the Commission and Member States has already made possible to bring into conformity more than 1000 bilateral agreements with 122 countries. Among them, horizontal agreements have been negotiated by the EU Commission with about fifty States, which have amended all the bilateral agreements between one of these fifty States and all EU Member States with which that third State has a bilateral agreement. The EU has concluded two horizontal agreements with other regional organisations, to wit, the West African Economic and Monetary Union (UEMOA)[234] and the Economic Community of West African States (ECOWAS).[235]

- A problem arises when bilateral agreements contain restricted capacity clauses. For instance, in the above example Air France can only use its rights based on its establishment in Rome if the prevailing capacity and frequency clauses laid down in the Italy-India bilateral agreement permit the operation of such extra services. In order to address this question the EU published EU Regulation 847/2004 on the *allocation of scarce traffic rights*, pursuant to which EU carriers must be able to receive traffic rights in EU States where they have an establishment in accordance with transparent and non-discriminatory procedures. Non-EU States may be reluctant to accept the designation of EU carriers following this EU policy as those carriers may benefit from 'Free Rider' opportunities used by non-designated EU carriers which were not agreed upon in the concerned bilateral agreement.[236]

- The Second Pillar concerns the *neighbourhood policy* of the EU. The objective of this policy concerned the creation, in 2010, of a European Common Aviation Area, henceforth also referred to as ECAA, encompassing the – then – twenty-seven EU States plus the States in the South Eastern part of Europe, that is, the Balkan area. The conduct of policy is different from the traditional negotiations between States as the South Eastern European States are requested to adopt and implement on a step by step basis the 'acquis' of EU air law in their national laws and external relations with EU States so as to contribute to the formation of an enlarged internal market with a level playing field for all carriers who are licensed in one of the States participating in the Common aviation area. Equivalent standards apply to the air transport legislation of the EU in the areas of liberalisation, competition, safety,

---

233. *See*, the website of the EU Commission: *Bilateral Air Services Agreements brought into legal conformity since the Court of Justice of the EU judgments of 5 November 2002.*
234. Members are: Benin, Burkina Faso, Côte d'Ivoire, Guinea-Bissau, Mali, Niger, Senegal and Togo.
235. Members are Benin, Burkina Faso, Cape Verde, Côte d'Ivoire, Gambia, Ghana, Guinea, Guinea-Bissau, Liberia, Mali, Niger, Nigeria, Senegal, Sierra Leone, Togo.
236. *See*, for a detailed analysis of this question, H.P. van Fenema, *EU Horizontal Agreements: EU Designation and the Free Rider Clause*, 31(3) Air & Space Law 172–195 (2006).

security, air traffic management, environment including noise and emissions and passenger protection. Currently, the said 'new' States are adopting and implementing the stricter EU norms.[237] Agreements with Mediterranean States, including Morocco (2006), Georgia (2010), Jordan (2010) and Israel (2013), are drawn up on a similar model. Negotiations with Ukraine, Tunisia, Azerbaijan and Turkey are placed in the agenda.

- The EU Commission also conducts *comprehensive* air transport negotiations also referred to as *'vertical mandate'* with key partners, encompassing all aspects of air transport, including competition, labour and consumer protection. The first agreement under this *Third Pillar* has been concluded by the EU and its – then- 27 Member States with the US in 2007 and created an 'Open aviation area', superseding bilateral ASAs between the US and EU States, which were for the greater part bilateral Open Skies agreements.[238] Those bilateral Open Skies agreements still contained the traditional nationality restrictions on substantive ownership and effective control. The agreement of 2007 was amended in 2010.[239] This agreement changes the fundamental basis upon which international operations in the world's major air transport market have been undertaken over the past sixty years. In 2009, the EU also made a 'vertical' agreement with Canada, which in terms of market access opportunities, goes beyond the EU-US agreement, and initialled an agreement with Brazil in 2011. Other candidates for such comprehensive agreements are the UAE, Qatar and the ASEAN States.

Relations with Russia remain somewhat uneasy, and do not fall under any of the above pillars as they are conducted on an ad hoc basis. Russia strongly opposed the EU ETS regime discussed in the previous section, whereas the EU Commission tried to take up the case of the EU airlines which had, and still have to pay high overfly charges when operating the route through Siberian airspace in order to reach Far East destinations. This state of affairs was settled by the adoption of a number of principles designed to gradually reduce the overflight charges,[240] but these have not yet been implemented.

---

237. *See,* for a more detailed analysis, P. Bombay and M. Gergely, *The 2006 ECAA Agreement: Centerpiece of the Euroepan EU's Aviation Policy Towards Its Neighbours,* 33(3) Air & Space Law 214–232 (2008).
238. A notable exception was the UK-US Bermuda II agreement (as amended), as to which *see,* section 2.1.1 of Chapter 2. As the UK insisted on limited access to London Heathrow airport as secured by the Bermuda II agreement it hesitated a long time to engage into an Open Skies regime.
239. *See,* section 10.3 of Chapter 2.
240. *See,* IP/06/1626 of 24 November 2006; *see,* J. Balfour, *EU-Russia Aviation Relations and the Issue of Siberian Overflights,* 35(3) Air & Space Law 225–248 (2010); E. Carpanelli, *The 'Siberian Overflights' Issue,* 11(1) Issues in Aviation Law and Policy 23–66 (2011), and J. Baur, *EU-Russia Aviation Relations and the Issue of the Siberian Overflights,* 35(3) Air & Space Law 225–247 (2010).

6.3 Evaluation

The EU's external policy is a fascinating legal exercise as it entails myriad multi-level jurisdictional questions mixed with long standing and forward looking policy objectives such as the introduction of the Freedom of establishment into air transport negotiations. The role of competition regimes is also articulated because of the open market approach adopted by EU policy makers.

In practice, the principal benefit of the EU clause concerns the acceptance of the EU air carrier as the third State cannot refuse that carrier on grounds of nationality. Thus, carriers who are part of a group such as KLM in Air France-KLM, and Swiss, SAS and Austrian in the Lufthansa Group, could continue to use traffic rights in markets where the EU had secured the including of the clause in the relevant agreements.

On the other side, the increased market opportunities are rarely used by EU carriers. Consequent upon the establishment of the Open Aviation Area between the EU and the US, several major EU carriers including British Airways, KLM, Air France and Lufthansa have commenced the operation of services from EU States where they had an establishment rather than a hub. However, they had to stop those operations because of lack of yields. It is hard to find a service operated for instance from Paris to Boston, New York or Los Angeles other than by the incumbent US or French carriers. This draw back applies in the first place to the operation of passenger services and less so to cargo services. As signalled in the discussion of the EU policy on horizontal agreements, such arrangements produce yet other hurdles in the area of allocation of traffic rights and the use of scarce capacity clauses under those agreements.

In its 'Aviation Strategy for Europe' (2015),[241] the EU Commission explains the main challenges ahead with respect to, among others, external relations. They concern the introduction of the 'fair competition' principle, which pursuant to EU Rules is deemed to include the regulation of State aid affecting such 'fair competing', and, as a corollary, the reconsideration of the effectives of EU Regulation 868/2004 on *the protection against subsidisation and unfair pricing practices*. Again, the EU Commission hopes that ICAO will take the lead in this respect, but ICAO also depends on the positions taken by many other Member States who may not have strong views on the regulation of State aid.

7   CONCLUDING NOTES

The field of air transport legislation in the EU is indeed a dynamic one. This dynamism is exemplified by three areas which expectedly will require intensive attention during the next decade, to wit Air Traffic Management, external relations of the EU and regulation of emissions while safety and security remain priorities of aviation policy-makers and legislators.

The internal market for the provision of air transport services was perceived by most people, and by most EU airlines, as being of positive benefit. It enabled national

---

241. COM(2015) 598 final of 7 February 2015.

airlines to compete in each other's markets whereas the provisions swept away at virtually a stroke most of the restrictive conditions pertaining under the old bilateral regimes.

Not only is there a growing body of air transport specific legislation but also the sector is significantly affected by legislation of a general nature. The internal market legislation, supplemented by competition law measures, including decisions on State aid, is inspired by EU Principles on the opening markets and the creation of a level playing field for undertakings by avoiding distortion of competition. The EU principles on consumer protection and improvement of environmental conditions have led to the adoption of EU measures in the concerned fields. The specificity and autonomy of international air law as laid down in the Chicago Convention, ICAO policies and bilateral ASAs are increasingly influenced by general EU law and policy principles, to begin with in relations between the EU States and third States as evidenced by the opposition against the EU ETS.

As the body of EU air transport law is growing and affects not only EU but also non-EU operators, its compatibility with international agreements is tested. Frictions between EU regulations and global arrangements are surfacing in a number of areas, including but not limited to the environment, passenger protection and nationality requirements for airlines. Understanding of EU law and international law is therefore indicated to understand the cause of such frictions.

CHAPTER 4

Contractual Air Carrier Liability under International Law

1 THE COMING INTO BEING OF THE WARSAW SYSTEM

The international legal framework for airline liability was initially formed by the Warsaw Convention for the *Unification of Certain Rules Relating to International Carriage by Air* of 1929 also referred to as the Warsaw Convention or WC29. The Warsaw Convention is one of the most ratified conventions in the field of international private law. 152 States are party to this Convention.[1] *Uniformity of law* was a major goal of the drafters of the Warsaw Convention as air services are often operated between various jurisdictions.

One of the major tenets was the limitation of the air carrier's liability for damage caused to passengers, baggage and goods, and also for damage caused by delay, after the analogy of the law of the sea. In the law of the sea, the liability of the owner/ operator of a ship was limited with a view of creating equal conditions for competition in the maritime sector. As aviation was perceived as a financially weak industry, and it also served the public interest, it needed protection in the form of limitation of liability. Thus, it would be easier to insure the risks inherent with the infant industry when liability was limited.

The rules of the Warsaw Convention on damage caused by delay are applied all over the world and have demonstrated their reliability and usefulness. The passenger knows that, wherever and whenever he/she flies, there is a certain degree of uniformity in the rules governing the carrier's liability, while the carrier, being aware of the extent of his liability, can make arrangements to insure himself against possible losses.

---

1. Per January 2017: 152; for a detailed list of contracting parties of the Warsaw Convention, which is necessary for the establishment of the applicability of the private air law conventions, *see*, the ICAO website, www.icao.int → Bureaus Legal → Affairs → Treaty Collection → Current lists of parties to multilateral air law treaties.

As time went by and aviation began expanding on a large scale, the Warsaw Convention had to be amended or added to in order to be kept up to date. The amendments and additions are the following:

(1) *The Hague Protocol of 1955*, henceforth also referred to as HP 55. It was added to the Warsaw Convention with the aim of adapting it to the demands of modern transport. The Protocol entered into force on 1 August 1963. As air transport was outgrowing its status as an infant industry in the post World-War II period, gradually and slowly there was a growing consciousness of the role to be played by consumer interests. The Hague Protocol had received 137 ratifications, a number which has been stable for the past years.[2] Most States are party to both the Warsaw Convention and to the Hague Protocol. For all of them, the regime of the Warsaw Convention, as amended by the Hague Protocol, governs their relationship in the present field, unless and until that relationship is governed by the provisions of the Montreal Convention of 1999. In rare instances, only the Warsaw Convention, or only the Hague Protocol, applies to this relationship.[3] The United States has refused to become a party to the Hague Protocol as it found the raise of the liability limits as produced by the coming into force of the Hague Protocol far from enough. The United States is only a party to the Warsaw Convention in its unamended form, and, as a consequence, has initiated the establishment of the Montreal Agreement of 1966 as to which *see* below.[4]

(2) *The Guadalajara Convention for the Unification of Certain Rules Relating to International Carriage by Air Performed by a Person Other than the Contracting Carrier* (1961). This amendment took the form of a Supplementary Convention because it was concluded to deal with a new subject-matter. It created a distinction between "contracting carrier" and "actual carrier." It has been in force since 1 May 1964.

(3) The *Guatemala City Protocol* (1971) was also meant to be an amendment to the Warsaw Convention. However, this Protocol has not come into force, and is not expected to do so.

(4) *Four amending Protocols* were concluded at Montreal on 25 September 1975, namely:

---

2. Per January 2017.
3. For instance, the Republic of (South) Korea only adhered to the Hague Protocol.
4. A US court held that the US did not consent to be bound by The Hague Protocol as a separate treaty amending the original Warsaw Convention by virtue of the US ratification of Montreal Protocol No. 4; *see, Avero Belgium Insurance* v. *American Airlines*; decision of 7 September 2005; 423 F.3d 73, 2005 WL 2143880. In a case involving a cargo carriage from Seoul to San Francisco, a US court determined that it was deprived of subject matter jurisdiction because the US and South Korea did not have treaty relations with regard to international carriage of goods by air, as the US had only ratified the original version of the Warsaw Convention, while South Korea had adopted the Warsaw Convention as amended by the Hague Protocol, but not the original Warsaw Convention; *see, Chubb & Son, Inc.* v. *Asiana Airlines*, 214 F.3d 301, 308 (2nd Cir. 2000).

- Montreal Additional Protocol No 1 (MAP 1), modifying the liability limits of the Warsaw Convention into Special Drawing Rights (SDR) of the International Monetary Fund (IMF).
- Montreal Additional Protocol No 2 (MAP 2), modifying the liability limits of the Warsaw Convention as amended by The Hague Protocol into SDRs of the IMF.
- Montreal Additional Protocol No 3, modifying the liability limits of the Guatemala City Protocol of 1971 into SDRs – which has no practical relevance.
- Montreal Additional Protocol No 4 (MAP 4), modifying the limits of WC 29 as amended by The Hague Protocol into SDRs and creating special provisions for the international carriage of cargo.

(5) The *Montreal Intercarrier Agreement* (1966) is an agreement concluded between International Air Transport Association (IATA) carriers flying from, via or into the United States and the US Civil Aeronautics Board (CAB), the predecessor of the current Department of Transportation (DoT), raising the liability limits for passenger injury and death under the Warsaw Convention, and creating a regime of absolute liability in that regard.

(6) In 1995, IATA introduced the *IATA Inter-Carrier Agreement* (IIA) as an *umbrella accord*, which means that individual carriers can implement it in their existing conditions of carriage, according to their own legal regime. IATA released the *Agreement on Measures to Implement the IATA Inter-Carrier Agreement* (MIA) one year later. According to IATA, these agreements could serve as temporary agreements to help saving the stagnated Warsaw System by waiving its restrictive limitation of liability.[5] The IIA should be seen as an interim solution in anticipation of the level of success of the latest official revision of the Warsaw system which was instigated and launched by International Civil Aviation Organisation (ICAO). This ICAO initiative brought the Montreal Convention, 1999, into being, as to which see below.[6] This IATA based regime is relevant for carriers operating in countries that have not ratified the Montreal Convention of 1999; examples are Garuda Indonesia which has signed the IIA whereas Indonesia has only ratified the Warsaw Convention, and Aeroflot which has signed MIA while the Russian Federation is a party to the Warsaw Convention as amended by The Hague Protocol.

---

5. Para. 1 of the IIA links the waiver of the limitation imposed by Art. 22(1) of the Warsaw Convention to the law of the domicile of the passenger. "… so that recoverable compensatory damages may be determined and awarded by reference to the law of the domicile of the passenger."
6. The US Department of Transportation granted 'Continued Discussion Authority' to IATA for the purpose of reaching an agreement among carriers to waive the liability limits of the Warsaw Convention, agreeing with IATA that the Montreal Agreement of 1966 must be brought up to date' as to which *see*, Department of Transportation, Order 96-1-25 of 23 January 1996, Docket OST-96-232.

(7) Finally, the *Montreal Convention 1999*, also referred to as MC99, became necessary because the Warsaw system no longer functioned satisfactorily. ICAO had chosen to modernise the liability system in order to maintain the coherence and uniformity of the international regime regarding air carrier liability.

For the present purposes, the 'Warsaw System', or the 'Warsaw Regime', consists of the Warsaw Convention of 1929, as amended by the Hague Protocol of 1955 as modified by the Montreal Additional Protocols No 1, 2 and 4, and as supplemented by the Guadalajara Convention, 1969. Its structure is illustrated in the below scheme.

Figure 4.1   The Warsaw System

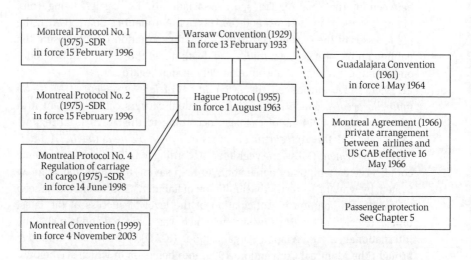

The list of legal instruments presented above demonstrates that it was high time for ICAO to take the lead again. Meanwhile, treaty relationships will be even further complicated in the interim period – which may last rather long – during which the treaties of the 'Warsaw System' exist next to the Montreal Convention, 1999.

2   THE OBJECTIVES OF THE MONTREAL CONVENTION, 1999

2.1   Modernisation and Consolidation

Pursuant to the provisions of Article 55 of the Montreal Convention, the entire Warsaw System is to be replaced eventually by this (Montreal) Convention. In case either the Warsaw Convention or one of the above instruments amending or supplementing this convention, and the Montreal Convention, 1999, apply to a carriage, the provisions of the Montreal Convention, 1999, prevail.

The principal reason for a new convention was based on the consideration that limitations of liability for death or injury of passengers as contained in the Warsaw System were increasingly questioned, in particular by the courts of several countries. Moreover, ICAO wished to restore uniformity in the patchwork of legal instruments governing international air carrier liability. Hence, it was desirable to have the Warsaw Convention replaced by a new uniform instrument prepared to be adopted by States world-wide.[7] However, this global coverage is far from being achieved because States, which are most prone to aviation accidents due to poor aviation regulation and safety records and thus most exposed to air crashes,[8] have not ratified this convention. Also, courts could rely on the enormous amount of case law made under the Warsaw Convention.[9]

The Diplomatic Conference for the establishment of the new convention was attended by 122 States and 11 Organisations; it adopted by consensus the *Convention for the Unification of Certain Rules for International Carriage by Air,* done at Montreal 28 May 1999. Also, States encouraged ICAO to draw up a "set of general principles or best practices on consumer protection."[10] The Convention entered into force on 4 November 2003. In January 2017, 123 States had ratified the Convention including the EU Member States, and the EU.

The principal objective of the drafters of the Montreal Convention, 1999 pertains to the adoption of the same or a similar approach regarding the use of terms of the Warsaw Convention of 1929, as amended by The Hague Protocol of 1955 and the Montreal Protocol no. 4. The drafters wished to preserve the interpretations of the terms made under case law during the past seventy years. It will be seen that many substantive terms of the Montreal Convention, 1999, are taken from the Warsaw Convention, 1929, and related instruments.

The sections below will first discuss the selected principal subjects of air carrier liability under the Montreal Convention, 1999, and, after that, under the Warsaw

---

7. As confirmed in: *Ehrlich* v. *American Airlines*, Inc. 360 F.3d 366, 371 n.4 (2d Cir. 2004); *Booker* v. *BWIA West Indies Airways Ltd.*, 32 Avi 15,134 (E.D.N.Y 2007); *Paradis* v. *Ghana Airways Ltd.*, 348 F.Supp. 2d 106, 110 n.4-5 (S.D.N.Y. 2004), aff'd 194 Fed. Appx. 5 (2d Cir. 2006).

8. *See,* Peter Neenan, *The Damaged Quilt: Inadequate Coverage of the Montreal Convention,* 37(1) Air & Space Law 51–64 (2012).

9. *See, Serrano* v. *American Airlines,* 32 Avi 16,385 (C.D. Calif. 2008); *Vigilant Insurance* v. *World Courier,* 2008 WL 2332343 (S.D.N.Y 2008); *Rafailov* v. *El Al Israel Airlines,* 32 Avi 16,372 (S.D.N.Y 2008); *Chubb Ins. Co of Europe, S.A.* v. *Menlo Worldwide Forwarding, Inc.,* 32 Avi 15,978 (C.D. Calif. 2008); *Kruger* v. *United Airlines* (NDCal) 32 Avi 15,703; *Baah* v. *Virgin Atlantic Airways Limited,* 2007 WL422993 (S.D.N.Y. 2007); *Paradis* v. *Ghana Airways Ltd.,* 348 F.Supp. 2d 106, 110 n. 4-5 (S.D.N.Y. 2004), aff'd 194 fed. Appx. 5 (2d Cir. 2006); *Kalantar* v. *Lufthansa German Airlines,* 402 F.Supp. 2d 130, 140 n. 10 (D.D.C 2005); *Jones* v. *USA 3000 Airlines,* 33 Avi. 17,442 (E.D.Mo. 2009); *Mansoor* v. *Air France KLM Airlines,* 33 Avi. 17,144 (C.D.Calif. 2008); *Best* v. *BWIA West Indies Airways,* Ltd., 33 Avi. 17,116 (E.D.N.Y. 2008).

10. *See,* ATConf/6-WP95 of 7/3/13 presented by Brazil promoting its own generous regulations on consumer protection as an example; *see also,* ATConf/6-IP/1 of 27/2/13 on the *Effectiveness of Consumer Protection Regulations,* presented by the ICAO Secretariat; and ATConf/6-WP/68 of 1/3/13 on *Consumer Protection: A Joined Up Approach Required by Governments and Industry,* presented by IATA, the Arab Air Carrier Organization (AACO), the Association of Asia Pacific Airlines (AAPA) and the Latin American and Caribbean Air transport Association (ALTA).

Convention, 1929, also referred to as WC 29. Other amending protocols and supplementary conventions will be mentioned when are specifically applicable to the subject matter.

3 AIR CARRIER LIABILITY UNDER INTERNATIONAL AIR LAW

3.1 Applicability

3.1.1 Applicability under the Montreal Convention, 1999

MC 99 applies to *international* carriage[11] of persons, baggage or cargo performed by aircraft for reward[12] and applies equally to gratuitous carriage by aircraft performed by an air transport undertaking.[13] Balloons and gliders are considered as aircraft.[14] The plaintiff has to supply evidence of the international character of the carriage.[15] States, including India,[16] Israel[17] and the EU States[18] apply, or are proposing to apply, the provisions of the Montreal Convention, 1999, also to domestic carriage. Furthermore, the Convention applies to carriage by air performed by a person other than the contracting carrier and to carriage performed by the State or by legally constituted bodies under the conditions of Article 1.[19]

---

11. As defined in section 3.1.2.1.
12. 'Leasing' qualifies as 'reward' under the Warsaw Convention according to the Tel Aviv District Court in *Chim Nir* v. *Ben Yitach*, CM 7913 in CF1444/06 so that this Convention is applicable to a helicopter flight operated under a lease contract for filming an advertisement.
13. In *Laveragne* v. *Atis Corporation* the court found that the provision of gratuitous air carriage in a private aircraft was not carriage by 'air transport' as defined in Art. 1 (1) of the Montreal Convention, as it declined to extend the definition of 'air transport undertaking' to the company owning the aircraft, which was operated under Part 91 of the US Federal Aviation Regulations governing flights for personal use. The German Federal Court decided (decision of 12 May 2012, I ZR 109/11) that a carrier can conclude one single contract of carriage by air even when a considerable part of the carriage is carried out by truck and not by aircraft; as to which see IATA Liability reporter 13 (2013).
14. *See*, a decision of the Court of Appeal of the Australian State of Victoria in *Mount Beauty Gliding Club Inc.* v. *Jacob*, [2004] VSCA 151 and the decision made by an English Court of Appeal in *Disley* v. *Levine*; 45 [2002] 1 WLR 785 (CA); these are WC29 decisions.
15. *See*, *Gerard* v. *American Airlines, Inc.*, 32 Avi 15,420 (Conn. Sup. Ct. 2007); on the application of the jurisdictional provisions of the Montreal Convention, 1999, to a journey from Australia to European cities, *see Tourni* v. *Scandinavian Airlines System*, unreported judgment of the District Court of New South Wales, Australia, dated 14 March 2007, per Judge Truss, as reported in the IATA Liability Reporter 6 (2008); the domestic leg Boston-Los Angeles of a round trip Boston-Puerto Vallarta, Mexico is 'international carriage' under the Montreal Convention, as to which *see*, *Gustafson* v. *American Airlines*, 658 F.Supp.2d 276 (D. Mass. 2009); Los Angeles was not an 'agreed stopping place.'
16. *See*, the Indian *Carriage by Air Act* (1972) as amended in 2009, designed ".... to make provision for applying the rules contained in the said Convention in its original form and in the amended form (subject to exceptions, adaptations and modification) to non-international carriage by air and for matters connected therewith."
17. *See*, the *Carriage by Air Law* of Israel.
18. By virtue of EU Regulation 889/2002 amending EU Regulation 2027/1997.
19. *See*, Art. 2 of the Convention.

Place of origin and place of destination are defined in the same fashion as under the Warsaw Convention, 1929. In a case of 2007, a US court found that there is:

[...] no reason to interpret the phrase 'place of destination' differently than courts have interpreted the phrase [...] in the Warsaw Convention. The 'place of destination' in the context of a round trip ticket is the ultimate destination specified by the contract of carriage between the passenger and the carrier, not the outbound leg of the trip. [...] moreover, the passenger's subjective intent regarding if or when the return trip would be made is irrelevant.[20]

The case concerned an interpretation of the term 'place of destination' as used in the provision on jurisdiction.[21] When the purchase for the international carriage, falling under the terms of the Montreal Convention, is separated from the purchase of the domestic transportation, as the concerned tickets where bought from different air carriers (United Airlines and Qantas) on their respective websites, the domestic transportation does not fall under the provisions of this convention.[22] In light of Article 1(3) of the Montreal Convention, 1999, a court observed that:

the Convention contemplates that an entirely domestic leg of an international itinerary will be covered by the Convention as part of one undivided [international] transportation – even if it is performed by a successive carrier and even if the various legs are agreed upon under a series of contracts – as long as it has been regarded as part of a single operation.[23]

---

20. *See, Baah v. Virgin Atlantic Airways Limited*, 2007 WL422993 (S.D.N.Y. 2007); thus a one way journey Bangkok-Los Angeles does not fall under the Montreal Convention, 1999 as Thailand is not a party to it; *see, Richards v. Singapore Airlines*, 36 Avi 15,291 (C.D. Cal. 2013).
21. *See*, Art.33(1) of MC99.
22. *See, Kruger v. United Airlines* (N.D.Cal) 32 Avi 15,703.
23. The courts have found a distinction between carriage entirely booked at the outset and carriage booked in separate stages, finding that the carriage will generally constitute a single operation if it is booked together prior to the departure of the trip, even if it is to be operated by separate carriers, *see, Bafana v. Commercial Airways (Pty) Ltd* 87 ILR 289 and *McLoughlin v. Commercial Airways (Pty) Ltd*, 602 F. Supp 29,33 (E.D.N.Y. 1985), where the Eastern District of New York held, "the law seems clear that where, as here, the parties arrange and pay in full for an international trip at the outset, each leg of the journey (even though some legs may be wholly domestic, covered by a separate ticket and carried on a separate airline) is within the Convention." The Courts have also found that where carriage is booked through a travel agent, the knowledge of the travel agent is imputed to the carrier, such that the carrier is deemed to be aware of the other bookings, *see, Haldimann v. Delta Airlines* 168 F3d 1324 (1999) where the Court of Appeals for the District of Columbia found that a flight booked through a Swiss travel agency called Lathion-Voyages, involving flights on Swissair for the transatlantic travel, and Delta for the domestic US travel, constituted a single operation. The court considered the wording of the Montreal Convention (1999) regarding the requirement that the carriage be conceived by the parties as a single operation, and determined that this was difficult to do, and that a series of cases had established that specific documentary indicia should be preferred over subjective intent (citing *Klos v. Polskie Linie Lotnicze; Swaminathan v. Swiss Air Transport Co; Sopcak v. Northern Mountain Helicopter Service* and *Petrire v. Spantax*). Similarly, in *Robertson v. American Airlines* 401 F3d 4999 (DC Cir, 2005), the same Court found travel on two different carriers when booked through a travel agent, Nancy Thompson of Gateway Travel constituted a single operation, and noting that "other district courts have held that a travel agent's knowledge of a plaintiff's travel intentions is imputed to the carrier, the district court resolved the issue by applying the same rule."

As under the Warsaw Convention, place of departure and place of destination are the same in case of a return ticket.[24] The Montreal Convention, 1999, provides that if a country of origin or destination is a party to various Conventions of the Warsaw System, and to the Montreal Convention, the provisions of MC99 prevail.[25]

Agreed stopping place, which is also mentioned in Article 1(2), must be distinguished from the *place of destination.* On a ticket Amsterdam-Rome-Amsterdam, Rome is an agreed stopping place and not the place of destination. It follows that, on a return trip, place of departure and place of destination will coincide. If the place of departure and destination is located in the same country, which is party to the Warsaw Convention, this Convention will be applicable, provided that the agreed stopping place is located in another country.

3.1.2 Applicability under the Warsaw Regime

3.1.2.1 Defining International Transportation

The Warsaw Convention, as amended, also applies to *international transportation.*[26] Article 1 of this Convention stipulates that place of departure and place of destination must be located in a State or in States party to the Convention. In the former case, that is, the case in which place of departure and place of destination are located within one State party to the Convention, the Convention applies if there is an agreed stopping place in a foreign State, even if that foreign State is not a party to the Convention.

The nationality of the carrier and of the passenger is irrelevant for the purpose of determining whether a journey is *international* or not. In the *Glenn* v. *Cubana* case of 1952, a US and a Cuban aircraft collided. The question was whether the Cuban carrier was protected by the limitation of liability as provided by the Warsaw Convention. Cuba was at that time not a party to the Warsaw Convention. The US Court ruled that the Warsaw Convention does not refer to the citizenship of the passenger or the carrier in order to be applicable. The applicability of this Convention is solely based on the character and the nature of the transportation as defined by Article 1 of that Convention.[27]

In the *Grein* v. *Imperial Airways* case, London, being the place of departure and place of destination, is located in a contracting State.[28] The ticket mentioned the journey London-Antwerp-London. The aircraft carrying the passenger crashed in Belgium. At the moment of the crash, Belgium was not a party to the Warsaw Convention.

---

24. *See, Jones* v. *USA 3000 Airlines*, 33 Avi. 17,442 (E.D.Mo. 2009); *Danner* v. *International Freight Systems of Washington LLC*; 2010 WL 329 (D. Md. 20 August 2010) and *Borges-Santiago* v. *American Airlines* (685 F. Supp. 2d 289 (D.P.R. 2010) in which cases the international character of the flight was denied.
25. Art. 55 of the Montreal Convention (1999).
26. The Hague Protocol of 1955 modified the term 'transportation' in Art. 1 into 'carriage.' The term carriage seems more appropriate from a terminological point of view.
27. *See, Glenn* v. *Cia Cubana de Aviation*, 102 F.Supp. 631, 3 Avi., 17,836 (S.D. Florida 1952).
28. *All England Law Reports* 1936, Volume 2.

The Convention applies, even if Belgium, the country in which there was an agreed stopping place, was not a contracting State. The English Court of Appeal defined *agreed stopping place* as a place:[29]

> [...] where according to the contract the machine by which the contract is to be performed will stop in the course of performing the contractual carriage, whatever the purpose of the descent may be and whatever rights the passenger may have to break his journey at that place.

Hence, the agreed stopping place must be evidenced by the ticket.

3.1.2.2 Domestic Flights

In the case of *Holmes* v. *Bangladesh Biman Corporation*, the UK House of Lords held that British national law governing aviation accidents claims – that is, the *Carriage by Air Act* (1967) – does not apply to a domestic flight in Bangladesh.[30] The US District Court for the Southern District of Texas ruled that the Warsaw Convention is not applicable to the claims for injuries sustained on a domestic flight where plaintiffs purchased tickets for international carriage from Italy to the US on one airline and separately purchased tickets for domestic carriage within the US during their stay on another airline.[31]

In *Robertson* v. *American Airlines* (2003),[32] the court found that the plaintiff's travel was a *single operation* under Article 1(3) of the Warsaw Convention, and that this Convention applied to all legs of her journey.[33] She had first booked a ticket for a Denver, Colorado, US – London, UK – Denver, Colorado trip, and then another one for a Washington DC – Denver, Colorado – Washington DC trip, whereas both trips were booked through the same travel agency. In addition, return travel from London to Denver and from there to Washington DC was coordinated on the same day. The plaintiff later booked a second return flight from London, UK, to Washington, bypassing Denver, Colorado, for the same day of travel. The accident caused burn injuries to the plaintiff on a journey from Denver, Colorado. The court examined the *documentary evidence*, on the basis of which the plaintiff's intention regarding international travel to be considered as a 'single operation', while taking into account:

- the successive carriers;
- the date and time of the plaintiff's travel bookings;
- the place of issuance of the plaintiff's travel bookings;

---

29. In *Weinberg* v. *Grand Circle Travel*, the court held that a hot air balloon voyage within the State of Tanzania did not include an agreed stopping place as referred to in the Warsaw Convention; *see*, Civil Action No. 11-11676-WGY, 2012 WL 4096611 (D. Mass. 19 September 2012).
30. All England Law Reports 1989 Volume 1.
31. *Santleben et al.* v. *Continental Airlines*, 2001 WL 1701469 (SD Texas 20 December 2001).
32. 277 F. Supp. 2d 91 (D.D.C. 2003).
33. As to which *see also*, *Kinzinger-Lignon* v. *Delta Airlines*, Civil Action No. 1-11-cv-2282-TWT, 2012 WL 1681863 (N.D. Ga 11 May 2012), and *Zhang* v. *Air China*, 866 F. Sup. 2d 1162 (N.D. Cal. 2012) in which the domestic legs were separated from the international journeys.

- the fact that the bookings were made by the same travel agent;
- the coordination of the different flights.[34]

A domestic leg of an international journey can very well fall outside, but may also fall within the scope, of international treaty regimes. The "objective manifestations of the party's intent" to consider or not to consider the domestic stretch part of an international journey is the determining factor. Factual evidence of the parties' intention and the objective facts of ticketing are decisive.[35] If parties cannot reach agreement on this, a court must establish that decision, taking into account all the elements of the case.[36]

3.1.3 Concluding Remarks

The agreement plays a fundamental role in achieving the objectives of the Warsaw and Montreal Conventions. As these conventions are designed to unify 'certain rules' pertaining to international carriage by air only, they must be supplemented by domestic provisions as indicated in these conventions.

The rights and obligations arising from the contract between the carrier and the passenger lay down said objectives, including the rules pertaining to the limitation of liability. Those rights and obligations must be known to the parties. Under the Warsaw regime, such knowledge enables the passenger beforehand to buy additional insurance in case of limited liability for passenger damage.

The term 'agreement' must be interpreted in a broad sense. The parties to the agreement must establish that the requisite contract is a promise, that is, an undertaking, on the part of the carrier to transport the passenger, and consent of the passenger.

For the Montreal Convention, 1999, and the Warsaw regime to be applicable, the carriage must be *international* as defined under those conventions and interpreted by courts. An increasing number of States make their provisions applicable to domestic carriage which is not international in terms of these conventions.

3.2 Documentation

3.2.1 Regulation under the Montreal Convention, 1999

This Convention has modernised rules on passenger tickets, baggage checks and other documentary requirements with the aim of achieving simplicity and compatibility with

---

34. *See also*, Court of Appeals in New South Wales, Australia, in *Gulf Air Company* v. *Fattouh*, (2008) NSWCA 225 where the claimant traveling on a return ticket Beirut-Sidney sought to establish jurisdiction in Australia by separating the two international legs of the single operation, that is, the return journey.
35. *See*, *Petrire* v. *Spantax*, 756 F.2d 263, 265 (2d Cir. 1985), and *Auster* v. *Ghana Airways*, 514 F.3d 44 (D.C. Cir. 2008); in this respect, travel agents may affect the establishment of these facts on the imputation of knowledge of agents on carriers.
36. *See*, *Coyle* v. *P.T. Garuda Indonesia*, 363 F.3d 979 (9th Cir. 2004), in which case the tickets for the domestic leg Jakarta-Medan mentioned the term: "DOMESTIK".

modern technologies. Electronic ticketing and electronic airway bills are valid and subject to Articles 3 and 9 of this Convention. Place of departure and place of destination are still required to be shown on the document of carriage or any other means which is designed to contain such information.

Failure to provide notice that the Montreal Convention applies[37] does not constitute a waiver of the statute of limitations defence under Article 35 of this Convention because, as follows from Article 3(5), non-compliance with the requirement of Article 3(4) does not affect the existence of the contract of carriage or the application of the Montreal Convention to limit liability.[38] This requirement is necessary because place of departure and place of destination determine the applicability of the Convention.

3.2.2   Case Law under the Montreal Convention, 1999

As MC99 has simplified documentation requirements, case law is hardly available. For MC99 to be applicable, the issuance of a ticket is not required.[39]

3.2.3   Regulation under the Warsaw Regime

Article 3 of the Warsaw Convention, 1929, contains the conditions for the passenger ticket. It must contain:

- An indication of the place of departure and destination.
- An indication of an agreed stopping place if place of departure and place of destination are located within the territory of one contracting State.
- A notice of the applicability of the Warsaw Convention, 1929, limiting damages as regulated by this convention.

Paragraph 2 of this provision imposes a sanction on the carrier in case the carrier has accepted a passenger without a ticket. Article 3 has been the subject of litigation. Baggage check – and air waybill – must contain a number of particulars, such as:

(a) the place and date of issue/execution;
(b) the place of departure and destination;
(c) the name and address of the carrier;
(d) number and weight of the carried items;
(e) the amount of the value of the carried items;
(f) a statement that the transportation is subject to the Warsaw Convention.[40]

---

37. Art. 3(4).
38. Following Art. 3(5); *see, Gustafson v. American Airlines*, 658 F.Supp.2d 276 (D. Mass. 2009) at 287.
39. *See, Kruger v. United Airlines*, 32 Avi. 15,705 (N.D. Calif. 2007).
40. *See*, Arts 4 and 8 of the Warsaw Convention.

The Hague Protocol simplified the above requirements by retaining conditions sub b) and f), while adding a condition pertaining to the agreed stopping place if the place of departure and the place of destination are located in the territory of the same State.

3.2.4 Case Law under the Warsaw Convention, 1929

The Warsaw Convention is not applicable if the carrier accepts a passenger without a ticket. In 2009, the French Supreme Court discussed the question whether the carrier carrying persons for free, so called *gratuitous* transportation or carriage, can rely on the liability limits of the Warsaw Convention as no ticket had been issued. The French Supreme Court confirmed that the non-issuance of a ticket results into the inapplicability of the limits laid down in the Warsaw Convention.[41]

The Supreme Court of Canada decided that the Warsaw Convention did not require any "notice" of the applicability of the limitation of liability in order for the limitation to apply. The protection of the limitation is only lost if the ticket has not been delivered. Even if the ticket has been delivered, but delivered 'irregularly', the carrier is protected by the limits of its liability as to personal injury.[42]

In comparable cases, US courts have reached different conclusions on the validity of an airline ticket. According to US courts, Articles 3 and 4 of the Warsaw Convention must be interpreted in such a way that, in any case, the passenger has the opportunity to protect himself against the limited liability of the carrier. One way to do so is to take additional insurance. This could be seen as a *teleological* interpretation, for the benefit of the passenger. Leading cases are *Mertens* v. *The Flying Tiger Line*[43] and *Warren* v. *Flying Tiger Line.*[44]

Most remarkable has been the ruling in the *Lisi* v. *Alitalia* case. A ticket had been delivered to passenger Lisi, including the notice as required under Article 3 of the Warsaw Convention, but this notice was "unnoticeable and unreadable" as the print was put in 'Lilliputian typography' so that the passenger's attention was not sufficiently drawn to the limitation of the carrier's liability. The 'Lisi' case was followed by the case of *Chan* v. *Korean Airlines* which was governed by the Montreal Agreement, 1966, concerning a flight of Korean Airlines, KAL, between New York and Seoul on 1

---

41. *See, Mme Y et Fonds de garantie des victims des actes de terrorisme et d' autres infractions* v. *Consorts X et Allianz*, decision of 25 June 2009; 252(4) Revue française de droit aérien et spatial 217–223 (2009). Although in a different context, Directive 2003/96/EC of 27 October 2003 restructuring the Community framework for the taxation of energy products and electricity' refers to the concept of 'private pleasure-flying' to exclude these activities from certain tax exemptions. This concept has been defined in the directive as "the use of an aircraft by its owner or the natural or legal person who enjoys its use either through hire or through any other means, *for other than commercial purposes* and in particular *other than for the carriage of passengers or goods or for the supply of services for consideration or for the purposes of public authorities.*"
42. *See, Ludecke* v. *Canadian Pacific Airlines Ltd.*, 98 DLR 3d 52 (Supreme Court Canada 1979).
43. 341 F.2d 851 (2d Cir.), cert. denied, 382 816 (1965).
44. 352 F.2d.494 (9th Cir. 1965).

September 1983.[45] This agreement provides that these airlines are committed to pay higher damages than those foreseen by the Warsaw Convention. The KAL Boeing 747 was shot down by a Russian military aircraft over Eastern Siberia. All crew members and passengers were killed. Mr Chan had been delivered a ticket in 8 point type. The representatives of Mr Chan based themselves therefore on the *'Lisi doctrine'*. According to this doctrine, a notice in a smaller letter print than the one which was prescribed by the Montreal Agreement (10 point type) amounted to inadequate notice. As a consequence, Article 3(2) would become applicable and the liability of the carrier unlimited. The US Supreme Court did not follow this line of argument in the Chan case.[46] It was of the opinion that the sanction for the carrier, as stipulated by Article 3(2), does not apply in cases where no "adequate" statement has been given. Consequently, the carrier could rely on the limitation of its liability.[47]

Article 4, referring to *Baggage check*, reads that if no baggage check has been delivered, or if this baggage check does not mention that the Warsaw Convention, including its liability rules, is applicable, the carrier may not invoke the limitation of its liability. In such a case, the carrier shall be liable without limitation of liability. In the case of *Cruz v. American Airlines*, the carrier had not recorded the weight of each suitcase that was checked in. The weight of the 'package' is one of the conditions which must be mentioned on the baggage check. Since the air carrier had not recorded this weight, it could not rely on the protection of limited liability limits.[48]

If a baggage check contains an "irregularity", the airline who issued the baggage check may nevertheless rely on the liability limits provided by the Warsaw Convention. On a round trip between Manchester and Los Angeles, claimants had left Manchester with two pieces of baggage but returned from Los Angeles with their pieces. The contents of the baggage were stolen. A UK Court of Appeal ruled that an incomplete baggage check is nevertheless a valid baggage check, albeit a baggage check containing an irregularity. There is nothing in this Convention that requires an airline to fill in a baggage check at every stopping place or stop over.[49]

In 2001, a US Court of Appeals held that the failure of an air waybill to *contain the place of execution*, even where the air waybill was prepared by the shipper, voided the carrier's limited liability and subjected the carrier to liability for the full value of the goods. The place of execution is a required particular under Article 8 of the Convention, and must be satisfied for a carrier to be able to invoke the limits of liability under Article

---

45. As a consequence, the Montreal Agreement of 1966 was concluded by the US Civil Aeronautics Board, and airlines flying from, to and via a point in the US contained a provision with respect to the size of the letter type, that is, 10 point letter type.
46. *See, Chan v. Korean Air Lines*, 490 US 122 (1989).
47. *See*, G.N. Tompkins, *The Road from Lisi to Chan – Notice of the Warsaw Convention Limits of Liability*, published in *Air and Space Law – De Lege Ferenda*, Liber Amicorum Prof. H.A. Wassenbergh, Pablo Mendes de Leon and T.L. Masson-Zwaan (eds) 135–147 (1992).
48. Affirmed by 356 F. 3d (United States Court of Appeals, District of Columbia Circuit, decision of 10 February 2004); *see also, Spanner v. United Airlines*, 177 F.3d 1173 (9th Circuit 1999), and: *Chan v. Korean Air Lines* 490 U.S. 122, 134 (1984), where the Supreme Court ruled: "But where the text is as clear, as it is here, we have no power to insert an amendment."
49. *See, Collins a.o. v. British Airways Board*, Decision of 19 November 1982; All England Law Reports 1982 Volume 1.

22. Even though the place of execution in this case was apparent from the other circumstances surrounding the air waybill, the court nonetheless held that the specific space for the "place of execution" must be completed.[50]

3.2.5 Concluding Remarks

The question of documentation plays a less prominent role under the Montreal Convention, 1999, than under the Warsaw regime as limits for passenger liability and requirements for documentation have been relaxed under the first mentioned convention. The applicability of these limits, and the provision on the mandatory information on these limits, failing which they would not apply, accounted for the relatively high number of cases under the Warsaw regime. That number has been substantially reduced under the Montreal Convention, 1999.

Under the Warsaw regime, notably US court decisions may give a strict interpretation of the rules regarding formalities pertaining to the transportation of baggage and cargo. All requirements stated in these provisions must be complied with. As said, failure to comply with specified requirements regarding the passenger ticket, baggage check and air waybill results in the inapplicability of the limitation of liability of the carrier.

3.3   Right of Action: The Parties

3.3.1   Regulation under the Montreal Convention, 1999

3.3.1.1   The Passenger under the Montreal Convention, 1999

A right of action lies with the *passenger*. Pursuant to Article 17 of MC99, the carrier is liable for damage suffered by the passenger. Neither WC 29 nor MC99 define the term passenger as to which see the next section.

The General Conditions of Carriage of IATA define a Passenger as:

> any person, except for members of the crew, carried or to be carried in an aircraft with the consent of the carrier.[51]

The passenger, or persons who are entitled to claim on his or her behalf, that is, a dependent of the passenger as determined by national law of the residence of the – deceased – passenger,[52] and/or the administrator of the estate of such a passenger will in the vast majority of the cases be the claimant or plaintiff.

---

50. *See, Republic National Bank* v. *Delta Airlines*, 263 F.3d. 42 (2d Cir. 2001), as reported in the Newsletter issued by Condon and Forsyth LLP, October 2001, at 1.
51. Article 1; another definition in IATA's Conditions of Carriage reads: "'Passenger(s)' means any person who is in possession of a Ticket, except members of the crew, who is carried or to be carried by plane."
52. As to which *see*, section 3.13.2 below.

As the term 'passenger' is not defined by any of the conventions, courts have interpreted it. A person accompanying the pilot of a helicopter conducting an aerial inspection of power lines was a passenger as he was not part of the crew.[53] This case was decided under Australian law, and not under MC99.

According to the Court of Justice of the EU, a passenger is "any person who is on a flight with the consent of the air carrier or the aircraft operator, excluding on-duty members of both the flight crew and the cabin crew." – irrespective of whether an individual or collective document of carriage has been issued. In the case before the Court of Justice of the European Union (CJEU),[54] the person in question was a passenger as he did not perform the tasks of the flight crew.

Only passengers, not animals, which are considered as cargo, can claim for damages under Article 17 of the Montreal Convention, 1999.[55]

Courts may allow for the submission of *class actions*. In a US case for the compensation of damage caused by delay, a class action was not allowed.[56] The Canadian Ontario Superior Court of Justice approved the settlement of a class action lawsuit against the defunct Skyservice Airlines. A class action lawsuit was commenced while defining two classes of plaintiff:

- passengers on the flight;
- non-passenger family members who were able to claim under local law for loss of care, guidance and companionship of the members of the first class.[57]

3.3.1.2 Regulation of the Air Carrier under the Montreal Convention, 1999

On the other side, the *defendant* will in most cases be the air carrier pursuant to the terms of MC99. MC99 does not define the term 'air carrier'.[58] Again, the term "carrier" is not defined under MC99.[59] Its Chapter V encompasses the provisions of the Supplementary Guadalajara Convention of 1961, making a distinction between the

---

53. Clyde & Co, Australian Aviation Newsletter at 9–10 (April 2016), *Who is a "passenger"?*, reporting the case involving the injured Mr. Edwards and Precision Helicopters Ltd.
54. *See, Wucher Helicopter GmbH and Euro–Aviation Versicherung AG v. Fridolan Santer*, Case C-6/14, judgment of the CJEU of 26 February 2015.
55. *See, Aya v. Lan Cargo*, 2014 WL 4672450 (S.D. Florida, 18 September 2014).
56. *See, Rambarran v. Dynamic Airways*, No. 14-CV-10138, 2015 WL 4523222 (S.D.N.Y 27 July 2015).
57. *See, Maggisano v. Skyservice Airlines Inc* [2010] ONSC 7169 (CanLII), reported by Carlos P. Martins, Newsletter of 2 March 2011, International Law Office, www.internationallawoffice. com; *see also*, Bersenas Jacobsen Chouest Thomson and Blackburn LLP, 'Air France Class Action Settlement Approved', Transportation Notes: *Legal Decision and Developments Affecting the Transportation Industry in Canada*, Volume 6(1) of January 2010; *Air France class action: important settlement made by the Ontario Superior Court of Justice*, case of *Abdulrahim v. Air France* (2011 ONSC 398), International Law Office, contributed by Gerard Chouest, www. internationallawoffice.com; Newsletter of 30 March 2011.
58. As compared with the Warsaw regime the carrier has become neuter under the Montreal Convention. The carrier was male under the previous conventions.
59. The same is true for the Warsaw Convention, as amended, as to which *see* below.

"contractual carrier" and the "actual carrier."[60] In the first place, the term "carrier" as employed in the Montreal Convention, 1999, must be understood as the "contractual carrier" as "the agreement" between the parties determines their understanding on applicability of certain provisions of the Convention.[61]

The term 'carrier' includes agents of the carrier. These terms have been explained in case law as to which see below. Since code-sharing has become an operational practice among air carriers, the study groups and committees preparing MC99 paid attention to the question of liability under code-shared operations.[62]

3.3.1.3 Case Law on 'Air Carrier' under the Montreal Convention, 1999

Actions for damages may be brought against the actual carrier or the contracting carrier, or both. If an action is brought against the contractual carrier only, that carrier may have recourse to the actual carrier pursuant to local law.[63] The broadened scope of the 'fifth jurisdiction' in relation to these arrangements has been briefly discussed above under the heading 'jurisdiction', as to which see, section 3.12.1 below.

In re Air Crash Near Rio Grande Puerto Rico on 3 December 2008, the court acknowledged that both defendants could be "carriers" under Article 39 MC99 regulating the relationship in terms of liability between the contractual carrier and the actual carrier because local law recognises joint liability of the two.[64]

In Best v. BWIA West Indies Airways,[65] the court was asked to interpret Articles 36 and 39 of the Montreal Convention, 1999. The court held that Article 39 of the Convention is designed to regulate liability in the context of code share agreements, and agreements under which a carrier leases the aircraft and crew ('wet lease' constructions) from another carrier for the provision of the carriage. However, Article 39 of the Convention does not apply to successive carriage. Moreover, if a carrier (BWIA) acts as an agent of another carrier (LIAT), the agent (BWIA) cannot be held

---

60. With the exception of Art. IX(3) of the Guadalajara Convention which has been deleted in light of Art. 43 of the Montreal Convention, 1999. See, ICAO Legal Committee, Report of the Second Meeting of the Secretariat Study Group on the Modernization of the Warsaw Convention System, LC/30-IP/1 of 4 February 1997 at 13.
61. See, McCarthy v. American Airlines, 32 Avi 16,472 (S.D.A.Fla 2008); see also, In re West Caribbean Airways, S.A, No. 06-22748-CIV, 2007 WL 5559325 (S.D. Fla 27 September 2007) for a more fine-tuned definition of the term contractual carrier who had engaged into charter agreement with Caribbean under which Caribbean leased its aircraft and crew to Newvac who was found to be the contractual carrier, whereas Newvac had also made a charter agreement with a travel agent, selling tickets to the passengers, and the flight was executed by Caribbean.
62. See, ICAO Legal Committee, 30th Session, LC/30-WP/4-2 of 31 January 1997 at 9.
63. See, Barthelemy Cousin and Jefferson Larue, Short Update on Use of the Montreal Convention, Association of Corporate Counsel, Lexology, 2 February 2010. See also, 'Who is a Contracting Carrier? The French Courts Decide'. Clyde & Co. Update (February 2012) commenting on Kuate v. Air France, Kenya Airways and others Paris Court of Appeals (2011) and Marsans International v. Air France Supreme Court in France (2012).
64. No. 11-md-02246-KAM, [2015] WL 328219 (S.D. Fla. 23 January 2015).
65. No. 06-CV-4589, 2008 WL 4458867 (E.D.N.Y. 29 September 2008).

responsible or liable for the actions of its principal (LIAT). Finally, the court decided that Article 36 of the Convention precluded the existence of an implied agency relationship between BWIA and LIAT. Article 36 provides that a successive carrier may be liable for an accident that occurs during another carrier's carriage, only "where, *by express agreement*, the first carrier has assumed liability for the whole journey." (*italics added*) In the present case, there was no evidence of assumption of liability.

As the theft of baggage is not an activity, which falls under the scope of the employment of an airline's employee who is an agent of the air carrier, Article 22(5) of the Montreal Convention, 1999 did not apply and claimant's damages were limited pursuant to Article 22(2).[66] Italian courts tend to treat providers of ground handling services as independent contractors rather than as agents of the carrier, thus making claims against them pursuant to international and European law inapplicable in these proceedings.[67] However, in 2016, the Italian Supreme Court changed this direction; it held that a ground handling service provider is regarded as an agent of the airline, following Article 30 of the Montreal Convention, 1999. The reasoning of this Supreme Court was among others based on the position that these service providers occupy under EU Regulation 96/67 on access to the ground-handling market at EU airports pursuant to which airlines can chose their own ground handlers.[68] Thus, a provider of ground handling services is regarded as an agent of the carrier.[69]

---

66. *See, Shah* v. *Kuwait Airways*, 653 F. Supp. 2d 499 relying on Art. 19:

> .....
>
> 2. In the carriage of baggage, the liability of the carrier in the case of destruction, loss. damage or delay is limited to 1,000 Special Drawing Rights for each passenger unless the passenger has made, at the time when the checked baggage was handed over to the carrier, a special declaration of interest in delivery at destination and has paid a supplementary sum if the case so requires. In that case the carrier will be liable to pay a sum not exceeding the declared sum, unless it proves that the sum is greater than the passenger's actual interest in delivery at destination.
>
> .....
>
> 5. The foregoing provisions of paras 1 and 2 of this Article shall not apply if it is proved that the damage resulted from an act or omission of the carrier, its servants or agents, done with intent to cause damage or recklessly and with knowledge that damage would probably result; provided that, in the case of such act or omission of a servant or agent, it is also proved that such servant or agent was acting within the scope of its employment. ...

67. *See*, IATA Liability Reporter 12 (2013), citing a case of the Milan court (Dec. no. 3405/2012)).
68. *See, SEA* v. *Ferrari SpA, KLM, Alpha Airport, Sea Handling*, Order no. 3361/2016 of the Italian Supreme Court of 19 February 2016, discussed by Laura Pierallini, *Recent Supreme Court case law regarding liability of ground handlers*, reported on 29 June 2016 on www.internationallawoffice.com, and G. Guerreri, *Air Cargo Liability Revisited in Italy*, 42(1) Air & Space Law 85–88 (2017).
69. *See, American Home Assurance* v. *Kuehne & Nagel*, 32 Avi. 16,185 (S.D.N.Y 2008), and *In re West Caribbean Airways, S.A.*, 32 Avi.15, 595 (S.D. Fla 26 September 2007), 32 Avi. 15,764 (S.D. Fla 9 Nov 2007), in which case the court of Florida dismissed the cases to Martinique (France) which is discussed in section 3.12.2, below.

3.3.2   Regulation under the Warsaw Regime

3.3.2.1   The Passenger under the Warsaw Regime

The injury or death must be sustained by a "passenger" but the Warsaw Convention has not defined the term passenger either. Hence, it is up to courts to give a definition.

The agreement with the carrier, as identified by the ticket, forms a decisive element for the identification of a person as a passenger.

3.3.2.2   Case Law on the Passenger under the Warsaw Regime

In the case of *Fellowes (or Herd) and another* v. *Clyde Helicopters Ltd.*, the relatives of a Scottish police officer who was killed on board a helicopter, which crashed during a snow storm, questioned whether the Scottish police officer had a contract of carriage with the defendant, that is, Clyde Helicopter. The police officer was found to be a passenger for the purposes of the Warsaw Convention. The UK House of Lords contended that the contract between Clyde Helicopters and the police authority, under whose authority the police officer came, was not a contract of carriage coming under the Warsaw Convention, as amended by the Hague Protocol.[70] In two Australian cases the judges arrived at a different conclusion. The persons in question were acting as 'observer' assisting the pilot, and hence, not passengers.[71]

Thus, a stowaway is not regarded as a passenger as he, or she, does not have a contract of carriage with the air carrier, nor does he have consent to be on board the aircraft, as required by the above definition of a 'passenger.'[72] Crew members on duty are not passengers but they may be considered as such when they are travelling as passengers as part of their employment, on so called 'dead heading' flights to an airport where they have to commence their duties as crew members.[73]

3.3.2.3   Regulation of the Air Carrier under the Warsaw Regime

Article 17 of the Warsaw Convention mentions the "carrier" as one of the parties to the agreement as referred to in Article 1(2) of the Convention. The question is who can be identified as a "carrier" being a party to the agreement. The Warsaw Convention does

---

70. *Fellowes (or Herd) and another* v. *Clyde Helicopters Ltd.*, Decision of the House of Lords of 27 February 1997, All England Law reports 1997 Volume 1.
71. *See, Edwards* v. *Endeavour Energy*, [2013] NSWSC 1899 [132] and *Stephenson* v. *Parkes Shire Council*, [2014] NSWSC 1758 [296].
72. *See also*, Art. 3 of MC 99, stipulating that "In respect of carriage of passengers, an individual or collective document of carriage shall be delivered ...", by the carrier. Thus, stowaways cannot claim under any of the conventions as there is no consensus made between the carrier and the passenger. We have not found case law confirming this state of affairs.
73. *See, In re Mexico City Air crash of October, 31, 1979*, 708 F.2d 400, 417–418 (9th Cir. 1983).

not define the term "carrier" but the Guadalajara Convention of 1969 does address the term, by making a distinction between "contractual carrier" and "actual carrier."[74]

Pursuant to Article 25 of the Warsaw Convention as amended and Article 22(5) of the Montreal Convention, 1999, the carrier is not entitled to rely on the provisions excluding or limiting liability if the damage is caused by the wilful misconduct of the carrier or of his agents acting within the scope of their employment.

Air carriers may include their 'servants and agents' which inclusion may have legal and other implications. While the definition of agent is a matter of national law, international law has made a contribution to its meaning as to which *see* below. For the defendant in a case governed by the Warsaw Convention, the advantage of being qualified as an agent is the protection of the liability limits. If the third party is not a servant or agent of the carrier, it stands in the same position as any other third party being sued in tort claims which may be governed by limited or unlimited liability regimes as determined by the applicable national law.

Being an *agent* of the carrier has relevance in the following situations:

- Article 20 of the Warsaw Convention, according to which the carrier is not liable if he proves that he and his agents have taken all necessary measures to avoid the damage.
- Article 25, under which wilful misconduct of an agent, acting within the scope of his or her employment, is equated with wilful misconduct of the carrier.
- The "place of business" of a carrier in the territory of a contracting state to the Warsaw Convention, may be interpreted as representing the "place of business" of an agent of the carrier, so that the court of such place of business is allowed under Article 28 of the Warsaw Convention to hear the claim.[75]
- Under code share agreements, making a distinction between the contracting carrier and the actual carrier, the actual carrier may be regarded as an "agent" of the contracting carrier; *see* next section.

Under EU Regulation 261/2004,[76] claims for damage caused by delay, denied boarding and cancellations must be exclusively directed against the *operating* carrier.

---

74. *See*, Art. I(b):

> (b) *"contracting carrier" means a person who as a principal makes an agreement for carriage governed by the Warsaw Convention with a passenger or consignor or with a person acting on behalf of the passenger or consignor;*
>
> (c) "actual carrier" means a person other than the contracting carrier, who, by virtue of authority from the contracting carrier, performs the whole or part of the carriage contemplated in paragraph (b) but who is not with respect to such part a successive carrier within the meaning of the Warsaw Convention. Such authority is presumed in the absence of proof to the contrary.

75. *See*, section 3.12.3 below.
76. *See*, section 2.2 of Chapter 5.

3.3.2.4　Case Law on the Air Carrier under the Warsaw Regime

An air carrier has been considered as *an agency of a State*.[77] This conclusion may have jurisdictional consequences because of the possible reliance of the carrier on State immunity, which the Warsaw Convention attempted to prevent by making the air carrier liable, whatever its status under national law.

According to a US District Court, an airline alliance, in the present case, the *Star Alliance*, does not qualify as a "carrier" under Article 17 of the Warsaw Convention.[78] The court found that, under this provision, a claim may be made against the actual operator of the aircraft involved in the accident, and any agent of that carrier whose conduct bears some causal connection to an accident falling under the scope of this Convention. The case formed yet another attempt to circumvent the restrictions imposed by the Warsaw Convention: a claim must be made against a carrier, pursuant to the rules established by Article 28 of this Convention. Consequently, neither Star Alliance as such, nor its creator/owner, United Airlines, could be held liable under Article 17 of the Warsaw Convention. The court recognised that a broad interpretation of the term "carrier", so as to include alliances in which the carrier involved in the accident participates, could have "profound consequences" on litigation under the Warsaw Convention. If viewed as a carrier, commercial airline alliances could be sued in the US by passengers of any participating airline for any accident coming under the said Article 17 throughout the world.[79]

The contracting carrier has been held 'vicariously' liable, that is, in tort, for negligent actions committed by the actual carrier under *code share* and *franchise agreements*. The contractual carrier is regarded as the 'principal', and the operating carrier as the 'agent' of the principal. The 'principal' airline can be held liable under tort for negligent actions of the operating carrier, acting as the agent, under an 'apparent agency' theory. Apparent agency exists when the principal airline, that is, the contracting carrier, holds out the agent, that is, the operating carrier, to the travelling public as possessing sufficient authority to act for the principal, and a third party is 'reasonably' entitled to rely on such authority of the operating carrier to act on behalf of the principal carrier. The interested third party, for instance, the passenger, could be misled while believing that there was such an agency relationship.[80] A bus company transporting passengers from the staircase of the aircraft to the terminal has been termed as an "agent" of the carrier.[81]

---

77. *See*, *Viktoriya Shirbokova* v. *CSA Czech Airlines, Inc.*, United States District Court District of Minnesota, Civil File No. 04-641, Decision of 24 August 2004.
78. *See*, *In Re Air Crash At Taipei, Taiwan, On October 31, 2000*, MDL: 1394 GAF (RCx) (C.D. Cal. 13 May 2002).
79. Reported by the newsletter of Condon and Forsyth LLP, July 2002, at 1–4; District Court of California.
80. *See*, Newsletter of Condon and Forsyth, July 2000.
81. *See*, *Yeomans* v. *Carbridge*, [2012] NSWDC 20, *see also*, section 4.1.5.

Ground handling companies may be considered agents of air carriers. *In re Air Crash at Taipei, Taiwan,* on 31 October, 2000,[82] the plaintiffs sued Singapore International Airlines (SIA) for damages resulting from an accident of that airline at Chiang Kai Chek Airport in Taiwan. At that airport, EVA Airways Corporation (EVA) was providing flight dispatch services to SIA for the flight in question at the airport of Taipei. The Court decided that EVA carried out *"essential flight services"* in *furtherance of the contract of carriage of an international flight.*[83] Thus, the court held that EVA was acting as SIA's agent and therefore entitled to the protection of WC29.

The English Court of Appeals found that the theft of bars of silver by an employee of a ground handling service provider was sufficiently closely connected to the purposes of his employment to hold the employer liable for the wrongful act of the employee.[84] Other decisions also explain that such service providers acting as employers must be vigilant to the risk of vicarious liability.[85]

An *airport security company*, assisting passengers in the process of embarkation, was *not* deemed to be an agent of the carrier for the purposes of applying the Warsaw Convention. A passenger had passed her carry-on bag containing about USD 100,000 worth of jewellery. The plaintiff sued Globe Airport Security Services and the three carriers operating out of the terminal in question. The US court agreed that the plaintiff was in the process of embarkation. In their final decision, the judges explained that Globe should not be considered an agent of the carrier (TWA) since the Warsaw Convention does not require security screenings.

According to the majority of the judges:

> [...] the services being rendered by Globe were not in furtherance of the contract of carriage for an international flight, but were basic airport security services required at all airports by domestic federal law, regardless of the flights destination and regardless of whether the person being screened was even a passenger.[86]

Aircraft overhaul and maintenance companies performing functions of the carrier are agents under the Warsaw Convention. Hence, they are protected by the liability limits. A federal court in the US dismissed claims designed to obtain punitive damages from an overhaul and maintenance company.[87]

---

82. Case No. 01-MDL-1394 (C.D. Cal. Dec 20, 2002).
83. The UNCTAD Secretariat has defined ground handlers as "Independent contractors with whom the carrier has contracted for the performance of a specific task."; *see,* UNCTAD Secretariat Report, *Carriage of Goods by Air: A Guide to the International Framework,* 40 at 158 (2006).
84. *See, Brink's Global Services Inc & Ors* v. *Igrox Ltd. & Anor,* reported in 2011 by Gates and Partners.
85. House of Lords in *Lister* v. *Hesley Hall* Ltd, and *Rustenberg Platinum Mines* v. *South African Airways.*
86. *See, Dazo* v. *Globe,* No. 00-15058, 2002 WL 1401934 (9th Cir. 1 July 2002).
87. *See, In re Air crash disaster near Peggy's Cove, Novia Scotia,* 2002 U.S. Dist. LEXIS 3308 (E.D. Pa 2002).

Travel agents or flight organisers are in most cases[88] not considered as air carriers, or as their agents.[89] If at all, they act, in fact, as agents of the passenger.[90] Interestingly, the knowledge of travel agents has been found to be imputed to carriers, which is a principal feature of an agency relationship. The courts have found that where carriage is booked through a travel agent, the knowledge of the travel agent is imputed to the carrier, such that the carrier is deemed to be aware of the other bookings.[91]

The liability of air carriers for damage which has arisen in the carriage of baggage and cargo is discussed in sections 3.10 and 3.11 below.

3.3.2.5 Lessor's Liability in Relation to the Use of the Aircraft

A US Federal Statute protects aircraft lessors from liability arising out of accidents caused by aircraft that they do not operate. This Statute reflects the principle that control and operation are essential factors in determining negligence. Under the law, owners can avoid liability if:

- the owner/lessor was not in control of the maintenance or operation of the aircraft at all relevant times leading up to the accident;
- the owner/lessor was not the employer of the operator or mechanic at fault;
- the owner/lessor had no knowledge of any dangerous condition or defect at the time control was transferred; or
- the owner/lessor did not entrust the aircraft to someone incompetent to fly it.[92]

A *lessor* can be held liable for negligent maintenance. It is generally the owner's responsibility to have a current airworthiness certificate, to maintain the aircraft and keep a record of that maintenance. However, in some lease agreements, the lessee has assumed responsibility for the safe operation and maintenance of the aircraft. Despite

---

88. But *see*, the role of Newvac which was found to be a contracting carrier, even though they effectively were only a flight organiser in *In Re West Caribbean Airways* which is discussed in section 3.12.2.
89. *See, Vaughn* v. *American Automobile Assoc.* (*AAA*), 326 F. Supp. 2d 195 (D. Mass. 2004); *see also, Sharlitt* v. *Flying Carpet*, CF 955/08, and *Iberia* v. *Dr Lorber*, CA 1346/05 (Haifa) International Law Office, contributed by Peggy Sharon and Keren Marco, www.international lawoffice.com; newsletter of 23 March 2011.
90. *See*, the website of Travelocity.com: "Welcome to the Travelocity.com website (the 'Website'). This Website is provided solely to assist customers in gathering travel information, determining the availability of travel-related goods and services, making legitimate reservations or otherwise transacting business with travel suppliers, and for no other purposes."
91. *See*, the *Haldimann* v. *Delta Airlines*, 168 F3d 1324 (1999) case cited in section 3.1.1 above.
92. 49 U.S.C. 44112(b) as confirmed in *Lu* v. *Star Marianas Air, Inc.*, No. 1:14-cv-00023, 2015 WL 2265464 and *Escobar* v. *Nevada Helicopter Leasing*, 2016 WL 3962805 (District of Hawaii, 21 July 2016).

the above Federal law, some states in the US hold lessors liable as they impose liability on owners or lessors by state law. Of those states, some limit the amount of liability that may be imposed, whereas others restrict liability only to non-passive owners,[93] that is, at any case, operators of the aircraft or by application of vicarious liability.

In 2000, an Air Philippines flight crashed during a domestic flight in the Philippines killing 124 passenger and seven crew members. Air Philippines could not be sued in the US, but the previous lessor/owner of the aircraft, AAR Parts Trading, and the lessor owner at the time of crash, Fleet Business Creditor, could. In this case, the claimants put forward that the law of the state of Illinois, where the lessors were based, and case law made in other states, did not prevent them claiming damages against their lessors.[94] When the court had decided that that Federal law of the US did not pre-empt the application of the state law of Illinois, and that hence, the lessor of the aircraft in question was not necessarily protected by Federal law, the case was settled out of court.[95]

3.3.2.6 Concluding Remarks

While neither the term passenger nor the term carrier have been defined under the Warsaw Convention or the Montreal Convention, the latter term has given rise to quite some case law, especially under the Warsaw Convention. A central question concerned the position of the agent in relation of that of the carrier. Case law has helped to clarify this relationship.

It cannot be excluded that in the future claimants look for other liable persons than the contractual or operating air carrier. Alliances and lessors have been sued as defendants in accidents involving the operation of aircraft, with a varying degree of result. Another potentially liable party is the manufacturer of the aircraft who has also been taken to court in aviation accident cases. However, the principle of exclusivity which will be discussed in the next section may prevent claimants from successfully litigating against those third parties. However, exclusivity does not prevent claimants from successfully litigating against third parties as it is argued that exclusivity applies only to carriers and their agents.[96]

---

93. *See also*, www.trial-law.com/aop/liability-of-aircraft-lessors#sthash.uQuczI3Q.dpuf.
94. On the theory of negligent entrustment.
95. No. 00 L 9599 (Il Cook Co. Cir.); *see also*, *Vreeland* v. *Ferrer*, Supreme Court of Florida, No. SC10–694; decision of 8 July 2011. *See*, however, *In re Lawrence W. Inlow Litigation*, 2001 U.S. Dist. LEXIS 2747 (S.D. Ind. 2001: "Federal common law generally does not provide a remedy for those injured in aircraft accidents. The word 'only' could have effect only if the statute preempts claims against lessors arising under state law.", and *Matei* v. *Cessna Aircraft*, 35 Fed. 3d 1142 (Fed. Cir. 1994). Affirmed in *Lu* v. *Star Marianas Air*, No. 1:14-cv-00023, 2015 WL 2265464 (D.N. Mar.I. 12 May 2015).
96. *See*, Peter Neenan, *The Effectiveness of the Montreal Convention as a Channelling Tool Against Carriers*, XI(1) The Aviation and Space Journal, January/March 2012.

3.4 Right of Action of the Claimant

3.4.1 The Concept of Exclusivity under Private International Air Law

A cause or right of action is an enforceable right under the applicable legal regime on the basis of evidence, indicating circumstances recognised by that law to create such a right for the plaintiff's benefit. The cause of action is especially relevant in common law jurisdictions. The legal basis of the action plays a far less dominant role in civil law countries, including France. In *civil law* countries, the legal basis of the action will be the *contract of carriage* as embodied by the ticket or the air waybill.

Liability of the carrier arises when he has not fulfilled his obligations under the contract. Otherwise, as under the Warsaw Convention, 1929, the Montreal Convention is "self-executing and creates a private right of action" in States recognising this self-executing effect.[97]

This section considers the application of the Montreal Convention to actions presented against the air carrier. Liability of other parties comes into play when such parties are not agents of the air carrier as discussed in sections 3.3.1.2 and 3.3.2.3 above, and in Chapter 8 on *Product Liability* and Chapter 9 on *Surface Damage*.

3.4.2 Exclusivity under the Montreal Convention, 1999

Where the Montreal Convention, 1999 is applicable to the carriage pursuant to Article 1, the carrier is either liable in accordance with the terms of the Convention or not liable at all. Otherwise said, when the Montreal Convention is applicable to the carriage in question but the liability rules as laid down in Articles 17–19 do not give rise to the liability of the carrier, the carrier is not liable, under that Convention or under domestic law.

The cause of an accident can lie with the aircraft manufacturer, the ATC agency or other third parties involved in commercial aviation. The drafters of the Article 29 of the Montreal Convention have chosen yet again for a regime based on exclusivity because Article 29 contains the *exclusive* legal basis of claims brought by a claimant against the carrier, including in respect of time limits.[98] This provision confirms the situation under Article 24 of the Warsaw Convention as to which *see* the next section. Hence, on questions regarding the conditions of international carriage by air and the liability of the carrier, there is no choice of law as the Montreal Convention, 1999 dictates the law. This Convention is designed to avoid conflict of laws, which may arise in other areas of private international law where the rules of such an area have not been unified.

---

97. *See*, Baah v. *Virgin Atlantic Airways Limited*, 2007 WL422993 (S.D.N.Y. 2007).
98. *See*, AIG *Property & Casualty* v. *Federal Express*, No. 15-cv-6316, 2016 WL 305053 (S.D.N.Y., 25 January 2016).

3.4.3   Case Law under the Montreal Convention, 1999

Thus, any action for damages, however founded, whether under the Convention or in contract or in tort or otherwise, can only be brought subject to the conditions as set out in the Convention.[99] A landmark case of 2014 concerned the language question spelled out in the case of *Thibodau* v. *Air Canada* which was handled by the Supreme Court of Canada.[100] Mr and Mrs Thibodau had complained about airline services which ought to be provided in two languages, that is, English and French, whereas the said on board services were rendered in English language only. The Supreme Court decided in favour of the airline and the exclusivity of the Montreal Convention by ruling that those damages did not fall under those which were protected by the Montreal Convention and this on an exclusive basis. Other than the CJEU in 261 claims, this court does not differentiate between 'damages' and 'damages'.[101]

An English court also affirmed the exclusivity principle in a dispute over injury suffered due to miss representation of a seat type on a particular service. The English court held that, pursuant to its Article 29, MC99 provided the claimant sole and exclusive cause of action and remedy in respect of any claim for loss, injury or damage sustained during the course of or arising out of international carriage by air. The court noted that:

> [...] whilst a conclusion which leaves the claimant without a remedy for an undoubted wrong is unattractive to those steeped in the common law, that conclusion is the result of a balance struck by the high contracting parties in the interest of certainty and uniformity.[102]

---

99. As confirmed in *Matz* v. *NorthWest Airlines*, No. 07-134447, 2008 WL 2064800 (E.D. Mich., 13 May 2008); *see also, Gubay* v. *South African Airways*, decision of the Manchester County Court, UK of 28 January 2008 (unreported); *Schaeffer-Condulmar* v. *US Airways*, (2009 WL 4729882; E.D.Pa 8 December 2008) addressing the split authority in the lower courts as to where the Montreal Convention completely pre-empts state law claims (answer in the affirmative); *Smith* v. *American Airlines* (Civ No. C 09-02903, 2009 WL 3072449 (N.D. Cal. 22 September 2009)); *Masudi* v. *Brady Cargo Services*, No. 12-CV-2391, 2014 WL 4416502 (E.D.N.Y. 8 September 2014); *Edem* v. *Ethiopian Airlines* (2009 WL 4639393 (E.D.N.Y. 30 September 2009)) in which certain claims were barred because Ethiopian Airlines was 'protected' under the Foreign Sovereign Immunities Act (FSIA) as a wholly government owned foreign company, and, in Canada: *O'Mara* v. *Air Canada*, 2013 ONSC 2931 (CanLII) in which the Ontario Supreme Court confirmed the exclusivity. In a case which was unrelated to MC99, namely, *Kuwait Airways* v. *Republic of Iraq*, (2010 SCC 40) the Canadian Supreme Court unanimously allowed a claim by Kuwait Airways against the Republic of Iraq to enforce a judgment of the English courts against the latter, despite the assertion of sovereign immunity, where the acts complained of consisted of the seizure of aircraft of the former by Iraqi Airways Company during the 1990 Gulf War. The Canadian Supreme Court found that Iraq had funded, controlled and supervised the litigation on behalf of Iraqi Airways, and that this involvement by Iraq fell within the 'commercial activity' exception to the international law doctrine of State immunity. The Court decided that, even though the original appropriation of the aircraft by Iraqi Airways Company was a sovereign act, the subsequent retention and use of the aircraft by Iraqi Airways Company constituted commercial acts and thus fell within an exception to the claim for sovereign immunity.
100. Decision of 28 October, 2014, 2014 SCC 67.
101. *See*, paras 80–82 of the *Thibodeau* decision.
102. *See, Gubay* v. *SSA*, decision of 28 January 2008, Manchester Country Court, UK; for a cargo case *see, Eli Lilly* v. *Air Express International USA*, 602 F. Supp.2d 1260 (S.D.Fla 10 March

In another case, the defendant airline had refused to admit a passenger because the airline felt that the passenger's picture was not the same as in the passport. Since the plaintiff did not base her claim on delay but on non-performance of the contract, the Montreal Convention did not apply.[103] On the other hand, in a US case, the court held that a claim based on denied boarding following a misinterpretation of the immigration requirements in the country of destination by the employees of the air carrier was pre-empted, and exclusively governed by the delay provisions of MC99.[104]

In *Tony Hook* v. *British Airways Plc*,[105] the English High Court ruled that disabled passengers cannot rely on EU Regulation 1107/2006 concerning the rights of disabled persons when travelling by air, to claim for hurt feelings after the carrier allegedly failed to make reasonable efforts to accommodate his seating requirements. The Court held that the Convention prescribes the only circumstances in which a carrier is liable for damages arising out of international carriage by air, and that the EU Regulation does not create a private law cause of action for damages. This is also true for discrimination cases which are pre-empted by the exclusivity principle as they are based on state law, and not on the Montreal Convention.[106]

A passenger who was injured during a transfer in Paris as a consequence of her falling from the van carrying her while being assisted by an employee of Passerelle, a local company engaged by Air France to assist passengers requiring wheelchair assistance, based a claim against Passerelle on domestic law. However, the event causing the injury occurred during the process of disembarkation, so that compensation could only be sought from Air France pursuant to the Montreal Convention, and not from Passerelle.[107]

A Tel Aviv Court argued that the exclusivity of MC99 does not rule out claims against a third party based on causes of action outside this Convention, in this case against Israel Airport Authority.[108]

However, *non-performance of the contract* does not pre-empt claims under local or state law. In this case the airline had failed to perform its obligation to perform

---

2009); *Garissi* v. *Northwest Airlines*, 2010 WL 3702374; *Magissano* v. *Skyservice Airlines*, 2010 ONSC 6203 and 7169. *See also, McAuley* v. *Aer Lingus Limited & Others* [2011] IEHC 89; *see also, Bridgeman* v. *United Continental Holding*, No. 4:12-cv-2848, 2012 WL 5989209 (S.D. Tex. Nov 29 2012) in which the court also held, that as a general rule, a claim for damages, arising out of the handling of baggage on an international flight, is preempted by the Montreal Convention, 1999.

103. *See, Kamanou-Goune* v. *Swiss International Airlines*, 2009 WL 8746000 (S.D.N.Y 27 March 2009).

104. *See, Lee* v. *AMR Corporation*, 36 Avi. 16,577 (E.D.Pa 2015).

105. [2011] EWHC 379 (QB).

106. *See, Naqvi* v. *Turkish Airlines*, No. 04-01066 (RJL), 2015 WL 757198 (D.D.C., 25 February 2015).

107. *See, Moss* v. *Delta Air Lines Inc.*, et al., Avi Cas. (CCH) 17,417 (N.D. Georgia, 31 January 2006).

108. *See, Goldrey* v. *Israel Airport Authority* (CF 5426-05-14. Goldrey sustained bodily injury while passing through the jet bridge. In *Batteries 'R' Us* v. *Fega Express, et al.*, (No.15-21507-CIV, 2015 WL 4549497 (S.D. Fla., 27 July 2015) the court found that the loss of the cargo had arisen during the period covered by "carriage by air" as formulated in Art. 18(1) MC99, confirming the exclusivity of this convention with respect to the claim.

carriage between Paris and New York under the contract.[109] In other cases US courts held that MC99 pre-empts contract claims that are indistinguishable from plaintiff's tort claims, however artfully pleaded, to avoid the application of this Convention.[110]

US courts decided that, in one of the plaintiff's state law claims for breach of contract involving compensation under EU Regulation 261/2004, the suit did not fall under the exclusivity of the Montreal Convention as this Convention does not pre-empt a breach of contract claim.[111] It mattered whether the carriers had (Iberia and the other EU airlines) or had not (British Airways, the US carriers) provided express reference to '261' compensation in their conditions of carriage as published on their websites. That is why British Airways could rely on pre-emption of the claim made by the passenger but Lufthansa could not. A similar approach – with respect to pre-emption – was adopted in the rulings concerning Continental and Delta.

In the *Giannopolous* procedure, two passengers also made claims for damages occasioned by delay against Iberia under '261'. Iberia tried to resist these claims by referring to the exclusivity of the Montreal Convention forbidding under Article 29 award of non-compensatory damages. However, as the delays were based on objective criteria such as length of the flight and length of delay, and the compensation was compensatory in nature rather than punitive, the court decided that there was no conflict with Article 29.

A Canadian Court observed that not all causes of action against an air carrier are subject to the provisions of the Montreal Convention, 1999. For instance, a claim arising from 'overbooking' does not concern the international carriage by air. Instead, the Court opined that this Convention should be interpreted "restrictively" creating room for the application of local law.[112]

Furthermore, a US court held that Article 29 of the Montreal Convention establishes that "not all damages actions involving the carriage of passengers, baggage

---

109. See, *Mullaney* v. *Delta Air Lines*, Civ No. 7324, 2009 WL 1584899 (S.D.N.Y. June 3, 2009); in *Nankin* v. *Continental Airlines* (2010 WL 342632 (C.D.Cal. 29 January 2010), the court also held that the Montreal Convention did not apply as this case was not based on the terms of the Montreal Convention but on non-performance of the contract. See also, *El-Zoobi* v. *United Airlines*, 2016 WL 868874 (Ill. App. Ct. 3 March 2016) in which an FAA officer relied on state law because of "tortious interference with a business relationship and intentional infliction of emotional distress", and *Benjamin* v. *American Airlines*, 32 F. Supp. 3d 1309 (S.D. Ga. 9 July 2014) dealing with breach of contract-based claims, which were not pre-empted by the Convention.

110. See, *Dogbe* v. *Delta Airlines*, 969 F.Supp.2d 261, 275 (E.D.N.Y. 2013 – breach of contract claims based on the same facts as the tort claim); *King* v. *American Airlines*, 284 F.3d 352, 356-57 (2d. Cir. 2002), in which the plaintiff's contract claim could not be distinguished from discrimination claims; and *Carey* v. *United Airlines*, 255 F.3d 1044, 1052–1053 (9th Cir. 2001) in which claims for emotional distress were combined with breach of contract claims arising from the same accident. For a cargo delay case see, *AGC* v. *Centurion Air Cargo*, 37 Avi. 17,242 (S.D.Fl. 2015).

111. See the 'Polinovski' cases against British Airways and Lufthansa (No. 1:11-cv-00779, 780), *Giannopoulos* v. *Iberia* (No. 1:11-cv-00775), *Volodarskiy* v. *Delta* (No. 1:11-cv-00782), *Gurevich* v. *Alitalia* (No. 1:11-cv-01890), *Lozano* v. *United Continental Holding* (No. 1:11-cv-08258), and *Bergman* v. *United Airlines* (No. 1:11-cv-07040).

112. See, *Carter* v. *Air Canada*, 2010 QCCQ 7590 decided by the court of Quebec; see also, *Hoffman* v. *Alitalia*, No. 14-5201, 2015 WL 1954461 (D.N.J., 28 April 2015), denying complete pre-emption of local laws in a case involving loss of baggage.

and cargo arise under the Convention."[113] The actions were based upon the California Civil Rights Act, breach of and interference with contract, defamation and intentional infliction of emotional distress. This statement can be difficultly rhymed with the language of the cited provision, as interpreted by other courts, and with the fact that a treaty which has been ratified by the US Congress superseding domestic laws on contract and tort. However, in another case the claim for emotional distress based on state law was dismissed because of the exclusivity of MC99.[114]

Latin American courts may adopt a broader interpretation of the exclusivity concept under the Warsaw/Hague Convention.[115] These courts follow that line of reasoning under MC99, at least as far as the Brazilian Supreme Court believes that the provisions of the Consumer Defence Code ought to prevail over the provisions of international treaties. In two other cases,[116] the defendant airlines, namely, Air France and Air Canada, argue that this approach infringes the Constitution of Brazil which states that international treaties have priority over domestic law. However, on 25 May 2017, the Brazilian Supreme Federal Tribunal decided in favour of the application of the Warsaw/Montreal regime in these cases.[117]

In short, it is difficult to signal an unequivocal trend to honour the exclusivity of MC99, even with the single jurisdiction of the United States where state courts have rendered different and sometimes even conflicting decisions on this question. The domestic regulations on which the claim is built in conjunction with the facts of the case and the interpretation of these two by the court will determine the outcome.

3.4.4 Regulation under the Warsaw Regime

Where the Warsaw regime is applicable to the carriage pursuant to Article 1 of either Convention, the carrier is liable in accordance with the terms of the Convention, or not liable at all. This state of affairs is confirmed under Article 24 of the Warsaw Convention.

Hence, on questions regarding the conditions of international carriage by air and the liability of the carrier, the Warsaw regime exclusively dictates the law. The Montreal Convention, 1999, thus maintained the exclusivity concept elaborated under the Warsaw Convention, 1929, and as explained in case law.[118]

---

113. See, Serrano v. American Airlines, 32 Avi. 16,385 (C.D. Calif. 2008).
114. See, Seshadri v. British Airways, 747 F.3d 1125, 1127 (9th Cir. 2014).
115. See, Sergio da Silva Couto v. Iberia (1996), reported in Clyde & Co Newsletter, February 2015, at 1.
116. See, Sylvia Regina de Moraes Rosolem v. Société Air France, and Cintia Cristina Giardulli v. Air Canada.
117. Reported by Clyde&Co, Insight/Update of 26 May 2017.
118. The wording was adjusted by the discussions at the Guatemala City Conference held in 1971, as to which see the end of section 3.5.2.3, which gave rise to the Guatemala City Protocol. At that Conference the wording now seen in the Montreal Convention was agreed, and the parties initially suggested the following wording: "The liability of the carrier as established under Articles 17 to 22 of this Convention shall be the sole and exclusive liability of the carrier under all circumstances in respect of damages arising out of an event giving rise to liability for the death or injury or delay of a person." The effect of this wording was understood at Guatemala

The conditions for liability under the Warsaw regime are that:

(1) the passenger is involved in international transportation by air, within the scope of Article 1 of this Convention, when the accident giving rise to the claim takes place;
(2) the accident causing the injury occurs during the course of embarkation and disembarkation or on board the aircraft, as formulated by Article 17;
(3) the accident causes a bodily injury to the passenger, as opposed to a purely mental injury.

If condition 1 is met, but either condition 2 or 3 is not, then the air carrier has no liability under the convention so the passengers are not entitled to rely on local or national law by virtue of the exclusivity of the convention as foreseen by Article 24 of the convention.

3.4.5 Case Law on Exclusivity under the Warsaw Convention, 1929

The highest courts in the UK, Canada, New Zealand, Singapore and India have also confirmed the exclusivity of the Warsaw Convention.[119] Such courts have held that the Warsaw Convention, as amended, pre-empts discrimination claims as well as based on, for instance, tort or illicit act.[120]

A leading case is *Sidhu v. British Airways*,[121] in which BA passengers made claims for damages occurred due to alleged negligence while in transit on a BA flight at Kuwait Airport. The plaintiffs claimed that the Iraqi government on 2 August 1990, on the day of the Iraqi invasion of Kuwait, unlawfully detained them. The question was whether the Warsaw Convention applied. The plaintiffs stated that their cause of action did not fall within Article 17 of the Warsaw Convention, which provided the only possible relevant claim under it. The plaintiffs argued that because:

City where, in response to a concern that, "...the Conference was more interested in protecting the carrier than in protecting others against whom suits might be brought as a result of the death or injury of a passenger...", raised by the Delegate of the United States of America, the Delegate of the People's Republic of the Congo stated: "No doubt one day there would be a Convention protecting the aircraft manufacturer. Meanwhile the conference was being asked to protect the carrier."

119. *See also*, the Rishon Le Zion Magistrates' Court, Israel, in *Sharlitt v. Flying Carpet*, CF 955/08, and *Iberia v. Dr Lorber*, CA 1346/05 (Haifa) International Law Office, contributed by Peggy Sharon and Keren Marco, www.internationallawoffice.com; newsletter of 23 March 2011.
120. *See also*, *Gibbs v. American Airlines*, 191 F. Supp. 2d 144 (D.D.C. 2002), and: *Watson v. American Airlines* [2002 U.S. Dist. LEXIS 11143 (D. Md. 2002)], in which case the court dismissed a claim concerning food poising, based on domestic law, because the Warsaw Convention pre-empts such claims.
121. 1 Aviation and Space Law Reports 217–219 (1994); the decision was confirmed in 1997 by the House of Lords as to which see 1 All ER 193 (1997). The National Consumer Disputes Redressal Commission of India followed the line of reasoning in a hijacking case which had occurred in 1999; *see*, *Indian Airlines Ltd.*, v. *Ashok Gupta & Anor* [30 April 2015], National Consumer Disputes Redressal Commission, New Delhi, No. 189 of 2009.

- bodily injury does not provide for compensation of mental injury; and
- there was no accident in the meaning of this provision.

Consequently, the plaintiffs concluded that the Warsaw Convention did not cover their claim. However, the judge in this case held in unambiguous terms that: "[...] it matters not whether the plaintiff brings his claim in contract..., or in tort, as in the present case..." and that "[...] the plaintiffs have no rights save under the Convention."

A French Court of Appeal confirmed that the liability of the air carrier can only be based upon the provisions of the Warsaw Convention. Consequently, an action against the travel agent designed to recover damages as a result of loss of baggage with a reference to domestic law for this purpose cannot be recognised.[122]

The tendency in US courts seems to be that the need for uniformity is a powerful argument for the exclusive applicability of the Warsaw Convention, in so far as the substance of the legal relationship between carrier and passenger/consignor is concerned.[123] In 1999, the US Supreme Court reached the following position in the *El Al Israel Airlines Ltd* v. *Tseng* case:

> [...] the Warsaw Convention precludes a passenger from maintaining an action for personal injury damages under local law when her claim does not satisfy the conditions of liability under the convention.[124]

Because the plaintiff, who had already checked in for the flight, could not convincingly argue that he found himself in the process of embarkation, Article 17 of the Warsaw Convention, 1929, did not apply. Consequently, his state claims against the defendant were not pre-empted by the exclusivity of WC29.[125]

In *Blansett* v. *American Airlines*, in which case the spouse of an injured passenger claimed loss of consortium under the law of Texas, the court decided that the Warsaw Convention does not pre-empt claims pertaining to loss of consortium brought under the law of Texas. The plaintiff relied on Article 24 of the Convention, which rules that the convention does not regulate who may bring lawsuit. The court decided in favour of the plaintiff, and dismissed the argument made by Continental Airlines based on the exclusivity of the Warsaw Convention.[126]

---

122. *See, Cour d'appel de Colmar*, Decision of 30 June 2005, Revue française de droit aérien et spatial 345–352 (2005).
123. *See also, Air Disaster at Lockerbie, Scotland, on 21 December 1988*, cited by Shawcross and Beaumont, *Air Law* VII/72.
124. 1999 Westlaw 7724 of 12 January 1999. This decision has been confirmed by various court decisions, including *Miller* v. *Continental Airlines*, 260 F.Supp. 2d 931 (N.D. Cal. 2003), *In re Air Crash at Belle Harbour, New York, on November 12, 2001*, 2003 WL 21032034 (S.D.N.Y 2003) and *Scully* v. *American Airlines*, in appeal from a Kentucky state court. The following was cited: "the passenger is bound by the Warsaw Convention where he was aware of the international character of the flight, even though he was injured on the domestic portion of the flight." *See also, Murillo* v. *American Airlines*, No. 09-22894-Civ, 2010 WL 1740710 (S.D. Fla, 29 April 2010).
125. *See, Hunter* v. *Lufthansa and Etihad Airlines*, 863 F. Supp. 2d 190 (E.D.N.Y. 202).
126. 204 F. Supp. 2d 999 (S.D. Tex. 2002).

The case made in Massachusetts, US, has been criticised.[127] The accident had taken place on an escalator in a terminal building while the passenger was changing gate and aircraft. The Court found that the accident did not occur 'during any of the operations of embarking or disembarking' under Article 17 of the Warsaw Convention,[128] leaving the door open for claims based upon domestic law.

'Complete non-performance of the contract', or cases where the airline has 'flatly refused to transport' a claimant, rather than "delay in transportation" may trigger non-applicability of the Warsaw or Montreal Conventions.[129] The facts of the case must show whether or not the contract for the carriage by air has been performed, or has been begun to be performed. If so, the Warsaw or Montreal Convention provides the exclusive cause of action for the passenger.

In 2011, *Sewer v. Liat, Ltd.*, a Court found that the Warsaw Convention pre-empted the plaintiff's discrimination claim.[130] The Court noted that every court which has considered if discrimination claims are pre-empted under the Warsaw Convention has confirmed that they are pre-empted, and thereby rejected the claim.[131]

Disabled passengers complaining of discriminatory behaviour of the airline in this regard are not entitled to rely on the provisions of the Warsaw Convention on the basis that the conduct of the airline has a discriminatory nature, with the result that they suffer personal injury. The following conclusion was reached in this respect by a US Court:

> Tseng and the courts which have addressed whether its teachings apply to federal discrimination claims focus on the Convention's goal of providing a comprehensive scheme of liability to endure predictability to signatories, and the goal of generally restricting the types of actions for damages which may be brought to ensure uniformity.[132]

Certain Latin American courts, especially in Brazil and Argentina, adopt a broader if not too broad interpretation of the exclusivity concept. For instance, the Federal Supreme Court of Brazil held in 2006 that award of moral damages in relation to delay of baggage is not limited by the ceiling set by the Warsaw Convention/Hague

---

127. By George N. Tompkins, in 32(3) Air & Space Law 226–227 (2007).
128. *See, Dick* v. *American Airlines, Inc.*, 31 Avi. 18, 636.
129. *See, Mizyed* v. *Delta Airlines*, No. 12-382 2012, WL 1672810 (E.D. La 14 May 2012).
130. For another discrimination claim which has been dismissed, *see, Salamey* v. *American Airlines*, No. 8:11 – cv – 2354, 2011 WL 5445129 (M.D. Fla 9 November 2011).
131. *See*, Civil Action No.: 04-76,2011 WL 635292 (D.VI. 16 February 2011).
132. *See, Waters* v. *The Port Authority of New York and New Jersey*, 158 F. Supp. 2d 415 (D.C.N.J 2001) at 430, as well as *Turturro* v. *Continental Airlines*, 128 F. Supp. 2d. at 180; H.R. Conf. Rep. No. 106-513, 2000 U.S.C.C.A.N. 80 § 128; *McIntyre* v. *City and County of San Francisco*. 2001 U.S.C. Dist. LEXIS 16944 (N.D. Cal. 12 October 2001); *DeGirolamo* v. *Alitalia-Linee Aeree Italiane*, S.p.A *and Continental Airlines*, Inc., 159 F. Supp. 2d 764 (D. N.J. 2001); *Glatfelter* v. *Delta Air Lines, Inc.*, 2002 Ga. App. LEXIS 30 (3d. Div 14 January 2002), in which case the court found that a delay of 15 to 20 minutes, caused by Delta's failure to provide wheelchair assistance to the passenger, as a consequence of which plaintiff missed a connecting flight, did not constitute a discriminatory act under US law.

Protocol. Brazilian courts prefer to apply the Consumer Defence Code rather than international airline liability agreements.[133]

3.4.6 Concluding Remarks

The concept of exclusivity is a principal pillar of the Warsaw and Montreal Conventions as it is designed to contribute to the unification of private international air law. Without it, their provisions would be explained without observing the uniform rules established by these conventions. In the light of the complexity of aviation cases, claimants benefit from a system of 'channelled liability' through the carrier, based on transparent criteria. However, these Conventions also contain limitations in terms of liability ceilings, time bars for legal procedures and the establishment of liability in case of accidents only. Moreover, the exclusivity of these conventions prevent passengers from choosing other avenues of liability, be it that courts are opening doors for these.

The scope of this concept cannot be easily determined. Claimants try to argue their cases under domestic law, or find other defendants than the air carrier, in order to escape the limitations set by the Warsaw and Montreal Conventions. However, the discussions held before the coming into being of the Guatemala City Protocol may indicate that the Montreal Convention was never intended to govern the relationship between a passenger and a manufacturer/other third party in which case a passenger has a right to bring a claim against any third party whose responsibility is involved with the cause of the damage, on the basis of breach of duty.

Thus, manufacturers and lessors have been sued for passenger claims with different degrees of success. Regretfully, those developments contribute to the carving out of this legal concept, and thus to the unification of this branch of law.

The tendency in United States courts seems to be that the need for uniformity is a powerful argument for the exclusive applicability of the Warsaw and Montreal Conventions, in so far as the substance of the legal relationship between carrier and passenger/consignor is concerned.[134] This logic has not been followed in other jurisdictions. Notable exceptions are Latin American courts, courts in the Philippines[135] and the Court of Justice of the EU, when testing the relationship between EU Regulation 261/2004 against these basic concepts of private international air law as to which *see* section 2.2 in Chapter 5.

---

133. *See, Sergio da Silva Couto* v. *Iberia* (1996), reported in Clyde & Co Newsletter, February 2015, at 1.
134. *See also, Air Disaster at Lockerbie, Scotland, on 21 December 1988,* cited by Shawcross and Beaumont, *Air law* VII/72.
135. The Supreme Court of the Philippines has chosen the same approach towards the limited scope of the exclusivity concept of the Warsaw Convention by holding that physical injuries and economic losses were exclusively governed by this Convention, but damages caused by humiliation are not. Hence, such damages should be awarded by virtue of local law, so that the time limit of two years within which an action must be brought before a court does not apply to claims for compensation of these damages; *see, Philippine Airlines* v. *Simplicio Griño,* G.R. No. 149547, 4 July 2008.

3.5 From Limited to Unlimited Liability, and Basis of Liability

3.5.1 *Towards Unlimited Liability under the Montreal Convention, 1999*

3.5.1.1 *The Establishment of a Two Tier Regime of Liability*

As proven in practice, it had become clear that unlimited liability is an achievable aim, also in terms of insurability. A treaty-defined, carrier-paid cover, which is not related to any monetary limit, is laid down in the Convention. Moreover, the term 'unlimited' liability could be misleading: liability is limited to the extent of *proven* and *recoverable* damages which are subject to different bases of liability. Since aviation accidents are often complex and involve technical difficulties, a presumed fault liability could be said to be preferable to fault liability, for the purpose of protecting consumer's interests, and limiting protracted court cases. This choice is also justified by a lack of access to evidence for passengers as a consequence of the regime set up by Annex 13 of ICAO.[136] The liability regime laid down in MC99, based on strict liability and presumed fault liability, meets this point.

Article 21 creates a *two-tier* liability system of compensation with a first tier up to 100,000, now, that is, until 2019,[137] 113,100 SDR, based on strict liability and a second tier starting at 113,100 SDR in which the carrier, it so chooses, may opt to avoid liability for such proven damages in excess of 113,100 SDRs by proving that the damage was not due to the negligence of the carrier or that the damage was solely due to the negligence of a third part for which the carrier is not responsible. The burden of proof has been placed on the carrier.

The passenger/claimant never has to prove fault of any kind to recover the proven damages sustained as a result of the bodily injury caused by the accident under Article 17 of the Montreal Convention. However, the carrier may choose to rely on one of the defences in order to escape liability for amounts above 113,100 SDRs. These defences, that are explained in the next section, are rarely invoked by the carrier, that is, principally the second defence mentioned under b) in the next section pertaining to the negligence of the passenger. Hence, assuming that all the requirements of Article 17 are met, if the damage claims is for 113,100 SDRs or less there is no defence to the liability of the carrier.

3.5.1.2 *Defences of the Carrier*

In order to escape the application of the *second* tier of liability, that is, for amounts exceeding 113,000 SDR, the carrier has to prove either that:

(a) such damage was not due to the negligence or other wrongful act or omission of the carrier or its servants or agents; or

---

136. *See*, section 5.1 of Chapter 6.
137. *See also*, ICAO Council – 188th session, C-WP/13478, 7/10/09; pursuant to Art. 24 of the Convention.

(b) such damage was solely due to the negligence or other wrongful act or omission of a third party, including that of the victim.[138]

Defence (a) could be met if the carrier proves force majeure which is generally difficult to prove in practice even with environmental events like storms and lightning because an aircraft is equipped with weather radar technology which could be used by the pilot to avoid the storm; failure to do so constitutes negligence. Likewise, it is doubtful whether the carrier can successfully rely on force majeure in case of terrorist attacks, where arguments can be raised about the security protocols for placing a bomb on board bomb or the route chosen as to which see the MH17 scenario where the aircraft was hit by an external missile.[139] A mechanical problem is not an event qualifying as force majeure in light of an airline's obligation to maintain its aircraft.[140] Defence (b) seems more unlikely to be invoked separately in many occasions, since the word "solely" would force the carrier to prove full negligence of a third party. Hence, failing such proof by the carrier, it is liable for all proven damages sustained by the passenger as a result of the death or bodily injury caused by such an accident. The carrier will very rarely rely on this defence in practice.

Carriers can invoke the defence of *contributory negligence* against claims arising under Article 21, both for claims up to 113,100 SDRs and for claims exceeding that amount (*see*, Article 20). Reference is made to case law coming under the Warsaw Convention, 1929, as discussed in section .3.5.2.3., below.

3.5.1.3 Insurance

A novelty in a treaty on the contractual liability of the air carrier is the mandatory insurance requirement for carriers covering their liability under the Convention.[141] The introduction of insurance provisions is not a novelty in private international air law treaties. The Rome Convention on *Damage Caused by Foreign Aircraft to Third Parties on the Surface* of 1952 is indeed designed to regulate requirements as to insurance. The Rome Convention of 1952 replaced the Rome Convention of 1933 and the Brussels Insurance Protocol of 1933.[142]

EU Regulations 785/2004 and 1008/2008 on air carrier licensing refer to insurance requirements to be imposed by the licensing EU Member States.[143] They must set

---

138. *See* Art. 20 of the Montreal Convention; thought could be given to situations in which a passenger drops luggage on his/her own head, he/she slips on the carpet, or drops boiling coffee on him/herself.
139. *See*, section 3.3.7.1.of Chapter 1.
140. *See, Mohammad* v. *Air Canada*, 2010 QCCQ 6858.
141. *See*, Art. 50.
142. *See* Chapter 9 on Surface damage; *see also*, the reference to EU Regulation 785/2004 in section 3.5.1.3 above.
143. *See* EU Regulation 785/2004 *on insurance requirements for air carriers and aircraft operators*, and Art. 11 of EU Regulation 1008/2008: "Notwithstanding Regulation (EC) No. 785/2004, an air carrier shall be insured to cover liability with respect to mail." According to Art. 2(10) of the same Regulation, and 'air carrier' means "an air transport undertaking with a valid operating license." *See also*, section 3.2.1 of Chapter 3.

conditions for insurance requirements. EU Regulation 785/2004 also applies to non-EU air carriers when flying from, into or through the EU.[144]

3.5.2 Limited Liability Regime under the Warsaw Regime

3.5.2.1 Reasons for Limitation

The Warsaw Convention sets limits of liability for passenger damage at 125,000 Gold francs, which amount was doubled under the Hague Protocol to 250,000 Gold francs. Two further clarifications were introduced into Article 22. *First*, the liability limits as foreseen by the Warsaw Convention as amended by The Hague Protocol, do not include the costs of the litigation, i.e., the costs of the court and other legal fees. *Second*, the conversion of gold francs into national currency was to be determined according to the value of gold at the date of the judgment, as to which see the last sentence of Article 22(5) of the Warsaw Convention. It remains an open question whether or not this is meant to refer to the official value of gold or to the market value of gold. When the Hague Protocol was established, the distinction between the two values did not yet exist.

The Warsaw Convention does not impose a compulsory insurance upon the carrier or the operator of the airline. Compulsory insurance was too great an obstacle for many countries, and prevented them from ratifying the mentioned Rome Convention of 1933.

Next to reasons for limitation of liability set out in section 1, above, it was anticipated that limited liability would speed up the settlement of claims. This also had the advantage that negative publicity would be avoided.[145] While the carrier was given the protection of limitation of liability, the passenger and the shipper of goods are granted reversal of burden proof. Once an accident has occurred, under the circumstances indicated in the Warsaw Convention, the carrier is presumed to be liable,[146] unless it can prove that it has taken all measures to avoid the damage, or that it was impossible for him to take such measures.[147] Case law under the Warsaw regime focuses on ways and means to break these limits, either by proving wilful misconduct on the part of the carrier,[148] or by putting forward that a ticket had not been issued.[149]

---

144. *See*, Art. 2(1) of Regulation 785/2004: "This Regulation shall apply to all air carriers and to all aircraft operators flying within, into, out of, or over the territory of a Member State to which the Treaty applies." (*italics added*)
145. *See also*, H. Drion, *Limitations of Liabilities in International Air Law* 12–44 (1954).
146. *See*, Art. 17 of the Warsaw Convention.
147. *See*, Art. 20 of the Warsaw Convention.
148. *See*, section 3.9.4.6 below.
149. *See*, section, 3.2.4 above.

3.5.2.2   Conversion of Gold Francs into SDRs Through MAP 1 and 2

Because the US unilaterally terminated the convertibility of the US dollar to gold in 1971, the price of gold, including gold francs was floating. This move necessitated the conversion of the amounts for liability in the Warsaw regime into a more stable currency. The Montreal Protocols are designed to create that stability.

Thus, the Montreal Protocols 1 and 2 of 1975 converted these amounts into 8,300 SDRs,[150] and 16,600 SDRs in the Hague Protocol. The equivalent of these latter amounts in Euros or USD varies every day in accordance with the wilful misconduct test designed to circumvent liability limits the value of the SDR but are nearly EUR 10,500/EUR 21,000 and about USD 11,500/USD 23,000.

Those limits were perceived as far too low by the US government, which was the principal reason why it did not ratify the Hague Protocol of 1955, and instead established the above-mentioned Montreal Agreement, 1966,[151] pursuant to which non-US carriers were obliged to adopt limits of liability for carriage to, from and via the US that were twelve times higher than under the Warsaw Convention and six times higher than under the Warsaw Convention as amended by The Hague Protocol. In exceptional cases, the IIA and the MIA as referred to in section 1 above may apply to carriage which does not fall under either the Warsaw Convention or the Hague Protocol or the Montreal Convention, 1999, if the carrier in question is a signatory of any of these IATA agreements.

If the plaintiff can prove that the carrier has committed an act, which resulted in damage caused by wilful misconduct, the limits of liability as foreseen in Article 22 are disregarded. The interpretation of wilful misconduct may vary from one jurisdiction to another, but a plaintiff must generally prove:

(a) a high degree of negligence which must deviate from the standard of care under an *objective* test; and

(b) that the carrier was aware that its behaviour may cause damage, yet, it was indifferent to this result under a *subjective* test.

Case law shows that courts tend to decide in favour of plaintiffs in case of severe losses incurred by the claimants even if the two above elements of proof could not be submitted by the claimant.[152]

---

150. That is, the currency of the International Monetary Fund (IMF).
151. *See*, section 3.5.2.3.below.
152. *See*, Peggy Sharon, Law Firm Levitan, Sharon & Co, Tel Aviv, in the Newsletter of 19 November 2008 of the International Law Office (www.internationallawoffice.com/Newsletter) reporting the cases *Olympic Airways* v. *Kalimi* (Supreme Court of Israel decision CA 74/81; *Ratz* v. *Euroswit Ukraine Airlines* (CC Tel Aviv 1668/06); *Riser* v. *Varig Brazilian Airlines* (CC Tel Aviv) 17738/06) and *Ben-Zur Nurseries* v. *Iberia* (CC Tel Aviv 33015/99). *See also*, the Nigerian Court of Appeal in *Air France* v. *Mrs. Brenda Akpan* [2015] LPELR-24648 (CA).

Carriers are not entitled to invoke the limits of liability in case of wilful misconduct, and neither in cases where they have committed a default which: "[...] in accordance with the law to which the case is submitted, is to be considered to be equivalent to wilful misconduct."

The first paragraph of Article 25 has been termed as "probably the most unhappy phrase of the entire Convention."[153] The unclear formulation has led to a variety of interpretations by national jurisdictions caused by the proper translation of the term "wilful misconduct" from the original, that is, the French text of the Warsaw Convention. The term 'wilful misconduct' is viewed to have a broader scope of application than '*dol*' which is the original term, as 'wilful misconduct' includes cases in which there was no intention to cause damage. '*Dol*' refers to intentional acts. In *Hennesy* v. *Air France*, the Paris Court of Appeal ruled, in 1954, that the passenger's death was caused by gross negligence of Air France. It concluded that the facts did not justify such a conclusion.[154]

A much debated and litigated question has been whether a wrongful act must be judged according to a subjective test, that is: did the aircraft commander personally have the intention to cause damage or at least that the commander had knowledge of the fact that the damage would probably result? Or, according to an *objective* test: does it suffice that, taking into account the normal behaviour of a good pilot, one can reasonably arrive at the conclusion that the commander had such knowledge?

The French Supreme Court (*Cour de Cassation*) adopted the *objective test* when it stated that the errors of navigation were based on a *subjective* appreciation of the facts and that this Court had not drawn the right conclusions from the facts, as stipulated in the Warsaw Convention, 1929.[155]

However, the *subjective test* has also been used, that is, in the *Tondriau* v. *Air India* case, which was ruled by the Belgian Supreme Court (*Cour de Cassation*) in 1977. The Court stated that:

> [...] the carrier or his agents had effective knowledge of the probability of damage and not simply that they ought normally to have had such knowledge.[156]

In the case of *Segala and others* v. *Pakistan International Airlines*, the Court held that the accident was caused by the deliberate conduct of the captain who must have been aware of the risks of his actions and omissions and, hence, of the likelihood that

---

153. *See*, H. Drion, *Limitations of Liabilities in International Air Law* 197 (1954); *see also*, *Pagnucco et al* v. *Pan Am*, reported in *Aviation and Space Law Reports*, May 1994, at 187.

154. *See*, *Hennessy* v. *Air France*, VIII Revue Française de Droit Aérien et Spatial 62–66 (1954).

155. *See*, *Emery* v. *Sabena*, XXII Revue Française de Droit Aérien et Spatial 193–194 (1968); *see also*, 2002 (3) SA 818 (W) (Witewaterstrand Local Division) in which a South African court also applied the objective test. In *Thomas Cook Group* v. *Air Malta*, [1997] 2 Lloyd's Reports 399], the court decided that claimants proved wilful misconduct on the basis of a balance of probabilities. A high degree of probability that a pilot intends to crash an aircraft is required to establish wilful misconduct.

156. XXXI Revue Française de Doit Aérien et Spatial 202 (1977); the translation is provided by Prof. Bin Cheng, *Wilful Misconduct: From Warsaw to The Hague and from Brussels to Paris*, II McGill Annals of Air and Space Law 61 (1977).

an accident would result so that Article 25 applies, and Pakistan International Airways (PIA) was not entitled to rely upon the liability limits of Article 22.[157]

A Hong Kong Court found that a pilot who had taken on too much fuel on board the aircraft, making it too heavy at the time of landing at which point it crashed at Hong Kong International Airport, demonstrated a particularly cautious attitude rather than reckless conduct. The Court took into account that the aircraft commander wanted to take sufficient fuel on board the aircraft to be able to divert should it become necessary, whereas the weight of the aircraft was high but still within the recommended limits for the aircraft.[158]

The *wilful misconduct* test not only covers an act, but also *an omission*. A member of the crew had omitted to perform safety test on the altimeter. A US Court of Appeals ruled:

"Wilful misconduct is the intentional performance of an act with knowledge that the performance of that act will probably result in injury or damage, or it may be intentional performance of an act in such a manner as to imply reckless disregard of the probable consequences of the act."[159]

Lack of application of security measures on the storage of consignments may amount to reckless conduct under Article 25. The fact that a consignment was kept in an office in an unlocked desk, located in an office where people come and go, and third parties could even sleep, contributed to the conclusion of the Court of Hong Kong that such handling system was ineffective. Limits of liability did not apply.[160]

Courts find that repeated and sustained actions falling below the standard of care constitute wilful misconduct.

The question, whether a certain conduct falls or does not fall below the standard of care depends on the circumstances of the case, as determined by the court.[161]

'Passive smoking', combined with certain other events, can constitute 'wilful misconduct' under the Warsaw Convention. A passenger travelling on an Olympic flight from Athens, Greece, to New York, US, had been exposed to a fellow passenger's smoking of cigarettes, while being seated three rows from the smoking section of the aircraft. As a result, he died from an asthma attack. The court found that the conduct of the carrier constituted 'wilful misconduct' under the Warsaw Convention, whereas the combination of the facts of the case constituted an 'accident' under Article 17. The family of the deceased passenger was awarded USD 1.4 million in damages.[162]

---

157. *See, Segala and others* v. *Pakistan International Airlines*, Tribunal Civile of Milan, Third Section, 3 December 2002.
158. *See, Kwok Kan Ming* v. *China Airlines*, Hong Kong Court of Appeals [2008] HKEC 1802.
159. *See, Pekelis* v. *Transcontinental and Western Air*, 3 Avi Cases 17,440; *see also, Goldman* v. *Thai Airways International Ltd*, All England Law Reports 1983 Volume 3 in which the subjective test was applied. The same test was used by the Irish Supreme Court, as to which *see* [2001] 4 IR 531.
160. *See, DFS Trading Limited and Anor* v. *Swiss Air Transport Co Ltd. and others*; High Court of Hong Kong Special Administrative Republic 24 May 2001; case law digest 26(6) Air & Space Law 362–365 (2001).
161. *See also, Koirala* v. *Thai Airways*, 126 F.3d 1205 (9th Cir. 1997).
162. *See, Husain* v. *Olympic Airways*, decision of the US District Court for the Northern District of California, affirmed by the Ninth Circuit Court of Appeals, 316 F.3d 829 (9th Cir. 2002, 71 U.S.L.W. 3612 (U.S. March 12, 2003).

The carrier being responsible for the loss of medicaments of a passenger who, as a consequence thereof, died eight days after arrival is liable under the 'wilful misconduct' test. The court also established the causation between the death and the event which satisfied the requirements of an 'accident' under Article 17 WC29.[163]

3.5.2.3   Defence of the Carrier

Similar to but not identical with the provisions of MC99, the carrier has two defences at his disposal under WC 29 in order to escape liability:

(1) the carrier, as the defendant in a suit, proves that he has taken all necessary measures to avoid the damage, or that it was impossible for him to take such measures (Article 20);
(2) the carrier proves that the damage was caused by or contributed to by the negligence of the injured passenger (Article 21(2)).

The defence of the carrier based on Articles 20 and 21(2) has hardly been invoked in court.

Contributory negligence was not acknowledged where a passenger took his attaché case from the luggage rack the passenger hurt another passenger after landing. The carrier was ordered to pay one third of the amount.[164]

When a passenger had spilled his coffee on his suit and body during a flight, he sued the airline. The airline relied upon the defence that it had taken all necessary measures to avoid the damage. The court agreed with the airline. Moreover, it held that the negligence of the passenger was the sole proximate cause of his injury.[165]

A German Court found that a passenger had contributed to the cause of the damage by failing to look at the information boards at the airport resulting in the missing of the flight. On the other hand, it also argued that the involved airlines should have correctly informed the passenger of their code share arrangement.[166]

A passenger who had omitted to fasten seat bells despite instructions thereto, and went to the door of the aircraft to say goodbye to a person in the terminal, fell from the aircraft on the ground expecting that the staircase was still there. The court held that the carrier had taken all the necessary measures to avoid the damage. Moreover, the damage was caused by, or contributed to, by the injured passenger.[167]

---

163. While also quoting Art. 21 of the Warsaw Convention; *see, Florence Prescod and others* v. *American Airlines and BWI,* United States Court of Appeals for the Ninth Circuit, No. 02-55097 D.C. No. CV-99-00496-CAS, *Per Curiam* Opinion, Filed 19 August 2004.
164. *See,* Court of Appeals of Aix en Provence, France, *Charpin & La Mutuelle Générale Française* v. *Quaranta & Société Inter,* 12 Air Law 205–207 (1987).
165. *See, Medina* v. *American Airlines,* Inc., 31 Avi 18,306 (S.D.Fla 2006), as reported by George N. Tompkins in 32(3) Air & Space Law 228–229 (2007).
166. *See,* Court of Frankfurt, *Landgericht Frankfurt,* 27 January 2005, case no. 2/26 O 416/03, discussed in 30(4/5) Air & Space Law 374–375 (2005).
167. *See, Chutter* v. *KLM,* US District Court, 27 June 1955, XXIII Journal of Air Law and Commerce 232 (1956); *see also,* the decision of the Tel Aviv Magistrat Court CF (Tel Aviv), *Sue Ellen YaFee* v. *Continental Airlines,* reported by Peggy Sharon and Keren Marco, www.

In a hijacking case, the French Supreme Court (*Cour de cassation*) found that the carrier had neither the right nor the ability to check security measures at embarkation. Consequently, appeal to Article 20 WC29 was justified.[168]

In the tragic '9/11' events the concerned airlines also relied on the defence that they had "taken all necessary measures to avoid the damage or that it was impossible for them to take such measures"[169] applicable to claims exceeding 100,000 (now 113,100) SDRs. The court noted that the defendant airline's ability to demonstrate this affirmative defence was 'high'. However, the court found that the claims for damages exceeding 100,000 (now 113,100) SDRs were "premature" as the airline should demonstrate that it had complied with all Federal regulations on security, and other regulatory obligations. Victims of the 11 September disaster claimed punitive damages from defendant airlines, airport operators, airport security companies and aircraft manufacturers. The court held that such damages are unavailable under local law as such damages cannot be recovered from insurers.[170]

Under the *Montreal Agreement of 1966*, the air carrier is not entitled to invoke the defence, if he has taken all measures to avoid the damage. This makes him absolutely liable under that Agreement.

The *Guatemala City Protocol* follows the regime of absolute liability in the same way as the above Montreal Agreement. There are two exceptions to this absolute liability rule applying to the carriage of passengers and baggage, namely:

- the damage solely results from a cause which is related to the state of health of the passenger or an inherent defect of the baggage;
- contributory negligence, or wrongful act or omission on the side of the passenger, causing or at least partly causing the damage.

The Montreal Agreement of 1966 has lost most of its significance since the entry into force of the Montreal Convention, 1999. The Guatemala City Protocol has not entered into force and is very unlikely to do so.

3.5.3 Concluding Remarks

One of the main achievements of the Montreal Convention, 1999, concerns the transition from limited liability to unlimited liability, that is, for passenger related claims. It had appeared that the increased safety record of airlines, combined with the achievement of consumer protection objectives justified such a move. That is why under this Convention the question of wilful misconduct in passenger liability cases has become irrelevant for personal injury cases as liability is unlimited in such cases, independently from the reckless intentions of the carrier.

---

internationallawoffice.com/Newsletter – dated 24 June 2015 in which case the court awarded damages to a passenger who had fallen despite the fasten seat bells sign being switched on; this case is more extensively discussed in section 1.2.6, above, on the notion of accident.
168. *See, Epoux Haddad* v. *Air France* XXVI Revue Française de Droit Aérien 342 (1982).
169. *See,* Art. 20 of the Warsaw Convention, as amended.
170. *See, In re September 11 Litigation II,* 494 F. Supp. 2d 232 (S.D.N.Y 2007) (Hellerstein, J.).

Claimants in delay and baggage cases may still rely on the argument that their damage resulted from an act of omission of the carrier, its servants or agents, "done with the intent to cause damage or recklessly and with knowledge that damage would probably result, provided that the claimant states and proves that the servant or agent was acting within the scope of his/her employment."[171]

The limits applying to carriage of cargo coming under the Montreal Convention, 1999 cannot be broken by proving wilful misconduct as there is no reference to such behaviour in cargo cases.[172]

The 'wilful misconduct' test played a significant role under the Warsaw regime as it enabled plaintiffs to go through the ceiling of the liability limits.[173] It has been frequently used in litigation, with varying degrees of success. Courts applied the subjective or objective test for determining wilful misconduct to reach a decision on the presence of 'wilful misconduct' whereby reference was made to the original French term '*dol*'.

Uniformity of international private air law, which is the main objective of the Warsaw Convention, is not supported by divergent interpretations. Courts have thus been granted the freedom to choose an interpretation which was most equivalent to '*dol*' or wilful misconduct. That is why it was concluded that Article 25 covers those acts, which are "committed deliberately or acts of carelessness without any regard for the consequences."[174]

The carrier has defences as its disposal to reject claims. However, hardly any use has been made of these instruments, at least in case law. It may be that carriers rely on these defences outside courts.

3.6   The Term 'Accident'

3.6.1   Regulation under the Montreal Convention, 1999

The wording of the compensable damages for passengers in the Convention is similar to but not identical with the wording of the Warsaw Convention: "damage sustained in the event of the death or wounding of a passenger or any other bodily injury suffered by a passenger" in the Warsaw Convention (Article 17) became somewhat more concise "damage sustained in case of death or bodily injury" in MC99 (also Article 17).

The damage must be caused by an accident. Hence:

- the facts of the case must establish whether there is an 'accident';[175]
- there must be a causal link between the damage and the accident.

---

171. *See*, Art. 22(5).
172. *See*, section 3.11.2 below.
173. See, section 3.9.4.6.
174. *See*, H. Drion, *Limitation of Liabilities in International Air Law* 203 (1954); *see also*, Prof. Bin Cheng, *Wilful Misconduct: From Warsaw to The Hague and from Brussels to Paris*, II McGill Annals of Air and Space Law 62–82 (1977).
175. *See*, *Buckwalter* v. *USAirways*, No. 12-02586, 2014 WL 116264 (E.D. Pa. 13 January 2014).

Again, reference is made to myriad cases made under the Warsaw regime, and the criteria which were developed there for the determination of the term 'accident.'[176]

3.6.2 Case Law under the Montreal Convention, 1999

The *behaviour of the crew* affects the identification of an event as an 'accident.' In a judgment from 2003, the court found that the airline employee's conduct did not constitute an accident. In 2007, a court determined that there was a question of fact whether or not the airline' behaviour could be termed an 'accident.'[177] Under the regime of the MC99, the presence of a discarded blanket bag on the floor of the aircraft which made a passenger slip does not constitute an 'accident' as it is not an unexpected or unusual event. According to the court, the crew had not violated standards of care.[178]

Being hit by a bottle of liquid falling from an overhead bin forms an 'accident.'[179]

On the other hand, the carrier's failure to equip the aircraft with an Automate External Defibrillator does not constitute an 'accident' under the Montreal Convention.[180] Moreover, "imperfect responses to medical emergencies" do not constitute an 'accident' if the crew's response is not 'unusual' or 'unexpected'. The analysis of these criteria must be based on, among others, industry standards and airline policies and procedures – which analysis lead to the qualification of an event as an 'accident'. In the present case, the court held that the deficiencies of the crew did not support the finding of an "accident."[181]

A passenger who had been downgraded from first class to economy class and pretended to have swollen knees caused by the lack of leg room could not claim under Article 17 of MC99 as the combined facts did not constitute an accident. Under the conditions of the carrier and public regulations, a passenger must advise the carrier at least 24 hours in advance of the journey if he or she needs a specific seat because of a disability.[182]

---

176. ICAO Annex 13 on *accident and incident investigation* defines an accident as: "An occurrence associated with the operation of an aircraft which takes place between the time any person boards the aircraft with the intention of flight until such time as all such persons have disembarked, in which: a) a person is fatally or seriously injured ... b) the aircraft sustains damage or structural failure ...." However, that definition is not used in private air law as to which *see* case law below.
177. *See, Watts* v. *American Airlines*; No. 1:07-CV-0434, 2007 WL 3019344 (S.D. Ind. 10 October 2007); *see also, Fulop* v. *Malev Hungarian Airlines*; F.Supp. 2d.- No. 00 Civ 1965 (VM) 2003 WL 202958 (S.D.N.Y. 29 January 2003) as discussed in section 3.6.4.
178. *See, Rafailov* v. *ElAl Israel Airlines*, 32 Avi 16,372 (S.D.N.Y. 2008); in the same vein, *Vanderwall* v. *United Airlines*, 36 Avi. 16,361 (S.D.Fla.2015).
179. *See, Smith* v. *American Airlines* (Civ No. C 09-02903, 2009 WL 3072449 (N.D. Cal. 22 September 2009).
180. *See, Aziz* v. *Air India*; 658 F. Supp. 2d 1144 (C.D. Cal. 2009).
181. *Singh* v. *Caribbean Airlines*, 13-220639 (S.D. Fla 18 September 2014); a similar case and outcome concerned *Safa* v. *Deutsche Lufthansa*, 2014 WL 4274071 (E.D.N.Y, 28 August 2014); the American Delta settled out of court a case with a passenger involving a spider bite on board aircraft as to which *see*, https://www.law360.com/articles/374225/delta-pays-passenger-for-in-flight-spider-bite.
182. *See, David* v. *United Airlines*, 2016 WL 1573423 (C.D. Cal., 18 April 2016).

Also, 'bumping' from a flight is not an 'accident' under the Montreal Convention.[183] The pilot's placing of his hand on the shoulder of a disruptive passenger accused of smoking on board is not an 'accident.'[184]

A US Federal Court broadened the notion of 'accident' by de-linking it to the operation of the aircraft. Plaintiff successfully argued that when she was hit by other passengers rushing to the wagon cart constituted an accident as an "out of the ordinary and unexpected event."[185]

In France, lower courts are reluctant to be too strict with the definition of 'accident' as they want to meet the concerns of the passengers who are regarded as a victim.[186]

The event must be *"unexpected or unusual"* in order to fall under the term 'accident' as used in Article 17 of MC99. A passenger who fell on an inoperable escalator which she was ascending has not sustained an accident under Article 17.[187] A passenger who hurt his foot against a piece of equipment which has been installed in the aircraft in accordance with public regulations has not been injured by an 'accident' under MC99 as the event was not "unexpected or unusual." According to the court, airlines are not liable for injuries coming from the regular arrangement of the seats.[188] An English Court of Appeal has ruled that a slip, trip or fall, unless caused by a distinct event independent of the passenger, does not qualify as an 'accident' within the meaning of Article 17 of the Montreal Convention, 1999.[189]

The plaintiff must give *proof of the facts* leading to an accident. However, courts conclude that a plaintiff will not necessarily be required to precisely the facts of the event that is claimed to be an 'accident' under Article 17 of MC99, and causing the bodily injury. Thus, it may be sufficient for the plaintiff to state that the injury was caused by an event that was external to the passenger and that it was unusual and unexpected.[190]

---

183. *See, Campbell* v. *Air Jamaica*, 760 F.3d 1165 (11th Cir. 2014).

184. *See, Glassman-Blanco* v. *Delta Airlines*, 2016 WL 117611 (E.D.N.Y., 25 March 2016).

185. *See, Arellano* v. *American Airlines*, 2014 WL 6682591.

186. French Supreme Court's decision of 22 February 2012, case of *Bomandouki* v. *Air France*, reported in Clyde and Co Aviation Bulletin 8-9 (2012).

187. *See, Ugaz* v. *American Airlines*, 32 Avi. 16,710 (S.D.Fla. 2008).

188. *See, Plonka* v. *U.S. Airways*, 37 Avi. 17,308 (E.D.Pa. 2015); *see also, Potter* v. *Delta Air Lines*, 98 F.3d 881,884 (5th Cir. 1996); *Zarlin* v. *Air France*, 2007 WL 2585061, at 4* (S.D.N.Y., 6 September 2007) in which cases a sudden reclining of a seat is unlikely to be called an 'accident'), and *Louie* v. *British Airways* (2003 WL22769110. At *6 (D. Alaska, 7 November 2003, regarding the operation of business class seat).

189. *See, Barclay* v. *British Airways*, [2008] EWCA Civ 1419; reference was made to the cases *Morris* v. *KLM* and *Saks* v. *Air France*, cited in section 3.1.6.

190. In the words of English and Australian courts: " .... a distinct event, not being part of the usual, normal and expected operation of the aircraft, which happens independently of anything done or omitted by the passenger." *See, Air Link Pty Ltd* v. *Paterson* [2009] NSWCA 251 ((2009) NSWCA 251); this case was decided under Australian law rather than under international air law.

3.6.3 Regulation under the Warsaw Regime

For the carrier to be liable, there must have been an 'accident' under Article 17 of the Warsaw Convention, and the Warsaw Convention as amended by the Hague Protocol. Said agreements do not define 'accident.' As said, the term 'accident' was maintained in the Montreal Convention, 1999, and has given rise to case law there.

The term 'accident' has also been analysed in case law coming under the Warsaw Convention and related Protocols. Principally, the US Supreme Court has given guidance on how to interpret this term. Proof for the qualification of an event as an 'accident' lies with the passenger.

3.6.4 Case Law under the Warsaw Regime

The US Supreme Court in the case of *Saks* v. *Air France* has given a 'classical' definition of the term 'accident.'[191] According to the US Court that delivered the judgements, an accident occurs:

> [...] when a passenger's injury is caused by an unexpected or unusual event that is external to the passenger.

Courts may adopt a lower standard for the assessment of the term 'accident.' If 'something happens' to a passenger, the event may be qualified as an accident. A passenger who fell in the lavatory of an aircraft as it was slippery because of the presence of residue of liquid soap of the floor has been qualified as an 'accident', entitling the passenger to claim bodily injury and suffering.[192] On the other hand, a passenger who had to step six inches down when disembarking the aircraft and suffered bodily injury from that stepping down did not receive compensation as there was nothing 'unusual or unexpected' about the incident.[193]

Courts have analysed an accident as *the product of a chain of events and causes.* The passenger must be able to prove that some link in the chain was an unusual or unexpected event external to the passenger. The link, however, must be attributable to the cause of the accident, not merely the occurrence itself. A woman who was sexually assaulted by a fellow passenger was not successful in her claim against the airline, that the assault was an 'accident' under Article 17. The court found that there was not an act or omission by the airline personnel which represented a departure from the normal, expected operation of the flight.[194]

Passenger behaviour on board aircraft has given rise to litigation under Article 17 of the Warsaw Convention. The accident must be the *proximate cause* of the injuries

---

191. 470 US 392, at 405 (1985); *see also*, *Balani* v. *Lufthansa*, 2010 ONSC 3003 (S.C.J.).
192. *See*, *Sharma* v. *Virgin Atlantic Airways*, 2006 WL 870959 (C.D. Cal. March 20, 2006); *see also*, *Cuartas* v. *American Airlines*, Civil Action No. 1: 10-cv-00390-LJM-TAB, 2012 WL 845543 (12 March 2012) in which the court decided that the jury might decide that an accident had occurred when a passenger fell on a slippery staircase when disembarking.
193. *See*, *Singhal* v. *British Airways*, decision made by the Uxbridge County Court in England on 2 November 2006 [unpublished].
194. 1999 WL 187213 (S.D.N.Y).

undergone by a passenger. Moreover, crew must respond 'adequately' to events on board aircraft which may give rise to damage, but the meaning of 'adequately' very much depends on the facts of the case. The interpretation of 'adequately' depends on the facts of the case..

The refusal of a passenger to leave the aircraft when immigration officials forced him to do so, with the approval from the crew, was considered as the proximate cause of his injuries. As a result, he was unable to recover under the Warsaw Convention.[195]

Agitation among passengers or between a passenger and crew, so-called humiliation of the passenger by the flight attendant, and psychological injury, and other behaviour falling under 'unruly passengers'[196] can constitute an 'accident' and, as a corollary, justify compensation if the other conditions of Article 17 WC 29 are complied with. The 'accident' must be *aviation-related*. The British Supreme Court of Judicature reached a different conclusion in the case of *KLM Royal Dutch Airlines* v. *Kelly Morris*,[197] in which the judges stated:

> We have no doubt that the accident that befell the respondent exemplified a special risk inherent in air travel and that, whatever the precise test may be, it constituted an 'accident' within the meaning of that word in Article 17.

A disabled passenger who was unable to stand upright and consequently fell on his hipbone sustaining injury cannot claim that the injury was caused by an 'accident' under Article 17 of the Warsaw Convention. As the UK Supreme Court states, the term 'accident' is not to be construed as including injuries caused by the passenger's particular or peculiar reaction to the normal operation of the aircraft. Indeed, the claimant fell as a result of his pre-existing medical situation. His appeal was dismissed.[198]

The *crews response* to the request from a passenger who needed medical assistance during the flight including an announcement on board, and continued observation of the passenger, but nevertheless had chest pains, did not constitute an 'accident'.[199] In the same vein, the death of a passenger which was caused by his asthma condition was not subject to Article 17 of the Warsaw Convention as the asthma conditions could not be identified as an 'accident' under this provision. During

---

195. *See, Cush* v. *BWIA International Airways Ltd.*, 2001 WL 1613978 (E.D.N.Y. 11 December 2001).
196. *See also,* Stephen R. Ginger, *Violence in the Skies: The Rights and Liabilities of Air Carriers When Dealing with Disruptive Passengers,* 23(3) Air & Space Law 106–117 (1998).
197. *See, KLM Royal Dutch Airlines* v. *Morris,* Court of Appeal – Civil Division, May 17, 2001, [2002] QB 100,[2001] CLC 1460, [2001] 2 All ER (Comm) 153, [2001] EWCA Civ 790,[2001] 3 WLR 351,[2001] 3 All ER 126.
198. *See, Chaudari* v. *British Airways,* decision of the Supreme Court of Judicature in the Court of Appeal (civil division) on appeal from Willesden County Court, CCRTI 9610229/G; *see also, Tinh Thi Nguyen* v. *Korean Air Lines Co,* in which the airline's failure to place the passenger in a wheel chair which was also caused by the passenger's lack of understanding of the Korean and English language is not an 'accident' under WC29; 2015 WL 7783806 (5th Cir., 2 December 2015).
199. *See, Fulop* v. *Malev Hungarian Airlines*; F.Supp. 2d.- No. 00 Civ 1965 (VM) 2003 WL 202958 (S.D.N.Y. 29 January 2003); in the same vein: *Sook Jung Lee* v. *Korean Air Lines,* No. SACV 10-01709-JVS, 2012 WL 1076269 (C.D. Cal. 21 March 2012), and *White* v. *Emirates Airlines,* Civil Action No. 11-20843, 2012 WL 4478446 (5th Cir., 1 October 2012); *Dabulis* v. *Singapore Airlines,* – in which the refusal to reseat a passenger was an "accident."

the flight, the crew and three doctors on board had done everything to save the passenger, who had experienced breathing difficulties, and suffered from a chronic pulmonary disease.[200]

Separation from relatives during a journey by air is not an 'accident'.[201]

Airlines may also be subject to liability in cases where a passenger contracts Severe Acute Respiratory Syndrome (SARS) in an aircraft cabin. Airlines must comply with international health regulations, as well as the laws of the countries to which they operate air services.[202]

In most cases, development of Deep Vein Thrombosis (DVT) has not been construed as an 'accident'. Hence, the carrier was not held liable for the damage related to DVT.[203] These cases are not argued anymore.

Circumstances on board aircraft such as the quality of meals and beverages, may lead to an accident. Under specified circumstances, passengers may be compensated for being served food causing bodily injuries. In such cases, the plaintiff must demonstrate negligence on the part of the air carrier.[204] Thus, a court found that mandatory disinfection of an aircraft and failure to warn passengers who had suffered from reactions to pesticides of allegedly harmful effects of such disinfection does not constitute an 'accident' under the Convention.[205]

A defective seat in an aircraft can also result in an accident, when the airline circumstantial evidence supports other elements constituting an accident. Such other circumstances can be the failure of the airline to remedy the uncomfortable situation, causing the damage.[206]

Weather circumstances have also been the subject of judicial decisions with different outcomes. While turbulence did not amount to an Article 17 accident in

---

200. See, Hipolito v. NorthWest Airlines, Inc., No. 00-2381, 2001 WL 861984 (4th Cir. 31 July 2001).
201. See, Sobol v. Continental Airlines, 2006 WL 2742051 (S.D.N.Y. 26 September 2006).
202. Pursuant to, amongst others, Art. 11 of the Chicago Convention.
203. See, In re Deep Vein Thrombosis Litig., NDCal 32 Avi 15,697; In re Deep Vein Thrombosis Litigation, 2006 WL 2547459 (N.D. Cal. 2006); Caman v. Continetal Airlines, Inc., 455 F.3d 1087 (9th Cir. 20060, cert. denied, US docket No. 06-804 (20 February 2007); Damon v. Air Pacific, Ltd., cert. denied, US docket No. 06 803 (20 February 2007); 1367 Aviation Law Reports (2007); UK House of Lords, Opinions of the Lords of Appeal for Judgment in the Cause Deep Vein Thrombosis and Air Travel Group Litigation, [2005] UKHL 72, Decision of 8 December 2005; see also, Dr Wolf Müller-Rostin, DVT Claim Dismissed by German Court, 27(2) Air & Space Law 151–156 (2002). The DVT case in Germany concerned Volander v. Lufthansa, District Court of Frankfurt am Main, 29 October 2001. For other DVT cases in which DVT was not considered an 'accident' under Art. 17 of the Warsaw Convention see, Ronald Schmidt in Case Law Digest, 29(1) Air & Space Law 67–68 (2004); French cour de cassation, no. 09-71303, 23 June 2011; for Argentina, see, File No. 10543/01, Federal Civil and Commercial Court of Appeals (Chamber III) Buenos Aires, 10/15/2009; McDonald v. Korean Air & China Travel (Canada), decision of the Ontario Superior Court of Justice of 18 September 2002; and an Australian case: Joanna Wilhelmina van Luin v. KLM Royal Dutch Airlines (District Court of New South Wales, 11 October 2002) Blansett v. Continental Airlines, No. 03-40545 (5th Circuit, decision of 21 July 2004); ElAl Israel Airlines v. David, District Court of Nazareth, decision of 7 July 2004. Edward Blotteaux v. Qantas Airways Ltd., United Airlines; Case 2:03-CV-00927 (decision made by John Walter of the Central District of California, on 5 September 2003).
204. See, Scala v. American Airlines, 249 F. Supp. 2d 176 (D. Conn. 2003) and Horvath v. Deutsche Lufthansa AG, No. 02 Civ 3269 (S.D.N.Y 11 July 2003).
205. Bankruptcy Court decision In Re UAL Corp., 310 B.R 373 (N.D. Ill. 2004).
206. See, Krum v. Malaysian Airlines System Berhad, [2004] VSC 185.

Margan v. Lufthansa German Airlines,[207] it could be an accident as held in *Brunk v. British Airways*.[208] The determination depends on, amongst other things, the severity of the turbulence. A light or moderate turbulence not necessarily has to be an 'accident' coming under Article 17 of the Convention. To determine this is a matter of fact.[209] The occurrence of an injury called whiplash, which was caused by heavy turbulence, can be identified as an 'accident' under Article 17 of the Convention.[210]

Hijacking has also caused airline liability under WC29 as it was deemed to be an "accident."[211]

The tragic '9/11' events have been settled by a special act, to wit the *Air Transportation Safety and System Stabilisation Act* of 22 September 2001,[212] under which claims could be made for personal injury or wrongful death.[213] The Act included the establishment of the '11 September Victim Compensation Fund of 2001, the purpose of which is to compensate eligible individuals who were physically injured or the families of persons who were killed as a result of the above tragedy. Claimants were entitled to receive compensation for *non-economic losses*. Most, but not all passengers were carried on domestic flights. Passengers who were travelling on *international* tickets on the flights of the 9/11 events were entitled to claim under the Warsaw Convention, as amended. However, the concerned airlines (United Airlines and American Airlines) flying under that regime had amended their conditions of carriage so that liability limits did not apply. The court decided that the hijacking events constituted an 'accident' under the Warsaw Convention, as amended.

3.6.5 Concluding Remarks

For an air carrier to be liable, the Warsaw regime and the Montreal Convention, 1999, require that the event giving rise to liability be an 'accident.' Not every event is an accident.

Under the Warsaw regime, airlines, who are the defendants, want an 'event' to be an 'accident' because they are protected by the limits of liability set forth by the Warsaw System. Conversely, under the Montreal Convention, 1999, airlines do not want an event to be an accident because they are fully liable if an accident occurs.

---

207. 181 F. Supp. 2d 396 (S.D.N.Y 2002).
208. No. Civ A. 00-00764 (HHK), 2002 WL 554536 (D.D.C. 15 April 2002).
209. *See, Magan v. Lufthansa German Airlines*, 339 F.3d 158 (2nd Cir. 2003); *see also, Girard v. American Airlines*, Inc., 2003 WL 21989978 (E.D.N.Y 2003).
210. *See, Van der Put v. Martinair*, President of the District Court of Amsterdam, 9 May 1996.
211. *See, Husserl v. Swissair*, 351 F. Supp. 702 (S.D.N.Y. 1972); *see also*, the National Consumer Disputes Redressal Commission of India followed the line of reasoning of the US Supreme Court in *Saks v. Air France*, in a hijacking case which had occurred in 1999; *see, Indian Airlines Ltd.*, v. *Ashok Gupta & Anor* [30 April 2015], National Consumer Disputes Redressal Commission, New Delhi, No. 189 of 2009.
212. Public Law 107-42.
213. The complete text of the Act as well as the debate, which took place in the US Congress, can be found at http://thomas.loc.gov.

Courts have given different interpretations to this term, especially under the Warsaw Convention. These interpretations have been followed in case law coming under MC99.

The Guatemala City Protocol of 1971 replaced the word 'accident' in WC29 by the word 'event.' The carrier is liable "[...] when the *event* which caused the death or injury took place [...]" (*italics added*). Hence, the liability of the air carrier is extended as more occurrences fall under the term 'event' than under 'accident.'

3.7   Process of Embarkation and Disembarkation

3.7.1   Regulation under the Montreal Convention, 1999

Under Article 17, the damage must arise between *embarkation* and *disembarkation*. The terms 'embarkation' and 'disembarkation' have been analysed in case law. For the air carrier to be liable, it must, among others, have been supervising the passengers as explained in the cases below.

3.7.2   Case Law under the Montreal Convention, 1999

In order to answer the question, whether the passenger had embarked, the following factors may be relevant:

  (1) the activity of the passengers at the time of the accident;
  (2) the restrictions, if any, on their movement;
  (3) the imminence of actual boarding;
  (4) the physical proximity of the gate.[214]

In the case at hand, the plaintiff, who had already checked in for the flight, could not convincingly argue that he found himself in the process of embarkation, because he "had ample time to roam freely about the public terminal before his flight was called." In conclusion, as Article 17 of the Montreal Convention, 1999, did not apply, it did not pre-empt his state claims against the defendant.

The *facts and circumstances of the case* are of crucial importance. Thus, a passenger who attempted to board a flight but missed it consequent to a disagreement about charges for excess luggage, is supposed to be in the process of embarkation. Hence, her claims were covered by the Montreal Convention, 1999.[215] However, a passenger located in the common airport area before receiving a boarding pass indicates that he/she has not yet embarked.[216] On the other side, claims arising from

---

214. *See, Hunter* v. *Lufthansa and Etihad Airlines*, 863 F. Supp. 2d 190 (E.D.N.Y. 202).
215. *See, Okeke* v. *Northwest Airlines*, No. 1:07CV538, 2010 WL 780167 (M.D.N.C. 26 February 2010).
216. *See, Beach-Mathrura* v. *American Airlines*, Order on Mot. Summary Judgement, No. 1:08-21925-CIV-UNGARO (S.D. Fla, 7 April 2009); and: *Tismanariu* v. *Air France*, 2014 QCCQ [Quebec Court] 2847 (2014).

accidents taking place in the baggage claim area are excluded by the definition of disembarkation.[217] A passenger who gets injured on an escalator while travelling between boarding gates does not find herself in the process of embarkation or disembarkation.[218] The concerned activity is not sufficiently close to the act of boarding an aircraft so that the Montreal Convention, 1999, is not applicable. However, a passenger who fell on an inoperable escalator after exiting the aircraft and while proceeding to the customs was found to the in the process of disembarkation.[219] An injury occurring on a moving walkway is not compensable under MC99 absent a 'close tie' between the accident and the disembarkation of the aircraft.[220] A claimant who was arrested upon finding his fire gun unattended on the conveyor belt was found to be in the process of disembarkation.[221]

3.7.3 Regulation under the Warsaw Regime

The terms 'embarkation' and 'disembarkation' have been taken from Article 17 of the Warsaw Convention, 1929, and remained unchanged in the Warsaw regime. A condition for applicability of the Warsaw Convention is that the accident, that caused the damage, took place between the process of *embarkation* and *disembarkation*.[222] They have been explained in myriad cases some of which are mentioned below.

3.7.4 Case Law under the Warsaw regime

In a *hijacking* case, passengers were waiting in Athens airport to board a TWA flight to New York were attacked by terrorists. The court had to address the question whether the passengers "[...] in the course of any of the operation of embarking [...]." It decided that, when Article 17 refers to:

- 'course', this means: moving in a certain direction, the act of moving forward;
- 'operations', this means: a series or course of acts to effect a certain purpose;

---

217. *See, Fedelich v. American Airlines*, 724 F. Supp. 2d 274 (D.P.R. 2010).
218. *See, Dick v. American Airlines*, 476 F. Supp. 2d 61 (D. Mass. 2007); *see also*, the case made by the *cour de cassation civile, première chambre*, of 8 October 2014, No. 13-24346, in which the French court held that the bodily injury of a passenger holding a baby on her arm, missing a step and injuring her ankle could not be attributed to the carrier unless the passenger had requested assistance. In the same vein, the bodily injury of a passenger whose knee which was stretched into the aisle got injured when the meal trolley rolled into his leg is compensable as the passenger did not contribute to the cause of the accident pursuant to Art. 21(2) MC99; *see*, http://www.internationallawoffice.com/Newsletters/Aviation/Israel/Levitan-Sharon-Co/El-Al-ordered-to-indemnify-passenger-for-injuries-sustained-during-take-off.
219. *See, Ugaz vAmerican Airlines*, 576 F. Supp. 2d 1354 (S.D. Fla 2008).
220. *See, Boyd v. Deutsche Lufthansa AG*, No. Civ A. 14-1260, 2015 WL 3539685 (E.D. La 3 June 2015).
221. *See, Seales v. Panamian Aviation*, Case No. 07-CV-2901, 2009 WL 395821 (E.D.N.Y., 18 February 2009); the airline had given assurances that the passenger was entitled to carry his fire gun if he followed the procedures, but had refused to provide an exculpatory statement on his behalf to the authorities.
222. *See*, Art. 17 of the Warsaw Convention: "The carrier shall be liable ... if the accident ... took place ... in the course of embarkation or disembarkation."

- 'embarking', this means: to go aboard.

The Court held that what is decisive is not where the passengers were, but what they were *engaged in doing*. As plaintiffs had completed the steps which the Court had identified as belonging to the process of embarkation, the Court decided in favour of plaintiffs. The carrier TWA would have refused the passengers if they would not have completed all the steps. Consequently, the carrier was liable under the Convention.[223]

In another judgment, the Court ruled that the following criteria are relevant for the determination whether, or not, a passenger is embarking:

(1) the passenger's activity at the time of the injury;
(2) the activity of the passenger when injured;
(3) The extent to which the carrier was exercising control or should have exercised control.[224]

Courts have also developed *the control or supervision by the air carrier* for testing whether or not the passenger is embarking or disembarking.[225] Passengers who have not yet checked in, have not yet received their boarding passes and have not proceeded through security check have not yet commenced the process of embarkation.[226] A French Court used similar criteria for the definition of 'embarkation.' A passenger who finds himself under the control of – agents of – the airline, while waiting in a room ('*salle d'accueil*') in order to be taken from there to the aircraft, is embarking. However, a passenger who has left this room without instructions from the agent of the airline, but who is near the aircraft, has not yet embarked. The Court took into account that the process of embarkation could start only a few moments before the departure of the aircraft because of the small size of the airport and the limited number of flights using this airport.[227]

In yet other cases, the Court confirmed that the process of embarkation can be interrupted by periods where the passenger is asked to wait before a flight is called, during which time the passenger is free to do what he/she wants without direction from the carrier and could not be regarded as undergoing any of the "operations of embarkation."[228] An event occurring at a place which was used by multiple airlines is not under the control of 'its' airline, but a passenger falling on an escalator while being

---

223. See, *Day* v. *Trans World Airlines*, 393F. Supp. 217, 13 Avi. 17,647 (S.D. N.Y. 1975), affirmed, 528F. 2d 31, 13 Avi. 18,144 (2d Cir. 1975), cert. denied (US Supreme Court 1976).
224. See, *McCarthy* v. *Northwest Airlines*, 56 F. 3d 313, 317 (1st Cir. 1995).
225. See, *Ong* v. *Malaysian Airline System* [2007] HKCU 1141; in appeal, see (2008) HKCA 88, in which the Hong Kong Court of Appeals gave a broad interpretation of the term disembarkation.
226. See, *Aquino* v. *Asiana Airlines Inc.*, 105 Call. App. 4th 1272, 130 Cal. Rptr. 2d 233 (2003).
227. See, *Mme Lowenton* c/ *GIE La Réunion et autres*, decision of 29 October 1992 of the *Cour d'appel de Paris* (7e Ch. B), published in 31 Recueil Dalloz Sirey 446-449 (1993).
228. Queen's Bench Decision of 27 March 2002, reported in Barlow Lyde and Gilbert Aviation News, Summer 2002, Issue 9 at 1; *see also*, *Astudillo* v. *Port Authority of New York and New Jersey*, decision, Sup. Ct. N.Y. Co. Index No. 101165/02 on 29 November 2004. Another accident pertaining to the provision of a wheelchair is analysed in *Balani* v. *Lufthansa* [2010] ONSC 3003 (SCJ); decision of the Superior Court of Justice, appeal made to Ontario Court of Appeal; *see*, Carlos Martins and Tae Mee Park, *Lack of Wheelchair at Aircraft Held to Be Article 17*

en route to boarding his flight may be in the process of embarkation. The passenger had asked to provide wheel chair assistance, which was agreed upon by the airline. The airline had started the process of embarkation from the moment the wheelchair was made available to the passenger.[229] Passengers in a transit phase are, according to a decision, "either disembarking ... or embarking."[230]

The term *disembarkation* has been discussed in cases where the passenger was injured when she fell on the 'down' escalator leading to the baggage claim and customs area. The court found that the carrier was not liable under the Warsaw Convention because she had already disembarked. The passenger was not directed into lines and no activities were required by the airline. She was injured on equipment negligently maintained by third parties.[231]

Similarly, passengers who have picked up their luggage, passed through customs control, gone down an escalator into the baggage claim area operated by a third (non-airline) party and walked to a nearby hotel while passing through airport areas which are commonly used by passengers from *all* airlines, have disembarked as they are outside the 'control' of their airline.[232] Thus, they fall outside the scope of Article 17 of the Warsaw Convention.[233]

3.7.5 Concluding Remarks

A condition for applicability of the Warsaw Convention is that the accident, that caused the damage, took place between the process of *embarkation* and *disembarkation*.[234] A broad interpretation of the words "embarkation" and "disembarkation" has been crucial for victims of terrorist attacks, or their legitimate representatives, at, for instance, airports, in order to receive compensation at all as other persons such as the terrorists, the airports or the security companies are no realistic alternatives. For instance, airports could hide behind exoneration of liability because of, for instance, immunity in case they belong to a State. In addition, claimants may have to prove fault of another defendant than the airline under local law. In such cases, the passenger has an interest to have a broad interpretation of the terms 'embarkation' and 'disembarkation.'

'*Accident*'; Newsletter of 22 December 2010, International Law Office, at: www.internationallawoffice.com and *Pacitti* v. *Delta Air Lines*, No. 04-CV-3197, 2008 WL 919634 (E.D.N.Y 3 April, 2008).

229. *See, Fazio* v. *NorthWest Airlines*, No. 1: 03-CV-808 (W.D. Mich., Decision of 15 March 2004).

230. *See, Murillo* v. *American Airlines*, No. 09-22894-Civ, 2010 WL 1740710 (S.D. Fla, 29 April 2010).

231. *See, Felismina* v. *TWA*, 13 Avi. 17,145 (S.D. N.Y. 1974).

232. *See, Muehlig* v. *American Airlines*, No. 02-5063 (WHW) D.N.J., decision of 6 July 2004).

233. However, *see KLM* v. *Tuller*, 292F. 2d 775, 7 Avi. 17,544 (D.C. Cir. 1961), cert. denied, 368 U.S. 921 (US Supreme Court 1961) in which the court held that the Warsaw Convention applied when a passenger was drowned after slipping from the aircraft's tail some hours after it crashed at sea.

234. *See,* Art. 17 of the Warsaw Convention: "The carrier shall be liable [...] if the accident [...] took place [...] in the course of embarkation or disembarkation."

On the other hand, when passengers are not in the process of embarkation or disembarkation, they may be entitled to sue the airline outside the Convention, under regimes which do not protect the airline by limitation of liability.[235] This 'third' avenue has of course become irrelevant under the Montreal Convention, 1999.

Courts have developed the test of control or supervision by the airline when determining the scope of 'embarkation' and 'disembarkation.' In this context, reference is made to Standard 3.45 of ICAO Annex 9 to the Chicago Convention on *Facilitation*, which dictates that the air carrier is responsible "for custody and care of passengers and crew members." Obviously, responsibility should not be confused with liability but the 'custody and care' elements are determining factors both in public and private air law.

3.8 Compensable Damages

3.8.1 Regulation under the Montreal Convention, 1999

3.8.1.1 Liability for Death and Bodily Injury

Under Article 17, the carrier "is liable for damage sustained in case of death or bodily injury of a passenger." Again, no definitions are given for either of these terms.

The term 'death' appears to be unambiguous, but national legislation may give different standards for it when persons are missed. This question arises in the tragedy of the Malaysian Airlines flight MH370 which has not yet been found. However, the question was resolved by the Malaysian Government issuing a declaration that all passengers were deceased in order to avoid that uncertainty. Under certain laws missed persons may be declared dead after for instance two years, in others the norm may amount to five years.[236]

More complex is the term 'bodily injury', which replaced the expression "wounding [...] or any other bodily injury suffered by a passenger" under the Warsaw regime. The term 'bodily injury' has been much debated in court cases as, again, no reference is made in the Convention to compensation of 'mental injury'. Compensation for 'mental injury' was mentioned in one of the first drafts of the Convention. The Legal Committee decided to delete an express reference to the term.[237] Importantly, the courts interpreting the term "bodily injury" under (Article 17 of) the Warsaw

---

235. Such persons can claim under national law, if their claim does not fall under the terms of Art. 17 of the Warsaw Convention as it forms an exclusive basis for liability claims as to which see the explanations on the concept of *Exclusivity* given in section 3.4.2 for the MC99 and section 3.4.4. for the WC29.

236. See, *Fatt* v. *Boeing Co.*, 2014 WL 6686651 (Ill. App. Ct., 26 November 2014); *see*, on the MH370, also: *MH370 passenger's family sue Malaysia Airlines and government* on the basis of negligence, The Guardian, 31 October 2014, and D. Kong and Q. Zhang, *Civil Procedure Issues in the Lawsuits of MH370 in China: Jurisdiction and Limitation of Action*, XV(1) The Aviation & Space Journal 2–11 (2015).

237. *See*, Report of the Second Meeting of the Secretariat Study group on the *Modernization of the Warsaw Convention System*, ICAO LC/30-IP/1 of 4 February 1997 at 6.

Convention could indeed rely on the more flexible term '*lésion corporelle*' which was the original term in the language in which the Warsaw Convention was drafted.

Again, mental injuries are not compensable, unless they are "caused by the physical injuries sustained."[238]

3.8.1.2   Advance Payments

The carrier *may* make advance payments to persons who are entitled to claim compensation on behalf of the victim.[239] Advance payments are designed to address the immediate needs of the persons who are entitled to such payments. However, it may be unclear who is going to decide what amount corresponds with the first economic needs, and who is entitled to claim on behalf of the victim. Identification of "immediate economic needs" and "persons who are entitled to claim" is not an easy task in the confusion, prevailing after an air disaster.

In practice, all or most airlines will make advance payments of between EUR 15,000 and EUR 30,000.

The carrier is only obliged to make an advance payment if he is required to do so under national law. EU law imposes such an obligation on Community air carriers up to the amount of EUR 16,000.[240] As this could not be decided at the 'multilateral treaty level', the drafters of the treaty were realistic enough to leaving the option of making advance payments open. ICAO Resolution A39-27 of 2016 upon its Contracting States to draw up legislation supporting victims of civil aviation accidents and their family members by the provision of, among other things, advance payments.

3.8.1.3   Punitive Damages

The Montreal Convention, 1999,[241] has specifically outlawed compensation of *punitive damages*,[242] thus resolving an issue which has been often the subject of litigation in the US. Also, punitive damages are not compensable in case of reckless of wilful misconduct of the air carrier.[243]

---

238. *See, Doe v. Etihad Airways*, 37 Avi. 17,281 (E.D. Mich. 2015); *see also, Bassam v. American Airlines*, 287 F. Appendix 309, 317 (5th Cir. 2008), citing the 'landmark cases' *ElAl Airlines v. Tseng, Eastern Airlines v. Floyd, In re Air Crash at Little Rock Arkansas, on June 1, 1999* and *Ehrlich v. American Airlines.*
239. Pursuant to Art. 28 of the Convention.
240. *See*, Art. 1(10) of EU Regulation 889/2002 amending the Annex of EU Regulation 2027/97.
241. *See*, Art. 29.
242. As confirmed in: *Booker v. BWIA West Indies Airways Ltd.*, 32 Avi 15,134 (E.D.N.Y 2007), and *Kruger v. United Airlines* (NDCal) 32 Avi 15,703; *see also, Aya v. Lan Cargo*, 2014 WL 4672450 (S.D. Florida, 18 September 2014).
243. *See, In re Air Crash at Lexington, Kentucky, 27 August 2006*, 32 Avi 15,235 (E.D. Ky 2007); *see also*, Barbara J. Buono, *The Recoverability of Punitive Damages under the Warsaw Convention in Cases of Wilful Misconduct: Is the Sky the Limit?*, 13 Fordham International Law Journal 570 (1989).

3.8.2 Case Law under the Montreal Convention, 1999

When a claim is made for bodily injury, there must be *evidence of injuries.*[244] Moreover, such injuries must be *caused* by an accident.[245] In a US case, a passenger was denied compensation because he had failed to provide sufficient *evidence of the facts* supporting his claim for "bodily injury."[246]

Thus, the compensation of *mental injuries* continues to be a source of litigation. In that respect, there has been no change from the original Warsaw system and the current trends in case law.[247] According to this decision, the question of whether damages are recoverable for a 'mental injury' when accompanied by a bodily or physical injury must be decided on a case-by-case basis as evidenced by medical reports. Hence, mental injury must be linked to physical injury.[248] Stand-alone mental injury is not compensable under MC99.[249]

---

244. *See, Seshadri v. British Airways*, No. 3:14-cv-0833-BAS, 2014 WL 5606542 (S.D. 4 November 2014) concerning purely emotional distress claims which were dismissed.

245. *See, Jacob v. Korean Air Lines*, Case No. 14-11663 (11th Cir., 20 March 2015).

246. *See, Labiad v. Royal Air Maroc*, 36 Avi. 16,256 (E.D.N.Y. 2014); similarly, a passenger had not established sufficient evidence of back injuries when claiming for compensation under MC99, as to which *see, Dibbs v. Emirates*, [2015] NSWSC 132, and *Narkiewicz-Laine v. Aer Lingus*, No. 14 CV 50098, 2015 WL 5009766 (N.D. Ill. 21 August 2015).

247. *See, Floyd v. Eastern Airlines*, 499 US.530 (1991), 23 Avi 17,367, *Vumbaca v. Terminal One Group Association*, 859 F. Supp. 2d 343 (E.D.N.Y 2012), and *Doe v. Etihad Airways*, 37 Avi. 17,281 (E.D. Mich. 2015).

248. *See, Booker v. BWIA West Indies Airways Ltd.*, 32 Avi 15,134 (E.D.N.Y 2007), and *Kruger v. United Airlines* (N.D.Cal 2007) 32 Avi 15,703; *Katin v. Air France-KLM S.A*, Civ No. 4:08-CV-348, 2009 WL 1940363 (E.D. Tex. 2 July 2009) in which claimant successfully argued that his concerns about eating foods after having eaten lobster which cracked his teeth, formed mental injury following bodily injury. The decision of the Superior Court of Ontario, Canada, approving the partial settlement of a class action for among others mental injuries caused by an Air France accident in Toronto on 2 August 2005 referred to maximum amounts allowed under Canadian law for the compensation of mental injuries, that is, CAD 100,000 – unless accompanied by evidence of physical injury in which case the maximum amount is CAD 175,000 – for a passenger claim; *see*, Bersenas Jacobsen Chouest Thomson and Blackburn LLP, *Air France Class Action Settlement Approved*, Transportation Notes: *Legal Decision and Developments Affecting the Transportation Industry in Canada*, Volume 6(1) of January 2010; *see also, Air France class action: important settlement made by the Ontario Superior Court of Justice*, Case of *Abdulrahim v. Air France* (2011 ONSC 398), International Law Office, contributed by Gerard Chouest, www.internationallawoffice.com; Newsletter of 30 March 2011; in Canada: *O'Mara v. Air Canada*, 2013 ONSC 2931 (CanLII) in which the court held that 'aggravated damages' were only recoverable as part of 'general damages'; according to the court, purely psychological damages are not recoverable, and neither are punitive or exemplary damages. In *Casey v. Pel-Air Aviation Pty Ltd.*, [2015] NSWSC 566, the New South Wales Supreme Court of Australia, referring to the evidence of chemical neurotransmitting agents which are important for brain functioning, held that Post Traumatic Stress Disorder (PTSD) is a form of 'bodily injury' under MC99; *see also, Kruger v. United Airlines* (N.D.Cal 2007) 32 Avi 15,703.

249. *See, Booker v. BWIA West Indies Airways Ltd.*, 32 Avi 15,134 (E.D.N.Y 2007).

3.8.3 Regulation under the Warsaw Regime

The regulation of passenger damages is only slightly different from that under the Montreal Convention, 1999. The carrier is not only liable for damages sustained in case of death or bodily injury of the passenger, but also for his or her 'wounding'.

The term 'punitive damages' is not mentioned in the Warsaw regime.

As said above, the concept of 'punitive damages' is especially relevant under US law.[250] In re *Korean Air Lines Disaster of 1 September 1983*,[251] the US Court of Appeals held that punitive damages are not recoverable in actions governed by the Warsaw Convention.

An obligation or an option for the carrier to provide an 'advance payment' to the passenger in order to meet the first economic needs has not been laid down either. The balance of benefits which the drafters of the Warsaw Convention sought to implement in 1929 did not yet take into account consumer protection trends including the provision of an advance payment.

3.8.4 Case Law under the Warsaw Regime

3.8.4.1 Assessment of Damages

Under the conditions laid down in Article 17 of the Warsaw Convention, the carrier must compensate damages sustained in the event of death, wounding or "[...] any other bodily injury sustained by the passenger [...]." The term 'bodily injury' has been clarified in court cases.

The damages must be *'legally cognisable'* which determination must be made under national law.'[252] A court found that the bumping of a passenger from the flight

---

250. Punitive damages are non-compensatory damages, which a defendant may have to pay upon conviction by a court, having in view the enormity of his offence rather than the measure of compensation of the plaintiff. Punitive damages are designed to punish the tortfeasor. *On the one hand*, they serve a social function as they must increase public safety, and the imposition of payment of such damages has a coercive remedial effect. Moreover, public policy dictates monetary punishment as a deterrent. *On the other note*, the imposition of payment of punitive damages may have disastrous effects on the financial condition of a company. Also, courts have stated that, if companies are permitted to shift the financial burdens to insurance companies, an award imposing payment of punitive damages would serve no useful purpose. *City Products Corp* v. *Globe Indemnity Co*, 151 Cal. Reporter 494 (Cal. Pp. 1979), and *Northwestern National Casualty Company* v. *McNulty*, 307 F2d 432 (5th Cir. 1962); see, however; *Lazenby* v. *Universal Underwriters Insurance Company*, 214 Tennessee 639, 383 S.W.2d 1 (1964).
251. 807 F. Supp. 1073 (S.D.N.Y 1992). There is more US case law confirming this position. The US Supreme Court refused to review the decisions given by the Courts of Appeals in these cases so that the ruling stands. The exclusion of punitive damages from damages was confirmed in *Razi* v. *China Airlines*, No. CV 03-08169 DDP (C.D. California, decision of 15 April 2004).
252. In *Zicherman* v. *Korean Air Lines Co*. 516 U.S. 217 (1996), the Supreme Court of the US ruled that: "... the Warsaw Convention permits compensation only for legally cognisable harm, but leaves the specification of what harm is legally cognisable to the domestic law applicable under the forum's choice of law rules ...". *See also*, *Lee* v. *American Airlines*, 2002 U.S. Dist. LEXIS 12029 (N.D. Tex 2002).

was not an 'accident' because it was not 'unusual' or 'unexpected' and that the plaintiff did not suffer legally cognisable 'bodily injury'.[253] Finding that no accident or bodily injury could be pleaded, no claim could proceed under Article 17 of WC29.[254] In a non-aviation case, the CJEU also ruled that the recovery of damages must be determined by national courts, in accordance with the applicable national law.[255]

For the *calculation of damages*, the Warsaw Convention refers implicitly rather than explicitly to national law. As the damage factors and the calculation of damages under the applicable law are significantly different for all claimants involved,[256] the persons suing the airline on behalf of passengers of an airline accident receive by way of settlement or by way of award after trial, whether by jury or by the court without a jury, the same amount of damages. Each damage must be evaluated by the court seized of the case or by insurers seeking to settle the case, upon the basis of the damage law applicable to each claim and the damage factors of each claim. Hence, the awards differ from case to case because the level of the award is determined by the law and the factual circumstances pertinent to the individual claimant.

In determining the value of the damages, courts take the view that the loss of property means "the actual value of such property taking into account the original cost and relative newness and the extent, if any, to which it had deteriorated or depreciated through use, damage, age, decay or otherwise."[257] Claims for loss of property must be supported by evidence of the value of comparable objects or by demonstration of the specific value of the artefacts.[258] Other criteria refer to 'the exercise of good sense and judgment.'[259]

The Supreme Court of Korea took into account the special circumstances in which aviation accidents take place, warranting higher damages resulting from other types of accidents such as motor vehicle accidents. This form of compensation must provide consolation for the dependants of the deceased passengers, and is separate from the compensation of economic losses.[260]

Non-economic damages are generally considered to be particularly high in the US because of the frightening manner of passengers' death or injury which every jury member can relate to. This is why most US claims are settled out of Court.[261]

---

253. In *Sewer* v. *Liat Ltd*, Civil Action No.: 04-76, 2011 WL 635292 (D.VI. Feb 16, 2011).
254. *See, Sobol* v. *Continental Airlines*, 2006 WL 2742051 (S.D.N.Y. 26 September 2006).
255. *See,* Case C-144/99 of the ECJ, *Commission of the European Communities* v. *the Kingdom of the Netherlands.*
256. Which impacts on the choice of competent court under the jurisdictional rules as to which *see* the section below.
257. *See also, Kodak* v. *American Airlines*, Inc., 9 Misc.3d 107, 110.
258. *See, Mohammed* v. *Air France*, 816 N.Y.S. 2d 697, 2006 WL 777076 (N.Y. City Civ Ct. 28 March 2006).
259. *See, MacGregor* v. *Watts*, 254 AD 904, 904 [2d Dept 1938].
260. *See, Nam* v. *Air China*, 2008 Da 3527; *Kwon & others* v. *Air China*, 2008 Da 3619; *Hee & Others* v. *Air China*, 2008 Da 3640 and *Gyo & Others* v. *Air China*, 2007 Da 77149.
261. *See also*, the Brazilian Seba and Lima judgments arising out of AF447. These were the amongst the highest ever judgments by a Brazilian Court for non-economic damages. The Court increased the previous Chamber of Indemnification judgment of 700 minimum salaries to 1000 minimum salaries per dependent.

Under US law, damage which involves an accident on the high seas may be subject to the provisions of the *Death on the High Seas Act*, also referred to as DOHSA. This act which was drawn up in 1920 is designed to cover accidents occurring on the high seas and to provide an exclusive cause of action for accidents covered by this act.

DOHSA excludes compensation of psychological injuries, including emotional distress and suffering, and punitive damages. Under it, *only* monetary claims can be awarded to widows and children of the deceased fishermen.[262]

On 3 March 1999, the US House approved a bill designed to amend the Federal Aviation Act in such a manner that airline accidents at sea are treated in the same way as accidents on land. Until the adoption of the bill, state tort laws applied to accidents occurring within the three miles coastal zone. Outside those limits, DOHSA applies.[263]

The Supreme Court of the Philippines found that the law of the country in which tickets were issued, that is, where the contract was made, and where the passengers were residents and citizens applies, rather than the law of the country where the tickets were handed – that country being the United States. The substantive law, or the *lex loci contractus*, pertained to rules on check-in requirements and overbooking.[264]

3.8.4.2 The Relationship Between Bodily Injury and Mental Injury under US Case Law

When a claim is made for bodily injury, there must be evidence of injuries, in this case caused, pursuant to the allegation of the passengers, by a falling bag.[265] Passengers suffering from traumas caused by the navigation of the aircraft through a hurricane, subjecting the passengers to 45 minutes of "physical battery and sheer terror of almost certain death" is not compensable as bodily injury as the passengers had not brought forward cognisable evidence of physical changes in their brains.[266]

US courts generally, but not always, conclude that 'bodily injury' is not intended to encompass purely psychological, mental or even psychiatric injury. Recovery of

---

262. *See, Zicherman v. Korean Air Lines Co.* which was yet another case arising out of the KE 007 crash, 516 U.S. 217 (1996): When DOHSA applies: " … neither state law, … nor general maritime law, … can provide a basis for recovery of loss of society damages." Hence, DOHSA provides the exclusive basis for the determination of damages.
263. Section 402 (b): *Death on the High Seas*: "In the case of a commercial aviation accident, whenever the death of a person shall be caused by wrongful act, neglect, or default occurring on the high seas 12 nautical miles or closer to the shore of any State, or the District of Columbia, or the Territories or dependencies of the United States, this Act shall not apply and the rules of Federal, State, and other appropriate law shall apply." And section 2(b)(1) of the *Compensation in commercial aviation act*: "If the death resulted from a commercial aviation accident occurring on the high seas beyond the 12 nautical miles from the shore of any State, or the District of Columbia, or the Territories or dependencies of the United States, additional compensation for non-pecuniary damages for wrongful death of a decedent is recoverable. Punitive damages are not recoverable. (2) In this Subsection, the term 'non-pecuniary damages' means damages for loss, care, comfort, and companionship."
264. *See,* IATA/Condon & Forsyth, 5 The Liability Reporter 24–25 (2002).
265. *See, Mumtaz v. Etihad Airways*, 2014 WL 7405216 (D.N.J. 30 December, 2014).
266. *See, Bobbian v. Czech Airlines*, No. 3-1262 (3d Circuit, decision of 29 March 2004).

physical injuries is allowed whether those injuries were caused by direct impact during the accident, or as a consequence of shock or mental injury afflicted by the accident, there being no doubt that the symptoms were covered by the term "any other bodily injury" as used in Article 17 of the Warsaw Convention.[267] A leading case on this subject is In *Eastern Airlines* v. *Floyd*,[268] in which the US Supreme Court held that mental or psychic injuries unaccompanied by physical injuries are not compensable under Article 17 of the Warsaw Convention. However, there were two types of injury for which recovery was undecided, namely, mental injury caused by physical injury, and emotional distress,[269] which resulted in organic damage, such as a stroke or heart attack following a shock.

Liability arises not only for "palpable objective bodily injury", but also for those injuries, that are caused by the psychic trauma of the accident and the mental suffering resulting from the bodily injuries. Not the trauma causing the skin rash, but the skin rash as a result of the psychic trauma of the accident is compensable, as well as the mental suffering caused by the skin crash. Non-bodily or behavioural manifestations of the trauma are not compensable.[270] However, in another case it was decided that mental injuries alone may be compensable, if the otherwise substantive law which applies provides an appropriate cause of action.[271]

Meanwhile, US Courts are divided on the interpretation of 'bodily injury' as exemplified by another frequently cited case, that is, *Husserl* v. *Swissair* (1975) in which the plaintiff stated that she had suffered bodily injury, severe mental pain and anguish resulting from her expectation of severe injury and/or death. Thus, the claimants could not recover pre-death pain and suffering.[272] There had been no bodily contact, but physiological manifestations as a result of mental and psychosomatic injuries caused by the trauma. The New York Court asked why the words "or any other bodily injury" were added in Article 17 if "wounding" already covers all bodily injuries. In other words, could "bodily injury" not be understood to encompass 'internal injuries'? In this context, reference is made to scientific findings stating that the mind is part of the body. As a consequence, the New York Court did not agree with the *Rosman* decision.

---

267. *See, Hammond* v. *Bristow Helicopters Ltd.*, [1999] S.L.T. 919, decided by a Scottish court of first Instance, relying on: *Eastern* v. *Floyd*, Aviation and Space Law Reports 49 (1994), and *Kotsambasis* v. *Singapore Airlines*, 148 American Law Reports 498 (1997) (N.S.W. C.A.).
268. *See*, the previous footnote.
269. Which was not recognised as 'bodily injury' in *Turturo* v. *Continental Airlines*, 128 F. Supp. 2d 170 (S.D.N.Y 2001).
270. *See, Rosman* v. *Trans World Airlines*, 13 Avi 17,231 (N.Y. Court of Appeal 1974).
271. *See, Husserl* v. *Swissair*, 13 Avi. 17,603 (S.D. N.Y. 1975); *see also, Georgopolous* v. *American Airlines*, Supreme Court New South Wales, (Judgement No. S11422/1993) 10 December 1993, Judge Ireland holding 'nervous shock' as a species of bodily injury.
272. *See, Dooley* c.s. v. *Korean Air Lines Co.*, US Supreme Court 97-704, 8 June 1998; S. Ct. 1998 WL 292072 (U.S.).

3.8.4.3 The Relationship Between Bodily Injury and Mental Injury under UK Case Law

The UK House of Lords ruled in the same vein in the case of *King* v. *Bristow Helicopters*. Here are the relevant conclusions of Lord Nicholls of Birkenhead:

2. There is a measure of disagreement ... on whether inherent in article 17 of the Warsaw Convention is an antithesis between bodily injury and mental injury, the latter being outside the scope of article 17. I can state my own view shortly.
3. The expression 'bodily injury', or *'lésion corporelle'*, in article 17 means, simply, injury to the passenger's body. The contrast is with absence of injury to a passenger's body. This simple meaning propounds a coherent and workable test. None of the submissions urged .... has persuaded me that this phrase should be given a different, more limited meaning. In particular, I see no occasion for limiting article 17 to bodily injuries which are 'palpable and conspicuous', whatever those two ambiguous expressions are taken to mean in this context. *The brain is part of the body.* Injury to a passenger's brain is an injury to a passenger's body just as much as an injury to any other part of his body. Whether injury to a part of a person's body has occurred is, today as much as in 1929, essentially *a question of medical evidence.* It may be that, in the less advanced state of medical and scientific knowledge seventy years ago, psychiatric disorders would not have been related to physical impairment of the brain or nervous system. But even if that is so, this cannot be a good reason for now excluding this type of bodily injury, if proved by satisfactory evidence, from the scope of article 17.
4. This does not mean that shock, anxiety, fear, distress, grief or other emotional disturbances will as such now fall within article 17. It is all a question of *medical evidence.* In *Weaver* v. *Delta Airlines* (1999) 56 F Supp 2d 1190 the uncontradicted medical evidence was that *extreme* stress could cause actual physical brain damage. The judge observed, at p 1192, that 'fright alone is not compensable, but brain injury from fright is.'
5. It really goes without saying that international uniformity of interpretation of article 17 is highly desirable. Like Lord Mackay of Clashfern, I have been much concerned that the interpretation of article 17 espoused by this House should, if possible, be consistent with the mainstream views expressed in leading overseas authorities. Most notable in this respect, given the important position of the United States in carriage by air, is the decision of the United States Supreme Court in *Eastern Airlines Inc v. Floyd* (1991) 499 US 530. I consider the view I have expressed above is consistent with *Floyd* and the other leading cases. I agree with Lord Hobhouse's analysis of the authorities.[273]

In short, while, on the one hand, it is acknowledged that the brain is part of the body, on the other hand, *medical evidence* must determine whether or not "bodily injury" includes mental injury.[274] A more literal interpretation was adopted in another case ruled by the British House of Lords in 2001:[275]

---

273. Judgement of 28 February 2002 [2002] UKHL 7; [2001] 1 Lloyd's Rep. 95, and www.public ations.parliament.uk/pa/g-1.htm.
274. *See also,* R. Garcia-Bennet, *Psychological Injuries under Article 17 of the Warsaw Convention*, 26(3) Air & Space Law 49–55 (2001).
275. Judgement of the British Supreme Court of Judicature, case no. B3/2000/3820, of 17 May 2001.

These considerations lead us to the firm conclusion that when those who drafted the Warsaw Convention used the phrase '*lésion corporelle*/bodily injury' they intended that phrase to have its natural meaning – physical injury. They did not intend that it would extend to a different type of harm, mental injury. The phrase had for the drafters a uniform meaning. Changes that have since occurred in the attitude of different jurisdictions to liability for causing mental injury cannot effect a change in the meaning to be accorded to the phrase in the convention.

Although the event was termed as an accident, the claim for compensation was dismissed because it did not justify the qualification of "bodily injury." In 2014, an Australian superior Court also arrived at the conclusion that pure psychological injury is not compensable.[276]

The English Court of Appeal dismissed the claim made by Miss Morris in *Morris v. KLM Royal Dutch Airlines*, referred to in section 3.6.4, above, because the natural meaning of '*lésion corporelle*' is physical harm. Miss Morris did not sustain any physical harm.[277] The House of Lords found that:

> For the purposes of Article 17, 'bodily injury' means physical injury to the body, and, accordingly, the Warsaw Convention does not permit recovery for any psychiatric condition (unless it is consequent upon physical injury or is proved to be an expression of physical injury to the brain, central nervous system or any other component of the body caused by the accident in question) or for any emotional upset (such as fear, distress, grief or mental anguish).[278]

In a claim which was based upon *breach of contract* rather than provisions of international airline liability conventions, the English High Court found that damages could include damages in relation to mental suffering, provided that the suffering was directly related to physical inconvenience or discomfort. The claimant was denied boarding on a flight from Nigeria to England as he was accused of having a fake passport.[279] The claim was not based on provisions of international conventions as the damage was not caused by an accident which took place between embarkation and disembarkation.

---

276. *See, Halime* v. *Singapore Airlines* [2014] NSWSC 1681 and *Stott* v. *Thomas Cook Tour Operators*, [2014] UKSC 15, in which the UK Supreme Court refused to admit a claim made by a handicapped passenger for personal, psychological damages caused by his treatment on board the aircraft. *See*, however, *Stephenson* v. *Parkes Shire Council*, [2014] NSWSC 1758 [296] in which case the New South wales Supreme Court held that a common law action for nervous shock could be introduced despite the seemingly exclusive nature of the domestic statute, relying on *South Pacific Air Motive Pty.* v. *Magnus* [1998] FCA 1107; [1998] 157 ALR 443.
277. [2002] UKHL 7, [2002] 2 All ER 565, [2002] 1 All ER (Comm) 385, [2002] 2 WLR 578, [2002] 1 Lloyd's Rep 745.
278. [2002] 2 AC 628, as confirmed by His Honour Judge Graham Jones in *Akehurst and others* v. *Thomson Holidays Ltd. And Britannia Airways Ltd.*, case No. CF103949 and CF 106685 of the Cardiff County Court.
279. *See, R. Wiseman* v. *Virgin Atlantic Airways*, decision of 13 June 2006, case HQ05X03112.

3.8.5   Concluding Remarks

Annoyance, irritation and discomfort, which may arise in case a flight is delayed or cancelled, have been put forward as 'bodily injury' under Article 17 of the Warsaw Convention. The principal question has thus become whether emotional and mental injuries fall under "bodily injury." How to assess these damages is a matter for national courts, interpreting national law regarding this subject matter.

The words "damage sustained in case of death or bodily injury" has been interpreted under national law taking into account the facts of the case and the state of affairs in medical science. Cultural differences may also account for the unequivocal interpretations which have been given by courts in this respect.

A principal question concerns the submission of emotional and psychic injuries under the term 'bodily injury.' Courts have set up long lines of reasoning to arrive at an equitable decision. In some instances, they stressed the arguments pertaining to the original wording of the Warsaw and the Montreal Conventions, in others they adopted a somewhat more liberal approach by stating that pursuant to research conducted in medical sciences the mind has to be regarded as part of the body; as a consequence, psychic damages should be compensable. However, it was more than once added that the harm must be 'legally cognisable'. A more generous attitude inspired by increased attention for consumer protection may further cement this approach.

3.9   Delay

3.9.1   Regulation under the Montreal Convention, 1999

Because passengers and shippers of cargo choose air transport among others because of its speed, the airline is held liable for damage occasioned by delay. The provision in MC99 for delay has the same wording as the Warsaw Convention of 1929, and the Warsaw Convention as amended by The Hague Protocol, with the understanding that the word "transportation" in the older Conventions is now replaced by the word "carriage":

> The carrier is liable for damage occasioned by delay in the carriage by air of passengers, baggage or cargo.[280]

The notion of delay implies that there is a discrepancy between the time when the airline's clients expect the performance of the carrier's duties and the time when these duties are actually performed. For this provision to become applicable, the delay must arise *in the carriage by air* as to which see case law discussed below.[281]

---

280. *See*, Art. 19 of the Montreal Convention.
281. *See*, sections 3.9.2.3 and 3.9.4. below.

This article has not been amended in subsequent treaties: The Hague Protocol of 1955, Guatemala City Protocol of 1971 and Montreal Protocols of 1975. However, delay has not been defined. To define delay is left to courts, which must decide whether there was an actionable delay, giving rise to compensation for a passenger.

Article 19 goes on by saying that the carrier is not liable for damage caused by delay if he proves that it and its servants and agents have taken all necessary measures that could be reasonably required to avoid the damage or that it was impossible for it or them to take such measures.[282] Importantly, under the Montreal Convention, 1999, a clear link is established between a claim for damage caused by delay on the part of the passenger, and an exoneration clause for the carrier.

Another important provision is the *limited liability for delay*, that is, to the amount of 4,150 SDR per passenger. This amount has been raised to 4,694 SDR, effective on 1 January 2010, till 2019, pursuant to Article 24 of the Montreal Convention, 1999.[283]

The 'wilful misconduct' test may still be applied in cases involving delay. Article 22(5) MC99 introduces the possibility of breaking the limits of liability for delay for passenger and baggage damage:

> if it is proved that the damage resulted from an act or omission of the carrier, its servants or agents, done with the intent to cause damage recklessly and with knowledge that damage would probably result.

This is the only instance in which wilful misconduct and similar behaviour may lead to breaking the limits of the Convention. Such conduct is only relevant for breaking the limits in cases involving delay in the carriage of passengers, and in cases involving destruction, loss, damage or delay in the carriage of baggage.

3.9.2 Case Law under the Montreal Convention, 1999

3.9.2.1 Liability for Damage Occasioned by Delay

A Canadian Court has defined delay as:

> [...] occurring when passengers, baggage or goods do not arrive at their destination at the time indicated in the contract of carriage.[284]

---

282. As explained in the case *Helge Management* v. *Delta Air Lines* (Civil Action No. 11-10299-RBC, 2012 WL 2990728 (D. Mass. 19 July 2012)), in which the court held that the airline had taken all reasonable measures to avoid the damage when passengers had to wait for a flight to Moscow on the next day, and *Klurfan* v. *LAN Líneas Aéreas y American Airlines* (C. Civ Com. Fed. Causa No. 6.966/09/CA1, 8 July 2014) in which case the defendant airlines were allowed to rely on bad weather conditions justifying the cancellation of the flight. The airline's defence was not honoured in *Perlman* v. *Brussels Airlines*, No. 2013-1386 N C, 45 Misc. 3d 127(A), 2014 N.Y. Slip Op. 51459 Op.(U), 2014 WL 4958218 – hence, the plaintiff's damages were awarded.
283. *See*, ICAO Council – 188th session, C-WP/13478, 7/10/09.
284. *See*, *Balogun* v. *Air Canada* [2010] O.J. No. 663 (Court of Ontario for small claims).

Damages must be substantiated, as held by the Supreme Court of Sudan.[285]

The Court of the EU addressed the question whether the right of action in the case for the compensation of damages caused by delay lies with passengers. The passengers were employed by an employer who claimed damage consisting of hours during which his employees, the passengers, had not worked, from the airline. The Court decided in favour of the employer in the light of the strict consumer oriented decisions given by this Court, but may have had a valid reason to do so because of a literal interpretation, referring to Article 31 of the *Vienna Convention on the Law of Treaties of 1969*, of the expression "any damage occasioned by delay" without indicating who has suffered that damage. Hence, MC 99 should therefore be interpreted as applying not only to damage caused to passengers, but also to damage suffered by an employer with whom a transaction for the international carriage of a passenger was entered into. The CJEU added that air carriers are however guaranteed that their liability may not be engaged for more than the limit applicable for each passenger as established by the Convention multiplied by the number of employees/passengers concerned.[286]

Generally, mental injuries must still be accompanied by physical evidence thereof.[287] However, courts have given different decisions on this matter.[288] The 'damage' condition does not permit a plaintiff to recover for emotional or psychological injuries, and missed opportunities which are difficultly quantifiable.[289]

3.9.2.2   Exoneration of the Carrier

A strike of re-fuelers has been regarded as an instance of force majeure, discharging the air carrier from liability.[290] However, a labour strike by the handling agent of the carrier

---

285. Decision of the Supreme Court of Sudan No. 197/2013, 23 March 2014.
286. C-429/14, decision of 17 February 2016, *Air Baltic Corporation v. Lietuvos Respublikos*.
287. *See, Campbell v. Air Jamaica*, Civil Action No. 11-cv-23233, 2012 WL 3562126 (S.D. Fla 17 August 2012).
288. Courts in the Ukraine (*Individual v. Aeroflot*, High Specialized Court of Ukraine, IATA Liability Reporter 15 (2013) have held that moral damages should be awarded. Spanish courts held that 'moral damages' are compensable under Art. 22(2) of MC99 for the loss of registered/checked baggage. The Barcelona Court held that, although 'moral damages' may be awarded, the total compensation may not exceed the carrier's liability of 1000 [now1,131] SDR per passenger. Cf. Section 15, rolls 645/07 – 2a Judgment 270. This decision was upheld on appeal: the court held that in line with the terms of the convention, moral damages could be compensated. The combined total for moral and material damages may not exceed that liability limits laid down in the convention; *see*, Uria Menéndez & Miguel Gordillo, International Law Office, 3 March 2010; In Argentinian cases governed by the Warsaw/Montreal Conventions, compensation of moral damage is accepted as a compensable item, as long as the total amount of recovery grants does not exceed the Convention limits, when applicable; as to which *see*, *Alvarez, Hilda v. British Airways*; Supreme Court of Justice, 10/10/2002.
289. *See, Lukács v. United Airlines*, 2009 Carswell Man 54, 2009 MBQB 29, [2009] 4 W.W.R. 512, 237 Man. R. (2d) 75, 73 C.P.C (6th) 385; reference was made to the case *Mullaney v. Delta Air Lines* and *In Re Nigeria Charter Flights Contract litigation* cited above; *see also*, *Vumbaca v. Terminal One Group Association*, 859 F. Supp. 2d 343 (E.D.N.Y. 2012).
290. *See, Tismanariu v. Air France*, 2014 QCCQ [Quebec Court] 2847 (2014).

was not.[291] According to a US Court, weather conditions do not give rise to a claim for delay. This may be different in Europe.[292]

In the case of the academic who had been told that his flight had been cancelled as a consequence of a mechanical failure, the Court decided this case pursuant to the provisions on delay, probably because none of the parties had put forward another argument. The Court was not convinced that the carrier had taken all reasonable measures to avoid the damage.[293]

3.9.2.3 Delay in the Carriage by Air as Opposed to Non-performance of the Contract

Cases involving delay must be distinguished from cases whereby passengers were not accepted to board a booked flight, and, as a consequence of such refusal, arrived later than foreseen by them at the place of destination. This phenomenon is also referred to as 'overbooking' which is covered by section 2.2.2 of Chapter 5 on Passenger Protection. In brief, 'overbooking' must be seen as a breach of contract, which falls outside the scope of the Montreal Convention, 1999.[294] Article 19 of the Montreal Convention, 1999, has been held applicable to a 'bumping claim.'[295] However, the carrier is not liable is late for the check-in of the flight.[296]

Similarly, the cancellation of a flight due to a labour strike may be regarded as non-performance of the contract of carriage, and not a delay under the Montreal Convention. Hence, the damage claims are not pre-empted by the Montreal Convention,[297] and may fall, for instance, under EU Regulation 261/2004 governing

---

291. Judgment of the Lisbon Court of Appeal of 29 October 2015; *see also*, the explanations given in the case *Helge Management* v. *Delta Air Lines* (Civil Action No. 11-10299-RBC, 2012 WL 2990728 (D. Mass. 19 July 2012)), in which the court held that the airline had taken all reasonable measures to avoid the damage when passengers had to wait for a flight to Moscow on the next day, and *Klurfan* v. *LAN Líneas Aéreas y American Airlines* (C. Civ Com. Fed. Causa No. 6.966/09/CA1, 8 July 2014) in which case the defendant airlines were allowed to rely on bad weather conditions justifying the cancellation of the flight. The airline's defence was not honoured in *Perlman* v. *Brussels Airlines*, No. 2013-1386 N C, 45 Misc. 3d 127(A), 2014 N.Y. Slip Op. 51459 Op.(U), 2014 WL 4958218.
292. *See*, section 2.3.8. of Chapter 5.
293. *See, Lukács* v. *United Airlines*, 2009 Carswell Man 54, 2009 MBQB 29, [2009] 4 W.W.R. 512, 237 Man. R. (2d) 75, 73 C.P.C (6th) 385; reference was made to the case *Mullaney* v. *Delta Air Lines* and *In Re Nigeria Charter Flights Contract litigation* cited above; *see also, Vumbaca* v. *Terminal One Group Association*, 859 F. Supp. 2d 343 (E.D.N.Y. 2012).
294. *See*, Legal Committee of ICAO, 30th Session, Report of the Second Meeting of the Secretariat Study Group on *the Modernization of the Warsaw Convention System*; LC/30-IP/7 of 4 February 1997.
295. *See*, section 3.8.4.1, above.
296. *See, Igwe* v. *NorthWest Airlines, Inc.*, 31 Avi. 18,431 (S.D. Tex 2007); reliance on *force majeure* caused by weather conditions was honoured in a decision on a flight delay made by the Prymorskyi Court of Odessa (case no. 2/522/7728/15).
297. *See, Mullaney* v. *Delta Air Lines*, 33 Avi. 17,819 (S.D.N.Y. 2009).

passenger protection in case of denied boarding, delay and flight cancellation.[298] The cancellation of a flight, resulting in ticketed passengers not travelling and with no alternative service arranged by the carrier, is not delay but also *non-performance of the contract*. Hence, passengers are entitled to sue the carrier under domestic law as they are not pre-empted to do so by the Montreal Convention, 1999.[299] Passengers who had checked in but were not in time at the check-in desk when the delayed flight departed have no right of compensation under MC99;[300] said passengers had to purchase new tickets.

3.9.2.4 Breaking the Liability Limits Through Wilful Misconduct

As said above, the 'wilful misconduct' test may still be applied in cases involving delay. Reckless conduct, if stated and proved by the claimant, does not make the other provisions of MC99 inapplicable.[301]

When the carrier can rely on air traffic management decisions in situations causing delay, there is no room for reckless or wilful misconduct by the air carrier.[302]

3.9.3 Regulation under the Warsaw Regime

The formulation of the provision on delay is the same as under the Montreal Convention, 1999. The only difference is that, where MC99 reads "The carrier *is* liable for damage occasioned by delay [...]" WC29 provides that "The carrier *shall be* liable for damage occasioned by delay [...]." (*italics added*) However, this difference does not appear to be an essential one.

The WC29 regime leaves the establishment of the link between a claim for damage caused by delay on the part of the passenger, and an exoneration clause for the carrier open for interpretation by national courts. There is no explicit reference in the provision on delay in WC29[303] to the exoneration clause for the carrier.[304]

The limits for damage caused by delay can be broken by proof of 'wilful misconduct' on the part of the carrier, in case of the Warsaw Convention, 1929, and reckless conduct under the Hague Protocol.[305] Case law necessitated a less open ended

---

298. *See*, section 2.2 of Chapter 5.
299. *See*, *In re Nigeria Charter Flights Contract Litigation*, 520 F. Supp. 2d 447 (E.D.N.Y. 2007); *see also*, section 5.3 for EU regulations and case law on this subject.
300. *See*, decision made by the Ukrainian Pecherskyi District Court on 8 May 2015, 757/36520/14.
301. *See*, *Bernfield* v. *US Airways*, 2016 WL 1583057 and *Booker* v. *BWIA West Indies Airways Ltd.*, 32 Avi 15,134 (E.D.N.Y 2007).
302. *See*, *Cohen* v. *Delta Airlines*, 2010 WL 4720222 (S.D.N.Y., 8 November 2010).
303. Art. 19 of the Warsaw Convention.
304. Art. 20 of the Warsaw Convention.
305. The main part of the new Art. 25, as amended under The Hague Protocol, reads as follows: "The limits of liability specified in Article 22 shall not apply if it is proved that the damage resulted from an act or omission of the carrier, his servants or agents, done with the intent to cause damage or recklessly and with knowledge that damage would probably result [...]".

and a more unequivocal text.[306] It would appear that the test for breaking the liability limits have become more severe under The Hague Protocol. Two conditions must be fulfilled:

- an act or omission designed to cause damage; and
- the intention to commit such an act or omission.[307]

The plaintiff must prove that the carrier, or his agents acting within the scope of their employment, possesses actual, or effective knowledge, and not knowledge, which they ought to have, taking into account all the circumstances of the cases. Delegates to The Hague Conference were not unanimous in their decision to raise the liability limits by 100 per cent. Actually, a number of representatives did not wish a higher limit than 60 per cent as compared to the limits set forth by the Warsaw Convention. The compromise achieved the following:

- a raise of the liability limit by 100 per cent, which is a concession in favour of the passenger/consignor;
- a strict formulation and application of the escape from the liability limits, which is a concession in favour of the carrier.

Hence, Articles 22 and 25 of WC29/HP55 are communicating vessels in the history of international private air law. What is added to one vessel is taken away from the other.

3.9.4   Case Law under the Warsaw Regime

3.9.4.1   Defining Delay

The Paris Court of Appeals set forth that a flight was delayed when the carrier realised its commitments for carriage in bad conditions and the arrival at the place of destination was later than foreseen. In addition, the court found that, when the flight has been delayed, the contract of carriage has been executed.[308]

By insertion of clauses into contracts with their passengers, airlines have sought to limit their liability for damage, which is the result of delay. Based on the previous version of the IATA Conditions of Contract, passenger tickets used to state that:

---

306. *See, Pekelis v. Transcontinental and Western Air*, 187 F.2d 122, 23 A.L.R.2d 1349, No. 39, Docket 21690, United States Court of Appeals Second Circuit. Decided 15 February 1951.
307. *See,* Prof. Bin Cheng, *Wilful Misconduct: From Warsaw to The Hague and from Brussels to Paris*, II McGill Annals of Air and Space Law 84 (1977). One case of interest on this point is the judgement of 9 September 1992, in the US District Court (E.D. NY) by Chief Justice Platt confirming three findings of wilful misconduct in relation to the Lockerbie crash.
308. *See,* Alexandre Job et Françoise Odier, *La responsabilité du transporteur aérien de personnes pour cause de retard,* Revue française de droit aérien et spatial 3-10 (2003), discussing the decision made by the Court of Appeals (*Cour d'Appel de Paris*) of 28 June 2002. The court stated that "il y a retard lorsque le transporteur réalise son obligation de transporter dans de mauvaises conditions et que l'arrivée à la destination se fait au-delà de l'instant initialement prévu."

Carrier undertakes its best efforts to carry the passenger and his baggage within reasonable dispatch. Times shown in timetables or elsewhere are not guaranteed and form no part of this contract.[309]

It can be questioned whether this IATA provision did not contravene the spirit, if not the letter of Article 19, in that it tends to relieve the carrier of at least a part of his liability. Reference is made to Article 23 of the Warsaw Convention. It is then up to national courts to judge whether or not the contractual clause, including that the carriage must be executed within a reasonable dispatch, is valid, or contrary to Articles 19 and 23 of the Warsaw Convention.[310] Passengers and shippers of cargo select carriage by air because of speed. Hence, courts did not allow airlines to escape liability by broad application of provisions such as the above-mentioned IATA General Conditions of Contract. Minor delays are permitted.

The carrier must perform the flight *within a reasonable time*, taking into account all relevant facts of the case submitted to the court.[311] Thus, a French Court did not accept the reliance by the air carrier on the indicative character of the times shown in the contract as a justification for the postponement of a consecutive flight, and hence, an exoneration of his liability.[312]

French Courts emphasise the deviation from the contract, whereas common law courts look at the reasonableness of the delay.[313] These attitudes are in line with the approach with respect to the interpretation of law in more general terms chosen by civil law and common law courts.

3.9.4.2   Scope of Damages

The damage must be quantifiable. Recovery for mental damages, including irritation, annoyance, inconvenience, uncertainty on the status of the flight and safety concerns, are not recoverable as they do not result into 'cognisable' economic loss.[314] Moreover,

---

309. Based on Art. X of the IATA General Conditions of Carriage. Full text:

> Carrier undertakes its best efforts to carry the passenger and his baggage within reasonable dispatch. Times shown in timetables or elsewhere are not guaranteed and form no part of this contract. Carrier may without notice substitute alternate carriers or aircraft, and may alter or omit stopping places shown on the ticket in case of necessity. Schedules are subject to change without notice. Carrier assumes no responsibility for making connections.

310. Art. 23:

> Any provision tending to relieve the carrier of liability or to fix a lower limit of liability than that which is laid down in this convention shall be null and void, but the nullity of any such provision shall not involve the nullity of the whole contract, which shall remain subject to the provisions of this convention.

311. *See also, Robert Houdin v. Panair do Brasil*, 24 Revue Générale de l'Air 285 (1961), and G. Miller, *Liability in International Air Transport* 155–157 (1977). *See also, Bart v. British West Indian Airways Ltd.*, l Lloyd's Reports 239 (1967).

312. *See, Souillac v. Air France, Tribunal de grande instance* of Seine, 26 June 1964, 28 Revue Générale de l'Air 18–19 (1965).

313. *See*, G. Miller, *Liability in International Air Transport* 158 (1977).

314. *See, Lee v. American Airlines*, 2004 WL 18008 (5th Cir. 2004); *see* however, *Ortuño Dora & others v. Iberia Líneas Aéras de España* (MJJ51024, 24 September 2009), and *B., N.J. & others*

they must be "occasioned by delay." Hence, there must be a link between the damage and the delay. This formulation gives room for *consequential damage*.[315] In 1984, a German case, the plaintiff argued that, due to the delay of his luggage, he had not enjoyed his holiday as he would have with his luggage having arrived in time. The court did not grant compensation for loss of enjoyment of the holiday.[316]

An American Court awarded damages for *mental anguish and emotional distress* caused by a delay involving a PIA flight. In this case, plaintiff had contracted for shipment by PIA of the remains of her husband to his burial place in his native village. Islamic doctrine requires that the corpse is being buried as soon as possible. PIA was aware of the urgency of the shipment to arrive in time. Several decisions made by the airline caused delay. The family of the deceased person suffered anguish and emotional distress. Not only did the court grant compensation for immaterial damages, but also ruled that the behaviour of the carrier amounted to 'wilful misconduct.'[317]

In Spain, compensations vary from payment of minor expenditures, which are directly related to the delay, to additional expenses including either a refund of the air ticket or the cost of a comparable carriage by air. Even immaterial damages have been awarded, in cases of delays of three to four hours and more. It is questionable whether such damages fall under the scope of the damages which are recoverable under the Warsaw regime or the Montreal Convention. Decisions on delay cases concerned amounts from EUR 300 to EUR 6,000.

A passenger may choose to base his claim on inconvenience leading to expenses incurred by rerouting of a flight after the first leg was delayed. Because Mr Malek's Venice-Paris flight was delayed, he missed his Paris-New York connection upon which he was rerouted to New Jersey. Rerouting and delayed arrival of his baggage plus broken items contained in his baggage caused him extra costs which were awarded by the court.[318]

Delay is a concern in China and other Asian countries. In 2004, the Civil Aviation Authority of China (CAAC) cleared the confusion surrounding compensation to be paid to passengers on delayed flights. The directive states that passengers are entitled to compensation from the airline. The airline may be exonerated from the duty to pay compensation in cases of external factors causing the delay, such as bad weather and

---

v. *Cubana de Aviación* (MJJ25936, 19 February 2008) and *De La Barrera Lucio J., & others* v. *Alitalia* (Lexis No. 70053490, 7 April 2009) where moral damages have been awarded in the exact same amount.

315. *See*, for instance, Art. 1(1) of the *Rome Convention on Damage caused by Foreign aircraft to Third Parties on the Surface* (1952), which states that there is "... no right to compensation if the damage is not a *direct* consequence of the incident ..." (*italics added*). *See also*, the 'New York' rule including that damage inflicted to a second house which burns as a consequence of an incident caused by an aircraft in flight is not covered by the said *Rome Convention* of 1952 as to which *see*, Ryan v. *New York Railway Co.* (1866) 35 N.Y. 210, 91 American Decisions 49.

316. *Amtsgericht* (District Court) *Dusseldorf*, decision of 15 October 1984 (47 C 470/84). The decision is summarised in 35 *Zeitschrift für Luft- und Weltraumrecht* 76–78 (1986).

317. 17 Aviation Cases 18,618; *see also*, section 3.9.4.6, below.

318. *See, Malek* v. *Societé Air France*, 31 Avi. 18,096 (CivCt. NY Cty 2006).

mistakes made by air traffic controllers. Amounts vary in accordance with the length of the delay, and may be paid in cash, air miles or ticket discounts. The CAAC did not determine standard amounts for compensation of delay, leaving this to airlines.[319]

3.9.4.3 Causes of Delay

For legal reasons, it is important to ascertain the cause of the delay. The *first* legal reason that the plaintiff must establish depends on the moment that the delay has arisen and whether or not Article 19 of the Warsaw Convention is applicable. The delay must be *occasioned* in the carriage by air, which is a matter of *interpretation* of the facts of the case. The *second* reason why it is important to determine the cause of the delay is that the carrier may have recourse to exoneration of liability if he can prove:

(1) either that he, the carrier, had taken all necessary measures to avoid the damage produced by delay, or that it had been impossible for him to take such measures;[320] *or*, alternatively;

(2) that the damage was due to the contributory negligence of the plaintiff, that is, the passenger, or to an inherent defect of the baggage or cargo.

As to the causes of delay, insufficient infrastructure facilities play an eminent role. Infrastructure does not only include ATC, but also delay in the allocation of airport infrastructure, that is, making available slots, bridges, gates and so forth. Other factors causing delay pertain to the following:

- administrative failures with respect to the reservation of seats, for instance, failure to make a reservation or double reservation of the same seats;
- deviations and omissions of stops for safety, security or meteorological reasons;
- failure to perform correctly baggage and cargo handling: for instance, baggage may be loaded into the wrong aircraft,[321] or failure to perform administrative handling of the cargo;[322]
- technical state of the equipment, that is, of the aircraft;
- administrative processing of the flight;[323]
- unfavourable weather conditions.

---

319. *See*, Xu Xiaomin and Miao Qing, *CAAC Guideline on compensation*, received by email on 23 July 2004.
320. Art. 20 of the Warsaw Convention.
321. *See*, H. Drion, *Limitation of Liabilities in International Air Law* 213 (1954).
322. *See*, for instance, delay of artwork at Milan airport due to Italian customs handling, in: *Weston v. Federal Express*, 29 Fed. Appx. 795; 2002 U.S. App. LEXIS 4723 (2nd Cir. 2002).
323. *See*, E. Mapelli, *Air carriers Liability in Cases of Delay*, I McGill Annals of Air and Space Law 119–115 (1976).

Thus, safety concerns can be related to the cause of delay. Passengers, who have solid reasons to believe that the aircraft on which they are booked is not safe, may be entitled to refuse embarkation into the aircraft. The operator of the aircraft, which passengers argue is unsafe, must compensate the damage, which is caused by the delay. This is the essence of a verdict rendered by the Amsterdam Court of Appeal in a claim which was raised by 42 passengers against Air Atlantis, a daughter company of the Portuguese flag carrier TAP. The flight from Amsterdam to Faro, Portugal, was severely delayed as a consequence of a number of technical incidents. Passengers had lost their faith in the safe operation of the aircraft, and returned on other aircraft. Passengers received compensation for both material and immaterial damage amounting to about USD 400 per passenger.[324]

These defences have been explained in court cases as to which *see*, section 3.8.4.5.

3.9.4.4 Non-performance of the Contract

Article 19 refers to the delay *in the transportation by air*, which has been modified in 'carriage by air' in the Hague Protocol of 1955 amending WC29. Delay arises as soon as passengers, baggage or cargo arrive at a later time than agreed between the airline and the client. Hence, the term 'carriage by air' has a different meaning than the period between embarkation and disembarkation[325] or the period specified in Article 18(2) of the same convention.[326] Even if a broad interpretation of the delay provision of the Warsaw Convention is justified from a systematic point of view, delay must be distinguished from *non-performance of carriage*.

Delay arises when the contract has been executed, but not timely. In the case of non-performance, the contract has not been executed at all. Non-performance on the part of the carrier is not covered by the Warsaw Convention but by applicable national legislation. In 1990, German courts had to decide on some cases in which the passenger arrived later than stipulated by the contract with his airline. In none of these cases, reference was made to liability of the carrier for damage resulting from delay.[327]

'Complete non-performance of the contract,' or cases where the airline has 'flatly refused to transport' a claimant, rather than 'delay in transportation' may trigger non-applicability of the Warsaw or Montreal Conventions.[328] The facts of the case must

---

324. *Consumentenbod* v. *Air Atlantis*, reported in Mr. de Pous, 1(1) Routertravel of February 2001, at 3.
325. Art. 17 of the Warsaw Convention.
326. In the same sense: H. Drion, *Limitation of Liabilities in International Air Law* 85–86 (1954). *See* however, Shawcross & Beaumont, Air Law VII/191. The broader interpretation is also advocated by G. Miller, *Liability in International Air Transport* 159–160 (1977).
327. Discussed by R. Schmid, *Which Are the Duties of an Air Carrier Who Does Not Execute an Air Carriage Contract as Agreed?* 15(1) Air Law 49–51 (1990).
328. *See, Mizyed* v. *Delta Airlines*, No. 12-382 2012, WL 1672810 (E.D. La 14 May 2012); *see also, Salamey* v. *American Airlines*, No. 8:11 – cv – 2354, 2011 WL 5445129 (M.D. Fla 9 November 2011).

show whether contract for the carriage by air has been performed, or has been begun to be performed. If so, the Warsaw or Montreal Convention provides the exclusive cause of action.

In the case of *Tumar v. Pan American World Airways*,[329] Pan Am could have relied on the defence provided by Article 20 WC29 if Article 19 was the basis of the action of plaintiffs. As the passengers were, according to the conditions of carriage with Pan Am, late for check-in they were not allowed to board. The court refused to grant damages because they were in breach of the contract with their carrier. The carrier did not need to invoke Article 20 WC29, but if it would have come so far, reliance on this clause might have been justified.

These cases show the interest of determining the *cause* of the delay. For damage caused by delay to be recoverable under Article 19 of the Warsaw Convention it must occur in the framework of the execution of the contract concluded between passenger and airline, or between airline and consignor or consignee. If this condition is fulfilled, the plaintiff is bound by the limitations drawn up by this Convention, namely, the cap on the carrier's liability[330] and the period of time within which he must bring a suit before the court.[331]

3.9.4.5 *Defences Available to the Air Carrier*

From the *first* defence it follows that a carrier is entitled to exonerate himself from liability if he can prove that the delay was reasonable. For instance, when the carrier was obliged to take another flight path resulting in delay for safety, including meteorological, reasons, he could argue that such a delay is reasonable. Not only speed, but also care for safety considerations in unforeseen circumstances is inherent to international carriage by air. In the case of *Komlos v. Air France*,[332] the court decided that the Convention only offers a *presumption of liability* because the carrier can escape his liability if he can prove that he has taken all the measures which were necessary to avoid the damage.[333] Consequently, the court to which the case has been submitted may, in accordance with its own national law, decide that the carrier is not liable, if the damage was caused by contributory negligence.[334]

Another French case illustrates this point of view. An aircraft operated by Air France was hit by serious mechanical problems so that the flight had to be cancelled. Passengers could be carried from Paris to New York on the next day only, which resulted into a delay of 16 hours. Since the mechanical problems could not be

---

329. 4 Aviation Cases, 18,152.
330. *See*, Art. 22 of the WC29, as amended by the Hague Protocol.
331. *See*, Art. 29 in conjunction with Art. 28 of the Warsaw Convention of 1929.
332. Cited by Shawcross and Beamont, *Air Law* VII/72 at note 1.
333. *See*, Art. 20.
334. *See*, Art. 21.

anticipated by Air France, were caused independently from its will,[335] and Air France had taken all necessary measures to avoid the damage, Air France's reliance upon Article 20 of the Warsaw Convention was successful.[336]

In Israel, courts have adopted the position that the carrier does not only need to prove that they did everything to shorten the delay, but also that they did everything possible to prevent the delay in the first place. In 2011, the Tel Aviv District Court ruled ordered the carrier to pay compensation for unreasonable flight delay resulting from damage on the cockpit window. One hour after take-off, the aircraft had to return to Vienna due to a crack in the pilot's cockpit window. The flight was cancelled, which resulted in a delay of approximately 33 hours. The Court found that the carrier did not prove that it took the necessary measures to detect the fault in advance, and that it failed to explain how, notwithstanding the actual maintenance and controls, the crack was caused.[337]

The *second* defence, that is, *contributory negligence* on the side of the passenger may arise when he has not followed the instructions of the carrier.[338] It may be difficult to ascertain whether the cause of the damage was produced by delay or by an inherent defect. The damage could be the result of the delay or by an illness, which the chickens had when they were shipped. Thus, expert tests are required to reveal the cause of the accident.

3.9.4.6   The Wilful Misconduct Test

The limits for damage caused by delay can be broken by proof by the claimant of 'wilful misconduct' on the part of the carrier, in case of the Warsaw Convention, 1929, and reckless conduct under the Hague Protocol.[339]

In one of the very few cases under this heading, the court, namely, the High Court of Singapore, was asked to apply wilful misconduct under the Warsaw Convention as amended by the Hague Protocol. The evidence was not unequivocal. Because

---

335. 'La défaillance du circuit électrique était imprévisible et indépendante de la volonté de la société Air France.'
336. A. Job and F. Odier, *La responsabilité du transporteur aérien de personnes pour cause de retard*, LVII Revue française de droit aérien et spatial 3–10 (2003), discussing the decision made by the *Cour d' Appel de Paris* of 28 June 2002.
337. *See*, P. Sharon, K. Marco, '*Flight Delay: Tel Aviv District Court Rules on Burden of Proof*,' available at www.internationallawoffice.com, 20 June 2012.
338. In 2012 the Port Authority of New York announced that it will start fining passengers who delay the planes. The fines are addressed to unruly passengers, as they will apply to cases where the passengers a) refuse to turn off electronic devices, b) being intoxicated an causing disruption, c) fighting with a flight attendant, d) lighting a cigarette or refusing to put one out, e) any kind of disagreement with a flight attendant.
339. The main part of the new Art. 25, as amended under The Hague Protocol, reads as follows: "The limits of liability specified in Article 22 shall not apply if it is proved that the damage resulted from an act or omission of the carrier, his servants or agents, done with the intent to cause damage or recklessly and with knowledge that damage would probably result [...]".

statements pertaining to the operational conditions under which the accident had taken place on both sides contradicted the court was not convinced by plaintiff's plea for wilful misconduct. Hence, defendant was entitled to rely on the liability limits foreseen in the mentioned Convention.[340] The court granted a judgment for unlimited compensation using the wilful misconduct test in a case were the defendant exposed the imported air cargoes to a huge risk of loss through theft or delivery to the wrong consignee and concluded that it had acted recklessly and with "knowledge that damage would probably result."[341]

In another case, it was ruled that damages for the wilful delay of passenger's baggage should be awarded in accordance with the applicable local law, that is, the laws of New York.[342]

3.9.5 Concluding Remarks

The most central provision, namely, Article 19 of the Warsaw Convention, provides no more and no less than a general framework within which the regulation of delay can be placed. That is why it should not be surprising that national jurisdictions will arrive at different solutions in comparable cases. A telling example forms the compensation for immaterial damages. Some courts have been willing to award on-material damages produced by delay, that is, up to the limits provided by this convention, whereas others have been reluctant to do so.

Delay in the carriage by air must be distinguished from non-performance of the contact. If the Warsaw regime does not apply, the plaintiff may be in an advantageous position in that the limits of this Convention do not diminish compensation. To what extent this is an advantage depends on the applicable national law.

Moreover, *the cause* of the delay must be established in order to determine whether or not the carrier has, or has not taken all necessary measures to avoid the delay. Secondly, for Article 19 of the Warsaw Convention to apply, the cause of the delay must occur in the context of "international transportation by air", or, as the case may be "international carriage by air." Thus, if such an occurrence falls outside the scope of the transportation by air, the action of the plaintiff should not be based on delay, but on the non-performance of the agreement.

In the EU, Regulation 261/2004 is designed to provide assistance to delayed passengers. As stated there, international law arguments may affect the scope of the measures foreseen in this regulation.[343]

---

340. *See*, The High Court of the Republic of Singapore, *Clarke and Others* v. *Silk Air (Singapore) Private Ltd.*, judgement of 24 October 200.
341. *See*, *Singapore Airlines Ltd & Anor* v. *Fujitsu Microelectronics (Malaysia) Sdn Bhd & Ors*, [2001] 1 SLR 241.
342. *See*, *Cohen* v. *Varig Airlines*, 62 A.D.2d 324, 333, 405 N.Y.S.2d 44, 48 (1st Dep't 1978).
343. *See*, section 2.3.1 of Chapter 5.

3.10   Baggage

3.10.1   Regulation under the Montreal Convention, 1999

MC99 sets a limit of 1,000, now 1,131 SDRs,[344] for destruction, loss, damage or delay of checked baggage per passenger rather than by reference to weight of the baggage, provided that the baggage is "in the charge of the carrier."[345] The claimant has to provide evidence of this requirement.[346]

As a general rule, a claim for damages arising out of the handling of baggage on an international flight, is pre-empted by the Montreal Convention, 1999.[347]

3.10.2   Case Law under the Montreal Convention, 1999

The term 'baggage' includes registered and cabin baggage. The carrier is liable for destruction, loss, damage or delay of baggage per passenger, excluding claims for emotional injuries caused by loss of or delayed baggage.[348]

The Conditions of Carriage of carriers generally contain the following condition:

> The checked baggage will be carried on the same aircraft as the passenger, unless the carrier decides that this is impracticable, in which case the carrier will carry the checked baggage on the carrier's next flight on which space is available.

On 1 August 2000, a Dutch civil court decided that baggage should be carried in the same aircraft as the passenger who carried the luggage. Said condition is part of the agreement between carrier and passenger, which imposes an obligation upon the carrier to carry the baggage on the same aircraft as the passenger.[349]

Article 22(2) of the Montreal Convention should be read in conjunction with Article 3(3) of that Convention and be interpreted as meaning that the right to

---

344. *See*, 188th session of the ICAO Council, C-WP/13478, 7/10/09. The new limit is effective on 1 January 2010, pursuant to Art. 24 of MC99, and is valid till 2019.
345. *See*, Art. 17(2) of MC99; *Thankgod Ekufu et al.*, v. *Iberia Airlines*, No. 12-cv-6669, 2014 WL 87502 (N.D. Ill. 9 January 2014); *Small* v. *America West Airlines, Inc.*, 32 Avi 15,878 (D.N.J. 2007), following case law made under the Warsaw Convention, as to which *see*, *Fuller* v. *Amerijet International* (273 F. Supp. 2d 902, 903 (S.D.) Tex. 2003), and *Wells* v. *American Airlines*, Inc., 1993 U.S. App. LEXIS 16990 (9th Cir. 1993).
346. *See*, *Malhotra* v. *All Nippon Airways*, No. 1:14-cv-02630-DLI-LB (E.D.N.Y. 17 August 2015); *El Hares* v. *Iberia Líneas Aéreas de España*, IJ-LXXI-895; 23 April 2014. A passenger claiming that personally carved pieces of art packed in checked baggage were lost in transit whereas there was no evidence of their market value, received the nominal value of 10 US$ as a matter of compensation; *see*, *Mohamed* v. *Air France*, 31 Avi 17,505 (N.Y. Civ Ct. Kings Cty 2006).
347. *See*, *Bridgeman* v. *United Continental Holding*, No. 4:12-cv-2848, 2012 WL 5989209 (S.D. Tex. Nov 29 2012). In *Calvo* v. *VRG Linhas Aereas*, Case 13237/10, Juzgado Nacional de 1o Instancia en lo Civil y Commercial Federal 11 Secretaria 22, reported by Elizabeth Freidenberg in International Law office of 3 April 2013 the court brought compensation for loss of baggage under local law rather than the Warsaw Convention as amended by Montreal Protocol No. 2.
348. *See*, *Bassam* v. *American Airlines*, 2008 WL 2725228 (5th Cir. 2008); *see also*, *Booker* v. *BWIA West Indies Airways Ltd.*, 32 Avi 15,134 (E.D.N.Y 2007).
349. *See*, *Opera Select* v. *KLM Royal Dutch Airlines*, case number 67216/KG ZA 00-425, District Court of Haarlem, the Netherlands; decision of 1 August 2000; *see also*, Annex 5.3 of EU Regulation 300/2008.

compensation and the limits to a carrier's liability of 1,131 SDR in the event of destruction, loss, damage or delay of baggage apply also to a passenger who claims that compensation by virtue of the loss, destruction, damage or delay of baggage checked in in another passenger's name, provided that the baggage did in fact contain the first passenger's own belongings. Therefore, each passenger affected by destruction, loss, damage or delay of baggage registered under somebody else's name shall be entitled to compensation within the limit of 1,131 SDR if he/she can prove that his/her belongings were in fact contained in the registered baggage. Each passenger must prove this satisfactorily before a national judge, who can take into consideration the fact that the passengers are members of the same family, have bought their ticket jointly or have travelled together.[350]

The Higher Regional Court of Frankfurt stated that, while the burden of proof for the loss of the carried item is on the passenger, the carrier must explain how exactly the baggage was treated.[351] Failing to do so resulted in the obligation to award damages in excess of the liability limit.

A US Court awarded limited damages for delay, that is, 1,000, now 1,131, SDRs per event – there were two delays cases – ruling that Article 29 of the Montreal Convention prohibits the award of non-compensatory damages.[352] However, the Lisbon Court of Appeals noted that moral damages deriving from the loss of baggage are not available under the terms of the Montreal Convention, 1999, except if the claimants can prove that the damage resulted from an act or omission of the carrier, its employees or agents, done with the intent to cause damage or recklessly and with knowledge damage would probably result. In the case of such act or omission of an employee or agent, it is also to be proved that such employee or agent was acting within the scope of his or her employment.[353]

On the other hand, two Spanish and Argentinian courts held that 'moral damages' are compensable under Article 22(2) of the Montreal Convention for the loss of registered/checked baggage. The combined total for moral and material damages may not exceed that liability limits laid down in the convention.[354]

The Barcelona Court held that, although 'moral damages' may be awarded, the total compensation may not exceed the carrier's liability of 1000, now 1,131, SDR per passenger. This decision was upheld on appeal: the Court held that in line with the terms of the convention, moral damages could be compensated. In Argentina, the

---

350. See, CJEU, Case C-410/11 *Espada Sanchez and Others* v. *Iberia Líneas Aéreas de España SA*; Press Release of the Court of Justice of the EU, No. 151/12 of 22 November 2012.
351. Decision of 26 February 2015, IATA Liability Reporter 23 (2016).
352. See, *Nastych* v. *British Airways*, 201 WL 363400 (S.D.N.Y. 2 February 2010).
353. Lisbon Court of Appeals, reported in the IATA Liability Reporter of February 2011, at 9–10; *see also*, the Lisbon Court of Appeal, 300/13.0YXLSB.L1-6, 25 September 2014.
354. See, Uria Menéndez and Miguel Gordillo, International Law Office, 3 March 2010; *see also*, Judgement of the Court of Appeals of Huesca dated 24 February 2010 (AC/2010/1142). This position was also followed by the Spanish Court of Appeal of La Rioja. The Court ruled that under Spanish law, passengers have the right to recover compensation for moral damages, but noted that the compensation could not exceed the limits established under Art. 22 of the Montreal Convention. *See* Judgement Number 299/2011 of 29 September 2011; in the same vein, the Italian *Corte di Cassazione*, Judgment No. 14667/2015, and *Alvarez, Hilda* v. *British Airways*; Supreme Court of Justice, decision of 10 October 2002.

jurisprudence elaborated by the Supreme Court of Justice states that in cases governed by the Warsaw/Montreal Convention, moral damage is accepted as a compensable item, as long as the total amount of recovery grants does not exceed the Convention limits, when applicable. In the same vein, the CJEU confirmed that the liability of air carriers for loss of baggage is limited to the amount of EUR 1,134. This limit is absolute and includes both material and non-material damage. The CJEU's reasoning was based on

- the ordinary meaning of "damage" under general international law;
- the objectives of the Montreal Convention, and, in particular, the fact that it imposes presumed liability on the carrier in return for the benefits of the liability limits;
- the fact that a passenger may make a special declaration of interest.[355]

The liability limit laid down in Article 22(2) also includes the amount which a passenger can claim in case checked wheelchairs or other mobility equipment has been affected by destruction, loss, damage or delay.[356]

Liability limits do not apply when a "special declaration of interest" has been made,[357] or unless the passenger proves:

that the damage resulted from an act or omission of the carrier, its servants or agents acting within the scope of their employment, done with the intent to cause damage or recklessly and with knowledge that damage would probably result.[358]

Such reckless conduct could not be proven by a passenger whose lap top was damaged because the stewardess spilling water on it while serving the passenger, resulting in limited liability of the carrier. A US Court proceeded thereby from the *subjective* test: the subjective knowledge of recklessness sufficed to state the claim for beaching the liability limits under Article 22(2) of the Montreal Convention.[359] Once the passenger and the airline have reached a "full and final settlement" of the claim no further damages can be claimed.[360]

There is no indication for the length of the delay upon which a passenger may claim damages for delayed baggage, and the period after which the baggage could be treated as lost. Mention was made of fourteen days and twenty-one days periods. The determination of such period is left to the discretion of courts.[361]

---

355. *See*, CJEU, Case C-63-09, *Walz* v. *Clickair* decision of 6 May 2010, para. 39.
356. *Ibid.*
357. Even if such a declaration has been made, the total amount to be paid out may be limited as per US airline policies. Upon payment of USD 2 for each USD 100 of purchase value the maximum amount which a US airline will pay is USD 5,000.
358. This argument pertaining to reckless conduct on the part of the carrier was not honoured in Thankgod Ekufu et al., V. Iberia Airlines, No. 12-cv-6669, 2014 WL 87502 (N.D. Ill. 9 Jan. 2014)
359. *See, Hutchinson* v. *British Airways*, 2009 WL 959542 (E.D.N.Y April 6, 2009).
360. *See, Coppens* v. *Aer Lingus*, No. 14-cv-06597-JFB-AKT, [2015] WL 3885742 (E.D.N.Y., 22 June 2015).
361. *See*, Report of the First Meeting of the Special Group on *the Modernization and Consolidation of the 'Warsaw System'*, ICAO Doc. SGMW/1 (1998) at 2–1/2.

3.10.3   Regulation under the Warsaw Regime

The regime governing liability for passengers, baggage and cargo can be found in Articles 18–22. The carrier is liable in relation to the person claiming compensation for destruction or loss of, or damage to, baggage and air cargo, as well as for delay in the carriage of baggage and air cargo.

Liability for the compensation of damage caused by 'wilful misconduct', or done with intent to cause damage or recklessly and with knowledge that damage would probably result, is unlimited. The carrier is not liable if it can prove that it and its servants and agents have taken all necessary measures to avoid the damage. The carrier can be exonerated from liability if the carrier proves that the claimant has caused or contributed to the cause of the damage. The person who is entitled to claim compensation for damage to or delay or loss of baggage or cargo is entitled to rely on the same benefits, which are granted to passengers in relation to the breakability of liability limits in case of wilful misconduct, possibly leading to unlimited liability under Article 25 WC 29.

As to documentation requirements, reference is made to section 3.2.

If the Warsaw Convention as amended by the Hague Protocol, or the Montreal Convention, 1999, is applicable to the carriage of baggage, the liability limit is (about) USD 20 per kilogram for *all* damages. As noted in section 3.10.2, certain courts, especially Spanish and Latin American courts, may include moral damages.

Article 18(4) of WC29, as amended by the Hague Protocol, provides that the carrier is liable for damage to baggage or cargo which finds itself "in the charge of the carrier, whether in an airport or on board aircraft."

The most essential change brought about by the Hague Protocol concerns the doubling of the liability limits for damage sustained by passengers. Liability limits for both checked and unchecked baggage, the latter being, baggage that the passenger carries himself, remained unchanged.

The word 'checked' before baggage was replaced by 'registered' in the Hague Protocol. 'Goods' in the Warsaw Convention was replaced by 'cargo' in the Hague Protocol. A new Article 22(2)(b) was added to the Warsaw Convention in order to define the weight of the registered baggage and of cargo to be taken into consideration in relation to the liability of the carrier.

3.10.4   Case Law under the Warsaw Regime

In Argentina, the constitutionality of the above limits has been acknowledged.[362] The carrier can be exonerated from liability if it proves that the claimant has caused or contributed to the cause of the damage.[363]

As said, the liability for damage to baggage is limited to baggage, which finds itself "in the charge of the carrier, whether in an airport or on board aircraft", or even

---

362. *See, A.C.* v. *Aerlíneas Argentina,*Cámara Federal de Apelaciones de Córdoba, Sec. Civil II, 4 August 2014.
363. *See* section 3.9.2.2.

"in the case of a landing outside an airport, in any place whatsoever." Hence, the liability of the carrier for damage to baggage and cargo has a broader scope than the liability of the carrier for bodily injury or death of passengers which is confined to the period between embarkation and disembarkation.[364]

A passenger who wanted to take his computer as hand baggage was refused to do so. It was unclear whether the Warsaw Convention or the Montreal Convention applied.[365]

A UK Court adopted a broad approach towards the responsibility and ensuing limited liability of the carrier for *baggage and cargo*.[366] Article 18(2) of the Warsaw Convention, as amended by the Hague Protocol, makes the carrier liable for damages sustained in:

> [...] the period during which the baggage or cargo is in charge of the carrier, whether in an aerodrome or on board the aircraft [...]

A carrier has to inform a passenger, or consignor of goods, that he/she can make a "special declaration of interest." In *KLM* v. *Hamman*,[367] a passenger, being informed by KLM staff that he could not carry a valuable item, namely a rifle, with him as hand baggage and that it would need to be checked, told the airline staff that the rifle was worth about USD 10,000. The passenger asked the airline staff to ensure the safety of this item. The rifle was stolen in transit. The court held that a declaration of interest sufficient to remove the limitation of liability had to be clear and had to mention a monetary value. The Warsaw Convention does not stipulate that such a declaration has to be made in writing. The court held that the passenger's failure to pay a supplementary sum did not affect his position, and neither did so the fact that there was no written agreement on the declaration of value. KLM should have demanded, or offered the opportunity for such payment.

3.10.5 Concluding Remarks

Liability for carriage of baggage has similar but not identical provisions under the Warsaw regime and the Montreal Convention, 1999. In light of the restricted number

---

364. As to which *see*, section 3.7.4; in *El Al* v. *British Airways*, Court of Tel Aviv, Israel, 38800-01-10, reported by Peggy Sharon and Keren Marco in International Law Office of 22 May 2013, the court held that the "occurrence which caused the damage" took place while the shipment was no longer under the control of the air carrier as it was stored in an airport warehouse where it should have been kept under refrigeration, which the air carrier should have told the storing company.

365. *See, Mezri* v. *Air France*, decision of the *Tribunal de commerce de Bobigny* on 20 October 2000 Air France was held liable for the loss of a computer but its liability was limited to 3151 French Francs as to which *see*, LV Revue française de droit aérien et spatial 138-147 (2001).

366. English court of first instance, Decision of 3 April 2000; *see*, BLG Aviation News at 15 (2000).

367. 2002 (3) All SA 484. In the cargo case of *Durunna* v. *Air Canada* [2013 ABPC 31 (CanLII)] a similar decision was taken. The Provincial Court of Alberta argued that the liability limits were inapplicable as the plaintiffs had provided sufficient evidence for the establishment of a special declaration of interest had been made, even when a supplemental sum had not been paid as this is not specifically required under the Warsaw Convention; reported in International Law Office of 17 April 2013.

of cases, the monetary limitation does not appear to be an essential problem. In exceptional cases, use has been made of the 'Special Declaration of Value' but this is, in practice, a rather unknown phenomenon.

Again, for an air carrier to be liable, *control* of the goods is a decisive factor. Reference is also made to the discussion on embarkation and disembarkation in section 3.7.4 above.

3.11 Cargo

3.11.1 Regulation under the Montreal Convention, 1999

The Montreal Convention of 1999 has incorporated the provisions of Montreal Additional Protocol (MAP) 4 as to which *see* section 3.11.4 below. Since the Montreal Convention, 1999, contains the provisions of MAP 4, ratification of this Convention by a certain State implies that the carriage of air cargo moving between that certain State and one or more of the States who are party to MAP 4 is governed by the same regime.

Under Article 34 of MC99, the parties to the contract of carriage of air cargo may agree that their dispute is settled by arbitration. The arbitrator or arbitration tribunal must apply the provisions of the Montreal Convention, 1999. This Convention does not indicate that arbitration is open for the settlement of passenger claims, which are subject to the mandatory and exclusive provisions of Article 33 MC99 as explained in section 3.11.1.

3.11.2 Case Law under the Montreal Convention, 1999

MC99 forms the exclusive basis for any claim for damages, even if the damage occurred during surface transportation, provided that the final destination on the surface is laid down in the air waybill and thus falls under the contract for carriage by air.[368] Only persons named as such in the air waybill, that is, consigner and consignee, can enforce rights under the contract of carriage[369] whereas, in the concerned case, the handling agent could not.[370]

The claimant, that is, the freight forwarder, shipper, and retailer, must *state* and *prove* actual damages.[371] A mere reference to the goods mentioned on the air waybill does not suffice as a matter of proof. The claimant must give more detailed evidence of the lost goods and timely and adequate notice[372] of damage or delay of the cargo

---

368. *See, Danner* v. *International Freight Systems of Washington*, 2010 WL 3294678 (D. Md. 20 August 2010), and *Masudi* v. *Brady Cargo Services*, No. 12-cv-2391, 2014 WL 4416502 (S.D. Fla. 8 September 2014).
369. *See, DHL Global Forwarding Management Unit Latin America et al.*, v. *Pfizer et al.*, Case No. 13-cv-8218, 2014 WL 5169033 (S.D.N.Y. 2014).
370. *See*, judgement of the Supreme Court of Portugal of 20 May 2014, 5808/09.9TVLSB.L1.S1.
371. *See, Masudi* v. *Brady Cargo Services*, No. 12-cv-2391, 2014 WL 4416502 (S.D. Fla. 8 September 2014), Supreme Court of Appeals of Turkey, 11th Chamber, judgment of 17 February 2014.
372. According to the Higher Regional Court in Munich, the purpose of a preliminary notice is to inform the carrier of damage, so as to enable the carrier to inspect the consignment and to

pursuant to the terms of Article 31 of the Montreal Convention.[373] Hence, this decision is favourable for air cargo carriers as it may reduce future amounts of compensation claimed by shippers. As dogs are considered as cargo, damages must be claimed under the cargo or baggage provisions, and not under Article 17 of MC99.[374]

The damage must be sustained 'during the carriage by air.' A US District Court held that the Convention does not apply to damage caused by the disappearance of the cargo after being delivered to the air carrier but before the carriage had actually started. In the case at hand, the claimant had not supplied sufficient evidence that the loss of cargo had taken place 'during the carriage by air.'[375] The air carrier, said the Court, was in the best position to confirm where the cargo was lost.[376] In the same vein, in case of an agreement for the carriage by air, Article 18(4) of the Montreal Convention proceeds from the rebuttable assumption that any damage to the cargo occurred during the carriage by air unless a proof is given for the contrary.[377]

For the carrier to be liable for damage of cargo, the cargo must be "in charge" of the carrier or its agent.[378] Cargo which is stored in the carrier's warehouse at the airport of the destination is meant to be "in charge" of the carrier, pre-empting State claims on this basis.[379]

When the cargo is deemed to be "in charge" of the air carrier, the carrier must follow the instructions for storage specified in the air waybill. If not it shall be liable up to the limits laid down in Article 22 of MC99 whereas in this case no wilful misconduct was found on the part of the carrier; hence the limits apply.[380]

---

clarify what exactly happened. If the carrier has in fact such knowledge, no further preliminary notice of claim is necessary as to which *see*, IATA Liability Reporter. Vol 15 (February 2012) at 16, and the decision of the Regional Court of Darmstadt, Germany, 27 June 2014.

373. *See*, German Federal Court of Justice, decision of 4 July 2008, reported in the Newsletter of International law office, Holger Bürskens, Law Firm Arnecke Siebold, *Compensation Claims for Lost Shipments*, 21 January 2009, at: www.internationallawoffice.com/Newsletters/; on the requirement of adequate notice, *see also*, UPS Supply Chain Solutions v. *American Airlines*, 646 F. Supp. 2d 1011 (N.D. Ill. 2009) and *Meteor AG* v. *Federal Express Corporation*; *see*, 2009 WL 3853802 (S.D.N.Y. 2009); *American Home Assurance Company* v. *Kuehne & Nagel*, No. Civ 6389, 2009 WL 3109839 (S.D.N.Y. 29 September 2009).

374. *See*, Aya v. *Lan Cargo*, 2014 WL 4672450 (S.D. Florida, 18 September 2014).

375. *See*, Han v. *Fedex*, 2015 U.S. Dist. LEXIS 116773 (E.D. Ill.2015); No. 15-cv-01582 (N.D. Ill. Sep 02, 2015).

376. *See*, Emirates Airlines v. *Aforka* [2014] LPELR-22626 (Court of Appeal, Nigeria).

377. *See*, judgement of the Supreme Court of Portugal of 20 May 2014, 5808/09.9TVLSB.L1.S1. When the air carrier charters a road carrier for part of the carriage without the consent from the consignor, MC99 is also applicable to the carriage by road; *see*, Cour d'appel Lyon (CA), 12 March 2015, No. 13/07108.

378. *See*, Danner v. *International Freight Systems of Washington*, No. ECH 09-3139, 2013 WL 78101 (D. Md. 4 January 2013 in which the court decided that the cargo was in the custody of the carrier (Cargolux) for the entirety of the time that they were lost. Hence, the damage had occurred during the period of 'carriage by air' as stipulated by Art. 18 of MC99.

379. *See*, Vigilent v. *World Courier*, 2008 WL 2332343 (S.D.N.Y. 2008), and *Certain Underwriters at Lloyd's London*, No. 12-cv-5078, 2014 WL 123488 (E.D.N.Y.) 10 January 2014.

380. *See*, French Cour de cassation [Cass.] decision of 30 June 2015, No. 13-28.846, thus abrogating French civil code provisions.

In case of destruction, loss, damage or delay of the cargo, liability limits are now fixed at 19 SDRs per kilogram,[381] and unbreakable.[382] A US Court of Appeals confirmed the unbreakability of such limits by removing cargo from the *wilful misconduct* exception.[383]

This amount will remain unchanged until the next review will take place in 2019.

Higher amounts may be awarded in case a *Declaration of Interest at Delivery* has been drawn up between the Parties. If the air waybill confirms that "no time is fixed for the completion of the cargo", a claim for damage caused by delay cannot succeed.[384] Only costs, not profits, which can or could have been made with the cargo can be recovered as the shipper can ship the goods again and make profits with the second shipment.

Time limits pay, or make you pay. A notice of arrival of a shipment of perishable food sent to the consignee nineteen hours after arrival is not adequate under Article 13(2) of the Montreal Convention, 1999. The carrier was held liable for the damage.[385]

3.11.3 Regulation under the Warsaw Regime

In cargo cases, the rights and liabilities of carriers and consignors are laid down in the airway bill. The carrier is entitled to require a consignor to draw up and deliver an air waybill which is prima facie evidence of the existence of the contract. For a third person to act on behalf of the carrier, it must have the *express authority* to act on behalf of the air carrier, in which case the carrier is bound by the contract which the agent has entered into and to receive the cargo on its behalf.[386]

Since the coming into force of WC29, carriage of cargo by air has been governed by what will be termed below *general* and *specific* provisions of this Convention.

The *general* provisions establish the liability regime applying to the carriage of passengers, baggage called "luggage" under the unamended Warsaw Convention, and cargo called "goods" under the unamended Warsaw Convention, including a provision on jurisdiction.

The *general* regime governing liability for passengers, baggage and cargo can be found in Articles 18–22.[387] The carrier is liable in relation to the person claiming

---

381. To be converted in national currency, as to which see, for instance, Supreme Court of Appeals of Turkey, 11th Chamber, judgement of 7 March 2014.
382. In Chile, the courts uphold a problematic criterion, according to which the indication in an air waybill of the monetary value of cargo is regarded as an act fulfilling the role of a Special Declaration of Value as described in Art. 22(2) of the Montreal Convention. Therefore, the carrier cannot avail itself in the liability limits established under the Convention.
383. *See, Morog* v. *Kuehne & Nagel, Inc.*, 56 Fed. Appx. 137, 2003 WL 329304.
384. *See, AGC* v. *Centurion Air Cargo*, 37 Avi. 17,242 (S.D.Fl. 2015).
385. *See, Wea Farms, Lima Peru* v. *American Airlines, Inc.*, 31 Avi 18,739 (S.D. Fla. 2007) as to which *see* Art. 13 of the Montreal Convention, providing that: "Unless it is otherwise agreed, it is the duty of the carrier to give notice to the consignee *as soon as* the cargo arrives." (*italics added*).
386. *See, Dilawari Exporters* v. *Alitalia* [2010] INSC 282, decision of 16 April 2010.
387. Loss of baggage by a passenger who wanted to take his computer as hand baggage but was refused to do so on a flight governed by the Warsaw Convention is examined in the case of *Mezri* v. *Air France*, decision of the *Tribunal de commerce de Bobigny* on 20 October 2000. Air

compensation for destruction or loss of, or damage to, baggage and air cargo, as well as for delay in the carriage of baggage and air cargo.[388]

Under Article 22 of the Warsaw Convention, the liability of the carrier is limited to two hundred and fifty Gold Francs per kilogram, unless:

- the cargo is loaded on board the aircraft with the consent of the air carrier without an air waybill having been made out, or if the air waybill does not include the notices required by Article 8 of the Convention; *or*
- the consignor has made, at the time when the package was handed over to the carrier, a "special declaration of interest", and has paid a supplementary sum if the case so requires.[389]

Under the Warsaw Convention as amended by The Hague Protocol, the limits of liability for the carriage of cargo are breakable of the claimant can proof wilful misconduct or reckless behaviour of the carrier, as to which *see* case law in section 3.11.5.5. The limits of liability for cargo that is, 17 SDRs per kilogram, under the Warsaw Convention as amended by The Hague Protocol and MAP4 are unbreakable.

However, limits as to carriage of cargo are *unbreakable* under the regime set forth by the specific regime laid down in Montreal Protocol No. 4, as to which *see* section 3.11.4, below.

Carriage of cargo is undertaken by a number of persons. The legal position of each of these persons must be analysed in order to identify the liability regime, which may be made applicable to their undertakings.

Finally, the provisions on successive carriage (*see*, Article 30) and on combined carriage (*see*, Article 31) also apply to carriage of cargo.[390] The same holds true for

---

France was held liable for the loss of a computer but its liability was limited to 3151 French Francs. *See*, LV Revue française de droit aérien et spatial 138–147 (2001). In *Shah* v. *Kuwait Airways* (653 F.Supp.2f 499 (S.D.N.Y. 9 September 2009) it was unclear whether the Warsaw Convention or the Montreal Convention applied. The court opted for the higher limits of the Montreal Convention.

388. The amount of damages and the compensation of immaterial damages were considered in *Avena Christian* v. *Aerolínas Argentinas* (Lexis No. 70052492; 3 March 2009). Damages include actual damages; accrued interest has to be determined in the course of the proceedings and is beyond the limits; *see*, *Buccic, Norberto & Others* v. *Aerolínas Argentinas* (305 Lexis No. 35031785, May 21, 2009.

389. As confirmed by the Supreme Court of Turkey in the case of *Guven Electronics* v. *Lufthansa*, Supreme Court of Appeals of Turkey, eleventh Chamber, 21 January 2011. In the case of *Durunna* v. *Air Canada* [2013 ABPC 31 (CanLII)] the Provincial Court of Alberta argued that the liability limits were inapplicable as the plaintiffs had provided sufficient evidence for the establishment of a special declaration of interest had been made, even when a supplemental sum had not been paid as this is not specifically required under the Warsaw Convention.

390. *See*, Dr M. Hoeks, *Multimodal Transport Law: The Law Applicable to Multimodal Contract for the Carriage of Goods* (2010); Dr George Leloudas, *Door to door application of the international air law conventions: commercially convenient, but judicially dubious*, Lloyd's Maritime and Commercial Law Quarterly 368 (2015); same author: *Multimodal Transport under the Warsaw and Montreal Convention Regimes: A Velvet Revolution*, in: Andrew Tattenborn and Baris Soyer (eds), *Carriage of Goods by Sea, Land and Air: Unimodal and Multimodal Transport in 21st Century* 77–110 (2014).

several other provisions of the Warsaw Convention, including but not limited to those on Jurisdiction (*see*, Article 28) and the general and final provisions.

Next to the *special* provisions on carriage of air cargo laid down in MAP 4, which are discussed in the next section, section III of Chapter II of the Warsaw Convention deals with "Documentation Relating to Air Cargo", containing requirements to the delivery and contents of the air waybill, as well as rights and obligations of the shipper (the Convention refers to "consignor") of cargo in his contractual relationship with the air carrier.[391]

The air waybill must contain a number of particulars, such as:

- the place and date of issue/execution;
- the place of departure and destination;
- the name and address of the carrier;
- the number and weight of the carried items;
- the amount of the value of the carried items;
- a statement that the transportation is subject to the Warsaw Convention.[392]

These particulars were simplified under MAP4 as to which *see* the next section under II.

3.11.4 The Special Regime of MAP No. 4 (1975)

On 25 September 1975, the Montreal Protocol No. 4 was signed in Montreal. MAP 4 changes *inter alia* provisions of the Warsaw Convention on carriage of air cargo.

The principal changes are the following:

I. *The introduction of the paperless air waybill*
While MAP 4 stipulates that the shipper must deliver an airway bill to the carrier, the carrier will be allowed to use "any other means which would preserve a record of the carriage performed", if the shipper consents.[393] If the shipper consents, he can then request a receipt for the cargo that will permit identification of the consignment and access to the carrier's computer records. This computerisation of the documents pertaining to carriage of air cargo, allowing for 'electronic air waybills', should save the carrier substantial administrative costs.

II. *Simplification and elimination of certain formalities*
The following formalities were simplified or eliminated by MAP 4:
a) the Warsaw Convention requires that the second part of the airway bill accompanies the cargo.[394] This condition has been eliminated by Article III of MAP 4.

---

391. According to the High Regional Court of Stuttgart, Germany, both the shipper and the consignee have the necessary right of action. However, the right of those parties is joint and several, as there cannot be double recovery against the carrier; *see*, judgment of 10 June 2009 (Court Ref. 3 U 12/09).
392. *See*, Arts 4 and 8 of the Warsaw Convention. The Hague Protocol simplified the above requirements.
393. *See*, Art. III of MAP 4, amending Art. 5(2) of the Warsaw Convention.
394. *See*, Art. 5(2).

b) where the carriage contains more than one package, the carrier can require the shipper to produce an air waybill for each package.[395] In a computerised transaction, the shipper can require separate receipts for each package.

c) As stated in the previous section, Article 8 of the Warsaw Convention includes a list of particulars which must be contained in the air waybill. Article III of MAP 4 reduces and simplifies this list so that the following pieces of information must be given in the air waybill

- the places of origin and destination;
- an indication of one stopping place in another State, if the place of departure and place of destination are located within the territory of the same State;
- an indication of the weight of the consignment.

III. *Maintenance of liability limits in case of failure to comply with formalities*

The carrier remains entitled to rely on liability limits of Article 22(2) of the Warsaw Convention, even if the notice requirements of Article 8 of the Convention have not been satisfied. The air carrier is not affected by sanctions in case these formalities have not been complied with by the parties to the contract.[396] Breakability of the liability limits in case of non-compliance with formalities in respect of carriage of air cargo has always been a source of litigation.

The limit now amounts to 19 SDR per kilogram. It applies to loss, damage and delay of the goods. The Montreal Convention, 1999, retains this regime.[397] The above provision does not affect the right of the consignor to make a *Special Declaration of Interest* pursuant Article 22 of the WC29 as amended.[398] Pursuant to the CMR regime,[399] cargo carried by road is subject to lower, but breakable limits.

IV. *Imposition of monetary sanctions in case of incorrect information*

The shipper is liable for damages when he has provided incorrect information to the carrier, either in the air waybill, or on the receipt. If so, the shipper must compensate the carrier for losses and damages suffered as a consequence of the provision of incorrect information. However, if the information supplied by the shipper is incorrectly written into the air waybill or into the electronic receipt by the carrier, the carrier is required to indemnify the shipper for the resulting damage.[400]

V. *Specification of defences available to the air carrier*

Under Article 20 of the unamended Warsaw Convention, the carrier is not liable if he can prove that he and his agents have taken all necessary measures to avoid the damage or that it has been impossible to take such measures. MAP 4 specifies the defences, which are available to the carrier.

The carrier is not liable for the destruction, loss of, or damage to, the cargo, if this resulted solely from:

a) inherent defect, quality or vice of that cargo;

b) defective packing of that cargo performed by a person other than the carrier or his servants and agents;

c) an act of war or armed conflict;

---

395. *See*, Art. 7 of the Warsaw Convention.
396. *See*, Art. 9 of the Warsaw Convention as amended by MAP 4.
397. *See*, Art. 22(3).
398. *See*, *KLM* v. *Hamman*, 2002 (3) All SA 484.
399. *Convention on the Contract for the International Carriage of Goods by Road/ Convention relative au contrat de transport international de marchandises par route* (CMR), Geneva (1956).
400. *See*, Art. 10 of the Convention as amended by MAP 4.

    d) an act of public authority carried out in connection with the entry, exit or transit of the cargo.

A carrier is not entitled to exculpate itself from liability for defective packing of cargo and improper loading. FedEx applied its conditions of carriage to a shipment which was defected during the process of loading. Since Article 18(4) of the WC29 extends the liability of the air carrier under that convention to the phases of loading, delivery and transhipment, FedEx was not entitled to enforce its conditions designed to exonerate itself from liability.[401] The defence regarding the taking of all necessary measures under the regime set forth by MAP 4, is only available to the carrier in the case of delay.

VI. *Conversion of Gold Francs into Special Drawing Rights*

MAP 4 converts the liability limits laid down in Article 22 of WC29, expressed in Gold Francs, into Special Drawing Rights (SDRs). SDR is the monetary unit of the International Monetary Fund (*IMF*), and is fixed by the combined values of certain national monetary units which are used in specified Member States of the IMF.[402]

VII. *Unbreakability of the liability limits*

The liability limits for carriage of cargo falling under the Montreal Additional Protocol No. 4 regime are *unbreakable*. This follows from the last sentence of Article VIII of Montreal Additional Protocol No. 4, modifying Article 24 of the Warsaw Convention:

> Such limits of liability constitute maximum limits and may not be exceeded whatever the circumstances, which gave rise to the liability, were.

    Under the regime of MAP 4, liability limits applying to carriage of cargo cannot be broken by:

- non-delivery of the necessary documentation; or
- proof by the claimant of wilful misconduct on the part of the carrier.

    Obviously, the carrier may have to pay higher amounts of compensation than the limit provided for in the Warsaw Convention as amended by the MAP 4 in case of a supplementary agreement between the carrier and shipper as reflected in a "special declaration of interest", and as foreseen in Article 22 of the Warsaw Convention, which has not been modified by MAP 4.

VIII. *Extension of period of complaint*

Article 26 of WC29 stipulates that the person entitled to delivery of the air cargo must complain to the carrier within seven days after receipt of the goods when damage has been inflicted to this cargo. The Hague Protocol of 1955 extends this period from seven to fourteen days; this extension is confirmed by MAP 4.

IX. *Right of recourse against third parties*

Article XI of MAP 4 stipulates that the air carrier has a right of recourse against third parties who caused or contributed to the loss or damage to the cargo for which the carrier is liable under the Warsaw regime. An identical provision has been inserted into the Montreal Convention, 1999.[403]

X. *Exemption of the carrier's liability in extraordinary circumstances*

---

401. *See, Sysco Food Services of Hampton Roads, Inc.*, v. *Maersk Logistics, Inc.*, 31 Avi. 18089 (S.D.N.Y. 2006).
402. 1 SDR is more or less equal to EUR 1.25; *see*, www.imf.org/external/np/tre/sdr/drates/0701. htm.
403. Art. 37.

The carrier is exempted from liability under Article 8 of the Warsaw Convention[404] for loss of or damage to cargo in the case of "carriage performed in extraordinary circumstances outside the normal scope of an air carrier's business."

XI. *Jurisdiction*

MAP 4 follows Article 32 of WC29 permitting arbitration clauses in contracts for the carriage of cargo. In a cargo case concerning jurisdiction, the German Federal Supreme Court concludes that the Montreal Protocols have no independent character as to the question whether a State is a Warsaw Convention party or not.[405]

XII. *Entry into force of the Montreal Protocol No. 4*

On 17 June 1998, MAP 4 entered into force. The changes it introduced can be implemented on the traffic moving between the more than 30 States who ratified MAP 4. It is expected that, due to the simplification of the rules, there will be far less litigation arising from baggage and cargo claims as a result of the entry into force of MP4, and its adoption by the US. Early July 2017, it has 60 States party.

3.11.5 Case Law under the Warsaw Regime

3.11.5.1 Liability of Persons in the Air Cargo Chain

The legal position of each of the persons working together in the 'carriage of cargo chain' may affect the applicability of the legal regime. For instance, a freighter forwarder may act as an agent for the client who wants his goods to be transported from A to B.

At other times, he issues an airway bill and undertakes to deliver the shipment from A to B, as a contractual carrier. In yet other cases, the freight forwarder may act as an agent of the air carrier.[406]

Under the *Himalaya Clause* in air waybills, the limits of liability protecting air carriers in cargo cases may be extended to ground handling agents of cargo carriers.[407] The handlers are *only* liable *in relation to the airline* if the damage arose from an act or omission of the handler done with the intent to cause damage or recklessly with the knowledge that such damage would probably result. This situation is the consequence of Article 8 of IATA's *Standard Ground Handling Agreement* concluded between airlines and their handlers.[408] Hence, each jurisdiction will have to decide when the

---

404. Under Art. 34 of the Warsaw Convention, as amended by Art. XIII of MP 4.
405. Although Germany is not a party to MAP 4, German courts are competent to hear cases arising from claims for compensation of damage of cargo. The competence of German courts is based on Art. 28 of the Warsaw Convention, even if MP materially – but not formally as Germany is not a party to MAP 4. MAP 4 is applied on the basis of German of Collision Law Rules, and the Choice of Law Clause; *see*, Federal Supreme Court decision of 22 October 2009 – I ZR 88/07.
406. *See* section 3.3.2.3 and 3.3.2.4, above.
407. *See*, *Central Insurance Co., Ltd., v. China Airlines, Ltd.*, 2004 WL 742916 (N.D. Cal. March 24, 2004).
408. Art. 8 of IATA's Ground-Handling Agreement reads as follows: "8.1 Except as stated in Sub-Article 8.5, the Carrier shall not make any claim against the Handling Company and shall indemnify it (subject as hereinafter provided) against any legal liability for claims or suits,

conduct of the agent is reckless misconduct, and may use the case law made under Article 25 of the Warsaw Convention as amended by the Hague Protocol.

In a case involving the cargo air carrier DHL International, Maman Cargo Ltd., an airport warehouse, DHL Israel, the forwarder, and Alon Gal who was employed at the time of the theft and had been convicted as the thief of the shipment, the Magistrates Court of Tel Aviv decided that Maman Cargo and DHL Israel were agents of the air carrier as they executed their functions in furtherance of the contract of carriage, but that Mr Gal was not. Hence, DHL and Maman Cargo were protected by the liability limits of the Warsaw Convention, whereas Mr Gal had to compensate the claimants for the full amount as he was not acting in his function as DHL employee when stealing the items. Thus, DHL could not be held vicariously liable for the compensation of damages.[409]

An air cargo carrier has been held liable to a shipper for the destruction of goods that were accidentally destroyed by a subcontractor who was trucking the shipment to the airport terminal. Consequently, the court found that the term 'carrier' included the trucker as the subcontractor of the carrier.[410] The air waybill permitted the carrier to substitute other carriers or other modes of transport. The term 'carrier' used there included *all* carriers.

The position of *freight forwarders* may vary. In certain cases, a freighter forwarder acts as an agent for the client who wants his goods to be transported from A to B. At other times, he issues an airway bill and undertakes to deliver the shipment from A to B, as a contractual carrier. In yet other cases, the freight forwarder may act as an agent of the air carrier. In a decision made by a Court in Israel,[411] it was held that in cases where the freight forwarder acts as a principal contracting carrier, its legal status is similar to that of the carrier. Hence, if the freight forwarder issued an airway bill and undertook the shipment, it could benefit from the provisions of the international airline liability conventions, namely, the Warsaw Convention as amended and the Montreal Convention of 1999. Depending on the facts and circumstances of the case, the freight forwarder may also act as an agent of the air carrier.

3.11.5.2 *Liability for Damage to Cargo in Charge of the Carrier*

Article 18(4) of the Warsaw Convention, as amended by the Hague Protocol, provides that the carrier is liable for damage to baggage or cargo which finds itself "in the charge

---

including costs and expenses incidental thereto, in respect of: (a) delay, injury or death of persons carried or to be carried by the Carrier; (b) injury or death of any employee of the Carrier; (c) damage to or delay or loss of baggage, cargo or mail carried or to be carried by the Carrier, and (d) damage to or loss of property owned or operated by, or on behalf of, the Carrier and any consequential loss or damage; arising from an act or omission of the Handling Company in the performance of this Agreement."

409. *See, Taga Electronic Components Ltd* v. *Worldwide DHL Express* (CF 19308-01), reported by Moshe Bady and Keren Marco in www.internationallawoffice.com on 3 September 2015.
410. *See, Corning, Inc.* v. *DHL Holdings* (USA), *Inc.* (EDKy) 32 Avi 15,694.
411. As reported by Levitan, Sharon & Co, *Court Considers Applicability of Warsaw Convention to Freight Forwarders*; *See,* Newsletter International law Office, dated 15 April 2009, available at: www.internationallawoffice.com/Newsletter.

of the carrier, whether in an airport or on board aircraft", or even: "in the case of a landing outside an airport, in any place whatsoever." The crucial factor is whether the damage was suffered as part of the *execution of the airway bill*, giving evidence of the contract for the carriage by air of cargo.[412] It is *assumed* that the damage occurred during the air transport. On the other hand, if the carrier can prove that damage was caused during the other forms of transport (road or sea) it would not be liable for the damage because it is outside the scope of the air waybill.

In *Siemens* v. *Schenker International (Aust) Pty Ltd.*,[413] a pallet in a shipment of telecommunication electric equipment, which was carried by air from Germany to Australia, was severely damaged when it fell from the truck to the roadway, while being taken from Melbourne airport to a warehouse. The warehouse was located just outside the airport boundary, approximately four kilometres from the airport's main gate. The damage occurred outside the airport boundary. Another court was not prepared to interpret Article 18(4) of the Warsaw Convention, as amended, extensively. Relying on the US decision *Victoria Sales Corp.* v. *Emery Air Freight Inc.*,[414] the Australian Court held that the damage had not occurred in an airport. Hence, and probably justified, the courts tend to adopt a literal interpretation of the term 'airport', by measuring precisely the boundaries of an airport in order to establish liability.

A US Court found that the carrier is liable as soon as it is "in charge of handling the goods", including loading and delivery.[415] Hence, the carrier is not only liable for the period during which the goods are on board the aircraft. If the claimant does not prove otherwise, the goods are supposed to have been delivered in the correct state.[416] The goods must have been delivered, and accepted by the person entitled to the goods. The intention of the parties – as manifested by the behaviour of such parties – define delivery, and answer the question whether the goods are "in charge" of the carrier, says a US court.[417]

If the moment of the damage or the loss cannot be determined, and absent proof to the contrary, the damage or loss is presumed to have been the result of an event, which took place during the carriage by air. A Canadian Federal Court confirmed that Article 18(3) of WC29 creates a legal presumption to this effect.[418]

A case involved a late arrival of the cargo and examination of the question of how long the cargo was 'in charge' of the air carrier, and whether the cargo was 'destroyed' possibly as a consequence of the late arrival of the cargo. Article 26 of the Warsaw Convention provides different timeframes for notice, depending on whether the cargo was lost, damaged or destroyed and that in the case of damage, the person entitled to

---

412. *See, Trimmings* v. *TAM Linhas Aereas*, C.N. Civ Com. Fed. Sala II Causa No. 5229/2010; 23 April 2014.
413. [2001] NSWSC 658 – The Supreme Court of New South Wales.
414. 917 F.2d 705 (2nd Cir. 1990).
415. *See, Fuller* v. *Amerijet Intl.*, 273 F. Supp. Ed 902 (W.D. Ky. 2003).
416. *See, Lufthansa Cargo AG* v. *Nationale Nederlanden, Fertiplant and SH. Saud Mohd Ali Al-Tani*, Decision of the District Court of Haarlem, of 17 December 2002, Case Number 71141/HA ZA 01-31.
417. In *Sompo Japan Insurance* v. *Nippon Cargo Airlines, Co., Ltd.*, 2004 WL 2931282 (N.D.Ill. December 15, 2004).
418. *See, Green Computer in Sweden AB.* v. *Federal Express Corp.*, 2003 FCT 587 CarswellNat 1323.

delivery must complain to the carrier forthwith after the discovery of the damage, and at the latest, within fourteen days from the date of receipt in the case of cargo.[419] According to the court in one of these cases, actual notice suffices, thus departing from the formulation of Article 26(2).[420]

Loss of cargo, which had arrived at a warehouse, did not fall under the Warsaw Convention. The loss occurred after the international carriage had been completed.[421] The carrier can however still be held liable if the incident took place on the *landside* of the airport, but the defendants were entitled to invoke the liability limits set forth by the Warsaw Convention.[422]

3.11.5.3 Damages

A New Zealand Court held that damage means losses sustained rather than physical damage only. Article 18(2) covers more than just physical damage. Freight costs made in order to repair physical damage may be part of the economic losses sustained as a result of the damage of the cargo.[423]

A US Court took the value of Russian paintings as confirmed by customs officials at USD 558 rather than awarding the claim made by the plaintiff for assessing the damage by reference to the advice made by the plaintiff's agent to insure the paintings for USD 60,000.[424] If the Warsaw Convention, as amended by the Hague Protocol, or the Montreal Convention, 1999, is applicable to the carriage of cargo, the liability limit is about USD 20 per kilogram for all damages.[425] A US Court determined that this amount should be used in order to determine damages occasioned by loss of cargo on a flight between Brussels, Belgium, and Tulsa, Oklahoma, Illinois via Chicago. Belgium is a party to the Warsaw Convention as amended by the Hague Protocol, whereas the US is a party to the Warsaw Convention as amended by the Hague Protocol as amended by Montreal Protocol No. 4. The US is not a party to the Hague Protocol, but the court took the view that when the US had ratified Montreal Protocol No. 4, the US acceded to the Hague Protocol.[426] Hence, Belgium and the US have treaty links on the basis of the Warsaw Convention as amended by the Hague Protocol.[427]

---

419. *See, Oriental Insurance* v. *BAX Global*, 2009 WL 229668 (N.D. Ill. 28 January 2009); *Maschinen-fabrik Kern* v. *Northwest Airlines* (562 F.Supp. 232 (N.D. Ill. 1983); *Olaya* v. *American Airlines* (2009 WL 32421116 (E.D.N.Y. 2009).
420. *See, Maschinenfabrik Kern* v. *Northwest Airlines* (562 F.Supp. 232 (N.D. Ill. 1983).
421. *See, Belik* v. *UPS*, reported in 38 Informa UK Ltd 15 (2002).
422. *See, Rolls Royce plc* v. *Heavylift-Volga Dnepr Ltd*, High Court of Justice, Queens Bench Division Commercial Court, 1999 Folio No.142, Judgement of 1 April 2000, where a Rolls Royce engine fell from a forklift being operated by the second defendant, Servisair. Servisair was the ground-handling agent for Heavylift, the carrier carrying the engines from East Midlands Airport to Seattle, where the Boeing factory is located.
423. *See, Vinotica Ltd.* v. *Air New Zealand Ltd*, [2004] DCR 2086; 2004 N2 DCR Lexis 38.
424. *See, Kesel* v. *UPS*, 2002 U.S. Dist. LEXIS 12350 (N.D. Cal. 2002).
425. *See also,* Tribunal of Marsala, case of *Titone Arini* v. *Eurofly*, decision of 14 April 2007.
426. *See,* 277 F.Supp. 2d at 267.
427. *See, Royal & Sun Alliance* v. *American Airlines*, Inc., 277 F. Supp. 265 (S.D.N.Y 2003).

A court in India calculated cargo limits at USD 20 per kilo. The court allowed this amount per kilo for loss of cargo in a case involving international carriage.[428] Once the goods have been delivered to the consignee mentioned in the airway bill,[429] the shipper is not entitled to claim loss of goods due to non-compliance with formalities laid down in Article 12 of the Warsaw Convention, provisions of the airway bill and misunderstanding among the parties to the contract.[430] If the air waybill contains a clause stipulating that the goods may be delivered to another person than the consignee to whom the goods must be delivered, that clause is null and void pursuant to Article 23(1) of the Warsaw Convention as the clause is intended to relieve the carrier of its liability in case of loss of the goods as a consequence of its reckless conduct ('*faute dolosive*').[431]

In Singapore, the court had to decide whether the limit of liability under Article 22 of Convention, as amended by the Hague Protocol, in the case of partial loss, had to be determined on the basis of the total weight of the shipped cargo, or upon the weight of the missing boxes. The shipper had shipped 1000 digital transceivers on the claimant airline in a single pallet which weighed 154 kilograms. The air waybill indicated that there was only one piece of cargo. When the shipment arrived in Hong Kong, four of the nine boxes containing 440 transceivers and weighing 60 kilograms were missing. The total value of the missing transceivers was USD 74,360. China Airlines argued that the liability limit set out in Article 22(b) was USD 2,974.80, which amount was based on the weight of the missing boxes, while the consignor claimed USD 7,635.32, which amount represented the value of the entire pallet. Article 22(b) requires the calculation to take into account "only the total weight of the package or packages concerned." Hence, the Singapore Court agreed with the consignor that the weight to be determined was the weight of the entire pallet.[432]

For a plaintiff to be entitled to compensation, he must show that there is *damage* pursuant to Article 26(2) of the Warsaw Convention. Damage may include loss. If the claimant shows that his suitcase has not only been damaged but that he/she also lost articles, he/she may attempt to recover the losses, that is, within seven days from the date of receipt in the case of baggage and fourteen days from the date of receipt in the

---

428. *See*, *Rajasthan Art Emporium* v. *Kuwait Airways*, *National Consumer Disputes Redressed Commission*, New Delhi, 21 May 2003, Newsletter of Barlow Glyde & Gilbert, Issue 15, Winter 03/04, at 4.
429. *See also*, *Oriental Insurance* v. *BAX Global*, 2009 WL 229668 (N.D. Ill. 28 January 2009), in which the court ruled that "the person entitled to delivery is the person to whom the cargo should ultimately be delivered, not the next company in the chain of carriers."
430. *See*, Pierre Frühling of the – then – law firm Field Fisher Waterhouse, Brussels, decision of the Belgium Courts of Appeal (*Cour de cassation*), decision of 10 April 2008, reported in International Law Office, *Court of Cassation Rules on the Meaning of 'Loss' under the Warsaw Convention*, Newsletter of 27 August 2008.
431. *See*, *Entreprise générale portuaire* (EGP) v. *Fedex*, French Court of Appeals (*Cour de cassation*), decision of 17 February 2009, published in 249(1) Revue française de droit aérien et spatial 108–111 (2009).
432. *See*, the Singapore Court of Appeal *China Airlines Limited* v. *Philips Hong Kong Limited*, the [2002] 3 SLR 367; on the calculation of damages and the compensation of lawyers' fees, *see also*, *Nissan Fire and Marine Insurance* v. BAX *Global* (2009 WL 1364870 (N.D.Cal. 2009).

case of cargo.[433] Such notice requirements may be fatal for the plaintiff. If the fourteen day notice requirement as laid down in the air waybill is not respected, the claim may fail.[434]

3.11.5.4 Limitation of Liability

Courts in Brazil, including the Superior Court, are reluctant to respect the treaty limits set forth by the Warsaw Convention of 1929 and the Montreal Convention, 1999. They argue that limitation of liability infringes the Brazilian Federal Constitution of 1988, providing for 'unrestricted indemnity' in its Article 5 and the Civil Code of 2002, stipulating that the indemnity should be quantified in relation to the 'extent of the damage 'in Article 944.[435] Moreover, the carrier must or should be aware of the high value of the cargo, even if a declaration of interest had not been made.

In the case of Ford v. *United Air Lines, Inc.*,[436] a passenger sued the airline for the severe damage which was caused to his bicycle. The carrier sought to rely on the limitations provided by the Montreal Convention, 1999, whereupon the carrier should have notified the passenger that its liability was limited. The carrier had failed to do so and its conditions of contract and carriage identifying such limitations on its website were not easily readable or accessible. The court found that the passenger had made a special declaration of interest when bringing the value of the bicycle to the attention of the airline. The airline could have offered the passenger to pay a supplementary sum in order to pay for coverage in excess of the Montreal Convention limits. However, no such offer was made. This belongs to the 'freedom of contract'.[437]

When the airline has not correctly packed the cargo, in this case a dog, it has failed to take all necessary measures all the necessary measures to avoid the damage, the condition required for exoneration under Article 20 of the Warsaw Convention as amended.[438]

---

433. See Art. 26(2) of the Warsaw Convention, as amended, as explained by the UK House of Lords in *Forthergill* v. *Monarch Airlines Ltd*, Decision of 10 July 1980, 1980 England Law Reports, Volume 2.
434. See, O'Gray Import & Export v. British Airways, No. 06-1020, 2007 WL 1378391 (D. Md. May 4, 2007).
435. See, IATA Liability Reporter 26 (2016).
436. 2006 APBC 103 (Provincial Court of Alberta, Canada, 1 June 2006).
437. See also, the case of KLM v. Hamman, 2002 (3) All SA 484.
438. See Court of Appeals of Argentina: Peiro v. Aerolinas Argentinas, MJJ5839, decision of 8 July 2010. Similarly, in Israel, the Acre Magistrates Court applied Art. 25 of the Warsaw Convention and determined that a baggage claim filed by an El Al's passenger was not subject the limitations of liability provided for in Art. 22 of the Convention, as a result of gross negligence from the carrier. The court found that El Al did not take the necessary measures to ensure that the content of the suitcase was appropriately packaged after a security check and by not doing so, El Al acted in gross negligence and with indifference to the possible results of its actions. The court therefore applied the provisions of Article 25 and ruled that the claim was not subject to the limitation amounts set in the convention; see, 39380-01-10 Rania Mugrabi v. EL AL Airlines Ltd. (2 November 2011).

3.11.5.5 Wilful Misconduct in Cargo Cases

A US Court stated that it was uncertain whether Article 25 of the Warsaw Convention, as amended by The Hague Protocol, as amended by the Montreal Protocol No. 4, applies to actions pertaining to the carriage of cargo. As Article 25 reads: "In the carriage of passengers and baggage [...]", the Court did not decide whether Article 25 also applies to the carriage of *cargo*, but that plaintiff failed to provide evidence for wilful misconduct on the part of the defendant airline.[439] However, a US Court of Appeals removed cargo from the wilful misconduct exception.[440]

When platinum boxes were stolen in the course of the loading of these boxes into the aircraft, the Court found that the act of theft by the people who loaded the goods amounted to wilful misconduct.[441]

3.11.5.6 Compliance with Customs Regulations

Compliance with requirements set by customs regulations is the responsibility of the consignor, and not of the air carrier, as to which see a case between the consignor and the air freight forwarder in a German case.[442]

3.11.6 Carriage of Mail by Air

Most airlines also carry airmail. Yet, the regulatory framework for cargo on the one hand and air mail on the other hand is completely different. Whereas international carriage of cargo falls under the terms of the Warsaw Convention, as amended – by, amongst others, MAP 4 -, carriage of airmail was explicitly excluded because of reasons related to the public interest. Carriage of postal times is excluded from the scope of the Warsaw Convention, as amended by the Hague Protocol. Article 2(2) reads:

---

439. *See*, *Chips Plus Inc.* v. *Federal Express Corp.*, 281 F. Supp. 2d 758 (E.D. Pa 2003); *see also*, the case of *Malenstein and others* v. *Korean Airlines Co. and Aero Ground Services*, decision of the District Court of Haarlem of 17 December 2002, Case No. 77078/HA ZA 01-1149 and 80725/HA ZA 02-151, "Rolnummer" (court case number) 77078, in which cargo case the court acknowledged wilful misconduct.
440. *See*, *Morog* v. *Kuehne & Nagel, Inc.*, 56 Fed. Appx. 137, 2003 WL 329304.
441. *Rustenburg Platinum Mines Ltd. and others* v. *South African Airways and Pan American World Airways*, Court of Appeals, decision of 10 and 11 July 1978, 1 Lloyd's Law Reports 19–25 (1979).
442. *See*, Darmstadt Regional Court Decision 7 S 227/11 of 18 April 2012, reported by Carsten Vyvers in International Law office of 22 August 2012; *see also*, The World Customs Organisation has an international convention on the simplification and harmonisation of customs procedures, the Kyoto Convention revised version (adopted on June 1999 and entered in force 3 February 2006), on matters pertaining to custom formalities. All States who are parties to the Kyoto Convention are bound by the provisions of the General Annex. Transitional Standard 3.21 states that: "The Customs shall permit the lodging of the Goods declaration by electronic means." This means that in all the States party to the Kyoto Convention, customs are bound to accept electronic messages or documents. The combined effect of MAP 4/Montreal Convention, 1999, and the Kyoto Convention results in an intensified development from the paper age into the electronic age, in which hundreds of millions of documents are progressively being replaced by cheaper and faster electronic records. *See also*, www.wcoomd.org.

This Convention shall not apply to carriage of mail and postal packages.

Carriage of postal items was considered to come under the regime of the Universal Postal Union (UPU), which was founded in 1874 in Bern, Switzerland, and is one of the oldest international organisations.

Meanwhile, the WC29, as amended by the Hague Protocol and MAP 4 provides in Article 2(3):

> In the carriage of postal items the carrier shall be liable only to the relevant postal administration in accordance with the rules applicable to the relationship between the carriers and the postal administrations.

Liberalisation, privatisation and cross border ventures affect the organisation of airmail on a national basis. Moreover, the cited Article 2(3) of MAP 4 is ambiguous. The division of responsibility – for the safe carriage of postal items – and liability between air carriers, national administrations and private postal service organisations is not clear, and requires further study.[443]

3.11.7 Concluding Remarks

Liability for damage to cargo is special as the carriage involves several persons who may be subject to different liability regimes. Cargo is carried through various modes to transport to its place of destination.

The current regime is based on the provisions of the Montreal Protocol, 1999, which is adhered to by sixty States. It aims at facilitating conditions for documentation and maintains an unbreakable liability regime.

Case law focuses on questions pertaining to the control of the air carrier, and the level of damages. This is not different from claims being presented in passenger procedures. The unbreakability of the limit was introduced by MAP4 and retained MC99.

A *specific* provision of the Warsaw Convention applying to air cargo concerns *arbitration*. Under Article 32 of the Convention, arbitration clauses in contracts pertaining to the carriage of cargo are allowed. However, this option is hardly used. The Montreal Convention, 1999, has a *separate* provision on arbitration, that is, Article 34, which, again, only applies to disputes in relation to carriage of cargo.

3.12 Jurisdiction

3.12.1 Regulation under the Montreal Convention, 1999

The Warsaw Convention of 1929 has listed four mandatory jurisdictions, which are competent to hear and decide on claims falling under its provision those being:

---

443. *See,* M.G. Schoonis, *The Entry into Force of the Montreal Protocol No 4, and Other Issues Relating to Cargo,* presentation made at a PAO seminar organised by the International Institute of Air and Space Law in Leiden on 6 November 2000.

- the court of the domicile of the carrier;[444]
- the court of the principal place of business of the carrier;[445]
- the place of business through which the contract has been made;[446]
- the court at the final destination;[447]

Any pre-incident agreements designed to alter the mandatory rules of jurisdiction laid down in the Montreal Convention are null and void.[448]

Article 33 of the Montreal Convention, 1999, introduces a so-called 'fifth jurisdiction" supplementing the above four jurisdictions that may be entitled to decide on an action for damages under the Convention. The 'fifth jurisdiction' has been controversial. The main supporter of the fifth jurisdiction, the United States, enumerated arguments for its introduction during the Conference, such as the fairness of the right of passengers or the persons representing them to claim in the 'home' courts of the passengers. These courts are best equipped to assess the damages based on local standards of living.[449]

The fifth jurisdiction gives access to the courts of the country of principal or permanent residence of the passenger in case of damage resulting from his death or injury if the cumulative conditions of Article 33(2) are met. Those conditions pertain to the following:

(1) the claim must result from the death or injury of a passenger; *and*
(2) the passenger must have his or her principal and permanent residence in the territory of the court;[450] *and*

---

444. Which refers to the corporation's headquarters, as to which *see Aikpitanhi* v. *Iberia*, 553 F.Supp. 2d 872, 876 (E.D. Mich. 2008).

445. Meaning the place of incorporation of the company, as to which *see*, *Swaminathan* v. *Swiss Air Transport Co.*, 692 F.2d 387, 390 (5th Cir. 1992) and *Smith* v. *Canadian Pacific Airways*, 452 F.2d 798, 800 (2d Cir. 1971).

446. That is, "the location where the passenger tickets ... were purchased", as to which *see Osborne* v. *British Airways*, 198 F.Supp. 901, 904–905 (S.D. Texas 2002); in *Cordice* v. *LIAT Airline* (2015 WL 5579868), the court found that LIAT's bank accounts and operation of flights to the US were not sufficient to render LIAT "essentially at home" in the US for a claim coming under MC99.

447. Which coincides, in a round trip, with the place where the journey originated, as to which *see*, *Swaminathan* v. *Swiss Air Transport Co.*, 692 F.2d 387, 389 (5th Cir. 1992).

448. *See*, *Avalon Technologies* v. *EMO-Trans, Inc., and Air Canada*, No. 2 :14-cv-14731-SFC-MJH (E.D. Mich., 29 April 2015); *see*, however, the decision of the Paris Court of Appeals of 2 June 2015 in which it held that it had jurisdiction for a case involving a shipment of Bordeaux wines from Bordeaux to China as Paris was at least implicitly the place where the contract was made (CA NO. 15/04938).

449. *See*, for arguments in favour of the 'fifth jurisdiction', George Tompkins, *The Future of the Warsaw liability system*, The Aviation Quarterly 38–76 at 46–47 (1999), and, for other arguments in favour of this concept, B. Cheng, *A Fifth Jurisdiction without Montreal Additional Protocol No. 3, and Full Compensation without the Supplemental Compensation Plan*, Air & Space Law 118–124 (1995); and: *A Shored-Up Warsaw Convention Plus a Contractual So-Called 'Fifth Jurisdiction'?* The Aviation Quarterly 18–30 (1997).

450. *See*, *Seales* v. *Panama Aviation*, 2009 WL 395821 (E.D.N.Y. 18 February 2009) in which the court found that the claimant's permanent residence was Panama – as testified by the claimant – rather than New York, and Paris.

(3) the court must be located in a state party to or from whose territory the carrier operates services for the carriage by air, either on its own aircraft or another carrier's aircraft pursuant to a commercial agreement; *and*

(4) the court must be located in the territory of a state in which territory that carrier conducts its business of carriage of passengers by air from premises leased or owned by the carrier itself or by another carrier with which it has a commercial agreement.[451]

This is one of the instances where the Convention recognises the conclusion of arrangements on code-sharing and franchising between carriers. The above conditions make room for the 'fifth jurisdiction' under such arrangements. However, the practical reality of these last two mentioned conditions is that most small carriers that are not part of a code sharing arrangement can avoid the fifth jurisdiction.

3.12.2 Case Law under the Montreal Convention, 1999

In *Hornsby* v. *Lufthansa*, the court analysed the term 'principal and permanent residence'. It referred to the definition laid down in Article 33(b) of the Convention, defining this term as:

the one fixed and permanent abode of the passenger at the time of the accident. The nationality of the passenger shall not be the determining factor in this regard.

The court sought to define the term "permanent abode" and found in the Black's Law Dictionary that this term must be understood as a "domicile or fixed home, which the party may leave as his interest or whim may dictate, but which he has no present intention of abandoning." Although the plaintiff was a resident of Germany, had bank accounts and doctors there, and had sold her house in the US, she declared that it was never her intention to become a permanent resident of Germany or any other country outside the US. The court found in favour of the plaintiff, arguing that her intent is the relevant factor. It held that it was more likely than not for the plaintiff to return to the US so that she could base her claim upon the 'fifth jurisdiction'.[452]

A similar case concerned Ms Choi who had regularly visited the US during a period of eight years, possessed a US driver's license, a social security card and bank accounts, while intending to live at some point in time in the US. However, the court held that she had not a "principal and permanent residence" in the US.[453]

---

451. Compliance with one of these options was denied by a US court in the case of *Razi* v. *Qatar Airways*, No. 4:12-cv-2073, 2014 WL 496654 (S.D. Tex. 6 February 2014) and *Fadhliah* v. *Air France*, 36 Avi. 15,287 (C.D.Cal. 2013); *see also*, *British Airways* v. *Gems Art Factory and others*, submitted to the National Consumer Disputes Redressal Commission of India, denying jurisdiction in Jaipur, India under the Montreal Convention; Case No. 81 of 2005.
452. *See*, *Hornsby* v. *Lufthansa*, No. CV07-07594, F.Supp.2d, 2009 WL 116962 (C.D. Cal.).
453. Pursuant to Art. 33(2) MC99; *see*, *Choi* v. *Asiana Airlines*, 36 Avi. 16,335 (N.D. California).

The Forum Non Conveniens (FNC) doctrine has been upheld under the Montreal Convention.[454] If there is an adequate alternative forum, and public and private interests favour referral to a foreign court, the court may exercise its discretion and refer the case to a forum abroad of public and private interests warrant such a referral.[455]

Claimants in the Air France (AF) 447 litigation[456] had argued that the FNC doctrine cannot be upheld under MC99 because:

- The *Hosaka* decision denied the FNC concept under the Warsaw Convention, 1929,[457] while the language for jurisdictional competence is the same under the Montreal Convention, 1999.

- The FNC concept is incompatible with the 'fifth jurisdiction' of the Montreal Convention, 1999, which is designed to provide claimants with the initiation of proceedings in their home State.

In the AF 447 litigation, the court considered various interests such as the preference for having local affairs, and the application of local law to be judged in the home country, the administrative difficulties flowing from court congestion, the availability of evidence and witnesses, translations and costs, and that FNC was considered in the *Hosaka* case, under the Warsaw Convention is different from FNC under the Montreal Convention because:

- The *Hosaka* decision was based on an analysis of the drafting history of the Warsaw Convention which is dramatically different from the drafting history of the Montreal Convention.

---

454. *See*, a decision form a judge in Northern California in the mid-air accident of Air France flight 447 in 2009, deciding that claims brought be victims of that accident cannot be filed in US courts, and reportedly places stringent limits on the damages they may expect to recover; *see*, www.cand.uscourts.gov message via internet dated 22 June 2011. The judge esteemed France a more appropriate venue partly because of French authorities' detailed ongoing investigation of the accident. Black boxes and cockpit voice recorders would be more accessible there.

455. *See, In re West Caribbean Airways*, S.A., 32 Avi.15, 595 (S.D. Fla 26 September 2007), 32 Avi. 15,764 (S.D. Fla 9 Nov 2007), in which case the court of Florida dismissed the cases to Martinique (France); *see also*, the accident of Flash Air arising out of the Boeing 737-300 crashing in the Red Sea after departure from Egypt in 2004; plaintiffs sued Boeing, US component manufacturers and the US leasing company in California but the Californian court dismissed the case to France on the basis of *Forum Non Conveniens* in June 2005. The French Court of Appeal decided in March 2008 that they did not have jurisdiction in the case, and that the US Court were more suited and sent it back to the US. Meanwhile, the French Supreme Court eventually ruled that the plaintiffs' jurisdiction challenge was premature, as to which *see*, for the US judgement: *Gambra*, 377 F.Supp. 2d 810; and for the French judgement: *Cour d'appel* [CA], regional Court of appeal, judgement of 6 March 2008, at 45–46.

456. AF flight 447 left Brazil with destination Paris on 1 June 2009, and crashed over the Atlantic Ocean. All 228 passengers and crew lost their lives. More than 70 claimants started proceedings against Air France, Airbus, and other manufacturers including Thales Avionics, and US component manufacturers. In the same vein: *Fortaner* v. *Boeing*, No. 11-56179 (9th Cir., 10 January 2013) pursuant to which decision the claim was dismissed to Spain on the basis of public and private interests.

457. *See, Hosaka* v. *United Airlines*, Inc., 305 F.3d 989, 1004 (9th Cir. 2002) in which the Court stated that "Article 28(1) of the Warsaw Convention precludes a federal court from dismissing an action on the ground of forum non conveniens"; *see also*, section 3.12.4, below.

- Several US courts have convincingly applied the FNC concept to cases coming under the Montreal Convention, 1999.

In view of the above, France had, all in all, a greater interest in judging the case. Hence, the application of the doctrine of FNC by American courts does not necessarily imply that the foreign forum referred will indeed accept to hear the case. In the above case, the French *Cour de Cassation* ruled that under the Montreal Convention, the selection of jurisdiction is an exclusive and imperative right of the claimant. Hence, decisions of American courts based on the doctrine of FNC cannot force French Courts to decide upon a case, when the United States is one of the available forums under the Montreal Convention.[458] However, the Court of the Southern District of Florida also believed that American courts cannot be forced to reopen a case based on the French interpretation of the Montreal Convention. That is why the Florida court denied the plaintiffs' motion to reopen the case in the United States.[459]

A clause in a shipping contract stipulated that US courts had exclusive jurisdiction with respect to claims made under the contract. This clause is invalid in light of Article 49 MC99 as this provision makes contractual clauses modifying the rules of jurisdiction invalid.[460]

Arbitration has been made possible for disputes arising out of the carriage of cargo within the jurisdictions of Article 33 (*see* Article 34). However, nothing in the convention seems to prevent carriers and passengers from reverting to arbitration. Whether or not arbitration for passenger claims is permitted depends on national law of the State concerned.[461] The Report on the *Modernization and Consolidation of the Warsaw System* states however: "Arbitration shall not be available in respect of the carrier's liability for the death of a passenger."[462] It seems, therefore, that this issue has yet to be clarified.

3.12.3 Regulation under the Warsaw Regime

Article 28 of the Warsaw Convention mentions four *fora*, which may be competent to hear an action under the terms of that Convention. The following may be relevant for the present discussion:[463]

(1) The relatively great number of jurisdictions among which the plaintiff may choose implies that Article 28 should be *strictly* interpreted.[464] The plaintiff

---

458. *Cour de Cassation*, French Supreme Court, judgement of 7 December 2011, No. Q 10-30.919.
459. *See*, EALA & Bird & Bird report of the 8th Munich Liability Seminar.
460. *See*, *Avalon Technologies* v. *EMO-Trans*, 36 Avi. 16,478 (E.D.Mich.2015).
461. *See*, Report of the First Meeting of the Special Group on *the Modernization and Consolidation of the 'Warsaw System'*, ICAO Doc. SGMW/1 (1998) at 2–10.
462. *See*, ICAO Legal Committee, 30th Session, LC/30-WP/4 at A-19, para. 5.4.22.
463. *See also*, A. Trimarchi, *An Analysis of the Grounds of Jurisdiction and Jurisdictional Issues of e-Ticketing in Light of the Warsaw/Montreal System*, in XV(1) Issues in Aviation Law & Policy (2016).
464. In *Alemi* v. *Qatar Airways*, the court in Baltimore, Maryland decided that it had no jurisdiction as the defendant was domiciled in Doha, Qatar, the plaintiff's ticket purchased in Teheran, and

may be tempted to 'forum shop'. According to this doctrine, the plaintiff selects a court without a sufficiently genuine link with   the case but which, as shown in other rulings, adopts a more favourable attitude towards the plaintiff when, for instance, the question of compensation of immaterial damages arises.

(2) Parties to litigation under Article 28 are not entitled to deviate from the options that are offered by this provision. That means that their suit may not be decided by alternative means of dispute settlement, such as arbitration. The rules on jurisdiction are *exclusive*.[465]

The plaintiff, for instance, the injured passenger, can choose any of the following four courts but is thus restricted by these four options. The court to which the case is submitted must at any rate be located in the territory of a contracting party.

(1) *The principal place of business of the carrier*
That is, the place where the management of the airline has its main seat and/or the place where the airline has its headquarters.

(2) *The court of the residence of the carrier, that is, in most cases of the defendant*
This is a rule of procedural law. As the air carrier is a company, the term "residence" does not seem to be suitable in the present context. The term "residence" refers to the place where natural persons live. Most probably and most logically it coincides with the term "principal place of business of the carrier."

(3) *An airline's place of business through which the contract has been made*
This option has given rise to most litigation. In this context, the plaintiff may refer his case to the court of the travel agency or a branch office of the airline, which has issued the ticket, or the air waybill. It is not self-evident to determine the place where the contract has been made, or, in other words, where the agreement has been concluded. The following examples may illustrate the uncertainty as to the determination of the place where the contract has been concluded.

(4) *The place of destination*
To identify the place of destination the two following factors should be taken into account. *Firstly*, reference may be made to what has been stated about this point in sections 3.1.1 and 3.1.2.1 with respect to "place of origin" and

---

the place of destination was also located in Teheran; 84 F. Supp. 2d 847 (D. Md. 2012); *see also*, *British Airways* v. *Atoyebi*, [2014 LPELR-23120 (Supreme Court of Nigeria).

465. The exclusivity of the jurisdictional rules of the Warsaw Convention in relation to the Brussels Convention of 27 September 1968 on *Jurisdiction and the enforcement of judgements in civil and commercial matters* were considered by the French Court of Appeal in a case involving several defendants, including an airline (Gulf Air) and a manufacturer (Airbus). This court recognised the exclusivity of the jurisdictional rules of the Warsaw Convention under the conditions *stated there M. Y...* v. *Gulf Air*, Cour de cassation, decision of 12 November 2009, 252(4) Revue française de droit aérien et spatial 447–451 (2009).

"place of destination." *Secondly*, what is relevant is not the real intention of the parties, but the intention of the parties as this appears from the contract. Both factors have been subject to litigation. Decisions have not always been unambiguous.

The jurisdictional rules laid down in Article 28 of WC29, are mandatory, and limit the choices of the plaintiff to the four fora laid down in it. No arrangements may be made between the plaintiff and the defendant for alternative fora, and other means of dispute resolution.

3.12.4 Case Law under the Warsaw Regime

Regarding the *principal place of business of the carrier*, the passenger may not bring the suit before the court of New Jersey when a passenger buys a ticket in Florida for a journey to Cuba, whereas the headquarters of the carrier are located in New York.[466]

The designation of the court of the residence of the carrier, that is, in most cases of the defendant is a rule of procedural law. As the air carrier is a company, the term "residence" does not seem to be suitable in the present context. The term "residence" refers to the place where natural persons live. Most probably and most logically it coincides with the term "principal place of business of the carrier."

The option pertaining to an *airline's place of business through which the contract has been made* has given rise to most litigation. In this context, the plaintiff may refer his case to the court of the travel agency or a branch office of the airline, which has issued the ticket, or the air waybill. It is not self-evident to determine the place where the contract has been made, or, in other words, where the agreement has been concluded. The following examples may illustrate the uncertainty as to the determination of the place where the contract has been concluded.

There must be a real connection, or *genuine link*, between the airline and the establishment, or place of business, of the airline in order to create jurisdiction under this provision. In 2006, the Italian Supreme Court decided that a travel agent who is not an appointee of the airline, but merely an IATA agent, cannot be qualified as the airline's place of business through which the contract was made, ruling out the jurisdiction of the Italian court.[467]

A passenger paid his ticket on an Air Jamaica flight through a travel agent in New York, and received against that payment a note confirming the advance payment. The branch office of Air Jamaica in Philadelphia arranged the ticket would be available for

---

466. This was the position of the Superior Court of New Jersey in *Tumarkin c.s.* v. *Pan Am*, 4 Aviation Cases, 18,152; *see also*, a Canadian case: *Ashad* v. *Lufthansa*, 247 CarswellOnt 7251.
467. *See, Reale-Mucelli* v. *Air New Zealand*, Court of Cassation, Joint Civil Chambers, 14 June 2006 reported by Giuseppi Guerreri in 33(2) Air & Space Law 175–176 (2008); *see also*, a Canadian case: *Ashad* v. *Lufthansa*, 247 CarswellOnt 7251.

the passenger in Jamaica, where the passenger collected his ticket. The ticket was issued in Jamaica. New York must be deemed to be the place where the contract was made.[468]

In *Polanski* v. *KLM Royal Dutch Airlines* the court found that the place where the contract was made was the place where the ticket was purchased, since that is the place where the acceptor completes his manifestation of his consent to be bound by the terms of the agreement.[469] This decision may mean that, in the case that the ticket was purchased and paid online in the house of the future passenger, the residence of the passenger may be considered as the place where the contract was made.

The following may serve to identify the 'place of destination.' *Firstly*, to define 'the place of destination', reference may be made to what has been stated about this point in sections 3.1.1 and 3.1.2.1 with respect to 'place of origin' and 'place of destination.' *Secondly*, not the real intention of the parties, but *the intention of the parties as this appears from the contract* is relevant. Nevertheless, both points have been subject to litigation. Decisions have not always been unambiguous.

Two residents of the United States had bought a return ticket Warsaw-New York-Warsaw, but they did not use the return section New York-Warsaw. They had bought the return ticket Warsaw-New York-Warsaw in order to comply with Polish Government's requirements. The two passengers had no intention whatsoever to return to Warsaw, and this was considered to be decisive by the New York District Court, the court of the place of destination as put forward by the 'subjective' intention of the passengers. The 'objective' intention of the parties as evidenced by the contract was not relevant in this case.[470]

Legal arguments based on Article 28(1) of the Warsaw Convention and public factors may lead to the conclusion that an action must be brought in a certain country.[471]

This situation has led to a number of court decisions under the doctrine of FNC, not only in the US, but also in France. In the US, the court can decline jurisdiction in circumstances, which are related to the familiarity of the court with the law it must apply. All kind of practical matters, including the lack of understanding of foreign laws because of language and other problems, may be a reason for a court to rule the FNC doctrine, which is frequently invoked before US courts when they find that a more appropriate court should handle the case.[472] The grounds for dismissing a case to another court may be the following:

---

468. *See, Campbell* v. *Air Jamaica* (1988), 21 Avi 17,755, and cases in which tickets were bought on the internet and potential jurisdictional questions arose but none of these made it to trial.
469. *See,* R. Tillery, *Polanski* v. *KLM Royal Dutch Airlines,* 71(1) Journal of Air Law and Commerce 91–98 (2006).
470. *See,* Shawcross and Beaumont, *Air Law* VII/137–143.
471. *See, In re Air Crash off Long Island,* N.Y., 65 F. Supp. 2d 207 (SDNY 1999), affirmed 209 F.3d 200 (2nd Cir. 2000).
472. *See, Piper Aircraft Co.* v. *Reyno,* 454 U.S. 235 (1981), and *Bhatnagar* v. *Surrender Overseas Limited,* 52 F.3d 1220 (3d Cir. 1995); *see also, In Re Air Crash Over The Taiwan Straigt On May, 25, 2002,* 331 F. Supp. 2d 1176 (C.D. Cal. 2004), reported in Condon & Forsyth LLP, September 2004, *In Re Air Crash at Taipei, Taiwan, on October 31, 2000,* 2004 WL 1234131 (C.D. Cal. 6 February 2004), *Zermeno* v. *McDonnel Douglas Corp.,* 2004 WL 1146192 (S.D. Tex. May 10,

- an adequate alternative forum is available;
- the balance of public, including the choice between the chosen and alternative forum, the administration of justice by a US court, the use and translation of foreign languages, and the availability of foreign law to US courts for adjudicating the case -, and private, that is, access to evidence, presence of witnesses, costs of the trial, interest involved with the case;
- the link between the case in terms of place of accident, nationality of airline, nationality of the victims, the application of the law of another State and the establishment of the Bureau investigating the accident in another State.

In the *Hosaka* decision,[473] the US Supreme Court upheld the decision of the US Court of Appeals in which this Court held that, where jurisdiction based on Article 28 of the Warsaw Convention is proper in the United States, a federal district Court is precluded from dismissing a case on the basis of the common law doctrine of FNC. This decision was contrary to earlier decisions made by US courts.

On 11 July 2006, the French *Cour de cassation* (Supreme Court) overruled decisions made by the same court (the *Cour de cassation*) in the case of *Kunze Bejon* v. *Pakistan International Airlines* (1998) (PIA) and by lower courts in the period following 1998, to the effect that there is no jurisdiction for claims against air carriers under the Warsaw Convention in suits with multiple defendants. Claimants sought jurisdiction of French courts. As Article 28 of the Warsaw Convention did not provide relief in terms of jurisdiction to plaintiffs, they sued non-airline parties, that is, the manufacturer of the aircraft (Airbus) before a court of Toulouse where Airbus has its principal place of business. The argument put forward by claimants for suing the air carrier in the same proceedings was that the Warsaw System does not provide guidance as to jurisdiction where there are multiple defendants, including non-carrier interests. Consequently, in the opinion of the court, reference should be made to the ordinary rules of French municipal law as to jurisdiction, so that the air carrier was found to be a necessary and proper party to the suit. Airbus was ultimately exonerated by the French court for the accident consisting of a crashing on approach to Kathmandu in 1992. In reaching its 2006 decision, the French Supreme Court argued that the rules of the Warsaw Convention had to be strictly applied and there was no room for variance. It also found that international conventions had precedence over French domestic law and in particular, the specific rules relating to jurisdiction.[474]

2004), *Lie* v. *The Boeing Co.*, 2004 WL 1462451 (N.D. Ill. 29 June 2004), and *In Re Air Crash Near Nantucket Island, Mass., On October 31, 1999* (2004 WL 1824385 (E.D.N.Y 16 August 2004), and *Viktoriya Shirbokova* v. *CSA Czech Airlines, Inc.*, United States District Court District of Minnesota, Civil File No. 04-641, Decision of 24 August, 2004.

473. *See, Hosaka* v. *United Airlines*, Inc., 305 F.3d 989 (9th Cir. 2002), cert. denied, 537 U.S. 123 S.Ct. 1284, 2003 U.S. LEXIS 1531 (24 February 2003).

474. As reported by Beaumont & Son Aviation at Clyde & Co in July 2006, *see*, www.beaumontclydeco.com in the cases of *Gulf Air* c/*Cie Airbus et autres*, and *Kenya Airways* c/*Cie Airbus et autres*.

The FNC concept has also been applied in product liability cases,[475] pursuant to which relatives of the deceased passengers sued the manufacturer of the aircraft and its component parts. In one case, the court explained that the involvement of Mexican authorities with the investigation of the accident and the availability of evidence in Mexico justified dismissal to that country.[476] In another one, the suit was governed by the substantive law of another State (Canada).[477] In *Frederiksson* v. *HR Textorn*,[478] the Court of Appeals took procedural factors including the availability of witnesses and evidence into account in deciding in favour of dismissal. However, claimants have also successfully instituted proceedings against the manufacturer, particularly in the state of Illinois in the US.[479]

The court must determine whether it has jurisdiction on the basis of the applicability of the Warsaw Convention. Hence, the damage must have arisen during *international transportation*. If not, Article 28 of the Warsaw Convention does not apply to the case.[480] In *Airbus* v. *Armavia*,[481] the French Supreme Court ('*Cour de cassation*') referred the case back to the Court of Appeals of Toulouse. This Court felt that the Court of Toulouse was the competent court because the litigation concerning a guarantee procedure initiated by the manufacturer Airbus which has its principal seat in that city. It was requested to pay damages to victims of an accident in which Armavia was involved, which was subject to the Warsaw Convention. However, the defendant Armavia has no connection with Toulouse nor had any of the passengers made a contract there.[482] Hence, this is a somewhat dubious decision.

3.12.5   Concluding Remarks

Jurisdiction is, next to the substantive law laid down in Article 17, a principal subject of the Warsaw regime and the Montreal Convention, 1999. Save for the addition of the so-called fifth jurisdiction at the insistence of the US, the formulation of the jurisdictional rules has stayed and its terms of reference have frequently given rise to litigation, not least in the US whose legal system has a relatively complex structure.

---

475. *See also*, section 5.3 of Chapter 8.
476. *See*, *Rolls Royce* v. *Garcia*, 77 So. 3d 855 857-858 (Fla. 3d D.C.A. 2012).
477. *See*, *Anyango* v. *Rolls Royce*, 971 N.E.2d 654 (Ind. 2012).
478. No. 3:08CV450, 2009 WL 295225 (D. Conn., 2 September 2009).
479. *See*, Air Philippines Flight 541 (Boeing 737, Philippines, 2000): *Ellis* v. *AAR Parts Trading* (2005); Transair Lockhart River (Fairchild Metro 23, Australia, 2005): *Thornton* v. *Hamilton Sundstrand Corp.* (2008); Tans Flight 204 (Boeing 737, Peru, 2005): *Vivas* v. *Boeing* (2009); Atlasjet Flight 4203 (Boeing MD-83, Turkey, 2007): *Arik* v. *The Boeing Company* (2008 affirmed by the Appeal Court in Chicago in 2011); XL Airways Flight 120 (cabin fumes intoxication, Boeing 767, 2007): *Sabatino* v. *Boeing* (2009); Mexico Interior Ministry private flight (Learjet, Mexico, 2008): *Björkstam* v. *Learjet* (2010); British Airways Flight BA038 (Boeing 777, England, 2008): *Stafford* v. *Boeing* (2011).
480. *See*, *Coyle* v. *P.T. Garuda Indonesia*, 363 F.3d 979 (9th Cir. 2004), in which case the tickets for the domestic leg Jakarta-Medan mentioned the term: "DOMESTIK".
481. Decision of the *Cour de cassation* of 4 March 2015, Arrêt No. 327 FS-P + B + I.
482. *See*, Pablo Mendes de Leon, *Jurisdiction under and Exclusivity of Private Air Law Agreements on Air Carrier Liability: The Case of Airbus versus Armavia Airlines*, in *From Lowlands to High Skies, Liber Amicorum* for John Balfour 261–274 (2013).

For a long time, the US has been and still is the leading jurisdiction when it comes to the settlement of aviation cases. Its courts have attracted cases from all over the world and had to adjudicate them because of the choices which are given in these jurisdictional rules, and their sometimes somewhat cryptic formulation.

This development has led US courts to construe the FNC concept, allowing them to send the case which is submitted to one of them to what they deem to be a more appropriate court abroad. This position has not always been understood by other courts, including civil law Supreme Courts, which prefer to depart from the mandatory rules laid down in the above conventions rather than adopting a relatively pragmatic approach.

This is one of the examples where common and civil law conceptions have to be married under private international air law. The case of *In re West Caribbean Airways* which has been sent back and forth across the Transatlantic Ocean shows that this can be a challenging and cumbersome task.

It also demonstrates the legal limits of the FNC concept as a foreign court is not obliged to accept the case, which is referred to it, and, with that, leaving the claiming possibly without a court.

3.13 Procedural Matters

3.13.1 Claims Against Third Parties

Whether necessary or not, Article 31 of the Convention confirms the rights of airlines to take action against third parties. Also, under Article 37 of the Montreal Convention, 1999, the air carrier has a right of recourse against third parties, whether or not a prior judgment has been made against the carrier on the matter of recourse.[483] This right was not mentioned in the Warsaw Convention.[484]

It follows that the carrier, operating under the scope of the Montreal Convention, 1999, expressly, and without restrictions, may reclaim paid damages with third parties. The air carrier may share the amount of damages with such another party if that other party is a claimant who has caused or contributed to the damage.[485] In practice, it is not easy for carriers to reclaim damages from third parties including but not limited to manufacturers, airport operators, security undertakings, ground handling providers, ATC agencies or the States, for contractual or statutory provisions limiting or excluding the liability of these third parties in relation to the airline.

---

483. *See, In re Air Crash at Lexington, Kentucky, 27 August 2006*, 32 Avi 15,235 (E.D. Ky 2007).
484. For case law coming under the Warsaw Convention, *see, In re Air Crash at Little Rock, Arkansas, on 1 June, 1999*, 291 F.3d 508, 516–517 (8th Cir.), cert. denied, *Lloyd v. American Airlines*, Inc., 537 U.S. 974 (2002).
485. *See,* Art. 20 of the Montreal Convention, 1999, and Art. 21 of the Warsaw Convention, 1929, as explained in *In re Air Crash at Lexington, Kentucky, 27 August 2006*, 32 Avi 15,235 (E.D. Ky 2007) and *Cortes v. American Airlines*, 177 F.3d 1272, 1305 (11th Cir. 1999).

3.13.2 Applicability of the Law of the State of the Claimant

The Warsaw Convention does not designate the persons who are entitled to claim damages under this convention. Article 24(2) states that an action for damages of a passenger in relation to the air carrier, exclusivity of the action which must find its legal basis in this Convention also applies:

> [...] without prejudice to the questions as to who are the persons who have the right to bring suit and what are their respective rights.

National law must deal with the persons who are entitled to bring an action for damages to the court.[486]

A related question concerns the *choice of law*. A court must assess damages in accordance with the law of the domicile of the passenger;[487] however, in practice, courts apply the *lex forum*. If there is a conflict between the law of the seat of the court, and the law of the domicile of the passenger, the seized court must apply the law of the state whose interests would be more greatly impaired if it were not applied.[488]

3.13.3 Civil Procedure Provisions

Questions of procedure must be governed by the law of the State in which the court hearing the case is located. Such questions include but are not limited to conditions on summoning the defendant, the use of a certain language and legal expressions as well as calculation of time periods which are mentioned under WC29, and MC99.[489] These provisions identify territorial jurisdiction. Each State party to either convention is free to administer justice in accordance with national procedural rules.

In the case of *Mehlman* v. *Swissair*, the Italian Court of cassation held that the "court having jurisdiction at the place of destination" refers to territorial jurisdiction, pursuant to which Italian law must identify the competent court.[490] In the words of the Ontario, Canada, Court of Appeals:

---

486. *See*, P.P.C. Haanappel, *The Right to Sue in Death Cases under the Warsaw Convention*, 6(2) Air Law 66–78 (1981).
487. *See*, Art. 1 of the IATA Carrier Agreement on Passenger Liability of 31 October 1995.
488. *See*, *In Re: Air Crash at Taipei, Taiwan, On October 31, 2000*; Case No. 01-MDL-1394 GAF (RCx) (C.D. Cal. 2002).
489. *See*, Arts 28(2) and 29 of the Warsaw Convention, 1929, as amended, and Art. 28(2) and Arts 33(4) and 35 of the Montreal Convention, 1999.
490. Court of cassation, Order of 26 May 2005 n. 11183, reported by G. Guerreri in 32(1) Air & Space Law (2006); *see also*, the decision of the Criminal Chamber of the French Supreme Court in *Association de defense des victims et familles du crash de Saint-Barthelemy (ADFV) – Fédération nationale des victimes d'accidents collectifs (FENVAC)* v. *Air Caribes* (decision of 3 June 2009; No. 08-83946) in which the French Supreme court decided that according to French procedural law, actions for damages can only be brought before the civil court, and not before the criminal court, irrespective of the question of whether the claimant is a passenger or a third party (deriving its entitlement to sue pursuant to domestic procedural law). This follows from Art. 24 of the Warsaw Convention.

[...] once a claim is issued within the two year period identified in Article 29 of the Convention, the Article 29 requirements have been satisfied and the claim is then governed by the procedure in the jurisdiction where the claim has been issued. Any subsequent procedural requirements, including those relating to the time for service or renewal of the claim, are governed by the rules of practice of that jurisdiction.[491]

The Court dismissed the appeal lodged by the air carrier. The notice of complaint must contain a complaint on damages. A preliminary notice merely referring to wet and deformed package but not stating the amount of damages does not meet the 'notice' standards under Article 26.[492]

3.13.4 Time Limits

3.13.4.1 Time Limits under the Montreal Convention, 1999

Again, time limits are of essence. Article 35 of MC99 sets forth the same two year period of limitation as contained in Article 29 of the Warsaw Convention. This limit must be strictly observed.[493] An action for lost or stolen baggage is barred if it is brought more than two years after the date of the intended arrival of the lost baggage.[494] Third party actions brought against the air carrier are not bound by this two years period as the text and the structure of the Convention do not create a right of action for contribution or indemnity and that such a right is not covered by the Convention, or Article 29.[495]

A Spanish court has held that, in certain circumstances, the two years' time limit may be broken. Examples occur in cases where the claimant sues the carrier before the wrong, that is, incompetent court whereas the claimant could not start the procedure as a result of causes lying outside the claimant's control. The result is that the time limit may be extended – but the case is under appeal.[496] In the same vein, a French Court of Appeals opined that the limitation period of two years may be interrupted when the defendant airline makes an offer for settlement which is not accepted by the

---

491. See, *Mosregion Investment Corporation* v. *Ukraine International Airlines*, 2010 ONCA 715.
492. See a case decided by the German Court of Appeals in Munich, reported by Mr P. Nikolai Ehlers: *Precision Pays*, 32(6) Air & Space Law 467–468 (2007).
493. See, *Cattaneo* v. *American Airlines*, No. 15-cv-01748-BLF (N.D. Cal. 24 September 2015), and *Awimer* v. *Yollari*, No. 15-cv-69 GEB-GSA, [2015] WL 5922206 (E.D. Cal., 9 October 2015).
494. See, *Small* v. *America West Airlines*, inc., 32 Avi 15,878 (D.N.J. 2007); *Chubb Ins. Co of Europe, S.A.* v. *Menlo Worldwide Forwarding, Inc.*, 32 Avi 15,978 (C.D. Calif. 2008), in which the court confirmed that the two year time bar also applied to carriage falling under Chapter v. – incorporating provisions of the Guadalajara Convention; *Onyekuru* v. *Northwest Airlines* 32 Avi 15,551 (N.D. Ill. 2007); see also, *Dickson* v. *American Airlines*, 2010 WL 331809 (N.D. Tex. 28 January 2010) and *Hall* v. *Heart of England Balloons* Ltd., Case No: 8BM10813, Birmingham County Court, 17 November 2009.
495. See, *Chubb Ins. Co of Europe, S.A.* v. *Menlo Worldwide Forwarding, Inc.*, 32 Avi 15,978 (C.D. Calif. 2008); *United Airlines* v. *Sercel Australia*, [2012] NSWCA 24; 2012 260 FLR 37; see also, *Allianz Global Corporate & Specialty* v. *EMO Trans California*, No. C 09-4893 MHP, 2010 WL 2594360 (N.D. Calif., 22 June 2010).
496. First Instance Commercial Court No. 7 of Madrid Judgment, 3 March 2007- (EDJ 2007/20138 as reported by Fernando Beteta in 32(4/5) Air & Space Law 380 (2007).

claimant.[497] US courts tend to decide that the application of local rules governing the limitation period undermines the goal of preserving uniformity of the provisions of the Montreal Convention, 1999.[498] In Canada, the court also opined that the provisions of Article 35 of the Montreal Convention were clear and rejected the proposition that the limitation period prescribed by the Convention could be extended by domestic law.[499]

Pursuant to Article 31(2) of MC99, passengers have twenty-one days to make a complaint as a condition for receiving damage occasioned by delay in the delivery of baggage. Passengers in cases involving Israeli airlines had conducted several conversations with the airline but had failed to formally require compensation within those twenty-one days. However, the court found that as a matter of fairness and because of the fact that the passengers had completed a form at the airport they were entitled to compensation.[500]

Under Article 31(2) of the Montreal Convention, in the event of damages, the person entitled to delivery must complain to the carrier immediately after damages are discovered, and, at the latest, within fourteen days of receipt of the cargo.[501] Any *written* statement giving a notice of the damage complies with the requirements of Article 31(2) MC99.[502] A court in Frankfurt held that only the reception of the goods is entitled to file a complaint to the carrier. A complaint made by the shipper does not satisfy the conditions of this provision. The court found that a contact between the air

---

497. See, Mr. and Mrs. Butin v. SARL Nessia and Royal Air Maroc, CA Paris, 21 October 2010 (No. 08/13968). As reported by Elizabeth Freidenberg, in Argentina Art. 18 of the Mediation Law (26.589/2010) sets forth that a mediation hearing called by claimants to recover damages may cause the time limitation to be suspended, in cases of either prescription or caducity. It remains to be seen what the interpretation of the Courts will be in the light of the provisions of the Montreal Convention. For further details see 'Mediation hearings may interrupt Montreal Convention Recovery Period' in http://www.internationallawoffice.com/newsletters In Italy, procedural time limits are suspended between 1 August and 31 August every rear, as to which see the Italian Law No. 742/1969.

498. See, Duay v. Continental Airlines, No. H-10-cv-1454, 2010 WL 5342824 (S.D. Texas of 21 December 2010); see also, Narayanan v. British Airways, 747 F.3d 1125 (9th Cir. 2014 where an action for damages was dismissed because it was introduced two years after the passenger's death rather than the flight's arrival as prescribed by Art. 35(1) of the Montreal Convention, 1999; see also, Schoenebeck v. Koninklijke Luchtvaart Maatschappij NV, No. CV 13-04992 SI, 2014 WL 1867001 (N.D. Cal. 8 May 2014), Halime v. Singapore Airlines [2014] NSWSC 1681 and Ireland v. AMR Corp., 20 F. Supp. 3d 341 (E.D.N.Y. 15 May 2014) – in which decision the court held that 'Chapter 11' of the airline does not stop the time limits set forth in the Montreal Convention.

499. See, Lemieux v. Halifax International Airport Authority. 2011 WL 1707079 (D.P.R. 9 March 2011).

500. See, Shmuel Gali v. El Al Israel Airlines Ltd. CFC (Ramle) 28128-10-13, and Barak v. Arkia Israeli Airlines Ltd., CF (Rishon Le Zion) 8423/04, see, www.internationallawoffice.com.

501. An oral complaint is not sufficient; the airline had sent a form to the shipper of the cargo who had not completed it within this period of 14 days, making his claim inadmissible under MC99; see, Mas & Sons Jardiners v. Florida West International Airways, 177 So. 3d 305 (Fla. 3d D.C.A. 7 October 2015); see also, Aya v. LAN Cargo, No. 14-22260-CIV-SEITZ, 36 Av Law Rep. 16,381 (S.D. Fla., 25 February 2015) where lack of written notice within fourteen days made the claim inadmissible.

502. See, Yoli Farmers Corp. v. Delta Air Lines, No. 15-Civ-2774 (BMC), [2015] WL 4546744 (E.D.N.Y. 28 July 2015). The Supreme Court of Turkey relied on the principle of good faith arguing that the carrier had become aware of the loss; see Supreme Court of Appeals, eleventh Chamber, 12 October 2015.

carrier and the recipient in the event of damages should be established, thus strengthening the position of the carrier and allowing it to inspect the cargo without delay.[503]

3.13.4.2 Time Limits under the Warsaw Regime

Time limits can kill an action brought under the Warsaw Convention, 1929, or the Montreal Convention, 1999. An action for damages must be brought within two years reckoned from the date of arrival at the destination, or from the date on which the aircraft ought to have arrived, or from the date on which the carriage stopped. Numerous actions have been lost because of the expiration of time limits.

In the case of *Ms Poonkam* v. *Royal Brunei Airlines*, the District Court of Queensland in Australia found that once the limitation period of two years has passed a claimant's rights are extinguished regardless of whether this would result in the plaintiff being left without remedy.[504] An Australian court put forward that the two years' time limit also applied to cases brought against agents of the carrier, in this case the bus company, preventing the claimant from relying on estoppel on the basis of Australian law.[505]

In the same vein, a District Court in Israel ruled that the two years limitation period under Article 29(1) of the Warsaw Convention cannot be extended on the basis of the provisions of the local law. The Court also analysed Article 29(2) of the Convention, which provides that: "[t]he method of calculating the period of limitation shall be determined by the law of the court hearing the case."

In this regard, the Court stated that Article 29(2) only refers to technical and insignificant exclusions of the calculation of the two-year period, that is, when the deadline for lodging a legal action occurs on a holiday.[506] However, also in Israel, a Court of First Instance has held that the two years' time limitation may be extended under specific circumstances. They include conditions under which a passenger/plaintiff initiates an action in a non-competent court, while returning to the competent court at a later stage, and conditions beyond the plaintiff's control preventing him/her to bring a claim within two years.[507]

Special facts of a case, including that the carrier acted in bad faith, fraud and concealed information, may also warrant an extension of this short period.[508]

---

503. *See*, Holger Burkens, *Court confirms That Notice of Complaint Can Be Filed Only by Recipient*, Newsletter of 22 December 2010, International Law Office.
504. Reported by the Aviation Law Bulletin of Ebsworth & Ebsworth, www.ebsworth.com.au, December 2006 at 4.
505. *See*, *Yeomans* v. *Carbridge*, [2012] NSDWC 91.
506. *See*, *NII* v. *Lipogan*, CF 54512-08.
507. First Instance Commercial Court No. 7 of Madrid, Judgment of 2 March 2007 [EDJ 2007/20138].
508. *See*, *Siberia Airlines* v. *The Estate of Alexander Grigorbaich*, Tel Aviv District Court decision of 27 July 2008, appeal denied on 23 February 2010, discussed by Peggy Sharon and Keren Marco, Levitan, Sharon & Co, International Law Office, 24 March 2010; *see also*, an Australian Superior Court in *Halime* v. *Singapore Airlines* [2014] NSWSC 1681.

3.13.5   Entry into Force

Early 2017, the Montreal Convention 1999 was ratified by 123 States and acceded to by one Regional Economic Integration Organization (REIO), namely, the EC/EU. In certain countries, international conventions must be implemented in national legislation in order to receive the force of law;[509] in other countries international agreements apply per se.

Regional Economic Integration Organisations are allowed to sign and ratify the Convention, as to which *see* Articles 53 paragraphs 2 and 3. On a European level, the Commission adopted a proposed Council Decision (2001/539), which provided for Community signature of the Convention.[510]

3.14   Concluding Remarks

So far, the Montreal Convention is a successful attempt to maintain the rich case law developed under the Warsaw regime and to continue to unify certain rules pertaining to the contractual relationship between air carriers on the one hand and passenger and consignors or shippers on the other side. For the time being one must be prudent: it is an attempt to achieve global uniformity. The coming years will reveal whether a sufficient number of States ratify the Convention, so that one can rightly speak of a global instrument.

Meanwhile a number of jurisdictions across the globe are unhappy with the protection, which MC99 is affording to airline passengers. Consumer legislation has made its way into private international air law, and questioned whether passengers are sufficiently protected in case of delay, and discrimination. Moreover, courts in various parts of the world find that personal rather than just 'bodily' injury should be compensated. Other than that, provisions have been drawn up for the grant of compensation in situations pertaining to overbooking and cancellation of flights which in most jurisdictions fall outside the scope of the MC99. Thus, courts do not give uniform decisions on the above questions whereas policymakers are also divided when they have to determine in favour of 'their' carriers rather than for the passengers or consumers generally. However, there is a distinct tendency to give the passenger a higher priority now. The next chapter will illustrate this tendency.

Hence, the choice is to leave MC99 as it is, or make an attempt to update it even further, taking into account the decisions made by courts as briefly explained in the above sections. ICAO has placed this dilemma on its agenda. For the time being, Resolution A39-9 (2016): *Promotion of the Montréal Convention of 1999* urges all Contracting States to support and encourage the universal adherence to the Convention

---

509. For instance, the provisions of the Montreal Convention, 1999, have been incorporated in the Indian Carriage by Air (Amendment) Act 2008 amending the Carriage by Air Act 1972; it was enacted by Parliament in February 2009 and notified in March 2009.
510. *See also*, the Chapter on the Community Regime. Under Council Decision 2001/539, Member States agreed that ratification of the Montreal Convention, 1999, would be effectuated "simultaneously" by Member States, once all their necessary ratification processes had been completed, and by the Commission, on behalf of the Community.

for the Unification of Certain Rules for International Carriage by Air, done at Montréal on 28 May 1999 and entreats all Contracting States that have not done so to become Parties to the Montréal Convention of 1999 as soon as possible. It also directs the ICAO Secretary General to provide assistance, as appropriate, with the ratification process if so requested by a Contracting State.

In 2015, the ICAO Council adopted *core principles for passenger protection*. They will be discussed in Chapter 5 on Consumer Protection.

Passenger Protection: With Special Reference to the EU

1 THE EMERGENCE OF PASSENGER RIGHTS

The previous chapter explained the principal goal of unifying rules pertaining to air carrier liability set by the Warsaw regime and the Montreal Convention, 1999. These conventions were geared to lay down a compromise between the economic interests of the airline industry on the one hand and the rights of the passengers on the other hand, and between the various regions in the world. The global reach of the said instruments necessitated such compromises but they have meanwhile been affected by local regulations such as EU Regulation 261/2004.

Various jurisdictions have introduced measures which are designed to provide more protection than that afforded by the global regime referred to above. The policymakers in those jurisdictions felt that the passengers deserved more protection than the global conventions could give them. Thus, they established legal measures, that is, acts, designed to enhance passenger protection.

The leading jurisdiction in this respect has been and still is the EU. This is one of the reasons why special attention will be paid to EU legislation and case law as it has served as a model in other jurisdictions. The relationship between such local legislations and global conventions will also be analysed.

2 PASSENGER PROTECTION UNDER EU LAW

2.1 The Coming into Being of EU Regulation 261/2004

In 1991, the EU – then EEC – had published Regulation 295/91 encompassing minimum rules for the protection of passengers who are denied access to an overbooked flight for which they had a confirmed reservation. It applied to flights departing from an airport located in the territory of a Member State, irrespective of the State where the carrier is established, the nationality of the passenger and the point of destination.

EU Regulation 261/2004 is the successor regulation of EEC Council Regulation 295/91 *establishing common rules for a denied boarding compensation in scheduled air transport.* Increase of flight delays, irritation about overbooking and cancellation, in conjunction with increased consumer awareness instigated EU policymakers to drastically extend the scope of Regulation 295/91 in Regulation 261/2004 establishing *common rules on compensation and assistance to passengers in the event of denied boarding, flight cancellations, or long delays of flights.* It repealed Regulation 295/91 and entered into force on 17 February 2005.

EU Regulation 261/2004 has been characterised as "the most litigated air transport legislation ever"[1] – which is not a good sign for the quality of the legislation. The list of cases provided in section 2.3 which is by no means exhaustive confirms this perception.

2.2 The Regime of EU Regulation 261/2004

2.2.1 General Conditions

As long as the passenger possesses a valid ticket and confirmed reservation for a flight departing from an airport in the EU, and has checked in timely, he/she is covered by EU Regulation 261/2004 on denied boarding, cancellation and long delay of flights.

The Regulation applies both to EU carriers and non-EU airlines operating from an airport in the EU. It may also impose obligations as defined below to EU carriers operating flights from a point outside the EU to a point in an EU State if the local law of the non-EU State from which the flights departs does not provide similar measures.[2] The obligations set out in this regulation apply to the *operating* carrier.

2.2.2 Overbooking

The system functions as follows in case of overbooking:

---

1. *See,* Conference organised by the European Aviation Club and the International Institute of Air and Space Law, Leiden University in Brussels on 14 and15 June 2012, at www.european aviationclub.com.
2. Art. 3(1), defining the scope of the Regulation, reads:
    1. This Regulation shall apply:
        a) to passengers departing from an airport located in the territory of a Member State to which the Treaty applies;
        b) to passengers departing from an airport located in a third country to an airport situated in the territory of a Member State to which the Treaty applies, unless they received benefits or compensation and were given assistance in that third country, if the operating air carrier of the flight concerned is a Community carrier.

(a) Airlines must call for volunteers to surrender their reservations, in exchange for benefits to be agreed upon between the carrier and the passengers, in which case such volunteers are entitled to:

- reimbursement of the ticket within seven days; *or*
- re-routing to the final destination at the earliest opportunity under comparable transport conditions; *or*
- re-routing under comparable transport conditions to the final destination at a later date at the passengers' convenience.

Passengers whose flights form part of a package can also take advantage of paragraph (a) above except for the right of reimbursement where such right arises under Directive 90/314/EEC regarding Package Travel as to which *see* section 4 below.

If the destination is served by several airports, the airline can offer the passenger a flight to an alternative airport, in which case the carrier must compensate the transfer costs from the alternative airport to the airport serving the flight for which the booking was made. The volunteer has a right to care (meals, phone calls, hotel accommodation), but does not have right to further compensation, for instance, compensation for delay under the Warsaw/Montreal Conventions, or national consumer protection law.

(b) If there is an insufficient number of passengers giving up a seat, the operating carrier may deny boarding passengers against their will; *and, if so*:

(c) the air carrier must immediately offer the passenger:

(1) care:

- meals and refreshments (care); *and*
- hotel accommodation when circumstances so require; *and*
- transport between the airport and the hotel when circumstances so require; *and*
- means of communication, as well as;
- reimbursement of the ticket; *or*

(2) re-routing to the final destination at the earliest opportunity; *or*

(3) re-routing to the final destination at a later date at the passengers' convenience; *and* anyway

(4) compensation in accordance with figures presented in the table below. Under EU Regulation 261/2004, passengers have the right to reimbursement or re-routing[3] as well as a right to care, that is, meals and refreshments, communications.[4] If the passenger is re-routed and the reasonably expected time of departure is at least a day after departure of the cancelled flight, the passenger is entitled to right to care and communications as well as hotel accommodation and transport between the airport and the hotel.[5]

---

3. *See,* Art. 8.
4. *See,* Art. 9(1)(a) and 9(2).

2.2.3 Amounts of Compensation

Regulation 261/2004 provides for the following amounts of compensation:

Compensation	Applicable to Flights	Distance Between Port of Embarkation and Destination
EUR 250	All	< 1500 km
EUR 400	Intra-Community flights	> 1500 km
EUR 400	Non-intra Community flights	> 1500 km, < 3500 km
EUR 600	All other flights	> 3500 km

If the passenger who is denied boarding against his will agrees to be rerouted, the carrier may reduce the compensation payable by 50 per cent so long as the arrival time of the re-routed flight does not, as compared with the arrival time of the original flight, exceed:

- two hours in respect of all flights of 1,500 km or less;
- three hours in respect of all intra-Community flights of more than 1,500 km's and for all other flights between 1,500 and 3,000 km's;
- four hours in respect of all other flights.

The passenger's acceptance of this offer constitutes an acceptance of liquidated damages but does not free the airline from claims on breach of contract.[6] As further explained in section 2.3.7 below, passengers who accept downgrading, for instance from business to tourist class, must be repaid the difference in price between the ticket at the business class price and that of tourist class.

Passengers who are denied boarding must also be provided with reasonable expenses for a telephone call, telex or fax to the destination, refreshments and meals which are reasonably related to amount of time spent waiting, and hotel accommodation, should it be necessary, in addition to any surface transportation which may be needed.[7] Thus, adequate compensation exists for passengers who were denied boarding.

---

5. *See*, Art. 9(1)(b) and (c).
6. This compensation is not an exclusive remedy, but rather an offer to liquidate damages. The passenger always has the option to refuse this offer of compensation and pursue a breach of contract claim in a competent national court, according to the terms of Art. 33 of the Montreal Convention, 1999; *see*, Art. 12 of EU Regulation 261/2004: Further compensation:

   1. This Regulation shall apply without prejudice to a passenger's rights to further compensation. The compensation granted under this Regulation may be deducted from such compensation. 2. Without prejudice to relevant principles and rules of national law, including case-law, paragraph 1 shall not apply to passengers who have voluntarily surrendered a reservation under Article 4(1).

7. The Regulation does not apply to flights that are part of 'packages.' *See also*, section 4 below.

2.2.4 Flight Cancellation

When a flight is cancelled, the passenger is entitled to the *assistance* consisting of:

■ reimbursement of the ticket within seven days; *or*

■ re-routing to the final destination at the earliest opportunity under comparable transport conditions; *or*

■ re-routing under comparable transport conditions to the final destination at a later date at the passenger's convenience;

and *care*, including:

■ meals and refreshments; *and*

■ means of communication;

and, in case of re-routing on at least the day after the planned departure time of the cancelled flight:

■ hotel accommodation when circumstances so require; *and*

■ transport between the airport and the hotel when circumstances so require;

and *compensation* according to the scheme laid down in section 2.2.3, above, unless:

■ he/she is informed at least two weeks before departure of the cancelled flight;

■ he/she is informed of the cancellation between two weeks and seven days before departure and is offered re-routing allowing him/her to depart within two hours before the scheduled departure time and to reach the final destination within four hours after the scheduled arrival time;

■ he/she is informed of the cancellation less than seven days before the scheduled departure time and is offered re-routing allowing then to departure no more than one hour before the scheduled departure time and to reach his/her final destination less than two hours after the scheduled arrival time.

Moreover, compensation is *not* due by the airline if it can prove that the cancellation is caused by "extraordinary circumstances" which could not have been avoided even if all reasonable measures had been taken as interpreted in case law as to which *see* section 2.3.8 below. The right to compensation for cancellation of the flight also depends on an assessment of the adequacy of the re-routing of the passenger.

2.2.5 Delay

If a passenger's flight has been delayed, that is:

■ for two hours or more in the case of flights of 1,500 kilometres or less; *or*

- for three hours or more in the case of all intra-Community flights of more than 1,500 kilometres and of all other flights between 1,500 and 3,500 kilometres; *or*
- for four hours or more in the case of all flights not falling under the above-referred two categories,

he/she is entitled to the following *care*:

- meals and refreshments; *and*
- means of communication;

And to the following other entitlements:

- hotel accommodation transport between the airport and the hotel when the expected departure time is at least twenty-four hours after the original departure time of the flight; *and*
- reimbursement of the ticket within seven days, when the delay is at least five hours.

Under Regulation 261/2004 a passenger whose flight has been delayed is *not* entitled to the compensation mentioned in the table of section 2.2.3, above. However, the Court of Justice of the EU (CJEU) has shed another light on this question, as it has done on other provisions of this regulation, as to which *see* the next section.

2.3 Case Law under EU Regulation 261/2004

2.3.1 The Relationship with the Montreal Convention, 1999

One of the very first cases was initiated by the International Air Transport Association (IATA) and the European Low Fares Airlines Association (ELFAA) who challenged the legality of Regulation 261/2004 on a number of grounds.[8] According to the claimants, it was incompatible with Articles 19 and 22(1) of the Montreal Convention. The European Court found the following:

> 44. It is clear from Articles 19, 22 and 29 of the Montreal Convention that they merely govern the conditions under which, after a flight has been delayed, the passengers concerned may bring actions for damages by way of redress on an individual basis, that is to say for compensation, from the carriers liable for damage resulting from that delay.
> 45. It does not follow from these provisions, or from any other provision of the Montreal Convention, that the authors of the Convention intended to shield those carriers from any other form of intervention, in particular action which could be envisaged by the public authorities to redress, in a standardised and immediate manner, the damage that is constituted by the inconvenience that delay in the

---

8. *See*, Case C-344/04, *IATA and ELFAA*; the Court rejected all of the arguments of the parties, and upheld the Regulation.

carriage of passengers by air causes, without the passengers having to suffer the inconvenience inherent in the bringing of actions for damages before the courts.

46. The Montreal Convention could not therefore prevent the action taken by the Community legislature to lay down, in exercise of the powers conferred on the Community in the fields of transport and consumer protection, the conditions under which damage linked to the above-mentioned inconvenience should be redressed. Since the assistance and taking care of passengers envisaged by Article 6 of Regulation No 261/2004 in the event of a long delay to a flight constitute such standardised and immediate compensatory measures, they are not among those whose institution is regulated by the Convention. The system prescribed in Article 6 simply operates at an earlier stage than the system which results from the Montreal Convention.

47. The standardised and immediate assistance and care measures do not themselves prevent the passengers concerned, should the same delay also cause them damage conferring entitlement to compensation, from being able to bring in addition actions to redress that damage under the conditions laid down by the Montreal Convention. Those measures, which enhance the protection afforded to passengers' interests and improve the conditions under which the principle of restitution is applicable to passengers, cannot therefore be considered inconsistent with the Montreal Convention.

The European Court has not, at least not correctly, evaluated the exclusivity of this Convention, and made a rather artificial distinction between damages under the Montreal Convention and damages under EU Regulation 261/2004. This is all the more striking as the Montreal Convention *exclusively* allows for 'compensable' damages, and forbids the provision of non-compensatory and other damages.[9] Moreover, by ratifying it, the EU has accepted the Montreal Convention as a single source of primary law because, "in the internal aviation market, the distinction between national and international air transport has been eliminated;" whereas "it would be impractical for Community air carriers and confusing for their passengers if they were to apply *different liability regimes* on different routes across their networks." (*italics added*)[10]

Unfortunately, those noble considerations laid down in the Preamble of Regulation 889/2002 amending EU Regulation 2027/97 have been severely violated by the EU legislator by adopting a regulation on a matter which is also covered by the Montreal Convention, that is, delay, in Regulation 261/2004, and, what aggravates the legal and practical situation, the decisions of the CJEU on this matter as to which *see* section 2.3.5 below. As a consequence, confusion has been caused by these – so called – legal acts among many who are involved with their application and analysis, as to which *see* the sources below.

The Court also refused to accept the arguments advanced by the claimants pertaining to procedural requirements, and infraction of the principles of legal certainty, proportionality and equal treatment.

---

9. Art. 29 – *Basis of Claims* "In the carriage of passengers, baggage and cargo, any action for damages, however founded, whether under this Convention or in contract or in tort or otherwise, can *only* be brought subject to the conditions and such limits of liability as are set out in *this Convention* without prejudice to the question as to who are the persons who have the right to bring suit and what are their respective rights. In any such action, *punitive, exemplary or any other non-compensatory damages shall not be recoverable.*" (*italics added*).

10. *See*, Considerations 8 and 13 respectively.

Thus, the CJEU did not find a conflict between the rules of the regulation and those of this Convention. This decision, and subsequent decisions affecting the exclusivity and other provisions of the Convention, have been severely criticised in literature.[11] Courts in EU States were also puzzled by the approach chosen by the court in Luxembourg in this, and following rulings, as to which *see* further below.

2.3.2 Scope of the Regulation

In an Information Document, prepared in 2008, the EU Commission clarified that the regulation is not applicable to an incident at a connecting point on the territory of a third country for a journey which started on the territory of the EU and whose next ticketed point is a third country.[12]

The CJEU held that Regulation 261/2004 does not apply to overbooking or cancellation of flights of passengers departing from a non-EU State to an EU Member State on a non-EU air carrier. On a return flight Düsseldorf-Dubai –Manila, the flight from Manila back to Düsseldorf was cancelled because of technical problems causing the passenger to depart two days later. The Claimant argued that the journey Düsseldorf-Dubai-Manila and back to Düsseldorf had to be regarded as a single flight so that Regulation 261/2004 became applicable as he had departed "from an airport located in the territory of a Member State to which the EU treaty applies", pursuant to the terms of Article 3(1)(a) of Regulation 261/2004. The European Court disagreed. The journey out of Düsseldorf – and back – "cannot be regarded as a single flight." The fact that the outward and return flights are made on a single booking does not affect that conclusion. Hence, the non-EU carrier was not obliged to pay compensation via the scheme set forth by Regulation 261/2004.[13]

The French Supreme Court (*cour de cassation*) regarded Annaba rather than Paris as the place of departure on a return trip Paris-Annaba (Algiers)-Paris. As the delay had been occasioned by the operating air carrier Air Algiers on the return trip Annaba-Paris, it was not obliged to provide compensation under Regulation 261/2004 as it is not an EU carrier.[14]

The distances mentioned in Regulation 261/2004 refer to the first leg and not to following legs of an international journey. A passenger travelling from Frankfurt via Amsterdam to Kilimanjaro, Kenya, is entitled to compensation for the Frankfurt-Amsterdam leg and not for the entire journey exceeding 3,500 km. Article 7(2) reads:

---

11. *See, for instance,* J. Wegter, *The ECJ decision of 10 January 2006 on the Validity of Regulation 261/2004: Ignoring the Exclusivity of the Montreal Convention,* 31(2) Air & Space Law 133–148 (2006); case note by K.St.C. Bradley (2006), Common Market Law Review 1101–1124 (2006) and J. Balfour, *Correspondence,* Common Market Law Review 555–560 (2007).
12. *See,* Information Document of the Directorate–General for Energy and Transport – Answers to Questions on the Application of Regulation 261/2004. For further details on the concept of 'flight' under the Regulation, *see,* M Chatzipanagiotis, *The Notion of Flight under Regulation (EC) No. 261/2004,* 37 Air & Space Law 245–267 (2012).
13. *See,* Case 173/07, *Emirates Airlines* v. *Dieter Schenkel,* decision of 10 July 2008.
14. Decision of 21 November 2012, reported by Benjamin Potier in Clyde and Co Aviation Report, 2013.

In determining the distance, the basis shall be the last destination at which the denial of boarding or cancellation will delay the passenger's arrival after the scheduled time.[15]

The distances laid down in Regulation 261/2004 refer to direct a point to point distance. Legs made between the point of departure and destination involving a stopover do not affect the distance. Hence, on a flight Rome-stopover Amsterdam-Munich, the distance between Rome and Munich, which is less than 1,500 km, is relevant for determining the compensation.[16]

2.3.3 The Parties in a Claims Procedure

- *Definition of a passenger:* Infants travelling on the arm of an adult and paying an administrative fee only rather than a fare are not passengers and, hence, are not entitled to receive amounts under the compensation scheme provided by Regulation 261/2004.[17] Article 3(3) of this regulation dictates that it shall not apply to passengers flying free of charge or at reduced fares which are not available to the travelling public.

  A passenger must have an accepted reservation by the airline. A confirmed reservation by a travel agent or tour operator is insufficient if the passenger is not booked on a specific flight.[18]

- *Claims against the operating carrier only:* Regulation 261/2004 entitles passengers to make claims against the *air carrier*, and not against a tour operator or travel agent. The regulation regulates 'pure' air transport agreements.[19]

  The German Federal Court of Justice held that if a journey consists of more than one flight, a term which has not been defined under EU Regulation 261/2004, the applicability of this regulation should be assessed for each segment of the journey separately, that is, for each flight carrying its own flight number. This principle also applies when the journey consisting of more than one segment is operated by the same carrier and booked as one

---

15. *See*, Case No. 30 C 21701/06-47, Court (*Amtsgericht*) of Frankfurt; decision of 16 February 2007. Hence the court should have awarded EUR 600 to the passenger; reported and criticised by Ronald Schmid in 32(3) Air & Space Law 234 (2007).
16. *See*, decision of the Landshut Regional Court of 16 December 2015 (13 S 2291/15), explained by Arnecke Sibeth, *Flight Distance Relevant to Amount of Compensation?* Published on www.internationallawoffice.com on 18 May 2015.
17. *See*, *Joshua Baldwin* v. *Ryanair Ltd*, decided by the Liverpool Country Court on 8 December 2015, unreported) and *Vago & Ors* v. *Ryanair Ltd* (2016), decision of 29 February 2016.
18. Decision of the Frankfurt Local Court, reported by Arnecke Sibeth, on 29 June 2016 on www.internationallawoffice.com "Burden of proof regarding airline booking acceptance lies with passenger."
19. Federal Court of Justice, Germany, reported by Arnecke Siebold, Delayed Flights: Federal Court of Justice Clarifies Scope of Passenger Protection, Newsletter International law Office, 12 November 2008, at: http://www.internationallawoffice.com/Newsletters/Aviation/Germany/Arnecke-Siebold/Delayed-Flights-Federal-Court-of-Justice-Clarifies-Scope-of-Passenger-Protection. /.

journey.[20] In a Dutch case, the claim was dismissed as the claim was directed against the mother company (KLM Royal Dutch Airlines) rather than against the operating carrier, being a daughter company of that airline.[21]

2.3.4 Denied Boarding

Denied boarding is not only caused by overbooking but also by any case of refusing passengers from being carried against their will[22] and operational reasons including the strike of airport staff making it necessary to reschedule the flight,[23] or, in case of connecting segments of a flight, a delay of the first leg of a flight.[24] In those circumstances the air carrier is not entitled to rely on the defence of 'extraordinary circumstances' – says the court.

A passenger who booked a flight with a carrier does not have to accept carriage with another carrier.[25]

Passengers are responsible for holding valid travel documents such as passports and visa, and air carriers have no duty to inform them hereof as they are not travel agents. If not the carrier is not liable for the compensation of damage in case of denied boarding.[26] A passenger who misbehaves may be denied boarding by the air carrier on the basis of the safety conditions laid down in the conditions of contract of that carrier,[27] despite the broad scope which the Court of the EU has granted to the concept of denied boarding under the Regulation.[28]

---

20. Decision of 13 November 2012 (X ZR 12/12).
21. District Court Amsterdam, decisions of 27 December 2012 (LJN: BY7874) and 10 May 2012 (LJN: NW5486).
22. *See*, Case No. 29 C 370/07, Court (*Amtsgericht*) of Frankfort; decision of 6 January 2007; [2008] *ReiseRecht Aktuell* 93, reported by Ronald Schmid.
23. *See*, Case C-22/11 *Finnair* v. *Timy Lassooy*, judgment of 19 April 2012.
24. *See*, Case 321/11, *Rodriguez* v. *Iberia*, judgment of 4 October 2012:

    the concept of 'denied boarding' includes a situation where, in the context of a single contract of carriage involving a number of reservations on immediately connecting flights and a single check-in, an air carrier denies boarding to some passengers on the ground that the first flight included in their reservation has been subject to a delay attributable to that carrier and the latter mistakenly expected those passengers not to arrive in time to board the second flight.

25. *See*, Case No. 16 U 216/06, Court of Appeals (*Oberlandesgericht*) of Frankfort; decision of 6 January 2007; [2008] *ReiseRecht Aktuell* 88, reported by Ronald Schmid.
26. *See*, Holman Fenwick Willan, *Denied Boarding*: *Passengers Responsible for Obtaining Necessary and Valid Travel Documents*, explaining the decision of 10 September 2015 (14-22.223) of the French Court of Cassation, published on www.internationallawoffice.com on 4 November 2015. The claim was based on provisions of the French Tourism Code and not on Regulation 261/2004; however the outcome would have been the same as Art. 2(j) allows a carrier to deny boarding to passengers when "there are reasonable grounds to deny them boarding, such as reasons of .... inadequate travel documentation."
27. *See*, Court of Appeals, Amsterdam, decision of 5 April 2016 (ECLI:NL:GHAMS:2016:1301).
28. *See*, Case C-22/11 *Finnair* v. *Timy Lassooy*, judgment of 19 April 2012, also cited above.

2.3.5 Delay

The actual arrival time of a flight corresponds to the time at which at least one of the doors of the aircraft is opened. That moment, that is to say, the moment in which the communication with the outside world is possible, is a decisive factor in determining the length of the delay.[29]

A flight may consist of various connecting legs, or segments of a flight. According to the CJEU:

> [...] in the case of directly connecting flights, it is only the delay beyond the scheduled time of arrival at the final destination, understood as the destination of the last flight taken by the passenger concerned, which is relevant for the purposes of the fixed compensation under Article 7 of Regulation No 261/2004.[30]

Again, the Court based its line of reasoning on the principle of equal treatment which it also adopted in its decisions concerning the distinction between cancellation and delay, and the treatment of passengers under EU Regulation 261/2004 in those events.

A German court ruled that in relation to claims for compensation under Regulation 261/2004, a delay can have the same legal consequences as a cancellation only if delays occur both on departure and on arrival. The claimants had booked two flights with the defendant airline. The plane left on time, but it arrived to the stopover destination three hours later than scheduled. This was due to an unforeseeable technical defect of the plane, which forced the crew to make an unscheduled stopover in Amsterdam. The claimants asked for compensation under Article 7 of the Regulation, referring to the *Sturgeon* decision. The Court denied the claim because there had been no delay on departure, and held that a delay should have the same legal consequences as a cancellation *only* where a delay occurs cumulatively on departure and arrival.[31]

A passenger arriving late at the check-in desk for the second part of a journey is not entitled to compensation from the carrier of the first leg pursuant to EU Regulation 261/2004 if his late arrival at the check-in desk is caused by the late arrival of the aircraft carrying him on the first leg of the journey.[32] In this case, a passenger had

---

29. *See, Germanwings v. Ronny Henning*, Case-452/13, decision of the CJEU made on 4 September 2014.
30. *See*, Case C-11/11, *Air France v. Folkerts*, judgment of 26 February 2013. In its judgment, the court speaks of 'stages' of a flight rather than of 'segments' of a flight. In the same vein, in Case 11, *Rodriguez v. Iberia*, judgment of 4 October 2012, the court found that "the concept of 'denied boarding' includes a situation where, in the context of a single contract of carriage involving a number of reservations *on immediately connecting flights* and a single check-in, an air carrier denies boarding to some passengers on the ground that the first flight included in their reservation has been subject to a delay attributable to that carrier and the latter mistakenly expected those passengers not to arrive in time to board the second flight."
31. *See*, Ulrich Steppler and Katharina Sarah Meigel, *Airline Compensation Claim Valid only If Delay Occurred on both Departure and Arrival* (9 May 2012) International Law Office, available at: www.internationallawoffice.com/newsletters/.
32. *See*, Case No. 30 C 1370/06, Court (*Amtsgericht*) of Hamburg; decision of 5 December 2006; reported by Ronald Schmid in 32(3) Air & Space Law 234 (2007).

booked a flight from Frankfurt to Bogotá via Paris. Due to weather circumstances and a congested airspace near Paris, the passenger arrived too late for the timely check-in for the Paris-Bogotá flight.

The German Federal Court of Justice found that EU Regulation 261/2004 does not entitle the passenger to compensation on the basis of denied boarding in case of a missed connecting flight due to a delayed earlier flight.[33] However, another decision appears to say that the cause of the passenger's late arrival at the check-in desk is irrelevant for determining his entitlement to denied boarding compensation. In the second case, this late arrival at the check-in desk was also due to the late arrival of the inbound flight.[34]

2.3.6 The Distinction Between Cancellation and Delay

A flight is cancelled and not delayed if the passenger is carried on a flight with a new flight number.[35] A flight is cancelled and not delayed if the passenger is carried more than 48 hours after the scheduled time of departure.[36] A flight which is delayed for more than twenty hours must be considered as cancelled, and not 'just delayed.'[37]

If passengers have to be carried by bus to a nearby airport because the aircraft in which they were supposed to be carried to their destination had a technical problem, they are not entitled to benefit from the entitlements of Regulation 261/2004 regarding passengers of cancelled flights as the operating carrier has performed the carriage by leasing an aircraft departing from that nearby airport. Hence, passengers did not occupy empty seats on another flight.[38] Moreover, the operating carrier was entitled to perform its flight by another carrier.[39]

An English court takes a different view.[40] A flight which has been delayed for more than twenty-four hours is a cancelled flight. Whereas a flight from Manchester to Vancouver cannot be regarded as a flight from London Stansted, in a previous case, where a passenger was to fly from Maastricht to Vancouver, Brussels Airport has been considered as a 'nearby' and, therefore alternative, airport. If a flight is delayed rather

---

33. Decision of the Federal Court of Justice of 30 April 2009 in case 118/2009. Reference was made to Arts 2(j) and 3(2) of this regulation.
34. Case No. 33 C 2/06, Court (*Amtsgericht*) of Offenbach, decision of 6 January 2007; 32(3) Air & Space Law 234 (2007).
35. *See*, Case No. 30 C 1370/06, Court (*Amtsgericht*) of Frankfurt; decision of 31 August 2006 reported by Ronald Schmid in 32(3) Air & Space Law 234 (2007).
36. *See*, Case No. 3 C 717/06-31, Court (*Amtsgericht*) of Rüsselsheim; decision of 31 August 2006; reported by Ronald Schmid in 32(3) Air & Space Law 234 (2007).
37. *See*, Case No. 3 C 1339/06-32, Court (*Amtsgericht*) of Rüsselsheim; decision of 6 January 2007; Court (*Amtsgericht*) Frankfurt/Main, decision of 12 October 2006 (30 C 1726/06-75) on the interpretation of the operating carrier and the distinction between delay and cancellation pursuant to the terms of Regulation 261/2004.
38. *See*, however the decision of the Court (*Amtsgericht*) Court Frankfurt of 31 August 2006: a change of flight number is relevant for the question whether a flight has been cancelled or delayed.
39. Decision of the District Court of Haarlem, LJN: AZ5276.
40. *See*, *David Hardbord* v. *Thomas Cook Airlines*, Addleshaw Goddard 2006.

than cancelled, the carrier is not obliged to supply the amounts foreseen for passengers whose flight has been cancelled.[41] This decision has to be related to the following, astonishing decision.

On 19 November 2009, the CJEU made yet another controversial ruling in the joined cases *Sturgeon* v. *Condor* and *Böck and Lepuschitz* v. *Air France*,[42] on references from courts in Austria and France, nowadays referred to, in short, as the *Sturgeon* case. After explaining the distinction between delay and cancellation, the CJEU opined that passengers on flights whose arrival at final destination is delayed by three hours or more are entitled to non-compensatory amounts as foreseen for passengers whose flights have been cancelled even though the terms of Regulation 261/2004 do not entitle passengers of delayed flights to the grand of such non-compensatory amounts. In other words, the CJEU amended Regulation 261/2004 and caused myriad critical comments.[43]

Meanwhile a number of courts in the EU, including but not limited to the British High Court of Justice[44] and the German Supreme Court (*Bundesgerichtshof*), as well as District courts in Germany, Finland and Belgium, are confused about the interpretation of EU Regulation 261/2004 regarding the obligation of air carriers to pay standardised, non-compensatory damages in the case of delay, and the consequent dilution of the distinction between remedies for delay an compensation which are clearly set out in

---

41. *See*, the Decision of the District Court of Haarlem, 20 December 2006 (LJN: AZ5276); 19 September 2007 (LJN: BB3974) and District Court of Amsterdam, LJN: BH 5037.
42. Joined cases C-402/07 and C-432/07; on 2 February 2016, the Bulach District Court in Switzerland decided that the *Sturgeon* decision does not apply in Switzerland; *see*, A. Frankhauser, *Does* Surgeon *Apply in Switzerland?*, posted on www.internationallawoffice on 4 January 2017.
43. *See*, J.M. Balfour, *Airline Liability for Delays – The European Court of Justice Re-Writes EC Regulation 261/2004*, 35(1) Air & Space Law 71–76 (2010); P.S. Dempsey and S.O. Johansson, *Montreal* v. *Brussels: The Conflict of Laws on the Issue of Delay in International Carriage by Air*, 35 Air & Space Law 207–224 (2010); Stephan Hobe, Rolf Müller-Rostin and Anna Recker, *Fragwürdiges aus Luxemburg zur Verordnung 261/2004*; 59(2) Zeitschrift für Luft- und Weltraumrecht 149–166 (2010); Kinga Arnold LLM and Pablo Mendes de Leon, *EU Regulation 261/04 in the Light of the Recent Decisions of the European Court of Justice – Time for a Change?*! 35(2) Air & Space Law 91–112 (2010); P. Mendes de Leon, *De vulkaan in IJsland en de Sturgeon zaak uit IJsland leiden tot uitbarstingen*, 19 Nederlands Juristen Blad 1218–1225 (2010) Stephan Hobe, Rolf Müller-Rostin, Anna Recker; *Fragwürdiges aus Luxemburg zur Verordnung 261/2004*; 59(2) Zeitschrift für Luft und Weltraumrecht 149–166 (2010); P.P.C. Haanappel, *Compensation for Denied Boarding, Flight Delays and Cancellations Revisited*, 62 Zeitschrift für Luft- und Weltraumrecht 38–54 (2013), at 39: "The European Court of Justice, *as so often*, in this and other areas, has consistently favoured the application of European Union legislation over other legislation, such as the Warsaw/Montreal system." (*italics added*); L. Giesberts and G. Kleve, *Compensation for Passengers in the Event of Flight Delays*, 35 Air & Space Law, No. 4/5, 293–304 (2010) 293; R. Lawson and T. Marland, *The Montreal Convention 1999, and the Decisions of the ECJ in the Cases of IATA and Sturgeon – in Harmony or Discord?*, 36 Air & Space Law, No. 2, 99–108 (2011); C. Thijssen, *The Montreal Convention, EU Regulation 261/2004, and the Sturgeon Doctrine: How to Reconcile the Three?*, 12 IALP, No. 3, 413–448 (2013); contrast C. van Dam, *Air Passenger Rights after Sturgeon*, 36(4/5) Air & Space Law 259–274 (2011).
44. Reference for a preliminary ruling from the High Court of Justice (England and Wales), Queen's Bench Division (Administrative Court) made on 24 December 2010 – *TUI Travel plc, British Airways plc, easyJet Airline Co. Ltd, International Air Transport Association, The Queen* v. *Civil Aviation Authority* (Case C-629/10).

this regulation. Several courts in Germany[45] refused to follow the implications of the *Sturgeon* decision until the CJEU had made a decision on the reference for a preliminary ruling made by the British High Court of Justice.

The CJEU has had the opportunity to come back to its controversial decision, as it had been asked to review the criteria adopted in *Sturgeon* in the joined cases of *Nelson* v *Deutsche Lufthansa AG* and *TUI Travel plc, British Airways plc, EasyJet Airline Co. and the International Air Transport Association*. On 15 May 2012, the Advocate General suggested the Court to confirm the decision made in *Sturgeon* based on the following arguments:[46]

- Articles 5, 6, and 7 of the Regulation should be interpreted in such way that passengers may rely on Article 7 for compensation if they are delayed by three hours or more on their scheduled arrival time.
- The carriers had not put forward anything new which might call into question the interpretation that the CJEU made in Sturgeon.
- The CJEU's interpretation in Sturgeon is compatible with the Montreal Convention 1999 as the type of damage covered by the Regulation is not covered by the Convention. It reaffirmed that Article 7 of the Regulation does not infringe the exclusivity of the Convention established in Article 29.
- The obligation to pay compensation is not disproportionate, and therefore it is compatible with the principle of proportionality.

On 23 October 2012, the CJEU confirmed its earlier decision on the subject by holding that:[47]

Articles 5 to 7 of Regulation (EC) No 261/2004 of the European Parliament and of the Council of 11 February 2004 establishing common rules on compensation and assistance to passengers in the event of denied boarding and of cancellation or long delay of flights, and repealing Regulation (EEC) No 295/91, must be interpreted as meaning that passengers whose flights are delayed are entitled to compensation under that regulation where they suffer, on account of such flights, a loss of time equal to or in excess of three hours, that is, where they reach their final destination three hours or more after the arrival time originally scheduled by the air carrier. Such a delay does not, however, entitle passengers to compensation if the air carrier can prove that the long delay is caused by extraordinary circumstances which could not have been avoided even if all reasonable measures had been taken, namely circumstances beyond the actual control of the air carrier.

Consideration of the questions referred for a preliminary ruling has disclosed no factor of such a kind as to affect the validity of Articles 5 to 7 of Regulation No 261/2004.

---

45. *See*, for instance, District Court of Nuremberg, Germany (*Amtsgericht Nürnberg*), decision of 9 June 2011, Case No. 36 C 600/11); District Court Cologne, Germany (*Amtsgericht Köln*); decision of 3 November 2010; Case No: 142 C 535/08).
46. *See*, Opinion of Advocate General Bot delivered on 15 May 2012; joined Cases C-581/10 and C-629/10.
47. Cases C-581/10 and C-629/10.

The above decision has yet again been severely criticised.[48] For the time being, it reflects the state of European law on the compensation of passengers whose flights have been delayed more than three hours. That said, the compensation is not due in case the said delay is caused by extraordinary circumstances which could not have been avoided even if all reasonable measures had been taken, namely circumstances beyond the actual control of the air carrier. Hence, that defence remains available in case of delay situations, even if this defence has been severely narrowed down by Court cases as signalled above.

It is highly regrettable that the CJEU is the author of new legislation. It has thus exceeded its mandate which is the application and interpretation, but not the creation of the law.

2.3.7 Entitlements of Passengers: Right to Care

Passengers are entitled to receive meals and refreshments free of charge even if the flight has been cancelled due to "extraordinary circumstances" as to which *see* next section.[49] One free drink in the case of a delay of 4.5 hour is sufficient to meet the conditions pertaining to care prescribed in Regulation 261/2004.

Entitlements because of downgrading are limited to the specific flight segment on which the downgrading took place, and not valid on other segments of the flight. The reimbursement for the down grading is limited to the 'bare' ticket price, excluding of taxes and charges.[50]

In 2013, the EU Commission proposed to limit the entitlements under the conditions outlined in its Proposal for a Revision of Regulation 261/2004. The claimants are entitled to the remedies listed in Article 8, and should seek further entitlements or compensation of – other – damages under national or international law. EU Regulation 261/2004 does not compensate moral or punitive damages.[51]

2.3.8 Extraordinary Circumstances

According to a German court, *technical failure* may be considered unusual but does not constitute extraordinary circumstances referred to in Article 5(3) of EU Regulation

---

48. *See*, Sonja Radoševič (adv LLM 2012–2013), *CJEU's Decision in Nelson and Others in Light of the Exclusivity of the Montreal Convention*, "…. Regulation 261 and the CJEU's 'judge made' law in *Nelson and Others*, by attempting to regulate the same substance and the same cause of action in an area which is explicitly regulated under the Montreal Convention, infringes the very wording of this Convention and its exclusivity", published in 37(2) Air & Space Law 95–110 (2013) at 102; C.-I. Grigorieff *Le régime d'indemnisation de la Convention de Montréal* in P. Nihoul C. Cheneviere C.Verdure, *Droits des passagers: états des lieux et perspectives*, 4 European Journal of Consumer Law 671–678 (2012).
49. *See*, Case No. 10 U 385/07, Court of Appeals (*Oberlandesgericht*) of Koblenz; decision of 11 January 2008.
50. *See*, *Steef Mennens* v. *Emirates*, Case C-255/15, judgment of 22 June 2016; the CJEU referred to Arts 10(2) in conjunction with Art. 2(f) of EC Regulation 261/2004, linking the terms 'ticket' and 'flight'; case note by K. Brecke in 42(1) Air & Space Law 71–84 (2017).
51. *See*, *Graham* v. *Thomas Cook*, [2012] EWCA Civ 1355.

261/2004.[52] In Holland, technical failure, for instance a leakage of kerosene, has been regarded as a safety issue and identified as an "extraordinary circumstance" exonerating the air carrier from liability.[53] However, evidence of adequate maintenance is not sufficient/enough to successfully appeal to the defence of 'extraordinary circumstances.'[54] A technical failure is only deemed to fall under the category of 'extraordinary circumstances' in the meaning of Article 5(3), if such failure can be attributed to external circumstances not falling under the responsibility of the airline as an entrepreneur.[55]

The CJEU has narrowed down the meaning of this term by finding that technical problems, which come to light during maintenance of aircraft or on account of failure to carry out such maintenance do not constitute, in themselves, 'extraordinary circumstances.'[56] However, it was not ruled out that technical problems may be covered by the term 'extraordinary circumstances' to the extent that they stem from events which are not inherent in the normal exercise of the air carrier. The CJEU decided that, since not all extraordinary circumstances confer exemption, the proof of their existence is on the party seeking to rely on these extraordinary circumstances by establishing that, even if the carrier had deployed all its resources in terms of staff, equipment and the financial means at its disposal, it would clearly not have been able to prevent the extraordinary circumstances with which it was confronted from leading to the cancellation of the flight.

After this CJEU decision, a German court held that the delay of a Ryanair flight due to a technical fault constituted 'exceptional circumstances' *ex* Article 5(3) of Regulation 261/2004. Hence, no compensation was made to the passengers.[57]

The UK Supreme Court has further narrowed down the meaning of 'extraordinary circumstances' caused by technical problems, in the cases of *Jet2.com* v *Huzar* and *Thomson Airways* v. *Dawson*, by upholding the Court of Appeal's opinion which reads as follows:

> [...] difficult technical problems arise as a matter of course in the ordinary operation of the carrier's activity. Some may be foreseeable and some not but all

---

52. *See*, Case No. 3 C 821/06-31, Court (*Amtsgericht*) of Rüsselsheim; decision of 8 November 2006; reported by Ronald Schmid in 32(3) Air & Space Law 234 (2007); *see also*, Commercial Court of Vienna (*Handelsgericht Wien*), decision of 29 May 2007 (10 C 1537/05 k), with note from Dr Renate Dirnbeck, in 56 Zeitschrift für Luft und Weltraumrecht 650 (2007).

53. *See*, Amsterdam District Court, *Plaintiffs* v. *KLM Royal Dutch Airlines*, Case No: 791233 CV Expl 06-19812, decision of 9 May 2007; *see also*, District Court of Haarlem, decision of 29 October 2009; LJN: BG2720 and District of Haarlem, decision of 3 October 2007, LJN AZ5828; *see also*, *Nas et al.* v. *Transavia*, District Court of Utrecht, decision of 27 June 2007, LJN: BE9027.

54. Court of Appeal of Amsterdam, decision of 16 February 2010; Case Nr 200.017.721/01.

55. *See*, Case No. 21 S 263/07, Court (*Amtsgericht*) of Darmstadt; decision of 1 August 2007; [2008] *ReiseRecht Aktuell* 88, reported by Ronald Schmid.

56. *See*, Judgment C-549/07, *Wallentin-Hermann* v. *Alitalia*, decision of 22 December 2007; Commentators argue that this may lead to a practically strict liability regime for airlines in case of cancellations. – *see also*, John Balfour, *Regulation EC 261/2004 and 'extraordinary circumstances'* published in 58(2) Zeitschrift für Luft- und Weltraumrecht (2009).

57. *See*, District Court of Lübeck, Ferghal O'Connor, www.businessandfinance.com., 4 May 2010.

are, in my view, properly described as inherent in the normal exercise of the carrier's activity. They have their nature and origin in that activity; they are part of the wear and tear.[58]

The scope of 'extraordinary circumstances' was again put forward to the CJEU in a detailed list of at least ten questions in the request for a preliminary opinion made by the District Court of Amsterdam to the CJEU at the end of 2014 in the case of *Van der Lans v. KLM*.[59] In its decision of 17 September 2015, the Court found that the 'extraordinary circumstances' defence is not valid in the case of a technical problem affecting the operation of the aircraft and which appear during the maintenance of the aircraft or because of failure to perform such maintenance.

The unexpected event, says the court, is inherent in the normal exercise of an air carrier's activity because air carriers are confronted as a matter of course with unexpected technical problems. The defence, holds the court, is applicable in two instances only – which instances should be considered as *exclusive* instances -, namely in the event of technical problems which have been caused by:

- a hidden manufacturing defect; *or*
- an act of sabotage or terrorism,[60] hence, where a third person is directly involved with the cause of the technical problem.

This decision is hardly surprising in the light of the Court's aspiration to promote consumer protection. Whether this position is in line with the drafters of EU Regulation 261/2004, as demonstrated by the considerations in the Preamble, and international jurisprudence based on the Montreal Convention 1999, is another question.

Damage caused to the aircraft by an aircraft staircase causing a delay in the operation of the service is not an 'extraordinary circumstance' although it could have been argued that the air carrier does not control such unexpected movements. However, the CJEU decided yet again in favour of the passengers by arguing that this kind of events falls under the normal activities of an air carrier and its control.[61]

(1) *Weather conditions as extraordinary circumstances: A Swedish court held that Ryanair could not rely on* the defence pertaining to 'extraordinary circumstances' as it had not investigated or been able to show that it had investigated whether it might have been possible to arrange for the passengers to fly home the next day with another airline. In this case, Ryanair had cancelled a flight because of bad weather conditions. The court also found that the passengers were entitled to the mandatory compensation provided by Regulation 261/2004, but not to the reimbursement of local travel expenses which they had

---

58. Decision of 31 October 2014.
59. *See*, Case C-257/14; in its decision of 26 February 2015, a Liverpool court refused to await the outcome of the van der Lans judgment in a case brought by Jet2.com, Ryanair and Wizz Air, as to which *see*, http://www.4kbw.net/news/26022015141611-airlines-denied-stays-of-flight-delay-claims.
60. Judgment in Case C-257/14, *Corina van der Lans v. Koninklijke Luchtvaart Maatschappij NV*.
61. *See*, *Sandy Siewert v. Condor Flugdienst*, C394/14, judgment of 14 November 2014.

incurred as they had to go back home from the airport. Both parties have appealed from this decision.[62] The passenger's victory however was short-lived. The ruling was overturned on appeal in May 2010 by a Swedish Appeals Court, which held that Ryanair proved that the flight was cancelled due to extraordinary circumstances.

Typhoons have been regarded as 'extraordinary circumstances'. A Brussels court ruled that the air carrier had sufficiently and convincingly proved exonerating extraordinary circumstances consisting of a typhoon at the scheduled arrival time, which prevented it from operating the flight as scheduled. The case involved the delay of a flight from Paris to Phnom Penh via Ho Chi Minh City. A passenger claimed EUR 600 in compensation for the late arrival at Phnom Penh. The court cited the air carrier's arguments regarding:

- US National Aeronautics and Space Administration documents, which established that the approach of the typhoon could cause severe safety issues at the time of the scheduled arrival; *and*
- the Belgian Royal Meteorological Institute, which defined a 'typhoon' as "a tropical cyclone with destroying powers developing in the north-western part of the Pacific Ocean."[63]

In addition, the court referred to several Dutch and French court rulings pursuant to which bad weather conditions, such as storms, were qualified as extraordinary circumstances exonerating airlines from compensating passengers for delay or cancellation. As a consequence, the air carrier could not be held liable under the Regulation and the court rejected the passenger's claim. Notwithstanding the generally strict and even incorrect application of Regulation 261/2004, the decision of the Brussels local court marks a rational and logical interpretation of the notion of 'extraordinary circumstances'.

The decision is in line with the CJEU ruling in *McDonagh* v. *Ryanair*,[64] in which the eruption of the Icelandic volcano was deemed to be an extraordinary circumstance exonerating airlines from compensating passengers, but not from their obligation to provide care. The EU Commission proposal to amend the Regulation contains a non-exhaustive list of events that shall be qualified as extraordinary circumstances, including "meteorological conditions incompatible with flight safety."[65]

Bird strikes are not 'extraordinary circumstances pursuant to a UK court. The judge referred to the fact that they happen several times per day so that it is not something beyond unusual.[66]

---

62. Decision made by the District Court of Nyköping, Sweden, report in Brussels Aviation Report of Beaumont and Son Aviation at Clyde and Co, London, of 30 April 2009.
63. Decision of 19 June 2013, reported by Mr P. Frühling and Holman Fenwick Willan, at www.internationallawoffice.com.
64. Case C-12/11, decision of 31 January 2013.
65. *See*, COM(2013) 130 final, 13 March 2013).
66. *See*, *Ash* v. *Thomas Cook Airlines*; case C-394/14 of the CJEU, order of 14 November 2014.

Whereas lightning strikes are an 'extraordinary circumstance' on the – non-binding – list established by the UK CAA, they are not in the view of Judge Melissa Clarke who ruled in favour of two passengers in an appeal case. The passengers were each entitled to EUR 600 compensation as a consequence of the delay caused by the weather conditions. The Judge stated that a light striking may well be an "unexpected flight safety shortcoming" but that does not make it an 'exceptional circumstance' which arises only "if it is not inherent within the normal exercise of the carrier's activity."[67] Hence, the carrier is responsible for the consequences of bad weather conditions causing extra safety checks – said the Judge.

(2) *Strikes as extraordinary circumstances:*[68] As *already observed, denied board-ing is no*t *o*nly caused by overbooking, but also by any case of refusing passengers from being carried against their will.[69] Among these non-commercial reasons are strikes put in place by airlines' employees, airport staff and by third parties, such as ATC or ground handling operators." Passengers who have been denied boarding because of strike of airport staff may be entitled to the remedies provided by Regulation 261/2004.[70] The German Federal Court held that passengers are not entitled to compensation for cancelled flights if the cancellation is due to a pilot's strike organised by the pilot's union.[71]

A Spanish court argued that passengers were entitled to a 'moderate compensation' under Regulation 261/2004, and also referred to the Spanish Constitution in order to underpin its decision.[72]

(3) *Bird strikes as extraordinary circumstances:*

A collision between an aircraft and a bird is an extraordinary circumstance within the meaning of Regulation 261/2004. In 2017, the CJEU found that any damage caused by a collision between an aircraft and a bird are not intrinsically connected to the usual operation of the aircraft, as such a collision is not by its nature or origin inherent in the normal exercise of the activity of the air carrier concerned and is outside its actual control. In light of this, the Court exonerated the air carrier from the obligation of paying compensation under the Regulation.[73]

---

67. Decision of Reading County Court, *Michael Evans and Julie Lee* v. *Monarch Airlines*, reported on 15 January 2016 on www.travelmole.com.
68. *See*, A. Trimarchi, *Strike as an Extraordinary Circumstance Under Reg. 261/2004*, The Aviation & Space Journal XV(4), (2016).
69. *See*, Case No. 29 C 370/07, Court (*Amtsgericht*) of Frankfort; decision of 6 January 2007.
70. *Finnair* v. *Timy Lassooy*, [2012] C-22/11.
71. Decision of 21 August 2012, [Case No. X ZR 146/11], reported in IATA Liability Reporter 46 (2013).
72. Central Contentious Administrative Court No 7 of Madrid, No's 871/2011; 693/2011; 863/2011; decision of 12 July 2012 in which cases the court found that the ATC strike was unforeseeable, that the passengers did not have a legal duty to bear the damage, that the strike did not amount to 'force majeure' and that under the Spanish Constitution all persons are entitled to compensation as a result of injuries suffered in their rights and assets.
73. *See, Peskova and Peska* v. *Travel Service* [2017] C-315/15. *See also*, CJEU Press Release No. 44/17 of 4 May 2017.

(4) *Reasonable measures to avoid the cancellation:*
In case an air carrier cancels a flight without checking whether that flight could have been operated to a nearby airport, that carrier has not taken "all reasonable measures" to avoid the cancellation of the flight, in which case it must pay the applicable compensation.[74]

2.3.9   US Case Law: Pre-emption by the Montreal Convention, 1999?

US courts decided that, if one of the plaintiff's state law claims for breach of contract involving compensation under EU Regulation 261/2004, namely the claim made by *Giannopoulos*, the suit does not fall under the exclusivity of the Montreal Convention as this convention does not pre-empt a breach of contract claim.[75] It mattered whether the carriers had (Iberia and the other EU airlines) or had not (British Airways, LOT from Poland,[76] the US carriers) provided express reference to '261' compensation in their conditions of carriage as published on their websites as "direct actions to enforce EU 261 rights are limited to courts in EU member states."[77]

That is why British Airways could rely on pre-emption of the claim made by the passenger (Polinovski) but Lufthansa could not. A similar approach with respect to pre-emption was adopted in the rulings concerning Continental and Delta. In the *Giannopolous* procedure, two passengers (Mr and Mrs Varsamis) also made claims for damages occasioned by delay against Iberia under Regulation 261/2004. Iberia tried to resist these claims by referring to the exclusivity of the Montreal Convention, which explicitly forbids award of non-compensatory damages under Article 29. However, as the delays were based on objective criteria such as length of the flight and length of delay, and the compensation was compensatory in nature rather than punitive, the court decided that there was no conflict with Article 29.

The claim in the case of *Gennadiy* v. *Delta Airlines*[78] was also dismissed by the US Court of Appeals as this court put forward that Regulation 261/2004 "is not judicially enforceable outside the court of EU Member States" as it is not incorporated into Delta's contract of carriage, so that it is not cognisable as a breach of contract.[79]

---

74. *See*, Case No. 232 C 3487/07, Court (*Amtsgericht*) of Dusseldorf; decision of 13 March 2008.
75. *See*, the 'Polinovski' cases against British Airways and Lufthansa (No. 1:11-cv-00779, 780), *Giannopoulos* v. *Iberia* (No. 1:11-cv-00775), *Volodarskiy* v. *Delta* (No. 1:11-cv-00782), *Gurevich* v. *Alitalia* (No. 1:11-cv-01890), *Lozano* v. *United Continental Holding* (No. 1:11-cv-08258), and *Bergman* v. *United Airlines* (No. 1:11-cv-07040).
76. *See*, *Dochak* v. *Polskie Linie Lotnicze S.A.*, 2016 WL 3027896 (N.D. Ill., 27 May 2016); the court found it plausible that the plaintiffs had valid arguments for compensation of delay under Art. 19 MC99.
77. *See*, *Bystka* v. *Swiss International Air Lines*, 2016 WL 792314 (1 March 2016).
78. Case No. 13-3521, decided on 10 April 2015 (7th Cir. 2015).
79. *See also*, the Case Report made by G. Tompkins of 40(6) Air & Space Law (2015).

2.3.10 Jurisdiction Including Procedural Matters

In 2009, the European Court delivered a decision in the area of jurisdiction in a cancellation case. Cancellation is not governed by the Montreal Convention, 1999. In *Rehder v. Air Baltic Corporation*,[80] the court held that the jurisdictional rules laid down in the Montreal Convention, 1999, are not applicable because:

> [...] the right which the applicant [...] relies on in the present case, which is based on Article 7 of Regulation No 261/2004, is a passenger's right to a standardised and lump-sum payment following the cancellation of a flight, a right which is independent of compensation for damage in the context of Article 19 of the Montreal Convention [...] The rights based respectively on those provisions of Regulation No 261/2004 and of the Montreal Convention accordingly fall within different regulatory frameworks.
> [...].It follows that, since it was introduced on the basis of Regulation No 261/2004 alone, the claim in the main proceedings must be examined in the light of Regulation No 44/2001.

The jurisdictional question which was posed to the CJEU concerned the choice of courts. The court considered this question in the light of EU law, that is, EU Regulation No 44/2001. This Regulation contains the principle of *proximity* for the establishment of the competent court. The CJEU held that the place of arrival and the place of destination of the flight are the places where the (air) services are provided, so that the courts of those places are competent to hear the claimant's claims. This choice does not affect the option of the claimant to bring the matter before the court of the defendant's domicile, as confirmed by EU Regulation 44/2001[81] and Article 33 of the Montreal Convention, 1999.[82] In short, this court chose the principle of proximity in terms of place of arrival and destination of the flight for establishing the competency of the court.

Passengers flying intra-EU flights are entitled to claim compensation by virtue of Regulation 261/2004 before the court of the point of departure or arrival. The principal place of business of the carrier is irrelevant.[83]

The exclusivity of the jurisdictional rules of the Warsaw Convention of 1929, the predecessor of the Montreal Convention, 1999, encompassing similar rules for jurisdiction, in relation to the Brussels Convention of 27 September 1968 on *Jurisdiction and the enforcement of judgments in civil and commercial matters* were examined by the French Court of Appeal in a case involving several defendants, including an airline (Gulf Air) and a manufacturer (Airbus). This court recognised the exclusivity of the jurisdictional rules of the Warsaw Convention under the conditions stated there.[84]

---

80. Case C-204/08, judgement of 9 July 2009.
81. *See*, Art. 2(1).
82. *See*, Peter Rehder v. *Air Baltic Corporation*, Case C-204/08, decision of 9 July 2009.
83. *See*, *Rehder* v. *Air Baltic*, Case C-204/08, para. 39 as it "does not have the necessary close link to the contract."
84. *See*, M. Y. v. *Gulf Air*, Cour de cassation, decision of 12 November 2009, 252(4) Revue française de droit aérien et spatial 447–451 (2009).

The period for bringing claims is not limited to two years as stipulated under the Montreal Convention, 1999 but by national rules of the EU Member States.[85] In the Netherlands, this period also amounts to two years. However, a Dutch court dismissed a claim brought by passengers within those two years as the passengers and not lodged their complaint "within a reasonable period of time" beyond which the claims arising from the imperfect performance of a contract cannot be enforced.[86] Regulation 261/2004 does not regulate statutory limitations because the time-limits for bringing actions for compensation under that regulation are determined in accordance with the rules of each Member State on the limitation of actions.[87]

EU Directive 2013/11 provides a mechanism for *Alternative Dispute Resolution for Consumer Disputes*. EU Member States were required to implement its terms in their national regulations by 9 July 2015. In the UK, the Civil Aviation Authority (CAA) has been designated as the competent authority for overseeing the implementation of this Directive. So far, British Airways and Thomson have subscribed to the services of bodies designed to resolve disputes regarding denied boarding, delay or cancelation of flights, destruction, damage, loss or delayed carriage of baggage, and of items while worn or carried by the passenger, and other disputes including those in which the treatment of disabled passengers is involved.[88]

Under Article 37 of the Montreal Convention, 1999, and Article 13 of Regulation 261/2004, air carriers have the right to recover damages from a third party should the circumstances of the case give reason to such an action. Obviously, carriers have such a right of recourse or redress anyway on the basis of applicable civil law. Carriers tried to recover damages paid in connection with delayed and cancelled flights from trade unions.[89]

2.3.11 Right of Regress

Under Article 37 of the Montreal Convention, 1999, and Article 13 of Regulation 261/2004, air carriers have the right to recover damages from a third party should the circumstances of the case give reason to such an action. Obviously, carriers have such a right of recourse or redress anyway on the basis of applicable civil law.

Carriers tried to recover damages paid in connection with delayed and cancelled flights from trade unions where those were caused by a strike of air traffic controllers based at Stuttgart Airport in Germany on the basis of German civil law provisions pertaining to liability in tort. However the court argued that the air carriers could not base their claims on the infringement of their rights to carry on their affairs.[90]

---

85. *See*, *Moré* v. *KLM* [2012] C-139/11.
86. District Court of 's Hertogenbosch, decision of 19 January 2012 (LJN: BV 1931).
87. *See*, CJEU, Case C-139/11, *Cuadrench* v. *Koninklijke Luchtvaart Maatschappij* (KLM).
88. *See*, Clyde & Co, Aviation and Airspace Newsletter at 13–16, June 2016.
89. *See*, section 2.3.7.
90. *See*, Decision of the German Federal Labour Court, explained by Arnecke Sibeth, *No damages to third party after unlawful strike?* Published on www.internationallawoffice.com on 14.10.2015.

2.3.12 Concluding Remarks

Regulation 261/2004 is by no means an easy regulation because it sets up a relatively sophisticated and complex regime for passenger protection. The entitlements vary in accordance with factors laid down in the regulation. It builds on the previous regulation whose scope was restricted to denied boarding.

Meanwhile the scope of this regulation has been expanded by subsequent decisions of the European Court for the benefit of consumer protection and equal treatment of passengers. Principal questions have been asked about the entitlements, the term 'extraordinary circumstances', the distinction between cancellation and delay, the geographical scope, and, last but not least, its relationship with the provisions of the Montreal Convention, 1999. While this Convention does not specifically deal with cancellation and denied boarding which are often but not always regarded under this convention as a 'non-performance' of the contract of carriage by air coming under national civil law rather than the exclusive provisions of the convention itself, this is not true for the matter of delay. Hence, delay is regulated by the mentioned Convention, and Regulation 261/2004.

The decisions made by the Court of the EU have been frequently criticised. They pertain in particular to the distinction between cancellation and delay, as discussed in section 2.3.6 above, and the notion of 'extraordinary circumstances, which has been examined in section 2.3.8. It would seem that this court prioritises European law, by following a sometimes artificial line of reasoning to justify its decision.

It is to be hoped that the anticipated revision of Regulation 261/2004 will bring more clarity on the questions which the current edition has provoked. In order to ensure common understanding and proper enforcement of the above decisions, the EU Commission has published interpretation guidelines on Regulation 261/2004.[91]

3 ASSISTANCE OF DISABLED PASSENGERS IN THE EU

3.1 EU Regulation 1107/2006 on the Rights of Disabled Persons

EU Regulation 1107/2006 concerning the rights of disabled persons and persons with reduced mobility when travelling by air provides principally that air carriers, their agents and tour operators must not refuse, on grounds of disability or reduced mobility, to accept a flight reservation or embark a person, obviously on condition that the person in question has a valid ticket and reservation, and has checked in timely, and must not require that that person can only travel if accompanied by another person who can give assistance. This point of departure knows the following exceptions. An air carrier may invoke that refusal:

---

91. See, *Interpretative Guidelines* on Regulation (EC) No. 261/2004 of the European Parliament and of the Council establishing common rules on compensation and assistance to passengers in the event of denied boarding and of cancellation or long delay of flights and on Council Regulation (EC) No. 2027/97 on air carrier liability in the event of accidents as amended by Regulation (EC) No. 889/2002 of the European Parliament and of the Council, C(2016), 3502 final.

- if necessary to meet applicable safety requirements; or
- if the size of the aircraft or its doors makes embarkation physically impossible,

in which case the air carrier, or its agent or the tour operator must make reasonable efforts to propose an acceptable alternative, and the person must be offered the right of reimbursement or re-routing as to which see the provisions of Regulation 261/2004 on denied boarding, delay and cancellation. The airline, its agent or the tour operator must give reasons for its refusal. Air carriers must make publicly available the safety conditions and restrictions applying to the carriage in question. Tour operators must make such rules and restrictions available in respect of flights in package holidays. In addition, airport managers must make the necessary announcements in the airports and provide assistance to disabled persons, provided that disabled persons have notified their arrival at the airport at least forty-eight hours before the scheduled time of departure of the flight.

3.2 Further Measures

Assistance may be subcontracted. The disabled persons may not be charged for the assistance, but other passengers may be required to make a contribution to a fund for the assistance, if the charge is reasonable, cost related and established in cooperation with airport users. Assistance must meet quality standards.

In 2008, the EU Commission published a Communication on the scope of the liability of air carriers and airports in the event of destroyed, damaged or lost mobility equipment of passengers with reduced mobility when travelling by air.[92]

3.3 Case Law

In 2011 the English High Court has ruled that neither EU Regulation 1107/2006 nor the Civil Aviation Regulations 2007, which give effect to the EU Regulation, allow an exception to the principle that the Montreal Convention provides a sole and exclusive cause of action for damages against a carrier. In *Tony Hook v British Airways Plc*,[93] the passenger who suffered from mobility and learning difficulties brought a claim under the Regulation for injury to his feelings after the carrier allegedly failed to make reasonable efforts to accommodate his seating requirements. In first instance, the Central London County Court dismissed Mr Hook's claim, as the liability of the carrier was governed solely by the Montreal Convention. Since the convention does not allow for recovery on the basis of hurt feelings, the Court decided that there could be no recovery.

The plaintiff appealed and requested to submit a question to the CJEU to clarify whether EU Regulation 1107/2006 permits a cause of action for recovery of damages

---

92. COM(2008) 510 final.
93. [2011] EWHC 379 (QB).

for injury to feelings. The High Court dismissed the appeal applying the criteria followed in *Sidhu* v. *British Airways* and in the ruling of the United States Supreme Court in *El Al* v. *Tseng*. It held that the Convention prescribes the only circumstances in which a carrier is liable for damages arising out of international carriage by air, and that neither the EU Regulation nor the UK Regulations create a private law cause of action for damages. The Court also rejected the request to refer the case to the CJEU, as it considered that the EU Regulation was clear.

4 THE PACKAGE TRAVEL DIRECTIVE OF 1990

4.1 Principal Provisions

Travellers in the EU whose journey is part of a package including, for instance, hotel, car rental and excursions, receive a legal protection under a special regulation, namely, the Council Directive 90/314/EEC of 13 June 1990 on *Package travel, package holidays and package tours*, henceforth also referred to as: Package Travel Directive, or the Directive. The purpose of the Directive is the approximation of the laws, regulations, and administrative provisions of the Member States relating to packages sold or offered for sale in the Community. This Directive applies mainly to travel agents and tour operators, although it could apply to airlines that arrange packages, including accommodations or excursions.

The organiser of the package is liable towards the consumer for the performance of the contract, regardless of whether or not the obligations are fulfilled by another party, such as a tour operator or other company. The organiser has his rights of recourse against this party. Similarly, the organiser is liable for damage, which results if the duties in the contract are not performed, unless it is through the fault of the consumer or the intervention of a third party or a force majeure. Compensation may be limited by the Member States in accordance with international conventions, that is, the instruments of the 'Warsaw System'. In short, the Package Travel Directive places a liability on tour operators for the performance of the package as defined under the Directive, and the tour operator cannot escape its liability by attributing it to its sub-contractors such as airlines.

The Travel Package Directive also lays down the link between travel organisers or retailers, on the one hand, and other service providers such as airlines in relation to consumer and passenger protection.[94] Member States are obliged to ensure that the tour operator remains liable, even in case of failure of other service providers such as insolvency of the airline.[95] In case of insolvency of the airline the tour operator still has an obligation for to "give prompt assistance to a consumer in difficulty". This clause

---

94. But national law may also play a role, as to which see the case on the transferability of airline tickets in relation to the provisions of the Package Travel Directive and Belgium consumer protection law, as decided by the Belgium Constitutional Court in a case submitted by the Consumer organisation *Test achats*. Report made by Pierre Frühling, Newsletter of 30 March 2011, International Law Office.
95. *See*, Art. 5 (1).

may apply to a consumer who is for instance stranded abroad as a consequence of the insolvency of a subcontracted airline.[96] In addition the tour operator must provide sufficient evidence of security for the refund of money paid over and for the repatriation of the consumer in the event of insolvency of the travel organiser or retailer.[97] It also provides for passenger protection in case of insolvency of package organisers and retailers, such as travel agents and tour operators.

The protection only regards consumers who have contracted the sale of a pre-arranged combination of:

(1) transport; and/or
(2) accommodation; and/or
(3) other tourist services not ancillary to transport or accommodation and accounting for a significant proportion of the package.

Consumers will only be covered where at least two of the above three elements are sold or offered for sale at an inclusive price and the service covers a period of more than twenty-four hours or includes over-night accommodation. Hence, passengers buying air tickets for a scheduled or non-scheduled service without the 'extra's' mentioned under (2) and or (3) above from an airline or from a tour operator are not covered by the protection afforded by the above Directive.

4.2 Explanation of Terms in Case Law

The term 'Package' has given rise to misunderstandings. The term 'Package' is often employed even though the terms and conditions suggest that the concerned services are not intended to be sold as a Package. Also services may be sold as 'flight plus hotel' suggesting that they do not constitute a package whereas in reality they could be deemed to fall under the terms of the above Directive.

The definition of when a holiday constitutes a package has been subject to litigation in the UK. In 2010, the UK Judge held that if the services are sold or offered for sale as components of a combination there is a package. If they are sold or offered for sale separately but at the same time there is no package. The Judge also opined that that the price for a "package" is not an 'inclusive' price where it is simply the arithmetical total of the component parts of the overall price, similar to the total price of goods at a supermarket checkout.[98]

In a judgment made in the UK in 2006, the England and Wales Court of Appeal further defined the terms of the definition of a Package. This court decided that this question is determined by the question whether the travel services are sold or offered

---

96. *See*, Art. 5(2).
97. *See*, Art. 7.
98. *See*, Mark Bisset, Clyde & Co, Newsletter of March 2010, reporting the judge of the City of Westminster Magistrates' Court in the case *Civil Aviation Authority* (CAA) v. *Travel Republic Limited* (RTL).

for sale as components of a pre-arranged combination or whether they are sold or offered for sale as separate travel services.[99]

In 2011, the CJEU interpreted the provisions of Article 7 of the Directive in the light of insolvency of a travel organiser caused by its own fraudulent conduct. Two travellers booked a package with a travel organiser, which declared itself insolvent before the start of the trip. The travel organiser guaranteed the travellers that the cost of the trip would be refunded in case of insolvency, as required by the Directive. Hence, the travellers presented a claim for reimbursement to the travel organiser's insurer. The facts of the case revealed that the travel organiser had no intention to organise the trip in question. The insurer refused to pay the claim, arguing that Article 7 does not cover a situation where the travel has been cancelled because of fraudulent conduct on the part of the travel organiser. The Court ruled that Article 7 did not attach any specific condition regarding the causes of the travel organiser's insolvency, and decided that the provision should be interpreted as covering a situation in which the insolvency of the travel organiser is attributable to its own conduct.[100]

As a corollary, the term 'pre-arranged' does, in the words of a European Court's decision,[101] not only apply to elements put together in advance, for instance, in a brochure, by the seller of the package but also to combinations of services as required by the customer., also referred to as a 'dynamic package', a 'shopping basket' or a 'virtual package' in the remarks made by TUI in relation to the Package Travel Directive. 'Pre' then refer to the period before the moment on which the seller (travel organiser) or purchaser reach agreement on the combination of services as composed by either party.

The CJEU decided that students-exchange programmes, under which students stay six months or one year abroad, during which period they stay free of charge with a local family as a family member, in order to attend classes in the concerned foreign country, do not fall under the scope of this Directive. This is so because the Directive requires the traveller to enjoy "accommodation" in the sense of the Directive. The Court found that 'hosting of students' cannot be described as 'accommodation' within the meaning of the Directive.[102]

4.3 Implementation

The above Directive has been implemented in Member States in their national acts on: consumer protection, trade practices, and acts or laws on tourism. A well-known

---

99. *See, The Association of British Travel Agents Ltd* v. *Civil Aviation Authority*, decision of 18 October 2006; [2006] EWCA Civ 1356.
100. Case C-134/11 'Reference for a Preliminary Ruling under Art. 267 of the TFEU from the District Court (*Landgericht*) Hamburg, Germany, made by decision of 2 March 2011, in the proceedings *Jurgen Blodel-Pawlik* v. *HanseMerkur Reiseversicherung AG*.
101. *See, Club-Tour, Viagens e Turismo SA* v. *Alberto Carlos Lobo Gonsalves Garrido*, Case C-400/00; [2002] ECR 1-4015.
102. Judgement of the Fifth Chamber of the Court, Case C-237/97 of 11 February 1999.

system is the UK Air Travel Organisers' Licensing (ATOL) scheme,[103] which has been used a number of times for covering expenses and adopting measures for the benefit of consumers coming under the terms of the above Directive.

5 PROTECTION OF PASSENGERS TRAVELLING ON OTHER MODES OF TRANSPORT

On 24 November 2010, the EU adopted a Regulation concerning the rights of passengers when travelling by sea and inland waterway. In some respects it resembles to the protection granted to passengers travelling by air, while in others it differs. This regulation (1177/2010) applies to passengers services from a point in the EU and between a point outside the EU and a point within the EU where the services is operated by an EU carrier; this is different from EU Regulation 261/2004 which must also be respected by non-EU carriers departing from an EU airport.

Member States may exempt services covered by public services obligations which is not provided for under EU Regulation 261/2004. Regulation 1177/2010 provides for remedies in cases of delay and cancellation. Amounts for compensation and other remedies are not the same as those afforded under EU Regulation 261/2004. Regulation 1177/2010 also provides for provisions on non-discrimination in respect of assistance to disabled passengers.[104]

6 PASSENGER PROTECTION IN OTHER JURISDICTIONS

Other jurisdictions are also taking steps designed to improve the position of passengers in cases of denied boarding, and delay and cancellation of flights. Claims are based on special regulations and/or on local civil law, that is, a general consumer's law.

For instance, countries in South America, including Brazil, Chile and Colombia now have special passenger protection regimes. Except for México, Guyana and Surinam, Central American countries do not have such special regulations. States participating in the Andean Community, including Bolivia, Colombia, Ecuador and

---

103. *See*, www.caa.co.uk/atol. In 2011, the UK CAA decided to reform ATOL to extend protection and improve clarity for holidaymakers. Included in the reforms is the introduction of 'Flight-Plus', ensuring flights sold with accommodation and/or car hire on consecutive days are financially protected. It also includes new ATOL certificates to help holidaymakers understand how their holidays are protected. In addition, agency agreements will see travel suppliers and agencies sign written agreements confirming their relationships. For further information about the reform, *see*, http://www.atol.org.uk/reform.

104. In a non-Warsaw-Montreal Convention case regarding the need for assistance during boarding the flight, an Australian court held that discrimination was established as the passenger was treated less favourably than fellow passengers without disability; *see, King* v. *Jetstar Airways*, [2012] 286 ALR 149; in another non-Warsaw-Montreal case, a New Zeeland court found that the provision of supplementary oxygen to a passenger who needed that when flying was not necessitated by applicable human rights provisions laid down in the laws of that State as to which see, *Smith* v. *Air New Zealand*, [2011] 2 NZLR 171; CA514/2009; [2011] NZCA 20.

Peru have a unified passenger regulation.[105] Colombia, Peru and México also have special enforcement bodies for the protection of consumers' rights.[106]

The Code of Federal Regulations in USA allows passengers to be compensated for being involuntarily denied boarding.[107] Furthermore, the regulations require air carriers to have contingency plans for lengthy tarmac delays. According to these regulations, all US and foreign air carriers operating to and from the US must ensure that their plans include providing passengers with adequate food and potable water, medical attention, lavatory facilities and notifications during a delay.[108]

New Zealand's Civil Aviation Act 1990, as amended in 2004, is intended to make an air carrier liable for damage caused by delay in the domestic carriage, unless the delay was caused by specified circumstances.[109] The air carrier is not liable if it proves that it, or its agents had taken all necessary measures to avoid the damage or that it was not possible for it to take those measures.[110] Unless the air carrier has acted recklessly or with wilful misconduct, the damages for delay are limited to the lesser of the amount of damage proved to have been sustained or an amount representing ten times the sum paid for the carriage.[111]

In 2010, the Government of India published rules designed to grant passengers compensation and full assistance in case of denied boarding. In addition, the airline is expected to arrange alternative transport for re-routing to their final destination at the earliest convenience and subject to availability, or offer a reimbursement of the full cost of unused ticket segments. This applies to passengers who check-in on time for any flight, including non-scheduled and charter flights.[112]

While the above-mentioned countries offer passenger protection by way of a special regulation, there are other countries that regulate this matter solely on the basis of their general consumer law. Thus, in Singapore passengers may seek assistance from the Consumer Association of Singapore or lodge a claim with a tribunal under the Consumer Protection (Fair Trading) Act for the air carrier's unfair practices.[113] Similarly, the Australian Consumer Law guarantees remedies for consumers if a business fails to provide a service or does not deliver the service as promised.[114]

In 2015, the International Civil Aviation Organization (ICAO) Council adopted core principles for passenger protection. The principles cover three phases of a

---

105. Decision 619.
106. Profeco (Mexico); Indecopi (Peru) and SIC (Colombia).
107. 14 CFR Part 250.
108. 14 CFR Part 259.
109. Part B, section 91Z, *Civil Aviation Act 1990*.
110. Section 91ZA.
111. Section 91ZC.
112. ALMT Legal, Ananjan Mitter, *Rules on denied boarding, flight cancellations and delays finally implemented*, Newsletter of 22 December 2010, International Law Office, at: www.internationallawoffice.com.
113. Part II of the Consumer Protection (Fair Trading) Act.
114. Chapter 3 of the Australian Consumer Law, as set out in Schedule 2 of the *Competition and Consumer Act 2010*.

customer's experience before, during and after travel – and will now be considered by ICAO's 191 Member States when they develop or review their applicable national regimes.[115]

Prior to travelling, the ICAO core principles recommend that passengers should benefit from sufficient levels of advance information and customer guidance, given the wide variety of air transport products in the market and associated legal and other protections which may apply. Product and price transparency is also recommended as a basic customer right.

During their travel, the ICAO core principles call for passengers to be provided regular updates on any special circumstances or service disruptions which arise, as well as due attention in cases of a service disruption. This could include rerouting, refund, care, and/or compensation. The core principles also call on airlines and other stakeholders to have planning in place for situations of massive disruptions characterised by multiple flight cancellations, and reiterate the fundamental right to fair access for persons with disabilities.

After travelling, the ICAO core principles stipulate efficient complaint handling procedures be established that are clearly communicated to customers.[116]

7 EVALUATION

Consumer protection in the EU is on the move. The legislator and the courts are doing their utmost to enhance passenger protection. It is questionable whether especially the Court in Luxembourg is balancing all the interests as it focuses on EU law principles, leaving aside the international law elements and the economic factors, that is, the solvability of airlines and the level playing field of EU and non-EU air carriers. In addition, the EU Commission is proposing a revision of Regulation 261/2004, based on case law which has been, in part, referred to in section 2.3.

At the same time, similar initiatives outside the EU are being taken to promote consumer protection. This is achieved by drawing up special legislation, along the lines of EU Regulation 261/2004, or by courts denying the pre-emptive effect of the Warsaw or Montreal Convention, or by applying more generous provisions of consumer protections and civil codes to international journeys by air, or by allowing claims based on other causes of actions, for instance product liability. Some of these regulations are applicable to incoming and outgoing flights, which coincides with the scope of EU Regulation 261/2004, that is, for EU carriers as concisely explained in section 2.2.1. Hence, such carriers may be subject to different and overlapping regulations which may give rise to confusion on the obligations of the carrier and the rights of the passengers.

---

115. *See*, a very interesting analysis made by V. Correia and N. Rouissi, *Global, Regional and National Air Passenger Rights – Does the Patchwork Work?* 40(2) Air & Space Law 123–146 (2015).
116. http://geteca.us/2015/07/09/icao-council-adopts-core-principles-on-consumer-protection-and-new-long-term-vision-for-air-transport-liberalization/.

In 2013, ICAO and IATA reacted. During the 39th General Assembly of ICAO held in 2016, States were urged to ratify the Montreal Convention of 1999 in order to preserve the unification of private international air law.[117] This was preceded by the 69th IATA Annual General Meeting (May 2013), calling upon States "to become parties to Montreal Convention 1999 as soon as possible", while "endorsing the IATA Core Principles on Consumer Protection as the Global industry position on best practice for national and regional passenger rights regimes."[118]

All of these movements affect the long awaited uniformity of rulemaking in international carriage by air. The only way out is the establishment of a new convention, or an amendment of the Montreal Convention, incorporating the various remedies for passengers as foreseen in the current patchwork of regulations. It is to be hoped that the EU bodies do not further aggravate the situation by introducing provisions infringing international law.

---

117. *See*, Resolution A39-9 (2016): *Promotion of the Montréal Convention of 1999* as alluded in in section 3.14 of Chapter IV.
118. *See*, www.iata.org/pressroom/pr/Documents/agm69-resolution-passenger-rights.pdf.

CHAPTER 6

Global Safety Regulation

1 THE RELEVANCE OF GLOBAL SAFETY REGULATION

This chapter examines aspects of the international safety system and the requirements related to its oversight. Safety is of principal importance for the operation of air services and airports as underlined by the provisions of the Chicago Convention of 1944, in this chapter also referred to as the Convention, and its Annexes which are updated from time to time in order to enhance safety by keeping track of new technological developments and methods. States, international and regional organisations,[1] airlines and their personnel, airports, air traffic controllers, manufacturers and maintenance companies each play an important role in fostering this objective. Their oversight and executive functions and tasks will be succinctly addressed in this chapter.

Accident and incident investigation also attracts increased attention, not least in the media. The role of the accident investigator in determining the causes of the accident in order to try and prevent a recurrence of the events leading to an accident will be considered. Consequent upon those considerations, the powers of the aircraft commander on board aircraft, the commander's possible criminal liability and the related topic of Search and Rescue of aircraft and victims after an accident will be briefly addressed. Also, the role of automation and the extent to which air navigation has become reliant upon it will be discussed; something about which there is a degree of concern amongst the pilot fraternity and their regulators.[2]

---

1. *See*, section 5 of Chapter 1 and sections 2 and 3 of Chapter 7.
2. *See*, section 3 below.

2 APPLICATION OF WORLD-WIDE STANDARDS

2.1 The Adoption of Standards and Recommended Practices (SARPs)

A fundamental principle of the Chicago Convention pertains to the adoption of uniform rules or standards with regard to all aspects of the safe operation of aircraft and of the system required to enhance the safety of international air navigation. Both 'Standards' and 'Recommended Practices', also referred to as SARPs,[3] have been defined by International Civil Aviation Organization (ICAO):

a) *Standard* – 'any specification for physical characteristics, configuration, material, performance, personnel or procedure, the uniform application of which is recognized as necessary for the safety or regularity of international air navigation and to which Contracting States will conform in accordance with the Convention; in the event of impossibility of compliance, notification to the Council is compulsory under Article 38 of the Convention;' and

b) *Recommended Practice* – 'any specification for physical characteristics, configuration, material, performance, personnel or procedure, the uniform application of which is recognized as desirable in the interest of safety, regularity or efficiency of international air navigation and to which Contracting States will endeavour to conform in accordance with the Convention.'[4]

This principle is reflected in Articles 12 and 37 of the Convention, both of which require that States shall adopt regulations uniform with those established under the Convention and the Standards adopted by ICAO, as embodied in the Annexes to the Convention. Amongst the most important elements of the system of air navigation and aircraft operation is the provision of infrastructure, including airports and air navigation control, to support the safety and reliability of civil aviation in order that the right to fly might be exercised with the minimum of risk to the safety of passengers, shippers of cargo and those on the ground.[5]

The technical standards required for aircraft and the issuing of certificates of competency and licences for its crew and other personnel are matters that have been made subject to uniform rules. As explained in section 3.3.6 of Chapter 1, SARPs are

---

3. For the establishment of SARPs, *see*, section 3.3.6 of Chapter 1, and for their implementation in national law, *see*, section 2.2 below.
4. ICAO Doc 7670 *Resolutions and Recommendations of the Assembly 1st to 9th Sessions (1947–1955)*, Montreal, Canada, 1956, Assembly Resolution A1-31 – *Definition of International Standards and Recommended Practices*, now consolidated into Resolution A36-13: *Consolidated Statement of ICAO policies and associated practices and associated practices related specifically to air navigation*, in Doc 9902, *Assembly Resolutions in Force* (As of 28 September 2007) at II-3; *see also*, ICAO, Assembly Resolutions in Force (as of 28 September 2007), Doc 9902, and J. Huang, *Aviation Safety and ICAO* (PhD Leiden), 58–59 (2009).
5. *See*, Art. 28 of the Chicago Convention: *Air Navigation Facilities and Standard Systems:*

> Each contracting State undertakes, so far as it may find practicable, to:
> Provide, in its territory, airports, radio services, meteorological services and other air navigation facilities to facilitate international air navigation, in accordance with the standards and practices recommended or established from time to time, pursuant to this Convention; [...].

laid down in the Annexes to the Chicago Convention. Their status under national law is not always as clear as one might wish, and has therefore given rise to court cases.[6]

Annex 1 contains rules on pilot certificates that were introduced for reasons of safety and uniformity, and constitutes an elaboration of Articles 32 and 33 of the Chicago Convention.[7] Article 32 of the Convention provides that an aircraft pilot must have a valid licence that is issued or validated by the State in which the aircraft flown by the pilot is registered.

The following Article 33 is essential for the safe and sound operation of *international* air transport: a license which is validated in one ICAO State must be recognised by all other ICAO States provided that such a license complies with the minimum requirements set by the relevant Standards of ICAO, in this case those of Annex 1 on *Personnel Licensing*. Pursuant to provisions laid down in bilateral air services agreements (ASAs), States are, following consultations, entitled to suspend, revoke or limit the operating permit of an airline, or indeed refuse a permit altogether, in case the applicable minimum safety requirements are not met.[8]

---

6. *See*, section 3.3.6 of Chapter 1; *see also*, section 1.2.1 of Chapter 2.
7. Art. 32 of the Chicago Convention reads:

> (a) The pilot of every aircraft and the other members of the operating crew of every aircraft engaged in international navigation shall be provided with certificates of competency and licences issued or rendered valid by the State in which the aircraft is registered.
> (b) Each contracting State reserves the right to refuse to recognize, for the purpose of flight above its own territory, certificates of competency and licences granted to any of its nationals by another contracting State.

Art. 33 reads:

> Certificates of airworthiness and certificates of competency and licences issued or rendered valid by the contracting State in which the aircraft is registered, shall be recognized as valid by other contracting States, provided that the requirements under which such certificates and licences were issued or rendered valid are equal to or above the minimum standards which may be established from time to time pursuant to this Convention.

This provision has been the subject of a court case concerning the – then – British airline British Caledonian against the US safety authorities, as to which *see*, section 3.3.6 of Chapter 1.
8. *See*, for instance, *Art. 8 – Safety, of the EU-US Agreement on air transport* of 2007, as amended:

> 1. The responsible authorities of the Parties shall recognize as valid, for the purposes of operating the air transportation provided for in this Agreement, certificates of airworthiness, certificates of competency, and licenses issued or validated by each other and still in force, provided that the requirements for such certificates or licenses at least equal the minimum standards that maybe established pursuant to the Convention. The responsible authorities may, however, refuse to recognize as valid for purposes of flight above their own territory, certificates of competency and licenses granted to or validated for their own nationals by such other authorities. [...].

This agreement is supplemented by *EU-US Cooperation Agreement in regulation of civil aviation safety* published 15 March 2011 (Council of Europe: Reference 8312/09) that entered into force on 1 May 2011 and which established the Bilateral Oversight Board (BOB).

Other principal subject matters addressed by SARPs concern the Rules of the Air (Annex 2), Airworthiness of Aircraft (Annex 8), Operation of Aircraft (Annex 6), Accident and incident investigation (Annex 13), Security (Annex 17), Protection of the environment (Annex 16) and Safety management (Annex 19). SARPs laid down in these Annexes are updated from time to time, as to which *see*, Chapter 1.

In addition to SARPs, ICAO also develops Procedures for Air Navigation Services (PANS), comprising practices as well as material considered too detailed for SARPs. PANS often amplify the basic principles in the corresponding SARPs to assist in their application.[9] Other than that, there are Regional Supplementary Procedures (SUPPS), supplementing PANS in certain regions regional air navigation plans,[10] and related manuals, circulars and guidance. They form constitute a comprehensive technical safety code for civil aviation.[11]

2.2 Implementation of SARPs in National Legislation

As noted above, Article 37 of the Convention requires that States must collaborate in securing the highest practicable degree of uniformity in regulations, standards, procedures and organisation in relation to aircraft, personnel, airways and auxiliary services in all matters in which such uniformity will facilitate and improve air navigation.[12] To that end, ICAO has adopted the SARPs contained in the Annexes, but it is the integration of such SARPs into the national regulations and practices of States, and their timely implementation that will ultimately achieve safety and regularity of air operations worldwide. Through the provision of national regulations States are expected to implement and enforce the SARPs.

The legal status of SARPs has raised questions in courts,[13] in literature[14] and in practice. Standards have been attributed binding force; this is especially so if national law treats them as part of the Chicago Convention and attaches them, for instance, to their national aviation codes as secondary regulations. Yet, in other cases they are

---

9. *See*, ICAO Doc 8143-AN/873/3, *Directives to Divisional-type Air Navigation Meetings and Rules of Procedure for their Conduct*, Part II, para. 3.
10. *See*, ICAO Doc 7030, *Regional Supplementary Procedures* (2008).
11. *See*, Dr J. Huang, *Aviation Safety and ICAO* 59 (2009).
12. ICAO Doc 9734, *Safety Oversight Manual* – (2006), para. 2.2.3.
13. On the applicability of ICAO Standards in domestic courts, *see*, *British Caledonian Airways Ltd* v. *Langhorne Bond, Federal Aviation Administration and others*, United States Court of Appeals, Decision of 2 September 1981; 665 F.2d 1153 (*British Caledonian v. Bond*, C.A.D.C. 1981); Cour d'appel de Colmar (Court of Appeals of Colmar), decision of 9 April 1998, case No. 09700470, Public prosecutor (*Ministère public*) c *Michel Asseline et autres*, on the Air France crash at the Mont Saint Odile; *De Vereniging Bewonersgroep tegen Vliegtuigoverlast* v. *Gemeente Rotterdam*, Rechtbank (District court) Rotterdam (The Netherlands), Case No: APV 98/2091-S1; *B.A.R. Belgium, NV Sabena and Deutsche Lufthansa* v. *De Gemeente* (Community) *Zaventem*; Raad van State (Belgium State Council), decision of 5 May 2005; Case Nos 69.837/XII-2441; 69.876/XII-2442; 74.820/XII-755; 74.821/XII-754; &76.712/XII-795; *see also*, L. Weber, *Convention on International Civil Aviation – 60 Years*, 53 Zeitschrift für Luft- und Weltraumrecht 298–311 (2004); *see also*, section 3.3.6 of Chapter 1.
14. *See*, M. Milde, *International Air Law and ICAO* 71–73 (2016); same author: *International Civil Aviation Organization – An Introduction* (2007) and J. Huang, *Aviation Safety and ICAO* 58–66 (2009).

regarded as guidance material or 'soft law' as States may choose not to comply with them. Indeed, Article 54(l) of the Chicago Convention dictates that the ICAO Council must as a matter of 'convenience' adopt SARPs and attach them to this Convention.

Moreover, it is sometimes believed that SARPs are *minimum* standards. However, that legal status only applies to the standards pertaining to airworthiness of aircraft which are drawn up in Annex 8, as dictated in the above quoted Article 33 of the Chicago Convention.[15] As explained in section 3.3 of Chapter 1, international, especially bilateral ASAs may specify the legal status of SARPs which must be read in the context of the agreement identifying such legal status.

Furthermore, ICAO stipulates that each State shall enact a basic aviation law that will provide for the development and promulgation of air navigation regulations which should be consistent with its acceptance of the Annexes. The State is required to make provision for the adoption of operating regulations and rules based upon the provisions of the Annexes.[16]

While the global implementation of ICAO standards is deemed by many, including ICAO, as necessary, the Chicago Convention also recognises, through Article 38 notification of differences mechanism.[17] Thus, although the legal status of SARPs is debatable, there is a 'conditional binding force'.[18] In other words:

> in accordance with Article 38, a contracting party must notify ICAO any time it fails to comply with a Standard in all respects; fails to bring its regulations or practices into full accord with any Standard; or adopts regulations or practices differing in any particular respect from the Standard.[19]

This also includes short term differences as, pursuant to Article 38, States must immediately notify ICAO of any differences, without exception. Other actions may be required from the Member State, such as the issuance of a NOTAM or Aeronautical Information Circular. The notification of differences does not mean that the concerned State is relieved of its obligations under the Chicago Convention.

Article 38 only sets out obligations for the notification of differences against Standards. ICAO has acknowledged that differences from Recommended Practices may also be important for the safety, regularity and efficiency of air navigation. Therefore, the ICAO Assembly has resolved that the Council should urge Member States to notify it of any differences, in addition to the date by which the State will comply with the SARPs.

---

15. *See*, more specifically, J. Huang, *Aviation Safety and ICAO* 67–68 (2009).
16. ICAO Doc 8335, Manual of *Procedures for Operations Inspection, Certification and Continued Surveillance* (2010), para. 3.1.2.1.
17. "Any State which finds it impracticable to comply in all respects with any such international standard or procedure, or to bring its own regulations or practices into full accord with any international standard or procedure after amendment of the latter, or which deems it necessary to adopt regulations or practices differing in any particular respect from those established by an international standard, shall give immediate notification to the International Civil Aviation Organization of the differences between its own practice and that established by the international standard."
18. ICAO AN 13/1.1-12/19 10 April 2012 Subject: Adoption of Amendment 43 to Annex 2, para. 7.
19. ICAO Doc 10055, *Manual on Notification and Publication of Differences*.

2.3 Safety Oversight

The achievement of the above objective, and the ability of an aircraft registered on another Members States' registry to exercise the right to fly in each other's airspace, is dependent upon States fulfilling the above obligations under the Convention. One such obligation is the performance of effective safety oversight of aircraft on a State's register and of those responsible for their operation and maintenance; as well as those who provide the services to support air navigation, such as aerodrome operators and air traffic service agencies and units.[20]

This obligation on the part of States is clearly expressed by ICAO in Part A of its Manual Doc 9734[21] and further amplified in ICAO Doc 8335.[22] The first-mentioned document establishes eight critical elements of a safety oversight system; the first such element being primary legislation and the second a code of regulations, that represents the means by which States implement the standards contained in the Annexes to the Convention. It is against those eight critical elements that ICAO conducts its safety oversight audits of States.

The ICAO Universal Safety Oversight Audit Programme (USOAP) has its origins in a Resolution (A29-13) of the General Assembly in 1992 and was first introduced on a voluntary basis in 1996. USOAP audits focus on a State's capability in providing safety oversight by assessing whether the State has effectively and consistently implemented the critical elements of a safety oversight system, which enable the State to ensure the implementation of ICAO's Standards and Recommended Practices (SARPs), and associated procedures and guidance material. Following a review by the ICAO Conference on a *Global Strategy for Safety Oversight* in November 1997, the programme became mandatory following a resolution of the General Assembly in 1998 (A32-11). Initially the audits were conducted only against compliance by States with Annexes 1 (*Personnel Licensing*), 6 (*Operation of Aircraft*) and 8 (*Airworthiness of Aircraft*) and began in January 1999. The reports of those audits were only partially made public. However, following further debate and a resolution of the 35th General Assembly in 2005 (A35-6) the audit programme was expanded to become a *Comprehensive Systems Approach* that covered 16 of the 18 Annexes; only Annexes 9 (*Facilitation*) and 17 (*Security*, which had its own audit) were excluded.[23]

The new audit programme began in 2005 and was completed by the end of 2010 and included audits of regional organisations such as European Aviation Safety Agency (EASA). This time the results are published in full on the ICAO Secure Website and partially, with the consent of States, on the public website. All States are therefore now

---

20. *See*, J.M. Clark, *Assuring Safer Skies? A Survey of Aeromedical Issues Post-Germanwings*, 81(3) Journal of Air Law and Commerce 351–376 (2016), and M. Milde, *Problems of Safety Oversight: Enforcement of ICAO Standards*, in: C.-J. Cheng (ed.), *The Use of Air Space and Outer Space. Cooperation and Competition*, proceedings of the International Symposium on the Use of the Air and Outer Space at the Service of World Peace and Prosperity (Beijing, 1995) 251–272 (1998).
21. ICAO Doc 9734-AN/959 *Safety Oversight Manual, Part A Establishment and Management of a State's Safety Oversight System*, Second edition (2006).
22. ICAO Doc 8335, Manual of *Procedures for Operations Inspection, Certification and Continued Surveillance* (2010).
23. *See also*, section 3.3.2.3 of Chapter 1.

able to access the reports on the other States and will use the results to determine whether or not to allow aircraft from those other States to use their airspace. The reports are used by, for example, the European Commission in determining which operators and States should be placed on the blacklist.[24]

ICAO Assembly Resolution A36-4 (September 2007) established a new approach to be applied to the USOAP beyond 2010 that is based on the concept of continuous monitoring, by which ICAO can identify safety deficiencies, assess associated safety risks and implement strategies for their mitigation and thus enhance States' safety performance. The systematic and more proactive conduct of monitoring activities in the new USOAP Continuous Monitoring Approach (CMA) is designed to make a more efficient use of ICAO resources and reduce the burden on States caused by repetitive audits.[25]

2.4 Enforcement under Bilateral and Other International Agreements

Bilateral and other international agreements, which States have concluded on the footing of Article 6 of the Chicago Convention on scheduled air services, regulate obligations of States to implement the minimum requirements adopted by ICAO in the form of SARPS and updated from time to time. A typical clause on Safety reads:

> All Parties shall recognize as valid, for the purpose of operating the air transportation provided for in this Agreement, certificates of airworthiness, certificates of competency, and licenses issued or validated by the other Party and still in force, provided that the requirements for such certificates or licenses at least equal the minimum standards that may be established pursuant to the Convention. All Parties may, however, refuse to recognize as valid for the purpose of flight above its own territory, certificates of competency and licenses granted to or validated for its own nationals by the other Party.

This provision reflects the purpose of Articles 31–33 in conjunction with Articles 37 and 38 of the Chicago Convention. Enforcement is not only left to ICAO and other organisations such as EASA, as to which *see*, Chapter 7, but also to States in the context of their international, traditionally bilateral agreements.[26]

In the words of a standard provision on Authorisation for the operation of the agreed international air services:

> A Party, on receipt of applications from an airline of the other Party or Parties, in the form and manner prescribed for operating authorizations and technical permissions, shall grant appropriate authorizations and permissions with minimum procedural delay, provided:
> The other Party is maintaining and administering the provisions set forth in Article [...] (Safety) and Article [...] (Aviation Security).

---

24. *See*, section 2.5.2 of Chapter 7.
25. *See also*, www.icao.int/safety/CMAForum/Pages/default.aspx.
26. *See*, for example the Canada-Mexico bilateral Agreement signed on 12 August 2011 that liberalises air services between the two countries but imposes strict compliance with the safety and security provisions.

The designated airlines of the other States are obligated to maintain minimum Standards drawn up by ICAO. If not, the Operating Permission may be withdrawn. Such a far going step, due to the political nature connected to such action and the potential economic consequences, is usually preceded by discussions in the form of consultations and negotiations between the competent aviation authorities of the concerned States.

The US FAA administers a system[27] pursuant to which it categorises foreign States under either Category 1 or 2 and under which it assists foreign States, their airlines and airports in improving the safety situation. States that are not yet in a position to meet the required international standards are listed as Category 2 States, whose airlines are forbidden to fly into US airspace or whose operations are severely restricted.[28] Until a new State, that is, one whose airlines have not previously flown to the US, has been audited under the programme and its level of compliance verified its airlines will not be permitted to operate to the US.

The EU has its own regime which will be explored in greater detail in Chapter 7.

2.5 Safety of Airports (Aerodromes)

2.5.1 Regulation under the Chicago Convention

The Chicago Convention addresses airports at several instances. For instance, Article 15 deals with airport charges,[29] whereas Article 68 allows each State, as a matter of a sovereign right, to designate the airport which is open for the operation of international air services.

For the present discussion, Article 28 of the Chicago Convention is most relevant as it states that each Contracting State, "so far as it may find practicable" must provide in its territory infrastructure including airports, and services "to facilitate international air navigation." The expression 'so far as it may find practicable' has caused confusion as it would seem that States are not obliged to provide airports and other facilities. In reality, however, ICAO and its Contracting States implement Article 28 through regional air navigation plans.[30]

Only airports which are used by aircraft operating *international* air services as defined in Article 96(b) of the Convention are subject to this provision, that is, Article 28, and must comply with the SARPs laid down in, principally, Annex 14 as to which *see* the next section.

---

27. International Aviation Safety Assessment (IASA) program established in 1992 and revised in May 2000 under 14 CFR Part 129.
28. *See*, FAA, 'Home Page', http://www.faa.gov/about/initiatives, and R.K. Seth, *The FAA Downgrade of Indian Aviation – What Went Wrong?* 14(1) Issues in Aviation Law and Policy 155–174 (2014).
29. *See*, section 6 of Chapter 2.
30. *See*, Dr J. Huang, *Aviation Safety and ICAO* 46 (2009).

2.5.2 Regulation under Annex 14 of ICAO

International law does not prescribe the method of ownership or management of airports. As there is no uniform type of management of airports, each State has its own airport regulations, implementing and supplementing the rules of Annex 14 of the Chicago Convention, containing technical rather than administrative, legal and economic matters.[31] The past decades have witnessed a major change in the structure of airport ownership with many States commercialising and even privatising those airports that were previously under direct governmental control and management.

Questions on privatisation of airports are left to States, also in the EU.[32] However, this development has resulted in ICAO recognising the need for certification by States of aerodromes (airports) used for international operations in accordance with the specifications contained in Annex 14 to the Convention and recommending the certification of other public use aerodromes.

2.5.3 Operation of Airports

There are two different kinds of airports: civil airports and military airports whereas there are also *dual use* airports.[33] The distinction between military and non-military airports is relevant because their legal status is different: military airports are subject to other rules and jurisdiction than those in force for civil airports. Civil airports must comply with the norms set forth in Annex 14 as implemented in national law whereas the operation of military airports falls under national law.

The operation of an airport may be related to the corporate structure of the airport which may be changed by way of corporatisation or privatisation of the airport. The establishment of charges by airport operators is a focal point of attention. Article 15 of the Chicago Convention prescribes uniformity and national treatment in this respect whereas economic regulation of airports may be affected by applicable competition law regimes, as airport operators generally tend to hold a monopoly or dominant position.[34]

Increasing attention is paid to compensation for environmental damages caused by the use of airports; environmental damages may be caused by noise or emissions. These external, environmental costs should be 'internalised', that is, reflected, in the airport or route charges. As a corollary, airports come under strict administrative scrutiny: public authorities are also mandated to protect the people living in the vicinity

---

31. *See*, section 2.5.5 of Chapter 7 on airport inspection in the EU.
32. *See*, S. Varsamis, *Airport Competition Regulation in Europe* 44–47 (2016).
33. *See*, R. Abeyratne, *Joint Use of Military and Civil Airports*, Law and Regulation of Aerodromes 223–256 (2014).
34. As to which *see*, section 3.3.2 of Chapter 2; *see also*, R.I.R. Abeyratne, *The ICAO Conference on the Economics of Airports and Air Navigation Services*, 34(6) Air & Space Law 218–238 (2009); *see also*, Marina Koester, *ICAO and the Economic Environment of Civil Aviation. The Impact of the Fifth World-Wide Air Transport Conference of 2003 on Challenges and Opportunities of Liberalisation*, 52 Zeitschrift für Luft und Weltraumrecht 322 (2003).

of airports. Hence, the civil liability of the airport operator for noise hindrance around airports comes under national law as it is not subject to an international regime.[35]

The legal relationship between the airport operator and its users, principally the airlines, as well as other service providers, such as providers of air navigation services and ground handling services, is a matter of increasing importance. The Single European Sky (SES) fosters the development of such relationships in a forward looking, innovative, environmentally friendly and cross border fashion.[36]

2.6 Transfer of Safety Oversight

Pursuant to the Chicago Convention, the State of registry is internationally responsible for the issuance of a Certificate of Airworthiness (CoA) of aircraft registered in its national registered, and of personnel licences serving on such aircraft.[37] In the decades after the conclusion of the Chicago Convention, international transactions concerning leasing, interchange or charter of aircraft from one operator to another, based in a foreign State, became an attractive method for meeting flexibility for the use of aircraft. Thus, an aircraft registered in one State was used in another. In turn, the State of registry of the aircraft was not capably of adequately carrying out safety oversight as it was used in another country or even in another part of the world.

This practice led to the adoption of Article 83*bis* of the Chicago Convention in 1980; it entered into force on 20 June 1997 for the States which have ratified it.[38] This provision has been considered as an exception to the 'genuine link' which normally, that is, via national law provisions, exists between an aircraft and the State of registry. The objective is to create the closest possible tie between the aircraft and the State overseeing its safety in order to avoid 'flags of convenience.'[39]

Article 83*bis* is also referred to as an 'Annex 6' delegation of safety duties as these duties pertain to the Operation of Aircraft as regulated by the SARPs laid down in this Annex. It delineates the limits of transferable responsibility to matters relating to only the rules of the air (Article 12), radio licensing (Article 30), airworthiness of aircraft (Article 31) and crew licensing (Article 32(a)).[40] Therefore, the transfer of

---

35. *See*, P.M.J. Mendes de Leon, *Liability of Airports for Noise Hindrance: A Comparative Analysis*, 11 The Korean Journal of Air and Space Law 169–202 (1999).

36. *See*, section 5.2 of Chapter 3; *see also*, D. Calleja Crespo and P.M.J. Mendes de Leon, *The Single European Sky: Prospects and Challenges* (2011).

37. *See*, Arts 31 and 32, as further explained in ICAO, Doc 9734 – AN/959, *Safety Oversight Manuel*, Part A – *The Establishment and Management of a State's Safety Oversight System* (2006).

38. 170 States per February 2017.

39. *See*, J. Huang, *Aviation Safety and ICAO* 42 (2009): 'The amendment to the Chicago Convention through Article 83*bis* reinforces the principle that the concept of 'flags of convenience' has no place within the ICAO system. Had 'flags of convenience' been acceptable, it would not have been necessary for ICAO to spend several decades in negotiating and adopting Article 83*bis* and to bring it into force.'

40. *See*, for instance, the Agreement between Aeronautical Authorities of the Russian Federation and Directorate General of Civil Aviation of the Republic of Turkey concerning *the transfer of regulatory oversight functions and duties including in the field of airworthiness* (2009) pursuant to which the Turkish aviation authorities shall be relieved of responsibility in respect of the functions and duties transferred to the Aeronautical Authorities of the Russian Federation, upon

responsibility is only within respect to these four Articles and their related Annexes. Articles 12, 30, 31 and 32(a) do not mention the transfer of jurisdiction. In the words of ICAO:

> Article 83*bis* is an umbrella provision, the ratification of which does not entail the automatic transfer of functions and duties from the State of Registry to the State of the Operator; it requires that such a transfer be expressly arranged through an agreement between the States concerned.[41]

Hence, the responsibilities contained in Articles 12, 30, 31 and 32(a) are not automatically transferred under Article 83*bis*. They must be *negotiated* and *agreed upon* between the concerned States, in which case one of the States may also refuse the transfer. Only that which falls under the Articles can be negotiated under Article 83*bis* and nothing more.

Annex 2, which is relevant pursuant to Article 12, refers to *jurisdiction*:

> The Amendment in no way affects the legal jurisdiction of States of Registry over their aircraft or the responsibility of Contracting States under Article 12 of the Convention for enforcing the Rules of the Air.[42]

Hence, it is clear that there is *no transfer of jurisdiction*, and that responsibility and jurisdiction are distinct legal concepts. This conclusion is supported by the work of ICAO in regards to 'Flag of Convenience.'[43] Thus, neither Article 83*bis* nor other provisions of the Chicago Convention provide for the transfer of jurisdiction.[44]

3 TECHNICAL REGULATION ON THE OPERATION OF AIRCRAFT

3.1 Aircraft Handling and Automation

With the increasing traffic density and a similar growth ratio in capacity and speed of present-day aircraft, the aircraft captain's duties have become more involved to the

---

due publicity or notification of this Agreement as determined in paragraph b) of Art. 83*bis*. Art. 2 limits the scope of the agreement to two aircraft Airbus A320 on the register of civil aircraft of Turkey and operated under leasing arrangement by the Russian registered operator, whose principal place of business is in the Russian Federation. Under Art. 3, the Parties agree that the Turkish authorities transfer to the Russian Authorities the following functions and duties, including oversight and control of relevant items contained in the respective Annexes to the Convention: Annex 1 – *Personnel Licensing*, issuance and validation of licenses. Annex 2 – *Rules of the Air*, enforcement of compliance with applicable rules and regulations relating to the flight and manoeuvre of aircraft. Annex 6 – *Operation of Aircraft* (Part I – International Commercial Air Transport – Aeroplanes), all responsibilities which are normally incumbent on the State of Registry. Where responsibilities in Annex 6, Part I, may conflict with responsibilities in Annex 8 – Airworthiness of Aircraft, allocation of specific responsibilities as defined in the attachment.

41. ICAO Circular 295 LE/2, *Guidance on the Implementation of Art. 83bis of the Convention on International Civil Aviation* (2003) at 5.
42. ICAO Annex 2 – *Rules of the Air* (2005) at v.
43. *See*, for instance, ICAO Secretariat, Study on the *Safety and Security Aspects of Economic Liberalization*, section 2.2.3.1 (2005).
44. For the situation in the EU, reference is made to section 2.4.2 of Chapter 7 discussing *Continuing airworthiness*.

extent that most flights can only be performed adequately with the aid of automation.[45] This may take various forms such as an automatic pilot; a computer for monitoring and correcting an aircraft's course; apparatus for avoiding collisions, for instance, Airborne Collision Avoidance System[46] (ACAS); a system for determining the aircraft's exact position;[47] telecommunication systems, including an automatic hijack alarm; automated landing instruments for adverse weather conditions, and so on. Many of these aspects of the automation and equipment requirements are mandated in the Annexes to the Convention.[48]

Thanks to modern navigational assistance provided by satellites, an aircraft's position can be determined largely independently and with reasonable accuracy. However, as the tragic case of Malaysia Airlines Flight MH370 shows, the system is not complete as aircraft can still go missing without any trace.[49] Nearly all major airports worldwide are already equipped with the 'Instrument Landing System', using radio signals and enabling safe landings to be made in all weathers. An improved version is the so-called 'Enhanced Vision System', which enables aircraft to land round the clock without any ground control assistance. The importance of these navigational aids is particularly relevant in regions where the infrastructure is not yet sufficiently developed.[50]

The automation devices have contributed to reducing the burden of a captain's responsibilities. However, the treatment of high-tech hardware as a panacea for all actions and problems must be resisted. As it is, the sheer volume and variety of instruments may well enhance the risk of errors being committed or extremely hazardous situations arising: the memory of the tragedy involving Korean Airlines flight KE007 in 1983, which inadvertently strayed into Soviet airspace probably due to faulty computer programming, exemplifies this point.[51] Also, the continuous availability of informative data may lead to an inadequate performance on the part of the pilot. Hence, it would be wrong to rule out the human factor: the captain's personal assessment and handling of the situation, his timely intervention remains paramount for a proper discharging of his duties and, consequently, the deciding element when it

---

45. *See also*, G. Contissa, G. Sartor, H. Schebesta, A. Masutti, P. Lanzi, P. Marti, & P. Tomasello, *Liability and Automation: Issues and Challenges for Socio-technical Systems*, 2(1–2) Journal for Aerospace Operations 79 (2013).
46. *See*, ICAO, *Airborne Collision Avoidance System* (ACAS) Manual, Doc 9863 AN/461 (2012).
47. *See*, Commission Regulation (EU) 2015/2338 of 11 December 2015 amending Regulation (EU) No. 965/2012 as regards requirements for flight recorders, underwater locating devices and aircraft tracking systems. *See also*, ICAO, *Global Tracking Initiatives*, http://www.icao.int/ safety/globaltracking/Pages/Homepage.aspx
48. *See*, in particular, Annex 6 on the *Operation of Aircraft*, Part I – International Commercial Air Transport – Aeroplanes, Chapter 6 (2016).
49. *See*, M. Thompson, J. Cooper and J. Harman, *The Search for MH370: Where Are We Now?* 41(6) Air & Space Law 459–474 (2016).
50. On the subject of air navigation satellite systems and the role of ICAO, *see*, T. Bribise, *Aeronautical Public Correspondence by Satellite* (2006), and I.H.Ph. Diederiks-Verschoor and V. Kopal, *An Introduction to Space Law* (2008), notably Chapter IV.B.4.
51. *See*, B. Cheng, *The Destruction of KAL Flight KE007, and Art. 3bis of the Chicago Convention*, in J.W. Storm van 's Gravesande and A. van der Veen Vonk (eds), *Air Worthy*, Liber Amicorum I.H.Ph. Diederiks-Verschoor 47–74 (1985).

comes to determining his responsibility.[52] In conclusion, as far as the pilot's legal position is concerned, new technology and automation has brought no fundamental change.[53]

3.2 Air Traffic Control (ATC)

For air navigation to reach the highest degree of safety an orderly movement of flights under the guidance of a control tower or centre is an absolute prerequisite. The control officers' duties may be compared with those of a ship's pilot: they issue instructions to all aircraft within range of their control area. In doing so they owe a duty of care in law to all of those who rely upon the information provided.

Annex 2 entitled 'Rules of the Air' specifies that an aircraft commander must follow the instructions of the control tower. Air traffic procedures are set out in detail in Annex 2.[54] Chapter 3 states that the aircraft commander is responsible for carrying out the directions of ATC. It also provides, however, that the aircraft commander is ultimately responsible for the safe operation of the aircraft.[55] In general, the commander will be bound by the instructions given by ATC. In certain cases, the commander may deviate from those instructions, for instance in an emergency. In such a situation ATC must be kept informed.[56]

This legal position may cause considerable uncertainty and confusion as to where to lay the blame in the event of an accident. Current practice has sought to resolve this problem by interpreting the relevant provisions to mean that the commander is bound to follow the controller's instructions except in an emergency. This position may, however, be conditioned by other factors. What is the position, for example, when the controller's instructions are in conflict with the advice provided by an on-board collision avoidance system or indeed the pilot's own visual observations? This was a very relevant factor in the accident over southern Germany in Überlingen in July 2002 that is referred to in section 2.4.7 of Chapter 7.[57]

Investigators pointed to failings on the side of Skyguide.[58] Other causes are related to confused rules and manuals, which led the Russian crew to make the wrong choices as the two aircraft sped towards each other. The Russian crew obeyed the controller's order to descend instead of heeding their on board collision warning

---

52. *See,* for example, UK CAA Paper 2011/03 (March 2011): CAA 'Significant Seven' Task Force Reports – Report 1 'Loss of control' report.
53. *See,* R. Schmid, *Pilot in Command or Computer in Command? Observations on the Conflict Between Technological Progress and Pilot Accountability,* 25 Air & Space Law 281–290 (2000).
54. *See,* F.P. Schubert, *Pilots, Controllers, and the Protection of Third Parties on the Surface,* XXIII Annals of Air and Space Law 185–200 (1998).
55. *See,* Standard 2.4 of Annex 2 (2005) on the *Authority of pilot-in-command of an aircraft:* 'The pilot-in-command of an aircraft shall have *final authority* as to the disposition of the aircraft while in command.' (*italics added*).
56. *See,* Report on the *Liability of Air Traffic Control Agencies,* ICAO Doc. 8582-LC/153-2, at 11–121, prepared by a sub-committee of the ICAO Legal Committee for the 15th session of this Committee at Montreal in September 1964.
57. For the product liability aspects, *see,* section 4.1 of Chapter 8.
58. *See,* Report of the Associated Press, *Swiss Co. Reaches Deal Over Collision,* 30 June 2004.

system to climb, putting the Russian aircraft in the path of the DHL aircraft which also was descending. On the Russian Cockpit Voice Recorder (CVR), a co-pilot was heard pointing out the conflict to the Skyguide staff. However, they apparently disregarded it and did not raise the point with ground control. Investigators also found that the Russians were unaware that, under international rules, instructions from the on-board collision warning system take precedence over orders from the ATC tower. One air traffic controller, a Danish national, present at the time of the accident was killed on 24 February 2003 by a Russian person whose wife, son and daughter had died in the crash.

In June 2004, the Russian families reportedly reached a – multi-million – deal with Skyguide. The settlement is based on the principle of equity and by negotiation between representatives of the parties involved, including but not limited to Skyguide, the Swiss and German government and their insurers, rather than on the application of strict rules, let alone international rules. Hence not all relatives and other persons entitled to claim will receive the same amount of compensation.

On 27 July 2006,[59] the District Court of Konstanz, Germany, made a decision on a case brought by Bashkirian Airlines against the Republic of Germany. Bashkirian Airlines requested the court to decide that Germany should compensate all damages which were caused by the accident and for which Bashkirian Airlines has been or could be held liable, whether by second parties – in particular, the survivors of the victims – or by third parties, for instance, people on the ground. The court found that the case had to be decided in accordance with German law – the *lex loci* (*delicti*). The court also explained that Skyguide was performing such services by delegation as the provision of air navigation services belongs to the sovereign competencies of a State. Germany (delegating competencies with respect to the provision of air navigation services to Skyguide) was responsible for the execution of such services in relation to third parties, including Bashkirian Airlines. Hence, the German State was held liable for all damages claimed by Bashkirian Airlines pursuant to rules of German law regarding State liability. The same District Court refused further compensation in a decision of 2008.[60]

Apart from the Chicago Convention and the rules made under it in the ICAO Annexes, no other internationally agreed rules exist in relation to this matter, which is so eminently suitable for that purpose. For any further regulations the domestic legislation has to be addressed.

Domestic law may imply that control tower personnel enjoy the status of civil servants;[61] a status that will determine their position in terms of rights, duties, working conditions and liability. They may in certain cases be exempt from civil and criminal liability under the law of the country in which they are employed, but this is a moving subject. Arguably, control tower officers carry a heavy burden of responsibility in their duties, depending in their operations almost entirely on advanced electronic equipment, perhaps even more so than a pilot: for example, they cannot observe their entire

---

59. Case Number 4 O 234/05 H (Fourth Chamber).
60. Judgement of 18 September 2008, in a procedure of the victims against the bankruptcy trustee of Bashkirian Airlines.
61. *See*, F.P. Schubert, *The Corporatization of Air Traffic Control*, XXII–II Annals of Air and Space Law 224–242 (1997).

control area or the movement of all aircraft with their own eyes. And yet, situations may arise in which a controller may be held responsible under national law rather than the pilot. Furthermore, that decision would stand quite irrespective of the role their equipment may or may not have played.

This was the case, for example, as a result of the tragic accident at Milan-Linate Airport in October 2001 when two aircraft collided on the runway during fog resulting in the death of 118 people. In that case, a corporate aircraft crossed the live runway as a SAS scheduled airliner began its take-off. The subsequent court proceedings against senior managers of the airport company, the air traffic services and the regulatory authority, as well as the duty controllers, held them liable for a series of failures to adequately mark the airport taxiways; to provide and maintain suitable equipment; and in the adoption of inadequate procedures. Several of the persons charged were sentenced to terms of imprisonment.[62] Ironically, such prosecutions almost inevitably lead to a reduction in the number of incidents being reported as those involved become more fearful for their own positions.[63] Also, reference is made to the discussion of the 'Just Culture' in section 5.2 below.

The tendency has become to keep one's head down instead of reporting incidents in the interests of improving safety as was noted by the Netherlands ATC agency following the prosecution in 2000 of three controllers as a result of a runway incursion at Amsterdam.[64] All of these cases have demonstrated that air traffic controllers and airport operators, and their senior management, must accept civil and criminal liability for shortcomings in performance of their functions regardless of the level of automation available to them. Again, modern technology does not seem to have altered the basic liability position essentially or resulted in a reduction of personnel liability, as it also contributes to enhancing transparency of the event giving rise to liability.

The ICAO Communication Navigation and Surveillance/Air Traffic Management system (CNS/ATM) has been investigating how airspace could be used more flexibly and efficiently, and so achieve better air traffic management, by more intensive use of satellites for communications, navigation and control purposes. Furthermore, aviation has already been and still is making use of a number of satellite navigation systems, notably Inmarsat, the US Global Positioning System (GPS) and the Russian GLONASS. The subject has thus become extremely complex. The ICAO CNS/ATM system will not be easy to implement: not only States but also various other organisations will have to be involved in what will be a long process of which the outcome is yet diffuse and

---

62. *See*, P. Alvintzi and H. Eder (eds), *Crisis Management*, in M. Catino, *The Linate Air Disaster: A Multilevel Model of Accident Analysis* (2010); *see also*, G. Brichi and Dr E. Carpanelli, '*Just Culture*', *and the Italian Approach Towards Aircraft Accident Investigation*, 62 Zeitschrift für Luft- und Weltraumrecht 19–73 (2013).
63. For the final report of this accident, *see*, http://www.ansv.it/en/Detail.asp?ID = 182.
64. *See*, comment in *Flight International*, 11–17 May 2004.

unpredictable.[65] As one of the first tangible results of the ICAO efforts, the Charter on the Rights and Obligations of States Relating to Global Navigation Satellite Systems (GNSS) Services has been drawn up.[66]

3.3 Aircraft Maintenance

3.3.1 A Coordinated Responsibility

Operating an aircraft requires continuous oversight of the 'technical health' of the aircraft. Modern maintenance methods and technology enable an aircraft to remain at the highest possible levels of reliability, performance and safety and kept in a state of airworthiness. The standards to be applied in achieving that level of airworthiness are determined by ICAO, which also lays down the methods for management of airworthiness and maintenance. The State of Registry is obliged to provide effective oversight by regular inspections of the aircraft and of those responsible for its operation and maintenance.[67]

Aircraft maintenance must always be performed in a coordinated manner that is largely determined by the manufacturer and the State of Design and Registration. This includes preventive maintenance, according to a designated and approved organisation by the aviation authorities in the country of registration of the aircraft 'maintenance program', and requirement-based maintenance. Thus, every part of every aircraft is regularly and thoroughly checked according to such approved maintenance programme that takes place on a regular, progressive basis.

Aircraft maintenance involves the application of internationally established standards embodied in national regulations. The regulations and the regulatory system that supports them contain a number of features:

- Strong regulation on the part of international and national bodies, aircraft-suppliers and manufacturers, combined with specific needs of the airlines/users.
- Solid education including basic, specialised and continuous training for technicians.
- Specific qualification requirements to ensure competence of personnel.
- High level of understanding on the part of personnel of, and compliance with, regulations.
- Adequate resources, given the high costs for trained personnel and specialised instruments.

---

65. See, B.D.K. Henaku, The Law on Global Air Navigation by Satellite. A Legal Analysis of the ICAO CNS/ATM System (thesis Leiden), 1998.
66. ICAO, Global Air Navigation Plan for CNS/ATM Systems, Doc 9750 AN/963 (2016); see, 25 Air & Space Law 139 (2000), XXIII Annals of Air and Space Law 322, 325–328 (1998) and also F. Bergamasco, GNSS Liability: Current Legal Framework and Perspectives for the Future from the International Aviation Point of View, XIII(4) Aviation and Space Law Journal 2–10 (2015).
67. See, ICAO, Safety Oversight Manuel – Part A (2006), para. 2.1.1 referring to oversight functions in Annexes 1, 6 and 8.

Regulations regarding maintenance, repair and overhaul are based on the standards contained in Annex 6 to the Chicago Convention and in requirements of bodies such as EASA.[68] Further binding regulations are provided in the domestic law of the State of Registry of the aircraft

3.3.2   International Regulation

Annex 6, Part 1, to the Chicago Convention, called 'Operation of Aircraft', contains the basis for regulations regarding the maintenance of 'Aeroplanes'. Chapter 8 of this Annex defines 'Aeroplanes' as aircraft including power plants, that is, engines, propellers, components, accessories, instruments, equipment and apparatus such as emergency equipment.

The following subjects are being dealt with in this Annex 6 (Part 1):

1. *Operator's maintenance responsibilities*
   Operators shall ensure in accordance with procedures acceptable to the State of Registry:
   - Each aeroplane they operate is in an airworthy condition;
   - The operational and emergency equipment necessary for an intended flight is serviceable;
   - The Certificate of Airworthiness of each aeroplane they operate remains valid.
   The operator shall not operate an aeroplane unless it is maintained and released to service by an approved maintenance organisation. The operator shall employ a person or a group of persons to ensure that all maintenance is carried out in accordance with a maintenance control manual. Maintenance of the aeroplanes must be in accordance with an approved maintenance program.
2. *Operators Maintenance Control Manual*
   The operator shall provide for the use by and guidance of maintenance and operational personnel concerned, a maintenance control manual acceptable to the State of Registry of the aeroplane. Amendments must be made as the need arises and copies of the manual must be issued to the authorities in the State of Registry and the State of the Operator.
3. *Maintenance Program*
   The operator shall provide for the use by and guidance of maintenance and operational personnel concerned a maintenance program approve by the State of Registry of the aeroplane. The program must also observe human factors principles.
4. *Maintenance Records*
   Operators have to maintain certain records concerning maintenance of their aeroplanes.
5. *Continuous Airworthiness Information*
   Operators shall monitor and assess maintenance and operational experience with respect to continuing airworthiness.
6. *Modifications and Repairs*
   All modifications and repairs shall comply with airworthiness requirements acceptable to the State of Registry.

---

68. *See*, section 2 of Chapter 7.

7. *Approved Maintenance Organisation*
Only maintenance organisations which are approved by the State may perform maintenance on aeroplanes.

8. *Maintenance Release*
The maintenance organisation shall issue a maintenance release certifying that the maintenance work on the aeroplane has been performed and completed satisfactorily in accordance with approved data and procedures as shown in the maintenance organisation's maintenance manual.

Again, the above standards must be implemented in national regulations and updated from time to time, as required by Article 37 of the Chicago Convention and explained in section 3.3.6 of Chapter 1 and section 2.1 of this Chapter.

3.3.3   National Regulations Regarding Maintenance, Repair and Overhaul

Apart from the afore-mentioned, as to which *see*, section 3.3.2., international rules concerning maintenance of aircraft, most States have national legislation or regulations regarding this subject. Often a CoA requires that the owner or operator of the aircraft carries out certain maintenance and that such maintenance is performed by an approved maintenance organisation or by qualified persons.[69] Maintenance must be performed following an approved maintenance program. Under certain conditions, the owner or pilot of an aircraft may personally perform specific inspections and maintenance on the aircraft.

Finally, sometimes inspections fail because employees carrying out maintenance are not held accountable for lax oversight or more serious infractions of rules and procedures. A further disturbing element is that the inspectors themselves sometimes lack complete training on the various aspects of the very aircraft and equipment they have to assess. Proper training programs and strict procedures are therefore essential, as well as teamwork by experts on the individual safety aspects.

3.4   Cybersecurity

One of the first reported cyber-attacks on civil aviation took place on 10 March 1997 when a teenager hacked into a Bell Atlantic computer system at the Worcester, Massachusetts airport, thus becoming the first juvenile charged with computer hacking in a US Federal Court. The attack disabled phone services; and safety infrastructure such as runway lights, and the airport fire department and the tower's radio transmitter.

While ICAO published the first edition of Annex 17 on 'Security' in 1974, it was not until 26 February 2014, around seventeen years after the Worcester Airport attack,

---

69. ICAO, Annex 8, Chapter 10 (2010).

that the Council adopted Amendment 14, as recommended by the Aviation Security Panel (AVSECP), which included Recommended Practices relating to cybersecurity.[70] Recommendation 4.9.1 states:

> Each Contracting State should, in accordance with the risk assessment carried out by its relevant national authorities, ensure that measures are developed in order to protect critical information and communications technology systems used for civil aviation purposes from interference that may jeopardize the safety of civil aviation.

It is not clear how 'interference' is to be interpreted within the context of the rest of the Annex, as Annex 17 predominantly refers to 'unlawful interference'[71] which is narrower as it only constitutes *illegal acts*. It is also not clear whether this refers to direct or indirect interference, or if it includes cyber-attacks that do not interfere, that is, monitoring and recording. Recommendation 4.9.2 then advances that Contracting States encourage their respective responsible entities to identify critical information and communications technology, and develop protective measures as appropriate. Thus, the Recommendation falls short of prescribing any concrete actions.

ICAO produced another document in the 1970s relevant to aviation security. The Security Manual,[72] which is in its ninth edition, is designed to assist Contracting States with aviation security issues. The document is, however, restricted so its content on cybersecurity cannot be further examined.

The dissemination of cybersecurity information, due to its link with national security and criminal law, and its commercial sensitivity, is often extremely limited. However, ICAO has been proactive in the past few years. One notable example being the agreement on a common roadmap to align their respective actions on cyber threats concluded in December 2014 between ICAO, Airports Council International (ACI),

---

70. ICAO, Working Paper, Assembly – 39th Session, Executive Committee, Agenda Item 16: *Aviation Security Policy*, A39-WP/2361 26 August 2016.
71. Annex 17, Chapter 1 – *Definitions*:

'Acts of unlawful interference'. These are acts or attempted acts such as to jeopardize the safety of civil aviation, including but not limited to:

- unlawful seizure of aircraft,
- destruction of an aircraft in service,
- hostage-taking on board aircraft or on aerodromes,
- forcible intrusion on board an aircraft, at an airport or on the premises of an aeronautical facility,
- introduction on board an aircraft or at an airport of a weapon or hazardous device or material intended for criminal purposes,
- use of an aircraft in service for the purpose of causing death, serious bodily injury, or serious damage to property or the environment,
- communication of false information such as to jeopardize the safety of an aircraft in flight or on the ground, of passengers, crew, ground personnel or the general public, at an airport or on the premises of a civil aviation facility.'

72. Aviation Security Manual (Doc 8973/9 – Restricted).

Civil Air Navigation Services Organisation (CANSO), International Coordinating Council of Aerospace Industry Associations (ICCAIA) and IATA.[73]

ICAO Resolution A39-19 (2016) *Addressing Cybersecurity in Civil Aviation* reiterates the relevance of concerted action with respect to combatting threats against the infrastructure of aviation, including its digital infrastructure. It calls on States to identify the threats and risks from possible cyber incidents on civil aviation operations and critical systems, to define the responsibilities of national agencies and industry stakeholders, and to encourage the development of a common understanding among Member States of cyber threats and risks, and of common criteria to determine the criticality of the assets and systems that need to be protected, including sharing of information, and to promote the development and implementation of international standards, strategies and best practices on the protection of critical information and communications technology systems for this purpose. The Resolution also aims at increasing collaboration:

> in the development of ICAO's cyber-security framework according to a horizontal, cross-cutting and functional approach involving air navigation, communication, surveillance, aircraft operations and airworthiness and other relevant disciplines.

ICAO has thus become active in the area of cybersecurity. However, more needs to be done, especially in the area of aviation *safety* and bridging this with *security*. The threat is real and thus necessitates the further regulation of cybersecurity in a proactive, effective and efficient manner. These efforts should be a priority for ICAO, because, while cyber-attacks on the aviation sector have so far been low-level and caused limited impact, the consequences of a malicious cyber-attack on civil aviation operations could potentially be catastrophic.[74]

3.5 The Passenger Name Record (PNR) Discussion Between the EU and Other States

A related subject is the on-going PNR discussion between the EU and the US. PNR is a record in the database of a Global Distribution System (GDS) containing the personal details of passengers when they book a ticket. Hence, it is a tool used by air carriers for monitoring their operations. PNR data include the details which an airline needs for making a reservation; the requirements may vary from one airline to another.

Both the EU and the US are committed to combat terrorism but they set different priorities when it comes to this subject.[75] In short, the US authorities grant an absolute priority to the protection of security, which may be caused by, among others, the

---

73. ICAO, *Aviation Unites on Cyber Threat*, http://www.icao.int/Newsroom/Pages/aviation-unites-on-cyber-threat.aspx.

74. ICAO, Working Paper, Assembly – 39th Session, Executive Committee, Agenda Item 16: *Aviation Security Policy*, A39-WP/2361 26 August 2016; *see also*, D.J.B. Svantesson, *The New Phenomenon of Cyber Law*, Proceedings of the conference *Air Law, Space Law, Cyber Law* – the Cologne Institute of Air and Space Law at Age 90, ed. S. Hobe, 123–136 (2016).

75. *See also*, M. Tzanou, *The War Against Terror and Transatlantic Information Sharing: Spill-Over of Privacy or Spill-Over of Security?*, Utrecht Journal of International and European Law 87–103

dramatic 9/11 attacks against the World Trade towers in New York in 2001, whereas the EU stresses the importance of maintaining human rights. In short, the US authorities demand more information on the passengers than the EU authorities are prepared to supply.

In 2016, the EU has adopted the *General Data Protection Regulation*,[76] and the 'PNR' Directive,[77] integrating the privacy legislation in these instruments.[78] The objective of this new set of rules is to give citizens back control over their personal data, and to simplify the regulatory environment for business.[79]

On the other side, the tradition of privacy protection in the US is less articulated. While the *Privacy Act* of 1974[80] provides individuals with a means to seek access to their records, and sets forth requirements for the responsible agencies its scope is restricted to US citizens only.

As a result of the above discrepancies,[81] and keeping in mind that transatlantic aviation must go on, the EU and the US have concluded agreements in 2004,[82] 2007 and

---

(2015), and R. Abeyratne, *Convention on International Civil Aviation. A Commentary* 353–361 (2013) and D. Korff and M. Georges, *Passenger Name Records, Data Mining and Data Protection: The Need for Strong.*

Safeguards, Report for the Consultative Committee of the Convention for the Protection of Individuals with regard to the Automatic Processing of Personal Data, Strasbourg, 15 June 2015.

76. EU Regulation 2016/679 on *the protection of natural persons with regard to the processing of personal data and on the free movement of such data*, and repealing Directive 95/46/EC (*General Data Protection Regulation*); it applies as from 25 May 2018.

77. EU Directive 2016/681 on *the use of Passenger Name Record* (PNR) *data for the prevention, detection, investigation and prosecution of terrorist offences and serious crime.* Member States, with the exception of Denmark, must bring into force the laws and administrative provisions necessary to comply with this Directive by 25 May 2018, as briefly commented by A. Masutti and Z. Török, *The EU Passenger Name Records Directive*, XIV(4) The Aviation and Space Journal 39–41 (2015).

78. On the same date (27 April 2016), EU Directive 2016/680 on *the protection of natural persons with regard to the processing of personal data by competent authorities for the purposes of the prevention, investigation, detection or prosecution of criminal offences or the execution of criminal penalties, and on the free movement of such data*, and repealing Council Framework Decision 2008/977/JHA was adopted, thus completing the new privacy/data protection framework.

79. *See*, W.M. Oude Alink, *The Regulation of Registered Traveller Programmes*, 13(2) Issues in Aviation Law and Policy 279–320 (2014), and T. Abeyratne, *Integrity of Travel Documents – The Wake Up Call from Flight MH370*, 63 Zeitschrift für Luft- und Weltraumrecht 238–249 (2014).

80. 5 U.S.C. § 552a; *see also*, the Freedom of Information Act (FOIA), 5 U.S.C. § 552. The US Department of Homeland Security is tasked to supervise these acts.

81. *See*, M.S.C. Taylor, *Flying from the EU to the US: Necessary Extraterritorial Legal Diffusion in the US-EU Passenger Name Record Agreement*, 19 Spanish Yearbook of International Law 221 (2016); K. Wilson, *Gone with the Wind? The Inherent Conflict Between API/PNR and Privacy Rights in an Increasingly Security Conscious World*, 41(3) Air & Space Law 229–264 (2016); P.M. Dupont, *Les données des dossiers passagers (PNR) dans le transport aérien*, 278(2) Revue française de droit aérien et spatial 111–128 (2016); R.I.R. Abeyratne, *Full Body Scanners at Airports – The Balance Between Privacy and State Responsibility*, 3(2) Journal of Transport Security 73–85 (2010) and sources mentioned there.

82. The compatibility of this agreement with EU privacy/data protection laws had been brought to the attention of the CJEU in 2006. The Court, however, annulled the Agreement on the ground of procedural reasons (Grand Chamber, judgment of 30 May 2006 – Joined Cases C-317/04 and C-318/04) as to which *see*, M. Nino, *The Protection of Personal Data in the Fight Against Terrorism. New Perspectives of PNR European Union Instruments in the Light of the Treaty of Lisbon*, Utrecht Law Review 73–74 (2010).

2012 in order to reconcile their positions, but they are not yet there.[83] It could also be envisaged that ICAO,[84] in close cooperation with IATA and the World Customs Organisations, work together for the creation of a solution in effort to enhance aviation security while respecting privacy rights.

However, given the absence of a global agreement, the incertitude of the status of the EU agreements concluded with a number of third countries which may have to be re-negotiated after the decisions of the CJEU and the adoption of domestic regulations by an increasing number of States PNR regulations, EU air carriers will find themselves 'trapped', that is, if they transmit the data they may be sanctioned pursuant to EU data protection laws; if they do not they may be sanctioned according to the third State's PNR legislation. Moreover, starting from 25 May 2018, non-EU air carriers operating flights to and from EU member States will be obliged to provide PNR data to specifically designated authorities of the Member State of landing/departure or stop-over according to the new PNR Directive. Thus, the risk of retaliation by third States will enhance in the absence of reciprocity.[85]

3.6 Unmanned Aircraft Systems (UAS)

A further development of automation that is increasingly being employed is that of UAS that is referred to in section 3.3.2.1 of Chapter 1 and in section 2.6.2 of Chapter 7.[86] The

---

83. The EU has also concluded PNR bilateral agreements with Australia as to which *see*, Council Decision 2012/381/EU of 13 December 2011 on the *conclusion of the Agreement between the European Union and Australia on the processing and transfer of Passenger Name Record (PNR) data by air carriers to the Australian Customs and Border Protection Service*, and Canada. The draft EU-Canada PNR agreement (2014) is pending waiting for the Opinion (1/15) of the CJEU requested by the European Parliament concerning its compatibility with EU treaties and the EU Charter of Fundamental Rights, especially Arts 7 and 8 on the right to privacy and data protection as to which *see also*, the preliminary Opinion of Advocate General Paolo Mengozzi of 8 September 2016 in which he argued that provisions of the draft PNR agreement with Canada are incompatible with EU primary law. This point of view may be relevant because other States requested the EU to negotiate a PNR agreement without which EU air carriers cannot provide data to third States with the risk of being sanctioned pursuant to EU data protection laws; however, negotiations were halted due to the pending Opinion. *See*, European Commission, Statement/15/5374, *Beginning of negotiations between Mexico and the European Union on PNR data transmission*, 14 July 2015. A reference to the requests submitted by the United Arab Emirates, South Korea, Brazil, Japan and Saudi Arabia is made in a question to the European Commission filed by a member of the European Parliament on 11 June 2015 (E-009612-15), to which Commissioner Avramopoulos replied that, "[in] addition to the negotiations already started with Mexico, the Commission has no plans at this stage to seek negotiation directives from the Council that would allow it to start negotiating bilateral PNR Agreements with any other third countries."
84. *See*, ICAO's Guidelines on Passenger Name Record (PNR) Data (Doc. 9944), and Annex 9, Recommended Practice 3.49 according to which contracting States requiring PNR data access should align with the ICAO Doc. 9944 and PNRGOV message implementation guidance material published by the World Customs Organization (WCO).
85. So far, third States have refrained from sanctioning EU air carriers for not providing PNR data. The author is very thankful to Dr Elena Carpanelli, University of Parma, Italy, for adding precious value to this section.
86. *See*, B. Scott, *The Law of Unmanned Aircraft Systems: An Introduction to the Current and Future Regulation under National, Regional and International Law* (2016); *see also*, A. Završnik, *Drones and Unmanned Aerial Systems: Legal and Social Implications for Security and Surveillance* (2016).

use of such systems is largely a domestic matter, rather than an international one at this moment in time and, therefore, does not fall within the remit of the Convention. However, States recognise the need for such systems to meet the same safety and operational standards as manned aircraft. Thus, UAS operations must be as safe as manned aircraft insofar as they must not present or create a greater hazard to persons, property vehicles or vessels whilst in the air or on the ground that are attributable to the operations of manned aircraft of equivalent class or category.[87] In its endeavours to ensure that UAS are under the mandate of ICAO, it has been vocal in its publications that Article 8 on Pilotless Aircraft encompasses UAS.[88] ICAO has however focused its efforts on a subcategory of UAS, namely remotely piloted UA, and published a Manual in 2015.[89]

Hence, the need exists to develop a system of UAS classification and appropriate regulation.[90] This work is on-going, for example, in Europe under EASA,[91] the European Organisation for Civil Aviation Equipment (EUROCAE), Working Group 73, and in the US.

4   AVIATION PERSONNEL

4.1   The Aircraft Commander

4.1.1   *Special Position*

One might compare the position of an aircraft commander with that of a ship's captain, but there are notable differences: generally, a journey by aircraft is shorter; passengers and crew are less numerous; and the freedom of movement on board is very much more limited. All these factors affect the relationships amongst those on board an aircraft, and contribute to making the aircraft commander's position quite different from that of a ship's captain.

The aircraft commander occupies a special position in aviation operations. Hence, it is most desirable that the rights and duties of a person in such a responsible position should be carefully defined as to which *see,* the next section.

---

87. UK CAA CAP 722 *Unmanned Aircraft System operations in UK Airspace.*
88. ICAO, *Unmanned Aircraft Systems* (UAS), Cir 328 AN/190 (2011).
89. ICAO, *Manual on Remotely Piloted Aircraft Systems* (RPAS) Doc 10019 AN/507 (2015).
90. *See,* A. Masutti, *Proposals for the Regulation of Unmanned Air Vehicle Use in Common Airspace,* 34(1) Air & Space Law 1–12 (2009); S. Kaiser, *UAV's: Their Integration into Non-Segregated Airspace,* 36(2) Air & Space Law (2011); S. Kaiser, *Legal Aspects of Unmanned Aerial Vehicles,* 55 Zeitschrift für Luft-und Weltraumrecht 344 (2006); J. Straub, J. Vacek and J. Nordlie, *Considering Regulation of Small Unmanned Aerial Systems in the United States,* 39(4/5) Air & Space Law 275–294 (2014); M. Ells, *Unmanned State Aircraft and the Exercise of Due Regard,* 13(2) Issues in Aviation Law and Policy 321–360 (2014) and A. Roma, *Remotely Piloted Aircraft Systems: Privacy and Data Protection Implications,* 13(1) The Aviation and Space Journal 22–34 (2014).
91. *See,* section 2 of Chapter 7.

4.1.2 Powers and Duties

The status of the aircraft commander continues to develop in the decades since 1980.[92] For instance, the above-mentioned role in the keeping of peace and order on board for the sake of safety of the flight has become a major subject of attention. No doubt this has to do with the emergence of 'unruly passengers' who engage in what is termed 'air rage', a subject that will be referred to in section 2.9 of Chapter 12. The position of the commander seems more and more to change from that of a mere pilot into that of a flight manager.

The powers and responsibilities of the aircraft commander may be categorised as follows. The first and foremost task concerns the responsibility for the condition of the aircraft and the welfare of the crew, the preparations for the flight and its successful completion.[93] This task includes the commander's duty to obtain the proper flight documents and the cargo manifests and to carry out pre-take-off checks, as laid down in Article 29 of the Chicago Convention. As a corollary, the commander must issue strict orders to crew and passengers. This role is especially important in the event of criminal offences being committed on board. Those powers in criminal law have been adequately defined in the Tokyo Convention of 1963, in particular Article 6 thereof, and The Hague Convention of 1970.[94]

In addition, the commander has the authority to undertake all necessary measures to ensure the safe completion of the flight.[95] The commander must have authority, for instance, to have repairs carried out when necessary, and to arrange for fresh supplies on behalf of the company by which he is employed.[96] When no airline officials are present in a particular country, the commander should be empowered to act as the official representative of the company.[97]

As the granting of such authority and duties is entirely at the discretion of the company it would be better to draw up international rules to cover this point, making it compulsory for contracting States to adapt their own legislation accordingly. The administrative duties of the commander include the registration of births and deaths on board an aircraft, the authority to perform marriages or to act as the competent authority for drawing up wills.[98] Also, the commander decides whether and in what way to render assistance in search and rescue operations in the event of an accident, in accordance with the provisions of the Convention.[99]

---

92. Study on the *Legal Status of the Aircraft Commander*, ICAO Doc. C-WP/6946 (26 October 1979).
93. ICAO, Annex 2 (2005).
94. *See*, section 3 of Chapter 12.
95. ICAO Annex 2, 2.4. *See*, E.E. Anderson, W. Watson, D.M. Marshall & K.M. Johnson, *A Legal Analysis of 14 C.F.R. Part 91 'See and Avoid' Rules to Identify Provisions Focused on Pilot Responsibilities to 'See and Avoid' in the National Airspace System*, 80(1) Journal of Air Law and Commerce 53 (2015).
96. On the retirement age of pilots under EU and German law, *see*, Case C-447/09 of the CJEU.
97. *See also*, P. Paul Fitzgerald, *Air Marshals: The Need for Legal Certainty*, 75(2) Journal of Air Law and Commerce 357–406 (2010).
98. *See*, Art. 7 of the Draft Convention on the *Legal Status of the Aircraft Commander*, ICAO Doc. 4006 (1947).
99. *See also*, Annex 12 of ICAO on *Search and Rescue* (2004).

4.2 Other Flying Personnel

This category includes anyone who normally performs duties during the flight and whose presence on board throughout the flight is essential: the co-pilot, other flight crewmembers, the flight attendants and potentially air marshals as security is increasing in importance.[100] Flying personnel may be categorised as persons in charge or command of the actual flying or technical matters during the flight, and persons performing ancillary services, for instance cabin attendants.

In terms of private international air law, the civil liability of aircraft operators and flying personnel is regulated by the Montreal Convention 1999 and the Warsaw regime which have been discussed in Chapter 4.[101] The aircraft commander and other crew members may be considered as 'servants' of the airline. Apart from these international agreements, general law and employment contracts govern liability.

4.3 Flight Duty Times

4.3.1 The ICAO Regime

This is an area of potential conflict as demonstrated by the continuing struggle and debate in relation to the formulation of norms for Flight Duty Times.[102] Annex 6 to the Chicago Convention (1944) requires that States shall establish regulations specifying limitations applicable to flight duty times, flight duty periods, duty periods and rest periods, based upon scientific principles and knowledge; thus ensuring that flight crew are performing at an adequate level of alertness.[103] This State responsibility is translated into an obligation under Annex 6 upon an operator to establish a fatigue management scheme or programme that is acceptable to the regulatory authority. How this Standard is implemented at the State level will depend to a certain extent upon the nature or type of operations conducted. For example, long-haul operations may require a different flight time limitation scheme from that applicable to multi-sector short-haul operations.

Similar requirements apply to personnel engaged in other areas of activity, such as air traffic controllers. These requirements represent a recognition that 'human factors' are frequently cited as causal factors in an accident investigation report and that, very often, such human performance levels may be influenced by lifestyle, work patterns and practices and tiredness on the part of flight crew and other personnel.[104]

---

100. *See*, 49 U.S. Code § 44917.
101. *See*, sections 3.3.1.2, 3.3.1.3, 3.3.2.3 and 3.3.2.4.
102. *See*, for example, Flight Global, *Fight over flight-time limitations kicks off*, 23 December 2010.
103. Annex 6, Part I, Chapter 4, para. 4.10 and Appendix 7 (2016).
104. *See*, N.N. DuBose, *Flightcrew Member Duty and Rest Requirements: Does the Proposed Legislation Put to Rest the Concern over Pilot Fatigue?* 76(2) Journal of Air Law and Commerce 229–252 (2011); *see also*, section 2 of Chapter 7.

315

4.4   Ground Personnel

The term 'Ground handling' covers a wide variety of services required by airlines in order to operate flights. These services include areas such as maintenance, fuel and freight handling. Ground handling also covers services like passenger check-in, catering, baggage handling and transport within the airport itself.

Since 1997, the provision of ground handling services in the EU is covered by Directive 96/67/EC. The Directive opened up ground handling services to competition. Prior to this, monopolies were the norms for ground handling services at EU airports and many airlines complained about high prices and poor quality service.

The legal status of ground personnel has hardly any basis in international law while,[105] at a national level, it enjoys the protection of rules applicable to aviation personnel generally only in isolated cases. Consequently, the position of ground personnel is at best covered merely by general provisions of domestic law and employment contracts. In this context the different interpretations given to the terms 'agent' and 'servant' in domestic and in the Montreal Convention, 1999, and the Warsaw regime and respectively are sources of legal problems.[106]

The category of ground personnel deserves a special mention in connection with the vital role played by the air traffic control (ATC) services, whose duty it is to ensure a safe and orderly flow of traffic. A strike action undertaken by this group of personnel may have the most serious consequences for thousands of people not even remotely involved in the conflict. Liability of their employer, usually a governmental authority, may be assumed and has been upheld in court on a number of occasions.[107]

5   ACCIDENT INVESTIGATION AND PREVENTION[108]

5.1   The Investigation

5.1.1   Basic Principles

Also included in the Chicago Convention are uniform rules relating to the investigation of and enquiries into accidents and serious incidents. These are to be found in Article 26, which reads as follows:

> In the event of an accident to an aircraft of a contracting State occurring in the territory of another contracting State, and involving death or serious injury, or

---

105. European Commission, *Air: Ground handling*, www.ec.europa.eu/transport/modes/air/ airports/ground_handling_market_en.htm. *See*, Council Directive 96/67/EC of 15 October 1996 on access to the *ground handling market at Community airports* as discussed in section 5.1.2 of Chapter 3; for a discussion of liability of ground handlers *see*, section 3.4 of Chapter 4.
106. *See*, sections 3.3.1.2, 3.3.1.3, 3.3.2.3 and 3.3.2.4 of Chapter 4.
107. *See*, A. Trimarchi, *Strike as an Extraordinary Circumstance under EU Reg. 261/2004: Some Considerations*, XV(4) The Aviation & Space Journal 2–13 (2016).
108. The author of this book is deeply indebted to Ms. J.M. Annemarie Schuite for her meticulous revision of this chapter and her expert efforts to update in particular materials on accidents investigation and enhance the quality of this section.

indicating serious technical defect in the aircraft or air navigation facilities, the State in which the accident occurs will institute an inquiry into the circumstances of the accident, in accordance, so far as its laws permit, with the procedure which may be recommended by the International Civil Aviation Organization. The State in which the aircraft is registered shall be given the opportunity to appoint observers to be present at the inquiry and the State holding the inquiry shall communicate the report and findings in the matter to that State.

The procedure for conducting such an investigation is set out in Annex 13.[109] This Annex is accompanied by ICAO guidance material, some of which will be discussed in the following sections. An explanation of the structure of an accident investigation authority and its responsibilities, the planning of the investigation, including the technical parts of it, distinguishing between major and small investigations, the notification of accidents and incidents, and manage actions at the accident site including initial responses and rescue operations, and conditions for the formulation of the final report, can be found in the *Manual of Aircraft Accident and Incident Investigation*.[110]

The sole purpose of an accident or incident investigation within the meaning of Annex 13 is the prevention of future accidents and incidents but not to apportion blame or liability.[111] This point comes back in the trend towards establishing a *just culture* in accident investigation as to which *see*, section 5.2, below.

Publication of the investigation report is also a requirement but Article 26 does not specify a time limit. This weakness is occasionally illustrated by the unwillingness of States to publish reports that might throw an unfavourable light on their aviation safety rules or practices.[112]

5.1.2 The Independence of the Investigation Authority

Proper, thorough and independent accident investigation, can foster aviation safety which can be achieved by an independent investigation authority conducting an in-depth investigation into the causes or probable causes of such an occurrence. The accident investigation authority has to be objective and impartial, and also perceived to be so. It has to withstand political or other interferences or pressures, and to be

---

109. Annex 13, *Aircraft Accident and Incident Investigation* (2016).
110. *See*, ICAO Doc 9756, *Manuel of Aircraft Accident and Incident Investigation*, Part I/*Organization and Planning* (2015); Part II/*Procedures and Checklists* (2012); Part III/*Investigation* (2012); Part IV/*Reporting* (2014).
111. Standard 3.1 of Annex 13; as to which *see* an interesting article from O. Rijsdijk, *A Particular Aircraft Accident Litigation Scenario*, 34(2) Air & Space Law 57–86 (2009); *see also*, C.A.S. Challinor, *The Decision of the English High Court in* Rogers & Anor v. Hoyle: *Clipping the Wings of the Principles of Air Accident Investigation*, 39(1) Air & Space Law 83–90 (2014); *see also*, S. Foreman, *Aviation Accidents and the French Courts*, 20(1) Air & Space Lawyer (2005).
112. *See*, H.L. van Traa-Engelsman, *The Dutch Parliamentary Inquiry into the Bijlmermeer Air Disaster – Lessons to Be Learned for International Air Transportation*, in: M. Benkö und W. Kröll (eds), *Air and Space Law in the 21st Century*, Liber Amicorum K.H. Böckstiegel 216–230 (2001).

separated from a State's aviation authority or other authorities that might interfere with the conduct or objectivity of an investigation.[113]

These basic principles were already set out in the first edition of the ICAO *Manual of Aircraft Accident and Incident Investigation*.[114] However, ICAO felt the need to strengthen these principles and emphasise the importance of an independent accident investigation authority. A new definition was introduced with the latest amendment of Annex 13.[115] An accident investigation authority is:

> The authority designated by a State as responsible for aircraft accident and incident investigations within the context of this Annex.[116]

The amendment also introduced a firm obligation for States to establish an independent investigation authority:

> A State shall establish an accident investigation authority that is independent from State aviation authorities and other entities that could interfere with the conduct or objectivity of an investigation.[117]

Functional independence of the State aviation authority can avoid a real or perceived conflict of interest, enhance the credibility of investigations and safeguard the integrity of the investigation authority. Furthermore the independency enhances the ability to properly and adequately identify the causes and contributing factors of the accident.[118]

States lacking resources to establish such an independent investigation authority, should consider implementation of a regional accident and incident investigation organisation.[119] States participating in such an organisation share human and financial resources. It will also allow investigators in the region to acquire experience, eliminate duplication of efforts, and achieve independence of investigations. ICAO's *Manual on Regional Accident and Incident Investigation Organization* provides information and guidance on how to establish and manage a regional accident and incident investigation organisation.[120] Agreements establishing such a regional organisation must be registered with ICAO.[121]

---

113. *See*, C.A.S. Challinor, *Accident Investigators Are the Guardians of Public Safety: The Importance of Safeguarding the Independence of Air Accident Investigations as Illustrated by Recent Accidents*, 42(1) Air & Space Law 43–70 (2017).
114. *See*, ICAO Doc 9756, *Manuel of Aircraft Accident and Incident Investigation*, Part I, Organization and Planning, Chapter 2: *The accident investigation authority* (2000).
115. Amendment 15 of Annex 13, as applicable since 10 November 2016; *see also*, ICAO Working Paper A39-WP/271, Assembly – 39th Session, Technical Commission, Agenda item 36.
116. Annex 13, Chapter 1, *Definitions* (2016).
117. Standard 3.2, Annex 13.
118. *See*, ICAO, Doc 9756, *Manuel of Aircraft Accident and Incident Investigation*, Part I, Organization and Planning, Chapter 2: The accident investigation authority (2015).
119. ICAO Doc 9946, *Manual On Regional Accident And Incident Investigation Organization* (2011).
120. For example, the *Grupo Regional de Investigación de Accidentes Aéreos* (GRIAA) established in Central America.
121. *See*, Art. 83 of the Chicago Convention.

In a number of States, separate accident investigating agencies for the various modes of transport are merged into a single national agency,[122] as exemplified by the US National Transportation Safety Board (NTSB) and the Dutch Safety Board including separate Chambers for the investigation of aviation, maritime and railway accidents.

While Article 26 of the Chicago Convention and Annex 13 identify the State of Occurrence as being responsible for instituting an investigation, Annex 13 also provides the possibility for that State to delegate the whole or parts of an investigation to another State or a regional accident and incident investigation organisation.[123] For instance, the investigation into Malaysia Airlines MH17 accident in Ukraine was conducted by the Dutch Safety Board upon the request of the Ukraine authorities.[124]

Besides the State leading the investigation, a number of other involved States have a right to play a role in the investigation. The State of Registry, State of the Operator, State of Design or State of Manufacture[125] are entitled to appoint an accredited representative to participate in the investigation.[126] Those accredited representatives can be accompanied by advisers.[127] The technical advisors appointed by manufacturers can furnish the necessary technical knowledge of the aircraft type, engines or avionics.

In the aftermath of an aircraft accident or incident various authorities are likely to be involved in the investigation. Thus, accident and incident investigation is governed by a number of principles which are listed below. Annex 13 stresses, in the *first* place, the need to coordinate the investigation with the judicial authorities,[128] but on the other hand it ensures full independence in the conduct of the investigation by the investigation authority.[129]

Secondly, Annex 13 recommends that 'any judicial or administrative proceedings to apportion blame or liability should be separated from any investigation under the provisions of this Annex.'[130] This principle is a corollary of the principle pertaining to the protection of Safety Information.

---

122. *See,* Griselda Capaldo, *Investigation of Aircraft Accidents and Incidents in Latin America,* Part I and II, 52 Zeitschrift für Luft- und Weltraumrecht 332, 513 (2003).
123. Standard 5.1 and 5.1.2, Annex 13.
124. https://www.onderzoeksraad.nl/en/onderzoek/2049/investigation-crash-mh17-17-july-2014 /onderzoek/1568/dutch-safety-board-investigation.
125. *See,* Chapter 1, *Definitions,* Annex 13.
126. Standard 5.18 of Annex 13.
127. Standard 5.19 and 5.20 of Annex 13.
128. Standard 5.10 of Annex 13.
129. Standard 5.4 of Annex 13; *see,* P.S. Dempsey, *Independence of Aviation Safety Investigation Authorities: Keeping the Foxes from the Henhouse,* 75 Journal of Air Law and Commerce 223 (2010).
130. Recommendation 5.4.1 of Annex 13; *see also,* ICAO Assembly Resolution A38-8 (2016) – *Conflict of Interest in Civil Aviation,* inviting States to examine the adequacy of national regimes designed to manage conflicts of interest with a view to ensuring and improving transparency and accountability.

5.1.3 Protection of Safety Information

Standard 5.12 of Annex 13 specifies types of records that are collected by safety investigation authorities. The main objective concerns safeguarding continued access by safety accident investigation authorities to essential information during the course of an investigation by preventing the misuse of the safety-related data. The use of investigation records for purposes other than accident and incident investigation, such as criminal, civil, administrative or disciplinary proceedings against involved organisations or personnel, may inhibit future availability of such records and therefore have an adverse effect on investigation activities.

The accident investigation authority is responsible for protecting the accident and incident records listed in Standard 5.12.[131] It concerns records generated or obtained during the conduct of an investigation instituted in accordance with Annex 13, such as Cockpit Voice Recorders (CVRs), Airborne Image Recorders (AIRs) and transcripts, statements, communication between persons involved in the operation of an aircraft, ATC communications, opinions and analyses generated by the investigation authority and the draft and final investigation report.[132]

Standard 5.12 does not explicitly stipulate the protection of the Flight Data Recorder (FDR) or its transcripts. However, provisions for the protection and use of flight recorder recordings in routine operations outside the scope of an Annex 13 investigation are contained in Annex 6 and Annex 19.[133] Furthermore, States may decide to apply Standard 5.12 on any other records obtained or generated by the accident investigation authority in the course of an investigation.[134]

The protection offered is not absolute but since the latest amendment 15 of Annex 13 the safeguards for safety information are strongly enhanced. States shall not make records available for purposes other than accident and incident investigation, unless:

> the competent authority designated by that State determines, in accordance with national laws and subject to Appendix 2 and 5.12.5, that their disclosure or use outweighs the likely adverse domestic and international impact such action may have on that or any future investigation.[135]

The right of decision-making granted to the 'designated authority' implies a subjective discretion as to when disclosure outweighs the likely adverse impact of non-disclosure on aviation safety. As a consequence, this provision creates uncertainty by leaving the final decision on the disclosure to the designated competent authority of the State. To decrease this uncertainty, amendment 15 to Annex 13 introduces a whole

---

131. *See*, Standard 5.4 (b) of Annex 13.
132. Standard 5.12 of Annex 13; *see also*, ICAO Doc 10053, *Manual on Protection of Safety Information*, para. 2.4 (2016).
133. *See*, Annex 6, *Operation of an Aircraft*, Part I – International Commercial Air Transport – Aeroplanes (2016), including *Amendment 40B to Annex 6* as adopted 2 March 2016 and applicable as of 7 November 2019; *see also*, Annex 19, *Safety Management* (2013), including Amendment 1 to Annex 19, as adopted 2 March 2016 and applicable as of 7 November 2019.
134. Recommendation 5.12.1 of Annex 13.
135. Standard 5.12 of Annex 13.

new Appendix 2 on the protection of accident and incident investigation records,[136] accompanied by the *Manual on Protection of Safety Information*.[137]

Appendix 2, part of the SARPS of Annex 13, intends to assist the designated competent authority in making a determination as required by Standard 5.12, by means of a balancing test to be administered on requests for disclosure or use of records listed in Chapter 5, Standard 5.12 in criminal, civil, administrative or disciplinary proceedings. This balancing test requires a weighing of factors, either in favour of protection or in favour of disclosure.[138] Prior to applying the balancing test the competent authority must determine if a material fact in question in the proceedings cannot be determined without that record.[139]

Meanwhile, courts are starting their own investigations in order to create transparency in the causes of the accident and to assist the victims in finding the appropriate remedies. For instance, in the Überlingen cases courts "went beyond the Accident Investigation Report's analysis of the technology."[140] It remains to be seen whether this instance will materialise in a tendency and, if so, which effects that tendency will yield with respect to the investigation conducted by the accident safety authorities.

5.1.4 *Reporting System*

Annex 13 requires the establishment of a mandatory incident reporting system to facilitate the gathering of information on safety deficiencies.[141] Further, the introduction of a voluntary incident reporting system to ensure the collection of information, which is not covered by the mandatory system, is also desirable.[142] In case the State decides to establish such a voluntary system, it is under an obligation to provide a non-punitive system and to implement measures to protect the sources of information.[143]

The ICAO *Safety Management Manual*[144] provides guidance in respect of mandatory and voluntary incident reporting. These aspects of Annex 13 are crucial in balancing the improvement of aviation safety on the one hand and the proper administration of justice on the other hand.[145] Establishing a *just culture* in accident investigation forms another crucial element, as to which *see*, section 5.2, below.

---

136. Annex 13, Appendix 2 on the *protection of accident and incident investigation records* (2016).
137. ICAO Doc 10053, *Manual on Protection of Safety Information* (2016).
138. Standard 4.2 of Appendix 2 to Annex 13 (2016).
139. Standard 4.1 of Appendix 2 to Annex 13 (2016).
140. *See*, Dr Hanna Schebesta, *Risk Regulation Through Liability Allocation: Transnational Product Liability and the Role of Certification*, 42(2) Air & Space Law (2017), section 3.
141. Standard 8.1 of Annex 13.
142. Recommendation 8.2 of Annex 13, now upgraded to a Standard.
143. Standard 8.3 of Annex 13.
144. ICAO Doc 9859, *Safety Management Manual (SMM)* (2013).
145. *See*, Mildred Trögeler, *Criminalisation of Air Accidents and the Creation of a Just Culture* to be published in Diritto dei Trasporti 2-44 (2011); *see also*, Yang, *Flight Accidents and Criminal Responsibility in China*, 34 Air & Space Law 393–402 (2009).

As explained in section 2.2 above, SARPs of ICAO have to be implemented in national or local law. Certain States have constitutional or other legal problems with the implementation of the principles mentioned above, and notify ICAO therefore of differences between their national rules and practices, and the relevant ICAO Standard, for instance, Standard 5.12.

The EU has adopted Regulation 996/2010 for this purpose, as to which *see*, section 4.1 of Chapter 7. This regulation is designed to achieve harmonisation among Member States in the matter of accident investigation.

5.2 Towards a 'Just Culture'

In July 2016, the eleventh edition of Annex 13 became applicable. Until then, Chapter 7 on Accident Prevention Measures contained a recommendation regarding the introduction and use of formal incident-reporting systems for accident prevention. Due to its non-mandatory nature, the unwillingness of States to comply with this recommendation has prevented the disclosure and dissemination of vital information. This norm was upgraded to a Standard with effect from 2001 and has been implemented in the EU Directive on Mandatory Occurrence Reporting.[146]

As said, a key element of Annex 13 concerns the independence of the investigating safety authority, also in relation to the judicial process. Unfortunately, many States find it difficult to achieve this objective either through lack of resources or because the State system accords precedence to the judicial authorities' investigative powers. This latter feature creates difficulty in fostering a 'just culture' regime in which people feel free to report matters of concern without the fear of self-incrimination.[147] The 'just culture' principles are reflected in the changes to Annex 13 in that additional safeguards against disclosure of statements and other sensitive data are introduced as to which *see*, sections 5.1.3 and 5.1.4 above.

The Just Culture aims to strike the right balance between the need to improve aviation safety and the recognition of the judicial system's legitimate right to investigate and prosecute criminal actions. This purpose is more critical at times when victims supported by media request transparency of the causes of the accident and sanctions in case criminal behaviour is at stake. Human errors are reported to be a principal cause of accidents. The number of cases regarding the behaviour of, principally, the aircraft commander, air traffic controllers and technical officers preceding the accident is therefore increasing.[148]

---

146. As to which *see*, section 4.1 of Chapter 7.
147. *See*, B.L. Ottley, *Airline Immunity for Reporting Suspicious Activities under the Aviation and Transportation Security Act: Air Wisconsin Corp. v. Hoeper*, 13(2) Issues in Aviation Law and Policy (2014).
148. *See*, ASDNews of 5 December 2010, *Human error to blame for Russian crash*; *see also*, tribunal of Bülach, Switzerland, on the criminal proceedings regarding the mid-air collision above Überlingen, Southern Germany, on 1 July 2002 (message of 4 September 2007); Sarah Langston with the blog faculty, *Brazil judge convicts two US pilots but suspends prison*, 17 May 2011; Message from Clyde and Co dated December 2010, *The blame game*; the Concorde criminal proceedings before the French court of Pontoise ruling that Continental Airlines and one of its

The Just Culture is based on three key principles:

Firstly, the determination of appropriate safeguards, which will ensure that individuals involved in safety investigations are not punished for their reported actions or omissions.

Secondly, that the protection granted shall not apply to cases in which unacceptable behaviour is involved, such as wilful misconduct or gross negligence.

Thirdly, the improvement of aviation safety should be achieved by encouraging full contribution to safety investigations.[149]

To ensure that the Just Culture concept can be applied in practice, its principles have to be laid down in a suitable regulatory framework providing the indispensable legal certainty. The balance between the various underlying objectives has not yet been formulated at the international level. European measures[150] shed a similar light on the subject as the matter is not only dictated by international rules but also influenced by national jurisdictions and policy objectives. Hence, practice will demonstrate how accident and incident investigation will be governed by the Just Culture concept. National law plays a predominant role there.

In conclusion the tendency in some States to 'criminalise' human error on the part of pilots and others undermines the legitimate efforts of the international community to achieve a truly just culture, to the possible detriment of the safety of passengers and others. Just culture aims at achieving the balance between the safety culture promoted by ICAO, and transparency of legal proceedings as mandated by national, including constitutional law.

6 CONCLUDING REMARKS

Uniformity of rulemaking helps to enhance safety, as an aircraft should be operated in any part of the world.[151] Equivalent standards, and adequate use of the same language, that is, English, are crucial for worldwide understanding of the navigation of international air services. Rules and instructions which apply in one State should be understood by the operators of every other State. This is the august objective laid down in the Chicago Convention which ICAO strives to implement by the establishment of SARPs and other norms.

---

engineers were guilty of involuntary homicide as a result of the investigation of the 2000 accident involving the Air France Concorde killing 113 people, as to which *see also*, Maud Marian and Sean Gates, *The Concorde Criminal Trial in France*, 36 Air & Space Law 121–128 (2011); *see also*, Regula Dettling-Ott, *Criminal Liability of Airline Pilots: Three Recent Decisions*, 13(1) Air & Space Law 4–17 (1988).

149. *See*, Mildred Trögeler, *Criminalisation of Air Accidents and the Creation of a Just Culture*, Diritto dei Trasporti 2–44 (2011).
150. As to which *see*, section 4.1 of Chapter 7.
151. *See also*, R.I.R. Abeyratne, *International Obligations as Regards Safety in International Civil Aviation*, The Aeronautical Journal of the Royal Aeronautical Society 457–466 (1997).

Realism dictates that States do not always comply with their commitments under the Chicago Convention. Lack of human and financial resources may prevent them from implementing and applying these global rules.

If the emergence of automation in civil aviation does not appear to have had much impact as far as the legal position of the carrier is concerned, this does not take away from the fact that there are a number of important related issues requiring closer attention in the near future. The *first* of these is the problem of jurisdiction with regard to cross-border data exchange. The *second* is the time lag between the moment of transmission and that of the receipt. *Thirdly*, who is to be held liable for faults occurring during the exchange? Will it be possible to exclude criminal liability in such cases? There are no uniform answers to these questions as they depend on national law, court decisions and development of views on the subject.

Also, air transport is increasingly dependent on high-tech equipment supplied by third parties which may be vulnerable for attacks, including cyber-attacks. However, such apparatus should be absolutely sound and serviceable. Failing that, suppliers may have to face serious claims for damages, for instance, under product liability legislation which is discussed in Chapter 8. In view of the magnitude of the interests at stake global action should be undertaken so as to arrive at an international agreement on this important matter.

Accident and incident investigation is a subject that will continue to be a matter of prime importance. Various organisations – including but not limited to ICAO, Eurocontrol, the European Commission and EASA[152] – are focusing their attention on the question of how to resolve the dilemma between the principal objective of promoting aviation safety and national policy and constitutional provisions designed to enhance transparency and to criminalise behaviour. That dilemma has yet to be resolved through the concept which has been termed 'Just Culture' which may evolve in the years to come.

---

152. *See,* section 2 of Chapter 7.

Regional Safety Organisations

1 FROM A GLOBAL APPROACH TO REGIONAL INITIATIVES[1]

This chapter examines aspects of different regional aviation safety systems that are in place around the world. Aviation safety is of key importance to civil aviation which is clearly reflected in international legal instruments, such as the Chicago Convention and its accompanying Annexes. The drafters of this Convention envisaged regulating aviation, especially aviation safety, at a global level as service providers and operators have to be understood in every corner of the world. However, in the words of Mr A. Berle, chairman of the conference leading to the adoption of the Chicago Convention in 1994:

> All agree that an effective form of world organization for air purposes is necessary. This does not exclude regional organizations having a primary interest in the problems of their particular areas; but no regional organization or group of regional organizations can effectively deal with the new problems resulting from interoceanic and intercontinental flying.[2]

These words explain perhaps why cooperation at a regional level is hardly provided for in the Chicago Convention. Apart from a permissive provision[3] and the operation of joint operating organisations requiring geographical affinity,[4] the Chicago Convention fosters the planning and development of air transport at a global level.[5]

---

1. The Editor is most grateful to Benjamyn I. Scott for this excellent and complete contribution on Regional Safety Organisations and for the invaluable feedback received from Rita Uva Sousa during the writing of this Chapter.
2. *See, Proceedings of the International Civil; Aviation Conference*, Chicago 1 November–7 December 1944, US Department of State Publication 2820 11 (1948).
3. *See*, Art. 55(a).
4. Chicago Convention, Art. 77.
5. *See*, the Preamble, and, among others, Art. 44(a).

While regional aviation safety is not a new phenomenon as examples can be found prior to the Chicago Convention, such as the Havana Convention (1928) that was ratified by sixteen American States,[6] the importance and growth of regional cooperation in the field of aviation safety took massive steps in the latter part of the twentieth century and has continued into the twenty-first century.

This chapter will principally present an overview of the advanced role that the EU, including European Aviation Safety Agency (EASA), henceforth also referred to as either EASA or the Agency, has adopted in this area. Regions in other parts of the world, while not being as legally advanced, also have been active in the promotion of aviation safety. Thus, the second part of this chapter will be dedicated to these, including the extensive work carried out by ICAO.[7] Finally, accident and incident investigation under EU rules will be examined as this plays a vital role in the advancement of aviation safety.

2 AVIATION SAFETY IN THE EU[8]

2.1 Introduction

The Joint Aviation Authorities (JAA), very much like many of the regional safety organisation discussed below, had a coordinative role, whereby it coordinated the activities of its Member States' national aviation authorities for aircraft certification.[9] Further to this, it also allowed the national aviation authorities to cooperate in other aviation safety-related matters, such as: licensing, operations and maintenance of aircraft. The JAA's main objective was then to develop and implement common safety regulatory standards and procedures to remove duplication between the participating Member States by encouraging the mutual recognition of these certificates.

The JAA was not a regulatory body as such competencies remained with the relevant national aviation authorities. As a result, this was not an ideal mechanism for 'achieving a uniform application and enforcement of aviation-related safety matters throughout Europe, including the obligations arising from the Chicago Convention.'[10] While EU regional aviation safety had been regulated since early 1990 with Regulation

---

6. American Convention on Commercial Aviation. The Convention was signed by twenty-one States and was finally ratified by sixteen: Bolivia, Brazil, Chile, Costa Rica, Cuba, the Dominican Republic, Ecuador, Guatemala, Haiti, Honduras, Mexico, Nicaragua, Panama, Uruguay, US, and Venezuela; *see also*, section 2.5 of Chapter 1.
7. *See*, M. Ratajczek, *Regional Aviation Safety Organisations: Enhancing Air Transport Safety Through Regional Cooperation* (PhD Leiden) (2014).
8. *See*, S. Hobe, N. Ruckteschell and D. Heffernan, *Cologne Compendium on Air Law in Europe* (2013).
9. *See*, R. Sousa Uva, *Legal and Regulatory Review: EASA's New Fields of Competence in the Certification of Aerodromes*, 5(1) Journal of Airport Management 60–71 (2010).
10. *See*, G. Boccardo, *European Aviation Safety Agency*, in: B. Scott (ed.), *The Law of Unmanned Aircraft Systems: An Introduction to the Current and Future Regulation under National, Regional and International Law* (2016).

3922/91[11] which, among others, introduced automatic recognition of certificates and legal source for Joint Aviation Requirements (JAR), it was felt that more than coordination is needed to be done in this area.

Thus, in 2002, the European Aviation Safety (EASA), was created as a specialised Agency of the EU by EC Regulation 1592/2002.[12] The legal basis for this in the EU is Article 100(2) of the TFEU[13] which gives the EU competencies for air transport. Regulation 1592/2002 could not dissolve the JAA, as it was established by the 'Cyprus Agreement' which was an international agreement,[14] rather there was a transition period, which included a temporary cooperation arrangement with the JAA, which ended in 2008 with the adoption of EC Regulation 216/2008.[15] Participation in EASA is more limited than the JAA as it only includes the 28 EU Member States and the four States of the European Free Trade Association (EFTA).[16] However, as membership is broader than the EU, it is possible, for example, for the UK to join under the Brexit scenario.[17]

2.2 Scope and Objectives

Pursuant to Article 2(1) of Regulation 216/2008, the Agency's main objective is to 'establish and maintain a high uniform level of civil aviation safety in Europe.'[18] In addition to this, Article 2(2) then sets forth a number of additional objectives.[19] From this list, four main areas can be identified: certification, rulemaking, standardisation and research and safety analysis.

---

11. EEC Council Regulation 3922/91 of 16 December 1991 on the *harmonization of technical requirements and administrative procedures in the field of civil aviation.*
12. EC Regulation 1592/2002 of 15 July 2002 on *common rules in the field of civil aviation and establishing a European Aviation Safety Agency.*
13. European Union, *Consolidated Version of the Treaty on the Functioning of the European Union.*
14. Arrangement Concerning the *Development, the Acceptance and the Implementation of Joint Aviation Requirements,* agreed on 6 December 1989 by Austria, Belgium, Cyprus, Denmark, Finland, France, Federal Republic of Germany, Greece, Hungary, Iceland, Ireland, Italy, Luxembourg, Malta, Monaco, The Netherlands, Norway, Poland, Portugal, Spain, Sweden, Switzerland, Turkey, UK and Yugoslavia.
15. EC Regulation 216/2008 of 20 February 2008 on *common rules in the field of civil aviation and establishing a European Aviation Safety Agency,* and repealing Council Directive 91/670/EEC, EC Regulation 1592/2002 and Directive 2004/36/EC.
16. Iceland, Liechtenstein, Norway and Switzerland.
17. *See,* Clyde & Co., *The EU Air Law Consequences of Brexit for the UK* (June 2016), and Lazar Vrbaski, *Flying into the Unknown: The UK's Air Transport Relations with the European Union and Third Countries Following 'Brexit',* 41(6) Air & Space Law 421–444 (2016), at 430–432.
18. *See,* EASA, *Preliminary Safety Review – 2017,* in which it is stated that one operator based in an EASA Member State crashed fatally in 2016, next to sixteen accidents and 100 serious incidents, that is, three and sixteen per million flights respectively. The most relevant key risk areas concern Aircraft Upset, Runway Excursion and Aircraft System Failure, in conjunction with associated safety factors, that is, flight crew awareness, monitoring of aircraft parameters, handling of technical failures and crew resource management (CRM).
19. Regulation 216/2008, Art. 2(2):

> 2. Additional objectives are, in the fields covered by this Regulation, as follows:

> (a) to ensure a high uniform level of environmental protection;

The Agency, while having a broad scope of competencies, is limited to *civil* aircraft.[20] For example, Article 1(2)(a) resonates Article 3 of the Chicago Convention, as it states:

> This Regulation shall not apply to: products, parts, appliances, personnel and organisations referred to in paragraph 1(a) and (b) while carrying out military, customs, police, search and rescue, firefighting, coastguard or similar activities or services.

The Member States shall nevertheless have due regard as far as practicable to the objectives of this Regulation, pursuant to Article (1)(2)(a), for such specified aircraft.

There are also a number of aircraft types that are listed in Annex II of Regulation 216/2008 which are also outside of the scope of EASA's competencies.[21] For example, Annex II(i) excludes 'unmanned aircraft with an operating mass of no more than 150 kg'. Due to the increased use of small UAS in Europe, the rationale for this inclusion in Annex II is no longer justified. Therefore, it is likely to be deleted during the next

---

(b) to facilitate the free movement of goods, persons and services;

(c) to promote cost-efficiency in the regulatory and certification processes and to avoid duplication at national and European level;

(d) to assist Member States in fulfilling their obligations under the Chicago Convention, by providing a basis for a common interpretation and uniform implementation of its provisions, and by ensuring that its provisions are duly taken into account in this Regulation and in the rules drawn up for its implementation;

(e) to promote Community views regarding civil aviation safety standards and rules throughout the world by establishing appropriate cooperation with third countries and international organisations;

(f) to provide a level playing field for all actors in the internal aviation market.

20. *See*, section 3.3.2 of Chapter 1; for further information on EU Agencies, EU, *Decentralised agencies: 2012 Overhaul* (2012).

21. Annex II:

    a. historic aircraft […];

    b. aircraft specifically designed or modified for research, experimental or scientific purposes, and likely to be produced in very limited numbers;

    c. aircraft of which at least 51 % is built by an amateur, or a non-profit making association of amateurs, for their own purposes and without any commercial objective;

    d. aircraft that have been in the service of military forces, unless the aircraft is of a type for which a design standard has been adopted by the Agency;

    e. aeroplanes, helicopters and powered parachutes having no more than two seats, […];

    f. single and two-seater gyroplanes with a maximum take-off mass not exceeding 560 kg;

    g. gliders with a maximum empty mass, of no more than 80 kg when singleseater or 100 kg when two-seater, including those which are foot launched;

    h. replicas of aircraft meeting the criteria of (a) or (d) above, for which the structural design is similar to the original aircraft;

    i. unmanned aircraft with an operating mass of no more than 150 kg;

    j. any other aircraft which has a maximum empty mass, including fuel, of no more than 70 kg.

revision of Regulation 216/2008.[22] That which is not within the scope of Regulation 216/2008 continues to be regulated by the relevant Member State at a national level.

2.3 Regulatory Powers

As part of its rulemaking tasks, as found in Articles 18 and 19 of Regulation 216/2008,[23] the Agency shall issue Opinions addressed to the EU Commission for it, then assess and adopt, upon approval, as new or amended legislation, notably Commission Regulations. This is often referred to as 'hard law'.

Furthermore, the Agency shall issue, what is referred to as, 'soft law':

(1) *Certification Specifications* (CSs) are technical standards adopted by the Agency indicating the means to demonstrate compliance with the Basic

---

22. Proposal for a Regulation on *common rules in the field of civil aviation and establishing a European Union Aviation Safety Agency*, and repealing EC Regulation 216/2008, COM (2015) 0613 Final. *See*, section 2.4.3.1, below.
23. Art. 18 – *Agency measures:*

   The Agency shall, where appropriate:

   (a) issue opinions addressed to the Commission;
   (b) issue recommendations addressed to the Commission for the application of Article 14;
   (c) issue certification specifications and acceptable means of compliance, as well as any guidance material for the application of this Regulation and its implementing rules;
   (d) take the appropriate decisions for the application of Articles Arts 20, 21, 22, 22a, 22b, 23, 54 and 55 including the granting of exemptions to holders of certificates it has issued, from the substantive requirements laid down in this Regulation and its implementing rules in the event of unforeseen urgent operational circumstances or operational needs of a limited duration, provided that the level of safety is not affected, that they are granted for a period not exceeding two months, that they are notified to the Commission and that they are not renewed;
   (e) issue the reports following standardisation inspections carried out pursuant to Articles 24(1) and 54.

   Article 19 – *Opinions, certification specifications and guidance material*

   1. In order to assist the Commission in the preparation of proposals for basic principles, applicability and essential requirements to be presented to the European Parliament and to the Council and the adoption of the implementing rules, the Agency shall prepare drafts thereof. These drafts shall be submitted by the Agency as opinions to the Commission.
   2. The Agency shall, in accordance with Article 52 and the implementing rules adopted by the Commission, develop:
      (a) certification specifications and acceptable means of compliance; and
      (b) guidance material;
      to be used in the certification process.

      These documents shall reflect the state of the art and the best practices in the fields concerned and be updated taking into account worldwide aircraft experience in service, and scientific and technical progress.

Regulation and its implementing rules, and which can be used by organisations for the purpose of certification.

(2) *Acceptable Means of Compliance* (AMC) are non-binding standards adopted by the Agency to illustrate the means to establish compliance with the Basic Regulation and its implementing rules.

(3) *Guidance Material* (GM) means non-binding material developed by the Agency that helps illustrate the meaning of a requirement or specification and is used to support the interpretation of the Basic Regulation, its implementing rules and AMC.[24]

Finally, EASA cooperates with the setting of international standards and assists with third countries with their own internal rulemaking when requested.[25]

The first rulemaking steps require the Executive Director to establish an annual five-year Rulemaking Programme after consultation with the Member States, Interested Parties' Advisory Bodies and the European Commission.[26] The five-year Rulemaking Programme lists the tasks to be completed in that year, while also setting out the rulemaking plans for the following four years.[27] The Agency can develop different types of regulatory material during this process, namely legislative proposals in the form of Opinions which may become 'hard law', and 'soft law', that is, AMC, guidance material and CS.[28] The main areas of the Agency's rule making activities will be discussed below in section 2.4.

Soft law is considered to be non-binding. If an entity, that is, an operator or a competent authority, wishes to deviate from an AMC, then it can file an Alternative Means of Compliance (AltMoC) as an alternative means of complying with the rule. This filing is, however, an obligation and it produces legal consequences. Therefore, the non-binding nature of an AMC is questionable as a whole. This also extends for CS because once they become part of the certification basis, they become binding on the concerned parties.

---

24. EASA, Management Board Decision 18-2015 replacing Decision 01/2012 concerning *the procedure to be applied by the Agency for the issuing of opinions, certification specifications, acceptable means of compliance and guidance material* ('Rulemaking Procedure'), 15 December 2015, Art. 2.
25. *See*, section 2.6.2, below.
26. Decision of the Management Board Amending and Replacing Decision 08-2007 Concerning the Procedure to be Applied by the Agency for the Issuing of Opinions, Certification Specifications and Guidance Material ('Rulemaking Procedure'), EASA Management Board Decision 01-2012.
27. The Rulemaking Programme for 2016 is governed by EASA Management Board Decision 18-2015 15/12/2015. *See*, Rulemaking and Safety Promotion Programme including the European Plan for Aviation Safety (EPAS) 2017–2021.
28. EASA, Management Board Decision 18-2015 'replacing Decision 01/2012 concerning *the procedure to be applied by the Agency for the issuing of opinions, certification specifications, acceptable means of compliance and guidance material* ('Rulemaking Procedure')', 15 December 2015.

2.4 The Regulatory Environment

2.4.1 Initial Airworthiness

Initial airworthiness comprises a significant and important part of the Agency's work.[29] In accordance with Article 5(5) and Article 6(3) of Regulation 216/2008, Regulation 748/2012[30] (as amended) pursuant to Article 1(1) lays down the common technical requirements and administrative procedures for the airworthiness and environmental certification of products, parts and appliances within the domains of:

(a) the issue of type-certificates, restricted type-certificates, supplemental type-certificates and changes to those certificates;
(b) the issue of certificates of airworthiness, restricted certificates of airworthiness, permits to fly and authorised release certificates;
(c) the issue of repair design approvals;
(d) the showing of compliance with environmental protection requirements;
(e) the issue of noise certificates;
(f) the identification of products, parts and appliances;
(g) the certification of certain parts and appliances;
(h) the certification of design and production organisations;
(i) the issue of airworthiness directives.

Part 21, as found in Annex I of the Regulation, then sets out the requirements and procedures for the above points.

2.4.2 Continuing Airworthiness

Following several amendments to EC Commission Regulation 2042/2003 on continuing airworthiness it was then repealed by EU Commission Regulation 1321/2014 as further amended.[31] The Regulation, pursuant to Article 1(1):

---

29. See, F. de Florio, *Airworthiness: An Introduction to Aircraft Certification and Operations* (2016).
30. EU Commission Regulation 7/2013 of 8 January 2013 amending EU Regulation 748/2012 laying down *implementing rules for the airworthiness and environmental certification of aircraft and related products, parts and appliances, as well as for the certification of design and production organisations*; EU Commission Regulation 69/2014 of 27 January 2014 amending EU Regulation 748/2012 laying down *implementing rules for the airworthiness and environmental certification of aircraft and related products, parts and appliances, as well as for the certification of design and production organisations*; EU Commission Regulation 2015/640 of 23 April 2015 on *additional airworthiness specifications for a given type of operations* and amending EU Regulation 965/2012; EU Commission Regulation 2015/1039 of 30 June 2015 amending EU Regulation 748/2012 as regards *flight testing*; EU Commission Regulation 2016/5 of 5 January 2016 amending EU Regulation 748/2012 as regards *the implementation of essential requirements for environmental protection*.
31. EU Commission Regulation 2015/1088 of 3 July 2015 amending EU Regulation 1321/2014 as regards *alleviations for maintenance procedures for general aviation aircraft*; EU Commission Regulation 2015/1536 of 16 September 2015 amending EU Regulation 1321/2014 as regards

establishes common technical requirements and administrative procedures to ensure:

(a) the continuing airworthiness of aircraft, including any component for installation thereto, which are:
  (i) registered in a Member State, unless their regulatory safety oversight has been delegated to a third country and they are not used by an EU operator; or
  (ii) registered in a third country and used by an EU operator, where their regulatory safety oversight has been delegated to a Member State;

Regulation 1321/2014 then contains a number of Annexes which set out different requirements that the addressees must meet in order to ensure the continuing airworthiness of the aircraft.

As to paragraph (a)(ii) above, reference is made to the discussion regarding the transfer of safety oversight in section 2.6 of Chapter 6 where it was concluded that neither Article 83*bis* nor the rest of the Chicago Convention provide for the transfer of jurisdiction, and that EU Regulation 216/2008 is harmonised with this in which Regulation similar wording is used.[32]

At the same time, EU Regulation 1008/2008 takes a somewhat cautious approach when imposing restrictions to the use of aircraft registered in non-EU States.[33] National legislation may also limit the transfer for a period exceeding six month in duration.[34]

Pursuant to Article 4, Part M sets out the requirements that shall be ensured for the continuing airworthiness of aircraft and components, including maintenance.[35] Pursuant to Article 5, Part 145 establishes the requirements to be met by an organisa-tion to qualify for the issuance or continuation of an approval for the maintenance of aircraft and components. Whereas, pursuant to Article 5, Part 66 defines the aircraft maintenance licence and establishes the requirements for application, issue and

---

alignment of rules for continuing airworthiness with EC Regulation 216/2008, *critical maintenance tasks and aircraft continuing airworthiness monitoring.*

32. *See*, next section (2.4.3.1); Art. 4(1) of Regulation 216/2004:

> Aircraft, including any installed product, part and appliance, which are: ...
>
> (d) registered in a third country, or registered in a Member State which has delegated their regulatory safety oversight to a third country, and used by a third-country operator into, within or out of the Community.

33. *See*, recital 8: "In order to avoid excessive recourse to lease agreements of aircraft registered in third countries, especially wet lease, these possibilities should only be allowed in exceptional circumstances, such as lack of adequate aircraft on the Community market, and they should be strictly limited in time and fulfill safety standards equivalent to the safety rules of Community and national legislation."; *see also*, Art. 13 allowing leasing among EU air carriers, and section.

34. *See*, section 31(1) of the UK *Air Navigation Order* (2016):

> The Secretary of State may, by regulations, adapt or modify the foregoing provisions of this Part as the Secretary of State deems necessary or expedient for the purpose of providing for the temporary transfer of aircraft to or from the United Kingdom register, either generally or in relation to a particular case or class of cases.

35. *See also*, for Part ML, EASA NPA, Light Part M, NPA 2015-08, 09 July 2015.

continuation of its validity. Pursuant to Article 6, Part 147 establishes the requirements to be met by organisations seeking approval to conduct training and examination as specified in Annex III (Part 66).

Finally, Part T establishes requirements to ensure that continuing airworthiness of aircraft referred to in Article 1(b) of Regulation 1321/2014 are maintained in compliance with the essential requirements of Annex IV to EC Regulation 216/2008.

2.4.3   Regulation of Air Crew

2.4.3.1   Scope of EU Regulation 216/2008

Regulation 216/2008, particularly Articles 7 and Annex III, covers the adoption of implementing rules necessary:

> for establishing the conditions for certifying pilots as well as persons involved in their training, testing or checking, for the attestation of cabin crew members and for the assessment of their medical fitness.

Commission Regulation 1178/2011[36] sets out the technical rules for aircrew including pilots and cabin crew, and those involved in their training and medical assessments.

The scope of the Regulation, as contained in Article 1, covers four main areas. *First*, pilots involved in the operation of certain aircraft, flight simulation training devices, persons and organisations involved in training and the testing or checking of those pilots have to comply with the essential requirements set out in Annex III to Regulation 216/2008. In some cases, certifications and licences are required. *Second*, medical fitness is extremely important for the safe operation of aircraft.[37] Therefore, 'pilots should be issued with a medical certificate and aero-medical examiners, responsible for assessing the medical fitness of pilots, should be certified once they have been found to comply with the relevant essential requirements.' Medical also covers the cabin crew. *Third*, the cabin crew are also responsible for the safety of the

---

36. EU Commission Regulation 1178/2011 of 3 November 2011 laying down *technical requirements and administrative procedures related to civil aviation aircrew* pursuant to EC Regulation 216/2008 (Amended); EU Commission Regulation 290/2012 of 30 March 2012 amending EU Regulation 1178/2011 laying down *technical requirements and administrative procedures related to civil aviation aircrew* pursuant to EC Regulation 216/2008; EU Commission Regulation 70/2014 of 27 January 2014 amending EU Regulation 1178/2011 laying down *technical requirements and administrative procedures related to civil aviation aircrew* pursuant to EC Regulation 216/2008; EU Commission Regulation 245/2014 of 13 March 2014 amending EU Commission Regulation 1178/2011 of 3 November 2011 laying down *technical requirements and administrative procedures related to civil aviation aircrew*; EU Commission Regulation 2015/445 of 17 March 2015 amending EU Regulation 1178/2011 as regards *technical requirements and administrative procedures related to civil aviation aircrew*; EU Commission Regulation 2016/539 of 6 April 2016 amending EU Regulation 1178/2011 as regards *pilot training, testing and periodic checking for performance-based navigation*.
37. As evidenced by, among others, the tragedy involving a pilot of the German carrier German-wings in 2015, as to which *see*, J.M. Clark, *Assuring Safer Skies? A Survey of Aeromedical Issues Post-Germanwings*, 81(3) Journal of Air Law and Commerce 351–376 (2016).

aircraft, having to perform the safety demonstrations and evacuate the aircraft in the event of a crash. *Fourth* and finally, the obligations of the Member States.

Regulation 1178/2011 then has several Annexes that set out the technical requirements which focus on the specific areas mentioned in Article 1: Part ARA (*Authority Requirements in Air Crew IR*), Part CC (*Cabin crew*), Part FCL (*Flight Crew Licensing*), Part MED (*Medical*) and Part ORA (*Organisation requirements for aircrew*).

2.4.3.2 Flight Time Limitations

EASA went through a lengthy procedure involving many institutions and organisations in Europe, some of which would appear to have little real understanding of the underlying rationale for the flight time limitations.[38] The new rules are designed to protect against the safety risks associated with aircrew fatigue, caused by long duty hours and short rest periods. However, pilots' unions and professional organisations argued that the new rules are well below the standards to be expected from a credible safety regulator and that, if not changed, will reduce safety standards currently in place in many EU countries.

Professionals argued that the new rules are designed to save the airlines money and that they allow pilots to fly aircraft for more hours per day than lorry drivers are allowed to drive lorries. At the same time the US FAA proposed rules that move in the opposite direction based upon experience in the US, particularly in the areas of commuter and air taxi operations.[39]

EU Commission Regulation No 965/2012 laid down the technical requirements and administrative procedures related to air operations which replaced Annex III to EEC Regulation 3922/91. However, this excluded Subpart Q on flight and duty time limitations and rest requirements. Article 22(2) of Regulation 216/2008 states that "the implementing rules shall include all substantive provisions of Subpart Q of Annex III to EEC Regulation 3922/91, taking into account the latest scientific and technical evidence". EU Commission Regulation 965/2012 was amended by EU Commission Regulation No 83/2014[40] to bring this into effect.

Article 8 states:

1. CAT operations with aeroplanes shall be subject to Subpart FTL of Annex III.
2. By way of derogation from paragraph 1, air taxi, emergency medical service and single pilot CAT operations by aeroplanes shall be subject to Article 8(4) of Regulation (EEC) No 3922/91 and Subpart Q of Annex III to Regulation (EEC) No 3922/91 and to related national exemptions based on safety risk assessments carried out by the competent authorities.
3. CAT operations with helicopters shall comply with national requirements.

---

38. EASA NPA, *Implementing Rules on Flight and Duty Time Limitations and rest requirements for commercial air transport* (CAT) *with aeroplanes*, NPA 2010-14, 20 December 2010.
39. 14 CFR Parts 117, 119, & 121.
40. EU Commission Regulation 83/2014 of 29 January 2014 amending EU Regulation 965/2012 laying down *technical requirements and administrative procedures related to air operations* pursuant to EC Regulation 216/2008.

Annex II Subpart FTL, which contains the flight and duty time limitations and requirements, was also added to the Air Operations regulatory framework. Such limitations do not stand alone and should be read in light of the other relevant EU and national rules, such as Council Directive 2000/79/EC[41] on working time of mobile workers. As of 18 February 2016, Commercial Air Transport operators subject to this Regulation shall have transitioned to Subpart FTL. To address concerns about the limitations, the Regulation proposes a review pursuant to Article 9a:

> The Agency shall conduct a continuous review of the effectiveness of the provisions concerning flight and duty time limitations and rest requirements contained in Annexes II and III. No later than 18 February 2019 the Agency shall produce a first report on the results of this review.

There is no doubt that this debate will continue for some time.

2.4.4 *Air Operations*

Article 8 of Regulation 216/2008 on *Air Operations* states that aircraft referred to in Article 4(1)(b) and (c) shall comply with the essential requirements set out in Annex IV and, if applicable, Annex Vb. In accordance with Regulation 216/2008, the Commission should adopt the necessary implementing rules for establishing the conditions for the safe operation of aircraft. This resulted in EU Commission Regulation No 965/2012.[42] The scope of this Regulation covers the detailed rules for air operations by

---

41. Council Directive 2000/79/EC of 27 November 2000 concerning *the European Agreement on the Organisation of Working Time of Mobile Workers in Civil Aviation concluded by the Association of European Airlines* (AEA), *the European Transport Workers' Federation* (ETF), *the European Cockpit Association* (ECA), *the European Regions Airline Association* (ERA) *and the International Air Carrier Association* (IACA).
42. EU Commission Regulation 965/2012 of 5 October 2012 laying down *technical requirements and administrative procedures related to air operations* pursuant to EC Regulation 216/2008; EU Commission Regulation 800/2013 of 14 August 2013 amending EU Regulation 965/2012 laying down *technical requirements and administrative procedures related to air operations* pursuant to EC Regulation 216/2008; EU Commission Regulation 71/2014 of 27 January 2014 amending EU Regulation 965/2012 laying down *technical requirements and administrative procedures related to Air Operations* pursuant to EC Regulation 216/2008; EU Commission Regulation 83/2014 of 29 January 2014 amending EU Regulation 965/2012 laying down *technical requirements and administrative procedures related to air operations* pursuant to EC Regulation 216/2008; EU Commission Regulation 379/2014 of 7 April 2014 amending EU Commission Regulation 965/2012 laying down *technical requirements and administrative procedures related to air operations* pursuant to EC Regulation 216/2008; EU Commission Regulation 2015/140 of 29 January 2015 amending EU Regulation 965/2012 as regards *sterile flight crew compartment* and correcting that Regulation; EU Commission Regulation 2015/640 of 23 April 2015 on *additional airworthiness specifications for a given type of operations* and amending EU Regulation 965/2012; EU Commission Regulation 2015/1329 of 31 July 2015 amending EU Regulation 965/2012 as regards *operations by Union air carriers of aircraft registered in a third country*; EU Commission Regulation 2015/2338 of 11 December 2015 amending EU Regulation 965/2012 as regards *requirements for flight recorders, underwater locating devices and aircraft tracking systems*; EU Commission Regulation 2016/1199 of 22 July 2016 amending EU Regulation 965/2012 as regards *operational approval of performance-based navigation, certification and oversight of data services providers and helicopter offshore operations*, and correcting that Regulation.

aeroplanes, helicopters, balloons and sailplanes, including ramp inspections; rules on the conditions for issuing, maintaining, amending, limiting, suspending or revoking the certificates of operators of certain aircraft under specific conditions; special operations; and high risk operations. Air operations within the scope of Article 1(2)(a) of Regulation 216/2008;[43] and the air operations with tethered balloons, airships and tethered balloon flights are not covered by the Regulation.

The Regulation has several Annexes that focus on the areas mentioned in Article 1: Part ARO (*Authority Requirements in OPS IR*), Part ORO (*Organisation Requirements for Air Operations*), Part CAT (*Commercial Air Transport*), Part SPA (*Specific Approval*), Part NCC (*Non-Commercial air operations with Complex motor-powered aircraft*), Part NCO (*Non-Commercial air operations with Other-than-complex motor-powered aircraft*) and Part SPO (*Specialised Operations*).

2.4.5 Air Traffic Management (ATM)/Air Navigation Services (ANS)

Traditionally, ATM in Europe was entrusted to and conducted by Eurocontrol.[44] In the twenty-first century, with Regulation 1108/2009,[45] the EU Commission and EASA also received competencies in this field, necessitating cooperation between the two organisations.[46]

EU Commission Implementing Regulation 1034/2011[47] established 'requirements to be applied to the exercise of the safety oversight function by competent authorities concerning ANS, Air Traffic Flow Management (ATFM), Airspace Management (ASM) for general air traffic and other network functions' to the activities of competent authorities and qualified entities. Commission Implementing Regulations (EU) No 1035/2011[48] laid down the common requirements for the provision of air navigation services.

---

43. Read in conjunction with Art. 4(5) of Regulation 216/2008 as Annex II aircraft fall within scope when engaged in commercial air transportation.
44. *See*, section 3.8 below, and section 5.2 of Chapter 1.
45. EC Regulation 1108/2009 of 21 October 2009 amending EC Regulation 216/2008 in the field of *aerodromes, air traffic management and air navigation services* and repealing Directive 2006/23/EC.
46. *See*, Pablo Mendes de Leon, *The Relationship Between Eurocontrol and the EC: Living Apart Together*, International Organizations Law Review 302–321 (2008).
47. EU Commission Implementing Regulation 1034/2011 of 17 October 2011 on *safety oversight in air traffic management and air navigation services*.
48. EU Commission Implementing Regulation 1035/2011 of 17 October 2011 laying down *common requirements for the provision of air navigation services* and amending EC Regulations 482/2008 and EU Regulation 691/2010; EC Commission Regulation 730/2006 of 11 May 2006 on *airspace classification and access of flights operated under visual flight rules above flight level 195*; EC Commission Regulation 1033/2006 of 4 July 2006 laying down *the requirements on procedures for flight plans in the pre-flight phase for the single European sky*; EC Commission Regulation 1794/2006 of 6 December 2006 laying down *a common charging scheme for air navigation services*; EC Commission Regulation 482/2008 of 30 May 2008 establishing *a software safety assurance system to be implemented by air navigation service providers* and amending Annex II to EC Regulation 2096/2005; EU Commission Regulation 255/2010 of 25 March 2010 laying down *common rules on air traffic flow management*; EU Commission Regulation 691/2010 of 29 July 2010 laying down *a performance scheme for air navigation services and network functions*

The requirements set out in EU Implementing Regulations 1034/2011 and 1035/2011 serve in particular to implement, at an initial stage, the essential requirements concerning the provision of air traffic management and air navigation services (ATM/ANS) set out in EC Regulation 216/2008, in particular to ensure compliance with Articles 8b and 22a, Annex Vb and to allow the commencement of standardisation inspections in accordance with Article 24 of EC Regulation 216/2008.

The requirements set out in EU Implementing Regulations 1034/2011 and 1035/2011, however, needed to be updated in light of technical progress. Therefore, Commission Implementing Regulation 2016/1377[49] repealed the two Regulations, which has since been repealed by Regulation 2017/373 and shall apply as of 2 January 2020. The new Regulation lays down 'common requirements for: (1) the provision of air traffic management and air navigation services ('ATM/ANS') and other air traffic management network functions ('ATM network functions') for general air traffic, in particular for the legal or natural persons providing those services and functions'.

2.4.6   Air Traffic Controllers (ATCs)

ATCs, and persons and organisations involved in their training, testing, checking and medical examination and assessment must comply with Article 8c and the relevant essential requirements set out in Annex Vb to EC Regulation 216/2008. In particular, they are to be certified or licensed once they have demonstrated compliance with the essential requirements. In light of the particular characteristics of air traffic in the Union, common competence standards for air traffic controllers employed by air navigation service providers should be introduced and effectively applied, ensuring air traffic management and air navigation services (ATM/ANS) to the public. This was in the form of EU Commission Regulation 805/2011[50] and then later EU Commission Regulation 2015/340.[51]

and amending EC Regulation 2096/2005 laying down *common requirements for the provision of air navigation services. See also*, EC Regulation 549/2004 of 10 March 2004 laying down *the framework for the creation of the single European sky*; EC Regulation 550/2004 of 10 March 2004 on *the provision of air navigation services in the single European sky*, also known as the *service provision* Regulation; *see also*, section 5.2 of Chapter 3, discussing the *single European sky*.

49. EU Commission Implementing Regulation 2016/1377 of 4 August 2016 laying down *common requirements for service providers and the oversight in air traffic management/air navigation services and other air traffic management network functions*, repealing EC Regulation 482/2008, EU Implementing Regulations 1034/2011 and 1035/2011 and amending EU Regulation 677/2011.

50. EU Commission Regulation 805/2011 of 10 August 2011 *laying down detailed rules for air traffic controllers' licences and certain certificates pursuant to EC Regulation 216/2008.* This Regulation is still in force in some States due to opt-outs contained in Regulation 2015/340.

51. EU Commission Regulation 2015/340 of 20 February 2015 laying down *technical requirements and administrative procedures relating to air traffic controllers' licences and certificates* pursuant to EC Regulation 216/2008, amending EU Commission Implementing Regulation 923/2012 and repealing EU Commission Regulation 805/2011.

The Regulation lays down the detailed rules for:

(a) the conditions for issuing, suspending and revoking air traffic controllers and student air traffic controllers' licences, associated ratings and endorsements, and the privileges and responsibilities of those holding them;

(b) the conditions for issuing, limiting, suspending and revoking air traffic controllers and student air traffic controllers' medical certificates, and the privileges and responsibilities of those holding them;

(c) the certification of aero-medical examiners and aero-medical centres for air traffic controllers and student air traffic controllers;

(d) the certification of air traffic controller training organisations;

(e) the conditions for validating revalidating, renewing and using such licences, ratings, endorsements and certificates.

This applies to student air traffic controllers and air traffic controllers exercising their functions under the scope of EU Regulation 216/2008, and persons and organisations involved in the licensing, training, testing, checking and medical examination and assessment of applicants in accordance with this Regulation.

2.4.7 Airspace Usage Requirements

Following a series of mid-air encounters in which safety margins were lost, including the accidents in Yaizu (Japan) in 2001 and in Überlingen (Germany) in 2002, it was decided that the airborne collision avoidance system software needed to be upgraded and harmonised at a European level. The legal basis for this was Articles 8(1), 8(5), and 9(4) of Regulation 216/2008.[52]

Implementing rules were subsequently put into place under the EASA regulatory system in the form of EU Commission Implementing Regulation 1332/2011.[53] This Regulation sets out the common airspace usage requirements and operating procedures for airborne collision avoidance to be fulfilled by operators of aircraft under Article 4(1)(b) and (c) of Regulation 216/2008 into, within or out of the EU; and operators of aircraft referred to under Article 4(1)(d) of Regulation 216/2008 within the EU or other areas where Member States apply EC Regulation 551/2004.

2.4.8 Standardised European Rules of the Air (SERA)

Pursuant to EC Regulation 551/2004 on *the organisation and use of the airspace in the Single European sky (SES)*,[54] and Articles 8 and 8b and Annex Vb of Regulation 216/2008:

the Commission is required to adopt implementing rules in order to adopt appropriate provisions on rules of the air based upon Standards and recommended

---

52. *See also*, section 3.2 of Chapter 6.
53. EU Commission Implementing Regulation 1332/2011 of 16 September 2011 laying down *common airspace usage requirements and operating procedures for airborne collision avoidance*.
54. *See also*, section 5.2 of Chapter 3.

practices of the International Civil Aviation Organisation (ICAO), and to harmonise the application of the ICAO airspace classification, with the aim to ensure the seamless provision of safe and efficient air traffic services within the single European sky.[55]

EU Commission Implementing Regulation 923/2012 (SERA), as amended by Commission Implementing Regulation (EU) 2016/1185, sets forth the rules on the rules of the air. Article 1 states that the objective of the regulation is to:

> establish the common rules of the air and operational provisions regarding services and procedures in air navigation that shall be applicable to general air traffic within the scope of EC Regulation 551/2004.

The regulation has a broad scope as it applies to aircraft operating into, within or out of the Union, and bearing the nationality and registration marks of a Member State of the Union, and operating in any airspace to the extent that they do not conflict with the rules published by the country having jurisdiction over the territory overflown. However, the rules do not cover all aspects of the rules of the air, therefore Member States may keep supplementary rules that complement SERA provided that they are not part of EU competence.

2.4.9 Aerodromes

Article 4(3a) of Regulation 216/2008 sets forth the applicability of EASA regarding aerodromes:

> 3a. Aerodromes, including equipment, located in the territory subject to the provisions of the Treaty, open to public use and which serve commercial air transport and where operations using instrument approach or departure procedures are provided, and:
>
> (a) have a paved runway of 800 metres or above; or
> (b) exclusively serve helicopters;
>
> shall comply with this Regulation. Personnel and organisations involved in the operation of these aerodromes shall comply with this Regulation.

Under Article 4(3b), Member States can exempt certain aerodromes from having to comply with Regulation 216/2008 and its Implementing Rules, notably EC Regulation 139/2014.[56]

As stated in Article 1 of EC Regulation 139/2014, it covers the issuance certification, conditions for operating an aerodrome, the responsibilities of the holders of certificates, conditions for the acceptance and for the conversion of existing aerodrome certificates, exemptions, prohibited and apron management services.

---

55. EU Commission Implementing Regulation 923/2012 of 26 September 2012 laying down *the common rules of the air and operational provisions regarding services and procedures in air navigation* and amending EU Implementing Regulation 1035/2011 and EC Regulations 1265/2007, 1794/2006, 730/2006, 1033/2006 and the Preamble of EU Regulation 255/2010.
56. EU Commission Regulation 139/2014 of 12 February 2014 laying down *requirements and administrative procedures related to aerodromes* pursuant to EC Regulation 216/2008.

The Regulation allowed for a transition period whereby national certificates would be valid. However, Aerodromes certified by EASA are required to convert their current national licences or certificates to an EASA certificate by 31 December 2017.[57]

2.4.10 Fines and Penalties

Regulation 216/2008 provides that EASA is responsible for the certification of certain products, persons and undertakings, which also provides the Agency with some oversight responsibilities. When the Agency identifies certain non-compliance with the rules and where these are not adequately resolved, then Article 25 of Regulation 216/2008 empowers the Commission, at the request of the Agency, to impose fines or periodic penalty payments on holders of certificates issued by the Agency:

1. Without prejudice to Articles 20 and 55, at the Agency's request the Commission may:
   (a) impose on the persons and the undertakings to which the Agency has issued a certificate, fines, where, intentionally or negligently, the provisions of this Regulation and its implementing rules have been breached;
   (b) impose, on the persons and undertakings to which the Agency has issued a certificate, periodic penalty payments, calculated from the date set in the decision, in order to compel those persons and undertakings to comply with the provisions of this Regulation and its implementing rules.

Pursuant to Article 25(2):

the fines and periodic penalty payments referred to in paragraph 1 shall be dissuasive and proportionate to both the gravity of the case and the economic capacity of the certificate holder concerned.

Article 25(3) then states that the Commission should develop detailed rules. This has been done via Commission Implementing Regulation 646/2012.[58]

Further to this, Article 68 of Regulation 216/2008 also imposes Member States to 'lay down penalties for infringement of this Regulation and its implementing rules' of which 'shall be effective, proportionate and dissuasive.'

2.4.11 Appeals

As an Agency of the EU, its acts and decisions are open to review. Firstly, the Boards of Appeal is responsible for deciding on appeals against the decisions referred to in Article 44 of Regulation 216/2008.[59] This means that an Agency decision taken

---

57. *See*, Art. 6 Regulation 139/2014.
58. EU Commission Implementing Regulation 646/2012 of 16 July 2012 laying down *detailed rules on fines and periodic penalty payments* pursuant to EC Regulation 216/2008.
59. EC Commission Regulation 104/2004 of 22 January 2004 laying down rules *on the organisation and composition of the Board of Appeal of the European Aviation Safety Agency.*

pursuant to Articles 20, 21, 22, 22a, 22b, 23, 55 or 64 are open to appeal to the Board of Appeal by 'any natural or legal person may appeal against a decision addressed to that person, or against a decision which, although in the form of a decision addressed to another person, is of direct and individual concern to the former.'

Pursuant to Article 50 of Regulation 216/2008, once all appeal procedures within the Agency have been exhausted, an appeal 'may be brought before the Court of Justice of the European Communities for the annulment of acts of the Agency which are legally binding on third parties, for failure to act and for damages caused by the Agency in the course of its activities.' Again, this is based on decisions taken pursuant to Articles 20, 21, 22, 22a, 22b, 23, 55 or 64. Such example includes *Heli-Flight GmbH & Co. KG v EASA* which concerned an approval by EASA of flight conditions, pursuant to point 21A.710(c) of the Annex to Regulation 1702/2003.[60]

Furthermore, the European Ombudsman has the right to investigate complaints by EU citizens about maladministration in the institutions and bodies of the EU. This does not include a right for the European Ombudsman to take a position or make a judgment on the content of an Agency decision. The European Ombudsman, upon a finding of maladministration, can simply address this directly to the Agency. If more is needed, then efforts are made to find an amicable solution to rectify the issue. Failing this, the European Ombudsman can make a recommendation to the Agency. Finally, it can draw up a special report to the European Parliament, which must then take appropriate action. While all of this is non-binding for the EU institutions, the European Ombudsman relies on persuasion and public pressure.

2.4.12 Fees and Charges

EU Commission Regulation 319/2014[61] regulates, *firstly*, the fees for certificates and approvals issued, maintained or amended by the Agency payable by applicants. A 'fee' is defined under Article 2(a) as 'the amounts levied by the Agency and payable by applicants for certification tasks'. *Secondly*, it regulates the charges for publications, handling of appeals, training and any other service provided by the Agency.

A 'charge' is defined under Article 2(b) as:

> the amounts levied by the Agency and payable by applicants for services provided by the Agency other than certification or, in the case of an appeal, by the natural or legal person lodging the appeal.

Finally, it regulates how these fees and charges are to be paid to the Agency.

---

60. Case T-102/13 and Case C-61/15 *P Heli-Flight GmbH & Co. KG v. EASA*.
61. EU Commission Regulation 319/2014 of 27 March 2014 on *the fees and charges levied by the European Aviation Safety Agency*, and repealing EC Regulation 593/2007.

2.5   External Relations

2.5.1   Third Country Operators

The European Parliament and the European Council tasked EASA in 2008 to establish a single European system for screening foreign air carriers' safety performance with the aim of streamlining the administrative process for these third country operators. This resulted in EU Commission Regulation 452/2014[62] whereby Annex 1 (Part TCO) contains the operator requirements and Annex 2 (Part ART) contains the authority requirements.

Under this Regulation, third country operators must gain an authorisation which demonstrates its compliance with ICAO standards if that operator wishes to perform commercial air transport (CAT) operations into, within or out of the EU. TCO authorisation is not required for overflight of the EU.

In order to comply with the streamlining ethos, the Agency takes a risk based approach to its assessment of the foreign operator. Once the assessment is successfully completed, the foreign AOC is validated by EASA by the issuance of a TCO Authorisation which is accompanied by Technical Specifications which include the scope of authorised operations with a thirty-month transition period. The TCO can then operate within the EU under the conditions of the authorisation.

2.5.2   'Blacklisting'

The phenomenon of 'blacklisting' legislation relates to foreign registered aircraft and is based upon a number of EU regulations.[63] These instruments are designed to avert the likelihood of European passengers being exposed to unacceptable risks of death or injury as a result of being carried on airlines that are perceived to be unsafe or which come from countries that are considered to be failing to provide effective oversight of their air operators/carriers.

The introduction of this measure in the EU was largely the result of the loss of the lives of French passengers as a result of the crash of an Egyptian airline, Flash Airlines Flight 604, that, unbeknown to the French, had been banned from Swiss airspace on safety grounds. The regulation system is also designed to ensure that all Member States

---

62. EU Commission Regulation 452/2014 of 29 Apr. 2014 laying down *technical requirements and administrative procedures related to air operations of third country operators* pursuant to EC Regulation 216/2008.

63. *See*, T.J. Lynes, J.C. Goldstein and S.B. Herman, *A Guide to the EU Blacklist*, Katten Muchin Rosenman LLP, 6 August 2015; for another approach, *see*, E. Hedlund, *Good Intentions, Bad Results, and Ineffective Redress: The Story of the No Fly and Selectee Lists and a Suggestion for Change*, 79(4) Journal of Air Law and Commerce 701–746 (2014).

are in possession of information regarding air carriers that are deemed unsafe or which come from countries where there is inadequate safety oversight.

Regulation 2111/2005[64] established EU rules on '*the establishment and publication of a Community list, based on common criteria, of air carriers which, for safety reasons, are subject to an operating ban in the Community*' and Regulation 473/2006[65] lays down the necessary implementing rules for Regulation 2111/2005.

Regulation 474/2006[66] then contains the list of air operators that are banned from operating in the EU. The Regulation is then amended every four months by the Commission to update the official list of banned air operators, which is then published in the Official Journal of the EU (*OJEU*).[67] The list contains the names of the individual carriers which operations are fully banned from operating within the EU and the names of airlines that may operate under restrictions and conditions. The Regulation does not ban operators from flying through the EU airspace. Any decision to ban or partially ban should primarily be taken on safety grounds, however due to the sensitive nature of this activity, of which operators could be state owned, political forces also play a role.

The principal Regulation also contains provisions requiring that passengers should be notified at the time of reservation, or as soon as it is known, that the air carrier upon which they will be carried pursuant to the contract of carriage is placed on the list. Third countries whose carriers are affected by this measure may receive assistance from the EU or its Member States for improving the situation.

The information derived by States from the ICAO Safety Audit Reports or the results of safety checks of aircraft at EU airports provide the basis for a decision as to the acceptability of an aircraft or air operator.[68] The EU Commission proposed that ICAO create a global blacklist for unsafe air carriers. However, the President of the ICAO Council was not convinced that the use of blacklists would help to enhance the safety record. ICAO is in favour of strengthening international compliance with its safety standards.[69]

---

64. EC Regulation 2111/2005 of 14 December 2005 on *the establishment of a EU list of air carriers subject to an operating ban within the EU and informing air transport passengers of the identity of the operating carrier*, and repealing Art. 9 of Directive 2004/36/EC.

65. EC Commission Regulation 473/2006 of 22 March 2006 laying down *implementing rules for the Community list of air carriers which are subject to an operating ban* within the Community referred to in Chapter II of EC Regulation 2111/2005.

66. EC Commission Regulation 474/2006 of 22 March 2006 establishing *the Community list of air carriers which are subject to an operating ban within the Community* referred to in Chapter II of EC Regulation 2111/2005.

67. Last updated 16 May 2016. *See*, Report from the Commission to the Council and the European Parliament on the application of Regulation 211/2005 *regarding the establishment of a EU list of air carriers subject to an operating ban within the EU and informing air transport passengers of the identity of the operating air carrier*, and repealing Art. 9 of Directive 2004/36/EC, COM (2009) 710 Final of 11 January 2010.

68. *See*, Report from the Commission to the Council and the European Parliament on the European Union SAFA Programme, COM (2011) 159 Final 31 March 2011.

69. *See*, section 3.3.6 of Chapter 1.

Pursuant to Regulation 2111/2005, Article 4(3):

Each Member State and the European Aviation Safety Agency shall communicate to the Commission all information that may be relevant in the context of updating the Community list.

EASA plays a role in this process as it provides technical information and support, and works in close cooperation with the Commission.

It is also vital for EASA to communicate with the Commission as TCO, meaning non-EU operators, pursuant to TCO.300 of Regulation 452/2014 shall apply for and obtain an authorisation issued by the Agency before operating into, within or out of the EU.[70] Regulation 452/2014 and Regulation 2111/2005 should be read together as, for example, TCO.320 specifically addresses TCO authorisation for operators that are subject to an operating ban.

EASA is further involved in this area as pursuant to EU Regulation No 965/2012, ARO.OPS.100 the 'competent authority shall issue the AOC when satisfied that the operator has demonstrated compliance with the elements required in ORO.AOC.100.' In order for an operator to be given an AOC, it must, *inter alia*, comply with Annex IV to Regulation 216/2008, Part ORO, Part CAT, Part SPA and Part 26 to EU Regulation 2015/640.[71] This adds another layer of safety protection as non-compliance to the EU aviation standards by operators with the competent authority in the EU results in an operation ban in the EU.

While Blacklisting, TCO and Air Operations provide three powerful mechanisms to the EU to ban or restrict air operations in the EU, there is fragmentation and even duplicity of efforts. For example, it does not necessarily follow that an operator which is denied a TCO authorisation for safety reasons will also be placed automatically on the Blacklist. This is especially the case as the official blacklist is only updated every four months which could result in a delay. Therefore, more could be done to harmonise this process to close the gaps and, thus improve safety.

2.5.3 Bilateral Air Safety Agreements with the US, Brazil and Canada

A Bilateral Air Services Agreements (BASA) allows for the mutual acceptance of findings of compliance by Technical Agents or Aviation Authorities between the EU and a Third Country. Under the EU legal framework, based upon Article 100(2) TFEU, the European Commission is responsible for conducting the BASA negotiations on behalf of the EU with Third Countries. As a result, the Agency shall provide technical

---

70. EU Commission Regulation 452/2014 of 29 April 2014 laying down *technical requirements and administrative procedures related to air operations of third country operators* pursuant to EC Regulation 216/2008.
71. EU Commission Regulation 2015/640 of 23 April 2015 on *additional airworthiness specifications for a given type of operations* and amending EU Regulation 965/2012.

support to the Commission, as required, leading to the adoption of a BASA. There are currently three in force, based on Article 12 of Regulation 216/2008: Brazil,[72] Canada[73] and the US.[74]

While a BASA is aimed at the mutual acceptance of findings of compliance, there are differences between the three existing ones. The negations of BASAs is complex and this has resulted in the BASA between the EU and US having noticeable differences from those concluded with Brazil and Canada, which are more similar in content and structure. Therefore, the specific BASA should be consulted in order to appreciate its scope and legal effect.[75]

It is likely that more BASAs will be concluded in the future as more States advance their international aviation manufacturing industries. Therefore, it is possible that China and Japan may also conclude a BASA with the EU in the future.[76]

2.5.4 Working Arrangements

According to Article 27(2) of EC Regulation 216/2008:

> The Agency may cooperate with the aeronautical authorities of third countries and the international organisations competent in matters covered by this Regulation in the framework of working arrangements concluded with those bodies, in accordance with the relevant provisions of the Treaty. Such arrangements shall have received the Commission's prior approval.

A Working Arrangement is usually signed between EASA and the authority of a non-EU country, a regional organisation or an international organisation. The Working Arrangement can cover any matter under the scope of Regulation 216/2008 and are subject to the Commission's prior approval.

The majority of Working Arrangements are conducted between EASA and ECAC non-EU Member States. This is understandable as these States are situated geographically close to the EU territory and have strong economic ties, including via aviation,

---

72. EU Council Decision 2011/694 of 26 September 2011 on *the conclusion of an Agreement between the European Union and the Government of the Federative Republic of Brazil on civil aviation safety Agreement between the European Union and the Government of the Federative Republic of Brazil on civil aviation safety.*
73. EC Council Decision 2009/469 of 30 March 2009 on *the signature of an Agreement on civil aviation safety between the European Community and Canada Agreement on civil aviation safety between the European Community and Canada.*
74. EU Council Decision 2011/719 of 7 March 2011 concerning *the conclusion of the Agreement between the United States of America and the European Community on cooperation in the regulation of civil aviation safety Agreement between the United States of America and the European Community on cooperation in the regulation of civil aviation safety.* See also, A.M. Oliveto, *FAA* vs. *EASA: A Comparative Analysis of the Disciplinary Systems Applied in Aviation Law,* 15(1) Issues on Aviation Law and Policy (2015), and M. Jennison, *The Future of Aviation Safety Regulation: New EU-US Agreement Harmonizes and Consolidates the Transatlantic Regime, But What Is the Potential for Genuine Regulatory Reform?* 38(4/5) Air & Space Law 333–350 (2013).
75. The most substantial differences are handled in the technical implementing procedures.
76. European Commission, *Aviation: EU to launch negotiations with China and Japan for new safety agreements,* 8 March 2016.

with the EU and its Member States. However, Working Arrangements also have a global reach as they include, *inter alia*, Israel, Japan and the United Arab Emirates.

2.5.5 Ramp Inspection Programmes

The EU's *Ramp Inspection Programme* focus is ramp inspections on aircraft used by third country operators under Safety Assessment of Foreign Aircraft (SAFA) or by EU operators under Safety Assessment of Community Aircraft (SACA). It involves 47 States, including all of the EU Member States and also several non-European States, such as Canada, Israel and Singapore.[77] The EU Ramp Inspection Programme replaced the EU SAFA Programme.

The Ramp Inspection Programme is regulated by EU Commission Regulation 965/2012 which provides the legal basis for inspection of aircraft at airports. The inspection is carried out either on aircraft suspected of non-compliance of either international or EU safety standards, or on aircraft where no suspicion of non-compliance is suspected, so to check that proper procedure is being followed.

Further to the Regulation, the Agency has produced AMC and GM to Part ARO, and Inspection Instructions on the Categorisation of Ramp Inspection (SAFA/SACA) Findings – INST.RI.01/002 approved on 18 November 2015 which are also applicable.

Aircraft in one of the Participating States, which are under the safety oversight of another Participating State, can be subject to a ramp inspection. The focus of these inspections is on the aircraft documents and manuals, flight crew licenses, the apparent condition of the aircraft and the presence and condition of mandatory cabin safety equipment. The applicable requirements are:

(a) ICAO international standards for aircraft used by third country operators.
(b) The relevant EU requirements for aircraft used by operators under the regulatory oversight of another Member State.
(c) Manufacturers' standards when checking the technical condition of the aircraft, and
(d) Published national standards (e.g., Aeronautical Information Publications (AIPs)) that are declared applicable to all operators flying to that State.[78]

Ramp inspections, pursuant to Subpart RAMP, are not designed to guarantee the airworthiness of the aircraft or to replace proper regulatory oversight, as they are limited to on-the-spot assessments and cannot assess everything. These inspections have a limited role in aviation safety. However, if non-compliance to the safety standards is found that has an immediate impact on safety, the inspector can demand corrective action to

---

77. Albania, Armenia, Austria, Belgium, Bosnia and Herzegovina, Bulgaria, Canada, Croatia, Cyprus, Czech Republic, Denmark, Estonia, Finland, France, Georgia, Germany, Greece, Hungary, Iceland, Ireland, Israel, Italy, Latvia, Lithuania, Luxembourg, Malta, Republic of Moldova, Monaco, Montenegro, Morocco, Netherlands, Norway, Poland, Portugal, Romania, Serbia, Singapore, Slovak Republic, Slovenia, Spain, Sweden, Switzerland, The former Yugoslav Republic of Macedonia, Turkey, Ukraine, United Arab Emirates and UK.
78. See, https://www.easa.europa.eu/ramp-inspection-programmes-safasaca.

be taken before the aircraft is allowed to leave. Therefore, depending on the finding and the individual inspector, ramp inspections could have a significant economic impact on the operator.

2.6 Draft EU Regulation 216/2008

2.6.1 Introduction

As part of the 2015 European Commission's 'Aviation Strategy to Enhance the Competitiveness of the EU Aviation Sector' the EU is in the process of revising Regulation 216/2008. The objective is to provide a new Parliament and Council Regulation, which builds upon the lessons learnt and experiences gained throughout the life of EASA, that can effectively regulate aviation safety for the next decade. As a result of this, much of the substantive content from the current Regulation 216/2008 will be maintained, perhaps with some editorial and format changes to reflect updates in legal drafting by the EU. However, there is also a desire from Member States and the EU bodies to expand the scope of EASA's competencies by taking them away from the individual Member States, such as the inclusion of a potential opt-in for state aircraft. Two key areas, which will be explored below, are unmanned aircraft Systems (UAS) and cybersecurity.[79]

It is unclear when Draft Regulation 216/2008 will come into force as there are many contentious matters.

2.6.2 Unmanned Aircraft Systems

There has been extensive growth in recent years of the civil UAS market.[80] As a result, regulatory bodies at a national, regional and international level are working to develop rules to regulate this developing technology. This rush to regulate has produced a varied mix of national regulations and a patchwork of international rules. The issues are exacerbated as EASA is currently barred by Annex II of Regulation 216/2008 from regulating civil UAS with a MTOM of 150 kg. Therefore, the EU rules cannot be harmonised as it is currently up to each individual Member State, in light of a lack of EU competencies, to regulate UAS.

As a result of this, the European Commission, supported by the Agency, is working to amend the scope and competences of the Agency through the Draft Regulation 216/2008.[81] The Draft Regulation 216/2008 has introduced two relevant definitions:

---

79. A developing area that, for example, is not specifically dealt with by the new text is 'roadable aircraft'. See, B.I. Scott, *Roadable Aircraft: An Analysis of the Current Legal Environment*, 40(3) Air & Space Law 255–270 (2015).
80. *See also*, section 3.3.2.1 of Chapter 1.
81. Riga Declaration on Remotely Piloted Aircraft (Drones), *Framing the Future of Aviation Done in Riga on 6 March 2015* (2015).

- 'unmanned aircraft' means any aircraft operated or designed to be operated without a pilot on board;
- 'equipment to control unmanned aircraft remotely' means any instrument, equipment, mechanism, apparatus, appurtenance, software or accessory that is necessary for the safe operation of an UA other than a part and which is not carried on board of that UA.[82]

These two definitions make the division between the aircraft (UA) and the system required to operate the aircraft (UAS) clear. This is an important distinction to make as the scope of the two is very different and this could have profound effects if the two are confused.[83] For example, creating such a distinction 'avoid[s] that the equipment to remotely control the UA be systematically part of the "certification" of the UA. Therefore, the unmanned aircraft covers only the flying element (the aircraft).'[84]

The current version of the Draft Regulation 216/2008 under Articles 45–47, while somewhat convoluted and likely to be amended following the consultation of the P-NPA[85] and NPA[86], contains three types of three risk-based categories:

(1) 'open' is a category of UA operation that, considering the risks involved, does not require a prior authorisation by the competent authority before the operation takes place;
(2) 'specific' is a category of UA operation that, considering the risks involved, requires an authorisation by the competent authority before the operation takes place and takes into account the mitigation measures identified in an operational risk assessment, except for certain standard scenarios where a declaration by the operator is sufficient;
(3) 'certified' is a category of UA operation that, considering the risks involved, requires the certification of the UA, a licensed remote pilot and an operator approved by the competent authority, in order to ensure an appropriate level of safety.[87]

---

82. Proposal for a Regulation on *common rules in the field of civil aviation and establishing a European Union Aviation Safety Agency*, and repealing EC Regulation 216/2008, COM (2015) 0613 Final, Art. 3 (29) & (30).
83. *See*, B. Scott, *Terminology, Definitions and Classification*, in: B. Scott (ed.), *The Law of Unmanned Aircraft Systems: An Introduction into the Current and Future Regulation of UAS under National, Regional and International Law* (2016).
84. *See*, G. Boccardo, *European Aviation Safety Agency*, in: B. Scott (ed.), *The Law of Unmanned Aircraft Systems: An Introduction into the Current and Future Regulation of UAS under National, Regional and International Law* (2016).
85. EASA, *'Prototype' Commission Regulation on Unmanned Aircraft Operations*, 22 August 2016.
86. EASA, *Notice of Proposed Amendment 2017-05 Introduction of a Regulatory Framework for the Operation of Drones: Unmanned Aircraft System Operations in the Open and Specific Category*, NPA 2017-05.
87. *See*, EASA, *Concept of Operations for Drones – A Risk Based Approach to Regulation of Unmanned Aircraft* (2015); EASA, *Advance Notice of Proposed Amendment 2015-10 Introduction of a Regulatory Framework for the Operation of Drones*, A-NPA 2015-10 (2015).

These three categories are then reflected in the draft rules published by the Agency which aim at introducing the implementing rules on Open and Specific category unmanned aircraft (UA) to the Draft Regulation 216/2008. The ethos behind the rules take 'an operation centric approach, where risk of a particular operation is made dependent on a range of factors. Concerning security and privacy aspects of UA operations, the consultation does not point to the need for new rules, but more to a better application of existing rules, with a closer collaboration between national aviation authorities and national data protection authorities.'[88] The success of this approach is questionable as the Agency has maintained weight limits, such as the 25 kg limit to the Open category.

Much more can be said for the work already conducted by EASA in this domain and a lot more awaits the Agency, such as the publication of soft law, issuance of certificates and oversight.[89] However, the work of the Agency is ambitious and complex in this area, and it must be congratulated for its work done as this is one of the most challenging rulemaking tasks that is has engaged in during its short history. Section 4.2 below explains how EASA is or may be involved with the investigation of accident and incidents caused by Unmanned Aircraft Systems (UASs).

2.6.3 Cybersecurity

With the advancement of technology, a new and potentially catastrophic 'security' issue is emerging, and this again has required the international community to react. Such reactions are directed towards 'cybersecurity' and include the amendments to ICAO Annex 17 and references being made in the Beijing Convention 2010 (*not in force*).[90]

Article 76(1) of the Draft Regulation 216/2008 provides EASA with competencies to cooperate with Member States and the Commission on security matters related to civil aviation. This cooperation includes cybersecurity. Furthermore, Article 76(2) provides EASA with the competencies to provide technical assistance to the Commission in the implementation of EC Regulation 300/2008. This strengthens the bridge between traditional aviation security matters, as governed by Regulation 300/2008 and aviation safety as governed by the Regulation 216/2008. As a result, the two legal texts must be compatible.

An example of an overlap between the two legal texts can be seen in 300/2008, Annex, point 11(1) on Staff Recruitment and Training:

> Persons implementing, or responsible for implementing, screening, access control or other security controls shall be recruited, trained and, where appropriate,

---

88. Proposal for a Regulation on common rules in the field of civil aviation and establishing a European Union Aviation Safety Agency, and repealing EC Regulation 216/2008, COM (2015) 0613 Final.
89. *See*, EASA, *Policy Statement Airworthiness Certification of Unmanned Aircraft Systems* (UAS), Doc E.Y013-01 (2009).
90. *See*, section 5.2 of Chapter 12, and section 1 of Chapter 1, and sources mentioned there; *see also*, D. Jeyakodi, *Cyber Security in Civil Aviation*, 14(4) The Aviation & Space Journal 2 (2015).

certified so as to ensure that they are suitable for employment and competent to undertake the duties to which they are assigned.

Those people named above could include aircrew. The training prescribed in 300/2008 to aircrew could be included in the EASA aircrew system resulting in their training being regulated by Regulation 216/2008 and EU Commission Regulation No 1178/201 on aircrew.

However, an important distinction that needs to be made is that 300/2008 deals with security in the traditional aviation sense, that is, 'unlawful interference' that is linked with national criminal law. Whereas, the Draft Regulation 216/2008 links cybersecurity with safety and, thus, does not require an unlawful act, and is instead broader. While EASA already had competences to deal with safety, and arguably security issues linked to safety, this makes it explicitly clear that safety related cybersecurity is under the scope of Regulation 216/2008.

Thus, Draft Regulation 216/2008 would arguably bring cybersecurity under the whole EASA safety regulatory system without much legal drafting. It is expected that amendments will be needed in the Implementing Regulations and Annexes to Regulation 216/2008.

3   OTHER REGIONAL SAFETY ORGANISATIONS

3.1   Introduction

Regionalism in aviation safety is complex as it involves different types of cooperation, varying safety related focuses and diverse stakeholders. Consequently, the purpose of this section is not to provide a comprehensive list of all regional aviation safety organisations nor is it to explore them in great depth.[91] The purpose is, however, to introduce the concept and some of the major regional safety organisations, in order to demonstrate their diverse and important role in global aviation safety.

While the Chicago Convention only marginally touches upon regional cooperation,[92] Article 37 of the Convention on the adoption of international standards and procedures states:

> Each contracting State undertakes to collaborate in securing the highest practicable degree of uniformity in regulations, standards, procedures, and organization in relation to aircraft, personnel, airways and auxiliary services in all matters in which such uniformity will facilitate and improve air navigation.[93]

A legal basis can, therefore, be implicitly found in Article 37 for States to collaborate with other States to ensure high standards of aviation safety through uniformity, whether this be bilaterally, through regional cooperation, fragmented global cooperation or world-wide cooperation.

---

91. For a detailed study on regional safety organisations *see*, M. Ratajczyk, *Regional Aviation Safety Organisations: Enhancing Air Transport Safety through Regional Cooperation* (2014).
92. *See*, section 1 above.
93. *See*, section 3.3.6 of Chapter 1 and section 2.1 of Chapter 6.

There is currently no internationally recognised legal definition of 'regional safety organisations'. This is not surprising as the concept is explicitly missing from the Chicago Convention. Furthermore, international cooperation, is either open to all States, such as the Chicago Convention, so they do not have a regional dimension. Alternatively, they have specific target States or regions, such as Regulation 216/2008, which has an EU/EFTA Member State focus. Therefore, there is typically no reason to define such a term in law. ICAO often refers to Regional Safety Oversight Organizations (RSOO) to cover:

> a number of legal forms and institutional structures that range from highly formalized international intergovernmental organizations, [...] such as the European Aviation Safety Agency (EASA) and the Pacific Aviation Safety Office (PASO), to less institutionalized projects established under the ICAO Cooperative Development of Operational Safety and Continuing Airworthiness Programme (COSCAP).[94]

It is then for the concerned States to 'determine the legal form and institutional structure that best fits the needs and characteristics of their specific region.'[95] As a result, this section will take a de facto approach, rather than a de jure one, that looks at the geographical location of the participating States, as opposed to legal character or organisational structure.

3.2 Cooperative Development of Safety Programmes

A Cooperative Development of Operational Safety and Continuing Airworthiness Programme (COSCAP) is a cooperative regional project set up under the auspices of ICAO.[96] They have 'the objective of improving aviation safety, including aircraft accident prevention, and enhancing the safety oversight capabilities of member States.'[97] Currently there are six in existence: CIS Project,[98] COSCAP-GS,[99] COSCAP-NA,[100] COSCAP-SA,[101] COSCAP-SEA[102] and COSCAP-UEMOA.[103]

---

94. ICAO *Safety Oversight Manual*; Doc 9734-AN/959, Part B, Forward.
95. ICAO *Safety Oversight Manual*; Doc 9734-AN/959, Part B, Forward.
96. *See also*, within the context of ICAO, Regional Aviation Safety Groups (RASGs) and Regional Accident and Incident Investigation Organizations (RAIOs).
97. ICAO *Safety Oversight Manual*; Doc 9734-AN/959, Part B, para 3.2.2.
98. Commonwealth of Independent States. Member States: Armenia, Azerbaijan, Belarus, Kazakhstan, Kyrgyzstan, Moldova, Russia, Tajikistan, Turkmenistan, Ukraine and Uzbekistan.
99. Gulf States – Harmonization of international and national safety oversight provisions, regulations and procedures. Member States: Bahrain and Kuwait.
100. North Asia. Member States: China, Democratic People's Republic of Korea, Mongolia and Republic of Korea.
101. South Asia. Member States: Bangladesh, Bhutan, India, Maldives, Nepal, Pakistan and Sri Lanka.
102. South East Asia. Member States: Brunei Darussalam, Cambodia, China, Hong Kong, Indonesia, Laos, Macao, Malaysia, Myanmar, Philippines, Singapore, Thailand, Vietnam and Timor-Leste.
103. Africa; Member States: Benin, Burkina Faso, Côte d'Ivoire, Guinea-Bissau, Mali, Mauritania, Niger, Senegal and Togo.

The participating States will create a relatively informal project or programme document that will contain: institutional structure, the objectives of the project, governance, sources of funding, and duties and responsibilities of all the parties including States and ICAO. Sometimes the project or programme document is preceded by Memorandum of Understanding (MoU), or appended MoC or Protocol Agreement.[104] As a result of the freedom left to the participating States in the establishment of the COSCAP, each COSCAP differs in respect to the five points listed above. Therefore, each COSCAP should be individually consulted in order to gain an extent of its role and responsibilities. However, each COSCAP shares certain common characteristics as they are born out of the ICAO *Safety Oversight Manual* Part B,[105] that is, they:

> can function only in association with ICAO [and do] not have a legal personality and therefore cannot conclude agreements with other entities, such as funding agencies, in its own right.[106]

Therefore, it can be seen that COSCAP, due to their objectives, global reach and somewhat harmonised approach play an important role in aviation safety.[107]

3.3 East African Community (EAC)

The EAC Civil Aviation Safety and Security Oversight Agency (CASSOA), which is headquartered in Entebbe, Uganda, is an autonomous body of the EAC that was established on 1 June 2007 following the signature of the Protocol for the Establishment of CASSOA by Kenya, Tanzania and Uganda on 18 April 2007.

Pursuant to Article 6 of the Protocol, there shall be a Board which governs CASSOA, Secretariat and any other establishment deemed necessary by the Board. In its role, the Board has established two necessary *establishments*, namely:

(a) The Technical Committee: This is responsible for all technical and regulatory issues relating to safety and security oversight.[108]

(b) Finance and Administration: This is responsible for the administration and management of resources of the Agency.[109]

---

104. ICAO *Safety Oversight Manual*; Doc 9734-AN/959, Part B, para 3.2.3.
105. "The objective of Part B of the Safety Oversight Manual is to provide guidance for States wishing to establish and/or participate in an RSOO. Establishing an RSOO, as well as ensuring its sustainability, entails the adoption of a regional strategy, bringing together the efforts of Member States, international and regional organizations, and other aviation stakeholders." ICAO Safety Oversight Manual; Doc 9734-AN/959, Part B, para 1.1.1.
106. ICAO *Safety Oversight Manual*; Doc 9734-AN/959, Part B, para 3.2.5.
107. *See*, A. Trimarchi, *From the Chicago Convention to Regionalism in Aviation. A Comprehensive Analysis of the Evolving Role of the International Civil Aviation Organization*, XV(1) *The Aviation & Space Journal* 26–36 (2016).
108. Airworthiness, Flight Operations, Air Navigation Services, Aerodromes and Ground Aids, Aviation Security, Personnel licensing, Aviation Meteorology and Centre for Aviation Medicine.
109. Human Resource and Administration, Finance, Information Technology and Office Management.

CASSOA works in cooperation with the civil aviation authorities of the participating States,[110] which are competent for regulating civil aviation activities in their respective territories. Pursuant to Article 4 of the Protocol, the primary objectives of CASSOA are to:

(a) Promote the safe, secure and efficient use and development of civil aviation within and outside the Partner States;
(b) Assist the Partner States in meeting their safety and security oversight obligations and responsibilities under the Chicago Convention and its Annexes; and
(c) Provide the Partner States with an appropriate forum and structure to discuss, plan and implement common measures required for achieving the safe and orderly development of international civil aviation through the implementation of international standards and recommended practices relating to the safety and security of civil aviation.

In pursuit of this, CASSOA has three major functions:

(a) Harmonising operating regulations to ensure that they meet international standards and recommended practices;
(b) Developing standardised procedures for licensing, approving, certificating and supervising civil aviation activities; and
(c) Providing guidance and assistance to Partner States including putting in place measures for resource sharing particularly for the technical personnel.[111]

While CASSOA is providing a common framework and mechanism to facilitate compliance with the Chicago Convention and its Annexes by the Partner States, it has faced problems with financing, and the retention of regulatory technical staff within the organisation and the shortage of regulatory technical staff in the Partner States.

Furthermore, CASSOA works in cooperation with the competent national aviation authorities, so it lacks enforcement powers to ensure compliance and it is not clear whether the political will exists to strengthen the organisation.

3.4 The Pacific Aviation Safety Office

The Pacific Aviation Safety Office (PASO) was established on 11 June 2005 by the Pacific Islands Civil Aviation Safety and Security Treaty (PICASST). The organisation is based in Port Vila, Vanuatu and is managed by the General Manager, who oversees the running of the office, and three aviation inspectors specialised in Airworthiness, Aviation Security and Flight Operations. The aviation inspectors provide technical assistance to the Party States within the respective areas. PASO has three types of members:

---

110. Burundi, Kenya, Rwanda, Tanzania and Uganda.
111. CASSO, *About Us* (2016).

(1) States which are party to the PICASST.[112]
(2) States which are not party to the PICASST.[113]
(3) Associate member organisations.[114]

Pursuant to Article 3, PASO is responsible for the regional aviation oversight for its members in the areas of airworthiness, flight operations, airports, security and personnel licensing. Furthermore, PASO is also involved in air navigation and accident investigation.

The benefits of a tailored regional organisations that reflects the special characteristics of the participating states are apparent in PASO. Due to the composition of its States, cost effectiveness and sustainability are of fundamental importance to the small island States. Therefore, these are central to PASO which 'aims to utilise coordinated and collaborative business and inspection methods to minimise the costs of safety and security oversight to participating states and the aviation industry.'[115] Thus, PASO must be credited as it provides a mechanism that allows small island states to meet their international obligations, therefore increasing aviation safety, while at the same time not unnecessarily burdening them.

PASO inspectors carry out audits and inspections within its scope of competencies, in accordance with the legal environment of the state of operation, including both national law and ICAO SARPs, and then submits the report to the competent national authority. If any non-compliance to a rule is found, then the inspectors recommend remedial steps and alternate remedial steps for the national authorities to take. Once such recommendations are accepted and enforced by the competent national authority, PASO continuously monitors their implementation until full compliance has been achieved. While there is a lack of legal enforcement mechanisms, as the competency remains with the national aviation authority to ensure compliance, continuing oversight by PASO provides political pressure to encourage the non-complaint state to rectify the safety issue.

3.5 The Caribbean Aviation Safety and Security Oversight System

The Caribbean Aviation Safety and Security Oversight System (CASSOS) was established by the Agreement which entered into force on 3 July 2008 in accordance with its Article XX and was officially launched in February 2009 at the Headquarters of the Caribbean Community (CARICOM) Secretariat in Guyana. Its mission is:

[t]o grow a safe, secure, vibrant and orderly civil aviation system, making a key contribution to the development of the Region through partnership.

---

112. Cook Islands, Kiribati, Niue, Nauru, Papua New Guinea, Samoa, Solomon Islands, Tonga, Tuvalu, and Vanuatu.
113. Australia, Fiji and New Zealand.
114. Asian Development Bank, Association of South Pacific Airlines, Pacific Islands Forum Secretariat, and US FAA.
115. PASO, *About Us* (2016).

There are three types of membership to the organisation:

(1) Member States that signed the Agreement.[116]
(2) States that acceded to the Agreement in accordance with Article XXI.[117]
(3) Associate members.[118]

According to Article 3 of the Agreement the primary objectives of CASSOS are to:

(a) assist its State Parties in meeting their obligation as Contracting States to the Chicago Convention by achieving and maintaining full compliance with the ICAO Standards and Recommended Practices; and

(b) facilitate and promote the development and harmonisation of civil aviation regulations, standards, practices and procedures amongst the State Parties consistent with the Annexes to the Chicago Convention.

While it can be seen from Article 3 that the focus of CASSOS is fixed on traditional safety goals, such as compliance with ICAO SARPs, it rightly targets these to the specific challenged faced by the participating State Parties. For example, it aims to reduce costs in the 'establishment of infrastructure and the implementation of development programmes, personnel training and establishing maintenance facilities' and with the 'standardization in the approaches to regional safety oversight in areas such as licensing, aviation security, certification, inspection and surveillance'.[119]

3.6 The Latin American and Caribbean Air Transport Association

The Latin American and Caribbean Air Transport Association (ALTA)[120] was established in Bogota, Colombia in April 1980 upon the initiative of eleven flag carriers.[121] Unlike the other regional safety organisations discussed in this chapter, ALTA is a private, non-profit organisation, rather than one that operates at a State level. ALTA has three types of membership:

(1) *Full members*: Latin American and Caribbean airlines with domestic and/or international services.[122]

---

116. Antigua and Barbuda, Barbados, Dominica, Guyana, Saint Lucia, St Kitts and Nevis, St Vincent and the Grenadines, and Trinidad and Tobago.
117. Haiti, Suriname and Jamaica.
118. *See*, the UK Air Safety Support International (ASSI) which has been an active participant since the early launch of RASOS and continues to participate in CASSOS.
119. Caricom, *Caribbean Aviation Safety and Securing Oversight System* (CASSOS) (2016).
120. Formerly the Latin American International Air Transport Association (AITAL).
121. Aerolineas Argentinas, Aeromexico, Aerope, Avianca, Ecuatoriana de Aviacion, Lacsa, Lineas Aoreas Paraguayas, Lloyd Aoreo Boliviano, Mexicana de Aviacion, Varig and Cruzeiro do Sul, and Viasa.
122. Aerolineas Argentinas, Aeromar, Aeromexico, Aaeromexico Connect, Avianca, Bahamasair, Boa, Caribbean Airlines, Cayman Airways, Copa Airlines, Copa Airlines Colombia, Cubana, GOL, InselAir, Latam, Latam Cargo, Liat, Sky Airline, Surinam Airways, Tame and Volaris.

(2) *Associate Members*: Airlines that are not based in Latin America or the Caribbean, but with interests or are doing business in these areas.[123]

(3) *Affiliate Members*: Airline-related organisations or companies that work closely with the industry in these areas.[124]

These member airlines represent over 90 per cent of the region's commercial air traffic.

The objective of ALTA is to coordinate the collaborative efforts of its members in order to facilitate the development of safer, more efficient and environmentally friendly air transport in the Latin America and Caribbean region. Its key areas of priorities are:

(a) Safety promote: Safer air transport in the region;
(b) Cost efficiencies: Develop a more cost efficient air transport industry in the region; and
(c) Environment promote: Environmentally friendly air transport in the region.

As this is a private organisation, commercial interests are naturally at the heart of this collaborative effort. However, the importance of safety cannot be overlooked as a safe and reliable air service is necessary for the success of any airline. Therefore, it is not surprising that safety is a core priority for ALTA, but this may be compromised for more pressing economic needs so caution is required.

ALTA examines the key challenges of the region's air transport, and provides recommendations and actions for improved solutions. ALTA has developed committees with different areas of competencies.[125] With the area of safety, the Safety Committee or AI-ST analyses trends and procedures that may be adopted to improve safety in this region.

3.7 The European Civil Aviation Conference (ECAC)

ECAC has been briefly introduced in section 5.1 of Chapter 1. It maintains relations with its sister organisations, namely, the Arab Civil Aviation Commission (ACAC), the African Civil Aviation Commission (AFCAC) and Latin American Civil Aviation

---

123. Air Canada, Air Europa, Air Transat, Delta Air Lines, Iberia, jetBlue, OAI, TAP, Turkish Airlines, United and UPS.
124. Aercap, Air Lease Corporation, Airbus, Amadeus, APG, Ascend, ATR, Boeing, Bombardier, CFM, Chubb, Embraer, Flight Global, GE Aviation, Hahn Air, Heico, Holland & Knight, ICG, ITC, Kellstrom Materials, Lufthansa Systems, Lufthansa Technik, Mercator, Mitsubishi Aircraft Cooperation, MTU Maintenance, OAG, Panasonic, Planetife, Pratt & Whitney, Rockwell Collins, Rolls-Royce, Sabre Airline Solutions, Safran, Safran Snecma, Satair Group, Seabury, SITA, Spencer Stuart, Superjet International, UATP, Wencor Group, Willis Lease and World Fuel Services.
125. Safety, Technical Purchasing, Fraud Prevention, Environment, Fleet Management, Fuel, Legal and Government Affairs, Airport and ATC Charges, and Technical Maintenance.

Commission (LACAC), and other governmental and non-governmental organisations in the civil aviation field, and with States worldwide, also in the field of aviation safety.

3.8 Eurocontrol

This organisation has also been concisely discussed in Chapter 1, namely, in section 5.2. It is mandated to supervise aviation safety by the management of a seamless system for air traffic operating in the airspace of its Member States, and States with which Eurocontrol has concluded agreements to that effect.

In the regulatory field, the tasks in this field are now gradually transferred to the EU, in particular the EU Commission and EASA. The two organisations now work together, in particular in the SES programme,[126] to enhance aviation safety in Europe.

3.9 Other Safety Related Organisations

Some other notable regional organisations that have an important role in aviation safety include: the AFCAC,[127] the Association of Southeast Asian Nations (ASEAN),[128] the Banjul Accord Group Aviation Safety Oversight Organisation (BAGASOO), the Civil Aviation Authorities of Africa and Madagascar (AAMAC), the Central American Agency for Aeronautical Safety (ACSA), the Civil Aviation Council of Arab States (CACAS),[129] *Corporacion Centroamericana de Servicios de Navigacion Aerea* (COCE-SNA), the Common Market for East and South Africa (COMESA),[130] the Interstate Aviation Committee (IAC), the Joint Authorities for Rulemaking on Unmanned Systems (JARUS), the LACAC,[131] the SADC and the South Asian Regional Imitative (SARI).

---

126. *See,* section 5.2 of Chapter 3.
127. This Commission is a branch of the Commission on economic, social, transport and communicational affairs, which is itself an affiliation of the Organisation of African Unity (OAU). Membership is open to African States which are members of the Economic Commission for Africa, ECA, or the OAU.
128. In Asia, the Association of South East Asian Nations (ASEAN) is becoming more active in the field of air transport as it promotes to the safety and liberalisation of air transport in the region. ASEAN is achieving this goal by drawing up intra-regional arrangements. *See,* A.K.J. Tan, *Aviation Policy in the Philippines and the Impact of the Proposed Southeast Asian Single Aviation Market,* 44(4/5) Air & Space Law 285–308 (2009), and *The 2010 ASEAN – China Air Transport Agreement: Much Ado over Fifth Freedom Rights?* 14(1) Issues in Aviation Law and Policy 19–32 (2014).
129. CACAS has translated the main air law treaties into Arabic and established the Arabic Services Transit Agreement as well as an agreement to create a Pan-Arabic airline.
130. In Africa EAC, SADC and COMESA aim at liberalising intra-regional air services and implementing competition provisions. These ventures are placed under the umbrella of the Yamoussoukro Decisions drawn up by the African Union and are designed to liberalise air traffic among its Member States and to achieve greater cooperation in the technical field. *See,* C.E. Schlumberger, *Open Skies for Africa: Implementing the Yamoussoukro Decision,* The World Bank (2010).
131. LACAC has held a number of conferences, concentrating on non-scheduled air transport tariff structures and a '*Code de la navigation aérienne latinoamericaine*'.

3.10 Concluding Note

There is a growing tendency among States to mandate regional organisations with safety related tasks. These pertain to operation, regulation, enforcement and supervision.

As remarked in the first section of this Chapter, ICAO is and will continue to perform as an umbrella organisation, drawing up rules, procedures, studies and advices for operations. As stated in Chapters 1 and 6, its enforcement powers are limited but increasing.

To bridge the gap between the mandate of ICAO on the one hand, and regional organisations on the other, cooperation between the two is needed.[132] For States participating in regional organisations, respect for the rules and procedures set forth by and under the Chicago Convention and its Annexes and other regulations should be of a primary interest in order to safeguard safety globally.

4 EUROPEAN ACCIDENT PREVENTION

4.1 The EU Dimension

The EU has also been active in harmonising accident investigation procedures among its Member States.[133] One of the earliest measures adopted in Europe was Council Directive 94/56[134] of 21 November 1994 establishing the fundamental principles governing the investigation of civil aviation accidents and incidents.

Directive 94/56 has since been repealed by EU Regulation 996/2010 which was then supplemented by Directive 2003/42/EC[135] of 13 June 2003 *on occurrence reporting in civil aviation*. This Directive required Member States to adopt regulations governing the mandatory reporting of occurrences which fall short of being accidents or incidents requiring investigation under Directive 94/56. The purpose of the measure was to require matters to be reported for examination and analysis to determine trends in mechanical or human performance with a view to avoiding or reducing the risk of accidents and incidents occurring.

EU Regulation 996/2010, which is in line with ICAO Annex 13, leaves the EU States room to apply 'just culture'[136] principles by reference to national law whilst, at the same time, allowing public prosecutors the right to access sensitive materials such as Cockpit Voice Recorders and Flight Data Recorders under certain specified

---

132. *See*, M. Ratajczek, *Regional Aviation Safety Organisations: Enhancing Air Transport Safety Through Regional Cooperation* (2014).
133. *See*, O. Rijsdijk, *European Guidelines for Aircraft Accident and Incident Investigations*, 20 Air & Space Law 196–200 (1995).
134. Council Directive 94/56/EC establishing *the fundamental principles governing the investigation of civil aviation accidents and incidents*.
135. Directive 2003/42/EC on *occurrence reporting in civil aviation*.
136. *See*, section 5.2 of Chapter 6.

conditions. The Regulation acknowledges a priority for the safety investigators without compromising the objectives of a judicial investigation.[137]

The Regulation emphasises the European dimension of the subject by providing for the establishment within Europe of a Network of Accident Investigation Agencies in order to enhance intra-EU coordination on accident and incident investigation and to secure greater cross-border cooperation; as well as sharing of expertise and resources in the process while stressing the role of EASA in preparing safety recommendations and carrying out safety tasks on behalf of EU Member States.[138] EU Regulation 996/2010 attempts to reconcile the safety interests governed by international air law with national policy objectives regarding transparency of information and the consequent criminalisation of behaviour; these national policy objectives are sometimes underpinned by constitutional provisions.[139] EU States have different views on that compromise, which are reflected in provisions of the Regulation.

On the 3 April 2014 the EU adopted Regulation 376/2014 *on the reporting, analysis and follow-up of occurrences in civil aviation*. Regulation 376/2014 repealed Directive 94/56 and amended Regulation 996/2010 by deleting Article 19.[140] The objective of the Regulation, as set out in Article 1, is:

> to improve aviation safety by ensuring that relevant safety information relating to civil aviation is reported, collected, stored, protected, exchanged, disseminated and analysed.

Thus, it has two clear objectives:

(1) to provide and facilitate the reporting; and
(2) allow the flow of such information to go to those who can improve on the safety.

As with ICAO Annex 13, the Regulation explicitly states that '[t]he sole objective of occurrence reporting is the prevention of accidents and incidents and not to attribute blame or liability', it conforms to the same overarching principle enshrined in aviation accident and incident reporting.

In order to be more proactive in this area, in-line with the obligations of Regulation 376/2014, the European Commission has a dedicated webpage where anyone can make an occurrence report.[141] This works in parallel to EASA's reporting system which covers occurrences within the scope of Regulation 216/2008 and its

---

137. *See*, for an excellent analysis, C.A.S. Challinor, *Accident Investigators Are the Guardians of Public Safety: The Importance of Safeguarding the Independence of Air Accident Investigations as Illustrated by Recent Accidents*, 42(1) Air and Space Law 43–70 (2017); *see also*, section 5.2 of Chapter 6 on Just Culture and sources mentioned there.
138. *See*, section 2.3 above.
139. *See*, section 5.2 of Chapter 6.
140. EU Regulation of 3 April 2014 on the *reporting, analysis and follow-up of occurrences in civil aviation*, amending EU Regulation 996/2010 and repealing Directive 2003/42/EC and EC Commission Regulations 1321/2007 and 1330/2007.
141. European Commission, *Aviation Safety Reporting* (2016).

Implementing Rules.[142] Both the Commission and EASA work together in this matter, and also cooperate with national competent authorities in and outside of the EU.

EU Commission Implementing Regulation 2015/1018[143] supplements this system by laying down a list classifying occurrences in civil aviation to be mandatorily reported according to EU Regulation 376/2014.

4.2 Application to UASs

Regulation 216/2008 is currently being revised as part of the 2015 European Commission's *Aviation Strategy to Enhance the Competitiveness of the EU Aviation Sector*. Article 125 of Draft Regulation 216/2008 sets out to amend Regulation 376/2014 in order to remove the requirement to report occurrences or other safety-related information involving certain UA unless death, serious injury or manned aviation is involved.[144] As small UAS are much more susceptible to crashing than manned aviation, this amendment attempts to strike a balance between mandating reporting to increase safety and to remove unnecessary requirements for UAS operators and the relevant competent authorities that would otherwise be overwhelmed by such reports.

The proposed rules on UAS provide more detail in this area. In both the 'Open' and 'Specific' categories, occurrence reporting by the operator is envisaged in compliance with EU Regulation 376/2014. In the case of the Open category under draft version UAS.OPEN.90 this is limited to fatal or serious injuries to person or when a manned aircraft is involved. In the case of the Specific category under draft version UAS.SPEC.120, the operator must report to the competent authority any occurrence that involves injury to any person or *damage to any property, vehicle* or another aircraft.[145]

---

142. EASA, *Report an Occurrence* (2016).
143. EU Commission Implementing Regulation 2015/1018 of 29 June 2015 laying down *a list classifying occurrences in civil aviation to be mandatorily reported* according to EU Regulation 376/2014.
144. Proposal for a Regulation on *common rules in the field of civil aviation and establishing a European Union Aviation Safety Agency*, and repealing EC Regulation 216/2008, COM (2015) 0613 Final. Para. 2 of Art. 3 of EU Regulation 376/2014 is amended as follows:

> 2. This Regulation applies to occurrences and other safety-related information involving civil aircraft to which Regulation [add ref. to the new regulation] applies.
>
> However, this Regulation shall not apply to occurrences and other safety-related information involving unmanned aircraft for which a certificate or declaration is not required pursuant to Article 46(1) and (2) of EU Regulation YYYY/N [ref. to new regulation], unless the occurrence or other safety-related information involving such unmanned aircraft resulted in a fatal or serious injury to a person or it involved aircraft other than unmanned aircraft.
>
> Member States may decide to apply this Regulation also to occurrences and other safety-related information involving the aircraft to which Regulation [add ref. to the new regulation] does not apply.

145. EASA 'Prototype' Commission Regulation on *Unmanned Aircraft Operations European Aviation Safety Agency* including Explanatory Note, 22 August 2016.

5 CONCLUDING REMARKS

Regional developments often express the specifics of the concerned region which is not always the case at a global level. Furthermore, they often produce standards much quicker, and provide stronger oversight and enforcement mechanisms, as compared with ICAO.

While a comprehensive global approach is much more suitable for this international industry, regional developments should be seen as a positive step in enhancing aviation safety across the whole world.

The efforts made at an EU level have contributed enormously to the current high standards of safety that is a pillar of the aviation industry, of which, the efforts of EASA must be on a whole congratulated.

Furthermore, the increasing number of regional organisations outside of the European context is testament to their vital role in aviation safety. While these are not as legally advanced as the EU system, it is possible for them to evolve into more substantial players in aviation safety.

While the regional organisations and aviation safety thinking has focused on traditional issues, such as certification, air operations, accident investigation and air crew, the scope of interest is expanding. This has been seen with the growing mandate of EASA in the areas of UA and cybersecurity. It is likely that such trend will continue.

The benefits for a harmonised global approach, most likely through ICAO, must be balanced against the success of regional safety organisations. While the short term appears to support the further growth of regional safety organisations, the long term is not so clear. Finally, the importance of other stakeholders, including national aviation authorities, manufactures and operators, must not be underestimated. Therefore, aviation safety is not the responsibility of one entity, but everyone involved in this global industry.

CHAPTER 8

Product Liability

1 INTRODUCTORY NOTE

The area of product liability in general and aviation in particular is vast. Therefore, this chapter is confined to an overview only of the general concepts that have evolved into the modern principles of product liability accompanied by specific aviation examples.

While most States now have enacted product liability regimes,[1] this chapter is largely confined to a review of English, American and European laws. This is because the specifics of products liability originated in the United States, closely followed by England, and then the EU took steps to codify product liability.[2] The relationship with aviation claims will obviously be addressed in the sections below.

It is generally agreed that product liability is the liability resulting from damage caused by defective products. A broader definition is given by Hursh, as follows:

Product liability is:

> the liability of a manufacturer, processor or non-manufacturing seller for injury to the person or property of a buyer or third party caused by a product which has been sold.[3]

There are three grounds for a successful product liability claim, to wit:

(a) a defective design;
(b) a defective construction;
(c) an inadequate instructions for handling a product put on the market.

---

1. *See also*, the attachment to this chapter.
2. EC Council Directive 85/347 on the *Approximation of the Laws, Regulations and Administrative Provisions of the Member States concerning Liability for Defective Products*, henceforth also referred to as the *EC Directive*; *see*, section 4.2 below.
3. *See*, R.D. Hursh and H.J. Bailey, *American Law of Products Liability* 2, 3 (1974).

Whenever a product turns out to be defective after it has been sold, under US and English common law principles there are two remedies available against the manufacturer, that is:

(1) a breach of contract warranty;
(2) a tort action based on negligence.[4]

An action for breach of warranty is usually only available to the direct purchaser on the basis of his contract with the manufacturer, which of course weakens its range and effectiveness. An action in tort offers the advantage of being available to third parties, who have acquired the defective product at a later stage and who have no contractual nexus with the original manufacturer.[5]

Historically, as aviation began to develop in earnest it became apparent that it was an important point of public policy that aircraft manufacturers bore a legal responsibility for product safety and reliability standards similar, or at least comparable, to those imposed by law on manufacturers of ordinary consumer goods.

In order to give effect to the desire to make manufacturers responsible the concept of the tort of negligence was developed, followed by strict liability and finally, in Europe, codification of the concept of strict liability. The US has considered codification but has not yet been successful.

2 THE EVOLUTION TOWARDS STRICT LIABILITY

2.1 Negligence as a Basis for Claims

The seminal cases in the development of common law products liability law were decided in 1916 in the United States and 1932 in the United Kingdom.

The US decision in *McPherson* v. *Buick*[6] of 1916 established the fundamental rules of liability based on proof of negligence. In Buick the court stated that liability would attach to a manufacturer "if the nature of the thing is such that it is reasonably certain to place life and limb in peril when negligently made." The court recognised the unsatisfactory situation in contract law which limited a breach of warranty claim to the contract parties. In its decision the court opened the way for a third party to receive compensation. In short, the court was looking for a way around the doctrine of *privity of contract.*

In 1932, the English courts set out the negligence test, in the now famous "snail in the ginger beer bottle" case of *Donaghue* v. *Stevenson*.[7] In the words of the court:

---

4. *See,* for a case centring on the subject of 'warranty': *Helicopter Sales (Australia) Pty. Ltd.* v. *Rotor-works Pty. Ltd.*, High Court of Australia; 1 Air Law 189–190 (1976).
5. *See,* I. Awford, *Some Recent Developments in Products Liability in Tort*, 10 Air Law 129–151 (1985).
6. *See, McPherson* v. *Buick Motor Co.*, 217 NY 382, 111 NE 1050 (1916).
7. *See, McAlister* (or Donoghue) v. *Stevenson* AC 562, HL (1932). The three partite test for negligence includes: (i) duty of care owed (ii) breach of that duty and (iii) damage caused by breach.

A manufacturer of products which he sells in such a form as to show that he intends them to reach the consumer in the form in which they left him with no reasonable possibility of intermediate examination, and with the knowledge that the absence of reasonable care in the preparation or putting up of the products will result in an injury to the consumer's life or property, owes a duty to the consumer to take reasonable care.

These two cases set out the foundation stones of liability based in negligence for aviation claims.[8] The resultant test established is:

(a) the damage had been caused by a defect inherent to the product;

(b) the defect already existed when the product left the producer; and

(c) the defect was due to negligence on the part of the producer.

These decisions afforded slightly better protection to third parties, but proof of fault was still required to succeed. There was an onerous burden of proof placed on the individual, who in respect of aviation cases, was the least likely to be able to discharge that burden.

The decisions that followed these two seminal cases first limited the duty of care on the part of the manufacturer who produced the entire product. However, with the rapid advances in manufacturing processes, it became clear that many products were manufactured by way of a collaborative multi-party process and/or the manufacturer did not actually sell the product in the traditional sense. Therefore, the duty of care was expanded to include: those who do not manufacture but merely assemble the product and put their brand on it for onward sale. Those installing, modifying and even repairers, in some circumstances,[9] all potentially owed a duty of care.

For example, it has been determined that air navigation charts are capable of being a product and not a service, thereby extending the duty of care.[10]

The negligence principles being developed can be summed up by stating that a party may be liable in negligence if they put 'into the stream of commerce' a product that is defective, even if that product is a demonstration, free sample or for sale.[11] Also a party may be liable if they fail to warn of a material operational issue or a defect that the user could not reasonably be expected to have had prior knowledge.[12]

2.2 Safety Supervision

Responsibility for safety and the quality of the product, hence, aircraft and liability in case of damages in case of a defective product, may be closely related in aviation. Thus, the question has been considered whether or not a manufacturer can avoid liability if

---

8. In the UK non-aviation cases tend to follow the seminal case of *Junior Books Ltd* v. *Veitchi Co Ltd* AC 520 (1983)], 3 All ER 201, HL (1982).

9. *See, Vrooman Haseldine* v. *Beech Aircraft Corp.* 183 F 2d 479 (10th Cir (1950).

10. *See, Saloomey* v. *Jeppesen & Co* 707 F 2d 671 (2nd Cir, 1983); *also see,* Shaw Cross and Beaumont discussion Chapter 12 *Liability in Torts* at para 192; *see also,* section 2.1 below.

11. *See, First National Bank of Mobile* v. *Cessna Aircraft Corp.* 365 So 2nd 966 (Ala, 1978).

12. *See, Farr* v. *Butters Bros & Co* (1932) 2 KB 606. CA (case about a defective crane).

a 'defective' aircraft has been approved by an airworthiness authority – even in circumstances where that approval was negligent.[13]

In two UK cases, supervision of safety standards also concerned the question, whether a duty of care is imposed upon a governmental body. Supervision of safety standards involves the grant, suspension, replacement or refusal of Certificate of Airworthiness (CoA). A small aircraft, a Piper Comanche, crashed one month after the grant of the CoA. The owner of the aircraft is responsible for the maintenance of the aircraft. According to the Court of Appeal, it is not fair, just and reasonable that the UK Civil Aviation Authority (CAA) has a duty of care towards the owner of the aircraft.[14]

In another case involving the UK CAA, this body had delegated its powers of supervision pertaining to inspection and certification of aircraft to a private body, namely, the Popular Flying Association (PFA). PFA is an association promoting the design and construction of light aircraft by amateurs. On the second flight made by plaintiff as a passenger next to Mr Collins as a pilot, the aircraft crashed; both persons sustained injuries. Mr Perret sued Mr Collins, the PFA inspector (*Usherwood*) and the PFA, arguing that the crash was caused by negligence of the defendants. At first instance, the court decided that defendants had a duty of care. On appeal, the Court of Appeal found that there would be a 'remarkable' gap in the law if it held that that the injured passenger had no remedy against the persons who had negligently certified the aircraft as to fit to fly because of the lack of duty of care. The court stated the following:

> Where the Plaintiff belongs to a class which either is or ought to be within the contemplation of the Defendant and the Defendant by reason of his involvement in an activity which gives him a measure of control over and responsibility for a situation which, if dangerous, will be liable to injure the Plaintiff, the Defendant is liable if as a result of his unreasonable lack of care he causes a situation to exist which does in fact cause the Plaintiff injury.[15]

Hence, in the above scenarios, governmental agencies may not be relieved from a duty of care, with consequences for the imposition of liability upon those agencies if the conduct of the governmental agency is negligent, taking into account all relevant rules and factual circumstances. These can include the supervision of the safety of the product that is the aircraft, the applicable law and regulations, the reliance of governmental agencies on the defence pertaining to sovereign immunity,[16] and the presence or absence of an *international* element: plaintiffs and defendants had the same nationality, whereas the accidents took place on domestic territory. It is difficult

---

13. *See,* Dr Hanna Schebesta, *Risk Regulation Through Liability Allocation: Transnational Product Liability and the Role of Certification,* 42(2) Air & Space Law (2017).
14. *See, Philcox v. the Civil Aviation Authority* (1995), decision of 25 May 1995; *unreported.*
15. *See, Anthony Perret v. Collins, Usherwood and the Popular Flying Association,* 2 Lloyd's Reports 225 (1998); *see also,* J. Korzeniowski, *Liability of Aviation Regulators: Are the Floodgates Opening?* 25(1) Air & Space Law 31–34 (2000).
16. In a Canadian case which was unrelated to product liability but concerned safety oversight by a governmental agency, *Chadwick v. Canada* (2010), reported by Carlos Martin, Newsletter of 26 January 2011, www.internationallawoffice.com, the Canadian Federal Court of Appeal dismissed the government's reliance on the exemption of governmental liability and found that this Transport Canada could be held negligent, while holding that it had a civil obligation towards the plaintiffs to exercise 'reasonable care in enforcing national air navigation regulations.'

to predict what the outcome would have been if the case would have had an international element where supervision of safety is regulated in Air Services Agreements (ASAs) under which airworthiness standards of aircraft are recognised as long as they comply with the minimum norms set by International Civil Aviation Organization (ICAO).[17]

2.3 Knowledge

The other possible defence available to an allegation of negligence is that of giving a sufficient warning or adequate instructions. The case law has developed to conclude a manufacturer can avoid liability if the user had

(i) prior knowledge; or
(ii) it could be reasonably assumed that the user could be expected to have prior knowledge.

In respect of the 'assumption of knowledge,' it was held in a Texas court that there was no failure on the part of the manufacturer to warn the pilot not to fly when the pilot seat was not properly secured as it was obvious that it was dangerous.[18]

If it can be shown that adequate instructions were given but not regarded then the manufacturer can also avoid liability. The case of *Kay v Cessna Aircraft*[19] provides an instance of adequate instructions playing a crucial role. The pilot of a Cessna Skymaster Model 337 had, quite unforeseeably, misused the aircraft by failing to follow the operating instructions in his 'Owner's Manual.' Had he done so, he would have received a warning prior to take-off that one of the two engines was out of order. The court admitted that the instructions could have been drawn up more clearly, but found that had the pilot followed them, he could have averted the accident. The pilot's failure to comply with the instructions was ruled to be not reasonably foreseeable by Cessna, who were exonerated.

2.4 Continuing Duty to Warn

Again, as safety of aviation is of prime importance it is highly regulated. Therefore, it will come as no surprise that there is a continuing *duty to warn*.[20]

Such warnings will be issued by the manufacturer by issuing bulletins and/or other instructions from time to time and supplemented by directives issued by the local

---

17. *See*, section 1.2.1 of Chapter 2.
18. *See, Argubright* v. *Beech Aircraft Corp.* 868 F 2d 754 (5th Cir 1989).
19. *See, Kay* v. *Cessna Aircraft*, US Court of Appeals (9th Circuit), 24 February 1977; [1977] USAvR 375.
20. *See, United Aircraft Corp.* v. *Pan American World Airways Inc*, 199 A 2d 758 (Del 1964); *see also*, S.M. Mitchell, *A Manufacturer's Duty to Warn in a Modern Day Tower of Babel*, Georgia Journal of International & Comparative Law 573 (2000).

aviation authority. Also, the manufacturer is usually contractually obliged to continue to provide updates as per the after sales agreement.[21]

Legal representatives of deceased passengers have sued manufacturers of aviation charts for allegedly misleading information or lack of information. In one of the many cases arising out of the crash of Korean Air 007 on 1 September 1983, a number of plaintiffs had raised the point that the charts made by Jeppesen did not containing a warning explicitly noting the possible consequences of flying through Soviet (now Russian) airspace. They argued that the absence of an explicit warning in those charts constituted negligence and resulted in an unreasonable dangerous product being released into commerce and that the place where the aircraft operated by Korean Air was shot down should have been designated as a "danger" or "warning" area on the Jeppesen chart listing "Airspace Restricted Areas".[22] The court considered the chart as a 'product' but declined to find that Jeppesen had a duty to warn civilian aircraft in the terms put forward by plaintiffs and decided that the chart did not cause the aircraft to deviate from its assigned course. Consequently, the claims against Jeppesen were dismissed.[23]

In the 2009 case of *United States Aviation Underwriters* v. *Pilatus Business Aircraft*, one of the many issues considered was whether or not the engine manufacturer (Pratt and Whitney) had a duty to provide warnings in the Pilot Operating Handbook (POH). Pratt and Whitney maintained that as the POH is published by the airframe manufacturer they were under no duty to include warnings in the POH. The 10th circuit disagreed and concluded that there was a duty on Pratt and Whitney to include such warnings in the POH.[24]

In summary, the traditional doctrine of *privity of contract* operated to prevent an injured third party from recovering for damages caused by a defective product. As a result the concept of tortious liability in negligence was developed. However, the injured party still had the onerous burden of proving that the manufacturer was indeed negligent. In order to remedy this unsatisfactory state of affairs there was a persistent

---

21. *See, Amiri Flight Authority* v. *BAe Systems Plc,* 2002 EWCH 2481 (Comm) (2003) 1 Lloyd's Rep 50 in which case it was held that a manufacturer, who has no contract with a maintenance provider, did not owe a maintenance provider a duty to warn of dangers which might cause the maintenance provider economic loss.
22. They pointed out that maps provided for the US Department of Defence contained an explicit warning that: "Aircraft infringing upon non-free-flying territory may be fired upon without warning." The warning printed on the Jeppesen charts was: "NAVIGATION WARNING – Pilots flying Northern Route between U.S. and Japan avoid approaching or overlying territory under Soviet control, specifically the Kurill Islands." Upon this argument, the defendant, Jeppesen, replied that: a) it had not violated any duty to warn; and b) there was no 'proximate cause.'
23. *See,* I. Awford, *Civil Liability Concerning Unlawful Interference with Civil Aviation,* in: P.M.J. Mendes de Leon/T.L. Zwaan (eds), *Aviation Security,* Proceedings of a conference held in January 1987, at 49 (1987).
24. *See, United States Aviation Underwriters, Inc* v. *Pilatus Business Aircraft,* Ltd, 2009 U.S. App. Lexis 25488 (10th Cir. 2009).

push in both the United States and England to allow the concept of strict liability to be introduced into products liability cases and therefore transfer the burden.[25]

2.5 Strict Liability

The trend in favour of applying strict liability to manufacturers, outside contracts, grew stronger and stronger in the United States, and finally, in 1963, it was adopted, for the first time, in the case of *Greenman* v *Yuba Power Products*.[26] The court ruled that:

> a manufacturer is strictly liable in tort when an article he places on the market, knowing that it is to be used without inspection for defects, proves to have a defect that causes injury to a human being.

Not long afterwards the principle was formally incorporated in the Restatement (Second) of Torts which was adopted by the vast majority of states.[27] In 1997, the Restatement (Third) of Torts restates strict liability but has not yet been adopted by most states.[28]

While this was a positive step, US law still requires the identification of the defective products and systems without access to the investigation or data obtained in the safety investigation conducted under the rules of ICAO.[29] These lay down that 'any judicial or administrative proceedings to apportion blame or liability should be separated from any investigation under the provisions of this Annex.'[30] Thus, the sole purpose of an accident or incident investigation within the meaning of Annex 13 is the prevention of future accidents and incidents but not to apportion blame or liability.[31] In the UK, since the decision of the Court of Appeal in the 'landmark' *Rogers* v. *Hoyle* case made in 2014,[32] the accident investigation report can now be relied on by an English Court to the extent that the report does provide facts or analysis which is relevant to the claim.

---

25. See, Nesselrode v. Executive Beechcraft Inc. and Beechcraft Aircraft Corp., Missouri Sup Court No.67428 (1986); 20 AVI 17,224 1986-8 the court stated that the concept of strict liability was justified on the grounds that the manufacturer or seller is better equipped than the consumer to obtain insurance and thus insulate themselves from economic damage.
26. See, Greenman v. Yuba Power Products Inc., 59 Cal. 2d 57, 377 P2d 897, 27 Cal. Reptr. 697 (1963).
27. American Law Institute, Restatement (Second) of Torts of 1965, Section 402-A, *Special Liability of Seller of Products for Physical Harm to User or Consumer. See*, S.L. Frank, *Strict Products Liability under California Law*, 5 Air Law 195–210 (1980).
28. American Bar Association, *Product Liability*, Law Business Research 207 (2010).
29. See, section 5.1 of Chapter 6.
30. Recommendation 5.4.1 of Annex 13, as to which see also, section 5.1.2 of Chapter 6.
31. Standard 3.1 of Annex 13 as to which see, an interesting article from O. Rijsdijk, *A Particular Aircraft Accident Litigation Scenario*, 34(2) Air & Space Law 57–86 (2009); see also, C. Challinor, *The Decision of the English High Court in* Rogers & Anor v. Hoyle: *Clipping the Wings of the Principles of Air Accident Investigation*, 39(1) Air & Space Law 83–90 (2014); see also, S. Foreman, *Aviation Accidents and the French Courts*, 20(1) Air & Space Lawyer (2005).
32. [2014] EWCA CV 257.

US civil procedure dictates that the claims be pleaded with particularity, which can be impossible without any firm evidence, and given limitation periods which are often shorter than the time that it takes for the official investigation to release its final report.

An even more dramatic illustration of the consequences of strict product liability is given in the crash of a Turkish Airlines DC-10 near Paris in 1974, where 346 people lost their lives as a result of the crash. Following take-off a door had burst open and the resulting explosive decompression had caused the floor to collapse. The facts made it clear that the manufacturers, McDonnell Douglas, were to blame. In addition, the modifications recommended by the McDonnell Corporation had not been carried out by Turkish Airlines on its aeroplane. In the ensuing proceedings, the manufacturers were sued on the basis of strict liability and were found liable.[33]

The *Greenman* decision was also restated in the 1975 case of *Berkebile v Brantly Helicopter Corp.*[34] On this occasion, the court decided 'that no current societal interest is served by permitting the manufacturer to place a defective article in the stream of commerce and then avoid responsibility for the damages caused by the defect'.

By the late 1970s the consumer had obtained some advantages but the new doctrine still imposed the burden on the claimant to prove that the defect causing the injury existed at the time the product left the seller's hands. The seller was not held liable if the product had been made unsafe by subsequent changes; hence, the claimant had to prove that the defect existed at the time that the product left the care and control of the manufacturer, that is, that the defect was not caused by changes made to the product by a third party after it had left the care and control of the manufacturer in an intervening event which caused it to be unsafe. Thus, this case concerns subsequent physical changes to the product in question and whether the defect existed when it was in the control of the manufacturers.

In *Bruce v Martin-Marietta and Ozark Airlines*,[35] the aircraft, a Martin 404 type, was built in 1952 and chartered by a team in the 1970s and crashed. As a result of the terrific impact the passenger seats broke loose from their attachments and were thrown against the bulkhead of the aeroplane, blocking the exit. Post impact the aircraft caught fire, and the accident resulted in thirty-two out of the forty passengers being killed. The manufacturers were sued for damages on three counts: 'negligence', 'implied warranty', and 'strict liability'.

The court stated that the manufacturer was not liable for the alleged defects in the adequacy of the seat fastenings and lack of fire protection in 1970 because the aircraft was not deemed to be defective by 1952 standards. Moreover the court concluded that

---

33. *See, Re Paris Air Crash,* US District Court, Central District of California, 1 August 1975, 14 *Avi* 17,207; US District Court, Central District of California, 10 February 1977, 14 *Avi* 17,737. *See also,* Judge Peirson M. Hall's, *Memorandum on the Choice of the Law re Damages re Paris Air Crash* (399 F. Supp. 732 (D.C.Cal. 1975)) and his extensive information about the statistics of the settlements in the 'Memorandum' in VIII *Annals of Air and Space Law* 615–64 (1978).
34. *See, Berkebile v. Brantly Helicopter Corp.,* 281 A.2d 707 (Pa. Super 1971); 311 A 2d 140 (Pa. Super 1971). Affirmed 377 A2d 893 (Pa. 1975); 13 *Avi* 17,878.
35. *See, Bruce v. Martin–Marietta Corp. and Ozark Airlines,* US Court of Appeals (10th Circuit), 24 September 1976; 14 *Avi* 17,472.

there was nothing to indicate that the ordinary consumer would expect a 1952 vintage aircraft to have the safety features of one manufactured in 1970.

This example relates to the *state of the art* defence as it concerns changes made to the body of knowledge of what is safe and unsafe, that is, what constitutes a defect, after the product had left the care and control of the manufacturer.

2.6 Crashworthiness

Today, there is a general expectation that we should survive certain accidents, and not to be killed or injured post-accident by things such as toxic fumes or an escape route being blocked. But, as the case of Bruce illustrates this was not always the case. The term 'lack of crashworthiness', for instance, was used in connection with a crash involving a United Airlines Boeing 727 near Salt Lake City in 1965,[36] where the death of most of the passengers had been caused not by the impact itself, but by toxic gases and disabling smoke forming as a result of the cabin interior catching fire.[37]

The concept of crashworthiness has developed as a response to the expectation to survive accidents and is based on strict liability principles and not negligence tests.[38] Briefly crashworthiness can be defined in at least three different ways:

(1) "Crashworthiness is the characteristic of a vehicle which protects its occupants from death in a survivable crash and otherwise protects its occupants from injury or cumulative injury."[39]

(2) Crashworthiness is "The ability of the aircraft structure to maintain living space for its occupants",[40] and

(3) A lack of crashworthiness is a design that aggravates the injuries caused by the original accident.

---

36. *See*, www.airsafe.com/events/models/b727.htm.

37. *See also*, the crash, without casualties, of Emirates flight EK 521; in the accident report, the GCAA of the United Arab Emirates reported in their initial accident report that none of the slides functioned fully with several not inflating at all, as to which *see*, GCAA, Air Accident Investigation Sector, Accident – Preliminary Report – AAIS Case No: AIFN/0008/2016, *Runway Impact During Attempted Go-Around*, issued on 5 September 2016; *see also*, the crash of Asiana Airlines flight 214 on 6 July 2014 where slides inflated inside the aircraft cabin, which was reported by CNN, *Asiana Airlines crash: At a glance*, 8 July 2014. Cases on crashworthiness have been against Robinson Helicopters arising out of the crashworthiness of their fuel tanks R44 and R22 helicopter that previously did not include a fuel bladder which meant that in very minor crashes where the occupants should have walked away, the helicopters were erupting into fire. After a series of cases, a Service Bulletin was produced requiring refitting of fuel bladders to all tanks to improve crashworthiness.

38. *See*, A.J Drago, *Crashworthiness on Land and in the Air*, 19 The Forum 435 (1984), and the crashes with Robinson helicopters, as to which *see*, R. Clayton, Is there a problem with Robinson helicopters?, www.stuff.co.nz published on 31 October 2016.

39. *See*, D. Donnelly, *Aircraft Crashworthiness – Plaintiffs Viewpoint*, 42 Journal of Air Law and Commerce 57–71 (1976).

40. *Glossary of Aeronautical Terms*, cited by G.I. Whitehead Jr., *Some Comments on Aircraft Crashworthiness*, 42 Journal of Air Law and Commerce 73–83 (1976).

3 PRODUCT LIABILITY DEVELOPMENTS IN THE US

3.1 Codification of Products Liability Law

There is no uniform federal product liability regime in the United States. However, it has been recognised that the variety of state laws, each with its own interpretation of products liability, is not a satisfactory state of affairs.[41]

The first attempt at a uniform code was the *Model Uniform Product Liability Act 1979*[42] and this was followed in 1986 by a bill produced by the Senate Commerce Committee which was a compromise between competing products liability bills. But so far there has been no success in agreeing a uniform position.

3.2 The General Aviation Revitalization Act (1994)[43]

In the United States persistent product liability litigation, against small, that is, general aviation manufacturers had a detrimental effect on these manufacturers and threatened their very existence. In response, the General Aviation Revitalization Act (GARA) was created to provide protection for general aviation manufacturers or manufacturers of new components, systems, sub assembly or parts that are more than 18 years old.[44] Though GARA is useful for the airframe manufacturer it is more difficult for the component manufacturer to gain protection under GARA because the 18 years runs from the date of installation of the component and not the date of manufacture of the airframe.

GARA provides four exceptions that allow a plaintiff to pursue a lawsuit after the mentioned 18 years. A plaintiff may avoid GARA if he or she pleads with specificity and then proves that a manufacturer knowingly misrepresented or withheld information from the Federal Aviation Administration (FAA) when the FAA requires the information for certification or other purposes and the information is causally related to the plaintiff's injury. GARA will not apply if an injured person was a passenger for purposes of receiving treatment for a medical or other emergency. GARA does not apply either if an injured person was not aboard the aircraft at the time of the accident. Further, the GARA limitation period does not apply to a lawsuit brought under a written warranty that would be enforceable if not for GARA.[45]

---

41. However, generally speaking products claims in the US are brought under strict product liability theory, tort (negligence or fraud) theory.
42. Model Uniform Product Liability Act, Department of Commerce, Federal Register, 31 October 1979, FR Doc 79-33253.
43. General Aviation Revitalisation Act of 1994 (108 Stat 1552), S2.
44. Section 2 of GARA stipulates that if an aircraft or component thereon is more than 18 years old there can be no civil claim for death, personal injury or damage to property against the manufacturer.
45. *See*, M. McGrory, *Protection for All the Pieces and Parts*, For the Defence 70, November 2013; Mr McGrory provides very insightful information on the operation of GARA in this article which can be accessed on the internet; *see also*, D.I. Levine & C.J.J.M. Stolker, *Aviation Products Liability for Manufacturing and Design Defects: Two Recent Developments*, 14 World Bulletin 93–94 (1998).

Interestingly, in the 2000 case of *Caldwell v. Enstrom Helicopter*[46] it was held that a flight manual can be a component for the purposes of GARA. However, in the case of *Burton v. Twin Commander Aircraft*, the court refused to extend the definition of component to include the maintenance manual. The court held that the FAA required the fight manual to be carried on board but the maintenance manual is not so required and is 'one means of compliance with FAA airworthiness obligations.'[47]

3.3 Evolution of Strict Liability in the US

The concept of strict liability has been continually extended. The evolution one may observe in US case law derives basically from a fundamental rationale that is the need to ensure that the costs resulting from defective products are borne by the manufacturers who put such products on the market, rather than by the injured persons who are powerless to protect themselves. An overriding motive behind this consideration has been the fact that the manufacturer is able to arrange for insurance:[48] he can spread his cost among the general public, because such expenditure can easily be offset by a modest price increase.

The doctrine of strict liability is consumer focused whereas the courts are usually not willing to extend it as between business to business dealings – when they have equal bargaining power and/or access to experts. This is well illustrated in the important case of *Kaiser Steel v Westinghouse Electric*.[49] The court established the following test to determine whether or not to apply the doctrine of strict liability in a particular situation. It ruled that (strict):

> Product liability does not apply as between parties who:
> 1. deal in a commercial setting;
> 2. from a position of relatively equal economic strength;
> 3. bargain the specifications of the product; and
> 4. negotiate concerning the risk of loss.

The significance of the *Kaiser* decision is evident in the case of *Tokio Marine v McDonnell Douglas* (1980). On 28 November 1972, a DC-8 aircraft manufactured by McDonnell Douglas and owned and operated by Japan Airlines (JAL), crashed during take-off at Moscow, killing fifty-two passengers and seriously injuring ten others. Tokio Marine, the insurers for JAL, sought relief from McDonnell for the loss of the aircraft, basing its action on grounds of strict liability. The Court of Appeals decided, however, that the doctrine of strict liability in tort was not to be applied in California in a case where the sales contract was between two large corporations, negotiating from a position of relatively equal economic strength.

In the case concerning the *Estate of Virgil Becker Jr. v. Forward Technologies Industries*, the Washington Supreme Court agreed with the defendants' argument

---

46. *See, Caldwell v. Enstrom Helicopter Corp* 27 Avi 18,167 (9th Cir 2000).
47. *See, Burton v. Twin Commander Aircraft*, LLC 148 Wash. APP 606 (2009).
48. *See,* M. Mildred (ed.), *Product Liability Law and Insurance* (1994).
49. *See, Kaiser Steel Corp. v. Westinghouse Electric Corp.*, 55 Cal. App. 3d 737; 127 Cal. Reptr.838 (1976).

holding that the plaintiff's state law claims are pre-empted by the Federal Aviation Regulations establishing federal standards of care.[50]

4 THE EC DIRECTIVE OF 1985

4.1 Scope

In 1985 the EC Products Liability Directive[51] was established and created a uniform code of products liability and at its heart is the concept of strict liability. It is beyond the scope of this chapter to go into great detail regarding; hence our comments will be restricted to review the basic principles only.

Article 1 "The producer shall be liable for damage caused by defect in his product."

The key words being producer, damage, defect and product the meaning of which will be reviewed below:

> Subject to specified exceptions which are not relevant here, a product is defined in Article 2 as all movables even though incorporated into another movable, for instance, a voice recorder, or into an immovable.
>
> Article 3 sets out a wide definition of a '*producer*' and includes the manufacturer of the finished product, the producer of raw material, manufacturer or any component part and any person who represents themselves as producer by putting his name or trademark to the product. Further any person who imports for sale or hire, lease for his business will also be deemed to be a producer. The EC Products Directive also anticipates circumstances where the producer cannot be identified and determines in such circumstances that each supplier of the product will be deemed to be a producer.
>
> Article 9 defines '*damage*' as death or personal injury and sets out limited recovery for damage to property.
>
> Article 6 defines a '*defect*' as a product that does not provide the safety which the person is entitled to expect taking all circumstances into account including the presentation of the product, the use to which it could reasonably be expected that the product would be put, and the time when the product was put into circulation. Article 6 makes it clear that a product will not be considered to be defective "for the sole reason that a better product is subsequently put into circulation."[52] Remarkably, the term 'putting into circulation' is not defined which could provide a fruitful area of legal discussion.
>
> Article 8 allows for a claim of contributory negligence to be considered in order to reduce or disallow a claim.
>
> Article 10 and 11 set out the limitation period which is three years to bring a claim with a longstop of ten years, at which point the claim will be extinguished.

---

50. 192 Wn. App. 65, 365 P.3d 1273 (Wash. App. 2015), review granted, 185 Wn. 2d 1040 (3 August 2016) reported on www.clydeco.com on 4 October 2016: *Washington Sate Supreme Court Grants Review of Aviation Product Liability Preemption Decision.*
51. *Products Liability* Directive (85/374/EEC); *see also*, D.J. Slijper, *Recent Developments Concerning Product Liability*, in: C.J. Cheng and P.M.J. Mendes de Leon (eds), *The Highways of Air and Outer Space over Asia* 203–247 (1992); *see*, J.-M. Fobe, *Aviation Products Liability and Insurance in the EU* (1994), A. Geddes, *Product and Service Liability in the EEC* (1992) and C. Mannin, *The Effects in Aviation of the EEC Directive on Product Liability*, 11 Air Law 248–252 (1986).
52. *See also*, as to these defences, sections 2.2, 2.5 and 2.7 above.

The EC Directive does not allow the producer to limit liability; however, Article 16 does allow the state to set limits of not less than EUR 70 million.

Finally, Article 12 makes clear that the rights under the EC Directive cannot be fettered or reduced by contract.

Finally, the EC Products Directive should be read in conjunction with EU Directive 2001/95 on general product safety. This Directive imposes an obligation on the producer to ensure that only safe products are placed into the market.

In the Überlingen case[53] before the Spanish Supreme Court reference was made to the above EC Product Liability Directive.[54] This court held that, among others, the manufacturers of the collision avoidance system technology used by Air Traffic Control (ATC) should be held liable for payment of some of the damages.[55] However, the accident was caused by a combination of factors which gave rise to a number of law suits.[56]

4.2 Defences

The EC Directive establishes a regime of strict liability and thereby offers some defences to a producer. Article 7 sets out the following defences, to wit:

(1) the producer did not put the product into circulation; or
(2) the defect did not exist when the product was put into circulation; or
(3) the product neither manufactured by him for sale or any form of distribution; or
(4) the defect is due to compliance of the product with mandatory regulations; or
(5) the state of scientific and technical knowledge at the time when the product was put into circulation was not such as to enable the existence of the defect to be discovered; or
(6) in case of a manufacturer of a component, that the defect is attributable to the design of the product in which the component has been fitted or to the instructions given by the manufacturer of the product.

Reference has been made principally to the defences mentioned under 4, above, in relation to the airworthiness of the aircraft and the state of the art at the time of production whereas the last mentioned defence may play a role in aviation litigation as an aircraft is composed of many instruments attached to it. These are also governed by

---

53. *See*, sections 3.2 of Chapter 6 and 2.4.7 of Chapter 7.
54. *See*, judgment of the Spanish Supreme Court of 13 January 2015, ECLI:ETS:TS:2015:181.
55. For a detailed analysis of this case, and the factual, institutional and legal circulates around the Überlingen accident, *see*, Dr Hanna Schebesta, *Risk Regulation Through Liability Allocation: Transnational Product Liability and the Role of Certification*, 42(2) Air & Space Law (2017).
56. *See*, G. Contissa, G. Sartor, H. Schebesta, A Masutti, P. Lanzi, P. Marti, & P. Tomasello, *Liability and Automation: Issues and Challenges for Socio-technical Systems*, 2(1–2) Journal for Aerospace Operations 79 (2013).

the contractual relations applying to the aircraft manufacturer and the manufacturer of such instruments. These defences are also briefly addressed in the next section.

The relationship between the aircraft manufacturer and airlines is more complex as it is not only subject to contractual relations but also conventions as to which section 5 below.

4.3 Jurisdiction

In product liability cases, the *Hague Convention on the Law Applicable to Product Liability* (1973) determines the applicable law. This convention is currently in force between fourteen European States.[57]

Pursuant to Article 6, the applicable law is the law of the principal place of business of the defendant, unless the claimant founds his or her claim on the law of the place of injury as a connection point. For this convention to apply, there must be a product and damage caused to natural or legal persons.

5 RELATIONSHIP WITH OTHER PARTIES AND LEGAL INSTRUMENTS

5.1 Channelled Liability in Air Law

The cause of an accident can also lie with the aircraft manufacturer or other third parties involved in commercial aviation. This section will principally look at the relationship between manufacturer and airline whereas other third parties will also be referred to.

As explained in Chapter 4, a system of channelled liability through the air carrier provides a simple route to compensation through the operation of the principle of exclusivity laid down in the Warsaw Convention (1929) (WC 29) as variously amended and in the Montreal Convention (1999).[58] Thus, the route is not only simpler but also mandatory;[59] however, case law is shedding a new light on this principle, and this mitigates the relationship in terms of liability between the manufacturer and airline.[60]

---

57. They are: Belgium, Croatia, Finland, France, Italy, Luxemburg, Montenegro, the Netherlands, Norway, Portugal, Serbia, Slovenia, Spain and the Former Yugoslav Republic of Macedonia.
58. *See*, sections 3.5.2 and 3.5.4 of Chapter 4, and Peter Neenan, *The Effectiveness of the Montreal Convention as a Channelling Tool Against Carriers*, XI(1) The Aviation and Space Journal, January/March 2012.
59. *See*, for an eloquent analysis of this subject, A.U. Kosenina, *Aviation Product Liability: Could Air Carriers Face Their 'Life and Limb' Being Placed in Peril for the Exclusivity of the Montreal Convention?* 38(3) Air & Space Law 249–268 (2013); the author signals at page 261 the following: ".... Manufacturers have become a preferential source for potentially greater recovery of damages for claimants as air carriers are protected under the Montreal Convention regarding jurisdictional and other limitations on the amount of damages that may be claimed."
60. *See*, sections 3.5.3 and 3.5.5 of Chapter 4.

5.2 Relationships Between Parties Involved with Aviation Accidents

5.2.1 The Legal Context of These Relationships

The liability aspects have always been a central aspect in contracts between producers in the aircraft chain, and other parties, with special reference to airlines. The reason for this is twofold. *Firstly*, in case of a product failure the potential damage is particularly high, whereas, *secondly*, the sales volume in terms of quantity in units sold is rather low in comparisons with other industries.

The two factors combined result in a very high exposure per unit sold. Insurers recognise this problem. Consequently, liability must be structured and managed by the parties involved in the contractual chain. A point of departure is that the manufacture is only liable for products, which are attributable to his manufacture. For instance, the producer of the manufacturer of the engine of an aircraft cannot be held responsible for malfunctioning of electronic equipment in the cockpit.

In the context of aviation accidents involving liability of the aircraft manufacturer, the following relations can be identified.

5.2.2 The Relationship Between the Manufacturer and Insurer

Depending on the relationship between the aircraft manufacturer and contractual terms between the two parties, the insurers may play a more or less active role in responding to the claim.[61] A further discussion of this subject falls outside the scope of this book.

5.2.3 The Relationship Between the Manufacturers in the Supply Chain

This is also a matter of contracts concluded between the aircraft manufacturer, for instance, Boeing, and other companies in the supply chain, for instance, the manufacturer of the aircraft's engines or information equipment such as aviation charts.

Under EEC Directive 85/374, the producer who is strictly liable for damage caused by a defect in his product is not only the manufacturer of the finished product, but also the producer of any raw material or the manufacturer of a component part.[62] The injured person must prove the damage, the defect, and the casual relationship between defect and damage.

---

61. *See*, R.D. Margo, *Aviation Insurance* 291–313 (2014).
62. *See*, Arts 1 and 3 of the EEC Council Directive *on the approximation of the laws, regulations and administrative provisions of the Member States concerning liability for defective products*, and: C. Mannin, *The Effects of the EEC Directive on Product Liability*, 11(6) Air Law 248–252 (1986).

5.2.4 The Contractual Relationship Between the Manufacturer and the Airline

The position of airlines has already briefly been mentioned in various sections above. Depending on the contractual terms the manufacturer may be liable as manufacturer for the end product, including the whole supply parts covered by the production chain, which is defective and therefore may cause damage to various parties, including airlines. Extensive examination and quality controls carried out both by the airlines and by government agencies, that is, in most cases, national civil aviation authorities accompany the delivery of aircraft. The examinations are governed by international rules which are updated from time to time by such organisations as ICAO, the US Federal Aviation Agency (FAA), and the European Aviation Safety Agency (EASA). Upon approval the national CAA delivers a *CoA* the legal implications of which have been described in section 2.2 on safety supervision, above.[63] Once the aircraft has been delivered, the operator must maintain 'Quality Assurance.' To this end, the manufacturer issues manuals for the use and maintenance of the aircraft as well as for the operation of the flight.

If an accident arises, the manufacturer conducts an 'Accident Investigation Procedure', in co-operation with the governmental authorities, which are governed by ICAO Annex 13 on *Aircraft Accident and Incident Investigation* and national regulations. Hence, the results of the investigation should be used to enhance safety but certain States, including but not limited to the UK, allow that the information coming from these reports made available to other civil procedures before English courts, in so far this relevant to the claim.[64]

5.2.5 The Non-contractual Relationship Between the Passenger and the Manufacturer

Obviously, next to the conditions of the prevailing contracts, are those relationships governed by national law and, in applicable cases, EEC Directive 85/374, and international conventions among which the mentioned private air law conventions.

In many States, injured persons can sue manufacturers and sellers of products even if the injured person cannot prove negligence by the manufacturer or seller. Reference is made to the sections on US and EU law above, and in particular to the case law explained in section 2.5 regarding the 'duty to warn.'

It depends on the circumstances of the case, including the jurisdiction under which the case is brought, whether or not the passenger can bring a claim against the manufacturer. A limited number of jurisdictions allow for the imposition of payment of punitive damages, as a matter of public policy, as to which see principally the US.

---

63. *See*, sections 1.2.1 and 1.2.2 of Chapter 2.
64. *See*, section 2.5 above where it refers to the *Rogers* v. *Hoyle* case.

Award of punitive damages must meet certain conditions established by the US Supreme Court. For instance, such damages must be proportionate with compensatory damages.[65]

5.3 Jurisdiction

When claimants benefit from actions against parties other than the airline, jurisdictional and other limitations described in the chapter on airline liability pursuant to the terms of the Warsaw and Montreal Conventions may not or do not apply in claims against, for instance, the manufacturer.[66]

The Forum Non Conveniens (FNC)[67] concept has also been applied in product liability cases, pursuant to which relatives of the deceased passengers sued the manufacturer of the aircraft and its component parts. In one case, the court explained that the involvement of Mexican authorities with the investigation of the accident and the availability of evidence in Mexico justified dismissal to that country.[68] In another one, the suit was governed by the substantive law of another State (Canada).[69] In *Frederiksson* v. *HR Textorn*,[70] the Court of Appeals took procedural factors including the availability of witnesses and evidence into account in deciding in favour of dismissal. However, claimants have also successfully instituted proceedings against the manufacturer, particularly in the state of Illinois in the US.[71]

In the case of Flash Air, arising out of the Boeing 737-300 crashing in the Red Sea after departure from Egypt in 2004. Plaintiffs sued Boeing, US component manufacturers and the US leasing company in California but the Californian court dismissed it to France on the basis of FNC, but the French court sent it back to the US.[72]

A complex jurisdictional question arose in the litigation between passengers of the crashed Armavia Airlines aircraft,[73] and Airbus. In *Airbus* v *Armavia*,[74] the French

---

65. *See, State Farm Mutual Automobile Insurance Co.* v. *Campbell*, 123 Supreme Court 1513, 71 U.S.L.W 4282 (2003).
66. *See,* section 5.13.4 of Chapter 4.
67. *See,* sections 3.13.2 and 3.13.4 of Chapter 4.
68. *See, Rolls Royce* v. *Garcia*, 77 So. 3d 855 857-858 (Fla. 3d D.C.A. 2012).
69. *See, Anyango* v. *Rolls Royce*, 971 N.E.2d 654 (Ind. 2012).
70. No. 3:08CV450, 2009 WL 295225 (D. Conn., 2 September 2009).
71. *See,* Air Philippines Flight 541 (Boeing 737, Philippines, 2000): *Ellis* v. *AAR Parts Trading* (2005); Transair Lockhart River (Fairchild Metro 23, Australia, 2005): *Thornton* v. *Hamilton Sundstrand Corp.* (2008); Tans Flight 204 (Boeing 737, Peru, 2005): *Vivas* v. *Boeing* (2009); Atlasjet Flight 4203 (Boeing MD-83, Turkey, 2007): *Arik* v. *The Boeing Company* (2008 affirmed by the Appeal Court in Chicago in 2011); XL Airways Flight 120 (cabin fumes intoxication, Boeing 767, 2007): *Sabatino* v. *Boeing* (2009); Mexico Interior Ministry private flight (Learjet, Mexico, 2008): *Björkstam* v. *Learjet* (2010); British Airways Flight BA038 (Boeing 777, England, 2008): *Stafford* v. *Boeing* (2011).
72. The French Court of Appeal decided in March 2008 that they did not have jurisdiction in the case, and that the US Court were more suited and returned it to the US. Meanwhile, the French Supreme Court eventually ruled that the plaintiffs' jurisdiction challenge was premature, as to which *see,* for the US judgement: *Gambra,* 377 F.Supp. 2d 810; and for the French judgement: *Cour d'appel* [CA], regional Court of appeal, judgement of 6 March 2008, at 45–46.
73. Armavia Airlines is the former national airline of Armenia.
74. Decision of the *Cour de cassation* of 4 March 2015, Arrêt No. 327 FS-P + B + I.

Supreme Court ('*Cour de cassation*') referred the case back to the Court of Appeals of Toulouse. This Court felt that the Court of Toulouse was the competent court because the litigation concerning a guarantee procedure initiated by the manufacturer Airbus which has its principal seat in that city. It was requested to pay damages to victims of an accident in which Armavia was involved, which was subject to the Warsaw Convention. However, the defendant Armavia has no connection with Toulouse nor had any of the passengers made a contract there.[75] Hence, this is a somewhat dubious decision.

6 CONCLUDING NOTE

With improved technology for the detection of the cause of an accident, the purpose of enhancing transparency with respect to these causes, and the quest for compensating the damages of the victims come the increased attention for product liability regimes. The complexity of the causes of an accident goes hand in hand with the legal remedies for victims.

Products liability claims are mostly based on strict liability. This concept has been stretched as consumer benefits had to be met. Moreover, insurance concerns can be normally addressed by the manufactures in business to business relations.

Also, the development of product liability law in aviation should be viewed through the lens of providing an alternative source of recovery for the injured passenger. However, because of practical difficulties, passengers are somewhat handicapped when pursuing their claims, since, unlike other product liability areas where the products are either in the possession of the claimants at the time of the accident or can be obtained from the police after their investigation, this is not the case for passengers and their representatives in light of the mandatory separation between the safety investigation and other proceedings. The Überlingen cases show however that courts "went beyond the Accident Investigation Report's analysis of the technology."[76]

Thus, the injured passenger may find damages limited by the operation of domestic and international carriage by air principles. Hence, depending on the choice of jurisdiction, in which, for instance, punitive damages may be available for the claimant, a product liability claim against the manufacturer may provide an obvious alternative cause of action and potentially greater damages recovery than against the airline.

---

75. *See*, Pablo Mendes de Leon, *Jurisdiction under and Exclusivity of Private Air Law Agreements on Air Carrier Liability: The Case of Airbus versus Armavia Airlines, From Lowlands to High Skies, Liber Amicorum* for John Balfour 261–274 (2013).
76. *See*, Dr Hanna Schebesta, *Risk Regulation Through Liability Allocation: Transnational Product Liability and the Role of Certification*, 42(2) Air & Space Law (2017), section 3.

ANNEX   PRODUCTS LIABILITY: SAMPLE COUNTRY OVERVIEW

Country	Statutory Causes of Action	Non Statute Causes of Action	Limitation Period – Approximately
Australia	Federal: Trade Practices Act State: various Fair Trading Acts	Breach of contract and tort (negligence)	The earlier of three years from when cause of action arose or ten years from date of supply
Brazil	Federal: Consumer Defence Code (CDC 1990) and Civil Code (CC2002).	General principles of tort. Strict Liability is available for products claims	three or five years depending on the cause of action.
China	No unified statute: General Principles of Civil Law, Product quality Law; The PRC Consumer Interest Protection Law and new Tort Law		two to ten years depending on cause of action
England	Consumer Protection Act 1987 which implements the European Product Liability Directive (85/374/EEC)	Breach of Contract and Tort (negligence) Strict Liability	Under the statute three years with ten year long stop Contract claims six years Tort (negligence) claims three years
Finland	Product Liability Act (694/1990) based on European Product liability Directive 85/374 and Tort Liability Act		three years with a ten year long stop
India	No specific statute but various including: The Consumer Protection Act 1986; Indian Contract Act 1872 and Sale of Goods Act 1930	Breach of Contract and/or Tort (negligence)	three years

381

Country	Statutory Causes of Action	Non Statute Causes of Action	Limitation Period – Approximately
Mexico	No specific Products Statute. But various including: Federal and State Civil Codes; Federal Consumer Protection Law; General Health Law; Federal Labour Law; Ecological Balance and Environmental Protection law	No cause of action for breach of contract/tort in the traditional sense is available	Two years
Russia	Consumer Rights Protection Act 1992 and Civil Code of the Russian Federation 1995		Three to Ten years depending on cause of action
U.S.A.	No uniform Federal statute. Each state has its own statue. But they tend to follow Strict Liability principles	Breach of Contract, Tort (negligence), Fraud, Conspiracy	One to Ten years depending on cause of action and state

Compiled by reference to Product Liability ABA Section of International Law 2010 Published by Law Business Research – adapted in 2017.

CHAPTER 9

Surface Damage and Collisions

1 DAMAGE CAUSED TO THIRD PARTIES ON THE SURFACE

1.1 The Coming into Being of the Rome Convention of 1952

The problems involved in cases of damage caused to third parties on the surface, as distinct from damage caused to passengers and shippers of cargo covered by a contractual relationship coming under the terms of the Warsaw regime and the Montreal Convention of 1999 as to which *see*, Chapter 4, were recognised as early as 1927. Studies on the subject were undertaken, culminating eventually in the Rome Convention of 1933 and its Brussels Insurance Protocol of 1938.[1] Neither effort can be regarded as particularly successful. The rules of the Rome Convention of 1933 were soon found to be lagging behind the rapid developments in aviation, and the Convention drew only a very limited number of ratifications.[2]

After the Second World War the matter was once again given attention, and at the instigation of the International Civil Aviation Organization (ICAO) Legal Committee, a sub-committee was established in 1947 to revise the Rome Convention (1952) of 1933 and to determine which objections had in fact prevented States from ratifying. The new Convention[3] also contained rules originating from the Brussels Insurance Protocol of 1938 concerning the obligation to arrange for insurance against possible injury to third party victims. The former Rome Convention of 1933 and its Brussels Protocol were superseded by the new Convention of 1952.

---

1. International Convention for the *Unification of Certain Rules Relating to Damage Caused by Aircraft to Third Parties on the Surface*, Rome, 29 May 1933; hereinafter also cited as the Rome Convention (1933). Additional Protocol to the International Convention for *the Unification of Certain Rules Relating to Damage Caused by Aircraft to Third Parties on the Surface*, Brussels, 29 September 1938; hereinafter cited as the *Brussels Insurance Protocol*.
2. Five States signed the Convention; only two the Protocol.
3. *Convention on Damage Caused by Foreign Aircraft to Third Parties on the Surface*, Rome, 7 October 1952; in this section also cited as the Rome Convention (1952) (1952) or the Convention.

The Rome Convention of 1952 is in force,[4] but it has not attracted many ratifications either. Only 49 (per 2017) out of the 191 ICAO Member States did ratify it; that number does not include major aviation powers.

The reasons for this lack of interest are summarised as follows:

- the limits for compensation mentioned in the Convention are considered too low;
- national legislation provides adequate safeguards for the interests of third parties on the surface: it was felt that there was no need for international rules on the subject;
- the Convention does not deal with problems such as noise, sonic boom or nuclear damage as to which *see*, section 2 below;
- there were objections against creating a *single forum*.[5]

The Convention came into force on 4 February 1958, but as early as 1964 suggestions were put forward for revision.[6] In 1978 a Diplomatic Conference was convened by the ICAO Council, where 58 States were represented whereas IATA, International Federation of Air Line Pilots' Associations (IFALPA) and the International Law Association (ILA) attended as observers.[7] A Protocol was adopted at Montreal aiming at amending the Rome Convention (1952) of 1952.[8]

The Montreal Protocol (1978) was opened for signature in September 1978 which entered into force on 25 July 2002, upon receipt of the fifth ratification.[9] So far it has received only twelve ratifications which number also remains stable and is not expected to increase dramatically.

The principal subjects of these conventions will be discussed in section 1.3 below.

1.2   Post '9/11' Developments: The 2009 ICAO Conventions

The unprecedented terrorist attacks of 9/11 of 2001 directed against the United States brought the intertwined issues of liability for and insurability of terrorist-related risks to centre-stage and on the agenda of States worldwide, particularly the United States.[10]

---

4. Since 4 February 1958, upon receipt of the fifth ratification.
5. *See*, A.J. Mauritz, *Liability of the Operator and Owners of Aircraft for Damage Inflicted to Persons and Property on the Surface* (PhD thesis, University of Leiden) 85–88 (2003).
6. *See*, G.F. Fitzgerald, *The Protocol to Amend the Convention on Damage Caused by Foreign Aircraft to Third Parties on the Surface (Rome, 1952) signed at Montreal, 23 September 1978*, IV Annals of Air and Space Law 29–73 (1979), at 32.
7. Minutes and Documents of the International Conference on Air Law, Montreal, September 1978; ICAO Doc. 9357 – LC/183. *See*, on this Conference, M. Milde, *Tenth International Conference on Air Law*, 4 Air Law 41–44 (1979).
8. *Protocol to Amend the Convention on Damage Caused by Foreign Aircraft to Third Parties on the Surface*, Montreal, 23 September 1978; hereinafter also cited as the Montreal Protocol (1978).
9. *See*, A.J. Mauritz, *Liability of the Operator and Owners of Aircraft for Damage Inflicted to Persons and Property on the Surface* (PhD thesis, University of Leiden) 92–107 (2003).
10. *See*, A.J. Mauritz, *Liability of the Operator and Owners of Aircraft for Damage Inflicted to Persons and Property on the Surface* 192–202 (2003).

Due to the limited availability of insurance coverage for risks related to war and terrorism for airlines worldwide after '9/11', States were immediately forced to step in with guarantees and other measures to prevent airlines from discontinuing their services altogether.[11]

These events helped to trigger recommendations to the ICAO Council by the Special Group on Aviation War Risk Insurance (SGWI) on an international mechanism under the auspices of ICAO whereby war risk coverage would be furnished by a non-profit entity to be backed by governments. These recommendations culminated in the ICAO scheme 'Globaltime', which aimed to provide third-party war risk liability insurance cover for all aviation industry entities of participating States.[12]

In the same period of time, ICAO received the responses to its questionnaire to States on the subject of modernisation of the Rome Convention (1952).[13] This led to a 'Draft Convention on Damage Caused by Foreign Aircraft to Third Parties on the Surface', which was prepared and considered by the ICAO Secretariat and ICAO Secretariat Study Group on the Modernization of the Rome Convention (1952) respectively in 2003.[14] The initial Draft, which contained specific provisions on general and terrorist-related risks, has ultimately been split into two separate Conventions which were adopted during the ICAO International Conference on Air Law in Montreal in May 2009.

The *Convention on Compensation for Damage Caused by Aircraft to Third Parties* deals with general risks, hereinafter also cited as the General Risks Convention (2009); and the *Convention on Compensation for Damage to Third Parties, Resulting from Acts of Unlawful Interference involving Aircraft*, henceforth also referred to as the Unlawful Interference Convention (2009), addresses terrorism-related risks. The latter now contains a *Supplementary Compensation Mechanism*, which forms an integral part of the Convention.[15] The presentation of two agreements offers States the advantage to become party to one or the other, or both.

---

11. War risk coverages including war, hijacking and other perils such as terrorism, have been reassessed and cancelled by insurers worldwide directly after '9/11' on the basis of the seven day notice clause contained in insurance policies as to which *see also*, section 5.5 of Chapter 10. This was the first blanket worldwide notice ever, in which airlines were offered a reduction of coverage for war related risks to USD 50 million aggregate for all passenger and third party claims under primary liability policies and reinsurance programs. On that basis, airlines would have been forced to ground their fleets entirely without government guarantees.

12. ICAO Council Study Group on *Aviation War Risk Insurance* (CGWI), First Meeting (Montreal, 16 April 2002), SWGI Proposal – Questions and Answers, Doc CGWI/1-WP/1.

13. ICAO State Letter LE 3/14.2-01/62 of 15 June 2001, *see also*, Report of the Rapporteur to the Legal Committee – 33rd session, LC/33-WP/3-4, 1.

14. ICAO Legal Bureau, Memorandum of 07/08/03 on the Third Meeting of the ICAO Secretariat Study Group on the *Modernization of the Rome Convention* (1952), Montreal, 3–5 September 2003 (SSG-MR/3).

15. For comments, *see*, M. Franklin, *Is a Successful New Convention on Airline Liability for Surface damage Achievable?* 31 (2) Air & Space Law 87–97 (2006); H. Kjelin, *The New International Regime for Third Party Liability*, 33(2) Air & Space Law 63–80 (2008), G.N. Tompkins Jr., *Some Thoughts to Ponder When Considering Whether to Adopt the New Aviation General Risks and Unlawful Interference Convention (2009)s Proposed by ICAO*, 38(2) Air & Space Law 81–84 (2008) and H. Caplan, *Liability for Third Party Damage on the Ground*, 33(3) Air & Space Law 183–213 (2008); R.I.R. Abeyratne, *The ICAO Conventions on Liability for Third Party Damage*

The ratifications of the General Risks and the Unlawful Interference Conventions of 2009 are also going slowly. Early 2017, seven States had become a party to the first mentioned convention and eight States to the second mentioned convention. For either of these conventions to come into force, 35 ratifications are required; no reservations may be made.[16]

Many States believe that national regulations or ad hoc arrangements are best equipped to deal with the matters governed by them. Practice appears to illustrate this point.

1.3 Principle Provisions of the International Conventions

1.3.1 Geographical Scope

The Rome Convention of 1952 is applicable to damage caused to third parties on the territory of a contracting State by an aircraft registered in another contracting State.[17] In Article 30, a territory of a State is defined as meaning:

> the metropolitan territory of a State and all territories for the foreign relations of which that State is responsible, subject to the provisions of Article 36.

It follows that when damage has been caused by aircraft registered in the State where the damage occurred, national law applies.

The Rome Convention (1952) applies only to damage caused by air collision to the extent that such damage is sustained *on the surface of the earth*: damage caused in the air is outside the scope of the Convention. One of the reasons was that the principle of risk liability had been adopted in the Convention as to which *see*, section 1.3.5 below. This principle could not be made applicable to air collision because such a collision involves two parties of equal strength in similar positions, a situation in which fault liability usually tends to be favoured.[18]

A comparable or similar provision on damage caused to aircraft in flight has not been included in either the General Risk Convention (2009) or the Unlawful Interference Convention (2009).

During the debate concerning the revision of the Rome Convention (1952) some States wondered whether installations like oil rigs should be mentioned, but the 1978 Conference rejected proposals to insert either the term 'floating construction', or the word 'installation'.[19]

Caused by Aircraft, 34(6) Air & Space Law 403–416 (2009); M. Milde, *Liability for Damage Caused by Aircraft on the Surface: Past and Current Efforts to Unify the Law*, 57 Zeitschrift für Luft und Weltraumrecht 532–557 (2008).

16. *See*, Art. 23 and Art. 40.
17. *See*, Art. 23 of the General Risks Convention (2009) and Art. 40 of the Unlawful Interference Convention (2009).
18. *See*, section 1.3.10 below, and G.F. Fitzgerald, *International Review – The Development of International Liability Rules Concerning Aerial Collisions*, 20 Journal of Air Law and Commerce 203–210 (1954), at 205.
19. ICAO Doc. 9357 – LC/183 at 107 ff.

On the other hand, the Montreal Protocol (1978) has widened the Rome Convention's scope by providing that it also applies when damage is caused by an aircraft, whatever its registration may be, whose operator has his principal place of business or, if he has no such place of business, his permanent place of residence in another contracting State.[20] This enhances protection for the injured party. A ship or aircraft on the high seas shall be regarded as part of the territory of the State in which it is registered.[21] The fact that the position of aircraft in flights above the high seas has been clarified is undoubtedly a step forward.

The General Risks Convention (2009) applies to damage to third parties within the territory of a State Party by an aircraft in flight on an international flight, other than as a result of an act of unlawful interference.[22] Notably, the aircraft that causes the damage need not be registered in another Contracting State, which extends the scope of this Convention considerably in comparison with the Rome Convention (1952).

In comparison with Article 2 of the General Risks Convention (2009), the scope of the Unlawful Interference Convention (2009) has been widened as to also include damage that occurs in a State non-Party which provides for financial support by an International Fund to the operator which has its principal place of business or permanent residence in a State Party and is liable for damage occurring in a State non-Party under certain conditions.[23]

If a State party so desires, the scope can also be expanded to apply in cases of non-international flights. Damage to a ship in or aircraft above the high seas or the Exclusive Economic Zone as well as drilling platforms or other installations permanently fixed to the soil in the Exclusive Economic Zone or the Continental Shelf is regarded as damage within the territory of the States concerned. Thus, a next step has been made to broaden the scope to such installations in comparison with scope of the Montreal Protocol of 1978.

1.3.2 Material Scope

The Rome Convention (1952) gives no definition of the term 'damage'. There is no jurisprudence interpreting the meaning of this term.

The Montreal Protocol (1978) excludes nuclear damage explicitly from its scope.[24] The reason for inserting this provision was that several international instruments on nuclear liability placed the liability squarely on the shoulders of the operator of the nuclear installation.[25]

The scope of the Unlawful Interference Convention (2009) relates solely to damage caused by an act of unlawful interference.[26]

---

20. *See*, Art. XII of the 1978 Montreal Protocol.
21. *See*, Art. 23(2).
22. *See*, Art. 2.
23. *See*, Art. 28.
24. *See*, Art. XIV.
25. *See*, M. Milde, *Tenth International Conference on Air Law*, 4 Air Law 44 (1979).
26. *See*, Art. 2.

1.3.3 Liability of the Operator of an Aircraft

Liability for compensation of damages attaches to the operator of the aircraft.[27] Under the Rome Convention (1952) the registered owner of the aircraft shall be presumed to be the operator and shall be liable as such unless, in the proceedings for the determination of his liability, he proves that some other person was the operator.[28] This provision demonstrates that the Convention places the burden of liability upon the operator rather than the registered owner.

The operator is defined in the same Article as "the person who was making use of the aircraft at the time the damage was caused." A person is considered to be making use of the aircraft, again according to Article 2, when he is using it personally or when his servants or agents are using the aircraft in the course of their employment, whether or not within the scope of their authority. The operator will usually be an airline company, but he may also be a private person using the aircraft for private purposes.[29]

In spite of the broad definition of the term 'operator', third parties are still exposed to the risk that their claims might be illusory, for instance when the charterer or the lessee of the aircraft turns out to be insolvent. For these and other situations, the Rome Convention (1952) provides for special provisions designed to protect third parties on the ground.[30]

Under Article 3 of both the General Risks Convention (2009) and the Unlawful Interference Convention (2009), liability is attributed to the operator.

The operator is defined as:

> the person who makes use of the aircraft, provided that if control of the navigation of the aircraft is retained by the person form whom the right to make use of the aircraft is derived, whether directly or indirectly, that person shall be considered the operator.[31]

Joint and several liability of operators for damage to third parties arises in cases where two or more of their aircraft have been involved in an event causing damage.[32]

One of the most striking characteristics of the General Risks Convention (2009) and the Unlawful Interference Convention (2009) is that they provide for an *exclusive remedy* for any action for compensation for damage to third parties which can only be brought under the conditions of the applicable Convention.[33] Actions can only be brought against the operator under both Conventions whereas all other persons or

---

27. *See*, Art. 2.
28. *See*, Art. 2(3).
29. For the legal relationship which may arise between owner and operator, *see*, section 3 of Chapter 11.
30. *See*, Arts 2(2)(a), 3, 4 and 7.
31. For specifications as to *the use* of the aircraft, *see also*, Art. 1(f) of both Conventions.
32. *See*, Art. 5 of the Unlawful Interference Convention (2009) and Art. 6 of the General Risks Convention (2009).
33. *See*, Art. 12 of the General Risks Convention (2009) and Art. 29 of the Unlawful Interference Convention (2009).

entities, such as owners, lessors, manufacturers of aircraft, Air Traffic Control (ATC) agencies, airport operators cannot be held liable.

Concerns against these provisions have been raised in relation to the Unlawful Interference Convention (2009) because of the fact that it is not justifiable that other entities who have acted negligently and contributed to the damage should benefit from such an exclusion of liability, particularly as they do not have to contribute to the International Fund under the Unlawful Interference Convention (2009), and victims cannot receive any compensation from such entities if the funds of the International Fund have been exhausted or the operator is insolvent.[34]

1.3.4 Damage Caused by an Aircraft

The very first prerequisite of Article 1 of the Rome Convention (1952) is that the damage must be caused by an 'aircraft in flight.' As the Rome Convention (1952) does not give a definition of 'aircraft', the original definition of the Chicago Convention (1944) is presumably applicable.[35]

Being 'in flight' for an aircraft means the period in time between the moment power is applied for the purpose of actual take-off until the moment when the landing run ends.[36]

Under the General Risks Convention (2009) and the Unlawful Interference Convention (2009) the damage must also have been caused by an aircraft in flight.[37] An aircraft is now considered to be 'in flight':

> at any time from the moment when all its external doors are closed following embarkation or loading until the moment when any such door is opened for disembarkation or unloading.[38]

The latter definition broadens the scope of liability of the operator of the aircraft. It has also been adopted in the Aviation Security Conventions which are discussed in Chapter 12.[39]

---

34. *See*, particularly the arguments against the channelling of liability in relation to the operator under the Unlawful Interference Convention (2009) raised by Germany in International Conference on Air Law, DCCD Doc. No. 7, 13.03.09'; *see also*, Peter Neenan, *The Effectiveness of the Montreal Convention as a Channelling Tool Against Carriers*, XI(1) The Aviation and Space Journal, January/March 2012.
35. 'Aircraft is any machine that can derive support in the atmosphere from the reactions of the air.' *See*, on the subject of definition of 'aircraft' section 3.3.2.1 of Chapter 1; aircraft lighter than air, for instance, balloons, are considered to be 'in flight' from the moment they become detached from the surface until the moment they become again attached thereto. *See also*, S. Kaiser, *Third Party Liability of Unmanned. Aerial Vehicles*, 57 Zeitschrift für Luft und Weltraumrecht 229–237 (2008).
36. *See*, Art. 1(2).
37. *See*, Art. 3(1) of these Conventions.
38. *See*, Art. 1(c) of these Conventions.
39. *See*, section 2.3 of Chapter 12.

1.3.5 Risk Liability

The traditional method of assigning liability for an act of tort is through *fault*, that is, the liability attaches to the person causing harm, either intentionally or negligently.[40] Another approach, though less common, is through *risk liability*. This is the type of liability incurred upon mere proof that the damage exists and that it has been inflicted by a particular person. No proof of intent or negligence is required here. The liability is incurred irrespective of the perpetrator's compliance with the required standards of care. It is the latter type of liability which has been adopted in Article 1 of the Rome Convention of 1952.[41] Hence, risk liability is attached to the 'operator' of the aircraft as discussed in section 1.3.3, above.

Certain States, including the US, is opposed to the principle of risk liability altogether: it did not sign the Rome Convention (1952) because in the event of damage being caused in a State party to it a US operator would be liable pursuant to risk liability principles.

Both the General Risks Convention (2009) and the Unlawful Interference Convention (2009) are based on risk liability of the operator as well, albeit under variations per liability regime. The principle of risk liability has also been adopted in the legislations of many countries.[42]

1.3.6 Causation

A causal connection between the damage and the act causing damage or injury is the second prerequisite. As it turned out to be impossible to agree upon a definition for an international Convention the meaning of causal connection is for the domestic tribunals to decide, in conformity with the intents and purposes of the Convention. The reason lies in the fact that in Article 1(1) of the Rome Convention (1952), damage caused by a person or thing falling from an aircraft is equated to and in fact ranks equal with the damage caused by the aircraft itself. It does not, indeed, seem to be fair to

---

40. For fine tuning the concept of risk liability, while checking it against absolute liability, *see*, B. Cheng, *A Reply to Charges of Having Inter Alia Misused the Term Absolute Liability in Relation to the 1966 Montreal Inter-Carrier Agreement in My Plea for an Integrated System of Aviation Liability*, VI Annals of Air and Space Law 3–13 (1981) and A.J. Mauritz, *Liability of the Operator and Owners of Aircraft for Damage Inflicted to Persons and Property on the Surface* 42–44 (2003).

41. Art.1(1): 'Any person who suffers damage on the surface shall, *upon proof only that the damage was caused by an aircraft in flight or by any person or thing falling therefrom*, be entitled to compensation as provided by this Convention.' (*italics added*); *see*, the Minutes of the Conference on Private International Air Law (Rome, September/October 1952), ICAO Doc. 7379 – LC/34, specifically at 12–15 and at 53–60; *see also*, A.J. Mauritz, *Liability of the Operator and Owners of Aircraft for Damage Inflicted to Persons and Property on the Surface* 42–44 (2003).

42. *See*, D. Goedhuis, *National Air Legislations and the Warsaw Convention* (1937); Minutes and Documents of the Fifth Session of the ICAO Legal Committee (Taormina-Rome, January 1950), ICAO Doc. 6029 – LC/126 281–296 (provisions of national law concerning the liability for damage to third parties on the surface).

restrict the meaning of 'damage' to damage caused exclusively by direct contact with the aircraft, but this is a point quite open to debate. Reference is made to the doctrine of *adequate causation* which has been a subject of much controversy over the years, and the adage of *res ipsa loquitur* (the case speaks for itself).[43]

Also, Article 1 of the Rome Convention (1952) and Article 3 of the General Risks and the Unlawful Interference Conventions (2009) state that no compensation is due if the damage results from the mere fact of passage of the aircraft through the airspace in conformity with existing rules of air navigation. The above point is illustrated by case law.[44]

The consequences of the lack of ratifications and the application of national law principles, including those pertaining to causation and other principles of liability, have been dramatically highlighted by an Israeli cargo aeroplane of ElAl crashing in the Bijlmermeer suburb of Amsterdam on 4 October 1992. Neither the Netherlands nor Israel is party to the Rome Convention (1952); hence Dutch law was applicable. Since Dutch law does not contain rules governing liability for damage caused by operators of civil aircraft, general rules regarding negligence had to be invoked. Here, strict liability is the standard rule for faulty objects, but an exception has been made for aircraft, which fall under the general rules of negligence, although specific regulation of the matter based on strict liability is envisaged in the Transport Section of the Dutch Civil Code.

Remarkably, someone who suffers damage caused by a remote-controlled model aircraft has the benefit of strict liability of the culprit, whereas victims of a full-scale Boeing 747 crash like the one in the Bijlmermeer have to prove negligence under Dutch Law.[45] That heavy burden of proof may be softened by the above *res ipsa loquitor* adage. Also, it has been emphasised that in the handling of emergency situations not only the safety of aeroplanes and passengers but also the possible risk to third parties should be taken into account.[46]

---

43. *See, Vincent d'Anna v. United States* (four cases), US Court of Appeals (4th Circ.), 11 April 1950; United States Aviation Reports 282 (1950); 3 Aviation Cases 17, 171.
44. *See,* section 2.2.2.2 below.
45. *See,* C.J.J.M. Stolker, *Compensation for Damages to Third Parties on the Ground as a Result of Aviation Accidents,* in: C.-J. Cheng (ed.), *The Use of Air Space and Outer Space: Cooperation and Competition,* proceedings of the International Symposium on the Use of the Air and Outer Space at the Service of World Peace and Prosperity (Beijing, 1995), 343–360 (1998); *see also,* P.M.J. Mendes de Leon and S.A. Mirmina, *The International and American Law Implications of the Bijlmer Air Disaster,* 6 Leiden Journal of International Law 111–122 (1993) and H.L. van Traa-Engelsman, *The Dutch Parliamentary Inquiry into the Bijlmermeer Air Disaster – Lessons to Be learned for International Air Transportation,* in: M. Benkö and W. Kröll (eds), *Air and Space Law in the 21st Century,* Liber Amicorum K.H. Böckstiegel 216–230 (2001).
46. *See,* F.P. Schubert, *Aircraft in Emergency: Pilots, Controllers, and the Protection of Third Parties on the Surface,* XXIII Annals of Air and Space Law 185–200 (1998) citing Netherlands Aviation Safety Board, Accident Report 92-11 (El-Al Flight 1862, Bijlmermeer, Amsterdam, 4 October 1992).

1.3.7 Exoneration from Liability

The Rome Convention (1952) contains three exceptions to the generally accepted principle of liability, that is, the operator can exonerate himself if:[47]

(1) he proves that the damage was caused solely through the negligence or other wrongful act or omission of the person who suffers the damage or of the latter's servants or agents, unless the person who suffers damage can prove that his servant or agent was acting outside the scope of his authority; in that case liability will be reduced to the extent that negligence or wrongful act or omission contributed to the damage;[48]

(2) the damage is a direct consequence of armed conflict or civil disturbance;[49] *or*

(3) the operator had been deprived of the use of the aircraft by act of public authority.[50]

These exceptions have been left unchanged by the Montreal Protocol (1978).

Under Article 10 of the General Risks Convention (2009), the defence of contributory negligence has been retained, and can be invoked if the operator proves that the damage was caused or contributed to by the negligence or other wrongful act or omission of a claimant, or the person from whom he or she derives their rights. The operator shall then be proportionately exonerated from its liability to the claimant to the extent to which negligence or the wrongful act or omission caused or contributed to the damage. Perhaps the most notable difference with the Rome Convention (1952) lies in the deletion of the criterion that the operator had to prove that the damage was 'solely' caused through the negligence or other wrongful act or omission of the person suffering damage or his servants or agents as the main rule to exonerate himself from liability.

The defence of contributory negligence can also be invoked by the operator, or dependant on the situation, the International Fund under the *Unlawful Interference Convention* (2009).[51] However, an important difference is made by the higher threshold that the act or omission of a claimant or the person from whom he or she derives his or her rights must now have to be done with intent and with knowledge that damage would probably result.

Similar to the Rome Convention (1952), the operator is not be liable if the damage is the direct consequence of armed conflict or civil disturbance under the General Risks Convention (2009).[52] Remarkably, that exoneration has not been adopted in the Unlawful Interference Convention (2009).

---

47. *See*, A.J. Mauritz, *Liability of the Operator and Owners of Aircraft for Damage Inflicted to Persons and Property on the Surface* 52–55 (2003).
48. *See*, Art. 6.
49. *See*, Art. 6.
50. *See*, Art. 5.
51. *See*, Art. 20.
52. *See*, Art. 3(8).

Under the Rome Convention (1952) the operator is liable for damage caused by bombs placed in an aircraft by third parties, notwithstanding the fact that neither the operator nor his servants or agents could have prevented such acts. Bombs are usually placed aboard aircraft for political motives; provisions dealing with such unlawful acts are contained in the aviation security conventions which will be examined in Chapter 12.

1.3.8 Limitation of Liability

Limits of liability are expressed in the Rome Convention (1952) in terms of weight, while gold francs are the units of account.[53] A scale of five weight categories has been adopted for this purpose, a number which has later been reduced to four in the Montreal Protocol (1978).

The Montreal Protocol (1978) has basically stuck to the same system as the Rome Convention (1952), but it has made some important changes including a sizeable upgrading of the compensation rates. As regards the limits of compensation for loss of life or personal injury, these were raised 375 per cent over those set forth in the Rome Convention (1952), namely to a maximum of 125,000 Special Drawing Right (SDR) (or 1,875,000 Monetary Units).[54] The limits of compensation include statutory interests, but not the costs of legal proceedings.[55] In comparison to the Rome Convention (1952) the limits have indeed been raised substantially, but important aviation States still consider these sums to be far too low, especially in relation to large transport aircraft.

Besides the schedule of limits of Article 11, there are two more instances of liability limits in the Rome Convention (1952). One of these refers to collision cases which will be dealt with in section 1.3.10 of this Chapter. The other applies in cases where two or more persons are liable.[56] There are also provisions for situation in which the total amount of the claims exceeds the limit of liability applicable under the provisions of the Convention.[57]

Roughly thirty years after the conclusion of the Montreal Protocol of 1978, the limits of the operator's risk liability have been raised substantially and identically in both the General Risks and Unlawful Interference Conventions (2009). Similar to the Rome Convention (1952) and the Montreal Protocol (1978), a correlation between weight of the aircraft based on mass of the aircraft and limit of liability has been maintained.[58]

---

53. See, Art. 11; see also, A.J. Mauritz, Liability of the Operator and Owners of Aircraft for Damage Inflicted to Persons and Property on the Surface 110–112 (2003).
54. See, H. Drion, Limitation of Liabilities in International Air Law (1954) para. 153.
55. See, Art. 20(10) of the Rome Convention (1952); see also, H. Drion, Limitation of Liabilities in International Air Law (1954) para. 102.
56. See, Art. 13(1). .
57. See, Art. 14 in conjunction with Art. 11(2); for speedier dispatch of claims, see, Art. 19.
58. Art. 4(1) of both Conventions now contains ten categories ranging from aircraft with a maximum mass of 500 kg to more than 500,000 kg with linked to limits of liability ranging from 750,000 to 700,000,000 SDRs. These categories are based on and correspond to the minimum insurance requirements per accident for air carriers and aircraft operators set out in Art. 7 of Regulation (EC) 785/2004 as amended by EU Commission Regulation 285/2010.

1.3.9 Unlimited Liability

The liability of the operator under the Rome Convention (1952) is unlimited if the person who suffered the damage proves that it was caused by a deliberate act or omission of the operator, his servants or agents, done with intent to cause damage, provided the servant or agent was acting in the course of his employment and within the scope of his authority.[59] Employees of the operator are persons whose duty it is to fly the aircraft, and persons performing services on the ground.

The severe threshold of having to prove a deliberate act or omission of the operator or his servants or agents done with the intent to cause damage has been lowered to the standard of negligence or wrongful act under the General Risks Convention (2009). The limits set out in Article 3 shall only apply if the operator proves that the damage was not due to his negligence or other wrongful act or omission or that of its servants or agents or was solely due to the negligence or other wrongful act or omission of another person.[60]

In effect, this creates a two-tier regime of limited absolute liability and unlimited liability based on negligence or another wrongful act or omission of the operator or his servants or agents per weight category of aircraft.

Therein lies a crucial difference with the three-layered liability regime of the Unlawful Interference Convention (2009). Under the first layer, the operator can be held liable based on risk up to the limit corresponding to the maximum mass of the aircraft with a maximum of 700 million SDR.[61] The International Civil Aviation Compensation Fund subsequently compensates damage which exceeds this limit up to a maximum of 3 billion SDR under the second layer.[62] The third layer of additional compensation can be claimed from the operator insofar as the total amount of damages exceeds the aggregate amounts of the first and second layer. The claimant must then prove that the operator or its employees have contributed to the occurrence of the event by an act or omission *done with the intent to cause damage or recklessly and with knowledge would probably result.*[63] Even in such a case, the operator cannot be held liable if the operator proves that an appropriate selection and monitoring system of its employees has been implemented.[64]

Furthermore, the senior management of the company of the operator shall be presumed not to have been reckless, if it proves that a system to comply with the applicable international security requirements has been established by the operator.[65]

These elements of the liability system of the Unlawful Interference Convention (2009) are controversial and have raised serious concerns amongst a number of States

---

59. *See*, Art. 12 of the Rome Convention (1952).
60. *See*, Art. 3(3) sub (a) and (b) respectively.
61. *See*, Art. 4.
62. *See*, Art. 18(2).
63. *See*, Art. 23(1) and (2).
64. *See*, Art. 23(3).
65. *See*, Art. 18(4).

in view of the fact that the capped liability system of the first and second layer is in effect unbreakable and contradicts fundamental principles of national systems of tort law because it even lowers the current level of protection of potential victims and claimants as provided by tort law. Arguably, it is unjustifiable that operators should benefit from limited liability in cases where for instance the operator or its servants or agents negligently caused or contributed to the damage.[66]

On the other hand, proponents of this system of liability have pointed out that operators of aircraft can only be adequately protected by such a regime in cases of unlawful interference, specifically if these amount to extreme damages, such as the events of '9/11' have proven.[67]

1.3.10 Mid-Air Collisions

Mid-air collisions are rare, but happen unfortunately from time to time. Among the causes of collision may be mentioned navigation errors, faulty construction and natural causes like icing and turbulence, interception and ATC errors.

In 1976, a tragic accident took place near Zagreb, Yugoslavia, when both crew and all the passengers lost their lives. The accident occurred at a time when the air traffic controllers were neglecting their duties, and their negligence was proved to be the cause of the collision which involved a Yugoslavia Airlines DC-9 and a British Airways Trident.[68]

On 12 November 1996, a mid-air Collision occurred over the village of Charki Dadri, near New Delhi, involving a Saudi Arabian Airlines Boeing 747-100B en route from Delhi to Dhahran, Saudi Arabia, and a Kazakh Airlines Ilyushin II-76 en route from Chimkent, Kazakhstan to Delhi, killing 349 people on the two flights making it the deadliest mid-air collision in history. The probable cause for the disaster was stated to be the unauthorised descending of the Kazak aircraft and absence of on-board Traffic Collision Avoidance System (TCAS). However, there were also shortcomings in the ATCs supervising the flights at the time of the accident.[69] A action suit for compensation filed in the Delhi High Court was rejected because Saudi Arabian Airlines was a State owned entity.[70]

Another dramatic accident occurred on 1 July 2002, when a total of seventy-one people died in a collision of a DHL cargo Boeing 757-200 and a Russian charter jet operated by Bashkirian Airlines, carrying children who were on holiday. The mid-air accident occurred in Southern German airspace, which is controlled by the Swiss air

---

66. See, more particularly the concerns raised by Germany in ICAO DCCD Doc. No. 7, 13/03/09 on the Draft Convention on compensation for damage to third parties, resulting from acts of unlawful interference involving aircraft.
67. See, P.Z. Binder, 9-11 & Airline Civil Liability (2002) – on line.
68. See, G. Thomas, Aviation on Trial, 39(9) Air Transport World 31 (2002).
69. See, M. Kingsley-Jones and D. Learmont, Collision Raises Doubts on ATC Routeings, in Flight International of 20–26 November 1996 at 8.
70. See, section 3.4.2.4 of Chapter 4.

traffic service provider Skyguide. In such cases, national law will be applied, that is, the law of the State where the damage has been produced. Generally, the owner, possessor and operator of the aircraft will be held liable. The victims and their survivors will receive compensation from them, with an important role offer the insurers of the liable parties and the solicitors representing the victims.[71]

Air collisions have practical as well as legal repercussions. From a practical point of view they result in extensive damage in terms of persons and goods.

The position of third parties suffering damage on the surface of the earth as a result of an air collision is quite different from that of persons involved in the collision itself. A third party on the ground is in a less favourable situation because he cannot protect himself by means of insurance: he does not participate in the risk involved in travelling by air.

In the legal sphere one would perhaps expect to find rules or guidance in the international Conventions on the liability of the carrier with regard to passengers and goods towards third parties on the surface of the earth. There is only one rule in international law referring to this knotty problem. Article 7 of the Rome Convention provides that:

> When two or more aircraft have collided or interfered with each other in flight and damage for which a right to compensation as contemplated in Article 1 results, or when two or more aircraft have jointly caused such damage, each of the aircraft concerned shall be considered to have caused the damage and the operator of each aircraft shall be liable, each of them being bound under the provisions and within the limits of liability of this Convention.

This provision, the only one with any relevance to the matter, is hardly adequate for the purpose. Comprehensive regulations on the subject do not exist, and will not be achieved until agreement is reached on an international level.[72]

Although Article 7 of the Rome Convention (1952) covers the subject only in very general terms, the operator of the aircraft may be held liable even when he is not guilty of causing the collision: the article is completely in line with the risk principle embedded in the Convention, and it affords maximum protection to third parties on the surface.[73]

---

71. *See also*, section 3.2 of Chapter 6.
72. *See*, N.A. van Antwerpen, *Cross-Border Provision of Air Navigation Services With Specific Reference to Europe: Safeguarding Transparent Lines of Responsibility and Liability* (PhD thesis, Leiden University) 176 (2007); C.W. Johnson et al., *Recognition Primed Decision Making and the Organisational Response to Accidents: Überlingen and the Challenges of Safety Improvement in European Air Traffic Management*, 47/6 Safety Science 853–872 (2009); *see also*, P. Brooker, *Reducing Mid-Air Collision Risk in Controlled Airspace: Lessons from Hazardous Incidents*, 43/9 Safety Science 715–738 (2005); S.R. Stegich and J.E. Demay, *Bashkirian Airlines Flight 2937-DHL Airways Flight 611 Mid-Air Collision: A Spanish Court Applies U.S. Law to Determine Liability and Damages – A Paradigm Shift As To Forum Non Conveniens Or Much Ado About Nothing?*, Condon & Forsyth LLP Newsletter 2–4 (2010); F. Schubert, *The Liability of Air Navigation Services Providers: Some Lessons from the European Sky*, in: D. Calleja and P.M.J. Mendes de Leon, *Achieving the Single European Sky: Goals and Challenges*, 51–64 (2011).
73. *See*, M. de Juglart, *La Convention de Rome du 7 octobre 1952* (1955), paras 70 and 71.

2 DAMAGE CAUSED BY NOISE AND SONIC BOOM

2.1 International Regulation

Excessive noise may be caused by:

(1) aircraft passing through the airspace;
(2) take-offs and landings affecting areas adjacent to airports; and
(3) test flights affecting those areas.

In 1952, the year in which the Rome Convention was concluded, the damage jet aircraft might cause on the surface could not be predicted which is one of the reasons why that Convention is not an appropriate instrument to deal with the problem.

The Montreal Protocol of 1978 did not provide a solution for noise and sonic boom either. It was decided at the Conference that without a considerable amount of additional information it would be premature to undertake the drafting of a new separate instrument.[74] As a result they were, rather reluctantly, left to domestic legislation, but with a recommendation that a separate instrument should, if possible, be created to deal with them.

To solve the problem on an international level two procedures have been contemplated. One was to amend the Chicago Convention; the other suggestion for a way out was to modify the Rome Convention of 1952. These approaches met with difficulties as States were believed to be hesitant to accept amendments of these conventions. ICAO has also discussed the matter but no international agreement has been reached as it is basically governed by national law.[75]

2.2 National Law and Jurisprudence

2.2.1 The 'Noise' Problem

In order to combat the effects of aircraft noise, especially in densely populated areas, legislative measures have already been introduced in several countries. Aircraft noise, including the effect of sonic boom, can cause damage to persons, especially to their hearing, and also to property. Besides, case law has played a useful role in providing relief for those suffering from excessive noise.[76]

'Nuisance', another legal ground used in connection with damage caused by aircraft noise, may be defined as:

---

74. *See*, ICAO Doc. 9357 – LC/183, at 19.; at 61–64 and at 72.
75. *See*, the Minutes and Documents of the 22nd Session of the ICAO Legal Committee (Montreal, October-November 1976), ICAO Doc. 9222 – LC/177-1 and 177-2.
76. *See also*, P.M.J. Mendes de Leon, *Liability of Airports for Noise Hindrance: A Comparative Analysis*, 11 The Korean Journal of Air and Space Law 169–202 (1999).

any act or omission which interferes with the enjoyment by another of his health, comfort, or convenience in the occupation of his land.[77]

Nuisance caused by noise is usually recognised by the courts only if it is continuous or repetitive and provided that sensible discomfort and annoyance have been caused to the owner of the property. The economic interests of the community as a whole are so considerable and air traffic has become such a common feature of modern life that it will be extremely difficult for a private action of an individual against aircraft operators causing him abnormal discomfort to be successfully upheld in court. Here again the law varies from country to country.

Claimants can sue an airline company for damages caused by aircraft noise. However, pursuant to public regulations regarding navigation of aircraft, airlines are obliged by law to land their aircraft on specially designated airfields. Another option would be to sue the operator of the airport, but he might defend his case by arguing that he is compelled by law to allow air traffic to use the airport, and that it is not the airport that has caused the noise anyway. A third possibility would be to sue the State, but this is obviously not a simple matter. The question here is whether the State can be or ought to be forced to grant compensation for acts that may be lawful in themselves. Similar claims could arise in connection with pollution.

As for persons wishing to claim compensation, they have to do so in accordance with the rules of national law, the Rome Convention (1952) not being applicable to such claims. Hence, both in the substantive and procedural field, national law play a predominant role as illustrated by the following cases.

2.2.2 Case Law in Selected Jurisdictions

2.2.2.1 France

In Nice (France) a high-rise apartment building had been constructed on the outskirts of the city, but the apartments were difficult to sell because of the noise produced by jet aircraft using Nice airport. The court decided that the operator of the aircraft was liable for the damage caused by manoeuvrings of the aircraft.[78]

A controversial noise related case concerned the inhabitants of a Paris suburb involving the airport of Paris (Aéroports de Paris, AdP), and the airlines Air France, Pan Am and TWA. The administrative court ordered the airlines to pay several hundred thousand USD to the inhabitants for noise hindrance.[79] The airlines appealed and the French Council of State (Conseil d'Etat) instructed AdP to cover the losses of the

---

77. E. Jenks, *The Book of English Law* 343 (1967).
78. *See, Cie. Air France* v. *Sté ERVE et al.*, Cour de Cassation (2e Ch. Civ.), 8 May 1968; Revue française de droit aérien 327 (1968); *see also*, R.H. Mankiewicz, *Airport Noise – Compensation of Adjoining Landowners under French Law: A Report on a Case and Some Further Consider-ations*, 35 Journal of Air Law and Commerce 238–244 (1969).
79. Air France: approx. EUR 186,000; PanAm and TWA: approx. EUR 13,000. These amounts are based upon the volume of traffic of each respective airline. This criterion can, of course, be challenged: the issue is not the amount of air traffic *per se*, but the noise that is produced.

airlines.[80] AdP was held liable regardless of the fact that unlawfulness could not be attributed to it as it had conformed fully with the rules. According to the court, the airport was the most directly involved party in causing the losses. On its turn, AdP has attempted to hold the French State liable as it has the exclusive authority to extend permits for the construction and operation of airports. The Council of State did not go beyond a marginal analysis of the government's performance: only if the French government would have acted in a blatantly unlawful manner in the sense of '*faute lourde*' or '*décision illégale*' could there be liability. There was no evidence of this.

2.2.2.2   United States

In the United States, proceedings have generally been based on one of the following three grounds: (1) trespass; (2) nuisance; (3) unconstitutional taking. Two landmark US Supreme Court decisions confirmed liability for aircraft noise hindrance. The main legal ground used in the US to obtain compensation is 'unconstitutional taking.'

It was used in 1946 in the first case of the *United States* v *Causby*.[81] The court held that frequent flights and the interference they caused equalled the taking of an easement for which compensation was due, but added that:

> The airspace, apart from the immediate reaches above the land, is part of the public domain. We need not determine at this time what those precise limits are. Flights over private land are not a taking, unless they are so low and so frequent as to be a direct and immediate interference with the enjoyment and use of the land.

The line taken in the *Causby* case was further qualified in the *Batten* case,[82] where direct overflight was made a requirement before compensation could be obtained. In only a very few states has compensation been granted for excessive noise affecting landowners. Whether repeated overflights do or do not constitute 'unconstitutional taking' on a particular property depends on three factors, according to the *Causby* judgment:

(1) the character of the land itself;
(2) the altitude of the flights;
(3) the frequency of the overflights.

In the case of *Duchemin* v *Pan American World Airways*, where there was a causal connection between the flight of supersonic aircraft and the collapse of a building, the court decided that the liability of the aircraft's operator in respect of

---

80. Decision of the French Council of State from 6 February 1987.
81. *See, United States* v. *Causby*, US Supreme Court, 27 May 1946; 2 Aviation Cases 14,189; United States Aviation Reports 235 (1946).
82. *See, Batten* v. *United States*, US Court of Appeals (10th Circuit), 10 July 1962; 8 Aviation Cases 17,101.

damage caused by the noise from the aircraft during take-off and landing was limited to damage and inconvenience over and above that normally to be expected in an urban environment.[83]

In 1962 the US Supreme Court confirmed that airports, including local airport proprietors, pilots or aircraft owners, including airlines, are liable for noise damage.[84] The California Supreme Court has been particularly clear on the question of liability.[85]

Claiming unconstitutional taking has been successful in American courts when the inconvenience was so serious that it was considered to equal the taking of an easement for which compensation was due. Regular low overflights in the airspace over the plaintiff's property have been construed as such, and damage, for instance, glass damage caused by sonic boom, may be caused purely incidentally as a result of aircraft noise.[86]

In the case of *Irving D. Aaron v City of Los Angeles*,[87] the operator of the international airport of Los Angeles (LAX) was held liable for the depreciation in value of real estate belonging to residents living in the direct vicinity of the airport, in the event:

> the owner of property in the vicinity of the airport can show a *measurable reduction in market value* resulting from the operation of the airport in such manner that the noise from aircraft using the airport causes a substantial interference with the use and enjoyment of the property, and the interference is sufficiently direct and sufficiently peculiar that the owner, if uncompensated, would pay more than his proper share to the public undertaking. (*italics added*)

In this case the plaintiffs did not sue the airport but the airlines that flew close to their houses. Plaintiffs claimed that airlines were causing an unreasonable infringement on the normal use of the said real estate. The California Court of Appeal found that the airlines flew entirely following the rules established by the government, meaning with valid airworthiness certification, and taking into account the existing safety measures.[88] The demand for compensation of damage from the airlines could not be honoured; the court added that this decision does not affect the rights of house owners in relation to the airport.

Hence, the criteria for liability claims in the United States are determined by asking whether or not there was real or substantial, in a disproportionate amount, loss

---

83. *See, Duchemin* v. *Pan American World Airways*, Cour de Cassation (2e Ch. Civ.), 17 December 1974; Revue générale de l'air et de l'espace 273 (1974); *see also*, Schoner's case law digest, 5 Air Law 52 (1980).
84. *See, Griggs* v. *Allegheny County*, 369 U.S. 84, 82 S.Ct. 531.
85. *See*, cases listed by Howard Beckman Attorney at Law, *Aircraft Noise Damages* (2013), available on the internet.
86. *See, Aaron* v. *City of Los Angeles* (1974): there is no federal pre-emption in the field of noise control for jet aircraft. Federal control of airspace is no defence for airport proprietor's failure to purchase adequate air easements and does not preclude landowners from seeking damages from municipal operators of airports for overflights that constitute a taking of property (Ct. App. 2nd Dist.; 40 Cal.App.3d 471, 115 Cal.Rptr. 162; cert. denied 419 U.S. 1122, 95 S.Ct. 806, 42 L.Ed.2d 822).
87. 40 Cal. App. 3d 471, 115 Cal. Report 162; *see also*, *Alleghenny Airlines et al.* v. *Village of Cedarhurst*, United States Court of Appeals, Second Circuit 238 F.2d 812.
88. The possession of a licence forms no exemption from a tort case.

incurred. The mere fact that planes are flying below a specified altitude, for example, 100 feet, is not reason enough for compensation to be offered. Also, compensation depends on the liability laws of the states.

2.2.2.3 Switzerland

In its decision of 12 July 1995, the Federal Court of Geneva decided that surrounding inhabitants of an airport may not, under strict stipulations, be refused the right to compensation.[89] Surrounding inhabitants have the option of a civil suit under Swiss law if the nuisance originates from a public service, for instance an airport, if in the process of creating the public service no right to compensation was incorporated, and if the public service necessarily involves nuisance.

With regards to liability suits in cases concerning nuisance caused by traffic on land the Swiss jurisprudence has developed a *tripartite test* over the years. The three prerequisites are the severity (*'gravité'*) of the damage; the special nature of the damage and the (un)foreseeable consequences of the act.

2.2.2.4 The United Kingdom

The *Civil Aviation Act* 1982 (as variously amended) confers immunity upon aircraft operators from any action in trespass or nuisance provided the conditions of the Act, including compliance with the *Air Navigation (Noise Certification) Order* 1990 are met. There could, however, be liability under the Act in respect of material loss or damage caused by an aircraft in flight, taking off or landing.[90] Immunity from actions in respect of nuisance by reason of noise and vibration caused by aircraft at certain aerodromes is also given by the Civil Aviation Act 1982. This immunity also depends upon compliance with the Air Navigation Order and regulations made thereunder.[91]

The problem of aircraft noise is dealt with in English law in two other ways, that is, by setting standards as to noise and by making special provisions to mitigate loss and hardship suffered by owners of property in the area of airports. The former implements both international and European legislation; makes specific regulations, orders, directions, notices and so forth for steps to reduce noise hindrance and fixes aerodrome charges. The latter primarily deals with issues governing compensation.

---

89. Decision of the Federal Court of Switzerland, Chamber for Public Law (*Tribunal Fédéral Suisse, Cour du Droit Public*), of 12 July 1995 in the attached cases E.40/1989, E.50/1989, E.22-24/1991, E.22/1992, E.50-52/1993, E.71/1993.
90. Civil Aviation Act 1982, section 76(2); *Greenfield* v. *Law* 2 Lloyd's Reports 696 (1955).
91. Section 77(2) Civil Aviation Act, and the Air Navigation Order 2009, SI 2009/3015, Art. 215 and the Air Navigation (General) Regulations 1993, SI 1993/1622, Reg. 13; *see Steel-Maitland* v. *British Airways Board* 1981 SLT 110. For the principles governing the extent to which statutory authority, for instance to operate an airport, provides a defence to an action based on nuisance *see, Allen* v. *Gulf Oil Refining Ltd.* Appeals Cases 1001 (1981), 1 All England Reports 353 (1981).

Thus, it has been concluded that:

> Individuals in other jurisdictions may well have greater access to more effective private actions and remedies against offensive noise levels from aircraft, but, certainly in the UK, such actions are limited due to the underlying acceptance that aircraft noise is a necessary evil emanating from increased air transport and the economic and social advantages it confers.[92]

In 1997, Hatton and others put a claim against the UK government before the European Commission for Human Rights (ECHR) on the basis of Article 8 of the European Human Rights Convention (EHRC) protecting the right on personal and family life. On 8 July 2003 the Grand Chamber of the ECHR decided in appeal that there had been no violation of Article 8 of the ECHR, because restrictions on the rights to respect private and family life are permitted under the said convention in the interest of the economic well-being of the country, and of the rights and freedoms of the others. Hence, it was legitimate for the UK government to have taken into consideration the economic interests of airline operators, other enterprises and the country as a whole.[93] Despite the absence of arguments supporting the interest of night flights for the national economy, the court decided that the government failed to strike a 'fair balance between the United Kingdom's economic well-being and the applicants' effective enjoyment of their rights to respect for their homes and their private and family lives' implying a violation of Article 8 of the EHRC. The UK government had to pay each applicant GBP 4,000 for immaterial damages, and GBP 70,000 for legal assistance. This court also decided that there had been a violation of an effective remedy, as guaranteed by Article 13 of the EHRC.

In a second case,[94] claimants also successfully demonstrated that the noise caused by low flying aircraft constituted an actionable nuisance. The court argued that the noise levels by the claimants from the jets were extreme. The noise affected the use and enjoyment of the claimant's country house causing a diminution of its market value. The claimants had made complaints for over fifteen years. Although there was an unreasonable interference, the court also found that there was an overwhelming national interest in the training of pilots flying low flying aircraft. It declined to make a declaration that the nuisance be stopped. However, because the claimants should now be required to bear the costs of the public benefit, the court awarded damages of up to GBP 950,000. The decision was based on common law nuisance, but the claims also referred to the Human Rights Act of 1998 and the European Convention on Human Rights. Also, if the claim on nuisance had failed, the claim based on infringement of human rights would succeed and be awarded with the same amount of damages.

---

92. *See*, P. Davies and J. Goh, *Air Transport and the Environment: Regulating Aircraft Noise*, 18(3) Air & Space Law 123–134 (1993).
93. *See*, Press Release 376 of 8 July 2003, Grand Chamber Judgment in the case of *Hatton and others v. the United Kingdom; see also*, Jurisprudence internationale, *Hatton et autres c. Royaume Uni*, Requête no. 36022/97, Arrêté du 8 juillet 2003, LVIII Revue française de droit aérien et spatial 89–92 (2004).
94. *See*, *Dennis* v. *Ministry of Defence*, reported by Barlow Lyde & Gilbert, Newsletter (2004).

2.2.2.5   Germany

It is not easy to make a civil claim for compensation in Germany. The main rule is that the sound pollution caused by aircraft must be tolerated.[95] This obligation to tolerate sound pollution is far-reaching and even exceeds the regular protection of property owners.[96] The otherwise open airspace can be confined by closing off[97] parts of it to air traffic and by establishing a hard deck. In case of flight contrary to such regulations, action could be taken.

A possible civil claim for compensation could be based on Article 33 of the German Civil Aviation Act ('*Luftverkehrsgesetz*'). This article lays strict liability on the operators of aircraft for personal and material damages to third parties on the ground by accidents.

By way of German jurisprudence, forms of psychological trauma also fall under the scope of this article.[98] The question now is if the article sufficiently covers problems caused by noise pollution, for instance, health problem, among which supersonic bang.

Liability of airports could be based on causes in the field of neighbourly rights of noise pollution.[99] The difficulty with this is that airports are only indirect sources of noise pollution. A causal connection is a prerequisite for liability.

It seems that air traffic must be tolerated when it is in accordance with the regulations of public law; in such cases the approach of civil law is relatively prospect-less. For this reason, the jurisprudence is concise on this matter.

2.2.2.6   Japan

In Japan, Narita airport has concluded an agreement with the users regarding the compensation of damage caused by falling of objects.

In 1981, the Japanese Supreme Court held that the Japanese government is liable under the State Tort Liability Act of 1947[100] as the damages caused by the noise and vibration of aircraft taking off and landing at the airport were caused by the negligence of the government when establishing and managing the airport in question. The

---

95. *See*, Art. 1 of the German Civil Aviation Code ('Luftverkehrsgesetz').
96. *See*, P. Wysk, *Ausgewählte Probleme zum Rechstshutz gegen Fluglärm*, Zeitschrift für Luft- and Weltraumrecht 19–20 (1998). The 'regular' protections are the guarantee of Arts 905 and 906 of the German Code ('*Bundesgesetzbuch*').
97. Prohibited or restricted areas ('*Sperrzonen*'); *see*, Art. 26 of the German Civil Aviation Code.
98. *See*, the decision of the District Court (*Oberlandesgericht*) of Oldenburg dated 27 October 1989, where the plaintiff had been awarded damages to the sum of 500 DM (appr. USD 250) for having suffered psychological trauma from passing NATO (North Atlantic Treaty Organization) aircraft. The verdict is published in 24 Versicherungsrecht 910 (1990) (Insurance Law).
99. *See*, para. 906 and 1004 of the German Code.
100. Act No. 125.

Supreme Court added that any person who has recognised the risk and tolerated the damages is not entitled to compensation, and that any future damage is not compensated in advance.[101]

3 CONCLUDING REMARKS

Surface damage has been regulated in global conventions. The limitation provisions may be regarded as an attempt to create a system affording the highest possible degree of legal security. The international regulatory framework for addressing liability for damage on the surface caused by an aircraft in flight has largely an academic value. The regime is in place, and is certainly interesting and worth studying but is hardly or has never been applied in practice.

Case law interpreting the provisions of the Rome Convention of 1952, and its amending Montreal Protocol of 1978, is basically absent. Publications made in the twenty-first century on this regime are scarce. However, there are, of course, comments on '9/11' and the Bijmer crashes but the international regime does not apply to those events.

This statement does not mean that studying the international regulatory framework does not make sense as the principles underlying these international agreements may be used for drawing up national regulations and arguing court cases. The principles of the Rome Convention (1952) may be used to draw up domestic law when a State perceives a need for it, or they may be used by courts when preparing their decisions.

Moreover, damage on the ground is not always substantial as evidenced by the crashes involving Eurowings, in a mountainous landscape, MH17, on agricultural terrain, and MH370, on the Indian Ocean. Notable exceptions are, again, '9/11' and the Bijlmer crash.[102]

Last but not least, damage claims which are made in this context are mostly settled out of court. All involved potentially liable persons, including but not limited to operators of airports and air navigation services, airlines and the States themselves, and their insurers, have a direct interest in settling the claims as swiftly and conveniently as possible. The tragedies following these accidents do not warrant complicated and lengthy judicial proceedings, whether based on national or international law. This conclusion applies even more to damage caused by mid-air collisions, which, fortunately, are rare.

More topical, more frequent and less dramatic is the question of liability for the compensation of damage caused by noise. Again, absent international or European regulations on the subject, national law as applied by national courts plays a predominant role here. A number of jurisdictions have produced interesting case law, especially so in the twentieth century.

---

101. Hanrei-Jiho No. 1025, at 39 ff.
102. *See also*, the crash of a Turkish cargo aircraft B747F on a residential area in Manas, Kirgizia, killing 37 people; *see*, www.upinthesky.nl of 23 January 2017.

These cases demonstrate the pragmatic approach which courts tend to adopt when arguing their decisions. Other environmental cases, in particular those involving questions pertaining to the liability for damage caused by emissions of aircraft, have not yet been put forward. It cannot be excluded that such claims will be submitted before courts in the next decade as they have been brought to the attention of courts in other sectors of economic life.

CHAPTER 10

Insurance

1 AEROSPACE INSURANCE IN CONTEXT[1]

1.1 Definition

There is no settled definition of what constitutes a contract of insurance. In very general terms, insurance transfers from an insured to the insurer the risks of financial consequences arising from whatever is covered by the policy, considered to be an event adverse to the interest of the policyholder. An insurance contract is sometimes defined by its characteristics and a useful definition is given in the case of *Prudential Insurance Co.* v. *Inland Revenue Commissioners* where, in return for premium, one party promises to pay the other party a sum of money or provide a benefit upon the occurrence of a specified event involving some uncertainty.[2]

Recognising the potential for catastrophe situations arising from aviation accidents or incidents, it becomes necessary to obtain financial protection for accidental loss or damage. As such, the insurance markets provide necessary support for the aerospace industry to help control the potential of wide ranging effects on private individuals, the general public, the operators and service providers. It is usually a mandatory regulatory requirement for aircraft operators. This chapter serves as an overview of the principal insurance issues at play.[3]

Insurance cover for airlines includes a wide range of property and liability risks involving the transportation of passengers and goods, use of and damage to the ever

---

1. This Chapter has been drawn up by Mr Nicholas Medniuk, Solicitor of the Senior Courts of England and Wales. The Editor in Chief is greatly indebted to the author of this chapter for his valuable contribution to this treatise.
2. *Prudential Insurance Co.* v. *Inland Revenue Commissioners* [1904] 2 KB 658.
3. For a fuller treatment on aviation subject matters *see*, R.D. Margo, *Aviation Insurance* (2014) and section IX, Chapter 40, C.N. Shawcross and K.C. Beaumont, *Air Law* (loose-leaf, updated); for insurance law in England & Wales, MacGillivray on *Insurance Law* (2016) is now regularly relied upon in courts.

expanding list of equipment, the buildings from which these services operate and even to the equipment manufacturers and various associated service and maintenance and repair organisations. A comprehensive insurance programme has become indispensable to all operators and service providers in the air transport industry, given the high market value of aircraft and the potentially huge financial liability flowing from their use. Well-crafted insurance should be considered as equally important to protect passengers as to those entrusting their goods to a carrier's care.

1.2 Historical Development

It is not known precisely when the very first aviation insurance policy was issued but the starting point seems to be around 1908.[4] After the First World War, aviation insurance was promoted as a specialist class of business by former military pilots entering the insurance industry. The expansion of commercial aviation in the inter-war period provided the impetus for increased demand for insurance and so during this period several insurers pooled their resources to spread the risk of the increasing exposure.

While insurance pools are not so prevalent today, the practice of sharing risks between insurers, generally known as co-insurance, remains just as strong and is a key feature of the current aviation insurance markets.

By the early 1950s,[5] London, notably Lloyd's of London, had established itself as the centre for placing aviation risks. Lloyd's had a long established system of syndication – a collective approach to providing cover but with 'several liability', meaning that each insurer is responsible for his own portion so that the risk was spread among a number of separate insurers. Today, while London remains an important insurance centre, as it is also for reinsurance, the aviation insurance market is now truly global. Jurisdictions include the United States, Bermuda, China, France, Germany, Switzerland and Japan, among others, providing significant insurance capacity. Most aviation policies will have cover provided by insurers from various countries either directly via co-insurance or by reinsurance.

Events that have touched the world, ranging from a difficult economic climate, changing oil prices, terrorist incidents and the evolution of the 'low cost' or budget airlines have all made their mark on the aviation industry, giving rise to the recent trend for consolidation. Coincidentally, this trend can also be seen for insurers as much as for airlines but for quite different reasons. In the mid-1990s it was possible to see a large list of insurers, perhaps forty to fifty, on an airline policy, each one taking a small percentage of the risk – sometimes less than 1 per cent. Today, perhaps ten to fifteen insurers will subscribe to a policy but each will commit a much larger share of the risk, for example, up to 20 per cent.

---

4. *See*, R.D. Margo, *Aviation Insurance* (2014) and *A Short History of Aviation Insurance in the United Kingdom*, Report H.R. 10 of the Historic Records Committee of the Insurance Institute of London (1968).
5. *See*, R.D. Margo, *Aviation Insurance* 3 (2014).

1.3 Nature of Aerospace Cover

Aerospace insurance is usually regarded as a 'catastrophe' type of cover as distinct from motor, homeowners or life insurance. This exposure to potentially very costly claims contributed to demands for substantial premiums to reflect the exposures. Pricing of risk has been quite closely linked to the level of received claims and thus costs have either risen or fallen significantly between the annual periods of cover. As a result, attempts have been made to reduce or stabilise the cost of insurance by using alternative risk transfer options.

In addition to the use of various financial instruments, some carriers formed their own 'captive' insurance companies while other airlines grouped together into consortia to spread the burden of paying premiums. However, these varying alternative methods achieved only limited degrees of success and traditional insurance remains the standard method of managing and transferring risk.

Underwriting decisions, that is, the process of analysing and valuing risk, have had to adapt to geopolitical changes and advancement in technology; for example, changes in governments have created 'no fly' zones as a result of trade embargoes or armed conflict, the continued development of jet engines and use of computers to actually operate aircraft, the use of composite materials rather than metals in manufacturing processes all adjust the inherent risk of operating a flying machine.[6] Insurers and operators continue to adapt to these changing profiles. Equally, changes in the law affecting the operations and liability of an insured may also prompt a review of the terms of cover.

Insurance law, which is essentially a specialist branch of contract, and corporate law provide the legal standards against which the policies may be judged. In common law jurisdictions, insurance law has historically been developed through the courts with minimal statutory involvement beyond codification of existing practice. However, particularly over the past few decades, insurance activity has been the subject of much regulation not just in the process of contract formation but also relating to the business environment in which insurance contracts are negotiated.[7] A number of civil law

---

6. *See*, section 3.3.2.1 of Chapter 1.
7. With London as one of the major centres of the aviation insurance market, the result of the UK's referendum on 23 June 2016 to leave the European Union will have consequences for the operation of both the insurance and aviation industries. The consequences are not yet determined but, broadly, the issues concern market access and regulatory equivalence across borders. Currently, the London market benefits from capital provided by the establishment of insurance branches by companies incorporated outside the UK but within an EU Member State, using passporting rights which is a licence for insurers to operate in all Member States if they fulfilled certain EU conditions. If branches of foreign insurers do not close, they will likely have to re-establish themselves as a UK entity but it is understandably difficult for a company to decide what to do while the regulatory position remains unclear. The flow of business may depend upon the regulatory regime continuing to be deemed equivalent with the EU regime called Solvency II. Accordingly, the UK risks losing some of its ability to offer insurance and reinsurance or, depending upon new arrangements, customers might find doing business elsewhere more attractive.

countries have developed specific codes governing insurance matters, which may periodically be updated.[8]

2 COMPULSORY INSURANCE

2.1 Provisions of International Conventions

The Rome Conventions of 1933 and 1952 sought to provide a regime for imposing an insurance requirement in respect of liability to persons or property on the surface.[9] However these conventions have only a small following States[10] and a relatively recent attempt by ICAO to revive this subject in the form of two proposed conventions[11] has, so far, failed to garner sufficient ratifications. Indeed, some argue that there is no need for such an international regime since most domestic law regimes adequately deal with the liability problem in most cases.[12] That said, these international initiatives do not address the question of the source of funds to pay for this liability.

Insurance for passenger, baggage and cargo/freight and for liability to third parties is a different matter. Where the Montreal Convention of 1999, henceforth also referred to as *the Convention*, applies,[13] Article 50 must be observed, as must EU Regulation 785/2004 on insurance requirements for air carriers and aircraft operators, henceforth the *EU Aviation Insurance Regulation*.[14]

The Convention imposes a simple obligation on States Parties to require that their carriers maintain adequate insurance covering liability under the Convention.[15]

---

8. For example Chile and Peru introduced new insurance contract laws in 2013.
9. *See*, section 1.3 of Chapter 9.
10. *See*, section 1.1 of Chapter 9.
11. In 2009 the members of ICAO completed work on the *Montreal Convention on Compensation for Damage Caused by Aircraft to Third Parties* and the *Montreal Convention on Compensation for Damage to Third Parties, Resulting from Acts of Unlawful Interference Involving Aircraft* as to which *see*, section 1.2 of Chapter 9. These conventions are not in force.
12. Under English law, *see*, the Civil Aviation Act 1982, section 76(2): Liability of aircraft in respect of trespass, nuisance and surface damage:

    (2) ... where material loss or damage is caused to any person or property on land or water by, or by a person in, or an article, animal or person falling from, an aircraft while in flight, taking off or landing, then unless the loss or damage was caused or contributed to by the negligence of the person by whom it was suffered, damages in respect of the loss or damage shall be recoverable without proof of negligence or intention or other cause of action, as if the loss or damage had been caused by the wilful act, neglect, or default of the owner of the aircraft.

13. *See*, section 3.1 of Chapter 4.
14. For English law, *see*, Civil Aviation (Insurance) Regulations 2005(SI 2005/1089).
15. *See*, section 3.6.1.3 of Chapter 4.

2.2   The EU Aviation Insurance Regulation

The EU Aviation Insurance Regulation,[16] applies to all operators flying within, into, out of, or over the territory of a Member State, is much more specific than the Convention.

Currently, insurance cover must provide for a minimum of 250,000 SDR per passenger in respect of passenger liability while in respect of liability to third parties the requirement is set as a range from 750,000 SDR to 700,000,000 SDR depending upon aircraft weight. The level of cover required for baggage and cargo has been updated by EU Regulation 285/2010 in line with the revised limits applicable under the Montreal Convention 1999 so that the level of insurance must be 1,131 SDR per passenger in respect of baggage and 19 SDR per kg in respect of cargo.

2.3   National Regulations

Most States grant their regulatory authorities the right to make the registration of aircraft and the right to engage in aviation activities contingent upon having a minimum amount of insurance cover, without making it mandatory in either case. Airlines cannot legally operate aircraft to most international destinations without providing evidence of sufficient insurance cover to protect third parties from bodily injury or property damage.[17]

In some countries, additional insurance is required for the benefit of the passenger.[18]

3   PARTIES TO THE PLACEMENT OF INSURANCE

3.1   Background and Focus

The formation of an insurance contract follows basic contract law principles where one party makes an offer for another to consider/accept supported by consideration (premium). However, given the complexity of the subject matter and the potentially large exposure at stake, the process of forming the contract known as 'placement', involves several parties, either actively or passively.

This section focuses on the London market, where many UK and international companies provide cover for aviation risks.[19] With the exception of the Lloyd's market, the placement process used in the London market is similar to markets in other countries.

---

16. *See also*, section 3.5.1 of Chapter 4.
17. *See*, section 3.6.1.3 of Chapter 4, in conjunction with section 1.2.1 of Chapter 2 on licensing conditions for carriers operating international air services.
18. For example, Austria, the German Federal Republic, Italy, Spain and Switzerland; *see also*, R.D. Margo, *Aviation Insurance* 30 (2014).
19. *See*, section 1.2 above.

3.2 Types of Insurers

Insurers come in two types:

(1) insurance and reinsurance companies (including captive insurance companies that enable an insured to participate in their own risk, and may be incorporated to cover risks that are unavailable in the market or perhaps to optimise tax advantages); and
(2) syndicates at Lloyd's.

Insurance companies who carry on insurance business in London are subject to English law which regulates and licenses the activities of the companies themselves and also key individuals who work within them. From a policyholder protection perspective, there is also an important requirement for insurers to maintain certain levels of solvency as measured against the volume of business, both premium and claims. These policies issued by the insurers are usually subject to the domestic law of the policyholders.

Lloyd's is not an insurer itself; the Corporation of Lloyd's provides and regulates a market place within which its members may transact insurance business. Individual members, known as 'names', may be persons or corporate entities and they group together into syndicates to provide insurance capacity. Several syndicates may be managed by an agent who conducts business on their behalf through an 'active underwriter'. Traditionally, each name had several and unlimited liability. The introduction of corporate members in 1994 created members with limited liability and individuals may now take a corporate membership. In practice, Lloyd's does not now operate unlimited liability for its members. Approximately, 90 per cent of Lloyd's capital is drawn from corporate entities rather than individual private names.[20]

3.3 The Role of Brokers

Brokers provide insurance consultation to insured persons and an intermediary service between the insured and the insurer. While the Lloyd's market requires that business be transacted with a broker licensed by Lloyd's for that purpose, the practice of using brokers is widespread but a potential insured may approach an insurance company directly. Some companies have established websites to offer cover for certain general aviation risks on-line.

Brokers typically act as an agent for the insured to whom they owe their primary duties but may also perform duties for an insurer in certain circumstances such as delivering the policy or insurance certificate and collecting the premium. The regulation of brokers is covered by the general law of agency while Lloyd's brokers must additionally observe Lloyd's Brokers Byelaw and its associated Code of Practice.[21]

---

20. *See*, www.lloyds.com.
21. *See*, *Bowstead and Reynolds on Agency* (2010).

3.4 Insurance Institutions

Insurance institutions offer supplementary services to the market as a whole. Several such institutions are representative bodies that seek to promote the interests of their members. The British Insurance Brokers Association (BIBA) represents brokers generally in the UK while the LMBC – a committee that now forms part of LIIBA, the London and International Insurance Market Broker's Association – serves Lloyd's brokers who are London centric with international business portfolios. Such dual representation is mirrored by representative bodies for insurers: the International Underwriting Association (IUA), representing insurance companies and LMA, Lloyd's Market Association representing Lloyd's underwriters. Each of these entities has aerospace sections.

The specific interests of worldwide aerospace insurance are represented by the International Union of Aerospace Insurers (IUAI) which seeks to:

> speak and negotiate on behalf of aerospace insurance interests, to provide a central office for the circulation of information between members, to cooperate for the better regulation and conduct of aviation insurance, and generally to do anything which may be beneficial to the development and conduct of aviation insurance.[22]

Premium levels are never discussed in the IUAI.

The Aviation Insurance Clauses Group (AICG) is a special entity set up to provide a forum for all interests to be represented when considering new wordings. It is tasked to consider and draft clauses for use as model wordings that are designed to have the support of the market, created through a representative spectrum of committee members incorporating views of policyholders and insurers.

4 UNDERWRITING AND THE CONTRACT OF INSURANCE

4.1 The Formation of the Insurance Contract

Some risks may be placed directly with an insurer; typically these are small general aviation risks. A proposal form is generally used, which is drafted by an insurer and seeks from the prospective insured information sufficient to consider the risk(s).[23] The normal process of placement for an airline risk or 'account' starts with the airline instructing a broker to procure insurance on its behalf. The broker prepares a document, known as a 'slip', containing the basic terms of cover sought. This slip is presented to insurers by the broker, who makes a presentation that will include factual information about the insured. Typically, the broker approaches an initial insurer to 'lead' the risk and once terms are agreed with the lead underwriter the broker will approach other underwriters, that is, co-insurers, until the risk is 100 per cent subscribed. The percentage of the risk subscribed by each underwriter constitutes a separate contract with the insured.

---

22. *See*, R.D. Margo, *Aviation Insurance* 54 (2014).
23. *See*, AVN 2A and AVN 2B.

After finalising placement, the broker may issue a cover note until a policy has been prepared. Pending production of the policy, the slip remains the contractual document. In recent years a process known as 'contract certainty' is operated which obviates the need for a cover note, as a policy is issued at inception of the cover. To foster efficient discussions between the broker and the underwriter, the introduction of a placing standard form – called the Market Reform Contract (MRC) – was developed. This encouraged consistency in the presentation of risks and aligned the contents of the agreement with the needs of contract certainty.[24]

Policies often run for a period of one year, many from 1 January to 31 December; so the 1st January renewal, colloquially known as '1,1', can be a very busy period, although some airlines renew at different points in the year. At renewal, the same parties might enter into a new contact on the same or similar terms but the principles related to contract placement will apply again at the point of renewal.

4.2 The Principle of Good Faith

Departing from the ordinary *caveat emptor* standard for contracts, parties to an insurance contract under English law are required to observe the principle of '*uberimae fidei*', that is, to deal with each other in the *utmost good faith*.

Predicated on the notion that an insured is the source of information about the proposed insurance, the duty of utmost good faith obliges the insured, or the broker on his behalf, to provide complete and accurate information to allow an insurer to fully assess the risk. This amounts to a duty to present all material facts that would influence the judgment of a prudent insurer in deciding whether to accept the risk and on what terms.[25]

4.3 The Impact of English Law

While English law no longer has quite the same influence on the world of aviation insurance, many contracts do adopt it as the governing law. As such, it remains significant and so recent reform of some fundamental principles of English insurance law merits mention.

The Consumer Insurance (Disclosure and Representations) Act 2012 applies to consumer contracts entered into on or after 6 April 2013. For aviation purposes, this means individuals who insure an aircraft mainly for purposes unrelated to the individual's trade, business or profession,[26] this would include an aircraft owned

---

24. *See*, www.londonmarketgroup.co.uk/mrc.
25. *See*, *Pan Atlantic Insurance Co. Ltd* v. *Pine Top Insurance Co. Ltd.* [1995]. Misrepresentation and non-disclosure are very technical areas of law. The duty of *utmost good faith* has been amended as to which *see*, section 4.3 about the impact of English law.
26. Section 1 of the Consumer Insurance (Disclosure and Representations) Act 2012 defines a "consumer insurance contract" as a contract of insurance between (a) an individual who enters into the contract wholly or mainly for purposes unrelated to the individual's trade, business or profession, and (b) a person who carries on the business of insurance and who becomes a party to the contract by way of that business (whether or not in accordance with permission for the

privately for leisure but used occasionally for business purposes. For non-consumer contracts, the Insurance Act 2015 applies. These two Acts update English law from rules favouring insurers in relation to contract formation (placement) and construction of insurance contracts by replacing the duty of utmost good faith with new rules and remedies.[27]

Consumers are bound by a less onerous duty to take reasonable care, taking into consideration all relevant circumstances, not to make a misrepresentation to the insurer.[28] Representations will likely be contained within responses to pre-contractual proposal forms such as AVN 2A[29] and AVN 2B.[30]

The Insurance Act 2015[31] provides a default regime but parties are able to contract out. Since the requirements of specialist markets, such as the aviation market, may not met by the default regime, it remains to be seen whether it will be adopted or in what situations the new rules might be set aside.

The rules relating to disclosure apply to non-consumer contracts only,[32] which will include reinsurance contracts. The Insurance Act 2015 introduces a duty of fair presentation, which retains the core elements of the duty of utmost good faith in the sense that the insured has the primary burden to disclose all material information[33] and any material representation of fact made by the insured must be 'substantially correct' plus any representation of expectation or belief must be made in good faith. A new second limb of the disclosure rule deals with the situation where an insured fails in its primary duty, then information provided may be sufficient to put a prudent insurer on notice that it needs to ask further questions. There is a new and separate duty on the insured to present a risk in reasonably clear and accessible fashion.

The Insurance Act 2015 introduces proportionate remedies. To be entitled to a remedy at all for a breach of the duty of fair presentation, the insurer has the burden to show that, but for the breach, (a) it would not have entered into the contract of insurance at all, or (b) it would have done so only on different terms. This will be known as a 'qualifying breach.' Whereas English law used to provide for a single

---

purposes of the Financial Services and Markets Act 2000); "consumer" means the individual who enters into a consumer insurance contract, or proposes to do so; "insurer" means the person who is, or would become, the other party to a consumer insurance contract.

27. Per Section 14(3) of the Insurance Act, section 17, Marine Insurance Act 1906 is amended to read: "A contract of marine insurance is a contract based upon the utmost good faith, and, if the utmost good faith be not observed by either party, the contract may be avoided by the other party."). The removal of the deleted words suggests that the principle of utmost good faith will be used as a guide to the construction of insurance contracts.

28. Section 2(2), Consumer Insurance (Disclosure and Representations) Act 2012.

29. Used for AVN 1C.

30. Used for AVN 1D.

31. The Lloyd's Market Association has provided a comprehensive guide on all aspects of the Act.

32. Defined by reference to section 1 of Consumer Insurance (Disclosure and Representations) Act (2012).

33. Section 7(3) Insurance Act 2015, a material fact is anything which "would influence the judgement of a prudent insurer in determining whether to take the risk and, if so, on what terms". Like the provision for (mis)representation, this codifies the pre-existing law.

remedy of avoidance *ab initio*,[34] avoidance is now only available if the insurer can show that the qualifying breach was deliberate or reckless.[35]

The remedy for other breaches depends whether the insurer can show that it would not have entered into the contract on any terms, in which case it may avoid the contract but must return the premiums paid, or if it would have entered into the contract but on different terms, unrelated to premium, the contract is to be treated as if it had been entered into on those different terms if the insurer so requires. If the insurer would have charged a higher premium, payment on claims may be reduced proportionately.

Bearing in mind that much of the aviation business written in London is reinsurance, it is important to mention the new rules in relation to what an insured ought to know to discharge the duty of fair presentation. A cedant, that is, a reinsured, owes the same legal duty as the primary insured to carry out a reasonable search for, and share with the reinsurer, material information and so may need to make enquiries of the primary insured if a question arises as there is now a duty not to turn a blind eye. A cedant therefore risks breaching the duty of fair presentation if it fails to pass on information which would have discovered by making enquiries of the primary insured because this would be considered information which "should reasonably have been revealed by a reasonable search".

The Enterprise Act 2016 introduces a new section 13(A) and 16(A) into the Insurance Act 2015 providing for an implied term that a claim will be paid within a reasonable period of time. The rule became effective from 4 May 2017 and will introduce a variety of new issues to consider. This may include questioning whether a valid claim has actually been made, as some policies prescribe what must be submitted. An insurer is permitted a "reasonable time" to investigate, which will clearly be a fact sensitive exercise and largely dependent on the size and complexity of the claim. However, even though some factors will be outside of an insurer's control, it will be no excuse to rely on a third party's inaction and so a note of caution arises from aviation claims handling when external agencies carry out investigations, for example under Annex 13 of the Chicago Convention; an insurer may be in a position to work out certain facts for themselves in relation to policy coverage and should be proactive in pursuing any third parties who cause delay (including claim handlers, loss adjusters and lawyers). The burden to show that reasonable grounds existed for taking longer than a reasonable time to investigate and pay a claim lies on an insurer and there is a defence where reasonable grounds for disputing the claim exist. Any claim for breach of this implied term must be brought within a year from when all sums are paid. There is no limitation on the amount recoverable and so particular care must be taken for

---

34. Section 18, Marine Insurance Act (1906). The remedy relieves a (re)insurer from any liability because the policy is deemed never to have existed. It is a remedy against the insured's misrepresentation and/or non-disclosure of material facts.
35. Per section 8(5), Insurance Act (2015), a breach will be deliberate if the insured knows that he is in breach of the duty and it will be reckless if the insured does not care whether he is in breach of the duty.

claims taking a long time to investigate or claims that will be resisted. Contracting out of this provision is possible only for non-consumer policies, save for deliberate or reckless breaches.

4.4 Underwriting Information

Underwriters seek to understand and rate risk. A great deal of statistical information is generally available and sometimes specifically collated or demanded by insurers. The fact that underwriting has been popularly described as a mixture of 'science and art' says something about how decisions are made. While many insurers operate with formal underwriting guidelines, the factors that determine whether to accept a risk will ultimately be a subjective appraisal made by the actual underwriter against general knowledge, technical underwriting guidelines and information provided by the insured through the broker.

For an airline, key pieces of information might include the number, type and age of the aircraft, the routes and frequency on which they are flown, details of who will maintain them and procedures in place for training pilots, staff and the programme of maintenance, the purpose of the flights and who or what will be carried. The costs of settlement of some nationals, for instance, US citizens can be notably higher than for citizens of other countries. Details of this type are highly relevant for insurers. The relevant legal jurisdictions that operations will have to deal with should also be important in the context of regulatory compliance and any possible claims/litigation. It is difficult to generalise since risks might amount to a single private light aircraft, a commercial air taxi service, up to a major international airline or group of airlines.

While no airline publically trades on its safety record, a loss history will be important to an insurer, who has a variety of methods to adjust premium accordingly. Working within the confines of the relevant regulatory system, an initially assessed premium may be partially refunded if no loss is suffered within the policy period or vice versa an initially lower premium supplemented in the event of a claim.

5 TYPES OF INSURANCE

5.1 Aviation as a Class of Insurance

The purpose of an insurance contract is to provide financial cover against a fortuity, which may be a number of risks/perils affecting persons or property. Accordingly, such contracts can be said to be contracts of indemnity as they do not deal with contingent events, as do life policies, where the insured receives no more than the loss actually suffered.

The heritage of the aviation market, which developed from marine insurance, is shown by use of common terminology. Indeed, many general principles of insurance law developed from marine insurance and apply equally to aviation insurance.

Nonetheless, aviation it is not the same as marine insurance,[36] for example, certain principles particular to marine insurance such as the doctrine of abandonment and constructive total loss do not apply as a matter of law to aviation polices, although they may be introduced as terms in the contract. Hence, aviation insurance is considered as its own class.

There are a wide variety of aviation risks depending on where an aircraft is geographically located, whether it is in storage/maintenance or in service and whether or not it is in flight. Cover can be provided in a single policy for hull and liability risks using the London Market model wording contained in AVN 1C and will be review below. A variant produced in 2014, AVN 1D provides similar cover and is also reviewed below.

Several other categories of insurance exist such as cargo insurance, manufacturers' and products liability insurance,[37] war and hijacking insurance,[38] and airport operations liability insurance. Separate policies can also be obtained to cover satellites, hovercraft, unmanned aircraft (UASs),[39] repossession and financial interests, and loss of licence.[40]

5.2 All Risks Cover

5.2.1 Principle of 'All Risks'

There are a number of policies available that provide cover for aircraft. One of the popular polices available on the London market is called AVN 1C, the London Aircraft Insurance Policy. It is of an 'All Risks' type limited by exclusions. This type of cover places an obligation on an insured to show that an insured peril has occurred, after which the burden of proof falls on the insurer to show that an exclusion applies.[41]

All risks covers seek to deal with loss, damage and liability arising out of an accident or incident. While it is a recognised wording, it may be amended by altering, replacing and/or supplementing its provisions for which there are several additional variable wordings, some of which are mentioned below. Indeed, airlines and their insurers often adapt their policies to suit the specific needs of the airline.

5.2.2 Hull Cover

Hull cover deals with the physical use and loss of an aircraft. Section I of the policy covers loss or damage to the aircraft and provides the insurer with an option such that the insured has no right to choose to abandon an aircraft to pay for, replace or repair,

---

36. *See, Kuwait Airways Corp.* v. *Kuwait Ins Co.* 1 Lloyd's Reports 803 (1999) and *Scott* v. *Copenhagen Re. Co (UK) Ltd.* Lloyd's Reports I.R. 696 (2003).
37. *See*, sections 2.5 and 3.3 of Chapter 8, and other sections of this Chapter.
38. *See*, section 5.5 below.
39. *See*, section 3.6 of Chapter 6.
40. *See*, section 1.2.1 of Chapter 2.
41. *See, Bond Air Services* v. *Hill* 2 Q.B 417 (1955).

accidental loss of or damage to the aircraft covered. Part 2 of section I sets out exclusions specific for hull coverage and includes wear and tear, deterioration, breakdown, defect or failure in any unit, for instance an engine, and the consequences of such defect or failure unless accidental loss arises.

Conventional hull insurance protects the insured regarding loss of or damage to the aircraft caused by such risks as fire, theft and collision.[42]

The meaning of the term 'collision' is given a very broad interpretation in the policies: any sort of physical contact with an external object comes within range of this word, and even damage caused by fire or ice formation may be included. Loss or damage caused by fire is sometimes brought under the heading of flight risks. In general, it is required that an 'incident' or 'occurrence' has taken place.

The amount that may be claimed is normally limited either to an amount agreed when the policy is placed which is often, the market value of the aircraft at that time, or the parties may agree on the value of an aircraft so that non-market value considerations may be taken into account. Such considerations are typically driven by the requirements and the amounts contained in finance agreements. A change in the market value does not affect the valuation agreed. In the case of damage, insurers impose on the insured an obligation to prevent further damage and retain a wide discretion as to how to respond to a claim, for instance they retain a choice as to whether repairs will be conducted. Under 3(c) of section I, deductibles may apply unless the aircraft is repaired or replaced but it is known that policies do not always provide for a deductible where a total loss has occurred.

A deductible is a specified amount that the insurance does not cover, sometimes described as an amount retained by the insured, that is, a financial interest to prevent a moral hazard arising and to remove nuisance value claims which are costly to administer. Where a deductible applies in respect of the hull, insurance for that deductible may be obtained to greatly reduce it but rarely to totally eliminate it.

Where an aircraft is destroyed, it will be clear that a loss has occurred. However, where an aircraft is lost, a claim cannot arise automatically as the aircraft must be 'unreported for sixty days' per 1(a) of section I. This gives rise to a principle of 'uncertainty of recovery'[43] so that aircraft need not actually be lost before a claim is paid and will be paid even if the aircraft is eventually found.

5.3 Legal Liability

Legal liability concerns the following:

(1) *Cover in respect liability to third parties* is dealt with by section II of AVN 1C and covers all sums for which the insured shall become legally liable to pay as a result of the operation of the aircraft as compensatory damages in respect of accidental bodily injury to persons other than passengers or property damage.

---

42. *See*, R.D. Margo, *Aviation Insurance* 233 (2014).
43. *See*, *Kuwait Airways Corp.* v. *Kuwait Ins Co.* 1 Lloyd's Reports 664 (1996).

The phrase 'legally liable' is important. It means that the insured is not entitled to claim for the voluntary assumption of responsibility.[44]

Further the liability must extend to the payment of 'compensatory damages'. As a matter of timing, an insurer is not only liable to pay once the insured is ordered to pay damages but when the insured is legally accountable to the third party.[45] Second, the requirement that damages must be compensatory appears to exclude cover for punitive damages, although the fact that punitive damages are not specifically excluded makes the position unclear.[46]

Wording different from AVN 1C which does not seek to limit cover to compensatory damages, may mean that punitive damages are covered unless domestic public policy intervenes[47] as being contrary to good order and interest. Simply put, punitive damages may be considered a fine and some jurisdictions ban the practice of insuring against being fined.

Exclusions apply to those acting in the course of employment or duties for the insured as well claims caused by noise pollution, contamination, electrical and electromagnetic interference.[48]

2) *Cover in respect liability to passengers* is dealt with by section III of AVN 1C and covers all sums for which the insured shall become legally liable to pay as compensatory damages in respect of accidental bodily injury to passengers whilst entering, on board or alighting from the aircraft; or loss or damage to baggage and personal effects arising out of an accident.[49]

The insuring clause obliges the insured to take measures to exclude or limit liability to the extent permitted by law prior to boarding and to do so by issuing any necessary documentation, for instance, a ticket or a boarding pass. In the electronic age, tickets are rarely issued and boarding passes or websites incorporate the Conventions' limits of liability.[50] This is normally done at the time of booking by use of terms and conditions in the contract of carriage. In this context, the wording of section III appears designed to get the benefit of the Warsaw/Montreal Convention regime.[51]

---

44. *See, Yorkshire Waters Services Limited* v. *Sun Alliance* 2 Lloyd's Reports 21 (1997).
45. *See, Lancashire Ins.* v. *IRC* 1 QB 353 (1899). Additionally many policies require an insured to refrain from admitting liability without the consent of the insurer. Also, in theory the implied term as to payment within a reasonable period of time applies to liability policies but a practical difficulty arises in determining when the insurer is actually liable to pay.
46. Indeed, across the United States, there is no uniformity between US states, *see*, Pamela C. Hicks, *Aviation Insurance: Coverage, Claims, and Controversies*, 81(4) Journal of Air Law and Commerce 611–630 (2016) at 620–621.
47. As a matter of policy construction, the *contra proferentum* rule favours the payment of such damages, even where the question is whether punitive damages can be considered compensatory.
48. *See*, AVN 46B and 47; separate cover may be arranged for liability arising for noise, vibration, sonic boom and associated phenomena; *see also*, section 2 of Chapter 9.
49. *See*, section 3.7 and other sections of Chapter 4, for instance, 3.10 on delay.
50. *See*, section 3.3 of Chapter 4.
51. Again, as explained in various sections of Chapter 4.

Because of the limitation of the insuring clause in section III which excludes the period before embarkation, it is not clear whether there is cover for delay;[52] such liability clearly arises for an airline and can occur after embarkation.[53] While no deductible applies to the liability cover, the policy will normally prescribe limits to each accident or aircraft.

Third party cover will have a combined limit for bodily injury and property damage while passenger liability may have a limit per passenger seat separately for bodily injury and for baggage/personal effects. Additionally, these will be subject to a further limit called a 'Combined Single Limit' where there is limit per accident for legal liability in respect of third parties and passengers combined. AVN 1C records these limits in a schedule.

5.4 Exclusions and Conditions

Conditions and warranties are very important terms in an insurance policy constituting provisions that benefit the insurer and control the behaviour of the insured. Section IV of AVN 1C carries three parts, that is, General Exclusions, Conditions Precedent and General Conditions; they are often replicated in other versions of aviation all risks policies. The effect of breach of these terms will depend upon the classification of the clause, but will range from discharging an insurer's liability on a claim to preventing the contract from coming into effect at all.[54]

While some exclusions are contained within a policy document, others may be incorporated by reference to model wordings. However, incorporation by reference, where an insured does not have the opportunity to read the exclusion, in some countries may render it unenforceable.

Supervision of aviation safety is regulated by and under the Chicago Convention pursuant to which every aircraft must possess a Certificate of Airworthiness (CoA) certifying that the aircraft fulfils the safety requirements in force and this is normally also a requirement for insurance cover.[55] Such a certificate does not prove that the aircraft is airworthy at the start of each flight. In the event of a dispute the possession of a certificate may be regarded by the courts as evidence in favour of the insured, but when, for instance, the maximum weight stipulated in the certificate is exceeded, the aircraft will not be considered as airworthy, irrespective of the presence of the certificate. The CoA does not extend to defects that the insured cannot be aware of such as latent defects or faulty construction.

In some countries loss or damage resulting from the insured's own fault have been excluded from the insurer's liability; in others the insurer may be held liable.

---

52. *See,* section 3.10 of Chapter 4.
53. *See,* section 3.8 of Chapter 4.
54. As to which *see,* general insurance texts such MacGillivray, *Insurance Law* (2016).
55. *See,* Art. 31 of the Chicago Convention: "Every aircraft engaged in international navigation shall be provided with a certificate of airworthiness issued or rendered valid by the State in which it is registered." and AVN 1C Section IV(B)2(a); *see also,* section 3.3.2.3 of Chapter 1.

Insurance against wilful misconduct or gross negligence is unlawful in some countries on the basis of the absence of uncertainty or fortuity. Different standards are applied in cases of wilful misconduct or gross negligence on the part of the insured's agents or employees.

Policies often cover flight risks but exclude ground risks. In general, insurers do not compensate for loss or damage resulting from

(1) starting the aircraft's engines without first making precautionary checks and procedures;
(2) revving up the engines in the hangar;
(3) leaving the aircraft outside the hangar insufficiently guarded and secured, unless such omission is due to force majeure.

Dependent upon the actual policy terms and the governing law, it is expected that examples (1) and (2) would probably be paid by the insurer.

Policies may exclude liability for experimental flights, aerobatics and other unusual activities such as record attempts and racing. It is possible to find coverage for these perils by special agreement.

The insured is obliged to notify the insurer immediately in the event of loss or damage. Most policies also include an obligation for the insured to undertake action to avoid or diminish any loss or damage.

The insurers are not obliged to pay until such time as the extent of the damage has been established to their satisfaction by experts.

5.5 War and Allied Perils

One addition to the list of exclusion clauses was occasioned by the Israeli raid on Beirut airport in 1968: it is the 'War, Hijacking and Other Perils Exclusion' clause.

Clause AVN 48 was first introduced in the London insurance market and later went on to form part of almost every hull and liability insurance policy outside of North America.[56] However, through AVN 52 cover the liability of the airline may be 'written back' into the policy. Even though hull cover is often provided under a separate policy, aspects of these perils may also be written back by AVN 51 which gives only a reduced cover.

The 1968 Israeli raid on Beirut airport and a subsequent spate of hijackings provided a catalyst for the insurance market to focus on the wording of the war risk exclusion. Now, as noted above,[57] airlines must consider their position with respect to compulsory insurance under the provisions of the above Montreal Convention 1999

---

56. *See*, R.D. Margo, *Aviation Insurance* 354 (2014). This clause was designed for and introduced on the London aviation insurance market; insurers elsewhere may thus have other clauses in their policies. *See*, the Appendix of Margo's book for the text of many model clauses.
57. *See*, sections 2.1 and 2.2.

and EC Regulation 785/2004. The latter establishes a specified obligation that a policyholder must carry certain minimum levels of cover for war, terrorism, hijacking, sabotage, unlawful seizure and civil commotion in respect of each and every flight.

The exclusion most commonly used today is AVN 48B, the language of which is replicated as an exclusion in AVN 1C,[58] although relatively recent alternative wordings AVN 48C and AVN 48D were developed by the AICG to reflect the enhanced threat represented by the use of tactical nuclear weapons and other Weapons of Mass Destruction ('WMD').

The interesting provision of the exclusion clauses, AVN 48C and AVN 48D, is subparagraph (b) where greater detail is given to excluded devices and substances. While both clauses exclude the act of "detonation of any device employing atomic or nuclear fission and/or fusion or other like reaction and any radioactive contamination or matter", AVN 48D further excludes "radioactive contamination and electromagnetic pulse resulting directly from such detonation." Subparagraph b(iv) deals with bio-chemical concerns. AVN 48D bars claims for a "*hostile* emission, discharge, or release" of bio-chemical substances, AVN 48C excludes "any use" of them, whether or not accidental, arising from a list of hostile situations and for political or terrorist purposes. In practice, there is likely to be little to choose between the two main exclusions because the real choice is in how excluded risks can, or cannot, be written back.

For extra premium, certain of the risks excluded may be 'written back' into an all risks policy as specified in Extended Coverage Endorsements. In the case of aircraft hulls, the risks which can be written back, that is, under AVN 51A, are only those specified in paragraphs (c), (e) and (g) of AVN 48B. This is clearly limited cover. 'Full' hull risks are often written by separate specialised war risks insurers using the standard wording contained in LSW 555B, C or D. These generally provide cover in respect of loss of or damage to an aircraft caused by, *inter alia*, war, invasion, acts of foreign enemies hostilities, strikes, riots, acts committed for political or terrorist purposes, and acts of sabotage, confiscation, nationalisation, seizure, restraint, detention, appropriation, requisition for title or use, and hijacking or unlawful seizure or wrongful exercise of control of aircraft.

---

58. AVN 1C, Section 4(A), exclusion 10 provides that the policy does not apply to claims caused by:

- (a) War, invasion, acts of foreign enemies, hostilities (whether war be declared or not), civil war, rebellion, revolution, insurrection, martial law, military or usurped power or attempts at usurpation of power.
- (b) Any hostile detonation of any weapon of war employing atomic or nuclear fission and/or fusion or other like reaction or radioactive force or matter.
- (c) Strikes, riots, civil commotions or labour disturbances.
- (d) Any act of one or more persons, whether or not agents of a sovereign Power, for political or terrorist purposes and whether the loss or damage resulting therefrom is accidental or intentional.
- (e) Any malicious act or act of sabotage.
- (f) Confiscation, nationalisation, seizure, restraint, detention, appropriation, requisition for title or use by or under the order of any Government (whether civil military or de facto) or public or local authority.
- (g) Hi-jacking or any unlawful seizure or wrongful exercise of control of the Aircraft or crew in Flight (including any attempt at such seizure or control) made by any person or persons on board the Aircraft acting without the consent of the Insured.

The difference between the alternative policies relates to the provision or exclusion of cover in respect of loss or damage caused by electromagnetic pulses or chemical, biological or bio-chemical materials.[59] Since the cover afforded by these alternatives represents a major difference in risk assumption, there is a corresponding difference in the level of premium charged.

In the case of liabilities, there are several versions of the write-back endorsement, AVN 52, the version used most commonly being AVN 52E, the later version introduced after 11 September 2001 attack on the World Trade Centre. Its immediate predecessor, AVN 52D, also a post-11 September 2001 iteration, introduced a sub-limit of USD 50 million in respect of third party bodily injury and property damage for any one occurrence and in the annual aggregate for any of the named perils excluded by AVN 48B. AVN 52E, was directed towards general aviation operators[60] which limits third-party liability to USD 10 million. AVN 48C and AVN 48D are partnered with bespoke write back clauses such that two categories arise:

(a) the provision of a war exclusion and write back that fully excludes so called WMD perils: AVN 48C partnered with AVN 52H for aircraft operators and AVN 52J for service providers; and

(b) the provision of an alternative that anticipates some level of WMD cover according to risk appetite: AVN 48D is partnered with AVN 52K for aircraft operators and AVN 52L for service providers.

A full review of the differences between the reinstatement provisions is beyond the scope of this work, however, the basic distinction is that AVN 52H and AVN 52J make it explicit that no WMD perils will be covered under the policy whereas AVN 52K and AVN 52L specifically offer WMD reinstatement cover up to pre-agreed sub-limits. Common to all reinstatement provisions, there is no write back in respect of the nuclear exclusion.

One advantage of a 'write back' of the war risk exclusion, is to prevent the insured from facing a dispute over whether the all risks or war risk policy covers the loss though such a dispute may occur at the reinsurance level. Policies often include a well-known provision, that is, the Provisional Claims Settlement Clause, known as AVS 103. This clause provides a preliminary sharing arrangement as between all risks and war insurers where each will pay 50 per cent of the loss to the insured and then arbitrate liability between themselves.

One well-known issue with war risks cover, from policy holders perspective, is that insurers reserve the right to give short notice of cancellation. Additionally, war risk cover may automatically terminate upon an outbreak of war between any of the major

---

59. LSW 555B: no exclusion for electromagnetic pulses or chemical, biological or bio-chemical materials. LSW 555C: specific exclusion for electromagnetic pulses or chemical, biological or bio-chemical materials, section 3(g)(ii) and (iii). LSW555D section 3(h) provides cover for such perils where such use originates solely and directly on board the aircraft whether on the ground or in the air.

60. See, Shawcross and Beaumont, *Air Law*, Chapter IX, para. 45.

powers, and upon the hostile detonation of any weapon of war employing automatic or nuclear fission and/or fusion whether or not the insured aircraft may be involved.

5.6 All Risks Variant: AVN 1D

5.6.1 *Structure*

Many policies follow the form or the content of AVN 1C, especially in the general aviation market. As noted, brokers may develop their own wording.

AVN 1D is a variant of AVN 1C, produced in early 2014. Like the earlier version, it will likely be used for general aviation risks placed on the London Market. The rationale for the revision was to simplify the contractual process and to allow for consistency with other clauses drafted since the introduction of AVN 1C.

The simplification comes from the policy structure. The policy schedule is located at the beginning, rather than the end, of the document and, while displaying similar pieces of information as required for AVN 1C, adds a jurisdiction and choice of law clause. Additionally, it notes that the schedule of aircraft may change subject to prior agreement by insurers; typically aircraft may be automatically added or deleted from cover. Given that airlines frequently arrange cover for the fleet of aircraft that they operate which can change during the policy period it is important for the parties to clearly understand which aircraft are covered and whether any premium is required to be paid or returned as a result of changes to the fleet. Typically, the accounting between insured and insurer will be handled via the broker.

In the definitions section[61] is an entry for 'aircraft' which, by its reference to the policy schedule and description of physical items such as engines installed on the aircraft, omits any reference to technical documents.[62] They should therefore be considered uninsured without further specific cover. Cover for technical documents is available as an endorsement to the policy, in a form called LSW 612, which covers "costs and expenses arising from loss of or damage to the Technical Records" relating to aircraft or spares that have been identified in the policy schedule.

5.6.2 *Cover*

The cover provided by AVN 1D broadly follows the format and the wording of AVN 1C.

AVN 1D makes clear that claims will be covered provided that they occur during the policy period, known as an "occurrence based" or "losses occurring" policy.[63] The claims process begins with giving notice of a claim and this is generally subject to a contractual term providing how and when notice must be made. In practice, such

---

61. The definitions are curiously not in alphabetical order.
62. Technical documents may be insured expressly in certain policies. On the legal status of aircraft engines, *see*, section 3.2.2 of Chapter 11.
63. To be contrasted with a 'claims made' policy, where the claim must be notified during the policy period.

notice is normally made by an operator to their broker, who will liaise with the insurers and, subsequently as may be necessary, any service providers such as loss adjusters and lawyers.

The question of what constitutes effective notice can be difficult and is generally controlled by a condition in the policy both as to promptness and likelihood of a claim. As to promptness, AVN 1C requires "immediate" notice, whereas AVN 1D requires notice "as soon as possible." As to likelihood, both variants require notice of "any event likely to give rise to a claim",[64] which means at least a 50 per cent chance of a claim.[65] Thus, there is a spectrum of situations within which notice could be made and it is for the insured to assess whether notice must be given against the factual circumstances and the requirements of the notice clause.

Both AVN 1C and AVN 1D contain requirements for what information must be provided to the insurer when giving notice – effectively full particulars of the circumstances. These provisions are expressed as a condition precedent to liability and so care must be taken to ensure compliance to ensure that a recovery on the policy is possible.

5.6.3 Exclusions

A section dealing with exclusions is bolstered in AVN 1D by attachments set out at the end of the policy providing the full wording for the following clauses:

(1) AVN 48B, War, Hi-jacking, and Other Perils Exclusion Clause (Aviation).
(2) AVN 38B: Nuclear Risks Exclusion Clause.
(3) AVN 46B: Noise and Pollution and Other Perils Exclusion Clause.
(4) AVN 2000A: Date Recognition Exclusion Clause.
(5) AVN 72: Contracts (Rights of Third Parties) Act 1999 Exclusion Clause.
(6) 2488AGM00003: Asbestos Exclusion Clause.
(7) AVN 111 Sanctions and Embargo clause.

This serves to underscore the importance of these particular policy terms and by setting out the full wording ensures that the terms are incorporated into the contract, which may be important if the policy is interpreted in jurisdictions which do not favour the incorporation of terms by reference.

5.6.4 Sanctions Cover

Both policyholders and insurers doing business in all classes of insurance with an international element need to consider whether trading restrictions imposed by

---

64. Under English law, *Rothschild Assurance Plc* v. *John Robert Collyear* [1999] Lloyd's Rep IR 6, this has been held by Rix J to mean that "there must be a real or material risk, something more than a *de minimis* risk, something more than a negligible, fanciful or speculative risk, that the circumstances notified might lead to a claim."
65. *See, Layher Ltd* v. *Lowe* [2000] Lloyd's Rep IR 510.

economic sanctions may affect their business. Such sanctions can be imposed by national governments[66] or international organisations, for example the United Nations or EU.

According to HM Treasury in the United Kingdom, examples of breaches of sanctions include deliberately channelling money to organisations or individuals subject to financial sanctions when their bank account or finances are frozen. The consequences can involve substantial penalties including fines or criminal prosecution and as such strict compliance is important. Aviation, as an international industry, obviously presents concerns since carriers may operate within embargoed countries or routes including such countries and may carry nationals of embargoed countries with the effect of preventing payments in the event of a claim.

Accordingly, AICG produced a wording that could be adopted, called AVN 111, to help insurers and policyholders deal with sanctions compliance. It provides that an insurer shall provide no coverage and have no liability to the policyholder where to do so would be unlawful. Where coverage is lawful but payment might be unlawful, an insurer is obliged to seek authorisation. If a rule of regulation takes effect during the policy period, an insurer or a policyholder has a right of cancellation upon giving thirty days' notice in writing, with return premium to be pro-rated subject to any claims.

An adapted version of the clause was produced for reinsurance purposes called AVN 111(R), which is an important additional clause, that is, rather than relying upon the existence of the version for insurance policies, because the nationalities of the corporate entities party to the reinsurance may be different from the parties to insurance.

Any policyholder under a composite policy operating illegally and in breach of sanctions will not prevent other insured persons from claiming.

6 CARGO

Carriers are liable for the loss of or damage to cargo[67] in their care for which the carriage by air will be only one part of the journey. The extent of such liability depends upon the applicable legal regime but the wide spread adoption of the Montreal Convention 1999 deserves mention for crystallising unbreakable limits of liability,[68] currently 19 Special Drawing Rights (SDR)s per kilogram,[69] unless a special declaration in writing has been made to the carrier, which is typically recorded on the air waybill.

Insurance provided to commercial parties for the carriage of cargo is provided by separate specialist markets and is beyond the scope of this chapter. The carrier's liability is typically covered by the aviation insurers but is not covered by the standard

---

66. Currently, per UK government website, the UK has over twenty-seven United Nations, European Union and domestic financial sanctions in place, covering just over 1,900 individuals, groups and countries.
67. *See*, Art. 18 of the Montreal Convention (1999); *see also*, Prof. M. Clarke & Dr George Leloudas, *Air Cargo Insurance* (2016).
68. The notion having been introduced by the Montreal Additional Protocol 4, 1975. This protocol was adopted by sixty States (per March 2017), as to which *see*, section 3.12.4 of Chapter 4.
69. *See*, Art. 22(3), Montreal Convention (1999).

wording of AVN 1C or D but it can be extended under an endorsement, called AVN 92, or by adding bespoke wording to cover cargo in the liabilities section of the policy. AVN 92 covers accidental physical loss of or damage to cargo whilst in the care, custody or control of the Insured for the purpose of carriage by air.[70]

Despite liability under the Montreal Convention 1999,[71] there is no specific cover for delay.

7 PRODUCT LIABILITY INSURANCE

7.1 Principles of Coverage

Manufacturers may procure product liability insurance against the risk of legal liability for damages arising from injury, loss or damage caused by a defective product or design or manufacture of a product forming part of an aircraft or the aircraft itself, including the failure to warn of potential hazards.

It is fundamental that there must be a liability, which is a question of law. Principles of liability will be determined against the law governing the use of the product and this is a complex area. Notably, an insurer is not necessarily bound by a decision on liability between the insured and the third party if the insurer can show that the basis for the determination was wrong.[72] A commercial settlement between an insured and the third party does not establish the insurer's liability.[73] However, any *ex gratia* payments made in consequence of a liability will be covered.[74]

That said, an insurer who declines to defend their insured upon being given notice will not be able to challenge the quantum of a genuine settlement.[75]

Further, an insurer who continues to defend their insured after discovering a breach of a condition or warranty may be taken to have waived the breach.[76] Insurers have a reasonable time to decide how to deal with a claim,[77] but in the case where there is doubt that a third party's claim is covered at all, an insurer who defends the claim anyway without contesting coverage may, both by its conduct and from taking control away from the insured, be taken to be estopped from later denying coverage.

Also, the nature of the illegality in question is a matter of public policy.

Under English law, in the case of *Lancashire County Council* v. *Municipal Mutual Insurance Ltd,*[78] the word 'compensation' was held not to exclude awards of exemplary punitive damages and that insurance against a liability to pay exemplary damages is

---

70. *See*, sections 3.12.1 and 3.12.2 of Chapter 4.
71. *See*, Art. 19, Montreal Convention (1999).
72. *See*, *Omega Proteins Ltd* v. *Aspen Insurance UK Ltd* [2011] Lloyd's Rep. I. R. 183.
73. *See*, *Smit Tak* v. *Youell* [1992] 1 Lloyd's Rep 154.
74. *See*, *Peninsular & Oriental Steam Co.* v. *Youell* [1997] 2 Lloyd's Rep. 136.
75. *See*, *Captain Boyton's World's Water Show Syndicate Ltd* v. *Employers Liability Assurance Corp Ltd* [1895] 11 T.L.R. 384.
76. *See*, *Evans* v. *Employers Mutual Insurance Association* [1936] 1 K.B. 505 and *Fraser* v. *B.N. Furman* [1967] 1 W.L.R. 898.
77. *See*, *McCormick* v. *National Motor and Accident Insurance Union Ltd* [1934] 40 Com.cas; *Liberian Insurance Agency Inc.* v. *Mosse* [1977] 2 Lloyd's Rep 560.
78. [1996] EWCA Civ 1345.

not unlawful; the insuring clause wording 'all sums which the insured shall become legally liable to pay as compensation' was found not to be clear as to its extent as so did not exclude exemplary damages.

7.2 Scope of Coverage

Subject to policy wording, cover typically relates to loss arising from a physical event during the policy period and potentially also external physical consequences and so would not include cover for the costs of investigations. Further, actual damage is required; a simple defective product is not sufficient to give rise to liability.[79]

Cover in the aviation market will likely depend upon the type of insured. Larger companies such as aircraft and engine manufacturers, and some component manufacturers, will likely have bespoke policies because the business is their product. Other insured's, whose business activity is not focused on manufacturing products, such as aircraft operators, maintenance and repair organisations, airports, may include a products type cover within a policy covering a broader range of risks.

In the United States, the Aircraft Builders Council (ABC) developed an insurance programme,[80] which is available internationally through a standard policy wording evolved over several decades by market participants (brokers, underwriters and policyholders) and is currently supervised by a committee made up of aviation brokers. A notable aspect of the programme is the insured's waiver of suit or claim against any other insured covered by an ABC policy, however a provision for arbitration is made within the policy.

7.3 Coverage by AVN 66

AVN 66 is titled the London Market Aviation Products Liability Policy Wording. This policy provides an insured with two principal covers:

(a) liability for damages because of bodily injury and property damage caused by an occurrence taking place during the policy period arising out of a products hazard;

(b) liability for damages for the loss of use of completed aircraft occurring after delivery to and acceptance by a purchaser or operator for flight operations caused by a grounding resulting from an occurrence taking place during the policy period and arising out of the products hazard.

---

79. *See, Pilkington UK Ltd* v. *CGU Insurance Plc* [2004] Lloyd's Rep I.R. 891.
80. Per the Aircraft Builders Council website: it was founded in 1954 at a time when aviation products liability coverage was in its infancy and not readily available on the open markets and helped develop a products liability insurance facility for the benefit of manufacturers in the aviation industry. Participants in the program may secure coverage limits of up to USD 1.5 billion.

The policy obliges the insurer to defend any claim or suit covered by the policy and also covers expenses incurred at the insurers request except loss of earnings and eliminating the cause of the loss. The policy defines a products hazard to mean the handling, use of, or the existence of any condition in an aircraft product, provided that such product has ceased to be in the possession or control of the Insured. Grounding means the complete and continuous withdrawal from all flight operations at or about the same time of one or more aircraft due to a mandatory order of the US FAA or the UK CAA or any similar civil airworthiness authority because of an existing, alleged or suspected like defect, fault or condition affecting the safe operation of two or more like aircraft.

7.4 Coverage by AVN 98

AVN 98 is a comprehensive aviation products liability policy which also provides cover in three sections. They include the following coverage:

(1) aviation products and grounding liability insurance, expressed in similar terms to AVN 66;
(2) working parties liability, covering work or the performance of any duty carried out by or on behalf of the insured and their business or operations away from the Insured's premises in connection with any aircraft product including liability for property damage to such aircraft product;
(3) aircraft third party and passenger liability insurance;
(4) airport liability insurance;
(5) aviation premises and hangarkeepers liability insurance.

It is possible to extend cover under section one for recalling aviation products and under sections four and five for personal injury.

A 'products type liability insurance' is provided as part of a comprehensive policy for airport operators known as the Ariel Form,[81] called *Airport Owners and Operators Liability Insurance Policy*, 48FLY00001. It covers bodily injury and property damage arising out of the possession, use, consumption or handling of any goods or products manufactured, constructed, altered, repaired, serviced, treated, sold, supplied or distributed by the insured or his employees but only in respect of such goods or products which form part of or are used in conjunction with aircraft, and then only after such goods or products have ceased to be in the possession or under the control of the Insured.

8   FINANCIAL INTERESTS

Since many airlines lack the financial resources to buy their aircraft outright, they look to banks or other finance houses to provide finance or to leasing companies for leased

---

81. Because it was drafted by the Ariel Syndicate at Lloyd's.

aircraft.[82] Owners and lessors, who may or may not be the same entity as to which *see,* Chapter 11, will want to ensure that their asset is adequately protected and, even though they will not normally have any operational interest, that any potential liability they could face either directly or indirectly[83] is insured.

Owners' and financial interests can be protected by inserting certain clauses into the policy itself, such as a loss payee provision. During the 1950s-60s leasing/ finance contracts often required the lessee to obtain insurance for the benefit of the lessor/ financier and so requests were made to insurers to provide cover. The underwriting process often involved the time-consuming practice of looking at the individual lease documentation and dealing with complex wording drawn from financial agreements, potentially at very short notice. So insurers responded and developed model wordings which were premised upon the common perception that underwriters should not be concerned as to whom a loss could be legally paid should an insured peril arise and that a lessor or financier must not expose an insurer to additional liability not contemplated under the original policy. One important issue was to avoid a possible double payment that is, one to the airline and one to the finance house.

The current form used is known as AVN 67B, which is actually a policy endorsement naming the contract parties, that is, the interested lessors and finance parties, as additional insured persons on the underlying policy. The presence of an additional party on the policy will normally mean that the policy is considered to be a composite policy, meaning that each party is considered to be separately insured.

This is a very important distinction if, for example, one party had breached the principle of good faith or, as has been seen a number of times, a lessee fails to return the aircraft; the lessor would still be entitled to the benefit of the policy.

9 REINSURANCE

9.1 Basic Principles

There is not sufficient space in this chapter to dedicate to reinsurance the important role it plays for the insurance industry in providing additional capital and further spreading of risk by allowing a 'cedant' insurer to reduce exposure to a given risk or risks. Through reinsurance, and subject to solvency considerations, a primary insurer can accept a higher proportion of risk, making them potentially more attractive to brokers and their clients and bringing greater efficiency into the placing or co-insurance exercise with corresponding benefits for all parties. For example, in some jurisdictions where it is a requirement to use national insurers for domestic risks, the reinsurers, again on a subscription leader/follower basis, will offer the expertise and capacity needed to cover the risk.

---

82. *See,* section 3 of Chapter 11.
83. A jurisdiction risk, that is, a concept of 'negligent entrustment' has arisen in the United States whereby an the person possessing a dangerous item, such as an aircraft, is under a duty to entrust it to responsible persons.

As noted above,[84] London is the major reinsurance market amidst a number of other key regions. Where such reinsurance also takes place locally within an airline's country, the reinsurance business may still reach wider markets under a further reinsurance contract known as a retrocession where the reinsurer spreads the risk even further.

There is no universal definition of reinsurance but it has been held to be 'insurance business'.[85] Accordingly, the principles of *utmost good faith* apply.[86] It is a separate contract from the original insurance such that there is no privity of contract between the original insured and the reinsurer.

9.2 Types of Reinsurance

There are many types of reinsurance and the terminology is very technical. The basic distinctions fall within two pairs of alternatives. A reinsurance policy may be 'facultative', where terms are negotiated for an individual risk, or a treaty reinsurance, which considers a portfolio risks; reinsurance may be proportional where the insurer and reinsurer share the risk and premium per a given ratio or non-proportional, that is, excess or stop loss, reinsurance where cover is arranged in layers. For proportional covers, the terms and conditions will normally be 'back-to-back' with the insurance, that is incorporate the terms of the insurance. In this instance, the governing law, if different, may prove crucial as to whether the cover is truly back-to-back.[87]

Non-proportional reinsurance has its own general terms and conditions and often will not be 'back-to-back' with the original or primary policy.

9.3 Other Terms

While a reinsurance contract normally responds to the net loss of the cedant, there can be significant issues in determining what constitutes a loss for the purpose of the reinsurance. Significantly, it is not necessarily fatal to a claim under a reinsurance policy that no claim has been actually paid under the insurance.[88]

In some cases, it may not be necessary for a paid claim to fall within the insurance at all for a reinsurance policy to respond if the policy includes a clause to 'pay as may be paid and to follow the settlements' of the reinsured.

In the event of a claim made against an aviation insurance policy, reinsurers may have rights to influence how the claim is handled under the terms of clauses known as AVN 25 (claims cooperation) or AVN 41A (claims control). The latter confers significantly greater rights to the reinsurer such as the right to appoint loss adjusters, lawyers, surveyors, etc., and to control settlement negotiations.

---

84. *See,* section 1.2 above.
85. *See, Re NRG Victory Reinsurance Ltd.* 1 WCR 239 (1995).
86. *See,* section 4.1.2 above.
87. *See, Wasa* v. *Lexington* UKHL 40 (2009).
88. *See, Boden* v. *Hussey* 1 Lloyd's Reports 423 (1988).

10 CONCLUDING NOTES

From its marine insurance roots, the aerospace market has established itself as a distinct sector of insurance business whose hallmark over its relatively short life is adaptability to rapidly evolving risk.

Given the global nature of the aviation industry, it is no surprise that political events throughout the world have an impact upon the market. With painful clarity, the events of 11 September 2001 serve very well to show how entwined insurance is to aviation operators, as the universal activation of review clauses in war risk policies forced a fundamental coverage reassessment, following which an international dialogue took place between all parties, including governments, as to how best to respond in the medium and long term to the new threats of terrorism to the aerospace industry and to wider society as a whole. Those discussions continue.

Meanwhile, political events like the planned departure of the United Kingdom from the EU can also change the shape of insurance industry. This will have implications for the availability and location of insurance cover for policyholders.

Innovations in technology, such as the use of composite materials, radar and computer technology, and the long term intention to introduce UA into the same airspace as manned aircraft, could dramatically change the risk profile of aviation operations. The constant striving for safety is mirrored by the tragedy that the aviation industry must occasionally face in the public eye, for example the collision of two aircraft over lake Konstanz, Germany in July 2002[89] and the losses in 2014 of two Malaysian Airlines aircraft in different but equally dramatic circumstances.[90] Many incidents and accidents do not attract worldwide media attention and, despite an ever safer industry, the potential for catastrophe has not been eliminated. This demands from underwriters a full consideration of the safety implications which different carriers bring to the market.

No doubt, more challenges lie ahead as technological development continues with a focus on energy efficiency and environmental protection. With the cost of all areas of business important for all insurance buyers, the rewards offered by insurers for those who implement such innovations which are empirically shown to operate effectively will continue to encourage a culture of safety. Such safety concerns include taking steps to ensure the reliability of computer systems in the face of the rise of cybersecurity concerns.[91]

With passenger traffic and the number of flights worldwide predicted to rise, the age old debate linking the number of accidents against the cost covering such an incident to premium levels will not quickly fall away but will continue to be hotly contested.

Let us express the hope that aerospace insurance can develop imaginatively and stay aligned to technological development and make the operation of aircraft ever safer.

---

89. *See*, section 2.4.7 of Chapter 7.
90. *See*, sections 3.1, 3.5 and 5.1.2 of Chapter 6.
91. *See*, section 3.4 of Chapter 6.

CHAPTER 11

Rights in Aircraft[*]

1 GENERAL INTRODUCTION

1.1 Rights, Consensual and Non-consensual Liens

This Chapter deals with rights in aircraft. The term 'rights' has many meanings, as it not only refers to rights of legal ownership but also to economic rights, such as the right of use of a lessee under a lease agreement or the grantee of a purchase option in respect of an aircraft. In addition the term 'rights' refers to liens and encumbrances, which covers a broad variety of rights: consensual liens, that is rights in aircraft created pursuant to an agreement between the owner and a third party creditor to secure payment obligations of the owner or another person towards the creditor, and non-consensual liens, that is, liens on an aircraft made without the consent of the owner. Consensual liens include mortgages, hypothecs, rights of pledge and other in rem rights as well as the rights of the conditional seller under a title reservation agreement.

There are many forms of non-consensual liens, ranging from rights of retention, that is, a creditor's right to retain possession of the aircraft until a certain debt is paid, rights of detention, that is, the right to detain an aircraft on the basis of statutory powers, precautionary or pre-trial arrest, arrest in execution and preferences such as the preferences pursuant to Article 4 of the *Convention on the International Recognition of Rights* of 1948, henceforth also referred to as the *Geneva Convention*, of claims in respect of compensation due for salvage of the aircraft.

International conventions such as the Geneva Convention (1948) and the *Convention on International Interests in Mobile Equipment* (2001), henceforth also referred to as the *Cape Town Convention*, together with the related *Protocol on Matters Specific*

---

[*]. This Chapter was written by Berend Crans, partner at Norton Rose Fulbright LLP, Amsterdam (The Netherlands); www.nortonrosefulbright.com.

to Aircraft Equipment, henceforth also referred to as the *Aircraft Equipment Protocol* (*AEP*) may provide a certain degree of comfort to owners, financiers and other beneficiaries of security rights in aircraft and engines, but it may highly depend on the laws of the jurisdiction where the aircraft is physically located at the relevant moment in time, for instance when the aircraft is made subject to precautionary arrest, whether the degree of comfort which a secured lender had, was indeed justified. It is next to impossible to deal with all scenarios and in this chapter we can only provide an outline of the various rights in aircraft, the international conventions aiming to protect such rights in Contracting States and how different rights may compete with each other.

Leasing has developed into the premier transaction structure in the aviation industry. Today, most airlines operate with leased aircraft and aircraft lessors are now the big fleet owners. In view of the importance of leasing and the different leasing structures which are available in the market, special attention is given to leasing in section 3 of this Chapter.

2   RECOGNITION OF RIGHTS IN AIRCRAFT

2.1   An Introduction to the Principal Conventions

2.1.1   A Brief History: Towards the 1948 Geneva Convention

As aircraft are by definition moveable and crossing borders on a daily basis, there has always been a need to develop an international system providing for the international recognition of rights in aircraft. The international recognition of rights in aircraft was one of the subjects examined during the International Conference on Private Air Law, held in 1925. It was the first time consideration was given to this problem on an international level. An expert committee, the *Comité International Technique des Experts Juridiques Aériens* (CITEJA), subsequently formulated two drafts which were accepted at the sixth plenary session of the CITEJA in 1931,[1] but an international convention to settle the matter never materialised at that stage.

The International Civil Aviation Conference held at Chicago in 1944[2] reopened the discussions on the basis of the two earlier texts. Following the end of the Second World War, the need for a convention on mortgage of aircraft became urgent due to pressure from several quarters aimed at facilitating the export of aircraft to developing countries while at the same time safeguarding the position of the seller by means of some form of security.[3] The reason why a new convention had a better chance of securing adoption than the previous drafts may well be attributed to the drastic changes in the social, economic and political environment prevailing at the time. New elements in the post-War situation are the following:

---

1. *See*, B. Hofstetter, *L'hypothèque aérienne* 211 ff. (1950).
2. *See*, section 3.2 of Chapter 1.
3. *See*, Hofstetter, *L'hypothèque aérienne* 218 (1950) and N.M. Matte *Treatise on Air-Aeronautical Law* 543–546 (1981).

(1) the valuable functions performed by aircraft had become more widely appreciated, and their value as a security increased accordingly;

(2) aviation safety had improved considerably;

(3) insurance policies reducing the risks of aviation had been perfected;

(4) special rules governing the ownership of aircraft were more readily accepted.

A final consolidated draft was presented to the second ICAO Assembly, meeting in Geneva in June 1948. On 18 June, the draft convention was approved, though with a few reservations. Following the ratification or accession by a sufficient number of states, the Geneva Convention entered into force on 17 September 1953. Per early 2017, the Geneva Convention has a total of eighty-nine contracting States.

The Geneva Convention has brought about consensus on the following important points:

- the creditor's interests are now adequately safeguarded in all Contracting States;
- priority claims have been defined; and
- their order of priority is determined by the law of the State where the aircraft is registered as to nationality.

Nonetheless some gaps remained: to begin with, the precise moment when a right in a registered aircraft is validly created has not been fixed; moreover, the Convention only protects consensual liens and does not cater for the recognition of non-consensual liens Finally, the Geneva Convention contains nothing on execution procedure or on entering an execution in the record of the Contracting State of the aircraft's nationality.

Against the background of the circumstances prevailing at the time when the Geneva Convention was concluded, no better result could probably have been achieved, and it may certainly be regarded as an important first step forward. The Geneva Convention is discussed in more detail in section 2.3 below.

2.1.2 *Towards the Cape Town Convention (2001)*

Leaving procedures regarding the exercise of rights subject to domestic laws implies a degree of uncertainty, in particular for lessors and security right holders, as to the time and expense involved with the repossession, de-registration and export of aircraft from certain jurisdictions. As it is fairly unpredictable where an aircraft will be located at the time a lease agreement is terminated, for instance because the lessee has failed to pay lease rent, or a loan agreement is terminated, for instance because the lessor/borrower failed to make a payment to the lender, lessors and lenders are never sure about the problems they may encounter in their efforts to repossess the aircraft or to exercise their rights and remedies under an aircraft mortgage in another jurisdiction. Such problems may not only be caused by inadequate domestic laws of the relevant jurisdiction, but also by non-transparent administrative procedures or a slow or corrupt judiciary.

The aviation industry's need for a uniform system regarding international interests in aircraft resulted in an industry initiative, supported by manufacturers, lessors and financial institutions. This initiative, initially driven by Unidroit,[4] resulted in a draft convention, the *Unidroit Convention on International Interests in Mobile Equipment* and a related *Protocol on Matters specific to Aircraft Equipment*, which fine-tuned the provisions of the Unidroit Convention for application to aircraft.[5]

This initiative led to a diplomatic conference in Cape Town in 2001 and the 2001 Cape Town *Convention on International Interests in Mobile Equipment*, henceforth referred to as the *Cape Town Convention*, and the related Protocol on Matters Specific to Aircraft Equipment, henceforth also referred to as the AEP.[6] The Cape Town Convention entered into force on 1 March 2006, following the deposit of the third instrument of ratification. By early 2017 the total number of Contracting States had grown to seventy-two. For more details, *see*, section 2.4 below.

2.1.3 Conflicts Between the Geneva and Cape Town Conventions

The Geneva Convention on the one hand and the Cape Town Convention together with the AEP, jointly the referred to as Cape Town Convention/Aircraft Equipment Protocol (CTC/AEP), on the other hand take a very different approach with respect to a variety of matters. The Geneva Convention has a civil law basis, whilst the CTC/AEP is clearly based on common law principles. The purpose of the Geneva Convention is the recognition by Contracting States of certain rights constituted in accordance with the laws of the Contracting State where the aircraft was registered as to nationality at the time of the constitution of such rights and regularly recorded in a public record of that Contracting State.[7] As a result the holder of such rights has the rights and remedies provided under the relevant laws of the state of registration. The central purpose of the CTC/AEP, however, is to create a new and sui generis interest which is not derived from, or dependent on, national laws as the CTC/AEP itself defines the rights and remedies awarded to the beneficiary of an 'international interest', as defined in the CTC/AEP. This feature makes the CTC/AEP quite unique.

---

4. International Institute for the Unification of Private Law.
5. *First Set of Draft Arts of a Future Unidroit Convention on International Interests in Mobile Equipment*, Unidroit Study LXXII, doc. 24 (1996). *See*, on this Convention, J. Wool, *The Next Generation of International Aviation Finance Law: An Overview of the Proposed Unidroit Convention on International Interests in Mobile Equipment as Applied to Aircraft Equipment*, 23 Air & Space Law 243–276 (1998) and Berend Crans, *The Unidroit Convention on International Interests in Mobile Equipment and the Aircraft Equipment Protocol: Some Critical Observations*, 23 Air & Space Law 277–282 (1998); *see also*, Berend Crans, *Analysing the Merits of the Proposed Unidroit Convention on International Interests in Mobile Equipment and the Aircraft Equipment Protocol on the Basis of a Fictional Scenario*, 25 Air & Space Law 51–56 (2000).
6. For a brief history of the Cape Town Convention and the Aircraft Equipment Protocol, *see*, Professor Sir Roy Goode, *Official Commentary* 5–7 (2013).
7. Art. 1(1) of the Geneva Convention.

In addition the Geneva Convention only relates to the recognition of rights in aircraft[8] and does not consider aircraft engines separately. The Geneva Convention considers engines as component parts of an aircraft.

The CTC/AEP on the other hand relates to 'aircraft objects', which term includes airframes, engines and helicopters. This apparent conflict between the Geneva Convention and the CTC/AEP where it concerns the status of engines often leads to undesirable consequences.[9]

2.2 Conflicts of Law

2.2.1 Limitations on the Choice of Law

There is a strong movement towards allowing the parties to an agreement as much leeway as possible to determine which laws shall apply to their contract as to which see, for instance, EU Regulation 593/2008 of 17 June 2008 regarding the law applicable to contractual obligations, generally referred to as the *Rome I Regulation*, which is based on the freedom of the parties to choose the law governing their agreement, subject to certain exceptions. The Rome I Regulation does not apply to specified matters, like the incorporation of trusts and the legal relationship between the incorporators, trustees and beneficiaries. In addition, certain types of agreements, like transportation agreements, consumer contracts, contracts of insurance and individual contracts of employment, are subject to additional rules. The Rome I Regulation contains certain other restrictions on the choice of law, in particular where it concerns the applicability of 'overriding provisions' of the laws of a jurisdiction with which the agreement has a close connection or where enforcement of the agreement would be contrary to the public order of the jurisdiction where enforcement is being sought.

The Regulation also provides that where the Regulation prescribes the applicability of the laws of a certain jurisdiction, this shall imply the applicability of the *substantive* laws of that jurisdiction, with the exclusion of the rules of private international law. This reflects the tendency in private international law to do away with the problems caused by *'renvoi'*. *Renvoi* may cause tremendous problems, if for instance the applicability of laws of State A, including its rules of private international law, leads to the applicability of the laws of State B. If the applicability of the laws of State B includes its rules of private international law, this could entail that the matter is referred to another jurisdiction or, even worse, back to State A, which would then again refer to State B.

---

8. The term 'aircraft' is defined in Art. 16 of the Geneva Convention and includes "the airframe, engines, propellers, radio apparatus and all other Art.s intended for use in the aircraft whether installed therein or temporarily separated therefrom." see also, section 3.3.2.1 of Chapter 1.
9. See, section 2.3.4 below and Berend Crans, *How Many Engines on a Boeing 737? An Analysis of Accession Rules in Relation to Aircraft Engines*, 38(3) Air & Space Law 229–248 (2013).

2.2.2 Conflict of Laws and Rights in Aircraft

When it comes to the transfer of title to an aircraft or the creation of security rights in aircraft, the parties generally do not have the liberty to elect the law governing such transfer of title or the creation of a security right. The question which property laws do apply is of course of utmost importance as for instance a transfer of title which is not compliant with applicable law will probably result in such transfer not being valid. When determining which property laws should apply to aircraft, various options can be considered:

- the *lex situs*, being the laws of the jurisdiction where the aircraft is physically located at the relevant moment in time;
- the *lex domicilii*, being the laws of the jurisdiction of the owner of the aircraft;
- the *lex actus*, being the laws applicable to the instrument of transfer;
- the *lex registri*, being the laws of the jurisdiction where the aircraft is registered as to nationality at the relevant moment in time;
- the 'proper law of transfer', which is basically the law chosen by the parties.

It would appear that various jurisdictions have chosen different conflict rules.

In the United States, the conflict rule for the transfer of aircraft is the *lex actus*.

In The Netherlands, conflict rules have been codified[10] and with respect to aircraft, the *lex registri* determines the applicable property law regime to the transfer and the creation of security rights in respect of aircraft.

In England, the *lex situs* is endorsed, also in relation to aircraft.[11] In some cases where conflict rules of relevant jurisdictions are different and lead to contradictory results, unsatisfactory judgments have been handed down. In England the 'Blue Sky' decisions of 2009[12] provide ample food for thought. This litigation arose out of transactions regarding the financing and leasing of certain aircraft in the light of US sanctions prohibiting the sale or lease of US manufactured aircraft to Iranian nationals. The first case dealt primarily with a claim against the operator of the aircraft for tortuous interference and the operator's counter-claims to the effect that title had been transferred to it or that the aircraft was held in trust by the legal owners. The second case concerned the question whether, with respect to two aircraft, valid mortgages were made. With respect to one of the aircraft, which was registered on the UK

---

10. *See*, Art. 127 of Book 10 of the Dutch Civil Code incorporating the Dutch Act on the Conflict of Property Laws (*Wet conflictenrecht goederenrecht*, which entered into force in 2008, and applies the *lex situs* to moveables generally but applies the *lex registri* to aircraft.
11. This has changed since the ratification of the CTC/AEP by the United Kingdom in 2015, but only where the CTC/AEP applies. Art. 6 of the implementing regulations, namely, the International Interests in Aircraft Equipment (Cape Town Convention) Regulations 2015, provides that "an international interest has effect where the conditions of the Convention are satisfied with no requirement to determine whether a proprietary rights has been validly created or transferred pursuant to the common law *situs* rule." *See*, M. Bisset, *Ratification of the Cape Town Convention by the United Kingdom*, 41 Air & Space Law 49–58 (2016).
12. *See*, *Blue Sky One Ltd. and Others* v. *Mahan Air and Another* [2009], High Court of England and Wales (EWHC) 3314 (Comm) and *Blue Sky One Ltd.* v. *Mahan Air and Another* [2010] EWHC 631 (Comm).

nationality register, an English law mortgage was executed. At the time of execution of the mortgage, the aircraft was located in The Netherlands. The English court held that the *lex situs*, that is Dutch substantive law without Dutch conflict rules, applied to the creation of the mortgage. As the English law mortgage would not meet formal requirements for an aircraft mortgage under Dutch law, it did not create a valid in rem right on the aircraft. If Dutch conflict rules would have been applied, the English law mortgage would have been valid, since Dutch law adheres to the *lex registri* and the aircraft was registered in the United Kingdom at the relevant moment in time. Similarly, if the case would have been brought before a Dutch court, the English law mortgage would have been found valid.[13]

The Geneva Convention (1948) contains a clear reference to the *lex registri*, but does not rule out 'renvoi', so that it does not provide a conflict rule.[14] It is regrettable that the Cape Town Convention (2001) fails to provide a clear conflict of laws rule.[15] The lack of a universal conflict rule regarding the property regime applicable to aircraft implies that uncertainty remains; the validity of a transfer of title or a security right may be assessed differently depending on the jurisdiction where the matter is being adjudicated.[16]

2.3 The Geneva Convention (1948)

2.3.1 *Recognition of Certain Rights in Aircraft*

Pursuant to Article 1(1) of this Convention, the Contracting States undertake to recognise the following rights:

(a) rights of property in aircraft;
(b) rights to acquire aircraft by purchase coupled with possession of the aircraft;
(c) rights to possession of aircraft under leases of six months or more;
(d) mortgages, *hypotheques* and similar rights in aircraft which are contractually created as security for payment of an indebtedness.

Article 1(1) further stipulates that the rights must:

(i) be constituted in accordance with the law of the Contracting State in which the aircraft is registered as to nationality at the time of their constitution; and

---

13. For a detailed description of conflict of laws issues relating to rights in aircraft, *see*, D. Osborne and J. F. Imhof, *English Conflict of Laws and the Transfer of Aircraft*, in: *Aircraft Finance – Registration, Security and Enforcement*, R. Hames and G. McBain (eds) (2011); *see also*, Berend Crans, *Aerial Conflicts of Law: An Analysis of Conflicts of Law Rules as Applied to Aircraft*, in *From Lowlands to High Skies: A Multilevel Jurisdictional Approach Towards, Air Law*, Essays in Honour of John Balfour (ed. Pablo Mendes de Leon) 215–226 (2013).
14. For more details on the conflict rule of the Geneva Convention, *see*, section 2.3.11 below.
15. For more details *see*, section 2.4.13 below.
16. *See*, H. Marren and A. Curtin, *Irish Cape Town Convention Mortgages – A Blue Sky Solution?*, supplement to *Air Finance Journal* at 18 and 19, September 2011.

(ii) be regularly recorded in a public record of the Contracting State in which the aircraft is registered as to nationality.

The term 'rights to acquire aircraft' covers not only purchase options in for instance (financial) lease agreements, but also hire-purchase and conditional sale agreements The term "rights to possession" typically refers to the rights of a lessee to possession of the aircraft during the term of the lease.

Article 1(2) of the Convention expressly states that the Convention does not prevent the recognition of any other rights in aircraft permitted by the laws of any Contracting State, but all Contracting States shall not admit or recognise any such other right as taking priority of the rights enumerated in Article 1(1). This applies, *inter alia*, to non-consensual liens like retention rights, which in some jurisdictions do have priority over consensual liens like mortgages.[17]

With respect to mortgages Article 5 of the Convention provides that the priority of a mortgage extends to all sums thereby secured, but that the amount of interest included shall not exceed interest accrued during the three years prior to the execution proceedings together with that accrued during the execution proceedings.

2.3.2 Priority Claims under the Geneva Convention

The Geneva Convention recognises two priority claims, described in Article 4, to wit:

(a) claims in respect of compensation due for salvaging the aircraft; and
(b) claims in respect of extraordinary expenses indispensable for the preservation of the aircraft.

Where such claims give rise, under the laws of the Contracting State where the salvage or preservation operations took place, to a right conferring a charge against the aircraft, such right must be recognised by Contracting States and shall take priority over all other rights in the aircraft. The effect of this provision is that for instance the rights under a mortgage may rank behind a salvage claim, in the event the jurisdiction where salvage was completed grants in rem effect to the right of that claimant.[18]

Salvage, in terms of the Convention, is not restricted to salvage at sea, although the American delegation would have favoured such a restriction. It argued that the provision was introduced in an analogy with maritime law: applying salvage law to

---

17. In England, for instance, possessory liens for repair work do take priority over mortgages; *see*, P. Farrell, in: Ravi Nath and Berend Crans (eds), *Aircraft Repossession and Enforcement*, Chapter on *England and Wales*, at 321 (2009). In connection with the ratification of the CTC/AEP, the United Kingdom made a declaration pursuant to Art. 39(1) of the Cape Town Convention preserving the priority of non-consensual rights over registered international interests; *see also*, M. Bisset, *Ratification of the Cape Town Convention by the United Kingdom*, 41 Air & Space Law 49–58 (2016).
18. In The Netherlands, claims in respect of salvage and extraordinary preservation costs do have priority over all other claims and privileges, except the costs of foreclosure, if salvage or preservation was completed in The Netherlands or another Contracting State; *see*, section 8:1317 Dutch Civil Code (*Burgerlijk Wetboek*).

land-based situations would create an element of uncertainty in the Convention, which would have repercussions on national legislations and give rise to a great variety of claims under the pretext of the Convention.[19] This priority claim faced objections mainly from States with great land masses.[20]

As mentioned above, the law applicable to the priority claims is the *lex rei sitae*, that is, the law of the place where the salvaging and preserving operations occurred. There is some doubt as to the applicable law in cases where the operations were carried out at sea; the general opinion seems to be that in such cases the law of the 'port of refuge' should be applied.[21]

According to Article 4(4) prerequisites for the exercise of the priority of these claims are

(a) that the claim must have been noted on the record within three months of the date of the termination of the operations, and that;

(b) within that period the claim has been settled out of court, or an action in court to enforce it has been commenced. In the latter case, the grounds for interruption or suspension of the three months' period will be determined by the law of the forum.

What precisely is to be understood by the expression 'extraordinary expenses indispensable for the preservation of the aircraft'? During the discussions on this Article it was agreed that preservation would mean keeping the aircraft in the condition in which it was found. The expenditure may include the costs of transportation to a safer place, or the costs of guarding the aircraft, but not the costs of repairs to put the aircraft in a better condition than it had been before the accident. In addition, the expenditure must be of an exceptional nature. According to Riese and Hofstetter the costs of repair may be included into this category provided they are of an exceptional character.[22]

2.3.3 Implied Priority Claims

In addition to the claims contemplated by Article 4, the Convention recognises four claims carrying an implied priority and listed hereunder, in the event of a sale in execution of an aircraft:

(a) a claim amounting to 20 per cent of the sale proceeds for persons suffering injury or damage on the surface in the Contracting State where the sale takes place, unless adequate and effective insurance is available (Article 7.5(b));

---

19. Minutes and Documents of the ICAO Legal Committee, 2nd Assembly, Doc. 5722, at 136 ff.
20. ICAO Doc. 5722 cited in the previous footnote at 133.
21. *See*, N.M. Matte *Treatise on Air-Aeronautical Law* 570 (1981), and B. Hofstetter, *L'hypothèque aérienne* 239 (1950).
22. *See*, B. Hofstetter, *L'hypothèque aérienne* 237 (1950); O. Riese, *Luftrecht* 293 (1949).

(b) claims in respect of costs legally chargeable in the Contracting State where the execution sale took place, provided such costs are incurred in the common interest of creditors in the course of execution proceedings leading to the sale (Article 7(6));

(c) claims arising from national laws 'relating to immigration, customs or air navigation' (Article 12);

(d) claims in respect of the sale of spare parts in the event the executing creditor is an unsecured creditor (Article 10(3)).

The terms of the Geneva Convention itself do not confer priority status on the claim referred to under (a), but the Convention does allow such priority, where the law of the state where the sale takes place does provide this type of protection to persons suffering injury or damage on the surface. This provision was dictated by the fact that third parties having suffered damage on the surface of the earth are not in a position to protect themselves in the same manner as creditors who have been forewarned by the entries in the record.

When the aircraft is properly insured against this type of liability the provision becomes superfluous and the entire proceeds of the sale goes to the creditors. An aircraft is considered to be properly insured if the insured sum amounts to the value of the aircraft when new.[23] This provision is particularly important with regard to fleet mortgages, where each aircraft is a part of the security for the total amount of the mortgage. Hofstetter considers it wrong to make priority status dependent upon insurance being proper or adequate.[24]

In a thesis in the Dutch language a clear and practical summary of the various claims is given in their order of priority: this order is particularly relevant because Article 4 creates a strong impression that its claims have priority over all others. The correct order is:

(1) claims based on Article 12, including but not limited to customs fines;

(2) claims based on Article 7(6) including but not limited to the costs of execution;

(3) claims based on Article 10 (spare parts);

(4) (a) claims based on Article 4 including salvage and preservation costs;
    (b) claims based on Article 7(5) that is, third parties on the surface;
    (c) claims based on Article 1.[25]

2.3.4 Definition of Aircraft

From the statements made by the French and British delegates during the preparatory stages of the Convention it is evident that the authors intended to create means of

---

23. Art. 7(5).
24. *See*, B. Hofstetter, *L'hypothèque aérienne* 253 (1950).
25. *See*, K. Rijks, *Het Verdrag van Genève* (PhD thesis Leiden University) 181–182 (1952).

financial support for the air carrier in the form of real security. Their idea was to create safeguards for the rights in aircraft intended to participate in international air traffic. Cable balloons, free balloons and gliders do not come under this category and the category of aircraft intended to be covered by the Geneva Convention is thus confined to aircraft intended to be used in international air transport.[26]

Article 16 of the Geneva Convention provides that 'aircraft' includes *inter alia* 'the airframe, engines, propellers, radio apparatus and all other articles intended for use in the aircraft whether installed therein or temporarily separated therefrom'. It is not entirely clear what the meaning and scope of this provision is and, in particular, whether the Geneva Convention intended to impose rules of accession to the effect that engines and other components of aircraft should be regarded as component parts of the aircraft and no longer as independent moveable objects.[27] In a number of jurisdictions,[28] property laws have similar accession principles or have been adapted to reflect Article 16. Obviously, accession rules – which could bring about that the owner/lessor of an engine may lose its ownership title if the engine is attached to an airframe owned by another lessor – are of great importance to lessors and financiers of engines and other equipment.[29] As indicated above accession rules may lead to commercially undesirable results.[30] The fact that engines are particularly expensive items of equipment and the fact that the property laws of many jurisdictions do already provide for the separate financing of aircraft engines has resulted in the Cape Town Convention specifically providing for engines being recognised as objects which can be separately transferred, financed and encumbered, even if attached to an airframe.[31]

No indication is given in the Convention as to the law applicable to aircraft under construction that have not yet been registered. It was thought impracticable to impose rules on aircraft even before they were able to operate internationally.

---

26. *See also*, section 3.3.2.1 of Chapter 1.
27. *See*, Cem Karako, *Separate Financing of Aircraft Engines* 61–63 (2010).
28. *See*, Ravi Nath and Berend Crans (eds), *Aircraft Repossession and Enforcement* 219 (2009), Chapter on Chile, at 273, Chapter on Denmark, at 346, Chapter on Finland, at 376, Chapter on France, at 617–619, Chapter on The Netherlands, at 785, Chapter on Russia, at 853, South Korea, at 958, Chapter on Sweden, at 992, Chapter on Switzerland, at 1023 Chapter on Thailand, and at 1134, Chapter on Venezuela; *see also*, Ravi Nath and Berend Crans (eds), II *Aircraft Repossession and Enforcement* (2010) at 197, Chapter on Italy, at 302, Chapter on Norway, at 363, Chapter on Poland, at 431 (Chapter on Turkey). Some of the afore-mentioned countries, including Denmark, Norway, Russia, Sweden and Turkey, have since then become a party to the CTC/AEP or are in the process of doing so which will result in the accession rules no longer applying.
29. *See*, Berend Crans, *Aircraft Finance Below Sea Level*, Supplement to Airfinance Journal at 38–39, July 2008, and B. Crans, *Selected Pittfals and Booby-Traps in Aircraft Finance*, in *Aircraft Finance – Recent Developments and Prospects* (ed. B. Crans) 5–7 (1995); *see*, for an analysis of how the Danish courts resolved a dispute arising from Danish accession rules based on Art. 16 of the Geneva Convention, Morten, L. Jakobsen and Lotte Bay Gabelgaard, *The Aircraft Engine Dispute in Denmark: First Judgment*, 39(3) Air & Space Law 215–226 (2014) and Morten L. Jakobsen and Morten Midtgaard Pederesen, *The Danish Aircraft Engine Dispute: The Sequel*, 40(6) Air & Space Law 421–427 (2015).
30. *See*, section 2.1.3 above and sources mentioned there.
31. *See*, section 2.4.2 below with respect to the status of aircraft engines under the Cape Town Convention.

2.3.5 Scope of the Convention

Article 11 provides that the provisions of this Convention shall in each Contracting State apply to all aircraft registered as to nationality in another Contracting State. This rule implies that states are not required to apply the Convention to aircraft registered in their own territory. Nonetheless several exceptions have been provided for:

(a) Article 2: "All recordings relating to a given aircraft must appear in the same record", which requirement is aimed at preventing double registration.

(b) Article 3(1): "The address of the authority responsible for maintaining the record must be shown on every aircraft's certificate of registration as to nationality", which is designed to ensure that the record entry can be traced by the public.

(c) Article 4, in conjunction with Article 11(2)(b) relative to compensation due for salvage of the aircraft or for extraordinary expenses indispensable for the preservation of the aircraft; these are awarded unless the salvage or preservation operations have been terminated within the state's own territory.

(d) Article 9, stating that "Except in the case of a sale in execution in conformity with the provisions of Article 7, no transfer of an aircraft from the nationality register or the record of a Contracting State to that of another State shall be made, unless all holders of recorded rights have been satisfied or consent to the transfer."

(e) Article 12, stipulating that "Nothing in this Convention shall prejudice the right of any Contracting State to enforce against an aircraft its national laws relating to immigration, customs or air navigation."

Aircraft used in military, customs or police services are excluded from the scope of the Convention, according to Article 13.[32]

2.3.6 The Record

There is no direct obligation for Contracting States to keep a record or registry for rights in aircraft, but in actual practice the benefits from the Convention will only materialise if a proper public record is maintained for the purposes of the Geneva Convention.[33] During the preparatory stages it had been suggested that Contracting States failing to keep a record would be obliged to recognise rights originating and recorded in other Contracting States, but would receive nothing in return.

---

32. See, section 3.3.2 of Chapter 1.
33. Art. 15 could, however, be interpreted as requiring Contracting States to maintain a record or other public registry, since many provisions of the Geneva Convention would be difficult if not impossible to apply in the absence of a record. See, for instance, Arts 4(4)(a), 7(2)(b) and 9 of the Geneva Convention.

The Convention does not provide detailed rules concerning the record, but Article 2 stipulates that:

1) All recordings relative to a given aircraft must appear in the same record.
2) Except as otherwise provided in this Convention, the effects of the recording of any right mentioned in Article 1, para. (1), with regard to third parties shall be determined according to the law of the Contracting State where it is recorded.
3) A Contracting State may prohibit the recording of any right which cannot validly be constituted according to its national law.

Unlike maritime law, where there is a central register separate from the national registers, air law, to the extent governed by the regime of the Geneva Convention only recognises national records. The CTC/AEP provides, however, for an international registry for the recordation of international interests on aircraft irrespective of such aircraft's state of registration as to nationality.[34]

Article 2(3) is of particular interest for two reasons. First of all, this provision appears to indicate that a Contracting State must not only recognise but also accept the registration in its record of a mortgage or other interest under foreign law, which was constituted in accordance with the laws of the jurisdiction where the aircraft was registered as to nationality at the time the mortgage was constituted. In other words, if with respect to an aircraft a valid mortgage was created under the laws of Contracting State A at the time the aircraft registered in Contracting State A's nationality register, Contracting State B, where the aircraft is subsequently registered as to nationality, shall accept the recording of the initial mortgage unless the laws of Contracting State B do not provide for a mortgage in respect of aircraft. On this basis, the Convention will only have effect provided national law has been complied with; for example, in jurisdictions where the equipment trust is not known, it may be inapplicable. Opposition to this rule initially came from IATA, which felt that it introduced a new element.[35] The Convention contains no indication at all as to the evidence value of the record, leaving yet another issue to be decided by national law.

2.3.7 The Procedure for Creating Mortgages

The procedure for creating mortgages is left to the national law of the State where the aircraft is registered at the time of their creation on the basis of 'registration equals nationality equals national law'. From the preparatory discussions it might be inferred that the drafters intended no deviation from this rule except for considerations of reasonableness or effectiveness. As discussed above,[36] several authors contended, however, that the domestic law of a State includes rules of private international law as

---

34. *See*, sections 2.4.1 and 2.4.8 below.
35. *See*, Minutes and Documents of the ICAO Legal Committee, 2nd Assembly, Doc. 5722, ICAO Doc. 5722 at 180 ff.
36. *See*, section 2.2 above.

well, which may include provisions referring to the laws of another jurisdiction as the applicable law. The Convention does indeed not provide a conflict rule.[37]

The manner in which rights in aircraft are constituted varies from country to country. In some instances they are established by agreement between the parties; in others they are created through the registration of the mortgage instrument with a public registry, as is the case in The Netherlands. The Convention presupposes that the rights are established by contract, irrespective of the recording.

When a mortgage is constituted by agreement, the holder of the rights will have to prove that the requirements of applicable law have been complied with. In the case of creation through registration of the mortgage instrument, the burden of proof may be lighter of one assumes that a state would not permit rights to be established if it is not compliant with the relevant provisions of its own laws.

The notion of creating rights in aircraft does not have the same interpretation everywhere. It would have been preferable to include some rules on the subject in the Convention, as was unsuccessfully attempted by the ILA.[38]

2.3.8   The Attachment of Aircraft

The attachment of an aircraft in execution is covered by Article 6, reading:

> In case of attachment or sale of an aircraft in execution, or of any right therein, the Contracting States shall not be obliged to recognize, as against the attaching or executing creditor or against the purchaser, any right mentioned in Article I, section (1), or the transfer of any such right, if constituted or effected with knowledge of the sale or execution proceedings by the person against whom the proceedings are directed.

The debtor's awareness of the sale in execution is a prerequisite: a notice on the record is not sufficient. The party against whom execution procedures have been brought must be aware that they have commenced. This provision tries to prevent the fraudulent transfer of an aircraft, that is, the creation of a claim by a debtor who knew that the aircraft was under execution.

Article 6 concerns not only the attachment of the aircraft itself, but clearly refers to the execution of a right in an aircraft, for instance a mortgage,[39] as well. With regard to the insertion of the words "any right therein", in some countries, for instance the

---

37. This is confirmed by R.O. Wilberforce, *The International Recognition of Rights in Aircraft*, 2(3) The International Law Quarterly, 421–458 (1948) at 439, the *Report on Recognition of Rights in Aircraft* (1950), *Report* of the 44th Conference of the International Law Association 241–242 (1950), and Calkins, *Creation and International Recognition of Title and Security Rights in Aircraft*, 15 Journal of Air Law and Commerce 156 at 164 (1948).
38. *See*, R.O. Wilberforce, *Report on Recognition of Rights in Aircraft*, Report of the 44th Conference of the International Law Association 233–254 (1950).
39. *See*, B. Hofstetter, *L'hypothèque aérienne* 46 (1950); *see also*, the annotation on Art. VI in 16 Journal of Air Law and Commerce 81 (1949).

United States and Portugal,[40] execution procedures may take place against a person other than the owner, for instance, the lessee of the aircraft. In such a case it is not the right of ownership that is sold or transferred, but the rights and interests in the aircraft held by the debtor. An obvious requirement here is that the sale involves a right in rem, a property right, and not a right in personam, a right enforceable only against the debtor personally. For States which do not recognise the execution of a right the provision of Article 6 is of course without relevance.[41]

Attachment and sale in execution are both subject to the laws of the Contracting State where they take place. Article 7 gives provisions to be observed in connection with the sale: the date and the place of the sale shall be fixed at least six weeks in advance; the executing creditor shall supply to the court or other competent authority a certified extract of the recordings concerning the aircraft; he shall give public notice of the sale at the place where the aircraft is registered as to nationality, in accordance with the law there applicable, at least one month before the day fixed, and shall concurrently notify by registered letter, if possible by air mail, the recorded owner and the holders of recorded rights in the aircraft and of rights noted on the record under Article 4, section (3), according to their addresses as shown on the record. The legal consequences of a failure to observe these rules shall be determined by the national laws of the Contracting State where the sale took place, but any sale in breach of these provisions may be annulled upon demand made within six months from the date of the sale by a person suffering damages as a consequence of such breach. In most cases, Contracting States have amended their domestic laws to reflect the above procedural provisions.

An exception to Article 7, section 4 is to be found in the earlier Montreal Draft of the Convention with regard to fleet mortgage, a form of security mentioned earlier in this Chapter.[42] In the United States, fleet mortgage is standard practice: it provides more security for the creditor and so makes it possible to borrow larger sums of money. On the part of the United States, serious objections were raised against excluding fleet mortgage: exclusion would have meant the end of it, as the difference between it and the regular standard aircraft mortgage would be eliminated. In view of the importance of fleet mortgage for international aviation the proposed exclusion was rejected.[43]

Article 8 provides that the execution sale of an aircraft in conformity with the provisions of Article 7 shall effect the transfer of the property free from all rights which are not assumed by the purchaser. Article 7, section 4, however, reduces the impact of Article 8 as it provides that no execution sale can be effected unless all rights having priority over the claim of the executing creditor in accordance with the Convention

---

40. *See*, Michael J. Edelman et al. and Carlos de Sousa e Brito, in: Ravi Nath and Berend Crans (eds), *Aircraft Repossession and Enforcement*, Chapter on the United States at 1103, and Chapter on Portugal at 751 (2009).

41. *See*, Minutes and Documents of the ICAO Legal Committee, 2nd Assembly, Doc. 5722, ICAO Doc. 5722 at 190–199.

42. *See*, Art. 8(4) of the Draft of Commission No. 4 of the 1st Assembly; *see also*, the Minutes and Documents of the First Session of the ICAO Legal Committee (Brussels, September 1947), ICAO Doc. 4635, at 197–201.

43. ICAO Doc. 4635 cited above, at 95–100; *see also*, N.M. Matte *Treatise on Air-Aeronautical Law* 564–565 (1981).

which are established before the competent authority, are covered by the sale proceeds or assumed by the purchaser. American delegates first objected to these rules. They would have preferred to see the rights in aircraft remain in place, as this would more or less force the holder of the mortgage to buy the aircraft himself. Moreover, it would not be fair if priority rights could be rendered illusory as a result of a sale in a country where foreign exchange control regulations prohibit the transfer of sales proceeds.[44]

2.3.9 The Transfer of Registration

Article 9 provides that, except pursuant to a sale in conformity with the provisions of Article 7, no transfer of an aircraft from the nationality register of one Contracting State to that of another shall be made, unless all holders of recorded rights have been satisfied or given their consent to the transfer.[45]

The provision was worded in the light of the risks a mortgage creditor may have to face when the mortgaged aircraft is sold to a purchaser in another country and registered in that other country. The British delegation objected to the condition which made de-registration subject to the consent of the holders of all recorded rights. It was argued that it was not the duty of the state to look after the security of the creditors: in addition, the clause was considered to constitute too much of an infringement on the freedom to contract. In spite of these objections the inclusion of Article 9 was held to be indispensable for an adequate protection of the creditors.[46]

Article 9 works in two ways: on the one hand it bars a Contracting State from deregistering an aircraft from its nationality register unless all holders of recorded rights have been satisfied or expressed their consent to deregistration and on the other hand it requires a new State of registration to refuse registration unless these conditions have been satisfied. In practice, a state will not register an aircraft in its nationality register, and subsequently in any public title register, unless it has obtained adequate documentary evidence that the aircraft is no longer registered on another state's register. This follows the principle of Article 18 of the Chicago Convention[47] and achieves compliance with Article 9 of the Geneva Convention.

2.3.10 Spare Parts

Article 10(4) contains a definition of the term 'spare parts', which mean 'parts of aircraft, engines, propellers, radio apparatus, instruments, appliances, furnishings, parts of any of the foregoing, and generally any other articles of whatever description maintained for installation in aircraft in substitution for parts or articles removed'.

---

44. ICAO Doc. 4635 cited above, at 110.
45. *See*, L.D. King, *Moving Toward Cape Town Confidence: A Proposal to Amend the Chicago Convention's Annex 7 and Bolster Reliance on the Cape Town Convention De-Registration Provisions*, 81(4) Journal of Air Law and Commerce 655–682 (2016).
46. *See*, Minutes and Documents of the First Session of the ICAO Legal Committee (Brussels, September 1947), ICAO Doc. 4635, at 112–114 and 118.
47. Art. 18 of the Chicago Convention reads: "An aircraft cannot be validly registered in more than one State, but its registration may be changed from one State to another."

According to Article 10(1), a recorded security right in an aircraft which, according to the *lex registri*, extends to spare parts stored in a specified place or places, shall be recognised by all Contracting States as long as these spare parts remain in the those specified places, provided there is a clearly visible public notice at those specified places specifying the name and address of the beneficiary of that security right, the type of security right and the record in which such security right is recorded. In addition, Article 10(2) requires that a statement describing the type and approximate number of the relevant spare parts shall be included in the recorded document. Such spare parts may be replaced by similar parts, without affecting the right of the beneficiary of the security right.

Sale in execution is provided for in Article 10(3); Article 7(1) and (4), as well as Article 8 are declared applicable. We note that Article 8 (2) and (3), governing the formalities of the sale and the sanctions, do not apply to the sale in execution of spare parts. Riese and Hofstetter strongly object to these rules which, in their opinion, are difficult for European legal minds to accept, while the American creditor still lacks adequate protection.[48] In today's practice, where most airlines have set up engine and spare parts pools, one rarely sees security rights created in respect of a particular aircraft which also cover stocks of spare parts.

2.3.11   Applicable Law

In a number of instances the Convention refers to the law of the Contracting State where the aircraft is registered as to nationality, the *lex registri*. A number of exceptions to the rule have nonetheless been incorporated in the Convention:

(1) Article 4, section 1, providing that the rights referred to in that section have priority provided that they are enforceable according to the law of the Contracting State where the operations of salvage or preservation were terminated, regardless of where the aircraft might find itself.

(2) Article 4, section 4(b), providing that the grounds for interruption or suspension of judicial action shall be determined by the law of the forum.

(3) Article 7, section 1, stipulating that the proceedings of a sale in execution of an aircraft shall be determined by the law of the Contracting State where the sale takes place.

(4) Article 10 section 3, containing a provision making Article 7, section 1 also applicable to the sale in execution of spare parts.

The exceptions listed above have clearly been inserted in order to ensure a more flexible application of the Convention's provisions. However, the Convention does not specify that the reference to the *lex registri*, the *lex fori* or the laws of the Contracting

---

48. *See,* O. Riese, *Luftrecht* 304 (1949); B. Hofstetter, *L'hypothèque aérienne* 262 (1950).

State where a sale takes place, only applies to the substantive laws of such state and not to the conflict rules. As a consequence, *'renvoi'* is not excluded.[49]

2.3.12 Miscellaneous Provisions

An interesting provision is set forth in Article 14 of the Convention which states:

> For the purpose of this Convention, the competent judicial and administrative authorities of the Contracting States may, subject to any contrary provision in their national law, correspond directly with each other.

This is probably the first time such a provision has ever been adopted in an international convention or agreement.

The rules for signature, ratification and denunciation have been laid down in Articles 18 to 23 of the Convention. Further, Article 23(1) authorises a State to declare, on ratification or adherence, that 'its acceptance of this Convention does not apply to any one or more of the territories for the foreign relations of which it is responsible.' Failure to do so will make the Convention applicable to such territories. In the event of a reservation being declared the state may adhere separately on behalf of such territories at a later stage. Besides separate accession, separate denunciation is equally allowable under the Convention. As such reservations do not affect the substance of the Convention they are not expected to give rise to complications.

2.4 The Cape Town Convention and AEP (2001)

2.4.1 A Different Approach and General Introduction

In 1992 the Governing Council of Unidroit set up a working group to assess the need for and feasibility of a uniform regime governing security interests in transactions relating to mobile equipment, in particular aircraft (objects), railroad rolling stock and space assets.[50] This initiative ultimately resulted in a diplomatic conference in Cape Town, co-sponsored by Unidroit and ICAO, in November 2001, and the Convention on International Interests in Mobile Equipment, also referred to as the *Cape Town Convention*, as well as the related Protocol on Matters specific to Aircraft Equipment, also referred to as the AEP. The AEP basically determines how the provisions of the Cape Town Convention apply to aircraft equipment. There is a consolidated text of the Cape Town Convention and the AEP, which is referred to herein as the CTC/AEP, unless indicated otherwise, article numbers used herein refer to the articles of the CTC/AEP.[51]

---

49. *See*, section 2.2.1 of this Chapter.
50. *See*, for a full chronology which goes back to 1988, Appendix XIII in Professor Sir Roy Goode, *Official Commentary*, published by Unidroit (Rome 2013).
51. For a table of concordance between the Art. numbers of the Convention and the Protocol and the Consolidated Text of the CTC/AEP, *see*, R. Goode, *Official Commentary* (Unidroit 2013), Appendix V.

The general purpose of the CTC/AEP is to facilitate the exercise of remedies by holders of 'International Interests' in aircraft equipment, that is owners, lessors and financiers, if the relevant debtor is in default under the relevant title reservation agreement, lease agreement or security agreement, in the jurisdiction where the relevant aircraft, helicopter or aircraft engines may be located at the relevant moment in time. As there are many horror stories about lessors being unable to repossess their aircraft, after the lessee consistently failed to pay lease rent, because the laws of the relevant country were inadequate or the court system was either corrupt or so clogged that it took years to get the aircraft back, which by that time was often hardly worth repossessing, there can be no doubt that there was, and is, a justified need for a new regime. The CTC/AEP not only addresses the position of the parties to transactions, but also requires the Contracting States to adapt their laws and legal systems to certain standards. Obviously, the benefits of the CTC/AEP expand with the number of ratifications, so that lessors and financiers can get more comfort that the CTC/AEP will apply if remedies are to be exercised.

By 31 December 2016, a total of seventy-two States has ratified or acceded to the CTC/AEP[52] and the number of ratifications and accessions is constantly growing. Although this number is arguably still not large enough to conclude that the Cape Town Convention provides for a global uniform regime, the ratifications include most important aviation states, including the USA, the UK, China, India and Russia. The drawback is that the CTC/AEP allows Contracting States to make declarations pursuant to Articles 52 and 53 relating to non-consensual liens, 61 relating to the relationship with the 1933 Rome Convention (1933),[53] 66, relating to internal transactions, 68, relating to territorial units, 70, relating to remedies, 71, pertaining to declarations in respect of certain provisions of the CTC/AEP, and 76, relating to pre-existing interests or rights.[54]

A Contracting State may also make subsequent declarations regarding the afore-said subjects, with the exception of declarations regarding pre-existing rights.[55] Allowing so many declarations does to a certain extent reduce the uniformity of the regime of the CTC/AEP. When looking at the status of the CTC/AEP[56] it is noticeable that almost all Contracting States have made one or more declarations.[57]

The CTC/AEP sets up an International Registry laying down an asset-based system, that is, registration against a uniquely identifiable asset rather than against the

---

52. This includes (i) the accession in 2010 by The Netherlands which, however only applies to the Netherlands Antilles (which no longer exist) and Aruba and (ii) the accession in 2009 by the EU, as a regional economic integration organisation. The impact the accession of the EU for the EU Member States is limited; *see*, Berend Crans, *The Implications of the EU Accession to the Cape Town Convention*, 35 Air & Space Law 1–7 (2010); for an up-to-date list of ratifications *see*, www.internationalregistry.aero.
53. *See*, section 5.4 below.
54. *See also*, Art. 73 of the CTC/AEP.
55. *See*, Art. 73 of the CTC/AEP.
56. *See*, Unidroit's website: www.unidroit.org.
57. The declarations listed on Unidroit's website refer to the article. number under the Convention rather than the consolidate text of the CTC/AEP.

name of the debtor. The International Registry does not constitute a title registration system, that is, a registry where owners can record their ownership title to an aircraft object, but only of security interests and of interests held by conditional sellers and lessors.

2.4.2 Sphere of Application

According to Article 2(1), the CTC/AEP provides for the constitution and effects of international interests in aircraft objects and associated rights. The term 'aircraft objects' relates to airframes, aircraft engines and helicopters. Certain restrictions apply to these terms. The term 'airframe' refers to airframes, other than those used in military, customs and police services, that, when appropriate engines are attached thereto, are type certified by the competent aviation authority to transport at least eight persons, including crew, or goods in excess of 2750 kilograms. The term 'airframe' includes all installed, attached or incorporated accessories, parts and equipment except aircraft engines and all data, manuals and records relating thereto.

The Cape Town Convention defines 'engines' as either jet propulsion engines with a thrust of at least 1750 lbs or turbine-powered or piston-powered engines having at least a 550 rated take-off horsepower. The term 'helicopter' refers to heavier-than-air machines supported in flight chiefly by the reactions of the air on one or more power-driven rotors on substantially vertical axes and which are type certified for the transportation of at least five (5) persons including crew or goods in excess of 450 kilograms. Helicopters used in military, customs or police services are excluded.

The term 'international interest' pertains to interests constituted under Article 10 CTC/AEP in airframes, aircraft engines or helicopters:[58]

    (a) granted by the chargor under a security agreement;
    (b) vested in a person which is the conditional seller under a title reservation agreement; or
    (c) vested in a person who is the lessor under a lease agreement.[59]

It is left to the *lex fori* to characterise the relevant agreement and to determine whether a certain interest falls under subsection (a), (b) or (c) of Article 2(2) of the CTC/AEP.[60] Article 10 sets forth the requirements for the constitution of international interests. The relevant agreement must be in writing and must relate to an aircraft object of which the chargor, the conditional seller or, as the case may be, the lessor has

---

58. According to Art. 2(4) of the CTC/AEP, an international interest in an aircraft object also extends to the proceeds of that aircraft object.
59. Art. 2 of the CTC/AEP.
60. *See,* R. Goode, *Official Commentary* (Unidroit 2013) at 45.

the power to dispose. In addition, the agreement must identify the relevant aircraft object[61] and, in case of a security agreement, allow for the determination of the secured obligations.[62]

Article 3 determines the sphere of application of the CTC/AEP and provides that it applies when, at the time of conclusion of the agreement creating or providing for the international interest, the debtor is situated in a Contracting State. Article 3(3) extends the sphere of application as it provides that the CTC/AEP shall also apply in relation to a helicopter or to an airframe pertaining to an aircraft which is registered in the nationality register of a Contracting State. If such registration is made pursuant to an agreement for registration of the aircraft, it is deemed that such registration is effective at the time of the agreement. The *situs* of the debtor is an important element for the question whether the CTC/AEP applies and Article 4 gives a broad definition: for the purposes of Article 3(1), the debtor is situated in any Contracting State:

(a) under the law of which it is incorporated;
(b) where it has its registered office or statutory seat;
(c) where it has its centre of administration; or
(d) where it has a place of business.

The last criterion appears to be a very broad one, but Article 4(2) determines that where the debtor has more than one place of business, only its principal place of business shall be taken into account. The location of the creditor is not relevant for the application of the CTC/AEP.

2.4.3 Rights Protected by the CTC/AEP

The Cape Town Convention protects seven different categories of rights or interests, namely:

(1) *International Interests*, as described in Article 2.
(2) *Prospective international interests*; this relates to an interest intended to be taken over identifiable aircraft objects as an international interest in the future, but which has not yet become an international interest, because, for instance, the debtor has not yet acquired title to the relevant aircraft object. In this connection one could think of the financing of a new aircraft yet to be delivered by the manufacturer to an airline. It is possible to register a prospective international interest in the International Registry prior to delivery of title to the aircraft so that it becomes an international interest upon delivery, but will be deemed to have become effective as of its initial registration. The concept of a prospective interest is quite unique, but the use thereof may be limited because it may be difficult to agree on the terms and

---

61. For purposes of identification of an aircraft object it is sufficient to state the name of the manufacturer, the manufacturer's serial number and its model designation (Art. 8).
62. There is no need to state a maximum sum secured.

timing of prospective interests between for instance a seller and an existing lender on the one hand and a buyer and a new lender on the other. A prospective interest can have an agreed limited validity in the sense that it will expire at a certain date unless it has ripened into an international interest in accordance with the terms of the agreement.

(3) *National interests*, being interests registered under a national registration system which would be registrable as international interests but for the fact that they ate created by internal transactions[63] in respect whereof the relevant Contracting State has made a declaration pursuant to Article 66(1) CTC/AEP, excluding the application of the Cape Town Convention to internal transactions.

(4) *Non-consensual rights or interests arising under national law and given priority without registration.* Pursuant to Article 52(1), a Contracting State may make a declaration specifying categories of non-consensual rights or interests which under national law would have priority over interests equivalent to international interests and which, to the extent specified in the declaration, are to have priority over registered international interests even though such non-consensual right or interest is not registered in the International Registry.

(5) *Registrable non-consensual rights or interests arising under national law.* Contracting States are entitled to make a declaration under Article 53 to the effect that non-consensual rights or interests arising under its national law may be registered in the International Registry, which will then be treated as a registered international interest. This category deals with 'registrable' rights or interests, as opposed to 'registered' interest. This distinguishes this category of non-consensual rights and interests from the previous category, that is those covered by a declaration pursuant to Article 52(1): registrable non-consensual rights rank for priority under the CTC/AEP only if registered in the International Registry.

(6) *Associated rights*, being rights to payment or other performance by a debtor under an agreement which are secured by or associated with the aircraft object.

(7) *Pre-existing rights or interests*, which are the subject of a Contracting State's declaration pursuant to Article 76 of the CTC/AEP. This article contains important transitional provisions. The starting point is that, except as otherwise declared by a Contracting State, a right of interest created prior to the 'effective date'[64] is not affected by the Convention and retains its

---

63. The term 'internal transaction' is defined as transaction of a type listed in Art. 2(2)(a) to (c) where the centre of main interest of all parties as well as the relevant aircraft object are located in the same Contracting State at the time of conclusion of the contract and where the interest created by the transaction has been registered in a national registry in that Contracting State which has made a declaration under Art. 66(1) of the CTC/AEP, pursuant whereto the CTC/AEP shall not apply to internal transactions.
64. Being the later of (i) the date the Convention came into force and (ii) the date on which the State in which the debtor is situated becomes a Contracting State; *see*, Art. 76(2)(a).

'pre-Convention' priority. Article 76(3) allows a Contracting State to make a declaration specifying a date, which is at least three years after the date on which the declaration becomes effective, on which the Cape Town Convention will become effective to pre-existing rights or interests. This implies that holders of pre-existing rights have at least three years to protect their pre-Convention priority through registration of their pre-existing rights in the International Registry.[65]

2.4.4 Remedies under the CTC/AEP: General Provisions

Articles 12 through 25 of the CTC/AEP describe the default remedies. Following the occurrence of an event of default as defined in Article 17, the *chargee* is entitled to exercise any one or more of the remedies listed in Article 12(1), that is to:

(i)   take possession or control of the aircraft object charged to it;
(ii) sell or grant a lease of the relevant aircraft object;
(iii) collect or receive any income or profits arising from the management or use of the aircraft object.

Pursuant to Article 19, the exercise of any remedy must be exercised in a commercially reasonable manner. Where a contract describes what 'commercially reasonable' is, this may determine the standard unless such provision is manifestly unreasonable.

These remedies are subject to any declaration made by a Contracting State pursuant to Article 70.[66] Alternatively, the chargee may request a court order authorising or directing any of the remedies set forth above.[67] A chargee proposing to sell or lease an aircraft object charged to it must give reasonable[68] prior written notice thereof to the debtor and any guarantor as well as to any person having rights in the aircraft object, provided such person has given notice of his rights to the chargee within a reasonable time prior to the sale or the commencement of the lease. Any sum collected or received by the chargee as a result of the exercise must be applied towards discharge of the amount of the secured obligations.[69] The chargee must, unless otherwise ordered by the court, distribute any excess proceeds among holders of subsequently ranking interests, which have been registered or which the chargee has been given notice of, and pay any remaining balance to the chargor. Article 13 provides that the chargee and

---

65. So far only Mexico has made a declaration under Art. 60 of the Convention, that is, Art. 76 of the CTC/AEP.
66. An 'Art. 70' declaration may provide that, while the charged aircraft is situated within or controlled from the Contracting State's territory, the chargee may not grant a lease in respect thereof in that territory and/or may provide that a remedy may only be exercised with leave of the court.
67. Art. 12(2).
68. According to Art. 12(4) a period of ten or more business days shall be considered 'reasonable.' The parties may, however, agree to a longer period.
69. This will usually include any costs and expenses incurred by the chargee and arising from the exercise of remedies.

all interested persons[70] may agree that ownership to an aircraft object or any other interest of the chargor in that aircraft object shall vest in the chargee in or towards satisfaction of the secured obligations. In addition, pursuant to Article 13(2) the chargee may request the court to order that ownership of, or other interest if the chargor in, an aircraft object covered by the security interest shall vest in the chargee in or towards satisfaction of the secured obligations. This order will only be given if the amount of the secured obligations to be satisfied by such vesting is commensurate with the value of the aircraft object, after taking into account any payments to be made by the chargee to any interested person.

The chargor or any interested person may, at any time after the default and prior to the sale of the charged aircraft object or the making of an order by the court pursuant to Article 13(2), discharge the security interest by paying the full amount of the secured obligations, subject to any lease granted pursuant to Article 12(1)(b) or ordered pursuant to Article 12(2). If the payment is made by an interested person, such interested person is subrogated to the rights of the chargee. As a result the 'new' chargee could exercise the same remedies permitted by the CTC/AEP.

Ownership to the aircraft object which is transferred to the chargee pursuant to section 1 or 2 of Article 12, shall be free from any other interest which is of a lower priority than that of the chargee as determined pursuant to Article 42 of the CTC/AEP.

Article 14 provides the remedies available to the conditional seller or lessor of an aircraft, being the right to terminate the relevant agreement and to take possession or control of the relevant aircraft object. The exercise of remedies may be subject to leave of the court if the relevant Contracting State made a declaration to that effect pursuant to Article 70.

2.4.5 De-registration of Aircraft and Export of Aircraft Objects

Following termination of a lease agreement or a conditional sale agreement or following an event of default under a secured loan agreement, the lessor, conditional seller or mortgagee of an aircraft object will want to be able to de-register[71] and export the aircraft object from the jurisdiction of the lessee, the conditional purchaser or, as the case may be, the mortgagor.

These remedies are provided by Article 15(1) CTC/AEP and enable the creditor to change the nationality of an aircraft and to move aircraft objects physically to another country. Article 15(1) provides that these remedies may only be exercised to the extent the debtor has at any time agreed thereto; Article 15(2) provides that these remedies may not be exercised without the prior written consent of the holder of any registered interest ranking in priority to that of the creditor.[72]

---

70. *See*, the definition of this term in Art. 1(z).
71. Since only aircraft and helicopters are registered, the de-registration from the nationality register only applies to such aircraft objects and not to engines.
72. Art. 15(2); the debtor and the creditor may not derogate from this provision as to which *see*, Art. 22.

Two routes are available to creditors: the route via the court or, where the relevant Contracting State has made a declaration pursuant to Article 71(1) that it will apply Article 25 CTC/AEP, the 'IDERA' route.

Article 20(7) of the CTC/AEP provides the trigger for action by the national authorities if the creditor elects the court route. A creditor invoking Article 20(7) must have obtained an order for advance relief under Article 20(1) CTC/AEP.[73] Once the creditor has notified the authorities of the grant of the relief, the authorities are to perform two obligations. The first is to make the remedies available within five working days after notification and the second is to expeditiously co-operate with and assist the creditor in the exercise of the remedies of de-registration and export in accordance with the applicable aviation laws and safety regulations, which are not set aside or otherwise affected by Article 20(7).[74]

The IDERA route leads to Article 15 via Article 25 CTC/AEP and applies only if the relevant Contracting State has made a declaration pursuant to Article 71(1) with respect to Article 25.

Article 15(3) is addressed to the Contracting States as it requires the registry authorities of the Contracting States[75] to honour a request for de-registration and export if:

(i) the request is properly submitted under a recorded[76] irrevocable de-registration and export request authorisation, commonly referred to as an 'IDERA'; and

(ii) the authorised party certifies to the registry authority that all registered interests ranking in priority to that of the authorised party have been discharged or that the holders of such interests have consented to the de-registration and export of the relevant aircraft object.

The IDERA is a creature of the AEP, and an instrument sui generis, and a format IDERA is attached to the AEP. IDERAs are to be distinguished from standard de-registration powers of attorney as they are not derived from or dependent upon national law. The concept is that an IDERA is a standing direction by a debtor, that is, a borrower or a lessee, addressed to the registry authority[77] to honour a request for de-registration made by the holder of the IDERA. To be effective, a debtor must agree to and sign and submit the IDERA for recordation to the registry authority.[78] If so agreed, signed and submitted, the IDEAR is binding and irrevocable.

---

73. The reference to Art. 15(1) in Art. 20(7)(a) CTC/AEP is incorrect and should be a reference to Art. 20(1). This a drafting error; see, R. Goode, *Official Commentary* (Rome 2013) at 184/185.
74. *See*, Art. 20(9) CTC/AEP.
75. This obligation is subject to any applicable safety laws and regulations.
76. *See*, Art. XIII of the Aircraft Equipment Protocol: this refers to recordation with the registry authority; the request must be substantially in the form annexed to the Protocol; *see also*, Art. 25 of the CTC/AEP.
77. The 'registry authority' is the authority which maintains the relevant nationality register; *see*, the definition of that term in the Aircraft Equipment Protocol.
78. *See*, Art. XIII (2) of the Aircraft Equipment Protocol and R. Goode, *Official Commentary* (Rome 2013) at 182 ff.

Where a chargee intends to de-register and export an aircraft otherwise than with leave of the court, Article 15(4) requires that reasonable prior written notice must be given to the interested persons specified in Article 1(z)(i), (ii) and (iii) CTC/AEP. In aircraft finance and lease transactions it is standard practice to require the chargor and, as the case may be, the lessee to execute an IDERA in favour of the charge, or the security agent, or, as the case may be, the lessor.

2.4.6 Additional Remedies and Interim Measures

In addition to the remedies referred to in the CTC/AEP, any additional remedies permitted by applicable law, including any contractually agreed remedies, may be exercised to the extent that they are not inconsistent with the mandatory provisions of Chapter III of the Cape Town Convention as set out in Article 22 CTC/AEP.[79]

The CTC/AEP also provides for interim measures as described in Article 20, subject to a Contracting State having made a declaration pursuant to Article 71(2).[80] If so, the relevant Contracting State must ensure that a creditor who adduces evidence of default by the debtor may, pending final determination of its claim and to the extent the debtor has at any time so agreed, obtain from a court speedy relief in the form of any one or more of the following orders as requested by the creditor:

(a) preservation of the value of the aircraft object;
(b) possession, control or custody of the aircraft object;
(c) immobilisation of the aircraft object;
(d) lease or, except where already covered by sub-sections (a)–(c), management of the aircraft object and any income arising therefrom; and
(e) if at any time expressly agreed between the debtor and the creditor, the sale and application of proceeds therefrom.

In most jurisdictions, the law provides for interim measures ordered by the court so as to prevent that the value of the aircraft is deteriorating pending the resolution of the question whether or not for instance the lessee was in default and indeed obligated to return the aircraft to the lessor. Where such provisions were lacking, the CTC/AEP provides a welcome addition to the remedies available to creditors, also because Contracting States, when making a declaration under Article 71(2) must specify what 'speedy relief' means, that is, how many working days will elapse between an application and the issuance of a court order.[81]

---

79. Art. 16; Art. 22 provides that it is not permitted to derogate from the provisions of Arts 12(3)–12(6), 13(3), 13(4) and 19 through 21.
80. Most, but not all, States have made a declaration under this provision which equals Art. XXX (2) of the Aircraft Equipment Protocol.
81. See, Art. 20(2).

As Article 20(1) provides that the seeking of a court order for interim measures is limited "to the extent that the debtor has at any time so agreed," it is advisable to include provisions to that respect in the relevant documentation so that the creditor will get the full benefit of this provision.

2.4.7 Remedies on Insolvency

Article 23 deals with remedies on insolvency and applies only where a Contracting State, which is the primary insolvency jurisdiction,[82] has made a declaration pursuant to Article 71(3).[83] With such a declaration the Contracting State may make a choice between Alternative A and Alternative B. Alternative A is often referred to as the 'hard' or 'rule-based' set of provisions which is particularly designed to meet the requirements of structured transactions. Alternative A requires the insolvency administrator or the debtor to

(a) give possession to the creditor within the earlier of:
    (i) the end of the 'waiting period';[84] and
    (ii) the date on which the creditor would otherwise be entitled to possession; or
(b) within the afore-said period cure all defaults[85] under the relevant agreement and agree to perform all future obligations under the agreement and the 'related transaction documents.'[86]

Unless and until the creditor is given the opportunity to take possession, Alternative A requires the insolvency administrator or the debtor, as applicable, to preserve the aircraft object and maintain it and its value in accordance with the terms of the agreement. The creditor is entitled to apply for any other forms of interim relief available under 'the applicable law.'[87]

Alternative A bars the insolvency court from preventing or delaying the exercise by the creditor of remedies beyond the contractually agreed cure period and in particular from staying or modifying a secured creditor's rights or remedies. The

---

82. The term 'primary insolvency jurisdiction' refers to the Contracting State in which the debtor's centre of main interests is situated; for the purpose of the CTC/AEP this shall be deemed to be the place of the debtor's statutory seat or, if there is none, the place where the debtor is incorporated or formed (unless proved otherwise).
83. Only a few Contracting States have not made a declaration pursuant to Art. XXX (3) of the Aircraft Equipment Protocol: Albania, Ireland, Malta, Spain, Sweden and the USA.
84. The 'waiting period' is the period which must be specified in the relevant declaration made by the Contracting State and refers to the period during which the exercise of remedies by creditors or beneficiaries of security interests may be suspended by an insolvency court. Waiting periods are usually either thirty calendar days (in some cases thirty working days) or sixty calendar days.
85. Other than a default constituted by the commencement of the insolvency proceedings.
86. The term 'related transaction documents' is not defined but is intended to include all documents, other than the agreement itself, that impose obligations on the debtor in respect of the transaction, for instance the related loan, a guarantee agreement or the participation agreement.
87. *See also*, Art. 20 of the CTC/AEP discussed in section 2.4.6 above.

creditors' protection under Alternative A is additionally improved by section 12 of Alternative A which preserves the priority of registered interests over other rights or interests other than non-consensual rights or interest covered by a declaration pursuant to Article 52.[88]

Alternative B is the 'soft' version. It requires the insolvency administrator or the debtor, as applicable, to state – at the creditor's request and within the period specified in the relevant declaration of the Contracting State – whether it will cure all defaults and perform all future obligations under the agreement and the related transaction documents or, alternatively, give the creditor the opportunity to repossess the aircraft object in accordance with applicable law. In the latter case, the applicable law may allow the court to require that additional steps be taken or that guarantees are provided, for instance to cover losses suffered by the debtor as result of the repossession order if the creditor's claim is denied in the substantive hearing.

The main differences between Alternatives A and B are first of all that in Alternative B the insolvency administrator only has to give notice that he will either cure all defaults or give the creditor the opportunity to repossess. In Alternative A, the insolvency administrator has to take affirmative action, that is either cure all defaults or give possession of the aircraft object to the creditor. Secondly, in Alternative B, where the insolvency administrator does not give the required notice or, if he has declared that he will give the creditor the opportunity to repossess, he fails to do so, the creditor cannot exercise any self-help remedies and must request a repossession order which may be subject to conditions.[89]

2.4.8 The International Registration System

Chapter IV of the CTC/AEP deals with the International Registry. As part of the implementation process of the Cape Town Convention and the AEP, the Secretary General of ICAO[90] set up a global tender for an organisation to establish the International Registry and act as Registrar of the International Registry. Aviareto Limited, a joint venture between SITA SC and the Irish government was selected.[91] The International Registry is established for registrations[92] of:

---

88. A declaration under Art. 52(4) may still lead to unpleasant surprises for the secured creditor who may find that the declaration entails that certain non-consensual rights have priority over an international interest that was registered prior to the date of the relevant declaration.
89. So far only one Contracting State, Mexico, has opted for Alternative B.
90. ICAO is the Supervising Authority referred to in Art. 27. In accordance with Art. 27(3), the Supervising Authority has established a commission of experts (CESAIR). See, Art. 27(4) for the Supervising Authority's role and Chapter VI of the Cape Town Convention for the privileges and immunities of the Supervising Authority and the Registrar. Chapter VII deals with the liability of the Registrar.
91. Pursuant to Art. 28, Registrars are appointed for a period of five years. For more information on Aviareto, please refer to www.aviareto.aero. See, Art. 28(3) as to the fee structure to be adhered to by Registrars.
92. The term 'registration' includes, where appropriate, an amendment, extension and discharge of a registration.

(a) international interests, prospective international interests and registrable non-consensual rights and interests;

(b) assignments and prospective assignments of international interests;

(c) acquisitions of international interests by legal or contractual subrogation under applicable law;

(d) notices on national interests; and

(e) subordination of interest referred to in any of the preceding sections.

A Contracting State[93] may designate one or more entry points through which information required for registration[94] shall or may be directly transmitted to the International Registry. Article 30 prescribes that the International Registry shall be operated and administered by the Registrar on a twenty-four hour basis.[95] Entry points are to be operated at least during working hours in their respective territories.

2.4.9 *Modalities for Registration*

Pursuant to Article 31, ICAO, in its capacity of Supervising Authority under the Cape Town Convention and the AEP, issued the Regulations and Procedures for the International Registry[96] which list *inter alia* the information required for the registration of aircraft objects with the International Registry.[97] A registration shall only be valid if made in conformity with Article 33, which prescribes which person is authorised to make a specific registration and whose consent is required for any amendment, extension or termination of a registration.

A valid registration is complete upon entry of the information required by the Regulations into the International Registry's database so as to be searchable. The term 'searchable' is defined in Article 32(3) in the sense that a registration shall be searchable when:

(a) the International Registry has assigned a sequentially ordered file number to the registration; and

(b) the registration information, including the file number, is stored in durable form and may be accessed at the International Registry.

If a registered prospective interest becomes an international interest, that international interest shall be treated as registered from the time of registration of the prospective international interest.[98] A registration remains effective from the date it is

---

93. So far only the United Arab Emirates have made such designation.
94. This does not apply to registration of a notice of a national interest or registrable non-consensual interests in each case arising under the laws of another State; *see*, Art. 29(1).
95. Entry points shall be operated at least during working hours in their respective jurisdiction.
96. ICAO Doc 9864.
97. The Regulations also cover matters like operational complaints, confidentiality and fees. The Procedures mainly address administrative items required by the Regulations as conditions to use the International Registry.
98. Art. 32(4); *see also*, section 2.4.3 above.

complete until discharged or until expiry of the period specified in the registration.[99] Article 38 deals with the formalities to be complied with in connection with the discharge of registrations when for instance the obligations secured by a registered security interest have been discharged. In that case the holder of the security interest is obligated to procure, without undue delay, the discharge of the registration after written demand by the debtor delivered to or received at the security interest holder's address as stated in the registration.[100]

2.4.10 Effects of International Interests

Article 42 provides the priority rules applicable to competing interests. Starting point is that a registered interest has priority[101] over subsequently registered interests and over unregistered interests. This priority even holds firm if the relevant registered interest was acquired or registered with actual knowledge of the unregistered interest. The buyer of an aircraft object under a registered sale is protected in the same way against subsequently registered interests or unregistered interests. The conditional buyer or the lessee of an aircraft object acquires its interest in or right over an aircraft object subject to interests registered prior to the registration of the international interest held by its conditional seller or lessor; this implies that conditional buyers as well lessees should verify whether there are any pre-existing registered interests. The CTC/AEP allows for the priority of competing interests or rights to be varied by agreement between the holders of those interest.[102] A party in whose favour subordination has been agreed should make sure that this subordination is registered with the International Registry so that it will be binding upon an assignee of the subordinated interest.[103] Article 42(9) specifically provides that ownership of, or another right or interest in an aircraft engine shall not be affected by the installation of that aircraft engine on an aircraft or the removal thereof from an aircraft.

The effects of insolvency on international interests are set out in Article 43. The main rule is that an international interest which was registered in compliance with the relevant provisions of the CTC/AEP prior to the commencement of the debtor's insolvency proceedings shall remain effective. This protection extends to non-consensual rights or interests under Article 53. Article 43(2) provides that this provision does not impair the effectiveness of an international interest which is effective under the applicable law. The wording is rather cryptic but implies that where under the applicable law the international interest is effective, even if it has not been

---

99. Art. 34(1); *see*, Art. 34(2) in relation to contracts of sale.
100. Under applicable law the term 'delivered to' may not be the same as 'received at'. Beneficiaries of registered international interests should at all times make sure that their current address for notices is stated in the registration.
101. The priority provided by Art. 42 to an interest in an aircraft object also applies to proceeds as to which *see*, Art. 42(7).
102. The question is, however, whether this is also permitted under the law applicable to the relevant security rights. In some jurisdictions it is not permitted that for instance mortgagees under aircraft mortgages vary their priority by agreement.
103. Art. 42(6).

registered prior to the commencement on the insolvency proceedings, then its efficacy is not impaired by Article 43(1). Finally, Article 43(3) provides that Article 43 does not in any way affect the rules of law applicable in insolvency proceedings relating to avoidance or fraudulent preference.

2.4.11 Assignment and Subrogation

Pursuant to the CTC/AEP there is a direct link between 'associated rights', being all rights to payment or other performance by a debtor under an agreement which are secured by or associated with the aircraft object, and the international interest which is intended to secure such associated rights. Article 44(1) provides that, except as otherwise agreed between the parties, an assignment of associated rights also entails the transfer to the assignee of the related international interest[104] as well as all the interests and priorities of the assignor under the CTC/AEP. Article 44(3) provides that 'the applicable law'[105] shall determine the defences and rights of set-off available to the debtor and the assignee.

Article 45(1) lists the formal requirements of assignment: an assignment of associated rights only transfers the related international interests if it is in writing and enables the associated rights to be identified under the contract from which they arise. An assignment of an international interest created or provided for by a security agreement shall not be valid unless some or all associated rights are also assigned. This provision also reflects the link between a security right and the obligations it secures.[106]

Various provisions of Chapter IX of the CTC/AEP deal with the assignment of associated rights by way of security.[107] Article 47 is of particular importance as it stipulates that in the event of default by the assignor under the assignment of associated rights and the related international interests, the remedies granted to a chargee pursuant to Articles 12, 13 and 15–21 shall apply in the relations between assignor and assignee, and in relation to associated rights, in so far as those provisions are capable of application to intangible property, as if references to:

(a) the secured obligation and the security interest were references to the obligation secured by the assignment and the security interest created by that assignment;
(b) the chargee or creditor were references to the assignee;

---

104. In most civil law jurisdictions there is an inseverable link between a security right and the obligations it secures: if the secured obligations are assigned by the creditor thereof, the assignee will – by operation of law – become the beneficiary of the related security right. The question is to what extent the CTC/AEP which allows the parties to agree otherwise would conflict with the property laws of jurisdictions where the security right 'follows' the secured obligations by operation of law, irrespective of what the parties agreed in that respect.
105. The term 'the applicable law' refers to the domestic rules of the law applicable by virtue of the rules of private international law of the forum State (Art. 5(3)). *See also*, section 2.4.13 below.
106. The remaining question is, however, what the status is of the associated rights which are not assigned together with the international interest. Will they then be totally unsecured? If so, the link between a security right and the obligations it secures is very loose.
107. Arts 44(5), 45(1)(c) and 47 CTC/AEP.

(c) the chargor or the debtor were references to the assignor;

(d) the holder of an international interest were references to the assignee and (e) to the aircraft object were references to the assigned associated rights and the related international interests.

With respect to the priority of competing assignments of associated rights, Article 48(1) lays down that where at least one of the competing assignments includes the related international interest and is registered, the provisions of Article 42 apply as if the references to a registered interest were references to an assignment of associated rights and the related registered interest and as if references to a registered or unregistered interest were references to a registered or unregistered assignment. An assignee of associated rights and the related international interest, whose assignment has been registered, only has priority pursuant to Article 48(1) over another assignee of the same associated rights if it follows from the contract from which the assigned associated rights arise that they are secured by or associated with the aircraft object. The priority only applies to the extent the associated rights are related to an aircraft object, which will be the case to the extent that they consist of rights to payment or performance relating to:

(a) advance payments for the purchase of the aircraft object;

(b) advance payments for the purchase of another aircraft object in which the assignor held another international interest, provided the assignor transferred that interest to the assignee and the assignment has been registered;

(c) the purchase price for the aircraft object;

(d) the rentals payable in respect of the aircraft object; or

(e) other obligations arising from a transaction referred to in (a) to (d).

In all other cases the priority of competing assignments of associated rights is to be determined in accordance with the applicable law. With respect to insolvency of an assignor, Article 50 provides that Article 43 applies to insolvency proceedings against the assignor as if references to the debtor were references to the assignor.[108]

Under Article 51(1), subject to Article 51(2), the CTC/AEP does not affect the acquisition of associated rights and the related international interest by legal or contractual subrogation under the applicable law. Pursuant to Article 51(2) the priority between an international interest acquired through subrogation and a competing interest may be varied by written agreement between the holders of these interests but an assignee of a subordinated interest is not bound by an agreement to subordinate that interest unless at the time of the assignment a subordination was registered relating to that agreement.

---

108. *See*, section 2.4.10 above.

2.4.12 Jurisdiction

Chapter XI of the CTC/AEP provides the rules relating to jurisdiction. This chapter does not apply to insolvency proceedings.[109] Pursuant to Article 54 the parties to a transaction have freedom to agree[110] on the jurisdiction[111] of the courts of a Contracting State in respect of any claim brought under the Convention, irrespective of whether or not the chosen forum has any connection with the parties or the transaction. In addition to the chosen forum, the courts of the Contracting State where the aircraft object is situated or where the aircraft is registered have jurisdiction to grant relief under Articles 20(1)(a), (b) and (c) and 20(7) in respect of that aircraft or aircraft object.[112] This concerns the relief pending final determination in the form of orders for the preservation of the aircraft object and its value, the possession control and custody of the aircraft object and immobilisation of the aircraft object and the remedies to procure the de-registration and export of the aircraft object pursuant to Article 15(1).[113] With respect to interim relief under Articles 20(1)(d) and (e) and 20(4) the chosen courts or the courts of the Contracting State where the debtor is situated will also have jurisdiction.[114] This deals with court orders regarding the lease or management of the aircraft object or the sale and the application of the proceeds thereof.

Pursuant to Article 57, waivers of sovereign immunity from the jurisdiction of the courts specified in Articles 54, 55 or 56 or relating to enforcement of rights and interest in respect of an aircraft object under the Cape Town Convention shall be binding and will be effective to confer jurisdiction and permit enforcement, provided the other conditions to such jurisdiction or enforcement have been satisfied. Any such waiver must be in writing and contain a description of the relevant aircraft object.[115]

In this connection the question arises whether this provision will indeed be effective in all circumstances. The effectiveness of a written waiver of sovereign immunity may depend on a number of other factors, such as the question whether the domestic laws of the relevant country do allow for such waivers and the capacity and authority of the person having executed the waiver.

2.4.13 Conflicts of Law

With respect to the contractual aspects, the Cape Town Convention allows the parties to agree on the law governing their contractual rights and obligations.[116] Such chosen law shall be the domestic law of the designated State, so that '*renvoi*' is excluded.

---

109. Art. 58 CTC/AEP.
110. Such agreement must be in writing or otherwise concluded in accordance with the formal requirements of the law of the chosen forum.
111. Which shall be exclusive unless otherwise agreed between the parties.
112. Art. 55(1) CTC/AEP.
113. *See*, section 2.4.5 above.
114. Art. 56.
115. Art. 57(2).
116. Art. 9(2); this is subject to the Contracting State having made a declaration pursuant to Art. 71(1).

Where it concerns proprietary aspects, the CTC/AEP's intent is that the international interest comprises an independent autonomous interest under its terms.

Unfortunately, no conclusive conflict rule has been drawn up. Instead there are various references to 'the applicable law', which is defined as the domestic rules of law applicable by virtue of the rules of private international law of the forum state. This does again exclude 'renvoi' but does not give a practical tool in international transactions. The outcome will depend on the guidance provided by the rules of private international law of the forum. This still leads to a substantial degree of unpredictability as it may be uncertain which forum will be involved, as is described in Articles 54 through 56 of the Cape Town Convention.[117] According to Article 2(3)(a), the applicable law determines whether an interest qualifies as a security agreement, a title reservation agreement or a lease agreement.[118]

Article 42(8) refers among others to the applicable law to determine whether or not rights in an object, not being an aircraft object, will continue to exist after such object has been installed in or on an aircraft object. Article 43 provides that the effectiveness of an international interest which is effective under the applicable law, shall not be impaired by insolvency proceedings.[119] Finally, there is a catch-all clause in Article 5(2) providing that questions regarding matters governed by the CTC/AEP and not 'expressly settled' therein, must be settled in conformity which the general principles on which it is based or, in the absence of such principles in conformity with the applicable law. Unfortunately, the references to 'the applicable law' will not provide the legal certainty which is so badly needed in this industry.[120]

2.4.14 Relationship with Other Conventions

Chapter XII of the CTC/AEP deals with the relationship with other conventions. The CTC/AEP shall:

(a) prevail over the United Nations Convention on the Assignment of Receivables in International Trade,[121] as it relates to the assignment of receivables which are associated rights related to international interests in aircraft objects;[122]

(b) for a Contracting State which is a party to the Geneva Convention, supersede that convention as it relates to aircraft as defined in the CTC/AEP, and to

---

117. *See*, section 2.4.12 above.
118. One could question whether this is conflicts with Art. 9(2) which refers to the chosen law and not the law determined through application of the rules of private international law of the forum state.
119. *See also*, the references to 'the applicable law' in Art. 23 (Alternative A as well as Alternative B) and section 2.4.7 for a description of the remedies on insolvency.
120. *See*, section 2.2 above.
121. This convention was opened for signature in New York on 12 December 2001.
122. *See*, section 2.4.11 above.

aircraft objects; with respect to rights or interests not covered by the CTC/AEP, the Geneva Convention shall not be superseded;[123]

(c) for a Contracting State that is a party to the Rome Convention (1933),[124] the CTC/AEP shall supersede that convention as it relates to aircraft as defined in the CTC/AEP;

(d) supersede the Unidroit Convention on International Financial Leasing[125] as it relates to aircraft objects.

The relationship between conventions is a complicated matter as it involves application of the law of treaties. Within the context of this book it would go too far to elaborate on these issues.

Particular attention must be given to scenarios where a Contracting State is a party to the CTC/AEP as well as to for instance the Geneva Convention and to what extent its obligations under the Geneva Convention towards other Contracting States to the Geneva Convention which have not ratified the CTC/AEP are affected by the CTC/AEP.[126]

3 LEASING OF AIRCRAFT AND ENGINES

3.1 Introduction to Leasing

3.1.1 Why Leasing?

If airlines need additional capacity they have various options: place an order with a manufacturer and wait until the ordered aircraft are delivered and prior to delivery arrange financing of the relevant aircraft. Financing aircraft with debt may have certain undesirable implications, such as the adverse effect on the airline's liquidity, the related increase of the airline's balance sheet total as well as an adverse change to its gearing ratio, that is, the level of its debt compared to its equity, which in turn may affect its credit rating and certain financial covenants under its existing credit facility agreements or other instruments.

Financial leasing has become the prime instrument to finance the acquisition of aircraft, as this does not materially affect the finance lessee's balance sheet, liquidity or gearing ratio.

Alternatively, in particular where an operator needs flexibility, *operational leasing* may be an attractive alternative to the financial leasing or ownership of aircraft. Today, the bulk of the world's fleet of commercial aircraft is not owned by the operators but by leasing companies, which have become the major fleet owners.

---

123. In this connection one can think of the recordable rights of lessee (rights of use and purchase option); *see also*, section 2.3.1 above.
124. *See*, section 5.4 and sources mentioned there.
125. Signed at Ottawa on 28 May 1988.
126. *See*, R. Goode, *Official Commentary* (Unidroit, 2013), sections 5.101 – 5.106.

Companies like GECAS[127] which owns or manages more than 1950 aircraft operated by 270 airlines,[128] and Aercap, with 1,607 aircraft owned, managed or on order,[129] are responsible for placing huge orders with Boeing, Airbus and other manufacturers, which are then leased to operators around the globe.

3.1.2   Operational Leasing

In essence there are two forms of leasing: *operational leasing* and *financial leasing*.

Operational leasing is characterised by the fact that the owner/lessor retains the economic risk in respect of the leased aircraft. An operating lease is usually for a limited period in time,[130] usually with extension options, and one would normally not find a purchase option in an operating lease. Following the expiry of the agreed lease term, the lessor will take the aircraft back and try to either sell or re-lease the aircraft to another operator. Subject to the initial lessee having complied with its obligations under the lease, including all maintenance and operational covenants and the return conditions, the lessor will bear all risks relating to the aircraft, including any reduction in market value. For airlines, operating leases provide enormous operational flexibility in comparison with purchasing aircraft, as purchase decisions must be made many years in advance. Downward trends in the global economy may entail that the airline, by the time the aircraft are delivered, no longer needs that capacity. In addition, operating leases do not require substantial capital expenditure and do not burden the airlines balance sheet. As the lessor remains the legal owner of the aircraft and carries all economic risks attaching to the aircraft, the aircraft will remain on the lessor's balance sheet, which is of course importance for tax and accounting purposes.

Operating leases come in many forms. For the mid and longer term, the most frequently used form of operating lease is the *dry lease*, that is, a lease where the aircraft is made available for use to the lessee, without crew, maintenance and insurance. The dry lessee is to provide its own crew and the lease agreement contains precise lessee undertakings regarding maintenance and insurance of the aircraft. For short term leases, airlines may elect *wet lease* arrangements where the lessor provides the aircraft including crew, maintenance and insurance.[131] Wet-leased aircraft are, as a rule, operated under the Air Operator's Certificate[132] of the lessor.

---

127. GE Capital Aviation Services.
128. *See*, www.gecas.com; last accessed on 9 January 2017.
129. *See*, www.aercap.com; last accessed on 9 January 2017.
130. Some operators enter into seasonal operating leases to meet peak demand during the holiday season.
131. This type of leasing, where a lessor provides an Aircraft including Crew, Maintenance and Insurance is also often referred to as an 'ACMI lease.' When the lessor provides less than the entire aircraft crew, for instance where cabin crew is provided by the lessee, the lease is often referred to as a 'damp lease' or 'moist lease.'
132. *See*, sections 1.2.1 and 1.2.2 of Chapter 2.

3.1.3 Financial Leasing

The distinctive feature of financial leases is that the lessor is the legal owner of the aircraft but the lease is structured in such a way that all economic risks attaching to the aircraft are transferred to the lessee. Financial leasing is primarily used as a financing instrument for airlines having purchased aircraft and looking for alternative forms of financing. Lessors operate as facilitators by assuming the airline's rights and obligations under the relevant aircraft purchase agreement with the manufacturer and by arranging for the financing of the purchase price. Following delivery of the aircraft to the lessor, the aircraft is leased to the operator/lessee.[133]

Financial lease agreements always provide for the transfer of ownership title to the lessee at the end of the agreed lease term,[134] be it automatically upon payment of the final rent instalment or upon the exercise of a purchase option. Such purchase option is structured in such a way that there is a strong economic compulsion for the lessee to indeed exercise the option. In most cases the purchase option price will be fixed and the payment thereof will result in the financial lessor having received, upon termination of the lease, full pay-out of the aggregate acquisition costs[135] of the aircraft as well as a fair margin. The fixed price purchase option implies that the financial lessee is taking residual value risk in respect of the aircraft.[136]

The fact that the lessee carries all economic risks attaching to the aircraft entails that the aircraft will be on the financial lessee's balance sheet. As a consequence, the financial lessee will be entitled to take depreciation on the aircraft in its profit and loss account, which will reduce its taxable corporate income.

3.1.4 Tax and Accounting Aspects

The different tax treatment of operating leases on the one hand, where the aircraft remains on the lessor's balance sheet with the operating lessor taking depreciation, and finance leases on the other hand, where the aircraft is on the financial lessee's balance sheet with the financial lessee taking the benefits of depreciation, resulted in a variety of cross border tax arbitrage transactions, that is transactions where the lease was set up in such a way that it qualified as an operating lease in the lessor's jurisdiction, allowing the lessor the benefit of depreciation, and as a financial lease in the lessee's

---

133. The structure usually involves single aircraft special purpose companies which attract funding from a financial institution to whom a mortgage on the aircraft is granted as security for the repayment of the loan.
134. This included expiry of the agreed term as well as early termination following the occurrence of a lessee event of default.
135. The lease rent payments and the purchase option price are calculated in such a way that the aggregate thereof provides full compensation to the lessor for the purchase price of the aircraft, all finance costs, administration and management fees and a profit margin.
136. This works both ways: if the purchase option price is less than the fair market value of the aircraft, the financial lessee will be able to realise a profit when he decides to sell the aircraft.

jurisdiction, allowing the lessee the benefit of depreciation too. This type of 'double dip' transactions is hardly available these days because of the tightening of tax and accounting rules across the world.

In addition, the IASB,[137] after many years of discussion with the aviation industry, issued new rules on the accounting treatment of leases, IFRS 16,[138] in January 2016. IFRS 16 replaces the previous rules[139] and wipes out the difference in accounting treatment between operational and financial leases in that there will be one type of lease instrument with certain specific accounting implications for lessors and lessees.[140]

Pursuant to IFRS 16, all leases will be treated the same way[141] in that leases are 'capitalised' by recognising the present value of the lease payments and showing them either as lease assets, that is, right-of-use assets, or as tangible assets, together with property, plant and equipment. If lease payments are to be made over time, the lessee shall also recognise a financial liability representing its obligation to make future lease payments. The most relevant exemption to this rule is that IFRS 16 does not require a company to recognise assets and liabilities for short-term leases with a term of twelve months or less.

3.1.5   Export Credit Agencies

Historically, certain countries have provided export credit finance to airlines that could not finance their orders in the commercial markets, because their financial condition was held to be too risky by commercial banks. Export credit finance is either direct financing provided by an Export Credit Agency (ECA) or a guarantee pursuant whereto an ECA assumes the default risk of the airline under loan agreements provided by banks to the airline for the funding of the acquisition of the aircraft.[142] As ECAs are usually government agencies of the exporting country, the commercial banks are able to rely on the sovereign credit of that country. The credit support provided by ECA guarantees enables commercial banks to charge relatively low margins and, although ECAs charge a fee for providing guarantees, this results in relatively cheap funding for the airline. This enabled manufacturers to sell their aircraft to customers which would otherwise have been unable to place orders. ECA support is often used in financial lease structures where the ECA guarantees the repayment of the loan[143] granted to the lessor for the acquisition of the aircraft.

---

137. International Accounting Standards Board.
138. IFRS stands for International Financial Reporting Standards.
139. IAS 17 Leases of the International Accounting Standards.
140. IFRS 16 becomes effective by 1 January 2019. For more information, *see*, the IASB website at www.ifrs.org.
141. In a way similar to the treatment of finance leases under IAS 17.
142. Usually the loan which is guaranteed by the ECA is provided by commercial banks to a special purpose company which acquires the aircraft and leases it to the relevant airline by way of a finance lease.
143. Usually one would see that the guarantee covers about 80 per cent of the loan amount.

In order to create a level playing field between aircraft manufacturers in the USA and the EU, an agreement was reached between the USA and the European Community in 1985 providing for minimum terms and conditions for loans or loan guarantees for the support by government ECAs of the export of aircraft with seventy seats or more, the Large Aircraft Sector Understanding (LASU). Later, this agreement was broadened to cover all commercial aircraft and LASU was incorporated as a sectoral annex to the OECD *Arrangement on Guidelines for Officially Supported Export Credits*.

Over time ECAs started to finance transactions involving airlines with better credits. This has resulted in complaints from airlines which could not get ECA guarantees because they were located in the same country as the relevant manufacturer[144] and from commercial banks as the attractive pricing for export credit finance was considered to make the commercial loan market uncompetitive. This resulted in stricter rules, making ECA supported financing less attractive for eligible airlines with access to commercial markets. The 2007 Aircraft Sector Understanding (ASU) provided for a steep increase in minimum guarantee fees to be charged by ECAs and more recently, in February 2011, even stricter rules and higher minimum fees were imposed by the New Aircraft Sector Understanding (NASU), which applies to all OECD countries and Brazil.[145]

3.1.6 Registration of Lessee's Rights

The Geneva Convention[146] provides for the recognition by the Contracting States of purchase options, coupled with possession of the aircraft, and rights to possession of aircraft under leases with a term of six months or more, provided such rights

(i) have been constituted in accordance with the laws of the Contracting State where the aircraft was registered as to nationality at the time of their constitution; and

(ii) are regularly recorded in a public record of the Contracting State where the aircraft is registered as to nationality.[147]

Some countries, like The Netherlands, do indeed provide for the recordation in a public registry of a lessee's purchase option and a lessee's right to possession of the aircraft,[148] which take effect as in rem rights.[149]

---

144. ECA credit support can only be provided where aircraft are exported from the manufacturing state. This implies that for instance Delta Airlines when ordering Boeing aircraft cannot obtain credit support from Export Import Bank of the United States, the U.S. ECA.

145. For a historical summary of export credit and a summary of the NASU rules, *see*, Airfinance Journal, February 2011, at 18 and 19.

146. *See*, sections 2.1.1 and 2.3 above.

147. Art. 1(1) subsections (b) and (c) of the Geneva Convention (1948).

148. Sections 8:1308 and 1309 of the Dutch Civil Code (*Burgerlijk Wetboek*).

149. As these recorded rights take effect as *in rem* rights, lenders requiring a first priority mortgage and total freedom in case of a sale in execution of the aircraft, should make sure that the lessees purchase option and possession rights are recorded *after* the recordation of the mortgage in the public register.

3.1.7 *Contractual Matters*

Describing in detail how aircraft lease agreements are structured would go beyond the scope of this book. Each lease agreement will be different but in general terms any lease agreement will contain the following provisions. The agreement will clearly describe when the aircraft is to be made available to the lessee and which conditions precedent must be met in order for the leasing of the aircraft to commence. Conditions precedent usually include the submission by the lessee to the lessor of a variety of documents including the lessee's constituent documents and its most recent accounts, corporate resolutions demonstrating that the lessee has taken all required corporate action, legal opinions, insurance certificate demonstrating that the required hull insurance and third party liability insurance are in place, copies of the lessee's air operating certificate and its operating licence, an executed de-registration power of attorney,[150] an executed 'Eurocontrol letter' which authorises Eurocontrol to inform the lessor about the status of any air navigation charges owing by the lessee and a certificate of acceptance executed by the lessee pursuant whereto it accepts the aircraft and confirms that the aircraft is in the agreed delivery condition.[151]

Obviously a lease agreement will also specify the term of the lease agreement, the expiry date and circumstances which can lead to early termination, such as the occurrence of a default or an event of default. Lease agreements will clearly specify the lease rent payable by the lessee, the commitment fee to be paid upon the execution of the agreement or prior to the lease commencement date as well as all other payments to be made by the lessee, such as security deposits and maintenance reserves. Where payments to be made by the lessee are subject to taxes which must be withheld by the lessee, the agreement will contain so-called 'gross up' provisions, which obligate the lessee to make such additional payment to the lessor as shall be necessary to ensure that the lessor receives the full amount due to it as if no withholding would have applied.

Any lease agreement will contain a limited number of lessor representations and warranties and a broad range of lessee representations and warranties, many of which must not only be true and correct on the date of the agreement and on the lease commencement date but also on each rent payment date. In addition, there will be a broad range of lessee covenants relating to hull insurance[152] and third party liability insurance,[153] the operation, maintenance and repair of the aircraft, the replacement of

---

150. Where relevant an IDERA; *see*, section 2.4.5 above.
151. *See*, N. van Antwerpen and D. Erni, *ACG Acquisition XX LLC v. Olympic Airlines SA*, 37 Air & Space Law 369–375 (2012).
152. The insurance policy must usually contain a 'loss payee' clause which provides that any payment in connection with damage to the aircraft will be paid to the owner/lessor rather than the lessee.
153. Generally, third party liability insurance arranged by the lessee must also provide coverage for the lessor and the financiers of the aircraft as co-insured parties.'

engines and parts, pooling of engines, the proper keeping of the aircraft records, maintaining the registration of the aircraft and the provision of certain information regarding the lessee.[154]

Lease agreements will also provide rules in relation to subleasing, the implications of a total loss in respect of the aircraft or an engine, assignment of rights and the collateral to be provided by the lessee.[155]

Finally, any type of lease agreement will describe in detail which events or circumstances will constitute a default or an event of default on the basis whereof the lessor is entitled to terminate the leasing of the aircraft and require the lessee to return the aircraft, including the aircraft books and records, to the lessor at the agreed redelivery location. The lease agreement will also require the lessee to return the aircraft to the lessor, be it at expiry of the lease agreement or following early termination, in the agreed redelivery condition failing which the lessee will continue to be obligated to pay the agreed lease rent without having the right of use in relation to the aircraft.[156]

3.1.8 Regulatory Requirements

Airlines wanting to operate with leased aircraft may have to comply with certain regulatory requirements, as the competent civil aviation authorities, in view of their responsibilities for the safe operation of airlines licensed by them, need to ascertain that the relevant aircraft are compliant with airworthiness requirements and other standards.[157] For instance, in the EU, Regulation 1008/2008[158] allows 'Community Carriers' to operate wet-leased aircraft subject to prior approval in accordance with applicable Community law or national law on safety. Where the wet-leased aircraft is registered in a third country, the approval of the competent licensing authority[159] will be required. Such approval may be granted if the airline demonstrates that all safety standards equivalent to those imposed by Community law or national law are met and the wet-leasing of the relevant aircraft is necessary because of the airline's exceptional needs, seasonal needs or to overcome operational difficulties.[160]

Other jurisdictions will have their own regulatory regime which in most will be inspired by the need for civil aviation authorities with oversight responsibility to

---

154. Such as the lessee's annual accounts.
155. Such as a security deposit, a parent guarantee, a bank guarantee or a letter of credit securing the obligations of the lessee under the lease agreement.
156. For an in-depth study of lease agreements, *see*, Dr D.P. Hanley, *Aircraft Operating Leasing: A Legal and Practical Analysis in the Context of Public and Private International Air Law* (thesis Leiden University, 2011, 2nd edition 2017), which also provides in a supplement a sample aircraft lease agreement.
157. Including noise and CO2 emissions and other environmental requirements.
158. EU Regulation 1008/2008 on *common rules for the operation of air services within the Community*, as discussed in section 3.2 of Chapter 3; *see also*, section 2.6/end of Chapter 6.
159. Being the civil aviation authorities competent under EU Regulation 1008/2008 to grant an operating licence to the relevant airline as to which *see*, section 3.2 of Chapter 3.
160. *See*, Art. 13.3 of Regulation 1008/2008.

monitor the aircraft which are operated by airlines in respect whereof such authorities have responsibilities and which are registered as to nationality in that jurisdiction.

Other regulatory issues to be considered are compliance by the lessee with applicable national and international sanctions. Sanctions imposed by the international organisations such as the United Nations and the EU as well as sanctions imposed by certain States, in particular the United States, are to taken into consideration so as to avoid problems for the lessor and its financiers.

Lease agreements must contain appropriate representations and warranties confirming that the lessee is not subject to any sanctions as well as covenants assuring compliance by the lessee with any applicable sanction legislation. US sanction legislation may affect lease agreements between non-US parties as the US Office of Foreign Assets Control contends that US sanction legislation already applies to a transaction where payments are to be made in US dollars.

3.2   Engine Leasing

3.2.1   *Historical Introduction to Engine Leasing*

The leasing of aircraft engines is a relatively new industry, which only started to develop in the early 1980s. The early engine lessors provided spare engines pursuant to short term lease agreements in order to fill the gap between the number of available spare engines owned by the airlines and their peak demand for engines. These gaps were often the result of engine failures or unscheduled engine maintenance or repair. When aircraft operating leasing became more popular in the late 1980s, when approximately 20 per cent of all aircraft in service were owned by leasing companies and aircraft engines became more expensive, leasing companies started to see economic sense in long term operating leases for aircraft engines. The demand for operating leases is also driven by the airlines' wish to free up capital which would otherwise be needed to maintain a certain stock of spare engines and to avoid having engines on their balance sheet. Also today, much of the rationale can be found in the rising cost of aircraft engines.[161]

In addition, the development of very large engines, with impressive rack prices in excess of USD 30 million, contributed to the growth of the engine leasing market. The current engine leasing market sees a number of large engine leasing companies catering to the needs of carriers or engine pools operated by a number of airlines.

Since the mid 1990s *engine pooling* has developed strongly. An engine pool typically covers one specific engine type. Usually an engine manufacturer or an engine lessor takes the initiative to set up an engine pool. Airlines sign up as members of an engine pool either by contributing their own spare engines to the engine pool or by buying into an engine pool. Through their membership, operators have access to the

---

161. The sticker price of a GE CF680-C2 engine rose from USD 6.5 million in 2000 to USD 13 million by 2010.

pool of spare engines to cover their needs for the duration of scheduled or unscheduled maintenance as well as in emergency situations where an aircraft is grounded due to an engine failure.

Some engine pools provide support to hundreds of aircraft.[162] Engine pools are usually administered by pool managers affiliated with the initiator of the pool.

3.2.2 The Legal Status of Aircraft Engines

In all cases, whether it concerns an airline wishing to acquire spare engines and obtain financing for that acquisition or the financing of the acquisition by an engine lessor of engines to be leased to operators or to be placed in an engine pool, financiers will require collateral including a security right over the relevant engines. This means that financiers must keep track of the location of the relevant engines so as to ensure that their security right is not adversely affected by non-consensual liens,[163] insolvency scenarios or even the loss of their interest by operation of property accession rules.[164] Similarly, engine lessors' ownership rights may be adversely affected by non-consensual liens, lessee insolvency and accession rules.

As the purpose of aircraft engines is to power aircraft, being extremely moveable objects designed to move between various jurisdictions, conflict of laws rules cannot be ignored when assessing the merits of an engine leasing or financing transaction including the position of the engine owner and the engine financier.

Unfortunately, there is no uniform approach as States have adopted different conflict of laws rules in relation to the question which property regime should apply to aircraft and engines and domestic laws with respect to the status of aircraft engines differ from jurisdiction to jurisdiction. In some jurisdictions aircraft engines are regarded as separate objects, irrespective of whether or not they are attached to an airframe, in other jurisdictions aircraft engines will be subject to accession rules and are regarded as component parts of the airframe to which they are attached.

This obviously does affect the position of the engine owner/lessor and its financier, who stipulated a security interest over the engine as collateral for the owner/lessor's indebtedness.

The legal status of an aircraft engine consequently depends on the property regime of the applicable law and this implies that an understanding of rules of private international law is crucial. Regrettably there is no uniform conflict of laws framework as explained earlier in this chapter[165] and, in addition, the Geneva Convention (1948) and the CTC/AEP take opposing views on the status of aircraft engines.[166]

---

162. Engine lessors like US based Willis Lease have set up engine sharing pools in the US and China respectively providing support to a total of one thousand aircraft.
163. The term 'non-consensual liens' not only refers to arrests of an aircraft but also to retention rights which for instance a repairman may exercise in respect of an engine in his possession.
164. *See*, section 2.3.4 above.
165. *See*, section 2.2 above.
166. *See*, section 2.3.4 above.

3.2.3   Risks Attached to Engine Leasing

Where the CTC/AEP applies, engine lessors who have made an appropriate filing of their interest with the International Registry will enjoy the protection provided by the CTC/AEP. If the leased engine is attached to an aircraft which is registered in a country which is not a party to the CTC/AEP, the status of the engine may change from independent aircraft object under the CTC/AEP to a component part if the property regime of the relevant country so dictates. As a consequence, the lessor of the engine may lose his title to the engine.

Similarly, where the engine lessor has granted a security right over the engine to a financier, such security right may extinguish in the scenario where the engine becomes a component part. Engine lessors and their financiers, but also engine lessees, aircraft lessors and operators should take due notice of the problems which may arise as a result of unanticipated accession as well as how the risks can be reduced by contractual arrangements between the various parties concerned.[167]

3.3   Subleasing

3.3.1   Introduction

Every lessee will stipulate the option to sublease the aircraft so as to obtain the necessary flexibility. If, during the term of the lease, the lessee experiences financial problems or wants to reduce its capacity for economic or strategic reasons and is unable to terminate the lease agreement without suffering severe consequences, subleasing may be a good option for the lessee to reduce its liabilities under the lease agreement. Lease agreements often provide that the lessee may sublease the aircraft to certain specified operators, the 'permitted sublessees'. Usually, the list of permitted sublessees is restricted to airline companies affiliated with the lessee. If there is no list of permitted sublessees, the lease agreement will usually provide that subleasing is only permitted with the express prior consent of the lessor. In all cases, there will be a list of conditions which must be met in connection with the subleasing of the aircraft.

Lessors usually show a pragmatic approach towards subleasing; subleasing the aircraft to a reliable and financially strong sublessee will be in the interest of both the lessee and the lessor. At the same time a lessor must identify certain problems which may arise in connection subleasing and make sure that it is adequately protected. Even though the lessee will remain fully liable for all of its obligations under the lease, subleasing may still lead to complications which must be identified and properly addressed prior to the entry into of the sublease agreement.

---

167. *See*, Berend Crans, *How Many Engines on a Boeing 737? An analysis of Accession Rules in Relation to Aircraft Engines*, 38(3) Air & Space Law 229–248 (2013) and Morten L. Jakobsen and Morten Midtgaard Pederesen, *The Danish Aircraft Engine Dispute: The Sequel*, 40(6) Air & Space Law 421–427 (2015).

3.3.2 Allocating Responsibility Between Sublessor and Sublessee

As between the sublessor and the sublessee there should be a clear allocation of responsibility with respect to a range of obligations arising from the leasing of the aircraft. The lease agreement contains a range of covenants with which the lessee must comply. This will include insurance requirements, operational restrictions, maintenance obligations, regulatory compliance and information covenants.

Following the commencement of the sublease agreement, the lessee will still be bound by these covenants and obligations towards the lessor. Thus, the lessee should make sure that the sublease agreement contains certain similar obligations for the sublessee, so that compliance with the terms of the lease agreement is not impaired. It is recommended that the lessee/sublessor stipulates inspection rights which will allow the lessee/sublessor to verify whether for instance the aircraft is maintained in accordance with the maintenance covenants of the sublease agreement and the corresponding covenants of the lease agreement.

3.3.3 Regulatory Conditions

Certain regulatory conditions are to be addressed in connection with any sublease agreement. These include the question whether the subleasing of the aircraft and the operation of the aircraft by the sublessee is in breach of any domestic or international sanctions. Again,[168] sanctions imposed by the international organisations like the United Nations and the EU as well as sanctions imposed by certain States, in particular the United States are to taken into consideration so as to avoid problems for the lessee/sublessor, the lessor and even for the lessor's financiers. Sublease agreements should contain appropriate sublessee representations and warranties confirming that the sublessee is not subject to any sanctions as well as sublessee covenants assuring compliance by the sublessee with any applicable sanctions.[169]

Obviously, it is in the interest of both the lessee/sublessor and the lessor that the sublessee is not a banned or restricted carrier which has no access to the European airspace[170] and that the sublessee is fully licensed under applicable laws to operate the aircraft.

3.3.4 Control over Sublease Payments

Lessors are well advised to get control over the flow of payments under the sublease. In particular in scenarios where the lessee turns to subleasing because it is experiencing financial problems, the lessor should stipulate that all sublease rent is paid to it directly, rather than to the lessee/sublessor. The lessor does not want to get caught in a situation

---

168. *See also*, section 3.1 above.
169. *See*, section 3.1.7 above.
170. *See*, EU Regulation 2111/2005 on *the establishment of a Community list of air carriers subject to an operating ban within the Community and on informing passengers of the identity of the operating carrier*, as discussed in section 2.5.2 of Chapter 7.

where the sublessee has duly paid sublease rent to the lessee/sublessor and the lessee failing to make the required payments under the lease agreement.

In addition, the sublessor's receivables under the sublease agreement should be assigned or pledged to the lessor as security for the lessee's obligations under the lease agreement.

Any collateral provided to the sublessor as security for the sublessee's obligations should be assigned to the lessor, again to secure the lessee's obligations under the lease. Thought could be given to guarantees provided by the sublessee's parent company, bank guarantees or letters of credit.

3.3.5 Other Concerns to Be Addressed

There is a range of other matters which a prudent lessor should identify and address. First of all, the lessor will require that the sublease agreement will explicitly state that the sublease is subject and subordinate to the lease and will terminate automatically in the event the lease terminates, whether through expiry of the lease term or following early termination by the lessor or the lessee. In addition, the sublease must contain a provision which obligates the sublessee to return the aircraft to the lessor at the agreed return location following the termination of the sublease.

Where the subleasing of the aircraft requires the aircraft to be registered in another country, the lessor should identify the potential implications of such change in registration. The change in registration may affect the remedies which the lessor may have under the lease agreement, such as the right to arrest the aircraft for the purpose of repossession. If, as a result of the change in registration, the Rome Convention (1933)[171] comes into play, the remedies of the owner/lessor may be severely restricted. If the owner has granted a mortgage or other security right over the aircraft to its financier, the remedies of the grantee of such security right may be affected similarly, triggering a default under the relevant finance agreement.

A change of registration may also entail that the aircraft becomes subject to a different property regime and an existing security right may no longer be recognised or enforceable as a result thereof. Again this may have serious adverse implications for the lessor if this qualifies as an event of default under the relevant finance agreement. A change of registration may also affect the status of the aircraft engines which may lead to complications if the laws of the country where the aircraft is registered as to nationality contain accession rules in relation to aircraft engines.[172]

The owner/lessor should also be aware of a potential increased vulnerability to non-consensual liens, including the remedies granted to ATC service providers, such as Eurocontrol, in certain jurisdictions.[173]

---

171. *See*, section 5.4 below.
172. *See*, section 3.2.2 above.
173. *See*, section 5.2 below.

4 CONSENSUAL LIENS

4.1 Introduction: Definition of Lien

Consensual liens come in many forms and shapes and a certain term may have a different meaning in different jurisdictions. In general terms a 'consensual lien' can be described as a form of security interest granted over an item of property by the owner thereof to secure the payment of a debt or the performance of other named obligations. The owner of the property is often referred to as the lienor or the grantor or the charger, and the beneficiary is usually referred to as the lienee or the grantee or the chargee.

Consensual liens can operate as rights in rem, which in general terms provides that the ownership title is retained by the grantor but allows the grantee to sell the aircraft if an event of default occurs, that is, typically non-payment of debt service under the loan agreement which was entered into to finance the acquisition of the aircraft and to take recourse on the sale proceeds, or as a conditional transfer of title, subject to the mortgagor's equity redemption.

With respect to the type of security interest available to a financier or other grantee, much will depend on the status of aircraft under applicable law.[174] In many civil law jurisdictions, aircraft have a special status so as to allow the creation of mortgages, being security rights which are typically reserved for real property, while in other jurisdictions aircraft are regarded as moveable property in respect whereof a different type of security right should be used.[175]

4.2 Creation and Perfection of Consensual Liens

In most jurisdictions, liens on aircraft will only be effective and can only be invoked against third parties if they are properly recorded in a public register. In some jurisdictions there is a separate public registry where ownership title can be registered and where consensual liens and non-consensual liens must be registered in order to be effective.[176] In other jurisdictions, the nationality register also serves as a register where consensual liens and non-consensual liens in respect of aircraft should be registered.[177] Yet other jurisdictions require that consensual liens must be registered with the company register as it relates to the grantor of the security right.[178]

---

174. For the conflict of law issues relating to the question which jurisdiction's property law regime applies, *see*, section 2.2 above.
175. For instance, Belgium; *see*, Mia Wouters, in: Ravi Nath and Berend Crans (eds), *Aircraft Repossession and Enforcement*, Chapter on Belgium at 125 (2009).
176. For instance, The Netherlands; *see*, Berend Crans, in: Ravi Nath and Berend Crans (eds), *Aircraft Repossession and Enforcement*, Chapter on The Netherlands at 611 (2009).
177. *See*, Patrick Hühnerwadel and Tanja Luginbühl, in: Ravi Nath and Berend Crans (eds), *Aircraft Repossession and Enforcement*, Chapter on Switzerland at 990 (2009).
178. *See*, Ian Wallace and Claire Forster, in: Ravi Nath and Berend Crans (eds), *Aircraft Repossession and Enforcement*, Chapter on Australia at 95 (2009).

Formal requirements may be light, requiring only a written instrument, to more demanding, requiring that the security must be created by way of a notarial deed,[179] that the instrument clearly specifies the mortgaged property, the secured obligations and the amount of the secured claim. No general rule can be provided with respect to the applicable formalities and in all cases the assistance of local counsel will be necessary.

Obviously, tax aspects are also to be considered. In many jurisdictions the granting of a mortgage or similar security right will trigger stamp duty or similar taxes[180] and it may be useful to consider whether other jurisdictions provide friendlier tax regimes.

5 NON-CONSENSUAL LIENS

5.1 Arrest of Aircraft

A distinction can be made between non-consensual liens, taking effect as an arrest of the aircraft, and non-consensual liens pursuant whereto possession of the aircraft can be retained or the aircraft can be detained in connection with specific debts relating to the operation of that aircraft. An arrest of an aircraft can serve different purposes and may have a different legal basis.

The main purpose of a precautionary arrest is to ground the aircraft in the relevant jurisdiction to ensure that it remains available for recourse by creditors and enforcement action in that jurisdiction. Precautionary arrest can, of course, also be used as a tool to persuade a debtor to pay amounts due to the person making the arrest. The main purpose of an arrest in execution is to have the aircraft sold, either in a private sale or in a public auction, and apply the sales proceeds to the amount owing by the owner of the aircraft to the creditor at whose request the arrest in execution was made.

An arrest in execution of an aircraft by a specific creditor does not guarantee that the relevant debt will be settled. An arrest in execution is usually a time-consuming and expensive exercise whereas a range of other creditors may crawl out of the woodwork with a variety of claims. In many cases arrest in execution will entail compliance with myriad formalities, waiting periods, verification of claims and proceedings between competing creditors and in the meantime the condition of the aircraft may deteriorate, while costs, including insurance costs, parking costs and preservation costs, will continue to add up. The Geneva Convention (1948) contains specific provisions which must be observed in the event of a sale of an aircraft in execution.[181]

---

179. This will usually be the case in civil law countries where the civil law notary is an independent official with statutory tasks, including verifying that the parties to for instance the notarial mortgage deed are duly present or represented by an authorised attorney-in-fact, that the granting of the mortgage was duly authorised (all corporate action being taken) and that the grantor of the mortgage is indeed the owner of the aircraft.
180. In some jurisdiction as high as 1 per cent of the amount secured by the mortgage.
181. *See*, section 2.3.8; Art. 7 of the Geneva Convention (1948).

5.2 Retention and Detention Rights

Rights of retention come in many forms, but can generally be defined as the right of a creditor, such as an aircraft maintenance facility, to suspend its obligation to return the aircraft and to retain possession of the aircraft until the amount owing to it in connection with the maintenance of the aircraft is settled. Detention rights also come in a variety of shapes.

For instance, in Canada most airports and NavCanada, which is the supplier of air navigation services, have a statutory right to seize and detain aircraft owned or operated by the airline owing them user charges, until such time that these charges have been paid.[182]

In the United Kingdom, the CAA is granted the right to detain and sell an aircraft; this power applies in relation to the non-payment of airport charges owed in connection with the use of various UK airport facilities[183] and unpaid air navigation charges payable for the supply of air navigation services provided by the UK National Air Traffic Services, the Danish and Icelandic authorities and Eurocontrol.[184]

Reference is made to the special rights of detention awarded to Eurocontrol to the effect that the UK CAA, acting as agent for Eurocontrol, may take all necessary steps to detain either the aircraft in respect of which navigation charges are outstanding or any other aircraft which is at that time operated by the defaulting operator.[185] In the UK special detention rights are also granted to the UK Environment Agency in relation to unpaid EU ETS[186] charges. The detention rights are aimed at operators and are consequently fleet-wide.[187] Other governmental authorities including customs or revenue services may also have special detention rights in respect of aircraft.

5.3 Observations on Precautionary Arrest of Aircraft

Most jurisdictions allow for the precautionary arrest of aircraft. Usually precautionary arrest can only be applied on the basis of a court order where the applicant must at least show that his request is based on reasonable cause. In some jurisdictions the applicant should also demonstrate that there is a reasonable fear that the debtor has the intention to evade payment of the debt by moving the aircraft to another jurisdiction.[188]

---

182. *See*, Richard Desgagnes, in: Ravi Nath and Berend Crans (eds), *Aircraft Repossession and Enforcement*, Chapter on Canada at 195 (2009).
183. S. 88 Civil Aviation Act 1982.
184. Reg. 4 of the Civil Aviation (*Chargeable Air Services Detention and Sale of Aircraft for Eurocontrol*) Regulations 2001.
185. *See*, Patrick Farrell, in: Ravi Nath and Berend Crans (eds), *Aircraft Repossession and Enforcement*, Chapter on England and Wales at 321 (2009). The same powers, including the 'fleet lien' are granted to the Irish Aviation Authority.
186. The Aviation Greenhouse Emission Trading Scheme Regulations 2010 (as amended); as to the EU ETS *see*, section 5.3.2 of Chapter 3.
187. *See*, Art. 16(10) of Directive 2003/87/EC as it applies to EU operators who are subject to an operating ban as to which *see also*, section 2.5.2 of Chapter 7.
188. *See*, Jan Dernestam et al., in: Ravi Nath and Berend Crans (eds), *Aircraft Repossession and Enforcement*, Chapter on Sweden at 941 (2009).

There are different grounds for a precautionary arrest; in addition to arrests requested by secured or ordinary creditors of the owner of the aircraft,[189] one can think of specific creditors of the operator and of an owner/lessor wanting to repossess his aircraft following the expiration of termination of the lease agreement. In most cases an application for precautionary arrest will be heard without the debtor being present so as to avoid that the debtor is given an opportunity to move the aircraft to another jurisdiction.

Given the impact of a precautionary arrest on the operations of the carrier, applicants must of course be aware of their potential liability for (substantial) damages, including substantial damages if a precautionary arrest is held to be frivolous; in addition, courts, when deciding on an application for precautionary arrest, will usually carefully balance the interests of the applicant and the operator of the aircraft.

In most jurisdictions, procedures have been put in place allowing an expeditious court review of the matter at the request of the operator of the aircraft and for immediate release of the aircraft if adequate security is provided by the owner or operator of the aircraft for the debt for which the arrest was allowed.

5.4 The Rome Convention on Precautionary Arrest of Aircraft (1933)

Although its importance is perhaps not evident at first glance, the *Convention for the Unification of Certain Rules Relating to the Precautionary Attachment of Aircraft*, signed at Rome on 29 May 1933,[190] in this section also referred to as the Convention, still plays a role in excluding commercial aircraft from precautionary attachment. The Convention is ratified or acceded to by thirty States, excluding however important jurisdictions like the United Kingdom, the United States, China, India and Russia.

The Convention enumerates the categories of aircraft which are exempted from precautionary arrest.

Article 3(1) provides that the following categories of aircraft are exempt:

a) aircraft exclusively appropriated to a state service, including the postal service, but excluding commercial service;
b) aircraft actually in service on a regular line of public transport, together with the indispensable reserve aircraft;
c) every other aircraft appropriated to the carriage of persons or goods for reward, where such aircraft is ready to start on such carriage, unless the arrest is in respect of a contract debt incurred for the purposes of the journey which the aircraft is about to make, or of a claim which has arisen in the course of the journey.

---

189. In principle, where a lessee has an assignable leasehold interest in an aircraft, such interest could also be subject of precautionary arrest; *see*, Michael J. Edelman et al., in: Ravi Nath and Berend Crans (eds), *Aircraft Repossession and Enforcement* (2009), Chapter on the United States at 1103.
190. Convention for the Unification of Certain Rules Relating to Precautionary Attachment of Aircraft, Rome, 29 May 1933, also known as the *Convention on Precautionary Arrest of Aircraft*; *see*, N. M. Matte, *Treatise on Air-Aeronautical Law* 497–501 (1981).

Article 2 of the Convention determines its scope of application. Article 2(1) defines what the term 'precautionary arrest' encompasses and gives a broad definition of that term.

Precautionary arrests by an owner[191] or any grantee of a *right* in rem in respect of the aircraft is prohibited, unless he can rely on an immediately enforceable judgment already obtained by ordinary process or upon any right of seizure equivalent thereto.

Article 2(2) provides an important expansion of the term 'precautionary arrest' as creditors' rights of retention under applicable law are assimilated to precautionary arrest and are subject to the rules of the Convention.[192]

Article 4 of the Convention stipulates that in all cases where arrest is not forbidden or where, although the aircraft is immune from arrest, the operator fails to invoke such immunity,[193] precautionary arrest can be avoided and the aircraft shall be immediately released if adequate security is provided by the debtor. This may be done by way of cash collateral or by way of an adequate third party guarantee. Security will be considered to be adequate if it covers the amount of the debt and costs and is assigned exclusively to the payment of the creditor, or if it covers the value of the aircraft in the event that this is less than the amount of the debt and costs.

The Convention further provides that all claims for release from precautionary arrest shall be dealt with in summary and rapid procedures. The Convention does not apply to precautionary arrest on the part of an owner disposed of his aircraft by an unlawful act[194] and to precautionary steps in case of insolvency or breach of customs, penal or police regulations.[195]

There is very little published case law on the Convention.[196] In one case, the Amsterdam Court of Appeal has given a strict interpretation to the exemption provisions. The Court considered that the flight plan of the arrested aircraft referred to a charter flight, which according to the Court fell outside the scope of 'regular line of public transport' as referred to in section (b) of Article 3(1) of the Convention,[197] and

---

191. *See*, however, the exception of Art. 3(2) applying to the owner "disposed of his aircraft by an unlawful act", further discussed below.
192. In some jurisdictions, the legislator has failed to take the provisions of the Convention into account. In the Netherlands for instance, section 8:1316 Civil Code provides that section 3:292 Civil Code shall not apply to aircraft registered in the Dutch Public Registry (being the register maintained pursuant to the Geneva Convention) and the public registers maintained in other Contracting States to the Geneva Convention. Section 3:292 Civil Code, however, only relates to the priority which a retentor has in relation to other creditors (including secured creditors like mortgagees) so that section 8:1316 Civil Code implies that the right of retention as such, which is a powerful pressure tool for creditors, is not prohibited. This is contrary to the provisions of the Rome Convention as well as the Geneva Convention; *see*, Ravi Nath and Berend Crans (eds), *Aircraft Repossession and Enforcement* (2009), Berend Crans, Rob Polak and Marie-José Blaak, Chapter on The Netherlands at 625 and footnote 111 on that page (2009).
193. This appears to indicate that a court cannot determine ex officio whether an aircraft is immune from arrest pursuant to the Convention.
194. Art. 3(2); *see*, Berend Crans, *Selected Pitfalls and Booby-traps in Aircraft Finance*, in *Aircraft Finance – Recent Developments and Prospects* (ed. Berend Crans) at 13–16 (1995).
195. Art. 7.
196. *See*, however, *Marian Kozuba Kozubski* v. *Aero-Transport*, Court of Haarlem (The Netherlands), 25 March 1964 and 8 July 1964, which can be found in F.A. van Bakelen and I.H.Ph.Diederiks-Verschoor, *Compendium Jurisprudentie Luchtrecht* 39 (1988).
197. Amsterdam Court of Appeal, 9 December 1993, *Schip en Schade* 1994, 91.

the fact that there are many more regular international flights in the present time than at the time the Convention was made. Thus, it held that there was no risk of a serious disruption of air services and allowed the pre-trial arrest of the aircraft.

Various attempts have been made to circumvent the Convention by way of a precautionary arrest in respect of the fuel present in an aircraft's fuel tanks, which in some cases proved to be successful.[198]

5.5 Other Restrictions with Respect to Precautionary Arrest

Where the Convention does not apply, it is, in general terms, advisable to determine whether bilateral air transport agreements contain any similar immunity provisions in this respect.[199] In addition, domestic laws may contain special requirements in relation to public service property, to the effect that certain assets are exempt from any form of arrest as this would impair public services.[200] There is hardly any case law on this subject.

5.6 Observations on Arrest in Execution of Aircraft

The term 'arrest in execution' covers, for the purpose of this chapter, the arrest of an aircraft as an enforcement action on the basis of an immediately enforceable judgment[201] against the owner of the aircraft or pursuant to the terms of a security right, such as an aircraft mortgage.

An arrest in execution will be subject to the civil procedure provisions of the jurisdiction where the aircraft is physically located when the arrest is made. This implies that attention must be given to a range of conditions, including the question whether indeed the judgment which is to be enforced will be recognised by the courts of the relevant jurisdiction. The recognition and enforcement of foreign judgments is only a given if there is a treaty or convention in force between the two relevant states providing for the mutual recognition and enforcement of final judgments rendered by courts in the Contracting States.[202]

---

198. President of the Haarlem District Court (in summary proceedings), 25 April 2003, *Kort Geding* 2003, 174.
199. Certain older bilateral air transport agreements contain reciprocal undertakings by each Contracting State to the effect that it shall procure that aircraft registered in the other Contracting State shall not become subject to precautionary arrest in its jurisdiction.
200. In The Netherlands for instance the Code of Civil Procedure (*Wetboek van Burgerlijke Rechtsvordering*) provides that property intended for public service (*goederen bestemd voor de openbare dienst*) cannot be made subject to any form of arrest. Commercial aircraft would normally not fall within the scope of these provisions, unless requisitioned for use by the government in emergency situations, for instance, war or natural disasters.
201. The term 'judgment' includes arbitral awards.
202. *See*, for instance, EC Regulation 44/2001, the *EC Civil Jurisdiction Regulation*, providing for the recognition and enforcement within the Member States of foreign judgments and, for arbitral awards, the New York *Convention on Enforcement of Foreign Arbitral Awards* (1958).

Failing such treaty, it will depend on the laws of the jurisdiction where enforcement is sought whether a new trial on the merits will be required. In many countries, however, a foreign judgment will be recognised and given effect to, without review of the merits of the case, provided:

(i) the jurisdiction of the foreign court was based on internationally accepted grounds;
(ii) the foreign judgment is the result of proper judicial procedures; and
(iii) the recognition of the foreign judgment and the enforcement thereof does not violate public order in the receiving State.

5.7 Public Sale Procedures

Compliance with the applicable civil procedure provisions requires proper preparation as these procedures are usually complicated, time consuming and expensive. This applies in particular to a sale in execution by way of a public sale.

Where the relevant State is a party to the Geneva Convention (1948), the procedures set forth therein,[203] including certain publication requirements and the requirement to notify the recorded owner of the aircraft as well as all holders of recorded rights as well as the observance of waiting periods, are quite cumbersome and can delay the process substantially. As the delays add on, the value of the aircraft may deteriorate quickly and costs to protect the aircraft against decay and cannibalisation may skyrocket.

Similarly, where the Cape Town Convention applies, the remedies set forth in the relevant provisions of that convention will be available to the charge.[204]

In some jurisdictions, the law allows for alternative methods of execution, that is, a private sale of the aircraft or that ownership of the aircraft shall vest in the chargee, subject to the value of the aircraft being applied towards satisfaction of the secured obligations.[205] Usually, the debtor is protected to the extent that a private sale can only take place with the permission of the competent court, which is to assess whether the proposed terms and conditions of the private sale, in particular the purchase price, is in line with market standards.

5.8 Rights of Third Parties

In the event of an arrest in execution, third party rights may play a role and may have to be observed. In this connection one should not only consider whether there are any recorded in rem rights pursuant to the Geneva Convention (1948) or International Interests, pursuant to and as defined in the CTC/AEP, but also whether any contractual obligations are to be observed. For instance, in financial lease transactions involving a

---

203. In particular Art. 7 of the Geneva Convention (1948).
204. *See*, section 2.4.4 above.
205. The Cape Town Convention also provides for this as to which *see*, section 2.4.4 above.

lessor/mortgagor, a lender/mortgagee and a financial lessee, the lender often provides a quiet enjoyment covenant to the lessee. This covenant basically says that the lender, where it would become entitled to take enforcement action pursuant to the mortgage, for instance because the lessor fails to make a required payment under the loan agreement, would still respect the quite enjoyment rights of the lessee under the lease agreement, provided the lessee has fully complied with its (payment) obligations under the lease agreement. This may still imply that the lender could arrange for a sale in execution of the aircraft, but only with the lease agreement staying in place.

6 CONCLUDING REMARKS

The subject matter of this Chapter is by its very nature complex, because of the international and multi-disciplinary character of transactions involving rights in aircraft. More often than not, parties to a transaction will have to deal with the domestic laws of the various jurisdictions as well as international conventions which may be based on different concepts. In addition, regulatory issues including environmental rules and regulations, tax and accounting aspects, insurance matters, liability issues and rules of private international law have to be taken into consideration.

International conventions like the 1933 Rome Convention and the Geneva Convention have provided guidance in the past, but may no longer be suitable in today's aviation industry.

As indicated in section 2.1.3 above, the aviation industry is not served by the parallel existence of two conventions based on entirely different principles and starting points. Uncertainty can arise for lessors and lessees, sellers and buyers as well as financiers of aircraft and aircraft objects, in particular if there is a change in the registration of an aircraft. There can be no doubt that the Geneva Convention no longer reflects the requirements of today's aviation industry. The CTC/AEP is the industry's response to the shortcomings of the Geneva Convention and its purpose is to facilitate the exercise by creditors of the main remedies, that is, the taking of possession or control of an aircraft object, the sale or lease of such aircraft object and the collection or receipt of income or profits arising from the management or use of such aircraft object. In my view, the interests of the aviation industry would be well served if more countries decide to ratify the CTC/AEP so as to create a truly uniform legal framework for rights in aircraft and engines.

Disputes in connection with aircraft finance or leasing transactions are often resolved through amicable settlements or private arbitration and this explains why case law on this type of transactions is relatively scarce.

According to the recent forecasts of the two major aircraft manufacturers, Boeing and Airbus, all economic indicators point at a substantial growth of the aviation industry in terms of passenger and cargo traffic in the short and medium term. As a consequence of increasing demands and the need to replace older aircraft, the world needs an astounding number of 39,620 new commercial aircraft over the period 2016–2035, requiring an aggregate funding of USD 5.9 trillion.[206]

In view of the size, scope and importance of the aviation industry and the constant changes to the regulatory environment and the development of new concepts of law to solve legal issues and facilitate transactions, the subject of rights in aircraft will remain topical and dynamic for many years to come.

---

206. *See*, Boeing, *Current Market Outlook 2016–2035*; www.boeing.com.

Criminal Air Law

1 BACKGROUND

1.1 The Regulatory Regime

Four international conventions currently govern this province of law, where introduction of new rules and sanctions had become so very urgent for reasons set out below. They are:

(1) The *Convention on Offences and Certain Other Acts Committed on Board Aircraft,* signed at Tokyo on 14 September 1963, hereinafter also cited as Tokyo Convention.

(2) The *Convention for the Suppression of Unlawful Seizure of Aircraft*, signed at The Hague on 16 December 1970 as amended by the Protocol Supplementary to the Convention for the Suppression of Unlawful Seizure of Aircraft, signed at Beijing on 10 September 2010.[1]

(3) The *Convention for the Suppression of Unlawful Acts against the Safety of Civil Aviation*, signed at Montreal on 23 September 1971 as supplemented by the Protocol for the Suppression of Unlawful Acts of Violence at Airports Serving International Civil Aviation, done at Montreal on 24 February 1988,[2] and

(4) The *Convention on the Suppression of Unlawful Acts Relating to International Civil Aviation*, done at Beijing on 10 September 2010, prevailing as between the States Parties over the instruments mentioned under 3 above.[3]

---

1. Hereinafter cited as the *Hague Convention,* and also known as the *Hijacking Convention*; the Supplementary Protocol may also be referred to as the '*Beijing Protocol*'.
2. Hereinafter cited as the *Montreal Convention* (1971) and also known as the *Sabotage Convention*; the Protocol amending this convention may be referred to as the '*Airport Protocol*'.
3. Hereinafter also referred to as the '*Beijing Convention*'.

The Conventions will be analysed hereunder in the order indicated above against the background laid down below. Other legal instruments and developments affecting the safety and security of air transport including the phenomenon of 'unruly passengers' will also be addressed.

1.2 Concepts of Jurisdiction

The international character of aviation makes it necessary to determine which State is competent to exercise jurisdiction in cases of criminal offences committed on board aircraft. Complications may arise when a State other than the State in which an aircraft is registered attempts to assert its jurisdiction with regard to offences committed on board such aircraft. Alternatively, a situation may arise where no criminal laws at all are applicable, for instance when an offence is committed above territories not subject to the sovereignty of any particular State, like the high seas, or when the place where the offence was committed cannot be determined. These situations can be examined in light of the following five theories:

- the *territorial* theory: the law of the State in whose airspace the offence has taken place will be applied by its courts. As it is not always possible to determine the exact position of the aircraft at the time the offence was committed it is impracticable for a State to base its jurisdiction solely on this principle;
- the *nationality* theory: according to this theory the law of State where the aircraft is registered is to be applied under all circumstances;
- the *mixed* theory: side by side with the law of the aircraft's nationality the law of the State over which the aircraft passes is enforceable whenever the security or public order of such State is threatened by offences committed on board;
- the theory of *the law of the State of departure*; and
- the theory of *the law of the State of landing*.

The last two theories confer jurisdiction on the State where the aircraft has departed and landed. Both have their own particular advantages: the former does not leave the commander any choice of jurisdiction, whereas the latter does allow his direct intervention. Because the commander can immediately inform the appropriate authorities by radio and alert the airport for assistance the necessary measures can be taken and an investigation started. This would preclude unnecessary delay in the flight schedule. A disadvantage of the last theory is that the pilot has full authority in selecting the State whose law will eventually be applied to the offence. The next place of landing will be that of the normal flight schedule or, if the commander is of the opinion that an emergency exists, the nearest possible place of landing.

1.3   Cases Illustrating the Need for a Convention

The need for international rules was illustrated by the notorious case of *United States* v *Cordova and Santano*.[4] An aircraft belonging to an American airline made a flight from San Juan, Puerto Rico, to New York on 2 August 1948, with sixty passengers and crew members on board, amongst whom were a Mr Cordova and Mr Santano. After an hour and a half of flying time, and while the aircraft was above the high seas, the two gentlemen became involved in an argument over a missing bottle. The stewardess made an attempt to calm them, but the two continued their fight in the rear section of the aircraft. This movement caused the aircraft, which was flying on automatic pilot, to climb steeply because of the weight increase in the rear section of the aircraft. The pilot took the appropriate measures to regain control of the aircraft, while being informed by the stewardess of what was going on. He thereupon handed control of the aircraft to the co-pilot and went to the cabin to stop the fight. Mr Santano calmed down, but Mr Cordova attacked the pilot, bit him on the shoulder and knocked the stewardess down. He was then overpowered by others and locked up for the rest of the flight. Prosecution was ordered against both Cordova and Santano, but the indictment against Santano was later dropped.

Although the District Court of New York was satisfied that violence on the part of Cordova had been proved it ruled that his acts could not be punished within the admiralty and maritime jurisdiction of the United States: the statute covering such acts was confined to offences committed on a 'vessel' upon the High Seas, and the court had to decide that an aircraft was not a 'vessel' within the meaning of the applicable statute. Moreover, the term 'upon the High Seas' could not be extended to include an aircraft in flight 'over the High Seas'.

Consequently, the court, finding Cordova guilty, had to arrest judgment of conviction since there was no Federal jurisdiction to punish him. Cordova was released from custody, and there was no way left to punish an offence committed above the high seas on board an American aircraft. In response to a wave of both domestic and foreign criticism, the United States Congress amended the Federal statutes, making maritime law applicable to offences committed on board aircraft over the high seas.[5]

A second case involved unlawful possession of drugs on board a British aircraft during a flight between Bahrain and Singapore. The case was brought before a British court pursuant to Article 62(1) of the British Civil Aviation Act 1949,[6] which reads as follows:

> Any offence whatever committed on a British aircraft shall, for the purpose of conferring jurisdiction, be deemed to have been committed in any place where the offender may for the time being be.

---

4. *See, USA* v. *Cordova (and Santano)*, US District Court, Eastern District of New York, 17 March 1950; [1950] *USA* v. *R* 1; 3 *Avi* 17,306; *see*, B. Reukema, *Drinking and Flying: Why the Two Do Not Mix Well on US Carriers*, IX *Annals of Air and Space Law* 133–147 (1984).
5. Public Law 514, 82nd Congress; [1952] *USA* v. *R* 437–439.
6. Civil Aviation Act 1949 (12 & 13 Geo. 6, c. 67).

Nevertheless, the court had to dismiss the case because the statutory offences of the law of England did not apply in British-registered aircraft outside British territory, unless specially so enacted. Article 62 of the Civil Aviation Act 1949 does not create offences because it merely asserts jurisdiction in England over offences created by common law or statutes.[7]

Added to other instances, the cases quoted above provided ample evidence that legislation was urgently needed to help clear up a most unsatisfactory situation. These cases led to international awareness on the need for an international criminal convention as to which *see* the following section.

2 THE TOKYO CONVENTION OF 1963

2.1 Scope and Purpose

The Tokyo Convention, in this section also referred to as the Convention, applies to:

a) offences against penal law;
b) acts which, whether or not they are offences, may or do jeopardize the safety of the aircraft or of persons or property therein or which jeopardize good order and discipline on board.[8]

Article 1(4) contains an exception for aircraft used in military, customs and police services. Following the formulation of Article 3 of the Chicago Convention, the main criterion is *the use* and not the ownership or registration of the aircraft.[9]

The objectives of the Convention are to:

- determine the criminal law applicable when an offence has been committed above territories not belonging to any particular State, such as the high seas, or in cases in which the place where an offence has been committed cannot be precisely located;
- define the rights and obligations of the aircraft commander in respect of offences and acts committed on board which jeopardise the safety of the aircraft;
- define the rights and obligations of the authorities of the place where the aircraft lands after an offence or an act which jeopardises the safety of an aircraft has been committed.

---

7. *R.* v. *Martin et al.*, Central Criminal Court (London), 22 March 1956; [1956] USAvR 141.
8. Pursuant to Art. 1(1).
9. *See*, H.J. Rutgers, *Conventions on Criminal Law Regarding Aircraft* 30–31 (1978); *see also*, R.P. Boyle and R. Pulsifer, *The Tokyo Convention on Offences and Certain Other Acts on Board Aircraft*, 30 Journal of Air Law and Commerce 305–354 (1964); G.F. Fitzgerald, *Offences and Certain Other Acts Committed on Board Aircraft: The Tokyo Convention of 1963*, 2 Canadian Yearbook of International Law 191 (1964).

2.2 Jurisdiction

Article 3 dealing with jurisdiction states that the Convention "does not exclude any criminal jurisdiction exercised in accordance with national law." This means that the jurisdictional rules contained in this Convention are of a subsidiary nature.[10]

Bearing in mind this important qualification, the same article stipulates that the State of registration is competent to exercise jurisdiction over offences committed on board. However, there are also cases in which States other than the State of registration have jurisdiction over such offences as is apparent from Article 4 of the Convention.[11] Offences against criminal laws of a political nature or those based on racial or religious discrimination are not subject to the jurisdictional rules of the Tokyo Convention save when the safety of flight is affected.[12] No such provision appears either in the Hague Convention or in the Montreal Convention, both of which will be discussed in sections 3 and 4 below.

2.3 Definition of the Term 'in Flight'

The Tokyo Convention applies from the moment when power is applied for the purpose of take-off until the moment when the landing run ends.[13] Yet, taken in connection with the authority of the aircraft commander, an aircraft is considered to be in flight:

> at any time from the moment when all its external doors are closed following embarkation until the moment when any such door is opened for disembarkation.[14]

---

10. *See*, J. Bailey, *Flying High Above the Law: A Discussion of the Law Concerning Criminal Offences Committed on Board Aircraft and the Associated Jurisdictional Confusion*, 22 Air & Space Law 89 (1997).
11. "A Contracting State which is not the State of registration may not interfere with an aircraft in flight in order to exercise its criminal jurisdiction over an offence committed on board except in the following cases:

    (a) the offence has effect on the territory of such State;
    (b) the offence has been committed by or against a national or permanent resident of such State;
    (c) the offence is against the security of such State;
    (d) the offence consists of a breach of any rules or regulations relating to the flight or manoeuvre of aircraft in force in such State;
    (e) the exercise of jurisdiction is necessary to ensure the observance of any obligation of such State under a multilateral international agreement."

    See, A.I. Mendelsohn, *In-Flight Crime: The International and Domestic Picture Under the Tokyo Convention*, 53 Virginia Law Review 509 ff. (1967).
12. *See*, Art. 2: "Without prejudice to the provisions of Article 4 and except when the safety of the aircraft or of persons or property on board so requires, no provision of this Convention shall be interpreted as authorizing or requiring any action in respect of offences against criminal laws of a political nature or those based on racial or religious discrimination."
13. *See*, Art. 3(1).
14. *See*, Art. 5(2).

The first definition was taken from the 1952 Rome Convention relating to damage to third parties on the surface, the second was added to the Tokyo Convention for practical purposes.

Under the first definition the time when the aircraft moves across the ramp area into position for actual take-off is left out of account: during that period the aircraft is not considered to be in flight, in terms of the Rome Convention. The same interpretation applies to Article 1(3) and so the national law of the State concerned is applicable. The safety of flight is more efficiently served when the aircraft commander can exercise his powers immediately after the external doors of the aircraft have been closed. This rule was prompted by the consideration that from the moment the aircraft has become a 'sealed unit', separated from the outside world, the commander should be in a position to take measures, internationally recognised, to protect the aircraft, the persons and the goods therein.

The two definitions serve to guarantee and ensure that at no time after the aircraft has become a 'closed universe' will it operate outside the scope of the Convention. It has therefore been provided that either the entire Convention will apply, or at least some of its important provisions like those of Chapter III concerning the powers of the commander as to which *see also*, the next section.

2.4 The Powers of the Aircraft Commander

Chapter III of the Tokyo Convention deals with the *powers of the aircraft commander*. The place where and the time during which the commander may exercise his authority are defined in the Convention, as is the liability for the measures taken by him or on his behalf. He may take 'measures of restraint' with regard to any person on board suspected of a criminal offence, disembark him in any subsequent State of landing or deliver him to 'competent authorities'.[15] The action taken by the commander is subject to *standards of reason*.[16] It may be difficult for him to decide just what constitutes an

---

15. *See*, Art. 6(2): "1. The aircraft commander may, when he has reasonable grounds to believe that a person has committed, or is about to commit, on board the aircraft, an offence or act contemplated in Article 1 paragraph 1, impose upon such person reasonable measures including restraint which are necessary; (a) to protect the safety of the aircraft, or of persons or property therein; or (b) to maintain good order and discipline on board; or (c) to enable him to deliver such person to competent authorities or to disembark him in accordance with the provisions of this chapter."

16. *See*, for US cases, *Azza Eid* v. *Alaska Airlines*, 2010 WL 2977727 (9th Cir. 2010); in appeal: *Eid, et al* v. *Alaska Airlines*, Ninth Circuit U.S. Court of Appeals; case number 0:13-cv-15668; *Cerqueira* v. *American Airlines*, 520 F.3d 1,14 (1st Cir. 2008); *Hammond* v. *Northwest Airlines*, 2010 WL 2836899; *Al Watan* v. *American Airlines*, 658 F. Supp. 2d 816; *Dasrath* v. *Continental Airlines*, 467 F. Supp. 2d 841 (S.D. Ohio 2003); *Al Qudhai'een* v. *American West Airlines*, 267 F. Supp. 2d 335; *Christel* v. *AMR Corp.*, 222 F. Sup. 2d 335 (E.D.N.Y. 2002); *Zervigon* v. *Piedmont Aviation*, 558 F. Supp. 1305 (S.D.N.Y. 1983); *Ruta* v. *Delta Airlines*, 322 F. Supp. 2d 391 (S.D.N.Y. 2004); for comments, *see*, Gerard Chouest, *Eid* v. *Alaska Airlines*, No. 06-16457 (9th Cir. 30 July 2010), in 36(4/5) Air & Space Law 335–338 (2011).

offence, but the ultimate decision is left to his discretion. This power may include the authority to refuse carrier to a passenger or goods if safety might be affected.[17]

The term 'offence' is not defined in the Convention due to the multitude and diversity of the national laws in the States party to it. This obstacle stood in the way of adopting a universally acceptable formula.

The aircraft commander and his crew enjoy immunity from criminal prosecution for their efforts to maintain safety on board by taking measures in regard to unruly passengers.[18] In 2006, a court in Israel found that the crew members had reasonable grounds to believe that the person in question had committed or was about to commit, acts on board aircraft forbidden by and under the Tokyo Convention.[19] However, that protection is not absolute and must be determined on a case-by-case basis. In 2011, the US Supreme Court held that the airline crew may have overstepped its discretion to maintain order and safety on board as the concerned crew member had acted in a hostile fashion against a passenger whose only 'crime' appears to have been getting on the airline worker's bad side by trying to stretch during the flight.[20]

2.5 Unlawful Seizure of Aircraft

Although this offence is covered in a general manner by Article 1, the Convention, in Article 11, has devoted a special Chapter to unlawful seizure of aircraft, a phenomenon which has become increasingly frequent since the late 1940s.[21] Such emphasis must be seen as a reflection of the deep concern of the authors of the Tokyo Convention and their wish to underscore the importance they attached to it. It may be argued that such emphasis was not quite commensurate with the effect they may have expected: not only does the Article fail to cover all forms of unlawful seizure, it also fails to prescribe any effective counter-measures, confining itself to imposing on contracting States the obligation "to take all appropriate measures to restore control of the aircraft to its lawful commander or to preserve his control of the aircraft." It is evident from the text of the quoted provision that hijacking is not adequately covered by it; moreover, it fails to prescribe any sanctions against the offence.

---

17. See, Art. 11 of the Tokyo Convention; as to national law see, for instance, 49 U.S.C. § 44902(b) of the US.
18. See, Art. 10: "For actions taken in accordance with this Convention neither the aircraft commander, any other member of the crew, any passenger, the owner or operator of the aircraft, nor the person on whose behalf the flight was performed shall be held responsible in any proceeding on account of the treatment undergone by the person against whom the action was taken."
19. See, M. Leshem, Court Analyzes the Elements of Air Carriers Immunity under the Tokyo Convention 1963: Zikry v. Air Canada, 32(3) Air & Space Law 220–224 (2007).
20. See, US Supreme Court, Case No. 10-962, Alaska Airlines v. Azza Eid, et al., Case No. 10-962; Corthouse News Service, Airline Still Faces Suit for Ejecting Passengers, reported on 29 July 2011; see also, M. Bennun and G. McKellar, Flying Safely, the Prosecution of Pilots and the ICAO Chicago Convention: Some Comparative Perspectives, 74(4) Journal of Air Law and Commerce 737–780 (2009).
21. See, A.F. Lowenfeld, Aviation Law, Documents Supplement, 1181 ff. (1981) (Worldwide Hijacking Statistics).

The lack of support in law for measures designed to combat aerial terrorism turned out to be one of the reasons for States to conclude a separate convention on hijacking, that is, The Hague Convention of 1970, which will be discussed in more detail in section 3 of this Chapter.

2.6 Obligations of States

Articles 12–15 draw up the powers and duties of the contracting States. The State where the aircraft has landed must take delivery of any person whom the aircraft commander delivers pursuant to Article 9(4) which allows him to deliver any person who he has reasonable grounds to believe has committed on board an act which, in his opinion, is a serious offence against the criminal law of the State of registration of the aircraft. The State of landing must immediately undertake a preliminary enquiry into the facts after it has taken into custody or imposed any other measures against a person of whom it has accepted delivery.

The State must also notify immediately the State of registration of the aircraft and the State of the nationality of the detained person and, if it considers it advisable, any other interested State. It must promptly report its findings to the said States and indicate whether it intends to exercise jurisdiction.[22]

The State may, if the person in question is not a national or a permanent resident of that State, return him to the territory of the State of which he is a national or a permanent resident, or to the territory of the State in which he began his journey by air.[23]

The provisions on extradition merit special attention,[24] as is pointedly illustrated in the *Soblen* case.[25]

The Hague Convention of 1970 contains more specific rules on extradition. The problems surrounding this delicate question will be reverted to in more detail in section 3.4 of this Chapter.

---

22. For a Chinese perspective *see*, Yang, *Flight Accidents and Criminal Responsibility in China*, 34(6) Air & Space Law 393–402 (2009).
23. Art. 14(1).
24. Art. 16: "1. Offences committed on aircraft registered in a Contracting State shall be treated, for the purpose of extradition, as if they had been committed not only in the place in which they have occurred but also in the territory of the State of registration of the aircraft. 2. Without prejudice to the provisions of the preceding paragraph, nothing in this Convention shall be deemed to create an obligation to grant extradition."
25. *See*, on the *Soblen* case, C.H.R. Thornberry, *Dr. Soblen and the Alien Law of the United Kingdom*, The International and Comparative Law Quarterly 414–474 (1963), notably at 444 ff.; G.F. Fitzgerald, *The Development of International Rules Concerning Offences and Certain Other Acts Committed on Board Aircraft*, I *Canadian Yearbook of International Law*, 230–251, at 248–249, note 36 (1963); XXXVIII *British Yearbook of International Law*, 479–483 (1962) and the Minutes of the 14th Session of the ICAO. Legal Committee (Rome, August–September 1962), ICAO Doc. 8302 LC/150-1 at 5.

2.7 Settlement of Disputes

The key Article governing this matter is Article 24 which states in paragraph 1 that in case of disputes between two or more contracting States there are three ways of reaching a settlement:

(a) through negotiation;
(b) through arbitration;
(c) by submitting the case to the International Court of Justice (ICJ).

According to paragraph 2, a contracting State may declare a reservation concerning the preceding paragraph.

2.8 Concluding Note

The Tokyo Convention entered into force on 4 December 1969. It has been ratified by 186 States in the world, that is, practically all States.

In spite of its imperfections the coming into force of this convention on offences may be regarded as a significant step towards establishing a moderate degree of legal order. It cannot be denied, however, that the final result shows a number of weak points such as: the absence of a definition of the word 'offence'; the restrictive approach to extradition, and imperfections in the field of jurisdiction necessitating the establishment of special rules applying to unruly passengers as to which *see*, section 6 below.

3 THE HAGUE CONVENTION OF 1970

3.1 The Need for a Convention

The reason why hijacking is so difficult to combat lies in the fact that aircraft are vulnerable. The hazards involved in such criminal acts are manifold and unpredictable. They have been aptly summed up by International Federation of Air Line Pilots' Associations (IFALPA) as follows: (1) a fight between the crew and the hijackers may cause a complete loss of control of the aircraft; (2) essential damage may be caused if weapons are used in the cockpit; (3) collisions may result from an aircraft being unable to observe traffic regulations; (4) fuel shortage may occur; (5) the crew may be unfamiliar with a particular airport and its approach procedures.[26]

In the 1960s and 1970s, hijacking activities focussed mainly on the Middle East and the Caribbean area, the latter centring on Cuba. In an attempt to combat hijacking in the Caribbean region an agreement was reached between the United States and Cuba in 1961, whereby US aircraft, crew and passengers would be returned under the

---

26. *See,* for IFALPA's actions *in re* hijacking E.E. McWhinney, *The Illegal Diversion of Aircraft and International Law,* 138 *Recueil des Cours* 261–372, at 287–289 and 335–337 (1973).

responsibility of the United States. The latter stipulation was agreed because the Cubans argued that the runways of their airports were too short for big jet aircraft to take off fully loaded forcing them to return passengers on smaller aircraft, a procedure involving long delays. As a result the US then assumed full responsibility for large jets taking off from Cuban airports with passengers.[27] As evidenced by the '9/11' tragedy in New York,[28] hijacking can now happen in all parts of the world.

At the end of the 1960s hijacking of aircraft increased with alarming frequency. This led to the conclusion, in December 1970, of the Hague Convention, which made hijacking an internationally punishable offence.[29] The Hague Convention, in this section also referred to as the Convention, further includes in its definition of aerial hijacking the following elements:

(a) the act must be unlawful;
(b) there must be some use of force, or threat of force;
(c) the act must consist of seizure of an aircraft and exercise of unlawful control over it or attempt thereat.

3.2 Scope of the Convention

The Convention is applicable irrespective of whether the flight is domestic or international.[30] The Convention further contains provisions on the pursuit and punishment of hijackers. It is applicable only to persons on board the aircraft in flight, but complicity and attempted hijackings are included as offences.

Unlike the Tokyo Convention, there is only one definition of the term 'in flight' in the Hague Convention: an aircraft is considered to be 'in flight' from the moment when all its external doors are closed following embarkation until the moment when any such door is open for disembarkation.[31]

3.3 Jurisdiction

Jurisdiction, according to Article 4, has been assigned to the following contracting States:

---

27. *See*, E.E. McWhinney, *The Illegal Diversion of Aircraft and International Law* 67 ff. (1975).
28. *See*, Committee on Homeland Security and Governmental Affairs, United States Senate, *Ten Years After 9/11 – 2011*, Senate Hearing 112–403 (2011); *see also*, section 1.2 of Chapter 9.
29. *See*, B. Cheng, *The Hague Convention on Hijacking of Aircraft 1970 – The Legal Aspects*, Aeronautical Journal 76 (1972); *see also*, P.S. Dempsey, *Aviation Security: The Role of Law in the War Against Terrorism*, 41 Columbia Journal of Transnational Law 649 (2002); and, from the same author: *Aerial Piracy and Terrorism: Unilateral and Multilateral Responses to Aircraft Hijackings*, 2 Connecticut Journal of International law 427 (1987).
30. *See*, Art. 3(3).
31. *See*, Art. 3(1).

(a) the *State of registration*, when the offence has been committed on board an aircraft registered in that State;

(b) the *State of landing*, when the alleged offender is still on board;

(c) the *State where the lessee of an aircraft without crew has his principal place of business or his permanent residence*;

(d) the *State in whose territory the alleged offender is found and apprehended* and which does not extradite him to any of the States previously mentioned.

Taking into custody or taking other measures to ensure the offender's presence have been made obligatory for the State where he is present, as well as making a preliminary enquiry into the facts,[32] but the Convention has stopped short of making the actual prosecution and trial mandatory.

Given this overall situation the Hague Convention has indeed introduced the principle of *universality of jurisdiction*,[33] which implies that an offender is liable to prosecution anywhere in the world, but with an important restriction: instead of fully honouring this principle, it has been made subject to the actual presence of the offender in a particular State.[34] Under the Convention not only hijacking itself,[35] but also the offender's use of force in connection with the seizure is covered by the jurisdiction.

3.4 Extradition

On the face of it, the Hague Convention seems to contain a reversal of the rules of Articles 15 and 16 of the Tokyo Convention on extradition. This impression could be inferred from Article 7.[36] The inspiration behind this Article is the well-known adage of *aut dedere aut judicare*.[37]

The reversal of policy, however, is not nearly as complete as it would perhaps seem. In Article 8(2) and (3) it is explicitly stated that extradition shall be 'subject to the other conditions provided by the law of the requested State.' The Convention, by this token, still contains no general rule making extradition obligatory. Extradition can only be effected in accordance with the laws of the requested State which, in turn, will reflect the rules of any extradition treaty that State may have concluded.

---

32. Art.6(1) and (2).
33. *See also*, I. Brownlie, *Principles of Public International Law* 467–471 (2012).
34. As an illustration *see*, A. Schaer, *Über den Abschuss von Passagierflugzeugen zur Terrorabwehr. Das Urteil des deutschen Bundesverfassungsgericht vom 15. Februar 2006* (Az. 1 BvR 357/05) *und die aktuelle Regelungen in Österreich und der Schweiz*, 56 Zeitschrift für Luft- und Weltraumrecht 551–558 (2007).
35. Art. 4.
36. "The Contracting State in the territory of which the alleged offender is found shall, if it does not extradite him, be obliged, without exception whatsoever and whether or not the offence was committed in its territory, to submit the case to its competent authorities for the purpose of prosecution. Those authorities shall take their decision in the same manner as in the case of any ordinary offence of a serious nature under the law of that State."
37. This principle has been applied to the rather curious case concerning the hijacking of a Polish airliner to West Berlin (*United States* v. *Tiede*): *see*, D. Schoner in 6 *Air Law* 43–47 (1981).

The Convention creates *quasi-territorial* jurisdiction for offences covered by it as not only States on whose territories the offence has been committed may extradite, but also States which have a link with the offence as established by Article 4(1) which has been referred to in section 3.3 above.[38] A distinction is made between States which make extradition conditional upon the existence of an extradition treaty, and the States which do not. The first category may or may not accept the Convention as a legal basis for extradition; the second shall 'recognize' the offence as an extraditable one.[39]

Also, the Convention is limited to offences as described in the terms of Article 1. This means that unlawful acts committed in connection with such an offence are not covered by its extradition provisions.

The Convention is silent on offenders claiming political asylum, although a ban on it had been contemplated during the preliminary discussions. Such a move would have meant an encroachment on the right of asylum. Consequently, when it comes to applying Article 7 much, if not all, will depend on the impartiality and integrity of the prosecuting authorities. Should they wish to ignore their obligation either to extradite or prosecute, then there is nothing to stop them. Herein lies the main weakness of the Convention: it cannot prevent States from granting political asylum to hijackers, if they so choose.[40]

However, the European Convention on the Suppression of Terrorism[41] has widened the range of extradition possibilities for acts of terrorism, including hijacking, by eliminating the area of what may be termed 'political' offences. In addition, the rule *aut dedere aut judicare*, which has also been included in the Strasbourg Convention, has been strengthened by contracting parties undertaking to enforce their own jurisdiction in the event of their refusing to extradite, for instance on the grounds of prosecution for reasons of race or religion. The last mentioned convention thus represents a significant step forward because offenders apprehended in the contracting States will not be able to escape trial.

3.5   Miscellaneous Provisions

The Hague Convention has adopted the provision in Article 11 of the Tokyo Convention safeguarding the right of passengers and crew to continue their journey and the

---

38. Art. 8: "The offence shall be treated, for the purpose of extradition between Contracting States, as if it had been committed not only in the place in which it occurred, but also in the territories of the States required to establish their jurisdiction in accordance with Article 4(1). The number of States to which extradition can be effected is increased accordingly."

39. *See*, the Minutes of the International Conference on Air Law (The Hague, December 1970), ICAO Doc. 8979-LC/165-1 at 125 ff.

40. *See*, the Minutes of the International Conference on Air Law (The Hague, December 1970), ICAO Doc. 8979-LC/165-1, notably the discussions on Art. 7 at 130–137 and 177–182. The 1978 *Bonn Declaration on Hijacking* (1978) may be used to impose an aviation blockade on countries giving asylum to air pirates as to which *see*, W. Schwenk, *The Bonn Declaration on Hijacking*, IV Annals of Air and Space Law 307–322 (1979).

41. Council of Europe, *European Convention on the Suppression of Terrorism*, Strasbourg, 27 January 1977.

return of the aircraft and its cargo to the persons legally entitled to it; this rule has been accentuated in the Hague Convention by adding the words 'without delay.'[42] Contracting States are obliged to promptly notify the International Civil Aviation Organization (ICAO) Council of any hijacking, the circumstances and the action taken in response to it.[43]

Finally, Article 12 prescribes that all disputes concerning the interpretation or application of the Convention shall be submitted to *arbitration*. So far, no use has been made of this method of settlement. When a settlement cannot be reached the dispute shall be submitted to the ICJ which has not yet happened for this convention.

This is the only provision in the Convention to which reservations may be made.

3.6 Concluding Note

For all the improvements achieved by the Convention, a few inadequacies still remain. One has already been referred to earlier in this section in connection with jurisdiction: there is *no obligation to prosecute*.

An important item not covered by the Hague Convention concerns the position of security agents on board aircraft and their powers to deal with hijackers. The issue has been discussed at the Diplomatic Conference, but IFALPA and the airline companies represented by IATA were opposed to the idea. Their opposition stemmed from their conviction that the presence of armed agents on board was dangerous, considering the vulnerability of an aircraft.[44]

4 THE MONTREAL CONVENTION OF 1971

4.1 Purpose

As the Hague and Tokyo Conventions were concerned exclusively with offences committed on board aircraft, another agreement was needed to combat other unlawful acts against the safety of civil aviation including acts of sabotage. These are dealt with in the Montreal Convention, in this section also referred to as the Convention, concluded in 1971, the year following the adoption of the Hague Convention.

A person commits an offence under this convention if he/she intentionally engages in an act of violence which is likely to endanger the safety of flight, by, for instances, placing substances on board aircraft or by destroying or damaging air navigation facilities or by communicating false information which may also affect the

---

42. *See*, Art. 9.
43. *See*, Art. 11.
44. *See*, H.J. Rutgers, *Conventions on Criminal Law Regarding Aircraft* 124–125 (1978); on the US 'Sky marshals', *see also*, P. Paul Fitzgerald, *Air Marshals: The Need for Legal Certainty*, 75(2) Journal of Air Law and Commerce 357–406 (2010).

safety of flight.[45] Attempts to commit such acts, as well as complicity, have also been made offences, pursuant to paragraph 2 of the same article. Unfortunately, the clause 'endangering the safety of the aircraft' in Article 1(1)(e), means that false bomb alerts, which cause only delay and no damage to the aircraft are not covered. False alarms thus remain outside the Convention's reach.

4.2 Scope

Again, the Convention is applicable to domestic as well as international flights if the point of take-off or landing, or both are situated outside the territory of the State of registration, or when the offence is committed in the territory of a State other than the State of registration. As for the word 'landing', this term is supposed to cover scheduled, intended and forced landings.

Special mention must be made of the words 'in service' for the purpose of the Convention. It is the first time that this expression has been used in a convention, and is deemed to be broader than 'in flight.'[46] It applies to the acts which are mentioned in section 4.1 above: those acts are also prohibited when they are committed against an aircraft 'in service.'

A proposal to make the carrying of deadly or dangerous weapons on board without permission from the carrier or his agent punishable was rejected.[47]

---

45. *See*, Art. 1(1):

> he unlawfully and intentionally:
>
> (a) performs an act of violence against a person on board an aircraft in flight if that act is likely to endanger the safety of that aircraft; or
> (b) destroys an aircraft in service or causes damage to such an aircraft which renders it incapable of flight or which is likely to endanger its safety in flight; or
> (c) places or causes to be placed on an aircraft in service, by any means whatsoever, a device or substance which is likely to destroy that aircraft, or to cause damage to it which renders it incapable of flight, or to cause damage to it which is likely to endanger its safety in flight; or
> (d) destroys or damages air navigation facilities or interferes with their operation, if any such act is likely to endanger the safety of aircraft in flight; or
> (e) communicates information which he knows to be false, thereby endangering the safety of aircraft in flight.

46. Art. 4(2):

> an aircraft is considered to be in service from the beginning of the pre-flight preparation of the aircraft by ground personnel or by the crew for a specific flight until twenty-four hours after any landing; the period of service shall, in any event, extend for the entire period during which the aircraft is in flight as defined in paragraph (a) of this Article.

47. *See*, the Minutes of the International Conference on Air Law (Montreal, September 1971), ICAO Doc. 9081-LC/170-1, notably the discussions on Art. 1 of the draft convention.

4.3 Jurisdiction

Contracting States have undertaken to impose severe penalties with regard to the offences listed above.[48] Article 5 states that each contracting State must take all such measures as may be necessary to establish its jurisdiction in the following cases:

(a) when the offence is committed in the territory of that State;
(b) when the offence is committed against or on board an aircraft registered in that State;
(c) when the aircraft on board which the offence is committed lands in its territory with the alleged offender still on board;
(d) when the offence is committed against or on board an aircraft leased without crew to a lessee who has his principal place of business or, if he has no such place of business, his permanent residence in that State.

Each State must take such measures in the event of the offender being found on its territory and not being extradited.[49] Another duty for contracting States is to take all necessary steps to prevent the offences mentioned in Article 1 in accordance with international and national law.[50]

4.4 Miscellaneous Provisions

Contracting States are required to supply each other with all relevant information when they have reason to believe that an offence mentioned in Article 1 is going to be committed.[51]

Finally, several provisions in the Montreal Convention are identical with those covering the same subjects in the Hague Convention. This applies to:

(a) the non-applicability of the Convention to military, customs and police aircraft;[52]
(b) the definition of the words 'in flight';[53]
(c) designation of jurisdiction in case if States operating joint and international operating agencies;[54]
(d) the final provisions, including settlement of disputes.[55]

---

48. *See,* Art. 3.
49. *See,* Art. 5(2).
50. *See,* Art. 10.
51. *See,* Art. 12.
52. *See,* Art. 4.
53. *See,* Art. 2(a).
54. Pursuant to Chapter XVI of the Chicago Convention; *see,* section 3.3.2.5 of Chapter 1.
55. *See,* Arts 13–16.

4.5 Dispute Settlement

4.5.1 The Iran-US Conflict on the Shooting Down of an Iran Air Aircraft

On 3 July 1988, an Airbus operated by Iran Air was shot down above the Gulf from the US marine cruiser 'Vincennes' killing passengers and crew. Iran brought the case to the attention of the ICAO Council who made a couple of recommendations purported to enhance aviation safety pursuant to Articles 54 and 55 of the Chicago Convention but it did not condemn the US for its actions.

Consequent upon the decisions of the ICAO Council, Iran approached the ICJ.[56] Before the ICJ could make a decision on the merits of the case, the two parties reached a final agreement on their views. The ICJ transmitted the files to ICAO while observing that Iran's claim had not been examined under Article 84 of the Chicago Convention.[57]

4.5.2 The Lockerbie Disaster

The Montreal Convention of 1971 has been referred to in the aftermath of the Lockerbie disaster. This serious accident involved the explosion on board and subsequent crash of a Pan Am aircraft over the Scottish village of Lockerbie in December 1988. Apart from all crew members and passengers, including many US citizens, a number of inhabitants of Lockerbie also fell victim to this disaster. The explosion was caused by a bomb that was alleged to have been brought on board the aeroplane by two Libyan nationals.

Their extradition to stand trial at a Scottish or US court was demanded by the UK and the US, which even led to a case before the ICJ as Libya proposed to judge the two men itself.[58] Extradition was unacceptable to Libya, which led eventually to the imposition of political and economic sanctions by the UN Security Council.[59] After seven years of these sanctions,[60] however, an agreement was reached by the UK, the US and Libya on a solution acceptable to all parties concerned. This comprised of a trial according to Scottish law to be held in a neutral country, that is, The Netherlands. This

---

56. *See*, International Court of Justice, *Case Concerning the Aerial Incident of 3 July 1988*, *Islamic Republic of Iran v. United States*, Volume II (2000).
57. *See*, section 3.3.8.3 of Chapter 1; *see also*, G. Guillaume, *Les affaires touchant au droit aérien devant la Cour internationale de justice*, in: M. Benkö and W. Kröll, *Air & Space Law in the 21st Century*, Liber Amicorum for Karl-Heinz Böckstiegel 80–81 (2001).
58. The International Court of Justice found that it has jurisdiction pursuant to Art. 14(1) of the Montreal Convention (1971), as to which *see*, International Court of Justice, *Preliminary Objections in the Case Concerning Questions of Interpretation and Application of the 1971 Montreal Convention Arising from the Aerial Incident at Lockerbie, Libya v. United States*, and, ICJ, Order of 14 April 1992, *Questions of Interpretation and Application of the 1971 Montreal Convention Arising from the Aerial Incident at Lockerbie*, 12 Hague Yearbook of International Law 153–157 (1999).
59. Pursuant to UN Security Council Resolutions 748 of 1992 and 883 of 1993.
60. Those sanctions were lifted in 2003.

country provided accommodation for the trial at a former military camp near the town of Zeist, located in the middle of this country, which for the duration of the proceedings was declared to be Scottish territory.

This solution to the problems raised by the '*aut dedere, aut judicare*' principle of the Montreal Convention was quite unprecedented and has led to an impressive range of books, articles and other publications.[61] Shortly after the start of the trial the University of Amsterdam held a most informative seminar in May 2000[62] where the following five aspects of the trial were discussed:

(1) the law applicable on the premises where the trial was held. This was in principle Scottish law, but the Agreement between the UK and the Netherlands stated that Netherlands law remained applicable unless provided otherwise;

(2) the transfer and extradition in 1999 of the accused from Libya to The Netherlands. Both were governed by Netherlands law, Scottish law, applicable treaties and UN Security Council Resolutions. These too were unprecedented procedures and the legal provisions used as a basis were not always adequate according to various commentators;

(3) the guarantees for a fair trial of the accused. Apart from Scottish law also the European Convention on Human Rights was applicable. A further point of interest was whether the Netherlands as the territorial State was (co)responsible for a fair trial;

(4) the legal assistance during the trial. Major problems could occur where evidence or witnesses from third countries were needed. Here too, Netherlands law, Scottish law and treaty law would be applicable; and

(5) the situation after the trial. If and when the accused were convicted and a custodial sentence was imposed, they would be transferred to Scottish territory. However, the legal arrangements made in connection with the trial did not allow their compulsory transfer: they could only be transferred if they agree so voluntarily.[63]

The Court pronounced its judgment on 31 January 2001. One of the accused was held to be guilty and will have to serve at least twenty years in a Scottish prison, the other was acquitted.[64] The former lodged an appeal against this verdict; this was

---

61. *See,* R. Black, *The Lockerbie Disaster,* 37 Archiv des Völkerrechts 214–225 (1999) and M. Kamminga, *Trial of Lockerbie Suspects Before a Scottish Court in The Netherlands,* XLV Netherlands International Law Review 417–433 (1998).

62. *See, The Lockerbie Trial. Legal Questions at the Commencement of the Trial,* a seminar organised by the Amsterdam Centre for International Law of the University of Amsterdam (Zeist, The Netherlands; 23 May 2000).

63. *See,* A. Klip and M. Mackarel, *The Lockerbie Trial – A Scottish Court in the Netherlands,* 70 Revue Internationale de Droit Pénal 777–819 at 815 (1999).

64. Case No. 1475/99.

however confirmed by the appeal court in February-March 2002. The criminal case against the second accused is now completely closed and cannot be appealed by the prosecution.

4.5.3   Other Cases

The scenario of the Lockerbie case may also play a role in the context of the prosecution of the MH17 perpetrators.[65] Various jurisdictional solutions are being discussed for bringing a suit against them, to wit a Court in Ukraine, the International Criminal Court, a court established by the UN Security Council and an ad hoc tribunal established by States on the basis of a special agreement thereto. Each of these options has its legal, and without any doubt, political advantages and disadvantages in terms of feasibility.

On 24 November 2014, the mother of one of the victims, a German citizen, has filed an application against the State of Ukraine before the European Court of Human Rights. The claimant alleges that the State of Ukraine has failed to ensure the right of life secured by the European Convention of Human Rights and the breach of Ukraine under the Chicago Convention to close only partially its airspace as the territory below was a conflict area. One of the questions which the European Court will have to face is whether all domestic remedies have been exhausted.[66]

4.6   The Airport Protocol of 1988

Following acts of sabotage directed against airports, ICAO has drawn up an *Instrument for the Suppression of Unlawful Acts of Violence at Airports Serving International Civil Aviation*. For that purpose a special sub-committee of the ICAO Legal Committee preferred the form of a Special Protocol to be added to the Montreal Convention.[67]

This addition was very useful to improve the safety at airports. While it has been widely ratified,[68] it has not been appealed to in legal or other proceedings even if such acts of violence have been committed at airports, not least in 2016 when, for instance, Brussels airport was seriously attacked by terrorists.[69] The situation was handled by applying national law, that is, the Belgian law.

---

65. *See*, section 3.3.7.1 of Chapter 1.
66. *See*, D. Pusztai, *MH17 Goes to Strasbourg: Some Remarks on Obligations of Prevention, Foreseeability and Causation*, on EJILTalk!, 9 October 2014, to be accessed on the internet.
67. This proposal was adopted at the ICAO Conference held at Montreal in February 1988. *See*, B. Cheng, *International Legal Instruments to Safeguard International Air Transport: The Conventions of Tokyo, The Hague, Montreal and a New Instrument Concerning Unlawful Violence at International Airports*, in T.L. Masson-Zwaan and P.M.J. Mendes de Leon (eds), *Aviation Security: How to Safeguard International Air Transport* (proceedings of a Conference held at the Peace Palace, The Hague, 22–23 January 1987) 23–46 (1987); *see also*, reports in 12 Air Law 50–51 (1987) and 13 Air Law 95–100 (1988).
68. Status: 174 States per December 2016.
69. *See*, BBC news, *Brussels explosions: What we know about airport and metro attacks*, 9 April 2016.

4.7 Concluding Note

Both the Hague Convention of 1970 and the Montreal Convention of 1970 have been widely ratified.[70] This shows the commitment of the international aviation community that States are seriously engaged with combating threats to aviation terrorism and acts of sabotage.

However, the Montreal Convention of 1971 suffers from the same weaknesses as the Tokyo Convention, and, in particular, the Hague Convention of the preceding year. Enforcement of the offences is dependent on the cooperation of States which may be dependent on the implementation and application of the provisions of this convention in the national laws of the contracting States and on the prevailing political and trade relations between States. The Lockerbie scenario forms a case study underlining the multifaceted aspects of an international aviation disaster.

All in all, the above may illustrate that treaty rules such as those of the Montreal Convention may cause more problems in their execution than was envisaged by their drafters.

Moreover, new techniques and new forms of conspiracies are being used to attack civil aviation including airports. The diplomatic conference held in Beijing in 2010 has recognised this trend by adopting the Beijing Convention and Protocol of the same year which will be discussed in the next section.

5 THE BEIJING CONVENTION AND PROTOCOL OF 2010

5.1 Background and Purposes

The devastating attacks of 9 September 2001 on the twin towers in New York and the terrorist threat of 2009 on a Northwest Airlines' flight from Denver to Amsterdam[71] prompted the aviation community to strengthen security measures such as the closing of cockpit doors, improvement of screening procedures and the establishment of watchlists laid down in ICAO Annex 17 on Aviation Security and national regulations, principally in the US, and to adopt the above two legal instruments. They underscore the need for continued supervision of aviation security and the strengthening of international legal regimes designed to prosecute terrorists. As evidenced above as to which *see*, the Lockerbie case discussed in section 4.5, political factors sometimes impede the enforcement of international rules.

This said, international cooperation evidenced by the adoption of the above conventions must contribute to an improved mechanism in the field of aviation

---

70. The Hague Convention of 1970: 185 States party; the Montreal Convention of 1971: 188 States party, as per December 2016, that is, the same numbers as five years ago.
71. On which occasion a passenger tried to ignite incendiary powder strapped to his leg. The passenger was prevented from committing his attack by a brave Dutch passenger. *See, Passengers' Actions Thwart a Plan to Down a Jet*, New York Times of 27 December 2009.

security.[72] Despite the above cooperative and regulatory efforts, ICAO reported no less than twenty-three instances of unlawful interference with civil aviation, including eight successful or attempted hijacks, one airport attack, one in-flight attack and two cases of attempted sabotage in the period 2001–2010.[73]

The diplomatic conference held in Beijing adopted on 10 September 2010 the *Convention on the Suppression of Unlawful Acts Relating to International Civil Aviation* and the *Beijing Protocol* to the 1971 Hague Convention on the Suppression of Unlawful Seizure of Aircraft which will be referred to as the *Beijing Convention of 2010* and the *Beijing Protocol*. They are designed to address the above concerns. In short, the two 'Beijing instruments' criminalise the act of using civil aircraft as a weapon and of using dangerous materials to attack aircraft or other targets, including airports.

5.2 The Beijing Convention of 2010

The Beijing Convention of 2010, in this section also referred to as the Convention, improves the provisions of the Montreal Convention of 1971, that is, the Montreal 'sabotage' Convention of 1971, including its Airport Protocol of 1988. The Beijing Convention prevails over the Montreal Convention of 1971 as amended by the Airport Protocol of 1988[74] as between States parties.

Interestingly, the Beijing Convention introduces the concept of dangerous materials which may be used for attacking civil aircraft engaged in an international, and in, specified cases, domestic flights.[75] The list of definitions specifying dangerous materials is rather long;[76] among others, it refers to chemical weapons, radioactive materials and nuclear materials which are also governed by other international conventions which prevail over the provisions of the Beijing Convention (1971).[77] Given the complexity of communication technology designed to serve civil aviation, the threat of cyber terrorism stays for further study on the agenda of the Aviation Security Panel of ICAO. In 2013, ICAO has added a Recommended Practice to its Annex 17 designed to combat cyber-attacks.[78] New guidance materials have been developed in support of these new SARPs.

The carriage and use of these materials, and their release from civil aircraft endangering the safety of the flight is prohibited under the conditions laid down in this convention. The persons performing such an act commit an offence under the Beijing Convention which is punishable by penalties as determined by the national laws of the contracting States. The offence is an act committed by a person using an aircraft in

---

72. *See*, the Declaration on Aviation Security made at the 37th session of the ICAO General Assembly of 2010.
73. *See*, ICAO, Annual Report of the Council, Table 11 (2010).
74. *See*, section 4.6, above.
75. *See*, Art. 5.
76. *See*, Art. 2.
77. *See*, Art. 7.
78. *"Each Contracting State should develop measures in order to protect information and communication technology systems used for civil aviation purposes from interference that may jeopardise the safety of civil aviation."*

service for the purposes of causing death, serious injury or damage to property or the environment.[79] Under the convention,[80] a person who destroys or damages air navigation facilities or interferes with their operation, if any such act is likely to endanger the safety of aircraft in flight, constitutes an offence under it. This provision covers cyber terrorism, and is the only instance where an aviation convention so does.

The Beijing Convention of 2010 is also taking stock of other new developments as it penalises the intentional, as opposed to the unintentional, carriage of biological, chemical and nuclear weapons and similar tools under its scope. It establishes a link between the proliferation of Weapons of Mass Destruction (WMD) and terrorism. States are required to cooperate in this respect as they must criminalise these acts under national law by virtue of international law.

The threat to commit an offence under the new instruments may give rise to criminal liability when the conditions dictate that the threat is a credible one. Remarkably, acts of conspiracy may also fall under the scope of the new treaties. While acknowledging fair treatment and human rights of any suspects, the Beijing agreements aim at enhancing cooperation between States in combating threats to aviation security.

Persons include natural and legal persons.[81] Natural persons managing legal entities may be made subject to civil, administrative and criminal liability in the State where the legal entity is established if they commit an offence under the Convention.[82]

States must take measures to establish their jurisdiction in accordance with the principles drawn up in the Beijing Convention.[83] Reference is made to the discussion of jurisdiction under the Tokyo (1963), Hague (1970) and Montreal (1971) conventions. The principle *aut dedere aut iudicare* is repeated in the Beijing Convention.[84]

The Beijing Convention enters into force when twenty-two States have ratified it.[85] Other international conventions designed to combat the use of nuclear, chemical and biological weapons prevail over the provisions of the Beijing Convention.[86]

The ICAO Assembly of 2016 urged States to accede to the Beijing Convention.[87]

---

79. *See*, Art. 1(f).
80. *See*, Art. 1(d).
81. *See*, Art. 3 in conjunction with Art. 1.
82. *See*, Art. 4.
83. *See*, Art. 8.
84. *See*, Art. 10.
85. *See*, Art. 22.
86. *See*, Art. 7 referring to the Treaty on the *Non-Proliferation of Nuclear Weapons* (1968), The Convention on the *Prohibition of the Development, Production and Stockpiling of Bacteriological (Biological) and Toxin Weapons and on Their Destruction* (1972) and the Convention on the Prohibition *of the Development, Production, Stockpiling and Use of Chemical Weapons and on Their Destruction* (1993), as between States parties to these conventions.
87. *See*, ICAO Resolution A39-10, *Promotion of the Beijing Convention and the Beijing Protocol of 2010*.

5.3   The Beijing Protocol of 2010

The Beijing Protocol widens the scope of the Hague – hijacking – Convention (1971) by amending it. The Hague Convention stays intact as between States Parties even if the Beijing Protocol enters into force.

Terrorist acts include acts which are carried out by technological means while using aircraft as a weapon.[88] Persons include, again, legal entities which organise, direct and finance acts of terrorism. They may be made subject to civil, criminal or administrative liability.[89] There are also new provisions on extradition, fine-tuning the provisions of the Montreal Convention (1971).

The Beijing Protocol also enters into force upon 22 ratifications.[90]

Despite the laudable purposes of the agreements, the ratification process of the above Beijing instruments is going rather slow.[91] It is premature to draw conclusions from this trend.[92]

6   THE PHENOMENON OF 'UNRULY PASSENGERS'

6.1   Appearance of the Phenomenon

In-flight violence has also become a major problem.[93] One of its causes is the abuse of drugs and alcohol by passengers. In spite of the existence of various international instruments discussed above problems regarding criminal jurisdiction frequently arise. Apart from drugs or drinking the feeling of the confined space of the aircraft, mental and emotional factors, the prohibition of smoking on board and lack of medication causes irritation triggered 'air rage' leading to unscheduled landings to disembark or deliver unruly passengers. Whereas in the period from 2007–2015 49,084 cases were reported, that number has increased 10,584 in 2015. The associated costs amount to USD 10,000 to USD 200,000 per landing.

Although the identity of unruly passengers and the relevant evidence can usually be established, there are many cases in which such passengers have to be released without being submitted to judicial process due to lack of jurisdiction of the State where the aircraft lands. The State of registration of the aircraft has the authority to apply its laws when a passenger misbehaves. Equally, the State in whose airspace the offence takes place also has jurisdiction, at least in theory. However, many States do not have legislation enabling them to deal with foreign nationals who commit an

---

88. *See*, Art. II.
89. *See*, Art. IV.
90. In accordance with Art. XXIII.
91. In December 2016, sixteen States had ratified the Beijing Convention and seventeen the Beijing Protocol.
92. That said, ICAO Resolution A39-10 (2016), *Promotion of the Beijing Convention and the Beijing Protocol of 2010* urges States to become a party to it.
93. Responses to a study by IATA member airlines showed that from 1994 to 1997 the number of reported incidents increased from 1,132 to 5,416 as to which *see*, ICAO Circular 288 LE/1, *Guidance Material on the Legal Aspects of Unruly/Disruptive Passengers*, June 2002.

offence on board a foreign aircraft outside their own airspace.[94] These shortcomings, and proposed and possible solutions, are discussed in the next sections.

6.2 The Regulatory Framework So Far

6.2.1 The Existing International Regime

Which rules are there to deal with such offenders? The Convention of Tokyo of 1963 applies to any act that is an offence under the criminal laws of a contracting State as well as to acts, which whether or not they are offences, may jeopardise safety, good order and discipline on board. Thus the acts of unruly passengers are covered.[95] As explained in section 2, above, the Tokyo Convention lays down an immunity rule in Article 10 by laying down that:

> neither the aircraft commander, any member of the crew, any passenger, the owner or operator of the aircraft nor the person on whose behalf the flight is performed, shall be held responsible in any proceeding on account of the treatment undergone by the person against whom the actions were taken.

The Montreal Convention of 1971 adds also rules on problems caused by wrongful acts.

6.2.2 Civil and Criminal Proceedings Against the Offender

Another solution may be found in starting civil or criminal proceedings against the offenders.

For instance, a passenger flying on Singapore Airlines forced a pilot to make an unscheduled landing in Northern Australia. The passenger was ordered to pay for the costs, and the fines calculated by a judge in Darwin, Australia.[96]

A US Federal court convicted an Iranian man who disrupted an Air Canada flight after the 11 September 2001 terrorist attacks with threats against Americans. His behaviour caused the flight to return to Los Angeles, escorted by fighter planes. The court confirmed the conviction of the defendant for interfering with flight attendants amid a verbal confrontation on the flight from Toronto, Canada, to Los Angeles in late September 2001. The Iranian man who was told to return to his seat when he was found smoking in a restroom said something like 'I will kill all Americans'.[97]

A man who had been dismissed as an employer of the Chinese airline Xiamen Airlines tried to disrupt the normal airlines' operations by speaking violently and

---

94. *See*, J. Balfour and O. Highley, *Disruptive Passengers: The Civil Aviation (amendment) Act 1996 Strikes Back*, 22(4/5) Air & Space Law 194–200 (1997); W. Mann, *All the (Air) Rage: Legal Implications Surrounding Airline and Government Bans on Unruly Passengers in the Sky*, 65 Journal of Air Law and Commerce 857–889 (1999–2000).
95. *See*, V. Nase and N. Humphrey, *Angry People in the Sky: Air Rage and the Tokyo Convention*, 79 Journal of Air Law and Commerce 701–746 (2014).
96. *See*, Dow Jones Newswires, 12 December 2003, *SIA AirRage Passenger to pay for Diversion Costs*.
97. As reported by Reuters, *US Court Upholds Unruly Passenger Verdict*, 28 March 2004.

threatening the airline, compensating his anger pertaining to the labour dispute. His former employer sent letters to other airlines and travel agents, and advised them to refuse him as passenger by blacklisting him in the interest of safety. The Beijing District Court found in favour of the 'blacklisting airlines' but held that a reasonable procedure should be followed when blacklisting individuals.[98]

In 2011, a flight from Paris to Boston had to be diverted to Gander, Newfoundland, Canada because one of the passengers had affixed newly discovered electronic devises to the wall of the aircraft cabin and refused to relinquish them when so requested by the cabin crew. The passenger pleaded guilty and was convicted on the basis of the Canadian Criminal Act as the flight in question was in flight and terminated in Canada. Among others, the offender pleaded that the flight terminated in Boston. The court found that whereas the term 'in flight' is defined, the term 'terminated' is not. The court distinguished between the ultimate destination of the flight and the termination of a flight segment. As the aircraft was no longer 'in flight' in Gander, Canada, the flight had terminated there establishing jurisdiction for the Canadian court.[99]

6.3 Response from ICAO

In order to address those lacunas, ICAO has drawn up a Circular (2008, in 2000) and established a Study Group under the Legal Committee proposing that States introduce national laws and regulations in accordance with the model legislation developed by the Study Group set out in ICAO Circular 288.[100] Many States have now introduced legislation giving them jurisdiction to deal with offenders on board an aircraft that makes its next landing in their territory on a complaint by the commander of the aircraft. The aircraft commander has authority to deal with the offenders.[101] Drawing up a 'black list' by air carriers could, however, give rise to conflicts with laws and regulations protecting privacy.

At the instigation of IATA, ICAO has paved the way for measures, including legal instruments. Among them are ICAO Assembly Resolution 33-4 (2009) and the establishment of a *Draft List of Offences Committed on Board Civil Aircraft*.[102] In 2010, the ICAO General Assembly has mandated the ICAO Secretariat Study Group on Unruly

---

98. District Court of Beijing, Decision of 11 November 2011, Deming Zhao, International Law Office, 28 April 2010.
99. *R.* v. *Minot*, 2011 NLCA 7, reported by Gerard A. Chouest, International Law Office (www.internationallawoffice.com) on 24 February 2011.
100. *See*, J. Huang, *ICAO Study Group Examines the Legal Issues Related to Unruly Airline Passengers*, 56 ICAO Journal 18 (2001).
101. *See*, S.R. Ginger, *Violence in the Skies: The Rights and Liabilities of Air Carriers When Dealing with Disruptive Passengers*, 23(3) Air & Space Law 106–117 (1998); R.I.R. Abeyratne, *Unruly Passengers – Legal, Regulatory and Jurisdictional Issues*, 24 Air & Space Law 46–61 (1999), and *The Fear of Flying and Air Rage – Some Legal Issues*, 1(1) Journal of Transportation Security 45–66 (2008).
102. *See also*, the *Report on ICAO's activities* in 25 Air & Space Law 136 and 140 (2000), T. Colehan, *Unruly Passengers: The Airline Industry Perspective on the Revision of the Tokyo Convention*, 9–22 Journal of Aviation Management 9–22 (2014), and R. Schmid, *Hooligans der Lüfte: Unbotmassiges Verhalten an Bord von Flugzeugen und die Rechtsfolgen*, in *Air and Space Law in the 21st Century* 181–200 (2001).

Passengers to consider the new issues relating to this subject.[103] ICAO, IATA and contracting States signalled the following shortcomings in the Tokyo Convention:

- The definition of 'in flight'.
- The definition of 'offences'.
- Jurisdiction, also in relation to leased aircraft.
- Protection of aircraft commander and crew from criminal proceedings.

whereas new provisions were laid down for the carrier's right of recourse and the supervision by In Flight Security Officers (IFSOs). The next section explains how these matters were dealt with in a new Protocol.

6.4 The Montreal Protocol of 2014

On 4 April 2014, a new Protocol amending the Toyo Convention of 1963 was adopted. It recognises the 'escalation of the severity and frequency of unruly behaviour on board aircraft that may jeopardise the safety of the aircraft or of persons or property therein or jeopardise good order and discipline on board.'

Between the contracting Parties to it, the Tokyo Convention and the amending Protocol must be read as a single instrument. It shall be known as 'the Tokyo Convention as amended by the Montreal Protocol 2014.'

It will enter into force on the first day of the second month following the deposit of the twenty-first instrument of ratification, acceptance, approval or accession. Per December 2016, eight States are a party to it.

A principal change concerns the *broadening of jurisdiction*. Under the Montreal Protocol (2014), mandatory jurisdiction may also be exercised by the State of the intended landing, or the scheduled destination and the State of the operator of the aircraft meeting questions in case of leased aircraft. In case the flight had to be diverted to a third State, that State is also competent to exercise jurisdiction.[104]

Under the Tokyo Convention, the term *'offences'* has been defined as offences 'against penal law and acts which may or do jeopardise the safety of the aircraft or good order and discipline.' The Montreal Protocol (2014) explains behaviour which is deemed to constitute an offence by identifying a physical assault or threat to commit such assault against a crew member or a passenger, and a refusal to follow lawful instruction given by or on behalf the aircraft commander for safety purposes as such.[105]

Proposals made by IATA to enhance protection of the aircraft commander and crew from criminal proceedings following their imposition of corrective measures were not adopted.[106]

---

103. *See*, https://www.icao.int/Meetings/a38/Documents/WP/wp049_en.pdf
104. Art. IV, which has become a new Art. 3 of the amended Tokyo Convention (1963).
105. Art. X, which has become Art. 15*bis* of the amended Tokyo Convention (1963).
106. *See*, on this matter, the cases of *Eid* v. *Alaska Airlines*, 621 F 3d 858 (9th Circuit, 2010) and *Zikry* v. *Air Canada*, Civil file No. 1716/05 A (Magistrates Court of Haifa of 2006); *see also*, M. Leshem, *Court Analyzes the Elements of Air Carriers Immunity under the Toyo Convention, 1963*: *Zikry* v. *Air Canada*, 32 Air & Space Law 220 (2007); G. Choust, *Eid* v. *Alaska Airlines*,

Annex 17 of ICAO defines an *IFSO*.[107] The aircraft commander may request but not require the assistance of an IFSO to restrain a passenger. However, the aircraft commander keeps the final authority for safeguarding the safety on board aircraft as IFSOs are not allowed to take precautionary measures against unruly passengers without authorisation from the aircraft commander.[108]

The Protocol gives carriers *the right to seek compensation from the offender*.[109] This provision is supposed to have a strong deterrent effect, as to which *see also*, section 6.2, above.

6.5 Criminalisation of Aviation People

This is becoming a sensitive subject. The term 'aviation people' includes persons who are working in air transport, that is, as airline executives, owners and operators of aircraft, aircraft commanders or crew, air traffic controllers, maintenance companies, representatives of civil aviation authorities and airport managers. They have become subject to the attention from public prosecutors following the call for transparency in relation to the aim of penalising people who have allegedly committed criminal acts. In so far as aircraft commanders and crew are concerned, this subject can be linked to the emergence of 'just culture' which has been briefly discussed in section 5.2 of Chapter 6.

International air law only marginally addresses this subject. ICAO Annex 13 prescribes that the investigation of an accident may not lead to criminalisation of people who were involved with the cause the accident.[110] Not all States have implemented this standard in their national legislation, paving the way for 'just culture', and crimination of those people, as to which *see*, below.

The Tokyo Convention grants a more explicit immunity from criminal and other judicial proceedings to the aircraft commander and crew, and other persons mentioned in this provision, including passengers.[111] Despite this provision, and consequent upon the *Eid* v. *Air Alaska* and *Zikry* v. *Air Canada* decisions in which the reactions from the aircraft commanders were tested in legal proceedings IATA has attempted to attach a

36(4/5) Air & Space Law 335–338 (2011) who starts his article by saying the following: 'An unfortunate decision from the US Court of Appeals for the Ninth Circuit undermines significantly the authority of the captain of an aircraft to maintain good order and discipline on board and ensure the safety of the flight.'

107. As 'a person who is authorised by the government of the State of the Operator and the government of the State of Registration to be deployed on an aircraft with the purpose of protecting that aircraft and its occupants against acts of unlawful interference.'
108. Art. VII, which has become Art. 6(3) of the amended Tokyo Convention (1963).
109. Art. XIII, which has become Art. 18bis of the amended Tokyo Convention (1963).
110. *See*, Standard 3.1: 'The sole objective of the investigation of an accident or incident shall be the prevention of accidents and incidents. *It is not the purpose of this activity to apportion blame or liability.*' (*italics added*)
111. *See*, Art. 10: 'For actions taken in accordance with this Convention, neither the aircraft commander, any other member of the crew, any passenger, the owner or operator of the aircraft, nor the person on whose behalf the flight was performed shall be held responsible in any proceeding on account of the treatment undergone by the person against whom the actions were taken.'

new provision to Article 10 of the Tokyo Convention, but that attempt failed.[112] In *Eid*, the US Supreme Court found that an aircraft commander's action under the Tokyo Convention should be held to a *standard of reasonableness* rather than the more deferential 'arbitrary and capricious' standard.[113] Authors point at the fact that the current state of affairs and law give little guidance to aircraft commanders as to how to act when they have to take action for the sake of safety, thus putting it at a risk because of doubt with respect to the legality of their behaviour.[114]

Here are a number of incidents which illustrate the above development:

- Upon the crash of the Air Inter flight on 20 January 1992 in the Vosges mountains located in the East of France killing eighty-seven people with nine people surviving the accident, employees of Air Traffic Control (ATC), the airline and the aviation safety agency have been acquitted from criminal sanctions.[115]
- In 1997, the US maintenance contractor Sabre Tech was found criminally liable for placing inadequately packed oxygen generators aboard aircraft thus illegally carrying dangerous materials on board aircraft causing its unsafe operation and the death of 110 people;[116] however, in appeal, the court held that that the charges and ultimate convictions against the company were not only improper but contrary to the law that the charges and ultimate convictions against the company were not only improper but contrary to the law that the charges and ultimate convictions against the company were not only improper but contrary to the law the charges and ultimate convictions against the company were not only improper but also contrary to the law.[117]
- Four Italian air traffic controllers have been convicted for manslaughter for their roles in a crash between a Scandinavian Airline System (SAS) aircraft and a private Cessna jet killing 118 people on 8 October 2001.[118]
- After the dramatic mid-air collision above Überlingen, South Germany, involving a DHL cargo aircraft and the Russian Bashkirian airlines aircraft

112. *See*, IATA's proposal for a new Art. 10(2) as formulated in a *draft* of the Montreal Protocol of 2014: 'The aircraft commander will be accorded a high degree of deference in any review of actions taken by him or her in accordance with this Convention and any actions taken shall be asses in light of the facts and circumstances actually know to him or her at the time that those actions were taken.'
113. *See*, Y. Hanlan, *Eid* v. *Alaska Airlines*: *The Great Divide*, 11 Issues in Aviation Law and Policy 479–499 (2011/2012), at 480.
114. *See*, Y. Hanlan, *Eid* v. *Alaska Airlines*: *The Great Divide*, 11 Issues in Aviation Law and Policy 479–499 (2011/2012), at 498.
115. *See*, Flight Global, *Six Accused in 1992 Air Inter Strasbourg Crash Acquitted, Airbus and Air France Ordered to Pay Compensation*, 7 November 2006.
116. *See*, R.A. Matthews & D. Kanzlarich, *The Crash of ValuJet Flight 592: A Case Study in State-Corporate Crime*, 33(3) Sociological Focus 281–298 (2000).
117. *See*, S.P. Prentice, *Justice Delayed*, USA v. *Sabre Tech*, 1 February 2002.
118. *See*, The Telegraph, *Controllers Jailed over Milan Air Crash*, 14 March 2005.

killing 71 people on 1 July 2002, a Swiss court gave three of the four managers of the Swiss ATC company Skyguide a suspended prison terms whereas the fourth controller had to pay a fine.[119]

- A former British Airways executive had to serve eight months in prison, and pay a fine of EUR 18,000, 'for his part in a conspiracy to fix air cargo prices' between 2002 and 2006.[120]

- A Swiss court sentenced a seaplane pilot to two years imprisonment and monetary penalties for criminal negligence on a flight causing the death of one person and injuries to himself on 23 September 2007.[121]

- While the pilot of the Germanwings flight which crashed on 24 March 2015 into the mountains of the French Alps did not survive the crash which reportedly had been caused by a suicide act of the pilot, Lufthansa, the parent company of Germanwings, and Germanwings, are being examined for their lack of supervising the mental health of the pilot in criminal proceedings.[122]

- In a complex legal and political case, a Polish military prosecutor charged in March 2015 two Russian air traffic controllers and two Polish air force officials for their lack of secure supervision of the landing of an aircraft carrying the Polish President and other high Polish officials on board on 10 April 2010 at the Russian Smolensk airport in foggy weather.[123]

- In June 2015, an airline executive and the director of maintenance of a US helicopter company were convicted to very long imprisonment following a helicopter crash killing two pilots and seven passengers whereas four people survived with severe injuries.[124]

- Fifteen Chinese air traffic controllers have been punished by the public authorities for their involvement in a runway incident which took place at a Shanghai airport in October 2016.[125]

- The Chief Executive Officer (CEO) of a Bolivian airline has been put in jail consequent upon a crash killing seventy-one people including the players of a Brazilian football team on 29 November 2016.[126]

---

119. *See*, swissinfo.ch, *Four Skyguide Employees Found Guilty*, 4 September 2007; *see also*, section 2.4.7 of Chapter 7.
120. *See*, The Telegraph, *Former British Airways Executive to Be Jalied over Cargo Price Fixing*, 1 October 2008; *see also*, section 3.3.3 of Chapter 3.
121. *See*, Baumgärtner Mächler, *Seaplane Pilot Found Guilty of Manslaughter*, published on 9 November 2016 on wwww.international office.com.
122. *See*, N.Y. Times, N. Clark, *France Opens Inquiry in Germanwings Crash*, 12 June 2015, at A9.
123. *See*, Wall Street Journal, P. Wasilewski, *Poland Charges Russian, Polish Officials Over Presidential Plane Crash*, 27 March 2015; *see also*, section 3.3.2 of Chapter 1.
124. *See*, U.S. Department of Justice, *Former Carson Helicopter Vice President Sentenced to Federal Prison*, 16 June 2015.
125. *See*, Flight Safety Foundation, Aviation Safety Network, *Controllers punished over near collision incident at Shanghai Airport*, China, 23 October 2016.
126. *See*, Reuters, *Bolivian Airline CEO to Be Jailed until Soccer Crash Trial Over*, 9 December 2016.

■ A French Court fined the British carrier easyJet EUR 60,000 because of its refusal to allow a disabled passenger to board for 'security reasons'.[127]

6.6 Concluding Note

While the Montreal Protocol is definitely an important step forward to address the behaviour of unruly passengers in an international context, it does not give 'full protection' to remedy the existing problems.[128]

Jurisdiction is not as mandatory as one might wish. States shall take measures '*as may be necessary*' to establish its jurisdiction – which necessity has to be judged by States.

States remain free to prosecute the offender, or not. There is no duty to do so, and so sanction in case a State refuses to prosecute an offender. States are merely encouraged to initiate proceedings.

Linked to this factor is the definition of 'offence' which is, in part, given by the Montreal Protocol but must be translated into concrete terms by State law as it is still vague. This may be confusing for airlines as the responsible aircraft commander, and the law enforcement officials, may not be sure whether the alleged unruly behaviour is a criminal offence in the State of disembarkation. Thus the offenders may be realised without charge, reducing the envisaged deterrent effect of the Montreal Protocol.

ICAO has started to update its Circular 288 – *Guidance Material on the Legal Aspects of Unruly/Disruptive Passengers* which is intended to facilitate the implementation of Resolution A33-4 of the 33rd Session of the ICAO Assembly: *Adoption of national legislation on certain offences committed on board civil aircraft* (unruly/disruptive passengers). The material covers three major aspects of the unruly passenger problem: the list of specific offences for inclusion in national law, extension of jurisdiction over such offences, and appropriate legal mechanisms available for addressing them.

Criminalisation of aviation people has been criticised in literature.[129] Authors argue that safety, and investigation into the cause of the accident, is not helped by

---

127. *See*, decision of 17 January 1917 of the court (*Tribunal correctional*) of Bayonne, France, referring to an earlier case in which easyJet was accused of discrimination of handicapped passengers, as to which *see*, the judgement of the Court of appeal (*Cour d'appel*) of Paris of 5 February 2013.

128. *See*, J. Donnelly, *Unruly passengers on board aircraft: a review of the current liability regime*, 24 Irish Criminal Law Journal 34 (2014); A. Piera, *ICAO's Latest Efforts to Tackle Legal Issues Arising from Unruly/Disruptive Passengers: The Modernization of the Tokyo Convention 1963*, 37 Air & Space Law 231 (2012); R. Abeyratne, *A Protocol to Amend the Tokyo Convention of 1963: Some Unanswered Questions*, 39 Air & Space Law 47 (2014); M. Jennison, *ICAO Adopts Flawed Protocol to Amend the Tokyo Convention of 1963*, 27(2) Air & Space Lawyer (2014).

129. *See*, G. Choust, *Eid* v. *Alaska Airlines*, 36(4/5) Air & Space Law 335–338 (2011); S.W. Dekker, *When Human Error Becomes a Crime*, 9(3) Human Factors and Aerospace Safety 83–92 (2003); R.M. Dunn, D. Hazouri and J. Rannik, *Criminalization Of Negligent Acts by Employees of U.S. And Foreign Companies*, 69 Defense Counsel Journal 17 (2002); R.H. Jones, *Criminal Prosecution of Civil Airmen Following Aircraft Accidents: A Dangerous Trend*, 1 Air & Space Law 3 (1984); P.J. Kolczynski, *The Criminal Liability of Aviators and Related Issues of Mixed*

criminal sanctions, and the publicity surrounding it. Meanwhile, airlines and also safety agencies such as EASA are taking more stringent measures for testing the mental health of pilots which tests have to be regularly conducted.

7 CONCLUDING REMARKS

In a meeting of the ICAO Legal Committee in Montreal in January 1973[130] proposals were submitted aimed at amending the Chicago Convention (1944) in such a way that States not complying with the Hague and Montreal Conventions would either be excluded from ICAO or refused the right of transit by the States party to the Chicago Convention. It was also proposed to convene a Diplomatic Conference which would set up a commission to monitor the facts and to advise on measures to be taken against States failing to comply. A Russian proposal suggested adding a Protocol to the Hague and Montreal Conventions requiring the extradition of the offender to the State of registration, if so requested, except when the offender is a citizen of the State receiving such a request. All these proposals failed to secure a majority at the meeting of the ICAO Assembly held in Rome in 1973.[131] However, the United States authorities and other States insist on an undertaking being given by their partners in bilateral agreements to the effect that the provisions of the three criminal Conventions will be applied.[132]

In the interest of safety of aircraft on land and in the air and of the passengers it is important that the Conventions reviewed in this Chapter and other legal instruments including but not limited to Article 3bis of the Chicago Convention, Annex 17 of ICAO and the ICAO *Convention on the Marking of Explosives for the Purpose of Detection* of

---

Criminal-Civil Litigation: A Venture in the Twilight Zone, 51(1) Journal of Air Law and Commerce 1–50 (1985); E.D. Solomon & D.L. Relles, *Criminalization of Air Disasters: What Goal, If Any, Is Being Achieved?* 76 Journal of Air Law and Commerce 407–456 (2011); A. van Wijk, *Criminal Liability of Pilots Following and Airline Accident: A History of the Issue Within the International Federation of Air Line Pilots' Associations* (IFALPA), 9(1) Air Law 66–71 (1984).

130. *See*, the Minutes and Documents of the 20th Session of the ICAO Legal Committee (Special Session, Montreal, January 1973), ICAO Doc. 9050-LC/169-1 and 169-2.

131. *See*, the 20th Session of the Extraordinary Assembly of ICAO (Rome, August–September 1973), ICAO Doc. 9087; *see also*, M. Milde, *The International Fight Against Terrorism in the Air*, in *The Use of Airspace and Outer Space for All Mankind in the 21st Century*, Proceedings of the International Conference on Air Transport and Space Application in a New World (Tokyo, 2–5 June 1993), Chia-Jui Cheng, ed., 141–158 (1995).

132. *See*, the following clause:

The Parties reaffirm that their obligations to each other to provide for the security of civil aviation against acts of unlawful interference (including in particular their obligations under the Convention of International Civil Aviation, done at Chicago on December 7, 1944; the Convention on Offences and Certain Other Acts Committed on Board Aircraft, done at Tokyo on September 14, 1963; the Convention for the Suppression of Unlawful Seizure of Aircraft, done at The Hague on December 16,1970; and the Convention for the Suppression of Unlawful Acts against the Safety of Civil Aviation, done at Montreal on September 23, 1971; and any other multilateral agreement governing aviation security binding upon the Parties) form an integral part of this Agreement.

199[133] are ratified by as many States as possible. During the ICAO discussions on how to impose sanctions on States unwilling to participate in the Conventions few results have been achieved due to political and economic implications.[134]

While rulemaking has reached a high standard, enforcement, implementation and application of those rules are still a matter of attention. States remain concerned about the conduct of their international relations affecting the maintenance of the august objectives laid down in international rules. The events following the Lockerbie disaster illustrate this point.

Also, the relationship between those regimes has yet to be established in terms of priority, subject matter and enforcement. The binding character of those rules may not always be clear. As shown by, among others, the Beijing Convention of 2010, non-aviation conventions must also be taken into account when remedying attacks against aircraft, airports and aviation generally. To study other fields of law is one of the challenges for lawyers interested in this field of air law.

---

133. *See*, the report and the text of a proposed Draft Convention in 15 Air Law 56–59 (1990), and also the report in 15 *Air Law* 162–163 (1990); The Convention entered into force on 21 June 1998. *see also*, I.H.Ph. Diederiks-Verschoor, *Responsibility for the Transportation by the Passenger of Dangerous Materials by Air*, in T.L. Masson-Zwaan and P.M.J. Mendes de Leon (eds), *Air and Space Law: De Lege Ferenda* 101–112 (1992) and R.I.R. Abeyratne, *Legal Aspects of Unlawful Interference with International Civil Aviation*, 18 Air & Space Law 262–274 (1993); J.V. Augustin, *The Role of ICAO in Relation to the Convention on the Marking of Plastic Explosives for the Purpose of Detection*, XVII Annals of Air and Space Law 33–69 (1992); and R.D. van Dam, *A New Convention on the Marking of Plastic Explosives for the Purpose of Detection*, 16 Air Law 167–177 (1991).

134. *See*, H.J. Rutgers, *Conventions on Criminal Law Regarding Aircraft* 176 (1978).

Bibliography

This list contains books which have been made in the field of air law. They include but are not limited to works which have been cited in this treatise. The list has been divided into five categories, to wit:

(A) *General air law*, including books referring to most if not all subjects pertaining to air law;

(B) *Public air law* including the operation of air services, safety and security, the protection of the environment, aviation commerce and competition regulation;

(C) *Private air law* including airline liability, insurance and product liability;

(D) *Rights in aircraft* including liens, aircraft financing and leasing, and

(E) *European air law* encompassing various aspects of air transport.

For other sources and publications such as treaties, international agreements, national legislations, European regulations, case law, air law magazines, articles, reports made by international organisations, newsletters from law firms, studies carried out by consultancy firms and websites reference is made to the sections which relate to the subject matter in question.

A. Air Law: General

Chia-Jui Cheng (ed.), *Regulatory Reform in International Air Transport: Henri A. Wassenbergh's Select Essays over a Period of Fifty Years 1950–2000* (2000).

Chia-Jui Cheng (ed.), *The Use of Airspace and Outer Space for All Mankind in the 21st Century*, Proceedings of the International Conference on Air Transport and Space Applications in a New World (Tokyo, 2–5 June 1993), (1995).

L.E. Gesell & P.S. Dempsey, *Aviation and the Law* (2005).

B. Havel & G. Sanchez, *The Principles and Practice of International Aviation Law* (2014).

P. Larsen, J. Sweeney and J. Gillick, *Aviation Law: Cases, Laws and Related Sources* (2012).

A.F. Lowenfeld, *Aviation Law* (1974).

N.M. Matte, *Treatise on Air-Aeronautical Law* (1981).

P.M.J. Mendes de Leon (ed.), *From Lowlands to High Skies*, *Liber Amicorum* for John Balfour (2013).

J. Naveau, M. Godfroid & P. Frühling, *Précis De Droit Aérien* (2006).

O. Riese, *Luftrecht* (1949).

M. Schladebach, *Luftrecht* (2007).

Shawcross and Beaumont, *Air Law* (loose leaf; updated) (1977).

J.W. Storm van's Gravesande & A. van der Veen Vonk (eds), *Air Worthy*, Liber Amicorum I.H.Ph. Diederiks-Verschoor (1985).

B.   Public Air Law

R. Abeyratne, *Competition and Investment in Air Transport: Legal and Economic Issues* (2016).

R.I.R. Abeyratne, *Aviation Security Law* (2010).

R.I.R. Abeyratne, *Convention on International Civil Aviation – A Commentary* (2014).

Ms. Angela Cheng-Jui Lu, *International Airline Alliances*: *EC Competition Law/US Antitrust Law and International Air Transport* (11 September 2002).

M. Benkö, *Air and Space Law in the 21st Century*, Liber Amicorum Karl-Heinz Böckstiegel (2001).

T. Buergenthal, *Law-Making in the International Civil Aviation Organization* (1969).

S. Calder, *No Grills: The Truth Behind the Low-Cost Revolution in the Skies* (2003).

B. Cheng, *The Law of International Air Transport* (1962).

C.J. Cheng & P.M.J. Mendes de Leon (eds), *The Highways of Air and Outer Space over Asia* (1992).

J.C. Cooper, *Roman Law and the Maxim 'Cujus est solum' in International Air Law* (1952).

P.S. Dempsey, *Air Commerce and the Law* (2004).

P.S. Dempsey, *Public International Air Law* (2008).

D.T. Duval, *Air Transport in the Asia Pacific* (2014).

R.J. Fennes, *International Air Cargo Transport Services*: *Economic Regulation and Policy* (1997).

P.P. Fitzgerald, *A Level Playing Field for 'Open Skies'* (2016).

A.D. Groenewege, *The Compendium of International Civil Aviation* (2003).

M.J. Guerro Lebron, *Los seguros aéreos*: *Los seguros de aerolineas y operadores aéreos* (2009).

P.P.C. Haanappel, *Pricing and Capacity Determination in International Air Transport: A Legal Analysis* (1984).

P.P.C. Haanappel, *Ratemaking in International Air Transport: A Legal Analysis of International Air Fares and Rates* (1978).

P.P.C. Haanappel, *The Law and Policy of Air Space and Outer Space*: *A Comparative Approach* (2003).

B.F. Havel, *Beyond Open Skies: A New Regime for International Aviation* (2009).

B.F. Havel, *In Search of Open Skies: Law and Policy for a New Era in International Aviation* (1997).

B. Havel& G. Sanchez, *The Principles and Practice of International Aviation Law* (2014).

B.D.K. Henaku, *The Law on Global Air Navigation by Satellite: A Legal Analysis of the ICAO CNS/ATM System* (1998).

S. Hobe et al. (eds), *Consequences of Air Transport Globalization* (2003).

S. Hobe (ed.), Proceedings of the Conference *Air Law, Space Law, Cyber Law – The Cologne Institute of Air and Space Law at Age 90* (2016).

J. Huang, *Aviation Safety and ICAO* (2009).

P.K. Lawrence, *Aerospace Strategic Trade: How the U.S. Subsidizes the Large Commercial Aircraft Industry* (2001).

T.L. Mason-Zwaan & P.M.J. Mendes de Leon, *Air and Space Law: De Lege Ferenda*, Essays in Honour of Henri A. Wassenbergh (1992).

T.L. Masson & P.M.J. Mendes de Leon (eds), *Aviation Security*, Proceedings of an International Conference held in The Hague (1987).

N.M. Matte, *De la mer territoriale à l'air 'territorial'* (1965).

N.M. Matte, *The International Legal Status of the Aircraft Commander – Le statut juridique international du commandant d'aéronef* (1975).

E.E. McWhinney, *The Illegal Diversion of Aircraft and International Law* (1975).

P.M.J. Mendes de Leon, *Cabotage in Air Transport Regulation* (1992).

J. Milligan, *European Union Competition Law in the Airline Industry* (2017).

M. Milde, *ICAO: A History of International Civil Aviation* (2010).

M. Milde, *International Air Law and ICAO* (2016).

A. Piera Valdés, *Greenhouse Gas from International Aviation: Legal and Policy Challenges – Essential Air and Space Law* (2015).

M. Ratajczek, *Regional Aviation Safety Organisations: Enhancing Air Transport Safety Through Regional Cooperation* (PhD Leiden) (2014).

N. Ronzitti & G. Venturini (eds), *The Law of Air Warfare: Contemporary Issues* (2006).

C.H. Schlumberger, *Open Skies for Africa: Implementing the Yamoussoukro Decision: Directions in Development* (2010).

W. Schwenk, *Handbuch des Luftverkehrsrechts* (1981).

W. Schwenk & R. Schwenk, *Aspects of International Co-operation in Air Traffic Management* (1998).

B. Scott, *The Law of Unmanned Aircraft Systems: An Introduction to the Current and Future Regulation under National, Regional and International Law* (2016).

U. Stepler, *Tarifbildung und IATA-Interlining im Luftverkehr Eine wettbewerbsrechtliche Betrachtung* (2007).

U. Steppler & A. Klingmüller, *EU Emissions Trading Scheme and Aviation* (2010).

J. Subilia, *L'utilisation des signaux satellitaires dans l'aviation civile internationale: Aspects institutionels et juridiques* (2009).

The International Bureau of the Permanent Court of Arbitration, *Arbitration in Air, Space and Telecommunications Law* (2002).

N.A. van Antwerpen, *Cross-Border Provision of Air Navigation Services with Specific Reference to Europe: Safeguarding Transparent Lines of Responsibility and Liability* (PhD thesis, Leiden University) (2007).

E. von den Steinen, *National Interest and International Aviation* (2006).

H.A. Wassenbergh, *Principles and Practices in Air Transport Regulation* (1993).

H.A. Wassenbergh, *Public International Air Transportation Law in a New Era* (1990).

H.A. Wassenbergh, *Reality and Value in Air and Space Law* (1978).

L. Weber, *Die Zivilluftfahrt im Europäischen Gemeinschaftsrecht* (1981).

L. Weber, *International Civil Aviation Organization* (2007).

G. Williams, *Airline Competition: Deregulation's Mixed Legacy* (2002).

G. Williams, *The Airline Industry and the Impact of Deregulation* (1994).

K. Ziolkowski (ed.), *Peacetime Regime for State Activities in Cyberspace: International Law, International Relations and Diplomacy* (2013).

C. Private Air Law

M. Clarke & G. Leloudas, *Air Cargo Insurance* (2016).

M. de Juglart, *La Convention de Rome du 7 octobre 1952* (1955).

P.S. Dempsey & M. Milde, *International Air Carrier Liability: The Montreal Convention of 1999* (2005).

H. Drion, *Limitation of Liabilities in International Air Law* (1954).

J.-M. Fobe, *Aviation Products Liability and Insurance in the EU* (1994).

D. Goedhuis, *La Convention de Varsovie* (1933).

D. Goedhuis, *National Air Legislations and the Warsaw Convention* (1937).

L.B. Goldhirsch, *The Warsaw Convention Annotated: A Legal Handbook* (1988).

M. Hoeks, *Multimodal Transport Law – The Law Applicable to Multimodal Contract for the Carriage of Goods* (2010).

Wu Jianduan, *The Evolution of Chinese Regulation in Light of the World-Wide Framework on the Contractual Liability for Air Carriers* (2003).

P. Larsen, J. Sweeney & J. Gillick, *Aviation Law: Cases, Laws and Related Sources* (2012).

R.D. Margo, *Aviation Insurance* (2014).

R.H. Manckiewicz, *The Liability Regime of the International Air Carrier* (1981).

A.J. Mauritz, *Liability of the Operator and Owners of Aircraft for Damage Inflicted to Persons and Property on the Surface* (PhD thesis, University of Leiden) (2003).

R.D. Margo, *Aviation Insurance* (2000).

M. Mildred, *Product Liability Law and Insurance* (1994).

G. Miller, *Liability in International Air Transport* (1977).

D.N. Stanesco, *La responsabilité dans la navigation aérienne/Dommages causés aux tiers à la surface* (1951).

R.C. Tester, *Air Cargo Claims* (1998).

G. Tompkins, *Liability Rules Applicable to International Air Transportation as Developed by the Courts in the United States* (2010).

A.T. Wells, *Introduction to Aviation Insurance* (1986).

D. Rights in Aircraft and Aircraft Financing

D. Bunker, *International Aircraft Financing* (2015).

V. Correia & C.I. Grigorieff, *Le droit du financement des aéronefs* (2017).

B.J.H. Crans & R. Nath (eds), *Aircraft Repossession and Enforcement: Practical Aspects* (2009).

R. Goode, *Official Commentary* [on the Convention on International Interests in Mobile Equipment and the Protocol thereto on Matters specific to Space Assets] (Unidroit, 2013).

R. Hames & G. McBain (eds), *Aircraft Finance – Registration, Security and Enforcement* (2011).

D.P. Hanley, *Aircraft Operating Leasing: A Legal and Practical Analysis in the Context of Public and Private International Air Law* (thesis Leiden University, 2011, 2017).

B. Hofstetter, *L'hypothèque aérienne* (1950).

C. Karako, *Separate Financing of Aircraft Engines: Legal Obstacles* (2010).

E. European Air Law

B. Adkins, *Air Transport and the European Union* (1994).

J. Balfour, *European Community Air Law* (1995).

M. Bartlik, *The Impact of EU Law on the Regulation of International Air Transportation* (2007).

V. Correia, *L'Union européenne et le droit international de l'aviation civile* (2014).

P.S. Dempsey, *European Aviation Law* (2004).

E. Giemulla & L. Weber, *International and EU Aviation Law* (2011).

J. Goh, *European Air Transport Law and Competition* (1997).

Hobe-von Ruckteschell-Hefferman, *Cologne Compendium on Air Law in Europe* (2013).

P.M.J. Mendes de Leon & D. Calleja-Crespo (eds), *Achieving the Single European Sky: Goals and Challenges* (2011).

R. Travis, *Air Transport Liberalisation in the European Community 1987–1992: A Case of Integration* (2001).

S. Varsamos, *Airport Competition Regulation in Europe*, Chapter 3 (2016).

Glossary[*]

Aerodrome – is another word for airport.

Aeronautical authority – a public body which is part of, or linked to, the Ministry of Transport of a State and which is responsible for policy making, regulation and enforcement of aviation related responsibilities such as safety oversight, the establishment of infrastructure including airports and air traffic control, licensing of air carriers, the conclusion and implementation of Air Services Agreement (ASA) and the conduct of relations with international organisations.

Agreed stopping place – term used in private air law conventions indicating the place on which the airline and its passenger of shipper of cargo agreed to make a stopover pursuant to the terms of their contract, as opposed to a landing for technical purposes in case of, for instance, emergency.

Air Service – 'Air service' means any scheduled air service performed by aircraft for the public transport of passengers, mail or cargo as to which *see* Article 96 of the Chicago Convention.

AOC – Air Operator's Certificate: the AOC is the key link to safety oversight. It attests to an airline's competence as to safe operation and it determines who is responsible for an airline's safety oversight.

ASA – Air Services Agreement: an agreement between States containing an internationally agreed legal framework upon which the agreed international air services are operated.

Bermuda I Agreement – original UK/US air services agreement signed in 1945; the original 'liberal' non-restrictive type of Air Services Agreement (ASA).

Bermuda II Agreement – UK/US air services agreement negotiated in 1977 which superseded Bermuda 1 in order to redress the balance of air service advantage, which at that time lay with the US, by limiting the number of airlines that could

---

[*]   The definition of the terms listed in this glossary give an indication of their meaning and not more than that; for more accurate definitions, reference is made to the legal acts in which they are drawn up including treaties, national legislations and other regulations.

be designated to operate on certain routes and the over-provision of capacity by some US carriers.

Blacklisting – regime of the EU listing carriers which are deemed to be unsafe in light of EU standards for aviation safety and therefore banned from entering the airspace of any EU Member State; the lists are updated regularly, that is, normally every four to six months.

C

Cabotage – the operation of domestic services in one State by a carrier of another State.

Charter – a non-scheduled flight operated according to the national laws and regulations of the country being served, as provided for in Article 5 of the Chicago Convention.

Civil Aviation Authority (CAA) – the name, or another name, of the Aeronautical Authority as to which *see* above.

Code Sharing – a marketing device whereby an airline places its designator code on a service operated by another airline. When selling a service, the marketing carrier is required to tell passengers that the service may be operated by another (operating) carrier.

CRS – Computerised reservation system used to store and retrieve information on tickets and other travel information for the purpose of distribution and selling; this system is now referred to as Global Distribution System (GDS).

Contracting State – a State that has consented to be bound by a treaty whether or not the treaty has entered into force.

Convention – a term used for international agreements between States; *see also,* Treaty.

D

Designation – nomination by a State of the airline or airlines to operate the agreed international air service(s). The bilateral partner can be informed of the nomination by letter, Diplomatic Note or inclusion of the details in a Memorandum of Understanding (MOU) /Agreed Record.

Dry lease – the lease of a basic aircraft without crew, insurance, maintenance, etc. and usually involves the lessee putting the aircraft on its own AOC and registering the aircraft on the register of its own State.

Drone – refers to an unmanned aircraft, and is also known as unmanned aerial system (UAS) or unmanned aerial vehicle (UAV).

Dual designation – the Aeronautical Authorities of each say may designate two carriers from operate the agreed international air services.

E

Effects doctrine – principle, and, in many cases, also a rule laid down in national legislation according to which the competition authority in a jurisdiction claims authority to judge a competition case because it has an effect on the market over which it has jurisdictional powers in accordance with its domestic legislation, even if the parties are located outside that jurisdiction and have made the concerned transaction abroad.

Exclusivity – in private air law, refers to the exclusive application of private air law conventions such as the Warsaw Convention of 1929 and the Montreal Convention, 1999, to the compensation of damages as regulated by the terms of those conventions.

F

FAB – Functional Airspace Bock, referring to a cross border arrangement between EU States designed to create an airspace block which is established in accordance with efficiency criteria rather than along national borders.

FIR – Flight Information Region: an airspace of defined dimensions within which air traffic services are provided by the named centre on behalf of a State.

FIS – Flight Information Service: a service provided to aircraft for the purpose of giving advice and information useful for the safe and efficient conduct of flights.

Flag of convenience – a maritime business practice whereby a merchant ship is registered in a State other than that of the ship's owners, and the ship flies that State's flag. Due to nationality requirements of aircraft in conjunction with compulsory safety oversight functions of the registration State this practice has not or not yet been implemented in aviation.

Flight Plan – information provided to air traffic service units about the intended flight of an aircraft.

Freedoms of the Air – reflect the rights of an air carrier to transit foreign airspace, make a technical stop in foreign territory and carry traffic on internationally agreed services.

G

GDS – Global Distribution System, *see*, CRS.

I

Implied powers – concept pursuant to which powers do not originate directly from provisions of the EU treaties but rather derive, implicitly, from general objectives laid down by the Treaties as interpreted by the Court of Justice of the EU.

Interlining – transportation on various segments of a journey operated by different airlines while using one airline ticket

International Air Service – an air service which passes through the air space over the territory of more than one state as to which *see*, Article 96 of the Chicago Convention.

L

Lease – an arrangement whereby an airline or another party (lessor) makes available an aircraft for the operation of services by or on behalf of an airline (lessee).

Leases can involve provision by the lessor of an aircraft only (dry lease), aircraft and crew (wet lease) or aircraft and flight crew (damp lease).

Lien – a security interest granted over an item of property, for instance, an aircraft, to secure the payment of a debt, for instance, pertaining to the payment of the purchase price or user charges.

M

Market investor principle – a principle according to which a public authority invests in an undertaking on terms which would be acceptable to a private investor operating under market economy conditions.

MOR – Mandatory Occurrence Reporting system which is a process for collecting, recording, acting upon and generating feedback regarding actual or potential safety deficiencies and hazards.

Multiple designation – the aeronautical authorities of each side may designate an unlimited number of carriers to operate the agreed international air services as to which *see*, for instance, 'Open Skies' regimes.

N

NOTAM – Notice to Airmen, that is a notice containing information about the establishment, condition or change in any aeronautical facility, service, procedure or hazard, the timely knowledge of which is essential to personnel concerned with flight operations. It is issued by the state's Aeronautical Information Service (AIS).

O

O & D – Origin and Destination of the traffic.

Operating Licence – granted by an Aviation Authority, attesting to the competence of an airline to operate air services. The criteria for granting a licence to EU air carriers are covered by Council Regulation (EC) No. 1008/2008, and relate principally to the place and nature of business; nationality of ownership and control; adequacy of financial resources; the holding of an Air Operator's Certificate (AOC); fitness; and passenger and third party insurance.

P

Pooling Agreement – an agreement between two airlines operating the same route to develop their traffic as profitably as possible. The revenues gained by the airlines on the routes covered by the agreement are placed into a common pool and shared out between the airlines in accordance with the terms of the agreement.

Predatory fare – a below-cost fare set by an airline with the intention of forcing competitors out of the market.

Privatisation – is the process of transferring ownership of specified property, for instance, shares of an airline, from the government or a public body to a private company or private national persons.

Privity of contract – The doctrine of privity in the common law of contract provides that a contract cannot confer rights or impose obligations arising under it on any person or agent except the parties to it.

PSO – Public Service Obligation: an obligation imposed on an EU air carrier to take, in respect of any route which it is licensed to operate by a Member State, all necessary measures to ensure the provision of a service satisfying fixed standards of continuity, regularity, capacity and pricing, which standards the air carrier would not assume if it were solely considering its commercial interest as to which *see*, Articles 16–18 of EU Regulation 1008/2008.

R

Route Schedule – an annex to an Air Services Agreement (ASA) setting out the routes that the designated airlines may operate. An open route schedule allows a carrier to operate via or to any point without restriction. The route schedule usually contains a condition requiring fifth freedom rights to be the subject of negotiation between the bilateral partners. This condition may be omitted with the effect that unlimited fifth freedom rights are permitted on the points on the routes set out in the route schedule.

Rules of the Air – term indicating the navigation rules drawn up by ICAO and laid down in, for instance, Annex 2 entitled Rules of the Air to the Chicago Convention, in order to promote the safe and efficient movement of civil aircraft in airspace.

S

Scheduled service – an air service operated on a regular basis by a carrier in accordance with a published timetable or with flights so regular or frequent that they constitute a recognisably systemic series.

SDR – Special Drawing Right, supplementary foreign exchange assets defined and maintained by the International Monetary Fund (IMF). Its value can be checked on a daily basis in newspapers and on websites including that of the IMF.

SES – abbreviation standing for single European sky, the initiative of the EU to synchronise air traffic management in the airspaces of its Member States, and other States who have made agreements thereto with the EU.

Single designation – the aeronautical authorities of each side may designate only one carrier to operate the agreed international air services

Slot – a particular time allocated to an airline to land or take-off from a particular airport. The allocation of slots at co-ordinated airports in the European Union is governed by EU Regulation 95/93 as variously amended which aims to provide for neutral, transparent and non-discriminatory slot allocation at the more congested Community airports through a co-ordinator independent of government, airlines and airports.

T

Tariff – the price charged for the public transport of passengers, baggage and cargo excluding mail, including the conditions governing the availability or application of such price and the charges and conditions for services ancillary to such transport.

Transit Passenger – a passenger who is passing through an airport for the express purpose of connecting with another flight.

Treaty – an agreement concluded in written form between two or more States or public entities such as international organisations having international personality, and governed by international law.

Index

543